SO-ACB-030

FLORIDA STATE
UNIVERSITY LIBRARIES

FEB 19 1993

TALLAHASSEE, FLORIDA

The Diary of Rexford G. Tugwell

Recent Titles in
Contributions in Economics and Economic History

THE DIARY
OF
REXFORD G. TUGWELL

The New Deal, 1932–1935

EDITED BY

MICHAEL VINCENT NAMORATO

Contributions in Economics and Economic History, Number 136
David O. Whitten, Series Adviser

GREENWOOD PRESS
New York • Westport, Connecticut • London

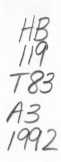

*HB
119
T83
A3
1992*

Library of Congress Cataloging-in-Publication Data

Tugwell, Rexford G. (Rexford Guy), 1891-
   The diary of Rexford G. Tugwell : the New Deal, 1932-1935 / edited
by Michael Vincent Namorato.
      p.   cm. – (Contributions in economics and economic history,
   ISSN 0084-9235 ; no. 136)
   Includes bibliographical references and index.
   ISBN 0-313-28017-7 (alk. paper)
   1. Tugwell, Rexford G. (Rexford Guy), 1891- . 2. Government
economists – United States – Biography.   I. Namorato, Michael V.
II. Title. III. Series.
HB119.T83A3   1992
330'.092—dc20   92-1166
   [B]

British Library Cataloguing in Publication Data is available.

Copyright © 1992 by Michael Vincent Namorato

All rights reserved. No portion of this book may be
reproduced, by any process or technique, without the
express written consent of the publisher.

Library of Congress Catalog Card Number: 92-1166
ISBN: 0-313-28017-7
ISSN: 0084-9235

First published in 1992

Greenwood Press, 88 Post Road West, Westport, CT 06881
An imprint of Greenwood Publishing Group, Inc.

Printed in the United States of America

The paper used in this book complies with the
Permanent Paper Standard issued by the National
Information Standards Organization (Z39.48-1984).

10 9 8 7 6 5 4 3 2 1

Copyright Acknowledgments

The author and publisher gratefully wish to acknowledge permission to reprint the following:

Excerpts from the articles " 'They All Laughed' " (July 3, 1933), " 'Goodnight, Goodnight' " (July 10, 1933), and " 'Same With Me!' " (July 17, 1933) from *Time*. Copyright 1933 Time Warner Inc. Reprinted by permission.

Arthur Krock, "Tugwell Defeats Peek," from *The New York Times*, December 8, 1933. Copyright © 1933 by The New York Times Company. Reprinted by permission.

Heywood Broun, "It Seems to Me," from *New York World Tribune and Sun*, December 18, 1933.

"The New Citizenship" (January 29, 1934) and "Land Control" (December 30, 1933) from *St. Louis Post-Dispatch*. Copyrights 1934 and 1933 respectively, Pulitzer Publishing Company, reprinted by permission.

"What the World Economic Conference Can Do" (April 12, 1933), "Brains Trust in Policy Clash" (July 1, 1933), "Industry Unites to Fight Food and Drug Bill" (February 3, 1934), and "Roosevelt Approves Program for Marginal Land Purchase" (February 28, 1934) from *New York Herald Tribune* © 1933 and 1934, New York Herald Tribune Inc. All rights reserved. Reprinted by permission.

Letter from F. Ryan Duffy to Franklin D. Roosevelt (May 6, 1933) and letter from Franklin D. Roosevelt to F. Ryan Duffy (May 16, 1933) from the President's private files, Hyde Park. Courtesy of the Franklin D. Roosevelt Library.

Letter from Edward J. Dempsey to F. Ryan Duffy, May 3, 1933. Courtesy of Timothy M. Dempsey.

Letter from H. Parker Willis to Carter Glass, November 19, 1933. H. Parker Willis Papers, Rare Book and Manuscript Library, Columbia University.

Memorandum for Governor Franklin D. Roosevelt relating to subjects discussed in conversation of November 17, 1932, by way of Professor Tugwell. James Harvey Rogers Papers, Manuscripts and Archives, Yale University Library.

Letter from Monte F. Bourjaily to Rexford G. Tugwell (December 11, 1933) and letter from George A. Carlin to Rexford G. Tugwell (January 26, 1934). Courtesy of United Feature Syndicate.

Letter from Harry E. Barnes to J. W. Darr. Courtesy Robert H. Barnes.

"Did Dr. Tugwell Commend 'Wine, Woman and Song?' " April 30, 1934. Reprinted from *The Baltimore Sun* © 1934, The Baltimore Sun Co.

Letter from Eleanor Roosevelt to Rexford G. Tugwell, March 3, 1934. Courtesy of the Franklin D. Roosevelt Library.

Grateful acknowledgment is also made to Grace F. Tugwell for allowing the use of various materials.

Every reasonable effort has been made to trace the owners of copyright materials in this book, but in some instances this has proven impossible. The author and publisher will be glad to receive information leading to more complete acknowledgments in subsequent printings of the book and in the meantime extend their apologies for any omissions.

To

Karen Ann, Michael John, and Rachel Marie

Contents

Foreword

Who was Rexford G. Tugwell? Not one in a thousand randomly chosen Americans will know the name. Younger citizens have never known it; their elders have forgotten. In the twentieth century's fast-paced second half the epochal events of the first have disappeared into history like the features of the earth photographed from a satellite plunging into space. What was once prominent becomes an indistinguishable blur in an absorbing contour. The World War, the Great War, the War to End Wars, faded into World War I as American school children struggled to remember that it came after the Civil War, not before. The Great Depression, the Brains Trust, the New Deal have either disappeared from the American history taught in public schools or become a few lines in a paragraph summarizing broader events, perhaps the career of Franklin D. Roosevelt--who is increasingly confused with the earlier president of the same surname.

Rexford Tugwell, for all his current anonymity, was a public man for his times, 1891-1979. He took three economics degrees from the University of Pennsylvania--B.S., M.A., Ph.D.--and rose through the ranks at Columbia University to professor of economics. Tugwell joined the Brains Trust in 1932, and served as assistant secretary of agriculture, undersecretary of agriculture, and director of the Resettlement Administration before becoming chairman of the New York City Planning Commission in 1938, Chancellor of the University of Puerto Rico in 1941, and Governor of Puerto Rico that same year. Who Tugwell was and what he thought and did have been set out in large measure by the man himself. In his able biography, Michael V. Namorato devoted ten pages to a listing of Tugwell's publications. The books and articles will serve only researchers concentrating on Rexford Tugwell. There will be few. What will be left to history? What will join the contours and what will be overwhelmed?

Namorato's biography and edited Tugwell diaries will enter history; the rest will be absorbed by it. Without Namorato's husbanding the Tugwell legacy would disappear under its own weight. Important people who leave few written records risk fading from view if the scant evidence is lost or overlooked. Those who leave vast writings overwhelm the capacities and willingness of archivists and librarians to maintain the record. Multiple volumes of autobiography and polemics repel researchers scanning an era, especially if the author promoted an unpopular position. Planning was Tugwell's panacea, but American society's poison. Tugwell would not be surprised by the fall of the communist economies; he promoted neither central committee plans nor enforcement by autocratic regimes. Cooperative planning for the benefit and with the support of society were his goals. If society generates millions of superannuated citizens who are financially unprepared for old age, planning for their care advantages everyone.

Tugwell promoted his political and economic positions with his pen. He published what he wanted others to read. What did he think? We can know only what he wrote for his own eyes. He was an academic, and who knows better than a professor that memory is unreliable? He prompted that memory with diaries, and Namorato has freed those writings from their private repository, edited them for publication, and entered them into the public domain. There is no better source of insight into the world and thinking of Rexford Tugwell.

David O. Whitten
Business Library Review
Auburn University, Alabama

Preface

It has been almost twenty years since I began working on Rexford G. Tugwell. Approximately 4 years ago, I thought a major landmark had been reached with the publication of Rexford G. Tugwell: A Biography (New York: Praeger Publishers, 1988). Yet, it wasn't enough. Even before the biography was released, I started working on editing the massive diary he had kept throughout his long life. Now, the diary is ready to be published and I can't say definitely that my work on Tugwell is over. It is for now or at least until another idea develops and my pursuit begins again.

To edit a diary such as this is a major undertaking. It is also one that can be completed only with the help of many individuals. Now is the time to thank those people who so patiently worked with me over these last 4 years. Grateful acknowledgment is given to David Whitten who encouraged me at those critical moments when completing a book seems almost impossible and who consistently talked about when the diary would be published instead of if it would.

Special thanks are also expressed to Dr. William Emerson and his staff (especially Ms. Elizabeth Denier and Mr. Paul McLaughlin) at the Franklin D. Roosevelt Library in Hyde Park, New York. As usual, their kindness and professionalism went a long way in making this undertaking a pleasant experience. Acknowledgment is also made to the Franklin and Eleanor Roosevelt Institute and the Liberal Arts Faculty Development Committee at the University of Mississippi for providing the financial support needed for this project.

Once the diary was identified, verified, and re-examined, support staff became indispensable. Dr. Robert Haws, chairman of the

Department of History at the University of Mississippi, was most helpful in providing the necessary clerical and graduate student assistance I needed. Phil Holman and Laura Boughton both worked assiduously in proofreading the entries and collecting information for the glossary. Dr. Royce Kurtz, University of Mississippi Reference Librarian, was instrumental in assisting with copyrights. There is no doubt that Ginger Delk, executive secretary in the history department, was a crucial element in bringing the diary to the stage where publication became a reality. Her cheery disposition, her calm demeanor, and her "we'll get it done, Dr. Namorato" attitude persistently convinced me that she knew more about what to do than I did. And, in her confidence, I came to believe the diary would see the light of day. Also helpful was Ms. Lucienne Bramlett Savell who assisted in the final stages of typing the manuscript.

Similarly, my gratitude is given to Ms. Cynthia Harris, Executive Editor at Greenwood Press. She was enthusiastic when the project started, patient as the deadlines came and passed, and supportive to the very end. Thanks are expressed as well to Ms. Julie LeGallee who led the editor through the production process with cheerful and friendly directions.

Finally, no listing of thanks would be complete without mention of the three individuals to whom this book is dedicated. To my wife, Karen, and our children, Mikie and Rachel, affection and gratitude for all. As always, they were there.

The Diary of Rexford G. Tugwell

Rexford G. Tugwell:
A Brief Sketch

Born July 10, 1891 in Sinclairville, New York, Rexford Guy Tugwell was the son of Dessie Rexford and Charles Tugwell. An only child for a good part of his youth, Tugwell grew up in a loving environment provided by his parents. His mother instilled in him a love of learning, reading, and nature while his father, a fairly prosperous businessman, taught him about business, profits, and laborers first hand. Growing up in a small town like Sinclairville and later Wilson, New York, Tugwell would always be attracted to the simplicity of small town life while simultaneously criticizing its glaring deficiencies in providing its citizens with opportunities to adapt to the modern world.

As a child, Tugwell suffered with asthma, thereby limiting his athletic inclinations. To compensate for that, he read avidly, a habit he nurtured throughout his long life. Bored with the formal education offered by the public schools he attended, he did as little as possible to pass his exams and keep his parents and teachers content. Reading, life experiences, and observing what was going on around him were more important means of learning in his thinking. By age 11, he began to apply himself more readily to a developing occupation with writing, another characteristic he nursed throughout his 88 years. Although done secretly at first, Tugwell started to display this talent as a newspaper reporter for the <u>Niagara Falls Gazette</u>. In 1909 after only 2 weeks at a military school in Virginia, the young adolescent decided to go to Masten High in Buffalo, New York. There, he met new people, experienced what it was like to live in a city, and decided he needed to go on to further his education. In 1911, he did just that when he enrolled in the Wharton School at the University of Pennsylvania.

At the Wharton School, Tugwell met a number of individuals who influenced him greatly. Scott Nearing and Simon Nelson Patten both affected his growing concerns about the American economic and business system. Patten was particularly important in this respect. Tugwell absorbed and accepted Patten's rejection of the classical economists, his endorsement and belief in an economy of abundance, his commitment to experimentalism, and his acceptance of technology. Patten, moreover, also served as a protector of his young student, doing much to help Tugwell secure teaching positions later on at Columbia University.

While at Wharton, Tugwell was also exposed to ideas which later impacted his own economic philosophy. Tugwell read and absorbed Thorstein Veblen's attacks on the classicists, Taylorism and its emphasis on planning, and institutional pragmatism. He was so impressed by each of these intellectual currents that he incorporated them into his own evolving outlook on the American economy and its potentiality.

It was also at Wharton that Tugwell married Florence Arnold in 1914. In 1915, he completed his B.S. in economics and, in the next academic year, he stayed on as an instructor of economics while finishing his M.A. From 1917 to 1918, he wrote on the issue of milk strikes in the United States and left the University of Pennsylvania to follow Carlton Parker to the University of Washington where he thought he was to study the application of psychology to economic issues. Instead, he found himself as an assistant professor of economics and marketing, writing lectures and teaching classes, a task Tugwell would always like when done in moderation. By 1918, Tugwell left the University of Washington and decided to contribute his services to the American war effort. Going to Paris, he headed the American University Union for university men. At the war's end, he decided to return to Wilson, New York and join his father in business.

While Tugwell's father was excited by the prospect of his only son returning home and undertaking family affairs, Tugwell himself soon changed his mind about what he was doing. Not much of a farmer and definitely feeling trapped in a small-town environment, he decided to return to his studies. Despite the lack of enthusiasm some of his professors expressed regarding his decision, Tugwell completed a Ph.D. in economics in 1922. With Patten's support, moreover, he had already secured an instructorship at Columbia University in 1920.

Columbia University, 1920 - 1932

Tugwell's tenure at Columbia University was probably one of the most productive and yet most difficult times in his life. During these years, he wrote prolifically, completing 4 books, serving as a joint author on a economics textbook, and writing over 45 articles in major journals and newspapers. In 1927, he travelled to the Soviet Union as a member of a trade union delegation, an event his critics never let him forget. In 1928, he served as an advisor to Governor Al Smith on agriculture during his campaign for the presidency, proposing his Advance Ratio Plan (ARP) as a solution to farm distress. Essentially, his ARP was an early attempt to plan agricultural production to meet consumer demand by scientifically determining how many farm goods were needed for the coming year. Tugwell even proposed a corporation be set up to administer any contracts and funds individual farmers would have to deal with. While Smith did not endorse the plan, the ARP at least showed Tugwell's own evolving thinking on farm distress.

In 1929, Tugwell travelled to France to study agriculture. On his return to America, he wrote about what he had seen. From 1930 to 1931, he also continued his writing and studying of America's educational system, eventually editing a major study entitled Redirecting Education. It was also during his Columbia years that Tugwell met and was influenced by John Dewey and Wesley Mitchell. In the former case, Tugwell's commitment to pragmatism was solidified while in Mitchell's case, Tugwell's adherence to quantitative economics was less important than his devotion to Mitchell who helped him with his Columbia colleagues.

Although successful from whatever view one takes, Tugwell did not receive his colleagues' support. Small-minded and petty in their own academic jealousies, they refused to recognize the contributions one of their own was making within the profession or on a national scale. Tugwell was disappointed and deeply hurt by what happened, but it was also a toughening experience and one that he later used in his New Deal days when attacks on him became quite commonplace.

The Columbia years were important for another reason as well. Throughout the 1920s, Tugwell wrote on a number of themes which dominated his thinking then and later. He persistently attacked the classical economics, arguing that they had no place in the modern technological society of the twentieth-century United States. He vigorously assaulted the American business system and the American businessman as being selfish, cruel, and indifferent to what America could achieve. Committed to an economy of abundance in which everyone shared the immense benefits of nature and America's ingenuity, Tugwell was appalled at business' greed and refusal to be "good sports." Planning, as a result, became all important in his thinking. Planning represented what could be accomplished for all of society instead of just the individual or the specific company. But, planning in the 1920s meant collaboration and cooperation, the service ideal, and a philosophical approach to America's economic problems, not a detailed blueprint of what had to be done.

Along these lines, Tugwell also defined the economist's role in American society. He was to provide the theory and the means to achieve the concert of interests and the economy of abundance which was easily within America's capabilities. With technology and all it could do, industrialists, in his opinion, had to think of consumers and workers, trying hard to provide the former with high quality products at good prices and the latter with safe environments and good wages. Here, Tugwell believed Taylorism could and would help, if given the chance. So too would redirecting America's education by placing more emphasis on experimentalism and studying alternatives.

One alternative that Tugwell studied in the 1920s was the Soviet Union. Neither then nor later did he ever endorse what Russia represented or was doing vis-à-vis planning. Enforced and regimented planning was anathema to the American way and Tugwell carefully and methodically discarded it. This was especially seen in his agricultural ideas of the normalcy era.

For Tugwell, the problem with agriculture was the farmer. He did not accept McNary-Haugenism which attempted to create an artificial price for American goods or tariffs designed to protect the American market for the American producer. Tugwell felt that neither offered solutions to the overproduction caused by the farmer himself. Farmers needed to cooperate, to plan, to think beyond themselves. A new approach was developing which might accomplish that -- domestic allotment. As time went on, Tugwell became a staunch champion of the idea and its implementation as a first step in the planning process. What is more important is that Tugwell soon had an opportunity to present this proposal to someone who could do something about it -- Franklin D. Roosevelt.

Brains Trust-New Deal, 1932 - 1936

In light of his growing reputation as an economist as well as his Columbia University affiliation, it was only natural for Raymond Moley to contact Tugwell and ask him to meet with Roosevelt's advisers in 1932. It was Moley who served as the nucleus and recruiter for Governor Roosevelt's coterie of advisers. After his initial screening by Sam Rosenman and Doc O'Connor, Tugwell was brought to meet Franklin D. Roosevelt himself. At that meeting, Tugwell articulated his own theories on what caused the Depression, why Hoover failed to address the crisis, and what needed to be done to overcome the deepening economic downturn. Roosevelt listened, was impressed, and decided to recruit the young economics professor into his inner circle --the Brains Trust.

As a member of the Brains Trust, Tugwell's job, along with Ray Moley and Adolf Berle, was to educate Roosevelt on the complex economic issues confronting him as a presidential candidate. Slowly and deliberately, they did just that, but always in the context and manner that Roosevelt wanted. This was most clearly seen in Tugwell's own disappointment with the pre-nomination campaign in which Roosevelt refused to commit himself openly to planning as Tugwell wanted. On a more specific level, Tugwell was assigned the task of working on agricultural recovery and industrial cooperation. For the latter, he proposed the last chapter of his Industrial Discipline as a solution to the industrial problems in the United States.

According to this proposal, associations within each industry would be set up to establish planning boards for that industry. These boards, in turn, would deal with all matters affecting that industry as well as assist in creating a central planning board to deal with interindustrial matters. The U.S. Industrial Integration Board would serve as an investigative and coordinating body, even exerting authority over prices and recalcitrant members of an industry. Cooperating with the federal government, an Industrial Reserve Fund would be set up and used to help cooperating businessmen. Essentially planning in Tugwell's view, its success depended on business-government cooperation. In the end, everyone was supposed to benefit. The most significant problem confronting the proposed solution, however, was how to go about implementing these ideas in practical, detailed ways. Tugwell did not pretend to have all the answers, but he was certain an experimental attitude and approach would provide the answers needed.

For agriculture, on the other hand, Tugwell worked on identifying the individuals associated with domestic allotment as well as understanding the content and specifics of the plan. He worked enthusiastically on both scores, becoming one of the leading spokesmen of domestic allotment among the Roosevelt advisers.

After Roosevelt's nomination was secured, Tugwell presented his own ideas for the campaign with a memorandum calling for the creation of a National Economic Council. Again, Roosevelt listened and even asked Berle to comment, but nothing came of it. As the campaign progressed, moreover, Roosevelt became more vague and ambivalent, frustrating Tugwell even more. It didn't matter, however. In November, Roosevelt won the election and preparations were begun for assuming the presidency.

From November 1932 through March 1933, Tugwell's role as a Roosevelt adviser changed again. As the diary will clearly show, he advised the president-elect on agriculture (specifically domestic allotment), industrial recovery, the London Economic Conference, the banking crisis, the Civilian Conservation Corps, relief, fiscal and monetary programs, the gold standard, and planning. In addition to domestic allotment, Tugwell spent a considerable amount of time and effort on the upcoming London Conference. Initially, he took a nationalist position and argued that it should deal with war debts, disarmament, and general regularization of commodity production. Tugwell wanted Roosevelt to support the payment of debts, isolate disarmament from the debt problem, and promote acceptance of bilateral agreements instead of tariffs. He definitely was opposed to any suggestions of free trade.

On the banking crisis, Tugwell suggested that Roosevelt make use of post offices, establish a corporation to issue script, and set up a national bank. Unfortunately, these ideas were overshadowed by Tugwell's own "faux pax" in the Rand incident. More an embarrassment than anything else, the incident showed Tugwell as naive and too outspoken. Tugwell had lunch with James H. Rand, Jr., chairman of the board of Remington Rand. Tugwell indicated that Roosevelt would let the banking situation develop on its own even if this entailed a collapse. Roosevelt would then blame Hoover and go about reconstructing the American banking system. Rand, of course, immediately told Hoover who, in turn, told the press who, in turn, denounced Tugwell. Fortunately, Roosevelt liked Tugwell so much that he ignored the incident and its political fall-out.

In spite of the Rand incident, as the inauguration approached, Tugwell's role in the administration was discussed. At one point, it looked as if he might be appointed assistant secretary of commerce, a position Tugwell was definitely attracted to. Events, however, had a different way of turning things around and he wound up in the United States Department of Agriculture.

After March 4, 1933, Tugwell again underwent an assignment change. He was now actively involved in the drafting and eventual passage of the Agricultural Adjustment Act and the National Industrial Recovery Act. Once the AAA was set up in May 1933, Tugwell played a key role in its implementation as assistant and later under-secretary of agriculture. While he initially supported George Peek as director, he came to oppose and actually contribute to his resignation in December 1933. To Tugwell, AAA was a first step towards a permanent land-use policy which included land withdrawal, resettlement, and eventual farm consolidation. Peek's emphasis on marketing agreements and his support of the large farmers and processors was too much for Tugwell. He also believed that Peek's refusal to fully endorse production quotas for farmers hurt the program. His resignation was, therefore, most welcomed by Tugwell.

If Peek's removal was a victory for Tugwell, it was short-lived. Peek's replacement, Chester Davis, while more sympathetic to domestic allotment, was not supportive of the liberal faction in the USDA which Tugwell was identified with. By 1935, Davis had had enough of their liberal interference with AAA policies. With Wallace's support, he fired Jerome Frank, Lee Pressman, and several others in the legal division. The "purge," as it was called, was a direct attack on Tugwell. Appalled by Wallace's support of Davis and determined not to stand by and let his friends and supporters be axed, Tugwell threatened to resign. It was only through the direct efforts of the President that he stayed on, although without any authority within or over the AAA. It was a bitter affair for Tugwell and one that he never forgot.

In addition to the AAA, Tugwell's activities in the USDA included reorganization, a project dear to him but without the support of Wallace or Roosevelt. He also worked hard to stop Lewis Douglas from cutting the research budget in the USDA. He played a role too in the early set-up of the Civilian Conservation Corps and served as a helper in the Surplus Relief Corporation. In the CCC, for example, Tugwell supported Roosevelt's efforts to place young men to work at reforestation projects while, in the Surplus Relief Corporation, he helped in providing food for those in need.

In 1933, in line with his responsibilities in the Agriculture department, Tugwell went on an extensive tour of ten western states in order to familiarize himself with the workings of the USDA and to meet with those working "in the field." He also worked, in 1934, on the sugar bill for Puerto Rico and travelled to Europe to present a paper at an international conference. While there, he met with American and foreign officials, one of the most important being Benito Mussolini. In 1934-1935, Tugwell also worked very hard to revise the Pure Food and Drug laws. Of all the activities he participated in, none caused him more grief and stereotyped him as a radical more than this. The food and drug industry went all out to attack him. The Copeland bill, or the Tugwell bill as it quickly came to be known, was designed to put more teeth into the 1906 Pure Food and Drug law as well as to extend its coverage to new areas such as cosmetics. Despite all he did for it, the bill, when eventually passed, was so watered down that Tugwell saw almost no advance in it.

Finally, by 1935, with his own influence in the USDA waning, Tugwell turned his attention to what became the culmination of his New Deal career -- the creation of the Resettlement Administration. Tugwell designed, organized, directed, and tried to salvage it before he left the New Deal at the end of 1936. A hodgepodge of several agencies' programs including the Federal Emergency Relief Administration and the Department of Interior, the RA was to conserve America's land by retiring poor land from agricultural use, to help farmers on submarginal land find new land to cultivate, and to construct suburban towns or garden cities in America. Recruiting an exceptionally able staff and dividing his organization into workable districts and functional categories, Tugwell made the RA a highly visible and effective New Deal program. In the end, the "greenbelt towns" would be attacked, the resettlement programs criticized, and the entire organization dismantled, but it still represented Tugwell's thinking on permanent land-use policies and his hope for planning within the American political and economic system.

All of these activities were extensive in scope and importance. But, they were not everything that Tugwell did. At the same time all of this was going on, he served as a spokesman and defender of the New Deal, writing articles and columns as well as giving speeches. He also took upon himself (although he said FDR wanted it anyway) to serve as a liaison between the president and the Congressional progressives, such as Robert LaFollette. The other major undertaking which he participated in was the creation of the National Recovery Administration and the eventual resignation of Hugh Johnson and demise of the NRA itself. Here, Tugwell was involved in the early organizing group efforts, the compromises reached before the NRA was set up, and the actual appointment of the director. Once the NRA was in operation, Tugwell was brought in at key moments to see what was going on and to determine what could be done to salvage the program, especially in terms of personnel. The Supreme Court, however, had another view of the NRA and acted in 1935 to completely overhaul it.

Tugwell was so angry at the Schechter decision that he appealed to Roosevelt to seek an amendment to the Constitution which would "clip the wings" of the overly powerful court. In the short-run, he also suggested his own Industrial Adjustment Act, a plan whereby Roosevelt would apply the principles of the AAA to industrial recovery efforts. Later, Tugwell endorsed Mordecai Ezekiel's Industrial Expansion Plan to replace the NRA. By then, Roosevelt had other things on his mind and none of these suggestions were taken seriously.

For Tugwell, 1935-1936 saw his own position declining to the point where he accepted the inevitable conclusion that his resignation was the only thing left. Blaming people like Ben Cohen and Tom Corcoran and the entire Brandeis anti-trust, atomistic approach to economic affairs, Tugwell left the New Deal without any bitterness or regret, seeing his tenure as a unique opportunity to serve FDR and the public.

New York/Puerto Rico, 1938 - 1946

In spite of his work in the New Deal and in many ways because of it, Tugwell was not welcomed to return to university life. Columbia University did not want him nor did any other academic community. Without a job and with a family to support, Tugwell accepted the generous offer of his friend, Charles Taussig, and became a vice president for the American Molasses Company. It was a short stay, however. By 1938, after a divorce from his first wife and a marriage to his former associate Grace Falke, Tugwell returned to public service. At the invitation of Fiorello La Guardia, he became the chairman of the New York City Planning Commission (NYCPC).

Recognizing LaGuardia's own lack of enthusiasm for the NYCPC, Robert Moses' staunch opposition, and the entrenched business and real estate interests in New York, Tugwell still thought much could be accomplished in his new role as chairman. It was, indeed, a hope he had, but one that did not materialize. Again, in spite of his best efforts in addressing problems in housing and zoning and in attempting to commit the city to a Master Plan, Tugwell encountered so much opposition that he began to look for a way out of a difficult position in the NYCPC. By 1940, one appeared due to the largesse of Harold Ickes.

Secretary of Interior Ickes asked Tugwell to investigate the 500-acre law in Puerto Rico. This was not as unusual a request as one might imagine. Tugwell was familiar with Puerto Rico since 1934 when he had worked on the sugar bill and his relations with Ickes had always been cordial and friendly. Tugwell's report on the 500-acre law eventually coincided with an opening for the Chancellorship of the University of Puerto Rico and governorship of Puerto Rico. Being at the right place at the right time surely paid off for Tugwell. By 1941, he was offered both the Chancellorship and governorship, a situation his enemies found so disagreeable that Tugwell was forced to resign the former.

As governor of Puerto Rico, Tugwell had to address the problems of World War II there, especially the threat of German submarines and the rationing of food and supplies. The years 1942 and 1943 were particularly difficult in both respects, but Tugwell pulled the small island through. He also worked very closely with the popular leader of the Populares Party, Luis Muñoz Marín. Together, both of them engineered a sweeping reform of Puerto Rico's political and economic system. By 1945, Tugwell had a long list of accomplishments including the creation of the Water Resources Authority, a budget bureau, a Development Bank of Puerto Rico, the Agricultural Company, an Institute of Tropical Agriculture, the Planning Law of 1942, revision of the Organic Act, and many others. It was an impressive feat, but it was also his last as a public servant. By 1946, Tugwell believed his time had come to resign as governor.

Academic Life Again, 1946 - 1979

Unlike 1937 when he was not a welcomed sight in academic circles, Tugwell returned to academe quite differently in 1947. A much sought after commodity, he served at a number of universities and in a number of different positions, ranging from consultant to visiting professor to director of programs. Like his pre-New Deal career, his post-Puerto Rico life was similar in how prolific he was. Aside from two "political" asides with the Wallace presidential campaign in 1948 and the Broyles investigation of all "suspect" Americans in 1950, Tugwell stayed in academe. From 1946 until his death on July 21, 1979, he wrote an enormous number of books, articles, books reviews, and newspaper columns. In all of it, though, four major themes emerged--the atomic bomb, national and global planning, Franklin D. Roosevelt, and the re-writing of the American Constitution. In almost every respect, the culmination of his evolving thinking on issues occurred. Seeing himself now as a political scientist and not a professional economist, Tugwell believed the atomic bomb represented the failure of his generation. He was so obsessed and depressed by it that he persistently wrote about it, seeking to understand why it happened and how to avoid its use in the future.

Now, planning on a national and global scale assumed even more importance. To Tugwell, planning was the only hope for mankind. As early as 1937, his writings on planning had taken a more fundamental and specific turn. No longer speaking of planning as a philosophical approach to problems, he now got down to its details in every conceivable way while developing a much more sophisticated theoretical and practical framework for it.

If planning was the world's only chance, another Franklin D. Roosevelt was America's only hope. Tugwell bemoaned over and over the leadership of the United States after Roosevelt's death. He addressed this persistently, searching and probing into who and what Roosevelt was and what he did accomplish and fail to do. Until such time as he appeared, Tugwell was afraid for America's future.

To confront that fear, he began to call earnestly for a rewriting of the American Constitution and a re-structuring of America's political system. Having lost all respect for the judicial and political branches of the U. S. government, Tugwell's constitution was based on a complete overhaul of America's values and politics. Although criticized by some as a "pie in the sky" academic exercise, Tugwell's new constitution represented a life-time of thinking, reflecting, and acting. In fact, Tugwell died in 1979 still concerned about how to implement it.

Final Thoughts

In the diary that follows, Rexford G. Tugwell will emerge as he was and not as others thought or wanted him to be. He was a unique, complex man. He consistently sought to learn about the world in which he lived by his reading, life experiences, and the people he came into contact with. In some ways, he was a paradox because he experienced tension between what he liked and what he wanted or thought needed to happen.

If the diary shows nothing else, it will demonstrate that Tugwell was a man who "wrote out loud," how he constantly probed issues and attempted to understand and refine his own positions on them. A personality will emerge too of a man who was strong-willed and self-confident, a man who often was too outspoken and sometimes too arrogant and condescending. Yet, beneath all of this, was a man who cared about people and about the world he lived in. He wanted so much for everyone to share in America's abundance, and he was angry and frustrated when they didn't. In those moments, Tugwell the so-called radical appeared. Bear in mind, though, that he was never a revolutionary, always an evolutionary. And, for himself, it all boiled down to service-- service to one's home, one's country, and, in the end, to mankind.

Rexford G. Tugwell Diary:
An Explanation

The Rexford Tugwell papers are located in the Franklin D. Roosevelt Library in Hyde Park, New York. The collection consists of 114 boxes and 9 scrapbooks. This represents Tugwell's original donation of papers to the library as well as a 1982 accretion given by his wife. The accretion was eventually interfiled in the original collection. The papers contain a wide variety of materials, including Tugwell's correspondence, writings, transcripts of speeches and interviews, photographs, newspaper clippings, and miscellaneous items. One of the most important parts of the collection is the Tugwell diary contained in boxes 30 through 42.

The diary begins in 1932 and continues through 1960. It is fairly representative in original entries during the New Deal years (1932-1935) and Tugwell's tenures as chairman of the New York City Planning Commission and governorship of Puerto Rico (1939-1946). After 1946, the diary is sporadic and inconsistent with entries centering on Tugwell's personal situation more than on his thoughts or opinions on events going on around him. The post-1946 diary, in fact, tends to be more a journal and series of personal notes (frequently handwritten) rather than a carefully composed work. In spite of this, the entire Tugwell diary, taken as a whole, is quite illuminating in scope and content.

Another important point to bear in mind is that Tugwell frequently relied on his diary in his own publications. There are four works in particular where he quoted, reproduced, or used it -- The Brains Trust (New York: Viking Press, 1968), Roosevelt's Revolution: The First Year, A Personal Perspective (New York: Macmillan, 1977), The Stricken Land: The Story of Puerto Rico (New York: Doubleday, 1947), and A Chronicle of Jeopardy, 1945-1955 (Chicago: University Press of Chicago, 1955). Within the Tugwell papers, moreover, there are some incomplete manuscripts dealing with his activities as a New Dealer in 1933-1934, extensive notes which he planned to use in drafting a manuscript on his

1934 trip to Europe, and even personal handwritten notes to scholars whom Tugwell expected would go through his papers. If nothing else, Tugwell not only made the most use of whatever he had written but he also was well aware of the importance of his own career.

In the pages that follow, Tugwell's New Deal diary is presented. There are actually two different New Deal diaries given. The first is the original which Tugwell kept during his years in the Roosevelt administration, specifically covering the period, 1932 through 1935. Given Tugwell's activities as assistant and undersecretary of Agriculture as well as his other duties such as serving on committees, public apologist for the New Deal, liaison with the progressives in Congress, and later director of the Resettlement Administration, it is understandable why he could not be as faithful to his diary as he may have wanted. Sometimes, when he was unable to keep a daily record of events, he would summarize the activities of the previous days in one entry. This explains, to a large degree, why some entries are longer than others. Unfortunately, however, there were still significant gaps, the most glaring of which is the period, June 1933 - March 1934. On a daily basis, this also explains why some months have only 1 or 2 entries and others have none. Tugwell simply was just too busy at times. He was very aware of this, so much so that he attempted to correct it later in his revised diary. Nevertheless, what does exist of the original diary is still quite impressive.

In 1952, Tugwell seriously thought about publishing his New Deal diary. As a professor of planning at the University of Chicago, Tugwell was concerned with his professional advancement and financial situation. The University Press of Chicago expressed some interest in the work, but nothing ever materialized. Although written twenty years later, the revised diary was and remains important because Tugwell tried to fill in the gaps in his original diary while he reflected on what had transpired during his days in the Brains Trust, the United States Department of Agriculture, and the Resettlement Administration. In the revised diary, he kept the original entries in tact, sometimes making only minor grammatical or word changes. He frequently added extensive footnotes to identify the individuals he was discussing or to explain why events occurred the way they did or at least the way he remembered them. A more frequently used technique in the 1952 diary was his inserting substantial amounts of a variety of materials, including detailed timetables, newspaper articles, correspondence, memorandum, and speeches he had given. He also worked assiduously to fill in the gaps in the original diary. This is especially important for the June 1933 - March 1934 time frame. While the revised diary needs to be assessed in light of the 20-year intervening period, it is still an important source on Tugwell as a New Dealer and on the New Deal itself.

Original Diary, 1932-1935

Between the time Tugwell entered the Brains Trust in 1932 until his resignation in 1936, he attempted to record the events in which he was involved. As will be seen, Tugwell was quite frank and outspoken in expressing his opinions on individuals he dealt with, legislation he worked on, or assignments either he took upon himself or which were given to him by Franklin Roosevelt. He invariably demonstrated the frustrations he confronted vis-à-vis individuals and/or events, the evolution of his own thinking on the issues he had to address, and the growing admiration and affection he had for Roosevelt. Throughout it all, Tugwell the professional economist, Brains Truster, governmental official, and New Dealer emerges.

In the original diary, Tugwell's entries were for the following periods: December, 1932, January, February, March, April, and May 1933, March, April, May, June, September, October, November, December 1934, and January, February, March, April, May, June, August, September 1935. In all, there are approximately 150 entries along with a few specific attachments Tugwell included such as personal letters or press conferences. Not surprisingly, the topics covered depended upon what Tugwell was doing at that time. In 1932, for example, the entries deal with Roosevelt's election, the Hoover-Roosevelt exchanges, the London Economic Conference, and Tugwell's growing interest and commitment to domestic allotment. The 1933 diary focuses on the depression, world economic conditions (especially tariffs, the gold standard, and debts), the Agricultural Adjustment Administration, foreign policy in the Far East and Europe, the banking crisis, reorganization in the United States Department of Agriculture, and revision of the Pure Food and Drugs laws. The 1934 diary centers its attention on Tugwell's trip to Europe, his work on Puerto Rico and the sugar bill, his speeches and writings, National Recovery Administration and its problems, USDA internal affairs, and agricultural problems generally. Finally, the 1935 entries address the purge in the USDA, Tugwell's own work in the Resettlement Administration, Pure Food and Drugs legislation, the Supreme Court, and Tugwell's relationship with Congressional progressives. Tugwell also consistently talked about individuals with whom he had any dealings throughout the New Deal diary.

Revised Diary

The 1952 diary attempted to elaborate on the original diary entries. Typically, Tugwell went through his original writings for the

New Deal years, occasionally making minor cosmetic changes in the writing or grammar while spending most of his time explaining what the original entries were about. He did this by putting together extensive timetables, detailed explanatory footnotes, and attaching specific newspaper articles, correspondence, or memorandum which he believed placed the topic of that specific entry in better context. In the selective portions of the revised diary which follow, the reader will see clearly how this was all done. In Tugwell's introduction, for example, he discusses the gap in his diary from the time he entered the Brains Trust until "some time after" Roosevelt was elected. He goes on to give insightful reflections on what he did in the early days of the New Deal and what he thought Roosevelt eventually accomplished. "The Hundred Days" and the "Addendum to the Hundred Days" is a good example of how Tugwell took his original diary entries and elaborated on them with footnotes, attachments, and a retrospective recounting of what he himself was doing in that period. "Monetary Preliminaries," "World Economic Conference," and "Intimations of CCC" each detail what the event or topic was about as well as what Tugwell's role was in each instance. Finally, "June 1933-March 1934" is a detailed account of what happened during this period and Tugwell's own activities in all of it. Here, Tugwell was specifically trying to fill in the gaps in the original New Deal diary.

Editor's Notes

In editing the Tugwell New Deal diary, every effort has been made to verify the entries and to keep them in tact. Except for obvious spelling or grammatical errors, the originals are reproduced as they had been written in the 1930s. Occasionally, the reader will encounter two conventions -- "...." and "sic." These are used respectively to indicate that Tugwell either forgot to include an attachment he referred to in the original or revised diary or his writing in that entry was exactly as it has been reproduced in this book.

Another stylistic change incorporated concerns Tugwell's footnoting scheme in the selected portions of the revised diary. Tugwell frequently numbered his footnotes by page only so that each page began with a new footnote 1. To assist the reader in following the diary as well as to accommodate the advances in word processing, a consecutive footnoting system has been employed.

Whether in the original diary or the selections of the revised diary, Tugwell persistently mentioned individuals, legislation, and events he encountered or saw going on around him. To facilitate the reading of the diary, an extensive glossary has been included at the end of the book. All individuals mentioned, specific legislation referred to, American and/or world events addressed by the diary are included in the glossary. The only exception to this procedure is when the diary itself identified or explained the individual or item under discussion.

Similarly, explanatory footnotes by the editor have been placed in the original and revised diary sections of the book. These have been used only when and in those instances where the text needed an additional comment so as to assist the reader in following the diary. Finally, a bibliography, specifically on the 1920s and 1930s, has been included to identify the writings Tugwell cites in the diary entries and to help those readers who might want to pursue any interest they may have in Rexford Tugwell.

ORIGINAL DIARY

1932

Memorandum
December 20, 1932

Attached to this there is the original draft of the telegram sent by
F.D.R. to Hoover in response to his request that Roosevelt join in
appointing members of the commission to examine the debts. The
background of this telegram is especially interesting. It goes back, of
course, to the situation which arose immediately after the election. On
November 10th and several succeeding days many of the countries which
owed us governmental debts presented notes asking for delay and
reexamination of their obligations to us. Mr. Hoover had not yet returned
from California where he went for Election Day. He telegraphed to
Roosevelt to cooperate with him in handling this matter, stating the
seriousness of the situation and suggesting the reconstitution of the Debt
Funding Commission.

It happened that on the day on which Hoover's telegram was
received at Albany I had come to see Roosevelt bringing H. Parker Willis
and James Harvey Rogers for a general discussion of proposed banking
legislation. After our interview the Governor asked me if I would not stay
that evening. I of course said I would. He was just recovering from a
rather serious attack of influenza. He lunched alone at his desk in the
study while the rest of us ate in the breakfast room as usual. (In all the
times I have been at Albany I have never yet eaten in the state dining
room. Roosevelt prefers the informality of the breakfast room.) After
luncheon on this particular day the Governor asked me to come in alone
before he talked with all of us together and he then told me about the

circumstances of the Hoover telegram and asked me to think over during the afternoon what ought to be done, suggesting that I stay until that night when Raymond Moley was to come to Albany. We then had our general conversation concerning the Glass bill for banking reform and Willis and Rogers left. I saw the Governor again for a few moments and he told me that he had determined to accept Hoover's invitation to come to Washington and said that he would do it on his way south to Warm Springs. He said also that he would take Moley with him to the conference. I was naturally very much pleased at this since it meant that the advice of academic people still continued to be valuable to him even though he was now in the position of President-elect and could, of course, command the advice and time of anyone in the country. He acted so quickly in this matter that he announced to the newspapermen at the afternoon press conference that he would take Moley with him to the conference with Hoover. Moley knew nothing about it until he arrived in Albany about ten o'clock.

The Governor was not feeling very well so that the only other caller he saw during that day was Cardinal Mundelein of Chicago with whom, however, he talked for a long time. After the Cardinal left we sat for nearly two hours between tea and dinner in the study before the fire and he came back again to the question of the depression and what could be done in the way of fundamental relief. I went over again my usual thesis that the policy for handling it ought to be determined on the selective basis and that we ought not to attempt to either inflate or deflate exclusively and that in certain instances deflation ought to be cushioned where genuine hardship was involved, as in the case of savings banks and insurance companies. I dined with him alone with Miss Tully and Miss Lehand and we afterwards spent the whole evening in further discussions of the economic situation in general, including the debt problem.

I had been expecting to go home that night. He then asked whether I would not stay and assist in the preparation for the conference. I felt at that time that all the problems before us ought to be included in the discussions of the conference: disarmament, intergovernmental debts, the problem of the stabilization of currency, the control of commodity production throughout the world, and tariffs. He was reluctant from the first to involve all these things in one general discussion and began to work out in his mind at that time the distinction which afterwards became so clear. This was that some problems are and remain economic but that some economic problems suddenly become political questions. He was not able at first to state this point of view very clearly and I did not at once grasp the distinction, but afterwards it seemed to me perfectly obvious. The immediate problem before us was that of the intergovernmental debts which we then began to study intensively, continuing in Albany until Saturday when the Governor left to go to Hyde Park and Moley and myself came to New York where we continued to study the problem almost night and day until the next Tuesday when the Governor and Moley left in the morning to go to the White House.

As we worked on the problem it became more and more clear that the debt question was more political than economic. Congress and the country in general were determined against cancellation. There was equal determination not to pay amongst legislators and others abroad. This situation became something of an impasse. It was our opinion all along that most countries were able to and would pay on December 15th which in the event was partially substantiated. Great Britain made her full payment, France, Belgium and some of the smaller countries refusing to pay.

After the White House conference the Governor and Moley went on to Warm Springs and I remained in New York. When they returned from Warm Springs we again took up the question of international economic relations which was once more becoming an immediate problem. The two delegates appointed to the preliminary meeting in Geneva on October 27th had been Dr. E. E. Day of the Rockefeller Foundation and Dr. John Williams of Harvard. I had talked informally with Day before he went and with Governor Roosevelt concerning the problems to be raised at the economic conference in Geneva. Nobody in the present administration seemed to have clearly in mind what the agenda ought to be. They had much more clearly in mind what they were determined not to have discussed which was, of course, the war debts and the tariffs. I told Day before he left that we were just finishing a campaign in which the problem of the tariffs had been one of the chief issues and that it certainly would be added to the agenda if we had anything to say about it.

While Day and Williams were attending the first preliminary meeting the campaign ended and Governor Roosevelt was elected. It became obvious at once that Hoover's restrictions on the agenda of the conference would need to be modified unless the conference were over and done with before March 4th when the Republicans were to go out of power. Immediately on his return, therefore, Day telephoned me and I went down to see him. He told me that the general results of the conference had been fairly futile. They had merely passed a pious resolution or two concerning return to the gold standard and had disbanded to meet again in January with the vague notion in mind that the conference itself, of which these meetings were only "organization" meetings, would meet in early April. Subsequently Moley and myself had another conversation with Day at the Harvard Club at which we explained to him our attitude toward debts. This was that they ought not to be cancelled and that even their writing down would require a considerable preparation of public opinion in this country; consequently the affairs of the Economic Conference, if we hoped it to succeed, ought not to be mixed up with all the emotional considerations which now surrounded the problem of the war debts. Otherwise, no one at the Conference would think of anything but war debts and we should never get beyond that discussion. He demurred. He thought the debts ought to be drawn into the pot along with other things, just as I had felt previously, until Governor Roosevelt convinced me that this was a political rather than an economic problem and that although we might think it better to forgive the debts, still what was the use if public opinion was dead set against it. Besides, I must confess that in going into it further I came to see it more and more clearly. I began to see that it was unnecessary to cancel the debts entirely and began to have a feeling that many of those Americans in the Middle West who were so bitter about cancellation had perhaps a shrewd conception of the right in the matter. If we should make the grand gesture of renunciation, as we were asked to do by the European countries, it would certainly not forward any of the other purposes we had in mind. They would smile at us as Clemenceau once smiled at Wilson in any generous gesture of this sort which we might make. The transfer problem, on closer study, seemed less and less impossible. It would seem particularly hard to explain how it was that interest and amortization payments on some fifteen to eighteen billion dollars of private debt could be transferred annually, an amount which it was difficult to estimate at less than five hundred million dollars a year, when it was entirely impossible, according to the arguments we heard so much, to transfer approximately half that amount for the account of the public debts. I think, also, that I was influenced a good deal in a severe way by the propaganda machinery which was immediately put in motion by all the foreign countries in the attempt to influence not only American opinion but especially the action of Governor Roosevelt with those of us who were known to be his close advisers. We never knew the source of the many approaches which were made to us (at least I never did) but it was not too difficult to imagine that most of them originated in New York City not far from the offices of the investment bankers who had so great an interest in the payments of the private debt. It was an easy inference that the forgiving of the public debt would make the private debts much more easy to collect. Both Moley and myself travelled about the same road in this respect. As we went further into the matter and as pressures were brought to bear from every side, our reaction was distinctly against cancellation and against any immediate move to postpone the payments due on December 15th. We therefore counselled Governor Roosevelt not to join with Mr. Hoover in any move of this kind. It was not so much that we felt it would be politically disastrous to the Governor as that we had been convinced, on examining the evidence, that the European countries, in spite of propaganda to the contrary, both could and would pay. We felt that the position of England warranted more leniency than that of any other country, she having made arrangements at a time when she was economically more prosperous than was France when her arrangements were made and consequently paid a rate of interest which was at least twice as high. This seemed to us something to be negotiated about in the future. In fact, we felt that we ought not to take a dogmatic stand about any of the future payments succeeding that of December 15th but we did feel that the problem ought to be approached by Governor Roosevelt himself through the ordinary diplomatic channels or by private negotiation and that so emotional a problem ought not to be mixed up with the deeper and more permanent affairs which would be involved in the discussions at the Economic Conference.

I similarly withdrew from my first position concerning disarmament. I had at first felt, as many other people did, that one of our main points of policy was the securing of disarmament in Europe so that we ourselves could lighten the burden of armament costs at home; and I thought that since international negotiation was something in the nature of a poker game we ought to further this policy by our ability to grant something concerning the debts. I became convinced on thinking it over, however, that even these two things ought not to be discussed jointly. The chief reason why I felt this way was that any forgiveness of the debts would be a permanent arrangement and that disarmament is a perennial matter. It is a victory which is never completely won. It requires constant negotiation. It is a thing in which we shall be involved for many years. We might make concessions on the debts and get in return concessions in disarmament but there would be nothing to prevent new crises in Europe from causing another race for armaments there.

Original Draft[1]

Dear Mr. President: I have given earnest consideration to your courteous telegram of December 17 and I want to assure you that I seek in every proper way to be of help.

It is my view that the questions of disarmament, intergovernmental debts, and permanent economic arrangements will be found to require selective, perhaps individual, treatment though with full recognition of the possibility that in the ultimate outcome the interrelationship of any two or of all three may become clear.

As to disarmament: your policy is clear and satisfactory. Some time, however, is required to bring it to fruition. Success in a practical program of limiting armaments, abolishing certain instruments of

[1]Handwritten by Tugwell.

warfare, and decreasing the offensive or attack power of all nations will in my judgment, have a positive and salutary influence on debt and economic discussions.

As to the debts: If the debtor nations desire to approach us they should be given earliest opportunity to do so. Certainly in preliminary conversations the chief executive has full authority either through the existing machinery of the diplomatic service or by supplementing it with specially appointed agents of the president himself to conduct such preliminary conversations or surveys without in any way seeking formal congressional action.

I am impelled to suggest, however, that these surveys should be limited to determining facts and exploring possibilities rather than fixing policies binding on the incoming administration. I wholly approve and would in no way hinder the making of such surveys.

As to the economic conference, I am clear that a permanent economic program for the world should not be submerged in conversations relating to disarmament and debts. I recognize, of course, a relationship, but not an identity. Therefore I cannot go along with the suggestion that the personnel conducting the conversations should be identical.

By reason of the fact that under the constitution I am unable to assume authority in the matter of the agenda for the economic conference until after March 4 next, and by reason of the fact that there appears to be a divergence of opinion between us with respect to the scope of the conference, and by reason of the fact that time is required to carry the conversations concerning debts and disarmament further toward solution, I most respectfully suggest that the final determination of the program of the economic conference, and the appointing of the delegates be held in abeyance until after March 4.

Meanwhile I can see no objection to further informal conferences with the agenda committee, or to the carrying on of preliminary economic studies which would serve an undoubtedly useful purpose. (Add two to American group making agenda.)

I feel it would be both improper for me and inadvisable for you, however much I appreciate the courtesy of your suggestion, if I should take part in naming representatives, who from the necessity of the case must be subject wholly to your authority and supervision. They could be responsible only and properly to you as President for the effective performance of their assignments, particularly in matters calling for almost daily touch with and direction from the Executive. I would be in no position, prior to March 4 to have that constant contact.

December 23, 1932

I have been ill for two days and out of things. In the meantime the exchange of telegrams between Hoover and Roosevelt has been made public together with two supplementary telegrams in which I had no part. It seems to me that these telegrams have made Roosevelt's situation perfectly clear and that for people who are new to the formulation of public policy we have come off fairly well in this exchange with a group who have been in charge of these matters for the government for a good many years. Our position is more clear-cut, the policy offers more hope of solution and our statement is made with more clarity and candor than was theirs. Governor Roosevelt is still puzzled to know why it is that Hoover insisted again and again on the setting up of a commission which would carry over from his term to another. I think my suggestion was the only tenable one in the circumstances. It is that Mr. Hoover is a different kind of man than Mr. Roosevelt; he is a business executive type and feels he must delegate everything which is why he cannot grasp the notion that the new administration will be run differently. The formal set up of governmental structure will, I imagine, never mean very much to Roosevelt. It means almost everything to Hoover which makes it all the more surprising that so little in the way of functional reorganization has been accomplished in Washington during the last four years. A good deal may be done in that way during the months to come but it will be because Democrats are pledged to economy and because some of the rest of us are interested in the reform of governmental structure rather than because Roosevelt believes it makes very much difference what kind of an administrative organization there is. Everything which has to do with policy will be filtered through his mind. The difficulty will be that he will not always be careful to have continuing advice. He is apt to take it from me at one time, from Moley at another time, and, perhaps if we are not handy, from some senator or congressman who happens to turn up at an opportune moment. An incident of this sort happened yesterday when, Justice Rosenman happened to be in Albany. Both Moley and I were ill. Rosenman either persuaded or advised him to issue a supplementary statement to the telegrams which seems to me to add nothing to our position and, in fact, to take away something from the clean, sharp division which we had set up between our policy and that of the Republicans. (Frankfurter, I have since learned, was also involved in this.)

I had a telephone call this morning from Day who reports having gone to Washington on Tuesday, December 20, and having come home without any great satisfaction in respect to policy. This is no wonder, of course, because at that time Mr. Hoover still hoped he might persuade Roosevelt to his view of policy. Day thought we had much the better of the exchange of views and that our policy was clearly correct. He said, however, that postponing of the agenda meeting still had to be arranged and that for this purpose he was returning to Washington today with

Norman Davis, Chairman of the Disarmament Delegation, who has just arrived from Europe. So far as the formalities go our delegates are supposed to sail next Wednesday for a meeting of the organizing committee for the Conference in London. It is our hope to postpone this until February and in the meantime have informal conversations with the British. Day expressed the hope that this can be arranged. He also said that in view of the Governor's expressed desire to have the preliminaries go forward in preparation for the Disarmament Conference he thought it would be desirable for himself and Williams to have another conference with the Governor some time in the near future to discover the scope of the studies and conversations which they ought to undertake; also whether anyone else ought to be associated with them. I told him that I thought we ought to arrange such a conversation in about a week and would attend to it.

December 24, 1932

My father and mother with little Betty (my sister's daughter - the only sister I had who died suddenly in 1929) motored to New York for Christmas with us. My father and I, with Robert Valeur, took the three girls, Marcia, Betty and Tanis[2], down to the Washington Market to buy a tree, "greens," mistletoe and general holiday trimmings. It seemed a poor excuse for taking the children into the woods to cut a tree and drag it home - as I should always do if I could get to the country - and if I had the children! Still we were quite gay and bought many things including some good cognac and rum at 57th Street at Fays' speakeasy where there was a divine smell of herby French cooking in preparation for an evening party, as Fay said, of "quarante deux Alsatiens." I should imagine forty-two Alsatians could be very festive. Anyhow, we brought the tree home across the fenders and the girls decorated it.

These small and homely festivals mean a lot to me. This one is the first to be complicated by quite so many worries. No one can live and work in New York this winter without a profound sense of uneasiness. Never, in modern times, I should think, has there been so widespread unemployment and the distress of sheer hunger and cold. I suppose I have done what I could both by way of protest against the system which caused the world's situation and by way of suggesting alternatives. It cannot be said now, either, that I have not done what I could to influence policy. My ideas are no longer purely "academic." By that I do not mean that I have had or am having much actual influence on public policy; I simply mean

[2]Marcia and Tanis were Tugwell's daughters from his first marriage to Florence Arnold.

that I have taken pains to argue for my views in the places where policy was being made and have sometimes been listened to. It has always been part of my philosophy that experimentalism is a process, not a book or an article; and my chief interest has always been in public policy. It cannot be said that I have neglected my first real opportunity to join in social experimentation.

This afternoon Day called. He had been in Washington again and I was anxious to know whether he had succeeded in getting a postponement of his trip to London for the organization meeting of the Economic Conference. I was the more anxious because Norman Davis (chairman of our delegation to the disarmament conference) on landing the other day said to reporters that the organization meeting would be held in January and the final conference in April. And, sure enough, Day reported his efforts at postponement futile, largely because of Davis' insistence. Day was puzzled to know what to do. On Sunday the Governor had been clear about desiring postponement; but apparently Davis had been talking with him too. Day feels as strongly as I do that a meeting now in London will come to nothing and will create a difficult situation since the British are sure to talk mostly about debts and to think about them even if they are not talked about. The more permanent matters which might move forward now will be submerged in this atmosphere. Davis may be thinking mostly of his central problem of disarmament which I suppose is threatened by the current irritation over the debts.

I got so worried about the situation of Day and Williams about to go off to London with no clear mandate from anyone and without an adequate background of our policies, that I called the Governor's house even if it was Christmas eve. He was not yet at Hyde Park and I left word that if he wanted to talk about business he might call me at home. He preferred, however, not to interrupt his family party - and I was foolish to do so too, I suppose.

December 25, 1932

Had a long talk with F.D.R. on the telephone and afterward with Day. Our plans for postponing the conference until the debt storm is over seem all to have gone wrong. Davis made a public announcement of a time schedule in today's paper without consulting anyone. I asked Day how it happened that Davis ran things with so high a hand and discovered him to have been much irritated at Davis' treatment of him. He had no intention of letting Day talk to the Governor, for instance, but expected to relay everything through himself. He even had Dulles call Day and arrange an appointment both before and after seeing F.D.R. expecting to get questions to ask and answers to bring back. Apparently Davis thinks he is to be Secretary of State and is beginning early. He has a lot to learn. I told F.D.R. something of all this and suggested the importance of seeing Day and Williams before they go if go they must just now. He asked me to bring them to Albany on Tuesday for a long talk saying that he would ask Davis to stay over. Perhaps we can have a better understanding of where we all stand if we can talk it out. As things are it is my belief that Davis is playing some game of his own although Day feels that his insistence on the January meeting against our desires is merely to save his face. He made the arrangement with the other diplomats without discussing the matter with the experts and now it is determined to see it through. I said it seemed a serious matter to sacrifice so much for so slight an amount of prestige but Day suggested the possibilities which we all know lie in rationalization. That may be all there is to it.

It was a rather nice Christmas. The whole family was together for the first time in several years. R. Valeur was with us. He seems to enjoy the family and I am always sorry for anyone who is a long way from home on Christmas. Coming through Columbus Circle there was a broad line of several hundred men. A nice festival for them! But at any rate things are moving a little. The dinner Morgenthau and I had with Senators Wagner, Costigan and LaFollette seems to have had some effect. That was about two weeks ago at the Mayflower in Washington. We talked about many things but mostly about relief. Just before dinner we were talking to F.D.R. from Henry Morgenthau's room reporting out brilliant success in consolidating the farmers. F.D.R. represented himself as greatly pleased and asked me to request Wagner to introduce a bill immediately for expansion of forestry work. This I did and also had a long talk with him about the desirability of rewriting the organization law for the R.F.C. A few days ago he made his speech about this and we may get the thing done at this session. The Corporation is not run as a relief financing institution but as a bank. Its present officers seem never to have heard the word emergency.

I talked with LaFollette about my ideas concerning industrial reorganization and found him much interested. He, of course, has been interested for a long time in planning. We have exchanged long letters since I came home.

Talking with the Governor today he asked me when I had got back. He evidently thought I had been in Washington again with Morgenthau. The first day I was ill I did have a wire from him saying he was called to Washington but he did not say that F.D.R. expected me to go too. Morgenthau, as a matter of fact, should never be trusted to do anything alone. I like him in many ways but he isn't long on brightness and he is so terribly ambitious just now that it is almost pathetic. I suppose he will get a Federal job but it will never be the Secretaryship. I'm sure F.D.R. knows him too well for that. I still hope it will be Wallace;

but I shall say nothing more to F.D.R. about it.

I understand there is much talk in Washington about Morgenthau and myself as envoys of F.D.R. in starting the legislative program. I do think we had some effect. But this session seems to me likely to be entirely futile in spite of all the bread lines and in spite of any prodding we can do. If we can only get some adequate relief going, the rest can wait. But we shall have a special session for some of the rest of it - farm relief, banking reform, a measure regulating stock selling, government reorganization, etc.

On the question of reorganization: on the way from Hyde Park to Albany last Sunday night, Douglas, F.D.R. and myself talked at length and freely about changes needed in Washington. Douglas very intelligent: liked him a lot and wondered at it in a congressman. Later discovered him to be an Amherst man, etc. We found a common admiration in Walter Wheeler Stewart. I must remember to take him to see the Governor. Some one has already suggested him as assistant for the Treasury. I should be glad to see him Secretary. In our conversation F.D.R. asked Douglas to attach a clause to the appropriations bill giving the President leave to reduce personnel, abolish functions, transfer, etc., his idea being that he might carry out a reorganization (which Congress will never do) and have it done months before Congress comes back. Members could then unload the burdens on him and simply recognize a fait accompli. A new President, he said, can do this and get away with it, if Congress will come through with blanket permission. Evidently Douglas took the mandate seriously for in today's TIMES there is a story foreshadowing such an action - evidently inspired by Douglas, since it mentions him - but showing his good faith. I must see him when I go to Washington. I am sure he can be worked with.

December 26, 1932

This was a rather confused day. A telephone conversation with Day at eleven confirmed our arrangements to go to Albany which I relayed by telephone to F.D.R. at Hyde Park (he being in the bath and the conversation relayed to him through Mrs. Roosevelt). Later, Day called again and said he had had a two-hour conference with Davis who objected strongly to the two delegates' projected visit to F.D.R. His grounds were that there would be attendant publicity and that they would arrive in Geneva expected to know Roosevelt's mind and to speak for him which they could not possibly do. This argument seemed to impress Day. But everyone knows that they have already seen F.D.R. and there seems to me more to be gained by a further acquaintance with his mind than can be lost by some people knowing to go to Albany since Davis had said he would arrange things that way with F.D.R. What will happen as a result of this I do not know. Day said also that he had pleaded with Stimson and Davis for two hours trying to get them to adopt the time schedule agreed on in Albany Sunday. Davis, however, was adamant. He must have reason for this opposition to F.D.R.'s views and probably will present them when they meet tonight. It will be interesting to see what they are.

I determined to go to Albany in the afternoon, hoping to arrive before Davis and to tell the Governor what I have been able to learn. But when I arrived at the executive mansion Davis was already closeted with him and I was told to come back at 9:30 in the morning. So the results are still confused.

It was more satisfactory to have had a conversation this morning with the son of David Lubin, the founder of the International Institute of Agriculture in Rome. This Lubin is a state official in California, is interested in agriculture (is opposed to our allotment plan) in Pan American relations and, of course, as a matter of family pride, in the Institute. He is a nice person without great ability, I should say, and is distinctly laissez faire. I succeeded pretty well in keeping the conversation to the Institute. I feel that our withdrawal from participation in its work was a mistake. It was a result of Asher Hobson's quarrel with the Italians. No doubt they ran things irritatingly in the early days of Fascism, but at least part of the fault seems to have been his. He was the American delegate to the Permanent Committee, as I understand, at that time, and Lubin says he was asked to withdraw. The U.S. then withdrew its support. This was a blow to the Institute and badly crippled its work but things have changed now. At the last Assembly meeting an arrangement with the League of Nations was ratified whereby the Institute takes over all agricultural work for the League - which is as it should be.

The Italians have settled down now, too, and we ought to explore ways of setting up relationships again. Our contribution could be saved many times over if we would stop trying to duplicate the Institute's work in our own Department. On this whole matter Lubin gave me a memorandum. It contains a letter from Easterbrook with practical suggestions for coordination. Lubin feels that we should go back to the Institute with only two conditions: that the Secretary-General should be elected by the Permanent Committee (which consists of a representative of each adhering government) with complete freedom. This is where, in the past, Italian domination has been felt and resented. And that there should be no nationalist bias in the selection of the staff. There are technicians anyhow and this should not be difficult.

The future greater service of the Institute depends, Lubin believes, on the discovery of better representatives for the Permanent Committee. At present only the English representative is of the old caliber; the rest are attachés of embassies or others appointed for reasons of economy or convenience.

December 27, 1932

At 9:30 I went to F.D.R.'s bedroom and found Davis there. F.D.R. apologized handsomely for not having me in on the conference of the night before, saying he wanted to make up his mind about Davis by letting him talk alone. I was naturally curious about whether Day and Williams were to be seen. They were not. Davis and I were to go to New York together and see Day at Davis' house; Davis has his way about this too. We talked about agenda for the conference, Davis showing me one of the financial aspects prepared by Loveday of the league. We talked about things in general for an hour or two and then Davis and I went to take a noon train. F.D.R. on leaving said that things on my end were going well in Washington but that he did not like the sudden talk of Congressional conversions to sales taxes which were being made to appear as coming from him. I suggested the alternative of lowering the income tax brackets and raising the rates and left him thinking that over. He asked me to go to Washington on the farm legislative business in a week.

What happened in the Davis affair was really a compromise. Davis had his way about the preliminary meeting of experts - Day and Williams are to sail tomorrow - and about their not seeing F.D.R. But he had to give way on his commitment for the conference meeting early in April. He told reporters last night it could not come until summer.

On the train Davis and I talked about numerous things. He complimented us on the campaign and produced an alibi for not being active, saying he had to be in Europe. Stimson told him, he said, that there was no Republican capable of handling the disarmament negotiations. I get a first impression of an able, resourceful man, but one whose motives I cannot quite understand unless there is personal aggrandizement of a special political sort in the back of his head. We talked about the debts and I suggested that here was a job for a trained diplomat - to discover a face-saving formula which could be agreed on by everyone. He said he would try to find it since he agreed that it stood in the way of any other international arrangements. The debts furnish a great barrier to trade, he said, because the exchange-controls of European nations are maintained in fear of losses - and some debt arrangement could give the reassurance needed. They would then give up restrictions of all sorts.

We left the train at 125th Street and went straight to his house. Day came there and we talked for an hour agreeing to meet next morning at eleven at Davis' office, when Williams could be present. Day still felt the debts ought to be included in the agenda as our strongest trading point. To this I would agree if I were sure F.D.R. could, in the time, reduce American opinion to sufficient flexibility so that we could use them to bargain with. But the June 15 payments are going to press him for some arrangement anyhow and he is going to have to try to loosen up opinion both here and abroad, a situation of which he is wholly aware.

December 28, 1932

What is more than anything else responsible for the continuance of this depression is, I am convinced, the persistent disparity among groups of prices. We often speak of ours as a price system but we seldom consider what this means. In the course of any period of stability we work out adjustments among various groups in the community. Each of them makes something or performs some service and this comes to have a price attached to it which will permit others to buy it with the prices which they have had attached to whatever they make. During a period of comparative stability in the price structure there are some disparities here but they are not serious and go unnoticed in the whole. When, however, there is a rapid change in the level of prices, all the individual characteristics of each group of prices is accentuated; some have far greater resistance to change than others. It is apparent that if all changed proportionately and at the same time the process of exchange would not be interrupted because the existing relationships would not be disturbed. The price of any single thing would buy as much as it was accustomed to do of every other thing. But when, as has happened since 1929, there is a violent recession of many prices and when, at the same time, many stay at their old levels, or fail to recede as rapidly, the buying power among those who divide up the proceeds of the fast-falling ones is diminished and is similarly enlarged among those who divide up the change-resisting ones. This is exactly the stage we are now in. Those who receive incomes from occupations whose goods continue to be priced at old levels are discovering how difficult it is to get the best of a system. They have succeeded in keeping up their prices and so have enhanced their own nominal power to command the goods of others. The difficulty is that people whose own price-receipts have fallen cannot purchase so many high value goods; and therefore their own receipts have fallen because of diminished demand. Everyone loses in this process; and everyone would gain from preservation of the old relationships to the general price level. An effective public policy at the present time which undertook to do something about the paralysis in trade would apply pressure to both sides. Some prices ought to go down; some ought to go up. Most obviously, all retail prices have resisted decline in comparison with wholesale prices.

But certain groups are worse offenders: for instance, public utility rates. And here we are frequently absurd when we are in a position to exercise control. For we refuse to require lowered rates because of declining income, not realizing that the reason for declining income is the refusal to reduce rates. Public service commissions are more capable of thinking in social terms, apparently, than any individual business man.

In our system we have no legal way of either raising or lowering prices; but nothing else will hasten the readjustment to a lower price level which is now proceeding so slowly and with so much resistance from those who would gain most from it. A little statesmanlike denouncing of retailers and public utility concerns might do something. Devices, like the domestic allotment plan for agriculture, ought to be really effective on the other side. But we shall in the future have to achieve either a stable price level or some means of public pressure toward adjustment to one which changes.

It seems to me obvious that in such a situation as the present one, general inflation will not procure the results we want because it will spoil the adjustments which during three years have already taken place and will make new readjustments necessary. It would improve the position of old debtors; but it would damage new creditors. It would be favorable to those groups which never adjusted themselves to the new price level; it would injure those who had done so. Many capital structures have been written down, many fixed costs reduced; all this would go for nothing and those who had refused to adjust would be protected in their refusal. All the problems of incidence would, in fact, be raised again. Whether the price level rises or falls the adjustments are equally difficult, only when it is rising we speculate for more rise and so create a false atmosphere of prosperity, and when it is falling we speculate for more fall and so create a depression which is more than reality. We therefore prefer prices to rise. It is change to which there has to be adjustment and which brings out the variety in resistance; it is this which needs to be overcome by control and planning.

In a situation like the present any emergency measures which will have the right effect are justified. Those who protect their prices need denouncing; those who suffer the worst declines need supporting. But all this is a poor substitute for general control of regularity.

The newspapers this morning carry the intimation from Albany that F.D.R. is wholly set against the sales tax. Now if he will come out for a revised and strengthened income tax structure!

December 29, 1932

A good deal of yesterday was spent in going over the material for the agenda of the Economic Conference with Day and Williams who are to sail tonight with Norman Davis. A new suggestion was made as a result of the talk Davis had with Mr. George Harrison, Governor of the Federal Reserve Bank of New York. This was that there should be a conference among the central banks of the world coincident with or perhaps previous to the World Economic Conference. This seemed to me to be a good idea. We went completely over the proposed subjects for the agenda making the point that, as the situation is, it should err rather on the side of inclusiveness than otherwise so that there should be no doubt about anything being available for discussion which we afterwards desired to bring up. I made the point again that debt negotiations would be going on meanwhile and that their position on this must be the assumption that some arrangement would be made before the Conference met.

I was rather pleased when I picked up the morning paper this morning to note that Mr. Davis has been the medium through which Mr. Hoover and Governor Roosevelt had been brought closer together in their foreign policy. The cleverness with which these diplomats learn to forward their own interest in the press is perhaps their chief accomplishment. In these particular negotiations Davis has been a disrupting influence rather than otherwise and yet through his connections he manages to come out with all the credit there is. In this whole negotiating process concerning the Economic Conference I am rather proud that my name has not appeared in the papers once.

This morning I had a talk with Moley reporting to him all that had been done on the Economic Conference affair. He said that he had urged the Governor to persuade Stimson to withdraw the appointments of Day and Williams and appoint Berle and myself in their place but that the Governor had refused to interfere to this extent. Moley still doesn't trust either of them with respect to our point of view abroad. He was very much disappointed about his failure to have his way in this matter and said that he was losing out in another respect which worried him just as much. The Governor seems determined to appoint Former Congressman Swager Sherley Director of the Budget. Moley has always felt that this position ought to be made more of; that, in fact, the Director of the Budget might become roughly analogous to the Chancellor of the Exchequer in Great Britain. Sherley's appointment will certainly not raise that position to any such level. It is true that Sherley was Chairman of the Appropriations Committee of the House during the War, but he has never been known as an outstanding man. Furthermore, he is an extremely sensitive person and there might be quite genuine difficulties of a personal sort in getting along with people.

December 30, 1932

I saw Moley for a half hour this morning. He had just come back from Albany rather discouraged at the kind of advice F.D.R. seems to be accepting. He cursed Felix Frankfurter heartily. There seems to be some bad feeling between them. He said F.D.R. asked him how F.F. would do for Assistant Secretary of State and he had said "My God, never!" Moley certainly has prejudices as well as dislikes. Yet he has intuitions too and sometimes is a lot nearer right than other people with better brains. He has terrible fits of temper, though I have only had one fight with him in all our association. The other day he had a seizure of this kind in talking to a certain Mr. St. Jean over the phone. This particular incident, however, I should call righteous indignation for St. Jean was certainly trying to capitalize on Moley's nearness to F.D.R. (He thinks I ought to be Undersecretary of Commerce. He, himself, will, I think, be either Undersecretary of State or Administrative Assistant to the President.)

I had another talk with Lubin who dithered on for a long time about some South American rapprochement scheme. I got some more information, however, about the Institute of Agriculture and he made the really good suggestion of getting an appropriation into the pending Department bill. I must try to work this out.

Had lunch with John Fennelley. I don't know what it was all about. He is Norman Davis' son-in-law. I think we respect each other but are as far apart in viewpoint as it is possible to get. He is one of those curious young men who seems to have been born with a sixty year old outlook. I was much relieved a few years ago when he resigned here as instructor; he has ability but so much starch in his mind that I think I could never have recommended him for promotion. We talked about farm relief and banking. I got one new slant on the wheat situation.

I had a telephone conversation with George Soule. Several months ago he approached me with a suggestion that I undertake a research project looking to the setting up of a private institute for the study of planning. I said I was interested and that curiously enough, something of the sort had been suggested by Day of the Rockefeller Foundation. He asked me to write the outline of a scheme of study which I did sometime in November. He wants now to see me about this next week and I am a loss to know what to say. Ought I to go into the government - if and when asked - or ought I to encourage this group to subsidize a year's study of planning? I shall try to put off having to decide as long as possible.

December 31, 1932

A quiet day alone in my office seems to be an opportunity for running back over my relationship to the farm relief bill (called the domestic allotment plan or price-parity plan) today reported out by Marvin Jones' Committee. My general interest in farm relief goes back a long way. Since my graduate-school days I have always been able to excite myself more about the wrongs of farmers than those of urban workers. It is partly, then, a matter of temperament.

The first serious study I gave to the problem was in 1922-23 in the course of writing the book on economics which never was published (I took Thor Hultgren in on the project. In 1928 he undertook to rewrite the Ms. and, as I learned on a recent visit to Washington, has done very little on it even yet). There was to be a chapter on Agriculture which, when I had written it seemed sufficiently timely to publish. It came out in the Political Science Quarterly in 1924; there was some discussion of it and it at once earned me an unwarranted reputation as an agricultural economist. But since that time I have had a special interest in that field, and especially the problem of public policy as it affects agriculture. I have done more writing on it, too. The longest work was my study of "Agricultural Policy in France" which appeared serially in the P.S.Q. during 1930. But the thing which most nearly expressed my views was an article written at C. L. King's request for THE ANNALS while I was in France. It is one of my best jobs, perhaps because I wrote it at leisure in that little study overlooking the Mediterranean at the bottom of the garden. That was when we lived on the Rue St. Jin Jin out on the Point de la Croisette in Cannes. (I should like another such leisurely opportunity to put things together in my mind; this working under continual pressure tends to get things done but it sometimes cramps the imagination. Any contributions to scholarship and literature I am likely to make will consist in the development of alternative suggestions - something strange and new - which I shall probably leave as mere suggestions rather than as finished tasks. I know myself that well at least; and I know therefore that looking at my career from the point of view of cultural history I ought to be loafing in a Mediterranean garden all the time with a pen and paper handy. In that way I might come through with creative ideas in a fairly steady stream. As it is, my activities tend to check and control their generation. I am aware that there is another side to this and I am not qualified, perhaps, to make so definite a commitment as I sometimes think. I have noticed that I sometimes generate creative ideas in very exigent situations and in the midst of confused activity. Perhaps the very pressure fuses solutions in the mind. It is a mysterious business at best. But my recent experience with the price-parity principle and the logical basis for it which seemed to pop into my mind without warrant or reason in the middle of a conference is a case in point. Within a week I had the thing all worked out and it is now accepted as the basis for agricultural price adjustment rather than the tariff basis which was formerly used. Perhaps I belong in the hubbub of controversy rather than in that Mediterranean garden. But I do desire tranquility with a deep desire and I never get it - or so it seems. Perhaps this desire is father to the thought that I should function best that way!)

When I first began to study farm relief as a public policy my critical sense rejected the McNary-Haugen ideas, although then I knew very little about background or the political considerations which were involved. So much can be seen from my writings. But the thing which always troubled me most and which still does was the insistence on restriction and negative planning rather than on the positive policy which I thought ought to be developed. This was first expressed in the ANNALS paper which I called "Farm Relief and a Permanent Agriculture." Nevertheless, I realize that, in agriculture, some preliminary restriction is necessary, especially in the export crops. The markets we have lost we are not likely to get back because the rest of the world has learned to do some of the things we expected to do for it. Restriction, of course, cannot be made to take place as it should, either. If we were to cut down our wheat crop 20%, most of the cut should be taken in the east. Wheatgrowing belongs to new, primitive countries, where spaces are wide and land is cheap. We shall not be able to do better than to restrict state-quotas (a simple percentage reduction from the past).

Restriction ought only to take place in the clear light of better alternatives. That would be rational. In an emergency, however, things are done in emergency ways. We are on the verge now of restrictive measures with only vague plans for the use of the abandoned land. This is a marvellous chance for setting our economy ahead and I hope it will be used better than I think it will. Both Wilson and Wallace are well aware of this problem. I hope both of them will be in the Department for if they are plans will surely go forward for positive betterment.

Meantime attention is centering on the domestic allotment plan. I cannot outline the history of this idea here; it obviously developed out of W. J. Spillman's scheme for outlook reports and voluntary reduction. I suppose M. L. Wilson is more responsible for its present form than anyone else; but, curiously enough, I am told by Wilson that its contractual feature was developed by H. I. Harriman, president of the U.S. Chamber of Commerce. At any rate the whole thing is very ingenious. It provides an excise tax on goods manufactured from agricultural commodities (wheat, cotton, tobacco, hogs - at present). This tax is to be used as a payment to farmers on a contract in which their consideration is an agreement to control their planting according to a plan. This plan is worked out by the Department on a basis of acreage needed to produce the total amount needed. States are then assigned quotas, then the counties; and within the counties local committees operate to fix the individual allotments. The whole thing is calculated to permit (even to compel) farmers to cooperate. It allows them to do together what they could not do separately.

I first heard of this scheme in its present form - though I was familiar with earlier variants - in the Spring when I was talking with B. Ruml in Washington at a meeting of the National Council on Education (I think it is) while I was working on my Social Objectives in Education for the General Education Board. Ruml evidently thought I should know about it and asked me whether I would come to a meeting of several people to discuss it. I later learned that this was a committee though of what organization I don't know. At any rate we missed connections and I never got to any meeting and did not see Ruml again, as a matter of fact, until one day late in November in New York. But I read over two versions of the plan which he gave me. They differed only slightly and I was not then interested in the administrative details, but the central idea appealed to me. It escaped the great difficulties with all plans of the export-debenture or McNary-Haugen sort, which were that production was not controlled and that "dumping" was involved. I therefore studied it some and talked with F.D.R. about limitation of production in general though I believe we never went over the plan carefully before I went to Chicago in June. In fact he had adopted as his policy the technique of making farm-leaders agree. He would adopt any plan, he said in effect, which they would center on. I said frankly that I did not like this. For one thing, this group would never invent anything new; for another whatever they did agree on would be purely farmer-biased and no better than class legislation always is. I said that we ought to make up our minds as to a workable plan, take it to the farm leaders and say to them, "You have fought among yourselves for fifteen years (which they had, the Grange, for instance, favoring the debenture plan, the Farm Bureau Federation favoring some equalization-fee plan, the Farmers' Union favoring outright price-fixing) and you have never agreed. If you had, some kind of relief would have been in effect by now. All this must stop. Here is our plan. If you will all join in supporting it we can put it over. If you don't you can be left outside and everyone can be told why." F.D.R. listened but said nothing, as I remember, except to ask "What plan?" I said (this was early in June) that there was to be a meeting of agricultural economists at the University of Chicago on June 23 and the days following, just preceding the Democratic convention, and that I might discover something if I went to that with my ears open. Anyway it was better to listen to the economists than to the politicians.

It was left this way while the speech of acceptance was being worked on by Moley, myself, Berle and some others (who were asked to do memoranda). I did go to Chicago and there I talked with Wilson and Wallace; but also with numerous others: Black, Davis, Tolley, etc. I soon discovered that the Wilson plan, as it was often called, was taken very seriously indeed and that I was not alone in supposing that it promised to meet the situation better than anything else. This was my first meeting with Wilson and we took to each other immediately. He knew even more of me than I of him. His interest in me was part of his interest in experimental philosophy and he seemed to regard me as its chief exponent in economics. I secretly felt that I was not only the chief but perhaps the only one; but all the same I welcomed a new recruit to my cause and was glad to offer myself as one to his. These were rather interesting meetings. I had intended to say nothing, having declined a formal invitation to speak, but finally was goaded by Black into talking about planning. Evidently this won over Wallace because from then on he warmed up to me.

I spent the following week-end at Urbana with Valeur at the home of the Wassermans'. I thought the thing out as best I could, and when I came back to Chicago for the Convention it was all straight in my mind. Moley and I stayed at the Drake and spent a good deal of time running back and forth between there and the Congress or Convention Hall. At the Congress the Business and Professional Men's League had rooms as well as those occupied by Farley and by Howe. Moley had the Ms. of the acceptance speech and we worked at it off and on as hopes rose and fell and as temperatures went up and down. The thing went on all week. We had very little sleep (none at all on one night). O'Connors had rooms close to Howes' and we spent some time there. There were frequent conversations with Albany over the phone. I, myself, early in the week called the Governor and told him we ought to put the principle of domestic allotment into the speech. He listened and asked many questions, but did not get it clearly. He had me tell it to Rosenman who did not get it either, he not knowing anything of agriculture. The next day I talked again to Roosevelt who got the hang of the thing this time, agreed to it, and asked me to send, I think, two or three hundred words in a telegram to be inserted in the speech.

About that time we hadn't much idea whether there would be a speech or not since the nomination was certainly in grave doubt. I labored over the statement, however, and sent it off. The next day and night, after talking with the Governor, Moley, O'Connor and I began to work rewriting the whole speech in fewer words since the Governor now saw that if the nomination came it would be after an exhausting week and that the speech would be made to a lot of tired delegates. We completed the job after long labor; I once went twelve hours without food just because I never thought of it. The next night the nomination came and we were glad we had done the job. But it all went for nothing. Our new version had been dictated to Albany over the phone and the Governor after one look at it went back to the original version. On the way out in the airplane, he cut it himself. Many things were consequently omitted; we had condensed but he merely cut. It seemed to me a very bad speech as I listened to it in the Coliseum but it did have the allotment principle clearly stated. The thing then, of course, as it was until the meeting with farm-leaders in Washington in December, was on a tariff basis.

Meanwhile I got Wilson to come to Albany to see Roosevelt and Moley and urged him to write the first draft of the farm speech we knew would have to be made. He did this and I went over it but it was mostly his work.

Here, then, was an idea with a long intellectual history, so to say, and the problem now was to see it embodied in legislation. A candidate for President had made commitment to it but everyone knew that this was a long way from seeing it become law. The indicated strategy was for the intellectuals to father it on some pressure group. This was indicated as well from Roosevelt's standpoint. The Governor had told the farm leaders that they must agree and had only indicated the principles within which the bill yet to be written must fall.

Things were complicated by each of the farm leaders' having a program of his own. This was true also of many agricultural representatives in Congress. I cannot recount in detail the ways of dealing with the farm leaders. They had to make speeches defending their own position, to read their own proposals (many of which were already in bill form - already introduced) but Morgenthau and I sat tight and listened. The general result after two days of this was that they agreed unanimously (thought some of them merely came in for political reasons and could hardly be counted on). F. P. Lee, a Washington attorney, who had been head of the Senate drafting service once and had written the McNary-Haugen measures, was engaged to draft and the thing was written.

A difficulty appeared immediately. Marvin Jones had already prepared a bill which was similar to the Norbeck bill which had been introduced the year before. This was intended to go into operation immediately and to give quick relief to farmers. The difficulty in this was that it did not give time to build up a Treasury surplus out of the processing tax and therefore threatened to be costly to the government. There were a whole year's supplies of both cotton and wheat in existence and Ezekiel and myself both saw the likelihood of an attempt to sell all this at once and receive the bonus. This would cost the Treasury far more than the tax receipts could be. The farm leaders, however, insisted that this should be Title 1 of the bill in spite of protests. The regular features of the domestic allotment plan were not to go into effect until the second year and even then there was one significant and other minor changes which were bad. The worst of these was the dropping out of individual contracts with producers and of state and county quotas for allotments. We realized that much manipulation would be required to make a workable measure but believed we would ultimately get what we wanted.

My contribution at the meeting of the farm leaders came in

suggesting the substitution of the price-parity base for the tariff principles which was adopted and written into the bill.

1933

January 4, 1933

The past few days have been extraordinarily tranquil: I have been able to work pretty regularly at my three most immediate writing jobs finishing the Industrial Discipline, going over the Ms. of Jared Eliot's Essays and working at the notes and introduction (this is the first of the Columbia University Series in Agricultural History of which Harry Carman and I are joint editors), and rewriting my essay on Social Objectives in Education. The C.U. Press is to bring out all three of these and I have been anxious to get the work done. It has been difficult with all the other things piling up. Two of the Ms. are already late and I have not been able to find the time, energy or requisite imaginative resources to finally finish them. So I have been glad of my free time.

Not all of it has been free, of course. I've had several talks with Moley, one with Lubin, one with Soule and one with Larry Cramer. Lubin and I are conspiring to get the U.S. back into the Institute of Agriculture at Rome. He wants to talk about a good deal else but I avoid it.

George Soule raised the question of the research grant for the preliminary study of an institute for planning. I was non-committal. I told him I could promise nothing. He wants some assurance that some foundation would be interested in financing such an Institute provided his group had financed the preliminary study. The only chance I know of would be Day and the Rockefeller Foundation. But Day cannot say in advance, I should suppose, that he can even interest his group. He and I have talked of this and I know that he is very much interested and hopes to move the Foundation in this direction. But there is nothing definite. I said all this and told him that he would have to be satisfied to talk with Day himself. I also said that I did not know that I ought to undertake the work. It was left this way. He is to try to get his group to lay aside a fund which can come to me provided we can see a possibility of using it profitably and the decision is to be deferred for a while.

The talk with Cramer was interesting. He used to be instructor of government here but was taken by Pearson to be his lieutenant-governor in the Virgin Islands. He has been there during the Hoover regime. He came to see me, I took him to Moley, and we sent him to see Howe and Senator Pittman. He was loyal to his chief and said he should be reappointed. We said no, to forget that. He said he had been approached by his politicos but had turned them down and that then they had favored Herbert Brown (of the Bureau of Efficiency). We encouraged him to look out for himself.

I am supposed to be in Washington but have hoped for more time here to work on my books. If I am not called I shall not go.

January 5, 1933

Things happened rapidly last night. Berle's office called me. Said La Guardia had wired him to persuade me to meet a group of Progressives today in Washington to discuss the farm bill. I decided I must go. I called F.D. and he said to go. After my seminar in the evening I went down to his house on 65th Street. He was cheerful-whistled me up up-stairs shouting "here, Rex, here Rex" and said his favorite dog had been called that. I told him I hoped Rex was still his favorite dog - all very merry! I asked him to tell the bunch of legislators he is meeting this evening to get on with the farm bills and to put the fund for the International Institute into the present appropriation bill. When we come to department reorganization, I told him, we will then be in a position to reduce our own activities by showing that they are already being done at Rome and that is part of our own program. He agreed and I left him a memorandum to use at the conference. (When I got to Washington in the morning I found note from Lubin, met him at the Mayflower, told him F.D. would raise the question at the evening conference, but said I thought Costigan who is well-disposed should then take the lead. He agreed and agreed to see Costigan).

F.D. tried out two ideas on me before Vincent Astor and a Mr. Franklin came in (son or nephew of P.A.S. Franklin). One had to do with the debts; he is evidently much worried about them. He said why not let Great Britain approach him and offer a settlement which he could make to appear reasonable; why not start by reducing the annual payments from sixty to forty years and make the annual meeting of these payments entirely flexible in any one year? They would be acknowledged but could be postponed without much formality. He would reduce interest for all debtors to about 1/2 of 1% - which is needed, he says for costs. I said some such formula was needed and that we could not settle the thing but ought to look forward to flexibility and negotiation. He is certainly going about this in an extremely intelligent way.

His other idea comes from Leon with whom Moley has consulted on the debts who is anti-British, believing they are using their power over exchanges to further their trade and injure ours. Pound declines: dollar rises in proportion: British buy dollars in Argentina and sell them in New York thus freeing pounds to buy British goods, depressing the pound and making the dollar higher. All very speculative and ingenious. But F.D. wants to know if the war-time law permitting the president to control gold in exchange is still in effect. I promised to ask Lee to look it up. He said I should go to Washington. I asked him what Morgenthau was up to because I did not want any conflict. There have been newspaper stories from Albany lately that H.M. was to be Assistant Secretary of Agriculture and I thought maybe F.D. wanted to turn all agricultural matters over to him. He said he thought H.M. was in Washington but for me to go and get in touch with him so that we should not conflict (This I did, calling him at 7:30 and having breakfast at the Mayflower with H.M. and Myers).

After breakfast I went to the Harrington and got in touch with Wallace and Wilson asking them to go with me to meet La Guardia's crowd in the p.m. We had a long talk about things in general. They seemed a little depressed. I left to do some writing and asked them to lunch with me at the Cosmos Club.

January 6, 1933

H. A. Wallace and M.L. Wilson came to lunch with me at the Cosmos Club. We talked about "What beside immediate farm relief." Wilson, Wallace and I see things nearly alike except that both of them are pretty determined general inflationists. What I am most interested in is the long-range planning of land utilization. Wilson has written a memorandum about it which he promises to send me. (It is important who has charge of this work in the D.A. of the new administration).

Wilson determined to go home in the afternoon and Wallace and I were left alone to go to the meeting of House progressives. I called Fred Lee, who is acting as counsel for the farm organization and who has drafted the bill in its successive stages. He said he would come.

Wallace and I then went to the gallery to hear the House debate on the bill. The gallery was so crowded we had to ask Jones to take us to the guest section. He had just finished his speech and was very tired. We heard part of one speech and then a very dramatic thing occurred. A message came from the President that Coolidge had just died. The House immediately adjourned.

Wallace and I talked for two hours over an ice cream soda and then went to the meeting. Lee spoke first on the administration of the bill. I then spoke for about half an hour and answered questions. There was intense interest. What I said was substantially as follows:

Economics of the Parity Plan

No desire to dictate: will use pressure to repel sinister influence but prefer reason for persuasion.

Domestic allotment plan is a part of the whole progressive scheme, one item in a long list of needed things. It ought not to be criticized because it does not do what it is not intended to do; it ought not to be expected to take care of situations to which it does not extend. Other measures are needed for other problems.

The whole conception into which it fits is that of a regulated and balanced economy. This depression is being prolonged by disparities. Groups cannot exchange for each other's goods because some are high and some are low. In this emergency some prices ought to be sharply lowered and some raised. Farm prices need raising. It is harder to get at the lowering process and probably can only be done for the most part by states though something should be possible for the Federal Government on mortgage rates, etc.

To raise farm prices it is proposed to use the taxing power. This is to get around the constitutional prohibition against fixing prices. This is not a sales tax, as has been said, it is an elevation of prices. We'll tell the Supreme Court it is a tax; but among ourselves it is not.

All the questions which interest an economist follow now:
1. Possibilities of substitution.
2. On whom will burden fall?
3. What will be the effect of redistribution of income
   in this way?

Such questions as these are the important ones; but like so many economic questions we shall probably not know the answers until we have tried the experiment; but not knowing them ought not to prevent our trying it out if there is some presumption of betterment. I think there is. When prices had these relationships we were better off all around but that does not mean it was because of price-parity; it means there was price-parity because an exchangeable balance existed. This is why we believe there cannot be any successful measure of this kind without a control of supply and this is basic to the idea.

But we also believe that supply can only be controlled by devising a mechanism through which farmers can bring the interests of all into concert with the individual interest of each. Under this plan it will pay farmers, for the first time, to be social-minded, to do something for all instead of for himself alone. We thus succeed, we think, in harnessing a selfish motive for the social good. We can even go further with this: we can make him contribute toward a long-run program in this way. We can plan for him and with him.

Wallace postponed his remarks until morning. There was so much interest that the members wanted to continue discussion then. I dined alone at the Cosmos Club.

January 7, 1933

Yesterday Wallace came to breakfast with me. We are in the course of making a friendship and are exploring each other's minds with a sort of delighted expectancy. We have much in common and our minds work somewhat in the same ways but we are both over forty -- he was born in 1889 and I in 1891-- and have been exploring the world independently up to now. This makes an amusing and valuable-but exhausting - interlude. Wilson's mind, though it is one of those poetic, intuitive ones, is far more elusive. He is much more difficult to get close to. Yet in many ways he is a great man. To know Wallace and Wilson well make a good deal of sacrifice worth while.

Wallace and I again spent several hours with La Guardia's progressive Congressmen. All but one or two of them are earnestly looking for the right answers to the country's problems; and they insisted not only on exploring the details and probable administrative procedures carefully but questioned me at length on the general economic implications. I have taken the line that I do not advocate the bill, but that I am glad to explore probable consequences. This procedure confused them at first: they are used to lobbyists' certainty. But they soon came to appreciate my method and to see that my way was the only possible way to discover an approximately right judgment. Mr. LaGuardia struck me as particularly honest and right-hearted. It seems a shame that he was defeated in November and will not be in the next Congress. Many feel that way about it. Several members told me they regarded him as the ablest or most useful member.

My view of the situation now is that the bill ought to secure its support through education rather than force. It will probably pass the House next week. There will be much argument for it and against it in the Senate; and then Hoover will veto it if it passes the Senate. In any case it will have to be passed in the Special Session after March 4.

There will therefore be continuous argument about it until that time. This I like and believe it will be a far better bill, as to administrative detail, as a result.

The change from "making the tariff effective" to "price parity" as a principle is somewhat confusing at first but I believe it is a better basis. I listened to debate in the House for a while in the afternoon. I was approached by Ed. O'Neal and Earl Smith, both, as to the Secretaryship but refused to say anything, saying that my relationship to Roosevelt precluded my never saying anything about appointments unless I were asked. I took the four o'clock train and got home at ten.

This morning I called Moley and told him our results at Washington and he told me what had happened at the conference in New York on the fifth. It was mostly on the budget. My advice - or maybe some one else's concerning the substitution of income for sales taxes seems to have resulted in something. Anyway F.D. told them that this was the way to get revenue. This a.m. the papers are indignant at talk of any more income taxes - that is the Times and Tribune. They talk, too, about a "revolt"" among Congressmen at the notion of lowering the brackets. But I think this is more propaganda. The income tax principle is right. F.D. should stick to it.

Moley said the International Institute of Agriculture matter came up and was agreed to. Senator Byrnes took Lubin's memorandum and the proper steps will now be taken.

I had a note from N. Peffer excitedly calling attention to the Far Eastern situation and to the probability that the Stimson position might lead us into war. I told Moley there seemed to be something here which we should explore. He said he was terribly busy but agreed that we should be informed. I wrote Peffer for more light and must see Shotwell and others.

Moley said he and F. D. R. had discussed Norman Davis at some length the other night. He feels Davis cannot be trusted. I feel the same way but for another reason: he is too close to the N.Y. financial crowd and I have no faith that any of them are ever disinterested about public policy.

January 11, 1933

There has been very little which was exciting in the past few days. I finished writing the Introduction to Jared Eliots' Essays in Field Husbandry. Carman had written one which I did not like because of its approach and because it was written too apologetically and too pretentiously. So I rewrote it at the risk of giving offence. This morning I signed the publishing contract.

Yesterday I lectured to the Contemporary Affairs group on Farm Relief using the attached outline.

There is just now a flood of opposition coming from interested sources. There is some, of course, which is not propagandistic but rather opposed because of different social theory. All those who hate government control as opposed to laissez faire are waking up to the bill's implications. (I attach a sample of each - interested and disinterested. Also the outline of my talk yesterday).

1. History of the plan.
   Spillman - outlook and intentions reports.
   Wilson and committee working under Rockefeller grant.
   The Wilson plan.
   1. The tax.
   2. Return of the tax in exchange for contract which required submission to planning.
   3. The basis of the tax: the tariff.
   4. Provision for referendum.
   5. The allotments.

2. The campaign commitment.
   1. Must be voluntary
   2. Must admit farmers to tariff benefits
   3. Must not be drain on budget
   4. Must reduce surplus

3. The short Session and legislative history
   1. Meeting with farm leaders.
   2. Consultation about commodities to be included.
   3. Change from tariff to price parity.
   4. Tax to be laid on processed commodities.

4. Economic picture into which plan fits.
   1. Present stage of the depression (Stalemate - difficult readjustments)
   2. Price disparities: when general level drops characteristic resistances develop
   3. Special difficulties with agricultural commodities which have very little resistance as over against such prices as (1) long term credits (2) utilities including railroad rates (3) taxes, etc
   4. Special justification at a juncture like the present for any attack on this problem of disparity: the allotment plan is one; there are others in view for readjusting mortgage rates, etc.
   5. But the wider implications are obvious. This is an attempt to plan. It is also an attempt to provide mechanism through which the interests of the individual can be made to run, for once with those of society.

January 12, 1933

I came to Washington again yesterday afternoon. The night before I spent an hour with F. D. R. Moley and Berle were there part of the time and we all stayed for a conference with Interstate Commerce Commissioners Mehaffy and Eastman, although this is out of my bailiwick and I have had nothing to do with the pending Railroad legislation.

The following up of the farm legislation has been somewhat annoying. Henry Morgenthau and I lost touch with each other and he came to Washington independently, working especially on the credit situation. (This is the most acute situation of all. With the fifty percent fall in prices in the last three years, the situation of long-term debtors has grown progressively worse. The farmers are worst off, of course, and are clamoring for legislation).

I had foreseen this during the campaign and it was I who persuaded F. D. R. to make the Springfield speech in which he promised to extend time for payment, hinted at writing down debtors' burden, and promised reorganization of the whole agricultural credit structure. And, of course, when there began to be riots about foreclosure proceedings in the Middle West, the situation got pretty warm for Congressmen.

Immediately after election I requested D. L. Wickens of the Department of Agriculture and M. Ezekiel of the Farm Board (economists) to make a study of both emergency and permanent measures. I also asked H. Parker Willis to contribute any ideas he had; in fact the post-election study began by my raising the question of farm mortgages at the Albany conference at which I introduced Willis and Rogers to the Governor. After this had been going on for some time I discovered that Henry Morgenthau was proceeding to a similar end with Wm. I. Myers of Cornell. I knew Myers and liked him but was well aware that he would have laissez faire notions (all the people at Cornell have) and believed that my people were better suited to the National situation. I was rather worried about conflict so I asked Morgenthau and Myers to come to a conference in Albany at which my people would also be present. This was held and it was agreed that we should all proceed together. But H. M. has steadily proceeded since to disregard that agreement. I can't go here into the differences of opinion involved in this. But it all came about again because F. D. R. is careless in his commitments. He tells several of us to do the same things and then forgets. This is all right when it involves study and reporting to him, but when it involves a political job the results are apt to be ludicrous. This is a case in point. The strategy on the farm bill was to have the farm leaders adopt it and promote it in Congress. The same thing was indicated here. F. D. R. told both H. M. and myself to see this through. Luckily we discovered this in time and worked together on the first trip to Washington when we got the farm leaders together on the domestic allotment plan.

At the end of that meeting, just before we left, I laid down the principles by which their discussions, and the formulation of their legislation, must be guided. This was at a luncheon with O'Neal, Earl Smith, John Simpson, Henry Wallace, etc. present, together with Morgenthau and Myers. H. M. thought I ought not to do this, but I knew the situation was acute, that there would be a lot of legislation introduced anyway, and that there ought to be some guidance from the Roosevelt camp. I therefore laid down these principles:

1. There must be centralization of administration, which includes liquidation of joint-stock banks.

2. The farmer must be able to find his credit sources in one place - whether long, middle or short term.

3. There must be arrangements for conciliation proceedings between debtor and creditor.

4. There must be an arrangement for preventing the dispossessing of farmers because of inability to meet mortgage engagements.

H.M. and I returned to N.Y. together after that meeting and agreed to keep closely in touch so that there should be no irritation. He did not keep this agreement but began to have meetings with farm leaders without consulting me. His excuse for this last night was that the Governor did not tell him to consult me. He knows, of course, this failing of F. D. R.'s and realizes that our own agreement was to prevent any trouble arising from it. At any rate it happened that way. I don't feel anything sinister about this at all except that H.M. wants so terribly to be Secretary of Agriculture and is willing to jeopardize policy for the sake of this ambition - but then I find most people willing to do that! The trouble is that Myers, on whom he depends, is allied with me. In this he is foolish. I am not his enemy and am only interested in the policy. I wish I could make him see that I don't even want any credit.

The situation became acute in the conference night before last with F.D.R. He asked me what was going on and I told him that Henry did not tell me and that I was afraid to mix in for fear of confusion. Moley and Berle were there. We told him our ideas about farm credits. After thinking it over F.D.R. asked Moley to act as a sort of chairman and draw the thing together. He thought there should be postponement for a week or two until things could be formulated and then we should all agree on emergency legislation, letting the permanent set-up go over until the Special Session. Meanwhile I was to come to Washington to see H.I. Harriman (president of the U.S. Chamber of Commerce) about farm relief and general business relations. Moley undertook to call H.M. off and to get a more general conference in which various views could be heard, perhaps under Senator Hull's aegis. However, last night I went down to the Harrington Hotel where, I had heard, the farm leaders were meeting and found Morgenthau and Myers in full blast. I told Wickens and O'Neal on the side that the Governor had said to go a little slow and to get the thing straight before proceeding too far. At least twenty bills (including a comprehensive one by J. Robinson) had been introduced and it was going to be a considerable job to reconcile all the views since they had crystallized so far.

After a while H.M. called me into the hall and said he had a conversation with Moley and that they had something of a row. He wanted to be frank, he said, and not to get into any mix-up. I told him he should do more consulting in that case but went on to say that I had no interest in this except to get the policy right and that he ought to consult the people I had working from the first. I said I was perfectly willing for him to handle matters. He said he had arranged for a meeting of a few Senators and Representatives in the morning at which there would be communicated to them the points of agreement amongst farm leaders and economists. He said he had told Moley and had been told to go ahead with this. This amounted, of course, to Moley's being let down.

I listened to the discussion for a while and came home. When I got to the Club a wire from Moley asked me to call him which I did. We agreed that things had gone so far there was nothing to be done but let H.M. go ahead. I imagine, however, Moley will have it out with F.D.R.

My chief interest here now is to see H.G. Moulton (Brookings Institution) and ask for a survey of the research activities of the government. I am afraid harm may be done in the pending reorganization unless this is done.

I must also see H.I. Harriman tomorrow and Congressman La Guardia. I ought also to see Marvin Jones and congratulate him on the passage of the bill in the House tonight (203 to 150).

January 13, 1933

I had conversations today with Moulton, Hall and Merriam of the Brookings Institution. I asked whether they would not prepare memoranda etc. concerning the research work of the various departments so that it could be used to best effect when reorganization came up. They were glad to be asked. They pointed out the distinction between the kind of reorganization which assimilates everything to functional categories and that which assembles functions about a needful job. There seems to be a quarrel in this field on this Institute of Government Research. The old director - Willoughby - seems to have held the categorical view. The new man - Hall - holds the opposite which is my own and, I suppose, would be Moley's.

There is not so much saving to be made in reorganization as most people think, I imagine. But with so much campaign talk about economy there is apt to be a good deal of slashing here and there. My concern is that this should be as intelligent as is possible under the circumstances. This group has long been studying the government and ought to help a lot in the quick decisions which will doubtless have to be made. This is always unsatisfactory to the academic person but the decisions will be taken anyway and he may as well help to make them as wise as possible.

They will go to work at once studying research which I asked for first, thinking that it may suffer most under undiscriminating attack and that it can least be spared in the long run. Doubtless there can be cutting done, but it ought not to injure the basic effort. But they will also try to meet any emergencies of judgment which may arise in the months to come with as good advice as they can find.

Henry Morgenthau had lunch with me. He said he had the agricultural credit situation well in hand, meaning that his group was ready with several decisions which have, however, to be drafted by Lee, and that the legislators are ready to push them. I shall keep out of this thing now as much as possible after the last experience. They are still undecided who ought to handle the bill in the Senate - Smith of S.C. the chairman of agriculture is a dodo and filled with big business propaganda. He would be hopeless. They are talking some of Norbeck. He may be the man.

I had a nice talk with Feis this afternoon about the economic conference. He said that things are going well in Geneva. This is contrary to press reports; but he had a telegram from Day which seemed to indicate it. The press has it that British reluctance to do anything about currency stabilization is hampering everything. It may be; but we, also, might meet them by going off gold, I suppose. It is worth considering at any rate. Feis was very agreeable and promised to keep me informed of everything in Geneva. As I was leaving he asked me if I were going into the new government. I said not that I knew of and that anyway I did not want to administer anything. He then asked if I would object to going to the Economic Conference. I said NO. He then intimated strongly that I might be appointed. But I had supposed this was to go over until F.D.R. came in. I wonder if when he and Stimson met the other day, they agreed to make appointments soon.

January 14, 1933

Irving Fisher has tried to see me a number of times this Summer and Fall. Except for one occasion when we met at the Executive Mansion in Albany early in Summer, much to his surprise, because he had hoped for an uninterrupted chance to present "reflation" to F.D.R., I have managed to avoid him. However, last night he caught me fairly at dinner at the Cosmos Club and proceeded to try to pump me as to my views and to impress me with his. I do not believe in outright inflation. Our policy has been shaped toward a pragmatic handling of prices. He wants, by some means, to bring the price level half way back to 1929. He believes that much can be learned from Swedish experience where they have succeeded in stabilizing for a year through the handling of the discount rate. I believe in stabilization too - that is in a managed currency and independence from the gold standard. But I am anxious first to straighten things out. There is more currency now than is needed. We need to correct disparities and inflation would not do that. I do not know how to manage the currency. I have some ideas about it; but correct management of it now, even if we had a plan, would not call for an increase in its amount. Fisher seems now to have abandoned his "compensated dollar" idea and to want to do it through the Federal Reserve, though he thinks the present Board would sabotage any such plan which, of course, they would. My view is that we ought to go off gold in international exchange so that we can manage internally. The Governor asked me some time ago how it could be done. He said some one had told him that a law giving the President power to regulate gold in international exchange in 1918 had never been repealed. If this is true it is important because then it could be done overnight by proclamation without long Congressional debate which would spoil the effect. I promised to look it up. So when Wickens came in to see me after dinner I asked him to do this secretly. Wickens and I also talked about farm credits, though nothing very new came out. He is an earnest, humorless chap I should trust utterly but he is apt to be a bore from lack of expressiveness and of terminal facilities.

This morning I called on Henry I. Harriman of the U.S. Chamber of Commerce and had a two hour conversation about a number of interesting things. He is mildly progressive and pulls a reluctant Board along with him pretty well. Wilson has told me a lot about him and took me to see him once before. This morning we were both more or less at leisure and I explained our policy to him quite fully concerning war-debts, the economic conference, price attitudes, etc. He made some suggestions about the Farm Bill which were well taken and agree with my notions.

All of us who were originally interested in the scheme feel that the bill as passed by the House has some fundamental defects which the Senate ought to remedy. The provision for state and county quotas has been lost, peanuts and rice have been included among the basic commodities, and the first period of operation promises, as it is at present, to cost the Treasury plenty. After talking about some other things with Harriman, I decided to go to see Senator Byrnes (S.C.) about these things. But first we discussed the applicability of the allotment principle to get it out of the way. Also I discovered that he liked W.W. Stewart and got him to dictate a letter in my presence recommending his appointment to F.D.R. for either Treasury, R.F.C. or Federal Reserve. He said also he had written to F.D.R. endorsing Wallace for Agriculture.

I got to Byrnes' office late and only had a few minutes before the Senate met. He had forgotten to take up the matter of the appropriation for the International Institute but promised to do so immediately. I got little chance to talk about Agriculture but we agreed to meet next week. He wants to help on it.

January 16, 1933

Several weeks ago, just as the lame duck session of Congress was opening, Walter Lippmann and I rode to Washington together and for several days saw a good deal of each other. I was anxious that he should have an idea of the intention of the domestic allotment plan as well as a better view of the contemplated economic policies as a whole. As a result of this he has written a number of intelligent and generally sympathetic articles.

I urged him at that time to use the academic draft of the allotment plan as a criterion and to come down hard on any departures from it. How well he is serving in this respect is illustrated by the attached article (sic). I took him to dinner with Wallace, Ezekiel and Morganthau. Wilson took him into camp as he does most people. I attribute a good deal of sympathetic consideration from people who would otherwise be opposed, to this meeting.

January 17, 1933

I had my first real difference of opinion with F. D. R. last night. The papers lately have made much of his agreement with Stimson on Far Eastern policy - the non-recognition of Manchukuo. He issued a statement concerning the sacredness of treaties, referring to the Kellogg-Briand and Nine-Power pacts and indicated his intention of going on with the present commitments. The effort has already been felt in a firmer stand in the League against Japan.

I sympathize with the Chinese too. But I firmly believe it is a commitment which may lead us to war with Japan. I said so and registered a vigorous dissent from any such position. He seemed very pleased at Stimson's cooperation with him; says he has called him on the phone every day lately and says he is quite prepared to see the policy through. He has a strong personal sympathy with the Chinese; and this added to a sudden trust in Stimson has carried him over. He admitted the possibility of war and said it might be better to have it now than later.

This horrified me and I said so: I pointed out that Japan was doing what countries in trouble at home always did -creating trouble abroad to divert attention and to work up patriotism which could be used to support the Military clique at home. I said that the budget was unbalanced, that there might be a financial crash there, and that things might fall of their own weight. He said he had pointed out the financial situation to Stimson and his answer was that Japan was really independent financially and moreover nearly self- sufficient. A crash would merely mean resort to token money and that they could carry on indefinitely that way. I said that this seemed to me nonsense, and pointed out that Japan would be glad to have war under these circumstances (at least the group of young militarists now in power would) and that we had better lean over backward not to be provocative. Both France and Britain have leaned toward Japan; we have sacrificed much in European policy to win even neutrality in our attempt to isolate Japan. We are hated for this and have lost much that we might have gained in forcing the removal of trade restrictions which is where our real interest lies. My arguments, I'm afraid, had no effect, though they may cause him to be more cautious in the matter. Moley was present but did not support me.

The agricultural situation did not get much discussion in view of their argument which must have gone on for an hour. While we were talking Stimson called on the phone to say that Hoover would like to see F. D. R. again on his way South (he is going tomorrow to Warm Springs for two weeks and then for his trip on Vincent Astor's yacht) about the debts. The British want to send a commission to negotiate and Stimson pointed out that the question of terms would come up within twenty-four hours of their coming. On this, he said, they could not act and needed cooperation from F. D. R.

F. D. R. agreed to go and said he would bring Moley, as before. We talked over the position to be taken, agreeing that only F. D. R. ought to negotiate terms. The British want to send a big commission, F. D. R. does not want the thing too elaborate: they can tell us no facts we have not got now. We agreed that Hoover should be told that their experts are not needed so much as some one who can negotiate for the government. Also we thought the thing might be done quickly, say in the two days F. D. R. plans to spend in Washington after his Southern trip, February 16 and 17.

On the farm question I asked if he had told Senator Smith (S. C. Chairman of Agricult. Comm) who had visited him the day before what the Senator is quoting him in Washington as saying: that our plan ought to be restricted to wheat and cotton. He said they had talked of such a thing but that he had not asked for the change. He thinks there are difficulties with hogs, and we all recognize that there are, I assured him we could work it with good administration. And as for dairy products, these ought to be included as much for political as for economic reasons.

If they are not we may have an enemy on every farm. To this he at once agreed.

I told him I felt the Jones bill should be changed in the Senate Committee in several respects:

1. We should get quotas back in for the neighborly self-policing reason if for no other.
2. We should make sure that the payments during the emergency period should not exceed receipts.

He agreed to this and asked me to see what Senators I could about it. He also asked me whether, if he spoke to Senator Huey Long on Thursday when he would see him in Washington, I would go to see him. I said I would. He has spoken of this a number of times; has the theory that Huey can be made use of but must be educated. He has been creating a great stir lately with his Senate filibuster against branch-banking in the Glass Bill. He got drunk with Vincent Astor the other night, so Vincent says, who reports that he intends behaving better when the new administration comes in. The Governor respects his possibilities for trouble and wants him worked on. I don't relish the task but will do the best I can.

His further instructions were these: get the Farm Bill through the Senate in better shape. Then have several farm leaders issue a manifesto congratulating Congress and anticipating all the arguments Hoover will use in his arguments - the business interests to be hurt. Call on all farmers for support. Hoover may then sign the bill, but if not this will contribute to a better opinion for it when it does become law.

He asked me to come to Warm Springs in about ten days to report what has happened.

January 21, 1933

The past three days have been crowded ones. Thursday, Moley and myself were taken by Bobby Straus down to the 23 St. Ferry. We crossed to Jersey City and caught F. D. R.'s special train. We arrived in Washington about three, were met by White House automobiles and taken to the Mayflower, where we stayed until Saturday morning. On the train in our group were William Woodin, Norman Davis, Moley and myself. Carey Grayson got on at Philadelphia to discuss inaugural affairs and had lunch and was photographed with us.

This group rode in F.D.R.'s own car - an observation car on the rear; the press were in a car ahead. We talked to F.D.R. in turn until lunch time and then we talked generally. For the last hour before reaching Washington F.D.R. rested. In the time I had with him I discussed the farm bill. I showed him a letter I had just written to Henry Morgenthau suggesting several necessary amendments on which all of us

ought to agree as a minimum when discussing the matter with Senators -
the bill was now before the Agriculture Committee of the Senate - and
so that there might not be the same lack of coordination which has been
so evident in the handling of the emergency farm credit bills (Ezekiel and
Wickens still complain that no attention is paid to their suggestions as
against those of Myers, but I am keeping out of it until the last minute.
I shall only intervene then if it seems absolutely necessary so that there
will be no trouble with Henry M. who I really do like and with whose
ambitions I should not like to interfere).

F. D. R. has been waking up gradually to the far-reaching
character of this legislation and asking some questions which show that
he has never seriously considered the proposed machinery at least in
detail. He had made some bad blunders in discussions with legislators and
has left thing indeterminate in his discussions with them until they have
begun to quote him on opposite sides of important issues.   In this
particular one he has been for operation only on cotton and wheat,for
operation on cotton, wheat, hogs and tobacco. He has been for Senator
Smith's plan and against it. All this is for two reasons: he has from the
first had the idea of following the lead of the farm leaders and not taking
too positive a line of his own, and, because of this, he has never got down
to rigorous study of the bill in its various forms and has not much
judgment of a positive sort.

The bill is before the Senate Committee now and will have to be
rewritten in many ways.

January 22, 1933

My account of the trip to Washington and what happened there
was interrupted to catch the New York train. This is Sunday morning in
my office.

It had been arranged that F. D. R. was to see Hoover during his
stop in Washington. Stimson has arranged this by a phone conversation
at which I was present during which F. D. R. said that he would take
Moley with him. I was naturally pleased at this because I had been afraid
that Davis' close connections with the State Department would have
operated to supplant Moley. When we arrived in Washington, Stimson
came to see F. D. R. and arranged about the White House meeting for next
day. It was not clear whether Davis was to go or not. In his interview
with the press on the train, F. D. R. had told the reporters that Moley was
to go with him and in response to a question about Davis' going had said
" No." Davis was called in at the Stimson conversation.

During the next morning I developed some differences of opinion
with Davis in conversations in his room. We agreed that the British had
to be allowed to present their case and that there had to be a connection

between debt-conversations and other mutual matters but I was insistent that we should not appear to concede anything beforehand in the way of reduction which would have been implied in a single commission to discuss all problems. Moley, in the Governor's apartment, also developed differences with Davis even more sharply, just before they were to leave for the White House for, it appeared, Davis was to go after all. The crux of the difference was that Davis wanted to trust matters to the present administration. He would have favored a single conference covering all subjects immediately. Moley was determined that nothing but preparation should take place before March 4, and that there should no suspicion of concession on the debts. Davis represents Wall Street, the State Department and the cancellationist attitude. Moley, I think, believes as I do too, that the debts are a big shadow in the background, affecting every international question; but he is against playing the Wall Street, republican game for cancellation. The Hoover administration are putting on pressure for immediacy which we suspect. If we let them move into commitments we will have to hold the bag with a hostile country and Congress after they are gone. Doubtless in time the debts are going to be whittled away to nothing; this, however, will be over a period of years. Meantime we shall have to carry on the struggle both with foreign nations and with opinion at home. The Hoover administration is trying, in my opinion, to move rapidly now, so that they can say they have started the thing off and so can claim credit for it, but so that they will have none of the grief associated with the struggle over arrangements. Davis is playing their game and Moley resents it bitterly as I do too.

I, of course, do not know what happened at the White House except at second hand. While this was going on I had a conference with Senator Byrnes and Carr of the State Dept. concerning the International Institute of Agriculture in which Carr was urged to speed things up and Byrnes agreed to make no moves in Congress until the State Department finished its negotiations over the conditions of reentry - the conditions seem only to be the resignation of De Michaelis.

What appears to have happened at the White House was that Hoover urged immediate action and Roosevelt said he would see the British after March 4. This being established they went on to the other things. Should the debts and other economic questions be considered together? Moley saved the day there, insisting on separate meetings against Davis and Stimson even against F. D. R.

In the afternoon Moley and I went to the State Department, he to call on Stimson as agreed at the White House to formulate the note to the British, and I to call on Feis for cables from Day and Williams. Feis was out and I returned to the hotel. Calling Feis in a short time, I was asked to come to the meeting with Stimson.

I went back immediately and found Moley, Feis, Bundy and

Stimson struggling over the formulation of the note. Stimson's proposal was wholly unsatisfactory. It completely ignored the points which had been established at the morning conference; it provided for a common meeting, it identified the questions and it clearly held out concessions on the debt as a return for currency stabilization. Before I came in Moley, who had been given power by F.D.R. to O.K. the note, had indicated that this was wholly unsatisfactory and had insisted that only one representative be asked to confer on the debt question and he with negotiating power; and that the representatives to discuss other questions should be mentioned separately. The problem was to indicate to the British that the two were so connected that we should insist on mutual satisfaction in both matters; but keep from any commitment.

When I came in all of them were working with pencil and paper trying to find a satisfactory formula. Stimson was irritable. He insisted that he was trying to protect F. D. R. in the coming negotiations by indicating a clear linking between the two sets of conversations. Moley was most conciliatory but very firm. I spoke up after a while saying that the Secretary did not seem to understand our reasons for separation. I said that the matters stood quite differently and that we should have been happier if there had not been such quick action nor such close linkage. Stimson turned on me with indignation and denounced me as trying to tear down everything he had been working for throughout his term. The connection was not quite clear. But evidently his little outburst was an accumulation of irritation at not having his way all day and at having to deal with people who must to him have seemed like sheer amateurs and upstarts. I was pretty angry and got red but managed to keep my mouth shut and take it out in glaring. Later I tried to explain. Stimson said that in all his conversations with the Governor there had been clear indication of intention to deal with both at once. Moley pointed out that they had been separated in the morning conversations and said that he had not understood what F. D. R. meant by saying that the sentences mentioning the "debts" and "other matters" were "twins." But that he could now see that he meant them to be treated together but separately and that this must be adhered to. I explained to Stimson that I had begun to talk with F. D. R. about the debts months ago and had first taken the position that not only debts but disarmament should be linked to other economic matters; that they should, for instance, be permitted to be discussed in the Economic Conference together. F. D. R. had immediately objected and had always maintained his objection; his arguments had won me over, I said, and then stated them:

> 1. To lay the debts on the table would be to admit that concessions were to be made.
> 2. Public opinion both at home and abroad was singularly determined: on the one side not to cancel, on

the other not to pay.

3. Other arrangements - monetary matters, tariffs,
etc. required very different handling of public opinion and
might be worked out whether or not the debts could be
reduced as rapidly as everyone hoped.

4. The kind of negotiations were different. The one
was now at the stage of plenary negotiation, the other a
matter for preliminary expert study and exchange of
opinion and the rate of progress might be very different.

I said that there seemed to be a fundamental misconception of
F.D.R.'s position; that there was no hurry and that if necessary we could
consult him before talking to Sir Ronald Lindsay.

Stimson kept talking about time. He had intended to meet the
ambassador early and then to have a press conference. Moley kept
working toward a formula as did Bundy and Feis. But Moley, though
agreeable, stuck to his position, rejecting everything that looked too
strong. Stimson snapped at Bundy and said "he'd better keep out of this"
when Bundy thought he had the formula. Stimson referred unhappily to
trying to be Secretary of State for two Presidents and also to trying to
protect a man more than he wanted to be protected. He gradually
regained his good humor and finally, under Moley's gentle persuasion,
accepted all that Moley required. After my rebuke and explanation I kept
pretty quiet, though Stimson came back to the matter again and said he
thought he knew the Governor's opinion better than Moley or I did. "In
fact," he said, "I have the aide memoire of a telephone conversation in
which the Governor agreed to joining the negotiation." He said Roosevelt
had used Leffingwell's illustration that with the debts and currency it was
hard to know which was the hen and which was the egg. Moley said this
was true and that we did not deny it but we differed on the procedure
indicated, that we could not now get in touch with the Governor and that
his (Moley's) say would have to be final. Stimson said he would have to
be governed by his own interpretation of Roosevelt's wishes, since he
believed he knew them. But Moley was firm and finally Stimson gave
way, went to a side table and wrote out a new note to be sent to the
British. To this, after emendation and correction, everyone agreed and
Moley and Stimson initialed it. It read as follows:

In our previous correspondence on this subject the British
Government has expressed a desire for a discussion in the near future of
the debts owed by that government to the United States. I am authorized
by Mr. Roosevelt, the President-elect, to say that he will be glad to receive
at Washington a representative or representatives of the British
Government for that purpose early in March, as soon as possible after his
inauguration.

Mr. Roosevelt wishes it to be understood that any discussion of the debt which the British Government may wish to bring up must be concurrent with and conditioned upon a discussion of the world economic problems in which the two Governments are mutually interested, and therefore that representatives should also be sent at the same time to discuss the ways and means for improving the world situation.

Stimson then told us that he felt compelled by our insistence on a course he did not agree with, to leave a memorandum in the State Department files registering his judgment that another course would have been preferable. He said, however, to Moley that he would cooperate in the future, asked him to call either in person or by phone whenever anything came up, and we came away feeling fairly satisfied at having established our point of view.

January 23, 1933

Saturday on the train coming home from Washington Moley and I ran into F. Trubee Davison, Assistant Secretary of War, with whom we had a long conversation concerning the state of the Republican Party. He also told us many useful things about the War Department and its possibilities of reorganization. Just about the time we were getting home I began to develop a sense of things which were likely to overtake us immediately as a result of the arrangements we had made in Washington and told Moley that it seemed to me that we ought to begin immediately to a make arrangements for receiving the British representatives who would be arriving in a little over a month and who would have to be met on a basis of equality. If we did nothing among ourselves, the matter of preparation would, of course, be left wholly to the State and Treasury Departments who might easily misunderstand or misinterpret the policies we wish to pursue. The two matters most prominent in this respect, of course, are the common arrangements concerning exchanges and the freeing of trade through new tariff rates. This last is likely to be difficult because of the Ottawa agreements entered into last summer between Great Britain and the Dominions, and the former will be difficult because of the reluctance of the British to take any step toward the stabilizing of the pound. The success of the Economic Conference will certainly lie in the preliminary arrangements which we are able to make in this first conference with the British. If we can go into the Conference with a united front, a long step will have been taken toward the Conference program which will aid in international recovery. Moley agreed with me but took a different attitude toward the kind of preparation we ought to make. He believed we should immediately confer with such people as Baruch and others and I felt that we ought to keep it strictly to those qualified experts we could assemble. We agreed, however, that we ought first to call Roosevelt and put the matter before him. We thought we ought to ask first, as to the part Davis was to play in the matter; second, the part the State Department was to play; and, third, what kind of a group of experts we ought to assemble. Moley called him at Warm Springs and he commended us for our conduct of the conference with Stimson and gave us a free hand to go ahead with the arrangement saying that we ought to keep the matter to a very few well-qualified experts letting the State Department work independently but cooperating with them and leaving Davis out of it entirely. I therefore immediately called Walter Wheeler Stewart on the telephone who said he could be called on for any purpose. I had him in mind for the international financial affairs because of the confidence he seems to command everywhere and because of his expertness as a delegate to the World Bank Committee and as American Advisor to the Bank of England. I also called E. Patterson of the University of Pennsylvania as the best person I could think of to talk about tariff matters. We arranged for a meeting on Tuesday afternoon. Moley was to call in James Warburg.

January 24, 1933

B. Ruml came to see me yesterday with a number of things on his mind. I regard him as one of our chief social inventors and was consequently glad to see him. He first offered to see whether he could approach the Packers informally and get them to help - as we persuaded the Millers to do - on the administrative details of the Allotment Plan. Their opposition will not be effective in preventing passage; but while they are opposing they might still help us on administration thus making the inevitable easier to bear. Since this is the way we handled the Millers and since Ruml is discreet and able, I told him to go ahead.

He then spoke about the Office of Education. The American Council members and official education in general is disturbed for fear Commissioner Cooper will be removed and a political appointment made. I expressed some doubt that Cooper was not a politician, now trying to protect his position by crying "no politics." Ruml admitted something of this. But I said I would speak to F. D. R. about letting Cooper continue for a while and then asking the American Council for recommendations provided they would agree in advance not to name some shell-back who would be provocative to our crowd. We agreed to handle this just between ourselves and say nothing to anyone.

He also called attention to the recommendation of Social Trends report of Hoover's Commission and suggested Roosevelt might take some notice of it. This was that the Social Science Research Council act as a kind of Planning Board. I suggested F. D. R. might ask the Research Council to make some study mentioning Social Trends. I must speak to him about this.

The newspapers are still reverberating with our debt note to Great Britain. The Britishers are apparently flabbergasted by our proposal. They think we are going to make return to gold our bargaining point in return for debt concessions. The chief point, that we are determined on an Anglo-American united front to make the World Economic Conference a success and to start world recovery if that is possible in that way, is ignored. If only American opinion on the debts can be loosened up much will be possible. We can then perhaps convince the British that we have new policies and that what we are after is not a bargain but steps toward recovery.

January 25, 1933

Tuesday afternoon Patterson, Warburg, Stewart and myself met in Stewart's office. I laid the whole problem before them and asked that they make themselves an informal board of advisers on the problems we shall have to meet in conversations with the British. Stewart and Warburg will necessarily concentrate on finance and currency and Patterson on tariffs with special reference to the Ottawa agreements.

It was agreed that we should work under cover. But Stewart is to see Day and make contact concerning the agenda meetings in Geneva from which he will be returning toward the last of the week. Meantime, I am leaving for a few days in Washington and then a visit to F.D.R. at Warm Springs to report on developments. In all probability Day and Williams will come to Washington and we can confer with them there.

The British reply to our note is published this morning. It accepts, but conditionally, saying that nothing can be settled in preliminary talks between the two nations alone which affect others and are on the agenda for the conference. This is a direct reply to our insistence on discussions of economic affairs coincident with debt negotiations. They are preparing to be insistent on cancellation. In fact Cabinet Ministers over there are making speeches which amount to lectures to us on elementary economics. The whole attitude is that we are inferior and illiterate - if we were not we should see that we ought to cancel all international obligations. I still favor only a write-down, though I think a moratorium for several years to enable all of us to pull out of the depression, ought to be arranged.

Other nations are rapidly approaching the State Department with proposals to talk about debts: F.D.R. has told Stimson over the phone that we will talk with any and all apparently including even those who did not pay on December 15th. For this I am glad. The question now arises whether we ought to discuss the economic questions of the Conference in a preliminary way with all of them. Stewart thinks we should since it seems clear that no bilateral treaties will be agreed to by Britain in advance of the general conference. I must ask F. D. R. his views on this and tell him Stewart's judgment.

In this same connection I must record a talk with Bogdanov night before last at his apartment. I discussed with him and Mirhalsky (I think) general conditions in Russia. (Several other persons were there). In a private talk with Bogdanov I told him what I had told Kellett several weeks ago and reported to F.D. R. that I believed recognition would come faster in an atmosphere of calm and quiet than in one in which agitation was being carried on. I repeated the request to Bogdanov that all pressure and agitation be avoided and he promised to assist in every way. Then I asked whether, if it seemed desirable, some Russian representatives could come for preliminary conversations before the conference. Russia is all-important to a wheat agreement; but since she owes us no debt there is no excuse for having her representatives here. He said he would be glad to take it up with Moscow and I promised to take it up with F.D.R.

A few days ago I sent my Industrial Discipline off to the Press. They intend to publish it in the Spring.

Yesterday I gave Forrest Davis of the World-Telegram a long interview for special articles. I thought it better to do this than to have him write one just from my printed work as he was instructed to do. It will be interesting to see whether he handles it fairly. I was frank about my view and hopes as to policy. We'll see if this is the best policy.

Last night I spent the evening with Mr. Kent, the architect of the new library, and Coss, Hawkes, Carman and Dick discussing interior decoration and arrangements of studies and books for the building now being built.

Moley and I agree this morning that in view of the British reply, we were even wiser than we then realized in our position or procedure at Washington last week. If there had been an identification of debt and other discussions the British would probably have refused altogether.

January 29, 1933

I have learned a lesson this week. When I arrived in Washington I discovered the local Scripps-Howard paper full of my interview. Davis had not played fair and had used my interview to forecast the new Administration's economic policies. There was a great furor over it embarrassing both F.D.R. and myself. I issued a statement disclaiming any official connection, etc. But it seemed best to keep away from Warm Springs, so after a day or two in Washington I came back to New York dodging reporters and attempting again to regain my anonymity. Moley was very helpful, never got excited, comforted me and explained everything to F.D.R. The whole thing may turn out to be a useful trial balloon but after this I shall never trust another reporter.

In Washington I had a long talk with Lewis Douglas and Moley and I met a group of inflationist Congressmen to see what was in their minds. They want to inflate by expanding Federal Reserve note issues through subscription to bond issues by the Treasury. Rather fantastic on the face of it though I resolved to look into the mechanism further.

I called at the State Department twice and saw Feis and Livsey (who was just back from the agenda meeting: Day and Williams were not to report at Washington until several days later) but could not make out much of what went on. Moley and I did a good deal of dodging of reporters, though we got out of this without much embarrassment.

Back in New York yesterday I got in touch with Day and we agreed not to meet until he had visited the State Department. But he asked that we communicate to F.D.R. the change in the British during the meeting in Geneva from pressing for an early Conference to pressing for a late one. This is the outcome of their determination to get the debt thing entirely out of the way first so that no bargaining on economic matters can include debt settlements. This we transmitted to the Governor by telephone, learning from him that he had invited Lindsay, the British Ambassador, to Warm Springs for a conference before Lindsay goes back to London to advise the Cabinet on our attitudes. I hope the Governor will speak frankly to him, for this whole matter threatens to become an impasse.

Stewart, Warburg and I had a long talk yesterday afternoon at Warburg's home. In organizing this new group there is a good deal of bringing up to date to be done. It is necessary for me to try to explain not only F.D.R.'s views but his pragmatic quality of mind, his Dutch persistence and his peculiar idealisms. We explored matters of domestic policy at some length as well as questions involving the projected conversations with the foreign nations who are coming here. I find Stewart a wise and open-faced man who is easy to like and trust; Warburg has very few of the qualities I expected to find in the son of his father. He knows a good deal but is not gifted in exploring implications, is a little naive, too, but wants to be liberal and is eager to help. I am sure there is the makings of a useful group here. To it Moley and I have decided to add Charles Taussig who has been sort of attached to the group all along and who has been working faithfully on tariffs; and a man named Romaine who is head of the Standard Statistics Company, one of the better of the commercial ventures in this field. He helped us a number of times in the exigencies of the campaign and will be very useful in furnishing statistics and in working on the commodity regularization phase of the program.

I feel strongly that Day ought to be added for the sake of continuation, believing also that he is not too committed to Hooverism, and that he is shrewd and able. I should not care to have Williams, but Day is of a different sort. Moley is much opposed to this but I think I shall persuade him.

Since I am not going to Warm Springs, and since F.D.R. will not be back in New York until February 18, I am sending the following memorandum by Moley of things I should have talked over if I had been there.

Memorandum for Professor Moley

1. Office of Education: American Council of Education requests temporary continuation of Cooper and leave to nominate an agreed-on successor.

2. Suggest letter to Social Science Research Council.

3. Following group of experts at work preparing for economic conversations: W.W. Stewart, E. M. Patterson, James Warburg, - Romaine, (E.E.Day?)

4. Get F. D.'s idea of preparatory work to be done; any ideas of agenda? Can they discuss anything at all? Shipping subsidies, for instance?

5. Suggest that Germany and Russia particularly are not to be here for debt conversations and that between them they will be extremely important in the Economic Conference. Our single greatest free market is Russia. Germany and ourselves have common interest there. Ought we to have pre-conference meetings with them as well?

6. Harriman and others are pressing for a falling back to a new line on farm relief.

7. To our group about the only way of compromise on the debts seems to be some variety of postponement. Our preparation will proceed, as far as possible, by leaving this factor unknown and regarding the matter as one of alternatives, with estimates of consequences.

8. It is opinion of our expert group that there will be a considerable liquidation with new lows all around in the spring - just when depends on debt settlements, progress of economic conversations, etc. We hope it may come in February but fear it as late as April. In view of that possibility overconfidence everywhere in possibilities of recovery under the new administration ought be discouraged.

9. As soon as Secretary of State is known, there ought to be better possibility of access to resources of State, Treasury and Commerce Departments for preparatory group in economics. Some formal designation will relieve the mystery and the curiosity of newspapers.

January 31, 1933

The Senate continues to dawdle about the Farm Bill, seeming neither to like the House version nor to know what to do about it. Harriman and Ezekiel have been urging me to come to Washington about it; but I have resolved to give all my time and attention to preparation for the coming economic conversations. They say Morgenthau is not trusted by the farm groups and that I am. All this trouble could have been avoided if there had been a clear responsibility for seeing it through. If F.D.R. would make up his mind about the Secretaryship it might yet be straightened out. As things are, various alternatives to the price parity-allotment scheme are being listened to and played with and nothing is getting done. Provided nothing happens in this Session, the Bill will have to be first in order at the new Session. I have told Moley all about it and he left last night for Warm Springs. What will be done immediately I don't know, but probably nothing effective. The trouble with the present situation is that the enemies of the bill are being given excellent opportunities for propaganda and are using them. The Press reports nothing favorable and much that is damaging.

On the economic situation, Moley is to consult F.D. for further instructions and let me know. I enlisted Romine yesterday for our group. He will be useful in many ways, but especially on the problems of commodity regularization. He is manager, also, of the Standard Statistics Company, and his group will be useful for compilations, etc.

Moley and I had a talk yesterday about our futures. I told him not to ask for any job for me from the new administration. I said, however, that I would always be glad to take hold of any emergency and do what I could. At present I an mainly interested in the legalization of the expert group which is to talk to the British. I advised Moley not to go further in his present anomalous role. He has much work, many responsibilities, and no authority. F.D.R. is certainly not treating him - or me, for that matter - fairly in requiring so much of us without any acknowledgement of our position. For myself, I shall go very cautiously until some regularization takes place.

Having been scared, for instance, by the close connection, in the public mind, between Roosevelt and a certain few of us, I arranged for the indefinite postponement of the publication of The Industrial Discipline. This may be overcautious, but the last chapter deals with the relation between Government and business and I don't want anyone to think that I am trying to force Roosevelt's hand or to get any additional prestige by association with him. It seemed best to arrange for postponement, which the Press agreed to.

It is about decided, too, that we will publish my educational material in two separate volume of about 100,000 words each. This seems best to the Press and it makes no difference to me.

February 4, 1933

Very little progress has been made this week on the matter in which I am most engaged just now - preparation for the economic conversations to come. At a meeting of the group - Stewart, Patterson, Taussig, Warburg, Romine - on Thursday, little could be done because everyone was uneasy about questions of procedure. F. D. is much too casual about delegation. If I had gone to Warm Springs I could have got him to define our present talk and indicate what is to be expected of this group in the actual conversations. Moley, of course, is there, but his mind is less on this than on other things and he probably does not see this situation as any different than so many which came up in the campaign when everyone worked with no reference to authority or commitment. But it is different. It is leading directly to international negotiations of a sort as serious as any ever undertaken. There must be preparation; but these must also be indications of limits and delegation of authority. Two rather worried calls to him at Warm Springs have left things as vague as ever. I think none of the group is at all unwilling to work. And none of them doubts my authority to ask it. But they feel uncertain where it comes out. Also we shall soon have to request cooperation from the government departments and I do not feel like going to Washington and requesting cooperation of that sort.

About all that was done on Thursday, aside from some general exploration of policy, was to hear from Day a report about the agenda meeting in Geneva.

Day is another source of uncertainty. I can't get an answer to the question whether or not he is to continue. Evidently Williams is not wanted; and I agree to that. But I have urged Day's retention.

I have had one or two private talks with Stewart. We disagree on domestic means to recovery, he believing it must come through expansion of equipment industries and I believing it can best be had by reconstructing purchasing power. He really is a wise and sympathetic person, however, and his great competence in a field where I am grossly ignorant disposes me to lean heavily on him. I should like to see him take the lead in the economic conversations. I believe he would organize the thing wisely and loyally. He refused to cooperate with the Hoover crowd; but is willing to do anything under the new auspices. If I can step out soon and turn the thing to him I shall do so gladly.

February 6, 1933

Stewart and I have been having some very satisfactory

conversations, one on Saturday in my office and yesterday at his apartment. Herbert Feis was present at yesterday's talk, having come from Washington on some other matters.

The problems facing us classify into: one, procedure, two, personnel, and three, policy. As to procedure we both feel that it may be better to keep things to a simple level in talking with the British rather than to get into a too-involved technical tangle which would lengthen things out. We feel that it may be better to test out crucial matters almost immediately: to test and be tested. For instance, a way might be devised to test the strength of the Empire sentiment. If Great Britain and the Dominions are determined to keep a preferential structure we may as well know it. It would be well, also, to discover whether our tariffs actually could be reduced.

As to personnel Moley said over the phone from Warm Springs that two others would need to be added to our group - who, I don't know, but suspect the Governor wants a silver man. This would be all right. We believe it is possible to do something with silver. Stewart believes it can be stabilized at 35 cents an ounce. It is now 25. This would be something for the silver countries. Otherwise, I should suppose the personnel will only be augmented by people from the government departments.

As to policy: on the assumption that we can give the British such a deal on the debts as it will embarrass them to refuse, we ought to try to do something on silver and wheat stabilization; to try to create purchasing power out of sterilized funds everywhere (our bank deposits in liquidation; the standstill funds); to try to lower tariffs and abolish exchange restrictions, and, perhaps, to do something on shipping subsidies. It is clear, also, that there ought to be a Conference of Central Banks coincident with the W. E. C and the British will probably agree to this.

The debts seem to us a lever with greatly impaired usefulness. It is probably only the British who will sacrifice anything to pay them. The others will, perhaps, not worry about default. It is, therefore, important to have an agreement with the British before June 15, but not so important with the others.

Feis has agreed to have certain studies begun in Washington on wheat, silver, commercial statistics, etc. These can be made use of later.

February 7, 1933

A meeting of the group considering the problems to be met and conversations with the British on economic matters yesterday afternoon was rather unsatisfactory in its outcome. Most of the group seemed to feel that the unsettled problems of policy, which none of us could answer, were such as to preclude further work until some authoritative word can be had.

The issue which seemed most important was the question of the maintenance of the gold standard as over against the possibility of inflation. This is a question, of course, which is deeply troubling to the country as a whole at the present time and I have taken the position that the President ought not to commit himself too deeply on either side of it until the necessities of the case have a chance to dictate their own policies. This seemed to Stewart wholly unsatisfactory as a basis of procedure. He feels that the President ought to say what his intention is with respect to this question very publicly and that our policy ought to be dictated by the answer. This seems to him a much more basic decision, for instance, than the question whether we are to raise or lower the tariffs. My position was that even this matter ought to remain for the moment in a flexible state and that we ought to be prepared to consider all kinds of improvised ways of meeting the exigent situations which I feel we are apt to find ourselves in during the next few months. The meeting, as a matter of fact, broke up on this note and how to proceed from here seems clear to none of us.

Before coming to this matter we heard something from Day concerning probable differences of opinion between ourselves and the British and thought that if we could assume a common desire to reach some stable basis of international exchange, the British might be willing, for their own sakes, to undertake the preliminary steps. More than that probably cannot be done. Day and Williams' plea for a de facto stabilization of the pound seems to us not only impossible from the British point of view but an undesirable way for us to bring pressure on the British.

We explored a good deal further the possibilities of doing something with silver both in a modified way and going over completely to international bimetallism. It was clearly the sense of the meeting that neither one ought to be tried which surprised me somewhat in view of Stewart's having previously said to me that he thought it might be possible to work out something in this field.

We explored also, in a general way, the field of the tariff, but here again could reach no conclusion because it is not clear what American policy is going to be. Our position as a creditor nation is what confuses all arguments of this sort. If we are to demand an excess of international payments to us it is logical that we should be prepared to receive an excess of imports over exports. Whether or not we shall be willing to accept the logic of this situation when it comes to working out the details of a tariff program, none of us knows; but it is certain to come up early in the conversations and we must have an answer to the question.

The whole affair, therefore, rests in this unsatisfactory state at the moment. Roosevelt will not be available for consultation for another two weeks. In the meantime we hope to get some authoritative word either from Moley or Hull. In my telephone conversations with Moley I asked him, in anticipation of these questions becoming crucial, to get the answers for me from the Governor if he could. So far he has let me know nothing and I cannot find out until he returns. Taussig is to visit Senator Hull tomorrow and possibly something may be learned from that since Hull has recently been in Warm Springs.

February 10, 1933

Since the rather unsatisfactory meeting on Monday the 6th matters relating to economic preparation have stood still waiting for Moley to get back from the South with some word from F.D.R.

He got back yesterday. F. D. R. wants Baruch to be chairman of the group and wants Judge Bingham of Louisville added. This last must be because he is to be Ambassador to Great Britain. Baruch carries sufficient prestige but may be hard to handle on other counts. Moley confirms my refusal to make commitment to a die-hard policy on currency. He agrees it is the only thing to do. How Baruch will be on this remains to be seen. Moley will see him first this morning and tell him of the commission and then I will have to bring him up to date. It is a relief not to carry this particular responsibility longer. But time is slipping by and the meeting with the British is less than a month off. I shall probably have to continue as one of the group.

Moley came back with word that Berle, Taussig and I were to have jobs in the new administration: Taussig, Tariff Commission, Berle, Federal Trade Commission, and myself Assistant Secretary of Commerce. But Berle and Taussig declined so Moley said I could have my pick of the three. I shall think it over for a while.

I was immensely pleased, however, that Wallace is to be Secretary of Agriculture with Wilson as Assistant - that, at least, is one hope come true!

February 12, 1933

The fact that Baruch is to be chairman of the group to prepare for the British conversations leave things in a bit of a mess with March 4 so short a time away. He cannot begin meetings until the 20th, according to Moley, and that will be pretty late. However, I am to see him this afternoon to tell him what has happened. Moley has heard from the Senate progressives, who were asked to name some one, and they want Senator Blaine (who goes out as a Senator on March 4). That gives us the following group: Baruch (Chairman), Blaine, Bingham, Stewart, Warburg,

Patterson, Day, Taussig and myself. I must try to arrange with Baruch for work to be done between now and the 20th. Nothing can be done about formal appointments or matters of protocol until F. D. gets back at the end of this week.

H.I. Harriman spent the morning with me yesterday and stayed to lunch. He came to give Moley and myself his idea of a program. Moley stayed for the first hour of our talk. I was especially interested to feel him out concerning the relations of government to business. Unless something can be done to bring business closer under government control and to change over from the old anti-trust law repressions to recognition and control of present trends and scale, I certainly would not be interested in becoming Assistant Secretary of Commerce. But he was rather encouraging about this, saying that he thought business would accept a good deal of control rather than continue with intermittent repression.

I have been playing with a suggestion of T. Blaisdell that the old Bureau of Corporations in Commerce be revived and the investigative staff of the Federal Trade Commission be moved over to it. Then, if some such scheme as I outlined in the last chapter of The Industrial Discipline could be worked out acceptably to Congress and to business, its administration could center there. The Federal Trade Commission has become so emasculated by court decisions that it might be better to abandon this line and start a new one. If this could be done it would be worth while to have a hand in it. But a lot depends on who is to be the Secretary of Commerce.

February 13, 1933

I thought today that I would make a new effort to get things started. Fundamental studies looking to conversations with the British ought to be begun. I did call Feis but after telling him to assemble what he could get from the Departments in Washington, Moley said that F.D. had said for us to keep clear of the State Department. I called him again and made it clear that all he did would have to wait until F.D. returns, as least it is not my responsibility and I have done what I could.

The more I think of it the less I enjoy the prospect of an official job. Integrity is an elusive thing; but there is no greater satisfaction than the feeling that it is protected. I am afraid of the eternal compromises I may be asked to make.

My talk with Baruch yesterday was not too satisfactory. He has an immense ego but not much knowledge. He will undertake the job but knows nothing yet of what is involved. He asked me to prepare the studies of background material - to arrange for them - but I am too limited in situation. No authority. Things will have to wait.

February 15, 1933

I saw President Butler yesterday and talked with him about two matters. First, I asked whether it would be possible for the University to provide $2000 in the budget next year for Donald Henderson who has been asked to leave at the end of this year. He said he would agree to it provided it was satisfactory to Hawkes, McBain and Fackenthal, and when I assured him that it had been agreed to by everyone, he asked me to tell Fackenthal to arrange it which I did. He agreed that it was a practical matter which was probably a good investment for the University, since, if we had dropped Henderson unconditionally at the end of the year, there would probably have been many protests from his friends among the Communists and the Social Problems Club. This ought to serve to keep them quiet though there is no particular justice involved.

Afterwards I asked him for some advice concerning the probability that I may be asked to do something in Washington during the coming administration. He said he thought it would be a mistake to make any formal official connection and cited his own experience of having been asked several times to be Secretary of State and Ambassador to Great Britain. He said for one thing, he would never take a job whose termination was unpredicted and, in the second place, he refused to be tied up by bothersome official annoyances which surround anyone in Washington. This would seem to me good advice if I were in the same position as he is. He is President of Columbia University and I am a professor, which makes all the difference. He said, however, that I could easily arrange for a leave of absence for a year if there was something for which I was needed in Washington.

Taussig called me last evening and asked me whether matters concerning economic conversations had made any progress. I told that they had not and that I was determined not to proceed any further without better authorization. He said he had talked to Moley just before Moley left Miami to meet the President and that Moley had asked me to call Judge Bingham and tell him that there would be a meeting of the entire group on Monday. This is the first I had heard of a meeting on Monday but perhaps Moley expects to arrange it with Roosevelt on the way home. As matters were left between me and Baruch, Baruch expected to notify me as soon as he came back from the South and I was then to arrange for a talk between the three of us before we called the group together but it may still be possible to carry out these preliminaries and still have the whole group meet on Monday.

There is still talk in the papers that MacDonald may come even before March 4. Ambassador Lindsay sailed for the United States yesterday with a financial adviser, which means probably that he expects to get in touch with the new administration immediately concerning preliminaries to our conversation.

I saw Berle yesterday and he did not seem so determined as he was formerly not to go to Washington. His reasons for not going are that he has assembled a whole group of his family around him in his law office and that they are dependent on him for their productivity, but I imagine this resistance may break down and March 4 may see the whole group assembled in Washington in some way or other.

February 17, 1933

Henry Wallace turned up yesterday and we spent the whole day together. He has had his letter of invitation from F. D. R. and is keeping under cover for the time being. He said the reporters became troublesome in Des Moines and he spent some time with his sister in Detroit and is now in New York waiting to see F. D. R. when he comes home. We congratulated ourselves on the Miami incident. There seems to be no way of protecting F. D. R. from actual danger now. He will simply have to expose himself less and trust to radio more though this is an unnatural procedure for him.

Wallace and I talked over nearly the whole range of problems we are facing. I got a good chance to lay many of my coordinating ideas before him with which he agrees. He read several chapters of The Industrial Discipline (I wonder if that book will ever see the light) and he was enthusiastic about the proposal for coordination in the last chapter. Much of our talk turned on reorganization of his Department. He seems to me very wise about it. He is especially interested to preserve the research and educational work but realizes fully how difficult it is to terminate any Federal function at all once it has started. Secretaries come and go but Bureau chiefs go on forever.

We talked about the past neglect of the function of economic control - how the Departments regard themselves, not as public agencies so much as special agents for the interests they represent. There is needed a new view of Commerce and Agriculture, for instance, as representatives, in special fields of the public, rather than representatives to the public of special fields. Given such a reversal of view, it would be possible to proceed toward entirely new policies in which a larger conception could be dominant. The interest of the public is in an agriculture suited to national needs; agriculture exists for the country; the country does not exist to support farmers. These ideas of mine Wallace agreed to wholly. I was interested to see that he appreciates his limitations as an administrator and that he hopes to remedy this by associating others with him for this purpose. We spoke especially of Earl Smith and Clifford Gregory. He is one of the most interesting people I know but he is wholly unworldly, not exactly impractical but moving more

freely among ideas than among situations. Yet he has a shrewd political
sense, too, and realizes the necessities of patronage. We went together
to lunch with Judge Bingham at the Park Lane. I brought him up to date
on the British conversation moves. He is an affable, well-addressed,
cultivated person. After seeing him I judge it likely that he may be the
Ambassador. And he may a be good one, too.

At night we went to see "Biography" at the Theatre Guild. In the
afternoon we had a long walk, talking ourselves hoarse.

February 19, 1933

The last two days have been interesting and lively; certain matters
have come finally to a head.

I saw F.D.R. on Friday for about two hours, going over many
issues. He seemed undisturbed by the attempt on his life and quite
disgusted with the zeal of the New York police in protecting him.

He O.K.'d arrangements for meeting myself and Baruch on
Sunday (today) and the whole group on Monday. I asked if I could now
request departmental assistance through Feis and he said "Yes." He made
the same answer to the question whether Feis should be included in the
Monday group.

He asked about Wilson as Wallace's Assistant Secretary. I was
opposed. I thought Wallace, not being strong on that side, should have an
able administrator. He agreed and asked for suggestions but I hesitated
to suggest anyone until I had talked to Wallace.

He expressed some indignation at what he spoke of as
Morgenthau's "campaign for the Secretaryship," and said that it had
merely irritated him; he had finally determined, he said, to offer him the
Chairmanship of the Home Loan Bank.

There was a tremendous pressure to do something about the
banking situation for everything is really going to pieces in Wall Street.
When I first came in Louis Howe was there and he was talking to Stimson
about Liberia. Afterward he laughed at Stimson's frank suggestion that
we should protect the Firestone investments there. Woodin came in
soon and he and Howe told F.D.R. how the banking situation had gone
to pot and how the bankers were all hysterical. All the big guns were
brought up.   Aldrich, Young, McKane, etc. were after him to do
something. He took it all smiling and could see no reason why he should
save these bankers; it was more important, he said to us, to save the folks.
I was proud of him. We discussed for some time various means of getting
currency out for business purposes if all the banks should close, which
now seems possible. I suggested the post offices and a liquidating
corporation for closed banks with power to issue script. This situation
is developing swiftly and may mean a tremendous change. But F.D.R. is

calm and sane about it. All the bankers now want their deposits
guaranteed by the government, something they fought for years. But he
sees no reason, as he said repeatedly, for specially protecting this interest
as against all others.

Saturday at noon I took H.A. Wallace to see F.D.R. We talked
about the general situation for some time and then I left them. When I
came back they both began to urge me to take the Assistant Secretaryship
of Agriculture. I said I thought I was to be in Commerce, if anywhere, and
urged that I was a university professor from New York City and that it
was most unsuitable politically and something I had not for a moment
contemplated. F.D.R. said what was most needed was skilled
administration for awhile until reorganization was complete. I said I
thought I ought to be outside somewhere where I could think and give
advice and do odd and confidential jobs. He said "Yes, but Wallace wants
you now and it seems a good thing to me." So I suggested that I go there
for a while to do H.A.'s surgery for him and start things off and that I
then leave and go somewhere else. F.D.R. saw that. It would, of course,
make it easier for Wallace if I did the reorganization work. He could
stand aside and say that of course he was helpless since I was so close to
the President. I could then get out and leave him with a clean situation.
So finally we all agreed on this. I now have my arrangements to make.
I rather bewilderedly woke up the way home to realize how casually
F.D.R. marshalled me into service.

February 20, 1933

Yesterday I took Baruch to see F.D.R. We talked over the
arrangements to meet the British and discussed current policy. Today I
assembled the whole group at F.D.R.'s 65th street house where he spoke
a few encouraging words and started the thing off. Cordell Hull was
unfortunately ill and so not present as we had planned but we made it
plain that he was to be Secretary of State and that our subcommittee men
were to work through him in getting work done by the government. The
work was divided into three major groups with Stewart in charge of
currency--exchange matters; Patterson in charge of tariff matters, and
Romine dealing with raw materials.

February 24, 1933

Planning for a change of life in these few days. It took some time
yesterday to put the quietus on the Smith cotton bill in the House. But,
at F.D.R.'s request I worked it through Marvin Jones who was
extraordinarily docile.

February 26, 1933

Day before yesterday Moley and I borrowed Bobby Straus' car and drove to Hyde Park where we spent the whole afternoon with F.D.

In the morning I had talked with Bobby and discovered that the whole Straus clan was in an uproar - not so much over the frustration of Jesse's ambition to be Secretary of Commerce as over the fact that old Henry Morgenthau had called him up and told him about it in a patronizing way. The Jewish first-family rivalry was involved. It happened because the Morgenthaus' were more pushing than the Strauses and because F.D. did not sense the situation. He is apt to forget a person who is out of sight, these days, with so much going on. And, indeed, no individual is so very important to him. He likes to talk to people but it doesn't much matter who and he makes up his mind almost regardless of advice.

The Straus matter will be fixed up by a few pleasant words from him but it ought not to have happened. If he were to be careless his secretaries ought to have caught it but they are not that sort. There is a charming carelessness about the whole household which has its advantages but also its faults. Perhaps things will take on a little more organization in the White House.

He spent some two hours reading photostat copies of a correspondence dealing with Henry Ford's attempt to get Muscle Shoals. It was explosive stuff and involved the Morgan outfit and Dwight Morrow - who, Walter Lippmann said to me, was the only first-quality statesman he had ever known! The whole thing revealed a cynical attempt to exploit the government for private advantage with no thought, apparently, on anyone's part that there was anything wrong about it. How the correspondence got into Louis Howe's hands none of us know yet. It was brought up by Jim Farley under seal and he stayed with us to hear it read but refused our offer to take him back to New York. He preferred the train.

I had never had much to do with him until that day. He is a good hearty Irish type. His ability is apparent as is also his lack of interest in any general ideas. He is frank and open as well as resourceful. It is impossible not to like him.

F.D.R., before we left, told me to come down to Washington to see Senator Hull (who has been announced for Secretary of State) and bring him up to date on the economic matters I have been pushing. I am to arrange for quarters for the group in the State Department building, to get Herbert Feis made executive secretary of the group and in general talk over policy. Baruch has gone off South again without starting anything and we think he is probably running out on us. This will be a delicate point in my conversation with Hull because we do not know exactly what his relations with Baruch are. So much Baruch money has been spread around - as campaign contributions and otherwise -that it never does to criticize him publicly. But F.D.R. is well aware of it and does not trust him. The attempt to have him act as chairman of this group is really a way of keeping him out of the cabinet. But he may cause us trouble. He and Smith run together naturally and as time goes on they will form a little group of their own as opposition within the party. We have discussed it several times and F.D.R. is quite prepared to have it happen.

The country's reaction to the cabinet is, on the whole, good. It is acknowledged to be a quiet, serious group, without prima-donnas but with a distinct progressive cast. Even the East is not too critical, Ickes was a surprise to me-as to nearly everyone. He was named by Hiram Johnson - which, of course, gives us firm support there. Roper was a personal choice which I am inclined to suspect is rather a grave mistake. However, that will appear soon enough.

I came to Washington last night. Today I am to see Hull and Feis -dining with the Feises. It is a bitter, windy day; the grand-stands across the park, ready for their bunting, are a rather arrant gesture toward a gaudier past. This is a serious business we are in and the inaugural gaieties will hardly lift the gloom even momentarily. F. D. struggles every day with the problems of a crumbling banking system, with a ruined railway system and a thousand other like matters. He is meeting them all seriously but with his head up and with a confidence I should like to share.

One of the first problems I shall meet at the Dept. of Agriculture I imagine, outside of the reorganization on which Wallace, Ezekiel and I are working, will be the Pure Food and Drugs administration which has been perverted by the attempt to protect business interests, forgetting those of consumers. Schlink, of Consumers' Research, says he has it on the present crowd there. I have asked for his stuff. I shall ask Lee to work it over; and if it pans out we'll blow them out of the water. I have long wanted this chance and shall make the best use I can of it, though I realize how much risk I shall run in doing it.

This morning I called on Senator Hull at the Carleton and we talked generally for a whole hour and agreed to meet late in the evening for a long talk. Ezekiel and I went over to the Dept. Agriculture building and looked over the offices. Mine is rather heavy but can be made liveable, I think, by simple decorative changes. At any rate it is ample for my purpose and I am prepared to like it.

I had dinner with the Feises and had a long drive into the country. Feis and I talked a good deal about the internal and international policies in prospect. We worked out the necessary procedure for getting the economic group to function: to assign quarters in the State Building and to ask Feis to act as executive secretary. Whether Baruch slips away or not we will now have a center of initiative on the job.

Hull and I explored the whole situation in the evening for two hours, mostly alone, but part of the time with W. Bullitt.

We cannot understand the British attitude except on the assumption that to them the debts are everything and the rest of the program of recovery nothing. He feels they want to drive us off gold to establish the pound as the world's monetary unit; I doubt this, thinking they stand to lose trade by it. But in any case we agree that trade restrictions are basic to the whole problem and that some economic diplomacy must be devised to break down barriers. The alternative is economic nationalism and the other nations should know that we are in the best position to play that game.

The British are stalling, working toward the June 15th payment date with nothing settled, in which case they will default probably and will then not have to join with us in a world program. I got Senator Hull to agree to ask Stimson to send a note to the British asking for immediate conversations both on debts and economic matters; but I then called F.D. on the phone and he vetoed this. Hull is to see Lindsay in the morning and is to say that if they insist on clean cancellation, nothing can be done. If they do not, then they must send plenary negotiators both on debts and economic matters.

Senator Hull and I would both of us rather force the matter, writing a note laying down a whole program of recovery and inviting the British to join, putting them in the wrong if they would not. Instead of that the present situation threatens to put us in the wrong because we are taking an absolute position on the debts. That, of course, may be done after March, but the question is whether it will. I am sure Hull wants to.

February 27, 1933

This was an extremely busy day. Early this morning I called on Hull and went over with him again the world situation in which the conversation with the British must be carried on. I urged him to convey to Lindsay our sense that the debts were adjustable matters although perhaps not immediately; also that this final settlement on which they are insisting is only a small part of a large program for world recovery in which we all must find a means of joint action. Hull agreed. He was really eloquent in stating the case for a new view of the world situation which should start with a truce in the economic warfare of recent years. He looks tired, pale and old. He has been suffering from an infected foot which has ill prepared him for the suddenly heavy burdens of these days. He looks- and is - a studious, retiring person, not suited to political hurly-burly.

Later I visited the Dept. of Agriculture. Neither Secretary was in but I arranged with some underling for Wallace's reception (and that of his Assistant Secretary) on Friday morning, the day before inauguration.

Subsequently Feis reported that he had traced the gold restriction law which I had asked him to look up a week before. He had asked Bell in the Treasury and they had the information on tap. Apparently they had thought of using it once before. Willis evidently asked for it, or Ballantine. I was satisfied that if we had to go off gold here was the means, but it needed a lawyer's exploration. I called F. D. R. and he said to get in touch with Walsh (who is to be Att'y Gen'l) and to get him to report on it. I tried, but Walsh was on his honeymoon (at 73 or so!) and would not be back for days. The situation is very acute with banks crumbling everywhere and with a greatly accelerated outflow of gold and this power might be needed at any moment. I called F.D.R. back and he said to get in touch with Pittman or Byrnes. I went to the Capitol and sent in my card to both but could locate neither. Finally, however, I found Pittman and asked him to study the thing. He saw its importance and agreed to do so and report to F.D.R.

This is an interesting thing. The power of the executive referred to occurs in a war measure, the Trading with the Enemy Act, and not in the Act itself but in an amendment. The first question was one of termination. There was a bracketed clause, in one section of the amendment, terminating the provisions at two years after the end of the war. But the Act itself was never repealed and apparently the termination clause did not apply to the gold control provisions. The various clauses were set off by semicolons and it is a nice question of construction altogether. There is needed also further investigation as to whether this war act was superseded by any other act or treaty, though that seems unlikely since a compilation and digest was made by the legislative service in 1928 which referred to none. I set the citation down for what interest it may have: Trading with the Enemy Act (as amended) (Together with the original act and the amendments thereto prior to Apr. 2, 1928) and the Settlement of War Claims Act of 1928. Prepared for the use of the Committee on Ways and Means of the House of Representatives by the office of the Legislative Counsel. (Government Printing Office, Apr. 2,1928) It will be interesting to see what comes of Pittman's research and what use is made of the act.

During the day I sandwiched in a talk with Lewis Douglas (now named Budget Director) covering departmental reorganization in general and the Dept. Agriculture in particular. I promised cooperation but urged him to let the initiative, as far as possible, come up out of the departments. This is a matter I feel very strongly. I think if I can be allowed to follow my own procedure I may be able to cut down our expenditure and to reorganize without incurring too much ill-will among my future colleagues. But not if a great hullabaloo is made about it and everyone is nervous and scared concerning his job. It will be a delicate piece of executive work and I look forward to it as I imagine many people do to a good game of some sort.

As I went to take the train at four o'clock I found O'Neal waiting on the platform saying that the Smith cotton bill was going to be called out and passed. The President had refused to intervene before and I did not see what I could say, so I got on the train and left him sorrowing. But just before the train started, the station master came in with a message saying that the State Department urgently wanted me. I got off and called. It was Feis. The Treasury people (Bell) had told him they had given him the wrong citation and he was much excited. I asked him to come to Pittman's office where, I said, we would go into the thing further.

Meanwhile I located Marvin Jones and tackled him about the cotton bill. He was determined to go ahead. I pointed out that it was as poor idea administratively and that besides it would drive a wedge between the West and the South just when we seemed on the verge of getting the first all-around legislation for farm relief in all the years of effort. But, I said, we would not intervene; it was up to him whether he would play ball with us or not. He thought there was little likelihood of passage but seemed pretty thoughtful over what I said.

Then I went back to Pittman's office where the Treasury people's excitement thinned out. Feis thought we were on the right track after all. But, he said, Bell had been so excited he had called Ballantine (undersecretary). Fearing a spread of rumor I counselled him to drop the thing, and to guard against tracing it beyond him to me. But I think it is known that I telephoned the information to Hyde Park. Anyway, I am leaving for N.Y. and have told Feis to forget it, leaving everything to Pittman.

This was a day! And, as we pass through Phila., I reflect that not for months have I slept more than four hours a night.

March 31, 1933

I have fallen so far behind in this record of events that it seems almost impossible to catch up. Yet we are doubtless in the midst of one of the most interesting periods in the history of the country and my recording ought to be kept up. It is the sheer pressure of decisions and responsibilities which prevents.

After the inaugural events we were plunged immediately into the banking crisis in which the presidential proclamation was based on the Trading with the Enemy Act of 1917 which I worked over for some time. This rather doubtful executive act was immediately validated by a scared Congress called into special session. Such wave of approval for F.D.R.

swept the country--so long disgusted with governmental inaction--that it seemed best to Wallace and myself to press for immediate farm legislation. To this F.D.R. agreed.

On the first Sunday night after inauguration it occurred to us that something like the broad powers assumed for banking might also be assumed for farming. But we rather gave this notion up since so much must in any case depend upon consent. We did, however, determine to call in the farm leaders for a conference. This was held within a few days. When the first leaders arrived they proposed broad general powers too, having reached this decision at a midnight conference on the train. We accepted the idea immediately provided they could get general agreement. At the conference next day, which was held in the Department, myself presiding, they secured this agreement. Next day a committee took it to the President and he told us to frame legislation on this basis. We engaged Fred Lee and set about drafting a bill. In a few days it was done and sent to Congress with a message (which I now have in original draft, F.D.R. having sent it to me). We had hoped to get the thing through before lobbyists of the processors could descend on Washington; but we immediately met with strong opposition. The packers, millers, and spinners are quite adequately represented in Congress. It seems impossible, in that group of small-town lawyers, to find anyone with the slightest interest in farmers or workers. They represent a wholly business interest for the most part. Our great difficulty was that the Chairmen of the agricultural committees in both House and Senate very definitely represented processors interests rather than farmers. We were able to bring enough pressure to bear to force the bill through the House in about four days. But as I write it is still in a Senate committee and we are busy night and day trying to save it.

It is an interesting bill in a number of respects which are unique. It declares the policy of restoring farm prices to parity but it allows us to approach this end gradually. It provides for a reduction of production but allows us to choose the method. It provides for the funds necessary to persuade land out of production but leaves us wide discretion in acquiring them. The processors tax is used but it can be applied gradually and with caution. But most interestingly, the section which was written to provide for licensing of processors (so that we might control them) turned, as we wrote it, into something with vast possibilities. It allows the Secretary to enter into agreements with associations of producers and processors on such terms as may be necessary to "eliminate unfair practices or charges that....prevent the effectuation of the declared policy" and the restoration of economic balance. This amounts, of course, to the suspension of the anti-trust acts for the food industries with broad regulatory powers lodged in the Department of Agriculture.

Our enemies read this with care. Some of them saw that they had

rom the power to agree than they had to lose from being
e opposition was, consequently, split. It is a bitter fight but
as it might otherwise have been. From the first H.A. and
it would eventually pass and it is true that the opposition
.... weaker as time has gone on and has come finally to
obstructionist and sniping tactics. The greatest handicap has been in not
having any real push in Congress. For real radicals such as Wheeler,
Frazier, etc., it is not enough; for conservatives it is too much; for
Jefferson democrats it is a new control which they distrust. For the
economic philosophy which it represents there are no defenders at all.
Nevertheless, in spite of everything it will probably become law.

While this rough-and-tumble fight has been going on I have been
working on two other major problems--beside, of course, getting
acquainted with my routine administrative duties. One of these has had
to do with the forestry bill and the other with departmental
reorganization.

The forestry bill, so far as I know, was conceived by the President
himself. He proposed to have 250,000 of the unemployed taken into a
kind of army which he called a "Civilian Conservation Army' who were to
be organized in groups and were to work in the forests and national parks
at a nominal wage. Opposition to it immediately developed from
organized labor which felt that it was an attack on wage standards. But
the unemployment problem is so tremendous that the opposition was not
sufficiently effective to prevent its becoming a law. It is being signed
today and the Department of Agriculture of course is to bear the major
administrative problems involved in its operation. The Forestry Service
I have found to be a very efficient organization and there is no doubt that
they will be able to carry out their part of this plan successfully. I have
worked on it a good deal in conferences with the Forestry people and
they are now at work on regulations to put it into effect. I have been
attracted to it because of my interest in long-run management of public
property and because it promises to do something almost immediately to
at least relieve the problem of unemployment. We expect to care for at
least 250,000 men in this way.

The other problem of departmental reorganization was really
more difficult than any. The Department is a good deal like a big
university. Many of its activities are of a research sort but intermixed
with these everywhere are more than forty regulatory acts which bring
us into contact, in mostly unpleasant ways, with the business community.
Many of the activities of the Department have been set up by statute from
time to time and the organization has become rather unwieldy and needs
reorganization. The problem of mastering the great mass of detail
involved in coming to definite functions and reducing them to some kind
of order has been tremendous but progress is being made and I have great

hopes of being able to simplify the administrative structure and putting the Department on a better functional basis. The details of this I suppose no one will be interested in later years. It is one of those immense and thankless tasks which necessarily fall to anyone who accepts administrative responsibility in times like these.

It has been greatly complicated by difficulties with the national budget. The Democratic Party has been pledged to make reductions in governmental expenditures and Lewis Douglas has been appointed Director of the Budget. It is a theory of his that research ought to bear the brunt of what he conceived to be necessary reductions, and very shortly he presented us with an ultimatum which required the reductions, of our activities by some sixty percent. This, of course, caused a rebellion and we are in the midst of a running fight with Douglas to see how much we can save of the Department's fundamental work. We refused to accept his first proposition and we are in process of making a new one to him on the basis of our reorganization plans which will reduce expenditures but yet, we hope, save the best of our activities. There is an immense amount of detail in working over these budgets.

Editor's Note

In order to avoid unnecessary duplication, the reader is referred to the section entitled, "The Hundred Days: March 31, 1933 to May 30, 1933" (p. 324). The following original entries are reproduced there: April 2, 3, 5, 14, 15, 21, 26, 1933 and May 3, 6, 30, 31, 1933. Although part of Tugwell's revised diary, the entries are just as they were written in 1933 except for Tugwell's adding of explanatory footnotes and miscellaneous attachments.

1934

1934[1]

Every little while some one says to me "of course you keep a diary", or "I wish I could see your journal" - something like that. But it usually has not seemed possible. Perhaps it may be again now; and I am willing to confess enough interest in written records to see why I ought to do it. It really is an experimental procedure which we are in the midst of too; and if enough of us wrote down our different impressions there might be real lessons in the whole record.

When I had to write a syndicated article each week, as I did for five months, together with articles and speeches averaging one or more a week, I should say, that was about all the writing I could do. My advocacy of the Food & Drug Bill lost me the syndicate last month and I am not so much in demand either for articles for the same reason. I may now have time for this record. I should like, even, to go back and record what I can of the events since I dropped it. From day to day I shall try to do that.

This is being written on the porch of a Miami Hotel. I flew down here day before yesterday and tomorrow leave by Pan American Airways for Puerto Rico-hoping also for a few days in the Virgin Islands. Charles Taussig was here in the hotel when I arrived. He explained to me his activities in the last two weeks as consultant to Governor Pearson. He also had some impressions of Puerto Rico and Governor Winship. He thinks the rum plant we have all worked for in the Virgin Island will be successful. I hope so. It can save the Islands, I believe. We had breakfast together too, then he and his wife left and I went out to spend a fascinating day with old Dr. Fairchild and the Superintendent of the

[1]No specific date given.

nt Introduction Garden at Coconut Grove.

This expedition came about in this way: in formulating the sugar bill, which I had a lot to do with engineering, I perceived the possibility of using the processing taxes on Puerto Rican sugar for the general improvement of the Island's agriculture rather than for specific benefits to producers, some sixty percent of whom are absentee. As I sized up the situation from Washington, the situation was that all possible profits from cash crops were being extracted for and by absentees. With funds available I thought some basic change might be brought about. I studied over it a good deal and became more and more convinced that we ought to try to do it. But first we had to know more. Lunching with the President one day I spoke to him about it. He urged me to see it through. I arranged with several Department people to come with me, got Secretary Dern to send me down officially, and am on my way. With me are John Carter, Silcox, the Forester, Dickey, a tobacco man, and Fred Bartlett. The last two went ahead on the boat. A day or two before leaving I discovered that Mrs. Roosevelt would be on the same Pan American plane out. It was pure coincidence; but it may not be so bad if the Politicos concentrate on her and leave me relatively free.

One thing I have had in mind is the possibility of recapturing some of the land using the subsistence homestead technique. On the whole I should think this might have to be the center of any rehabilitation scheme. But I don't like to prejudge.

Incidentally there has been a scheme floating around for a long time for a Pan American Experiment Station at Puerto Rico. It seemed to me that this was a possibility - a place with free facilities (Library, laboratories, etc., and some real scientists for staff) to which resort might be had. Dr. Fairchild was a little discouraging - said Panama was more central and had real tropical conditions. So some doubt this has come up in the beginning. Perhaps merely an enlargement of our own and the Islands' tropical agricultural work will be all that will seem justifiable.

At any rate it is swell to sit in the sunshine this morning after weeks of snow and cold and my usual winter coughs and sniffles. There is that about it any way even if it all comes to nothing.

March 6, 1934

Last night I took Mr. and Mrs. Carter to dine at the Miami-Biltmore. I had never been in it before and was interested in seeing how the lavish spenders carried on in depression. Of course Miami is by way of forgetting the depression anyway. There are great crowds of tourists here, prices are outrageous, and although everyone grumbles, they seem to like this particular paradise well enough to pay them. The Biltmore had two orchestras and a floor show . There was a room-full even on

Monday night. The same middle-aged and elderly men and women who can be seen straining their digestion and their vitality in New York restaurants of the same sort were there, the women languishingly admiring the Cuban musicians and gigolos, the men living through it and waiting for tomorrow's golf. It is an astounding thing, really, in the midst of depression. But these people couldn't do anything about that; some, of course, wouldn't if they could. The thing is, though, that they have no conviction of sin whatever, and no expectation of change. There's no hope in them.

This is being written in the Pan American Sikorsky flying out of Miami for Cuba where we fuel and go on to Haiti for the night. Silcox turned up last night late and when we were having breakfast this morning, Mrs. Roosevelt came in with her crowd. Lorena Hickok is with her and half a dozen newspaper women. But there was very little turmoil about getting away this morning and the plane is very comfortable aside from the noise. I'm anxious for a talk with Miss Hickok again. She knows more about a great many things than anyone I know. She is Harry Hopkins' eyes and ears and all of us read her reports from the country regularly. One reason the President is always surprising the country with his local knowledge is that he reads her stuff regularly.

I hope Mrs. Roosevelt can make this trip in some comfort and peace. She wants, she says, to make use of the years between now and sixty and this trip will show whether she can do it. Everyone is decent to her; but privacy of any sort is something else again.

Visually this is a lovely trip. The patches of vivid blue in the sea are incredible, the typical Caribbean light across the sky and the soft clouds against the horizon make everything contrast sharply with Northern prospects. In such a climate and with such fertile islands it seems incredible that this part of the world should be so ridden with poverty.

March 7, 1934

In the air again over Haiti after an over night stop at Port-au-Prince. Travelling with Mrs. Roosevelt is something of a task although Lorena Hickok takes up most of the slack. She and Mrs. Roosevelt, Carter and General and Mrs. Little (Commandant of Marines), it was all very nice. Armour strikes me as the best career diplomat I've seen. We had a talk about Haitian politics and economies. The sugar business is parlous here as else where. In general our trade relations are unsatisfactory. We buy little from them: they, much from us. Armour has been asked to start negotiations for a new commercial treaty with no assurances to offer except logwood - and they with denuded hills badly wanting reforestation.

I greatly enjoyed the coffee but found that almost none of it comes to us. It is not cultivated but grows wild in the hills and tastes like imagined coffee - as it should always have been but never was. Just, I suppose, as wild strawberries teach one what flavor is. We do not take it at home because the big companies demand standardization and there is too great a difference in year to year crops for them to use it in blending. I avoided talking to our man Baker in favor of seeing him on the way home; he is working mostly, I think, on long staple cotton. Armour says the realists here recognize that the economic future of the island lies with us, though the more dramatic talk a good deal still about the cultural tie with France.

It was strange to use a little French so really close to home. We slept in a little guest house the Armours have in their yard and had a swim before dinner and another before breakfast in a little bath house which was a relic of French colonial days. The Armour house was like so many in Port-au-Prince, very Swiss somehow, with high ceilings, tiled floors, and no glass - only shutters - in the windows. All very charming. Mrs. Armour is Russian, a good diplomatic wife, I should say, with a surface ease in conversation and many sharp perceptions.

We were up before dawn and flew away just precisely as the sun rose. The reason for exactitude - about which much was made -I am told is the mails. The Pan American is evidently afraid they may be next to have their contracts cancelled. The Eastern Air Transport on which I came down from Washington certainly has a low enough morale -closing many small ports, firing employees, etc. But I hope the army keeps the mails. There is a lesson needed for elegant grafters - and, anyway why should this service not be public? At any rate we're flying on time - just now above the lovely central Haitian valley - the cul-de-sac, and soon we land in the Dominican Republic.

Later

There was a good deal of the musical comedy about our landing at San Pedro de Macoris. We circled back over Santo Domingo several times and had a good look at the town; but there is no smooth water and the airport is 40 miles away. We were conducted from the landing stage by Arthur Schoenfeld, the Minister, up to a thatched reception tent where the President and his wife waited to receive. He looks somewhat like a dictator ought to - as though he might not mind a good deal of blood. His Foreign Minister must have weighed 300 pounds. They both wore formal clothes and silk toppers - all very grand. The populace stood around outside a barbed-wire stockade and clapped dutifully. Prominent ladies presented flowers - all very swell. I'm told the ambition of all Haitians and Santo Dominicans is a government job, largely because motor cars go with them. The President and cabinet in Haiti are fitted out with Packards - and so they were here. It was a little comic to see a huge brass plate on one of them marked "Wife of the President." She was a large chocolate-colored lady, very handsome. Dictators may lead precarious lives, but they evidently live them well. From what can be seen flying, Santo Domingo is far less attractive than Haiti. The city itself lies on a flat plain - and must be hot as Hades. Port-au-Prince climbs the hills and is charming. I hope I can go there again.

Everywhere we are seeing the light green squares of sugarcane - the stuff I've been worrying so much about in getting the sugar bill ready. But very little of this comes to us. Mostly to England and France.

March 8, 1934

This is noon - at the end of a busy 24 hours. I left the plane at San Juan, Mrs. Roosevelt and her party going on to St. Thomas. Gov. Winship brought me to the palace - La Forteleza - to stay. I have a room looking over the harbor and off to the hills on two sides. The Governor had his entire cabinet with their wives in to dinner; this morning I called on the Commissioner of Agriculture and the Chancellor of the University. Both are interesting and intelligent people. But I am just listening. Politics here, everyone says, are devious and I want mostly to make an economic-political judgment of possiblilites.

Everyone here seems to be quite aware of the possibilities involved in the expenditure of yields from the sugar processing tax; and it may be difficult to put through a plan even though we devise one which is good. Politicians are the same everywhere in jockeying to get whatever is to be done anyway. This is all right if they help rather than obstruct; but frequently they are stupid about their own interests. Governor Winship is a fine old army man with many years experience in Cuba, the Philippines and Liberia, with what appears to be a nice mixture of tact and firmness. He seems to have people's confidence here and I am sure that the game will be to work through him. I've had several long talks with him and he seems very anxious to play the game our way. He resents exploitation and has several little wars on with gasoline companies, public utilities, etc., who have exploited people here for years. He is threatening just now to set up a government gasoline station and a very good thing too.

This is a fascinating city, very foreign, rather poor, most of it, and some squalid.

March 9, 1934

Greatest emergency need here undoubtedly for housing.

Thousands of families squatting in marshes. Sent off cable today to Ickes asking for housing funds. This, of course, is not basic. There is over-population for a wholly agricultural community and nothing will do but industry. Have urged governor to start some by government if necessary. He seems receptive. There are several possibilities which I outlined. Am also urging formation of council under governor of emergency representatives here. AAA, NRA, FCA, FERA, etc., would help greatly in coordination.

Spent yesterday at Insular Experiment Station and at Forest headquarters - later drove through cocoanut country.

March 10, 1934

A long motor trip yesterday from 8:30 to 6 through the Eastern cane region to Fajardo, where we lunched with the paternalistic Senor Bird (whose grandfather was an Englishman) at his son-in-law's house - a long, heavy and rather trying lunch. After that we drove up into the forest with Barbour, the Forester, and saw the Puerto Rican version of C.C.C. Forest possibilities are considerable, especially for the quick-growing hardwoods in the high country where the rainfall sometimes runs to 150 inches and, with cover, will always keep the streams full.

Variations in rainfall are one reason for the great contrasts on so small an Island. In an hour we passed through regions ranging all the way from 25 to 150 inches. There is not so much erosion as I expected to see, though the streams running brown after heavy rains show that there is some. The soil is a heavy clay which compacts. Then, too, contour plowing is generally used, which helps. But too many very steep slopes are cultivated all the way to the top, especially with cane. Removal of cane from cultivation certainly ought to concentrate, if possible, on these, although it will be difficult with the individual benefit payment mechanism to do anything territorially selective.

Last night I had a conference with Muñoz Marín & Barcelo of the Liberal party, just to give them a chance to air their views. They have a kind of complicated scheme for taking over the properties of the United Puerto Rican Sugar Company, exchanging 50 acre plots for marginal holdings elsewhere, then getting land division, reduction of cane acreage and abolishing one absentee owner. It will bear looking into further.

March 11, 1934

My persistent cold - I had had it nearly all winter - has nearly disappeared under the influence of the soft warm air and the continuous sunshine. There's that much gained anyway.

Yesterday Bourne - the relief administrator, called a kind of general economic conference. It is planned to make an economic survey of the Island with Civil Works funds. About 50 people were there - officials, the two Bishops, businessmen, relief workers, etc. Each had a chance to put forward his pet projects. I learned a good deal about people and ideas here.

Wednesday, March 14, 1934

Sunday night the Governor had a big formal dinner for the Cabinet which was pretty dull, I being between two of the wives, one of whom spoke only a little English and one none at all. I expect it was even duller for them than for me.

Monday morning early six of us set out for a kind of Island tour, the general objective being to size up the Department's work at Mayaguez, the work of the second-unit schools (a combination of agricultural work with elementary education, fostered by Commissioner Padin, which seems to me wholly good) and a look at the sugar-cane and coffee country in the mountains and to the West.

The first day we lunched at the Isabella irrigation headquarters. That night and the next one, Fred Bartlett and I spent at McClelland's (Director of the Experiment Station at Mayaguez). The others went to a hotel in town. Barbour, our Forester, took his car and Menendez Rumos (Commissioner of Agriculture) took his. It was all very interesting and different in this tropical land. Wednesday we set out and drove all day in the mountain coffee country. This was a new view of things. Narrow, twisting roads but well kept by the Caminero system. I especially admired the road-side planting - oranges, almonds, avocados and ornamentals such as the flamboyante (Poinsettia royale). We slept in the desert country at Coamo Springs. It was one day I shall remember as long as I live for being full to running over with productive beauty, with color and movement and varied interest. The coffee grows in the mountains - from 2000 feet up. There the air is lively and sometimes almost cold. The slopes are rich with vegetation. Coffee needs cover which is furnished by banana trees among others, their light green being in contrast with the heavy green of the coffee trees underneath. Some of the other cover-trees are flowering ones - and when a tropical tree has flowers there is no restraint in the matter whatever. The so-called African tulip is perhaps the most spectacular one here. It stands out from a coffee "finka" like a flame in a darkened room.

The people up here are neither so numerous nor quite so squalid. It is from these mountains that workers have gone to the cities following destructive hurricanes and created those swamp-slums which seem so dreadful to a northern eye - and actually are, of course. I've been talking to some of the public health doctors, especially to the Commissioner of

Public Health. Their report of tuberculosis, malaria, hookworm, various parasitical diseases and general malnutrition is frightening. But this, of course, is part of the same economic picture as the slums and unemployment. It is aggravated here by the tropics which favor parasites, and mitigated by the absence of cold which is so often added to hunger in the North.

The whole presents a peculiar problem. Population increases by about 40,000 every year. It is almost, I think, the densest per acre population in the world. But the soil is deep clear to the hill-tops and subsistence - as apart from a higher standard - almost falls into a family's lap. It is a starchy subsistence. It makes the children potbellied and gives them too few growth-foods. They need milk and meat, lacks difficult to meet because of the parasites which attack animals.

These people, through cash crops, sugar, coffee, tobacco, have been made part of a world economy. They live mostly on imported rice, beans and codfish, only supplemented by the tree and root crops here. But their mobility is less than that of their products. Their excess drifts to the cities on the coasts and into the slums but stops there instead of being drawn into industry as the rural population on the continent is. The barriers are high costs of transportation and a language and cultural difference which keep them at home. Some hundred and fifty thousand are in New York City but they do poorly there. The obvious solution is either to make them self-contained and stop their increase in numbers or to make them a real part of the U.S. economy. But both alternatives are difficult.

March 22, 1934

Five days in the Virgin Islands were as good as five years for understanding. They are so small and their problem so relatively simple because of that. Puerto Rico, with its tremendous fecundity, is quite different and far more demanding.

The Virgins, lying East of Puerto Rico and having no mountains are hot and dry. A rainfall of 45 inches, which is about their average, in the continuous heat, and in a porous soil, makes them altogether different. The possibilities are fewer. They had an economic life of two sorts once - sugar in the old days when there was slavery and acting as an entrepot for the Islands all about. This was the life of St. Thomas and there is no agricultural tradition there at all. St. Croix has some because of the lie of the land. St. Johns has grown up to bush, and failing the development of bay oil on a larger scale than seems probable, will remain that way.

We went over last Friday, Silcox, Carter, Fred Bartlett and myself. I went to stay with the Governor. Saturday we went to St. Croix and stayed with Larry and Aline Cramer. Sunday afternoon I talked to the leaders of their opposition and later we went back to St. Thomas. Next day we explored St. Thomas and Tuesday went across to St. Johns, landing at Coral Bay and riding horseback over the trails back to the fishing club where we spent the night. Next morning we went back to St. Thomas where I addressed a gathering of the prominent citizens. (Had already talked briefly to the Council on Monday) and took the plane back to San Juan. In the evening Winship gave a kind of a farewell dinner. Beside our crowd he had Chardón, Menendez-Ramos, Dominguez (Director of the Insular Experiment Station), McClelland and Hern. During the evening I met a dozen of the big sugar producers, who had a little special pleading to do, ran away from all other appointments, packed, and was up at 4:30 to fly to Miami. We are aloft now, between Puerto Rico and Santo Domingo, a rough, stormy day so far, disappointed because our plan to stop over in Haiti blew up (Pan American is running full and couldn't carry us two days later). We had it all fixed for a Marine captain to fly us up over San Souci and the Citadel. We should land in Miami tonight, sleep there and land in Washington tomorrow afternoon.

I seem to have a certain faculty for running into trouble. I found myself landed in the Virgin Islands in the midst of a quarrel over the charter of the Virgin Islands Company. Their scheme arose from a suggestion the President made a long time ago that one way to attempt rehabilitation there was through reviving good old Cruzian rum. I've talked it over many times with Ickes, Chapman and others. Out of all the discussions arose the idea of a Government Company. Pearson thought it would be nice to get a charter in St. Croix but ran straight into the bourgeoisie. A lawyer or two, an auctioneer and a couple of merchants, thought they ought to be bought off, or that they might not be able to exploit the new set up, and set out to oppose it. I found Larry Cramer in a stew about it with a crucial meeting of his Council only a few days off. At his request, I met five leaders of the opposition. I think it did no good, except possibly to strengthen Larry's hand, because I rather obviously lost my temper at the pettiness and self-seeking which came out frankly.

Pearson was to have gone up to the States with us but Ickes wired instructions for him to stay until the Charter matter was settled, saying that unless a St. Croix charter was passed, the whole matter would be dropped. This was just like Ickes. He would get mad at three or four grocery store owners and sacrifice a whole island population because of their opposition. I expect a radio today telling me how Larry came out last night; but I hope these few detestable morons don't stop everything.

March 24, 1934

We landed at Miami after an uneventful 12 hour flight from San Juan at 5 Friday. The weather cleared over Santo Domingo. The plane was full, the seats uncomfortable, and the noise annoying; so that we arrived pretty tired and went to bed early. My radio from Pearson confirmed my fears - the St. Croix council did not pass the charter. The grocers won. They suggest, says Pearson, that the charter be got elsewhere. Well, they made that suggestion to me - which means they want a free hand to oppose and no responsibility. But Ickes ought to take this way.

We took off from Miami at 7 on a cool morning. We were switched to an old Stinson at Jacksonville. The pilot had trouble with it but nothing was said to us until Charleston when he said we should probably not get beyond Florence - there was sleet and snow North of us. He was right. They put us off at Florence and we took the train. Consequently we got to Washington at 2 in the morning instead of 5 in the afternoon.

I find things here no better. Many Congressmen hate the New Deal worse than ever and I am still at the center of the sniping. The President is caught between workers and employers in the automobile industry on the open shop issue. He is trying to compromise and I believe he will succeed since he is so competent in reconciliation. But the industrialists are getting back confidence rapidly and spoiling for a fight. The thing to do of course is to put off the issue, but I don't know how long it can be done.

Yesterday Jim Rand showed his colors. Testifying before a House Committee he read a letter into the record from some person named Wirt who seems to be a public school executive in Gary. Wirt alleges a traitorous conspiracy of the "brains trust" to deliver the U.S. to - somebody. He says some brain truster told him that F.D.R. was "only the Kerensky of this revolution." As a matter of fact I've heard F.D.R. make cracks about that himself. He may have made them to someone else less discreet, and given him ideas which he elaborated. The Congressional snipers have taken it up, anyway, and McGugin who has frequently denounced me on the floor in recent months intimated pretty clearly that I was the traitor. I attach the account in this evening's Star as an interesting exhibit in Congressional tactics.(sic)

Ernest Lindley and others who ought to know told me about two months ago that I was to be the center of the season's attack. This was just after Mark Sullivan visited Palo Alto and it is all supposed to be on Hoover's orders. It is interesting for me but a mistake on their part. It must rest on the belief that I really think for F.D.R., an incredibly naive assumption, and that he would be seriously crippled if I should be driven out, which is equally humorous. They're wasting a lot of energy on me which they might use more effectively; but from our point of view it does draw fire from Henry W. and the President. Of course, F.D.R. is so embedded just now in people's loyalties that no one dares attack him. But I am completely vulnerable and they can let themselves go on me. This doesn't hurt me and it does the cause good so I guess it is all right in spite of my dislike for publicity of any sort and a certain human desire which I naturally share with others to have my efforts meet appproval. This attack was so bad in December that an article in the Nation called it "Anti-Tugwell month". It seems to be coming to some kind of crisis. A Congressional investigation would not be at all surprising.

March 26, 1934

Had a long talk with H.A.W. over things which have happened since I left. He is much discouraged about the whole governmental system. It seems never to function for national purposes, only for sectional ones. Responses to local pressures cancel themselves out. It is difficult to break into the system with any program genuinely designed for the general good. I share his disquiet about the representative system, but pointed out to him that our device of permissive powers to the executive have gone some way toward breaking down Congressional power to obstruct and to force action for selfish interests.

We also talked over the sugar bill. This, in a way is an instance in point. The quotas are arranged to let all exist. But every means and weapon have been used to break down our arrangement, Cuba and our possessions being peculiarly defenseless. The beet sugar people have been ruthless and wholly selfish. But the bill on which we have worked so long seems to have a chance under Presidential pushing. Of course F.D.R. has given away on some points - and H.A.W. was unhappy about that and wondering whether he ought to fight even the President on it. I reminded him that nothing could be done at all unless we hung together under a leader and that we had no real right to make judgments. I also reminded him that much has to be set down to education in the hope that the education would prove useful later.

In the afternoon we went out to Beltsville, taking J. Darling with us. Went all over the property, marking out a possible place for a wild-life experiment Ding wants to make. Got stuck in the mud twice and had to push and dig the car out.

Had dinner at the White House and found the President in good form. He had compromised the threatened automobile strike after three days of continuous effort. He kidded me a good deal about Wirt el at, but seemed genuinely glad to see me back. It is easy to like him beyond the point of being critical. Loyalty is not difficult under such circumstances.

March 28, 1934

The past two days have been at least amusing. The great Wirt incident has given the whole country a laugh. Apparently the old fellow

did come to Washington last summer and did talk to some one. But this
of course was all stirred up by Jim Rand. It is evidently an attempt to
divert attention from the Stock Exchange Regulation bill which, by the
way, I haven't had anything to do with. The whole thing could be set
down as a mistake in strategy by now if there weren't so many
congressmen who would be glad to see all the administration intellectuals
handed over to the the wolves. (See especially the Baltimore Sun for
today - Farmer Murphy's piece - and Ernest Lindley's piece in the
Tribune).

I spent last evening with Hopkins, Bourne (F.E.R.A. of Puerto
Rico) and Silcox talking over possibilities. I pleaded for an immediate
housing program and for the formation of a company similar to the Virgin
Islands Company which should be able to start new industries.

There was great excitement yesterday afternoon when the House
overrode the President's veto on the Veterans' and Government pay bill.
Farley got H.A.W. to call up some Senators to try to stall similar action
in the Senate. But H.A.W's. heart wasn't really in it and he quit after
calling a few progressives who told him frankly that they didn't agree.

After Public Works meeting this afternoon I talked with Ickes,
Chapman & Taussig. Ickes agreed to go ahead and charter the Virgin
Islands Company in the District of Columbia and start operation right
away. He agreed without argument for which I was very glad.

Taussig and I at lunch talked over the Virgin Islands situation
and also things in general. He seems to share my feeling that N.R.A. is
proceeding very unrealistically. I have always felt that a sharp distinction
should be made between those businesses which are necessarily big and
those which lend themselves to decentralization well. And they ought to
be treated in different ways. What seems to me likely to happen in the
long run is that the New Deal will be wrecked by the grocers, the real-
estate dealers, etc. For the moment they ought to be treated very gingerly
and won over to the control and planning of the big businesses. Their
consent is absolutely necessary politically and they ought to be placated.
Besides they are not very important to us now. N.R.A. treats them all
pretty much alike and the small business men are being alienated
unnecessarily. A new blue eagle campaign at this time would be unwise,
it seems to me, for this reason. I believe I was thoroughly justified, in the
event, in opposing the original drive. And a new one would be even worse.
Taussig broached the idea of a new secret "brains trust," bringing in
Sumner Welles' name. I was a little surprised and non-committal. I
should think we'd had enough of this group business. What we really
need is the organization of a large movement in support of our policies
and I said so. In that way we might get some pressure of our own.
Taussig has been working on something like the "youth" movement
abroad, has organized a lot of study groups and is to have a radio

program. This is all good and I encouraged him in it.

I later talked over this thing with Waldo Stevens and gave him a rather enthusiastic blessing. He is to carry out the program.

March 30, 1934

Wallace, Ickes and I had a meeting today that, I think, may settle some very old controversies and bring credit to everyone concerned. The old quarrel, which has by now become historic, between Interior and Agriculture has been threatening to break out all over again. H.A.W. has been all steamed up to go for Ickes. The land office and the forestry people have been threatening each other. There was trouble over the Taylor grazing bill; there has been trouble over the policy of bringing in lands under reclamation and taking them out under our crop reduction program. Altogether I dreaded the interview all week.

Ickes opened up by proposing to assemble all land activities in Interior; H.A.W. countered by telling him he might as well suggest making Agriculture a bureau of Interior. The air was full of electricity for a few minutes. I then said that too much was at stake for Ickes and Wallace to get into an administrative quarrel. "You both," I said, "need to work together all the time against mutual enemies. And we must find a compromise." Ickes went on to sketch out the advantage of setting up in Interior a whole group of related activities under an Undersecretary, preferably me, if Henry would let me go. I was thinking as fast as I could and suggested that everything having to do with the surface of the land might come to agriculture; and everything of a construction, engineering or recreation sort might go to Interior. They both listened to this and began to suggest trades - Ickes saying just that - that a horse-trade might be worked out. I persuaded Henry not to be too stiff about Forests as such, saying we might take over Public Lands together with all grazing activities in the Forests. This caught on. Henry offered Roads; Ickes offered Reclamation. I saw that the chief problem was settled. The quarrel between the East and West would be solved in favor of Agriculture if we had Lands and Reclamation in Agriculture. I suggested that we have Subsistence Homesteads and Soil Erosion. Ickes readily agreed, saying that Subsistence Homesteads was all grief anyhow, which I guess is true. At the last minute H.A.W. tried to bargain for Indian Affairs but Ickes was adamant and I indifferent. But I did suggest that along with forests he ought to have wild life. So Biological Survey was understood to be going to him as we broke up. This will bring us Reclamation, Public Lands, Soil Erosion, and Subsistence Homestead; together with a new Grazing Service to be set up. It will take away Roads, Forests and Biological Survey. For my part, I think it is a grand compromise.

April 2, 1934

Lunch with Sir Stafford Cripps the other day was interesting both to get the views of a laborite on the left side and to hear his report of the activities of Walter Elliott. Without question Elliott is heading toward social control of English Agriculture. He is apparently the ablest, most charming and most aggressive member of the present government. Cripps says he told him that within five years one or the other of them would be governing England. Of course Elliott is Tory. He hopes to make landlords prosperous. But in a country where agriculture has lost so much it seems impossible that he should succeed.

Saturday night the mysterious Democratic dinner came off. It turned out to be a field day for the Old Guard. It centered about the promotion of the Jefferson Islands Club. There was a good deal of persiflage among themselves; but a good deal also of thinly disguised bitterness against the influence of the young and more liberal group. Robinson was especially nasty. These are our real enemies and will get rid of us if they can. This, also, is what makes the possibility of the Wirt investigation serious instead of comic. If we had only old-guard Republicans to fight it would not be so bad. It is working inside an organization whose senior places are in such hands that makes life discouraging.

I had a talk with Ernest Lindley about all this last night. He is inclined to think as I am that F.D.R. has done marvellously in working through the old crowd to get our legislation. The question is how far can this sabotage go without a break. It is evident that the time has not yet come; but meanwhile we have to take it on the chin without much backing. And people like Robinson and Harrison are discovering more and more that we can be attacked with impunity. These attacks will certainly increase. Life looks harder in the immediate future than it has for a long time.

Sunday, April 8, 1934

This week has been full of comings and goings about the Wirt incident. The Democrats, even those who are jealous and disgruntled at the rise of younger and more liberal men, have discovered that the old-guard Republicans are fishing in muddy waters. There seems to be a dampening of enthusiasm for investigation. But a Committee has been appointed and Wirt will be here Tuesday. What will come of it no one knows. If there is genuine strength in the present reaction, we may be thrown overboard. Personally, I should not be sorry. No one could be exactly happy under the attacks which I am getting now. Still I am comparatively serene about it since I have no doubts at all about the cause being sufficiently just.

I have spent a good deal of time this week over a speech to be made to the American Society of Newspaper Editors on the 21st. It has to be good, the way things are now.

In our own work, the milk problem worries me most, together with some remaining disloyalty to the cause in A.A.A. centering in Tolley and Tapp who have charge of marketing agreements and seem determined, for some reason, that the public interest shall be sacrificed to special ones. I am coming to believe that the rarest phenomenon in this world is a disinterested public servant.

The sugar bill is being turned, so far as I can see, into a refiner's bill. The great and rich lobby has forced into it just about all they want, in spite of all I have been able to do and in spite of the President's expressed wishes. I am afraid it is going to freeze refining in our old obsolete plants and shut out any possibility of developing the industry in Puerto Rico. It does give us quotas of raws but on the other points, the thing seems lost. It has gone the way of the Food and Drug Act and under the same kind of wholly selfish pressures.

There was a pleasant visit on Friday with Hugh Dalton. He says he has a nice place in Wiltshire which would make a good place to spend the term of a political exile. I may need it.

Wednesday, April 11, 1934

The great Wirt episode came to a climax yesterday in the Committee hearing. On the whole it was well handled and the country is laughing at Wirt without the Committee having made itself ridiculous. For this something is owning to Turner Battle who comes from Bullwinkle's state and who took him to see Steve Early. The Democrats came through all right and refused to allow an old-guard field day. Even the Herald-Tribune and the Washington Post who were out particularly to get me - ran my name in headlines and all that - have had to pull off. Neither one had an editorial about it this A.M. Yesterday Felix Morley had a particularly nasty one about young men experimenting and it was a serious come down for him.

Not much work was done around here all day. We listened to the hearing over the radio in the morning and discussed strategy a good deal the rest of the day.

I had a talk with Ickes today. He is much elated because a man he backed won in the Illinois primaries. So did Rainey, in spite of Wirt's testimony, by the way. Also had a long talk with Hull, trying to find out what he has in mind and whether, as Taussig insists, there is any use of trying to work with him. It is pretty thin. He is shrewd about politics - says, for instance, that we ought not to scare people about reforms - just do them. He is willing to go very slow; and really doesn't want much more than liberal democrats usually want. I doubt whether it is worth while hiding behind him to get respectability but something of the sort may be necessary. The present attack is getting pretty vicious. The Wirt thing has apparently been a complete flop; but it has not ended the attack. I shall make a speech next week stressing the Democratic and experimental nature of the program, which I can do with good grace. I'm a convinced Democrat anyway - that is, I believe people have to be carried along, and that we cannot step out beyond them. But I shall not give anything away to the enemy. I see no reason for compromise.

April 13, 1934

Taussig and Welles have very firmly fixed in their minds the idea that Hull can be brought far enough over to the liberal point of view to be useful. There is this about it, he might help to keep hold on certain old-fashioned liberals, though I doubt if he is willing to go through with a really modernized program which makes liberalism workable. We argued all this over at lunch at Welles' house. It was good to talk things over with Berle again. He came out to the house for the evening too and we went over the situation pretty thoroughly, agreeing:

1. That we will not get much more recovery on the present policy.
2. That we will be left with 8 to 10 million unemployed for whom provision must be made (a) in the emergency through relief, and (b) through a brave beginning of rehabilitation plans - resettlement, decentralized industry, subsistence farms, etc.
3. That no further fundamental progress is possible except through changed policy in N.R.A. ((This is the same point that I fought over so long and fruitlessly last summer. (See reports of N.I.R.A. Board in files). I finally brought the thing to a head in Cabinet, H.A.W. being away, and found the President determined to get all inside the code structures pretty much regardless of how)). The changed policy must be in two directions (a) concentration on the industries now raising prices and making the present maladjusted situation worse; and leaving the others outside or taking measures to raise their prices, thus enlisting their support for price reducing measures in the others; and (b) Perfecting a series of industry boards which can then have a council among themselves for creating policy. This will result in a long run in adjusting 75% of the maladjustments - the other 25% being consumers for whom the government must look out through regulation. I told Berle that so far as strategy goes, and helping F.D.R. in it, there were two existing agencies which might do long planning without being suspect - Hopkins' Relief

organization, because of its responsibility for people; and Frank Walker's Emergency Council. He said it had been suggested that he might go in with Walker. I urged him to do it. He is the best brains we have, and N.Y. is too far away.

Moley has an interesting article on the brains trust in Today which is reasonably accurate - a good thing to publish just now.

Lunched with Roy Howard and Lowell Mellett of the News. Talked about things in general. Found them strong in support and unafraid. Outlined my speech and found them favorable. Howard thinks the air-mail business the first real chink in F.D.R.'s armor.

Had a long talk about N.R.A. with Clay Williams. He can't see far, but service on N.R.A. is opening his eyes.

Monday, April 23, 1934

This has been a busy and rather exciting week. Saturday, a week ago, I went up to New York for a dinner Moley had at the Biltmore with Powell, Swope, McCrea, Wilkie, Rogers and some other Columbia people. On the train we had our first long talk in some time. He has, for some months, been sulking in his tent, his conversation full of recrimination and bitterness. He seems to have got over that a good deal, has his sense of humor back and is doing some work around here again. He sees the President often - helped him with the proofs of "On Our Way" and is working hard on the passage of the Fletcher-Rayburn Bill.

Corcoran and Lindley rode as far as Baltimore with us. Moley put forward the notion of reviving a group like the old brains trust, citing as reasons for it the present lack of discipline, legislative chaos, etc. Everybody seemed agreeable and I agreed, although I repeated the doubts I had to Taussig. This would at least bring the Corcoran group and ourselves together. We discussed who ought to be included. It was agreed that the following list was about right: Moley, Corcoran, Landis, Hopkins, Riefler, Frank, Lindley and myself. The objective would be to try to present another legislative program in 1934-35 which should be as sharp, as clear and as impelling as our first one was in contrast with that of this session. This would mean some group meetings over summer, some discussion of basic policies, and agreement on legislative priorities. Besides there is the Fall on which some common strategy would be desirable. Moley said he would have a dinner in Washington soon and get the crowd together for a preliminary talk.

Sunday I began work on my Dartmouth speech which I decided to call "On Life as a Long-time Enterprise" borrowing the phrase from Irwin Edman. By Monday night it was pretty well finished. The fellows around here didn't like it much - too much contrast with the one I just wrote for the publisher's dinner, "Return to Democracy", perhaps.

Anyway I worked it over pretty carefully and fancy it pretty much myself. Besides I had to work out a speech for Buffalo - I've decided to go over there from Dartmouth to speak on Saturday night.

I had dinner with Gov. Pearson and a group one night, at Herridge's another night, etc. It's almost as much effort to keep up this sort of thing as to do my job.

On Saturday night I gave the speech to the Editors. They didn't receive it any too well, I thought, but it got a wide distribution - the only New Deal speech to be carried in full by A.P. except the President's, so the boys say. And I think the effects have been wholly good. All through the Wirt business I made no defense. This enabled me to take the offensive again after the enemy's flop. We went to the White House to supper Sunday night. I approached the meeting with F.D.R. in some fear and trembling, for I had planned the strategy of the speech without consulting him. It was spread all over the Sunday papers and he couldn't fail to comment one way or the other. He came directly at it and gave me some really generous praise. It set me up a good deal and gave me courage to go on to another I have in mind.

Talking with Mrs. R. and Harry Hopkins after supper, I was surprised to discover how tense Mrs. R. has become about the present situation. She seems to think some radical change is imminent and is afraid we have not done much to get the country ready for it. I put forward my old notion about choosing which course we should follow, not in the terms H.A.W. used in his "America Must Choose" but in my own industrial terms. Shall we have a closed, restrictive industrial system in which businesses maintain high prices, manipulate their production to maintain them; and in which taxes are imposed to take care of the unemployed through various relief agencies; or shall we maintain, by governmental direction, probably, a balance in the price system which will enable each group to buy from every other, keep industry going, wages flowing and purchasing power equal to prices? Basic propaganda on this choice seems to me as good a thing as could be done just now and I seem to be a good one to put it out. The enemies have built up a good audience for me and use may as well be made of it.

There is no question but that most of us would follow the second alternative (with an important exception which I shall refer to in a minute) but, so far, all our efforts in that direction have been defeated. Price disparities have been made worse by N.R.A. and consumer purchasing power dried up by that much. We have done nothing, really, to correct basic maladjustments except by the A.A.A. program and there we have had more defeats than victories.

This is so conspicuous that there is no concealing it and the reason is probably (1) that Johnson bit off more than he could chew in getting all the industries in, instead of just the largest (Jerry Frank says he suffered from code in the head acquired in the draft) (2) that he has proved to be so poor an administrator.

Anyway it is probably a good time to restate the alternative objectives and try to do some basic educating on the choice to be made. I'll be working on that for some weeks probably.

Our report on Puerto Rico was completed on Saturday. I sent it over for Mrs. R. to read and hand to the President.

April 26, 1934
On train to Hanover, N.H.

The other day Brandeis sent word, in effect, that he was declaring war. It came through Gardner Jackson to Jerry Frank and myself. He, of course, does not believe the government ought to try to do so much; he believes in small units, in competition, etc. In a way the policy up to now has been a compromise between the old "Honesty in business" principle that he appproves - securities act, stock exchange act, food and drug bill, etc - and recognition and control of the trend toward large scale machine processes, together with an enlargement of government functions. This last he is against. Tom Corcoran, who is sincere, adroit and a little of a schemer, represents his point of view. So does Landis to a less degree. There are no differences here we cannot compromise. We need a good deal of regulation in the decades to come; but it is important to get a real start in overhead planning and government ownership. The development will necessarily be slow and will be inefficient at first, but it must go on.

I called in Ernest Lindley and asked him to get at Corcoran and after Cabinet yesterday (HAW being in Nebraska making a speech) asked FDR to get hold of Brandeis and butter him some. He said he would. Jerry Frank also succeeded in postponing the prosecution of an oil code case in conference with all the big-shot govenment lawyers on the theory that with Brandeis feeling as he does we ought not to take the case up. Ickes was inclined to be indignant (the oil administration is under him) so I told him about Brandeis. He said he hadn't realized that Brandeis was so intransigent. I think few people do; but it is so and Jerry and I have seemed to fail in working on him. Frankfurter shares his prejudices but doesn't fell so strongly about it.

Some progress is being made on the departmental exchange. I had Silcox in to see Ickes. Silcox persuaded him of the danger in an amendment to the Taylor Bill and Ickes authorized him to oppose it in his name. Afterward Silcox suggested that Ickes was a real conservationist and I seized the occasion to suggest the new set-up to him under pledge of secrecy. He seemed to like it.

FDR said he liked the Puerto Rico report very much. He has consented to calling Winship in with Chardón, Menendez-Ramos, and

Garcia and working out an emergency council under the government for all federal agencies. This will be done immediately. The sugar bill will be signed in a day or two which makes action imperative. I have consented to C. Davis' suggestion of Dalton as sugar chief, Weaver being needed for rice and anyway not exactly the type, though, in my opinion, a good man. Weaver and Prew Savoy have done excellent work on the bill; it is not their fault that it is such a bad one. As matter of fact it is not much better than the stabilization agreement we turned down last summer. Its treatment of the Islands is outrageous; and the refiners, by the means they always use, have got most of what they wanted into it. But I suppose it has to be accepted as better than nothing.

The same is true of the F & D bill which I understand is about to come up in the Senate. FDR has sent a note to Joe Robinson so I guess it will soon be on the calendar.

Editorials and comments on my speech are still coming in, together with considerable mail. It seems to have been the right strategy.

Yesterday I attended a long meeting at the Treasury on silver. Pittman had a man named Trent in to put the thing in a new way. Morgenthau, Oliphant, Coolidge, Viner, Warren and myself were there. I know Pittman's views backward and forward, of course, from hearing them in the discussions so many times preliminary to the London Conference. I have no special interest in silver. I do want a dollar based on the largest possible number of commodities and silver would be more - thru its tie-up with copper, etc. - really several more. So I am for acquiring some, but not at a price to enrich a lot of speculators. In a little talk with Oliphant and Viner afterward, Oliphant and I, at least, agreed that we could not stop much short of complete government ownership of the whole financial works. Viner was skittish of this - says he is afraid of treasuries. I pointed out that he ought not to be, so long as they were willing to keep men like himself around. Well, he thought that was only temporary and maybe it is. But Oliphant and I fell back on democratic dogma. We agreed that the people were entitled to a rotten financial system if they wanted it; and certainly they couldn't have a good one if they had no power over it. We left it like that.

April 30, 1934
On train - Buffalo to Washington

Well, it was a strenuous few days. Hanover is a difficult place to get to and we arrived at 2 in the afternoon, having had a ham sandwich and coffee for breakfast. Young Hess and another student met us at the train. After lunch I went to see the Orozco frescoes and then to call on Hopkins, the President. He seems to think he did something remarkably liberal in letting Orozco paint in the sacred library (basement). Hopkins strikes me as a spurious liberal but is certainly popular with his students. Why, I don't know for they say they never see him. Hopkins told me solemnly that he was taking an active part in Republican politics as a way of boring from within. I think he might like to be a senator or something. I don't know why I instinctively dislike and distrust him but there is no doubt about the sensation.

Dartmouth struck me again, as it has so often, as an anachronism which ought to be liquidated rather quickly along with all the other liberal arts colleges. I suppose it might be turned into a useful prep school or rest home, but its present function of sterilization of minds is dangerous and ought to be stopped. It really is a dreadful thing that we should let New England specialize in education - probably the worst place in the country for it.

The livelier boys at Dartmouth see the situation rather clearly; but it is as hard for them as for others to escape from the spurious but clinging sentiment in which every freshman is bathed. They take it out in staying on and agitating mildy "against war" or "for labor." The editor of the paper evidently expected something else than he got from my speech. He headed his editorial "They asked for bread and he gave them cake."

May 10, 1934

A rather quiet week came to a climax yesterday in three vists to the White House which gave us decisions on three matters; marginal land plans for the utilization of the $25 million I worked so long to get out of Public Works, what to do to make good on the government's obligations under the forestry code, and the signing of the sugar bill.

Lansill has done an excellent job in planning out the use of the $25 million for submarginal land purchases; we expect to put $15 million into purchases in submarginal areas, $5 million into purchase of recreation sites, and $2 1/2 million for Indian lands.

May 15, 1934

Dinner at the White House was interesting last night because at dinner there was a discussion of taxation, of armaments and of agricultural plans. We are framing a bill to carry out the old notion of reserved granaries. FDR has had this in mind for a long time. His wisdom in it has been shown by the recent hysteria over wheat shortage in view of the drought in the Northwest. Of course we have quite sufficient carryover; but recent dust-storms reaching even into the East has scared a good many people. I went to Cleveland and Oberlin, making speeches over the week-end, and flew through dust all the way out. After dinner Davis and FDR went into the oval room with Hull to discuss the prospective burial of the disarmament conference. Mrs. Roosevelt, Lorena Hickok and I discussed relief, temporary and permanent, all evening.

The Thorp matter has demanded some attention lately. I found Dickinson about to resign the other day in consequence of FDR's withdrawal of Thorp's name. There has been a lot of political skullduggery about this. I can't make out what Senator Stevens had to gain in opposing him. But he did and FDR gave in. Dickinson was placated by giving him temporary direct charge of Thorp's bureau. I called Moley and asked him to look after the thing when I had go to Cleveland.

President
(Secretariat)

Cabinet (18)
Executive Committee (7)

State, Agriculture, Interior,
Public Welfare, Treasury,
Budget & Planning, Industry

Cabinet Secretariat under
a director

****

State
War
Navy
Justice
Post Office
Interior
      Indian Affairs
      Mines
      Coast and Geodetic Survey
      Weather
      Power
      T.V.A.
      Petroleum Administrative Board
      Coal   "   "
                  etc.
Treasury
      Customs
      Internal Revenue

Mint
Engraving and Printing
Coast Guard
Narcotics
Unemployment Ad. Funds

Labor

Labor Statistics
U.S. Employment Service
U.S. Mediation Board
National Labor Relations Borad
Woman in Industry

Agriculture

Animal Industry
Dairy   "
Plant Industry
Chemistry and Soils
Entomology and Plant Quarantine
Agricultural Engineering
Agricultural Economics

Agriculture (cont)

Soil Erosion Service
A.A.A.

Commerce (out)

Census and Domestic Commerce - to Commercial Relations
Shipping Board - to communications
Navigation & Steamboat Inspection, and Lighthouses - to Navy

Public Works

Public Roads
Reclamation
Local Government Works
Federal Works (from Procurement)
Housing Adminstration

Industry

Federal Trade Commission
National Recovery Administration
Federal Alcohol Control Administration
Securities Board
Grain Futures Administration

Commercial Relations
        Foreign commerce
        Tariff Commission
        Export and Import Bank
        Commercial Treaty in Preparation
        Domestic Commerce

Public Welfare
        Federal Emergency Relief Administration as
        Unemployment Insurance Administration (to standards)
                        (Treasury as to funds)
        Old Age and Health Insurance Administration (as to standards)
                        (Treasury as to funds)
        Rural Resettlement
        Immigration and Naturalization

Standards and Health
        Education
        Fine Arts
        Childern's Bureau
        Food and Drug Administration
        Public Health
        Vocational Education

Standards and health (cont)
        Bureau of Standards
        Home Economics

Public Lands
        Forestry
        Parks
        Public Domain
        Fisheries
        Geological Survey
        Acquisition and Transfer
        E.C.W.

Communications
        T.C.C.
        Radio, Telephone, Telegraph and Cable
        Aeronautics
        Busses and Trucks
        Shipping Borad

Budget Planning and Procurement
      Budget Bureau
      National Planning Board
      Government Procurement

State	State (State, War, Navy, Com. Relations)
War	
Navy	
Treasury	Treasury (Treasury, Credit)
Post Office	
Justice	
Interior	
Labor	
Agriculture	Agriculture (Agriculture, Public Lands)
Public Works	
Credit	Public Welfare (Public Welfare,
Industry	Standards & Health)
Commercial Relations	
Public Welfare	
Standards and Health	Industry (Industry, Communcations,
Public Lands	Labor Interior)
Communications	
Budget	Justice
	Public Works (Post Office, Public Works)
	Budget

May 19, 1934

    Last night Mrs. R. asked me to bring Chardón, Menendez-Ramos and Garcia, to the White House for dinner. My admiration for her grows all the time. She is always concerned in good causes and has boundless energy in furthering them. These three have been here working at my request on a rehabilitation plan for the Island. Winship made a mistake in coming up with the sugar crowd and leaving the impression with the President that all P.R. was against the sugar bill. I was glad to have Chardón tell him just who these people were and reassure him, since he is to visit there the last of next month. He went off for his weekend on the Sequoia early, but at least we had a little talk. I think they are working out something pretty good; it centers on buying the South Puerto Rico properties and comes pretty high but it may be a good scheme.

    I have spent a good deal of time on a speech this week. It is to be given before the Social Service workers in K.C. on Monday. I had expected to leave today for Reedsville and catch a Saturday plane in Pittsburgh, but I was disappointed; the speech was not quite done, arrangements for furthering the F.& D. act were not complete, and the Secretary is away for three weeks. Altogether it seemed best to postpone going. I'll take a plane from here tomorrow or Monday.

There has been a good deal of discussion this week about whether to press the F.&D. bill now or to let it go over. I got Ray to talk to Rayburn, which was a little disappointing, (Rayburn is Chairman of the House Committee which will handle it) and interested Lindley and Corcoran. Meanwhile, it came up in the Senate and got a discouraging reception. Whether it has a chance I don't know. I was half-disposed to let it drop for now but on earnest representation from Campbell backed up by Cavers who insist that 75 percent of all we asked is still in the bill, I decided to get it by if possible. I asked the President about it again yesterday and he said to press it. I wish it could be got out of the way now.

Baruch came to see me yesterday and we had a talk about things in general. He and I agree that there is considerable deflation which still has to be undertaken. Municipalities have to have their debts written down; and the farm mortgage situation is still pressing. We agreed to work together on this and I had Jerry Frank explain his idea of a possible modus operandi. It is now perfectly clear, I think, that Berle and I were right in wanting to follow a conservative money policy and proceed to relieve debts by writing down rather than attempting to restore 1926 prices by manipulating gold and thus making the debt burden easier. We talked also about Johnson's situation and N.R.A. The N.R.A. is in great disfavor just now, largely among smaller people, so much so that it was decided yesterday at Cabinet not to ask for a renewal of licensing powers for fear of opening up a tirade. We agreed that the focus of policy ought to be on low prices and volume production and that Johnson ought to concentrate on getting prices down in those industries which have been taking advantage of the codes and making maladjustments in the system worse instead of better. Jerry and I asked him to convey our best wishes to Hugh and offer our help. He has got himself into the situation we, here, foresaw so very clearly last September and October and which we tried to prevent. It resulted, at that time, in the discreet disbanding of the Industrial Recovery Board because they all agreed with my contentions and Johnson would not listen but insisted on going around us to the President. At that time he was anxious above all to get all industries under the codes and so let everything get by with the idea, so I thought, of revising afterward. I knew this to be an error of the very gravest sort and protested as violently as I could, so much so that Johnson and I nearly had a personal row. It seems perfectly clear now that the mistakes of this sort will have to be gone back over and corrected. It will be twice as hard to do it right now as it would have been to do it then. Baruch is an intelligent man who knows a fact when he sees one. So now I find myself in substanital agreement with him on what must be done.

It is interesting that earlier in the week when La Guardia and Joe McGoldrick came to lunch with H.A. and myself, Berle came along. Afterward we had a talk and he told me that Johnson had asked him to work with him in N.R.A. I urged him to do it and we talked over possibilites, centering again on the necessity for price control and for abandoning the very wide spread of N.R.A. which creates so much resentment among small people.

Yesterday, also, I had lunch at Mary Rumsey's. Stacy May was there, who has been asked to take Thorp's place; Paul Douglas and his wife; and Thorp. There is a scheme now to take Thorp on as Frank Walker's Chairman of Consumers' Advisory Counsel. It may do for the time. Thorp shows a fine spirit, not disgruntled as he might well be and willing to go on doing anything for the cause. We have some accounts to settle with the Democratic Bourbons some day.

All week I have been bothering everyone about LaFollette. Jim Farley hadn't done anything up to yesterday and I tackled him at Cabinet meeting. What Bob is to do in this Fall's election is being settled out in Wisconsin today and I wanted him to come out for him. He belongs in our camp and I don't want a bunch of conservative democrats in Wisconsin to run away with the Administration's Prestige. What will come of it, I don't know; but Farley is incorrigibly regular and will probably make the obvious mistake; though I must say Cummings and Swanson spoke up immediately for Bob and Farley seemed impressed.

May 25, 1934

When Secretary Wallace, with myself as Assistant Secretary, took over the administration of the Department of Agriculture in March of 1933, we were concerned by numerous problems having to do directly with the emergency need for raising farmer's incomes. We also discovered very soon that the Department had other responsibilities which had to be met. One of these was the duty of protecting the American consumers.

It can be argued - and often has been - that the Food and Drug Administration does not belong in our Department. But it happens to be there; and there is no better logic for moving it to the jurisdiction of any other existing agency. It would be a mistake also to set it up as an independent office since coordination is largely obtained in our government through the Cabinet and any agencies out-side a Department are severely handicapped in securing representation in the administration. Mr. Douglas, among others, has argued that the whole field of consumer protection is sufficiently important to warrant a cabinet position and full departmental status. There is much to be said for this, especially in view of the great and neglected interest consumers have in the recovery effort. For the present, however, it remains in Agriculture, and it is our duty to further this interest to the extent of our ability. In pursuit of this it seemed necessary almost at once to recommend rewriting the basic law which controls the functioning of the Adminstration.

The reasons for this have been told many times. The question has been how to get a bill passed. F.D.R. directed me to have a draft made when we first started in. Cavers, Lee and Handler worked on it with Campbell and the others from the F. &D. Administration. We got it ready just as the Session was closing last year. It ran over the Summer, although Copeland introduced it on the last day. There were squeals from all those affected. And it immediately became the Tugwell bill - a kind of a symbol of government interference in private affairs. The adverse propaganda was very effective but so was ours. Just before the present session, hearings were held and the lobbyists succeeded in getting a good many emasculating amendments. It has been up for discussion in the Senate but there was not much interest -the liberals all felt that it was pretty well emasculated and the others didn't want a bill of any sort. It is so late now that it will probably go over again. I tried to get something done but without much success. Anyway it will probably be better for some more discussion.

May 31, 1934

In spite of an invitation to go with F.D.R. to the Naval Review in New York harbor, there were so many pressing things here that I decided to stay on the job. H.A.W. is still in the West (he has been gone two weeks) and as Acting Secretary there are many added trouble for me.

Senator Smith still has my nomination to be Under Secretary sequestered. His Committee has to report it before it can be acted on and he is refusing to call a meeting of the Committee. There has been a good deal of fuss about it. F.D.R. called him in some time ago and gave him a talking to but it seemed to do no good. Senator Byrnes is in charge of the thing and I have done nothing whatever in the matter. I understand the liberals are thinking of moving to discharge the Committee and so get action on the floor. Smith is the one we could do nothing with when we were trying to get a bill passed before inauguration. He is both stupid and reactionary; it was a mistake to have let him be chairman of the Committee on Agriculture where he can do the maximum damage. He is also obstructing the passage of our amendments to the AAA act; and he will continue to be as obstructive as he can. Unfortunately he was elected in 1932 and so has a clear term ahead of him. But Jimmy Byrnes has pretty much come out in the open against him. He and I have promised to go together to make speeches at Clemson College in August.

I have been anxiously trying to line up the Administration with Bob LaFollette - talked to Farley and F.D.R. and think something will be done. We need these Progressives with us. There is no hope of building up the Democratic party in the Middle West and if we did it would be so reactionary as to be of no use. Surprisingly enough Garner, Cummings and Swanson spoke up for it also when I tackled Farley about it just before Cabinet meeting the other day. F.D.R. by executive order, transferred Puerto Rico to Interior from War the other day. This, I think, should make the economic plan Chardón and the others are working out, easier to put into effect. Certainly a P.R. Company similar to the V.I. Company will be favored by Ickes and Chapman.

Saturday, June 1, 1934

Governor Winship turned up today. I asked to have him come. I am anxious to have him work on the economic plan so that he will be committed to it. His natural conservative tendencies make him feel sympathetic with the demands of the big sugar people. But he has a good head and it is necessary to work him over to a broad plan. In this way we may drive a wedge between him and the "big people".

Monday, June 3, 1934

The drought is absorbing all our energies just now. We are moving cattle out of the area and feed and water in. We are preparing to face the worst if it should spread. It seems almost certain to me that - this being an election year - the Old Guard will preach "God's displeasure" all over the Middle West and it may make agricultural adjustment very difficult. For this reason I am planning to speak at Brookings, S.D., on "Nature and Agricultural Adjustment", later in the month.

We are working up an Emergency Drought Program for the President, including money to buy and process or store animals, set aside measures of seed, furnish relief to destitute families, probably through work-relief mostly, and to buy submarginal lands. The proposal will amount to some 500 millions.

Later

At a conference this morning F.D.R. approved our drought program adding only one item; 50 million for extension of CCC camps. I had urged this item before, knowing he had it in mind, but the others had thought it ought not to be included. Davis, Hopkins, Westbrook and

Myers were present. We went over the whole situation and F.D.R. agreed to meet a group of Congressmen and Senators from the drought states tomorrow for which we are to prepare the data - we are also to prepare a message to Congress including items totalling 525 millions. The best thing in this, in my opinion, is 50 million for land purchase and improvement. This will fatten our land retirement program and be the only bit of permanent work we are likely to do as a result of the emergency, though Hopkins has had some practical processing bids from the packers and swears he will build a lot of community abbattoirs, storage and processing plants. Maybe he will, as a part of his works program.

I ran into Gov. Pinchot waiting to see F.D.R. at the White House and had him to lunch with Silcox, Hopkins, and Eric Biddle (Relief Director in Pa). We talked about relief in Pennsylvania. In view of the steel strike which will probably be called on the 16th, and Harry agreed to feed all the strikers, regardless, though they are having a quarrel as to whether the States are to be expected to carry any of the relief load. In this I believe Pinchot has a good argument in saying that where the states carry it, the little fellows pay a larger share of the taxes.

However, the thing which Silcox, G.P. and I talked about was the possibility that Interior might get the Forest Service. This prospect stirs all the conservationist's wrath. G.P. suggested a counter attack - the attempt to bring Public Lands and Reclamation over here. I told him I had thought of that and he seemed satisfied. As a matter of fact, I spoke to F.D.R. about it this morning and he said he favored passage of the Taylor grazing bill now and would prevent Ashhurst's amendment from passing - this threatened amendment was for the transfer of the Forest Service to Interior - but I personally doubt whether the Taylor bill will pass and hope it doesn't in present form. I think next session we might get a better bill.

This whole matter seemed so acute last week that Ickes asked me to see F.D.R. with him, which I did. Ickes was torn between the desirable immediate prospect of getting the forests and the charge of breaking his agreement on transfers with us. I urged the desirability of postponing everything until after election; and cited the dangers of stirring up the conservation quarrel now. The whole value, I said, of the deal we had worked out, lay in the division of the West. Once we let all their piratical interests get concentrated in Interior, we should never get the rest of the deal done. Evidently F.D.R. is now intending to hold off things for the present in this matter.

He talked over a list of "must" legislation with Harry and myself and brought up the matter of my confirmation saying that he was to see Smith tomorrow. On Sat. Malcolm Lovell (My class at the Wharton School and co-editor of the Pennsylvanian) came to see me and said that he knew Federal Judge Glenn in S.C. who was the real support of Smith there. He said there were certain reasons why Judge Glenn would do something for him. I said if it were not improper he might find out how matters were. He called Judge Glenn and afterward reported that Smith's opposition to me was the result of a patronage row with Byrnes, which seemed to point to a political error in letting Cummings and Byrnes handle negotiations with Smith. Smith, it seems is jealous of Byrnes anyway, since Byrnes has had much more confidence from the administration. Anyway, Glenn rounded up, over Sunday, a lot of Smith's supporters in S.C. and had them bring pressure to bear on him. I told F.D.R. this and intimated that he would fight the whole matter out with Smith tomorrow. Last week he made a kind of joke of saying that he had "traded me for two murderers" - by which he meant marshalls in S.C. who seems to have been pretty free with fire-arms. But evidently the trade didn't work. I told him that it seemed not to be a marshall but a new judge which all the trouble was about. He made a note and said he would look into it.

Wednesday, June 6, 1934

I had a long and very satisfactory talk yesterday after cabinet meeting with F.D.R. in which he outlined what he felt ought to be the next great drive. Toward security, he said, he thought it ought to be. And his idea is a comprehensive program of social insurance. We have talked of this before in connection with my objection to Frances Perkins' present unemployment insurance scheme. My point was that any adequate fund would be so big that it would raise numerous fiscal and theoretical questions which ought to be thoroughly explored. I was sure, I said, that the fund ought to be Federally administered and that it ought to be used to expand and contract activity - inflation in time of depression. Frances disliked all this - she has no financial mind at all - and wanted a purely state scheme. I agreed with her theoretically that it ought to be non-contributory; but F.D.R. insists on that - 50-50 employees and employers. I haven't been able to shake him in this by saying that the source is the same in any case and that the technical job of collection and disbursement is made very difficult.

He is about to send a message to the closing Congress on this, which, as he said, will be the Democratic campaign document and he "hopes the Democrats will recognize it." What he has in mind is a 50-50 contributory scheme, the States to manage collection and disbursement, the fund to be managed by a board of trustees appointed by the President. The funds' investments are to be of three sorts (1) U.S. Goverment bonds, (2) State and Municipal bonds (under severe supervision), and (3) the warehouse receipts of the ever-normal warehouses-when established.

This last was my suggestion. He snapped at it and saw the implications at once. It moved us toward a new fiscal policy. In fact, the whole affair would make the deepest kind of changes in American life. I suggested that he not only send the message to Congress but talk about it over the radio before election so that he gets a kind of mandate. This he seemed already to have in mind.

He will appoint a committee to work over summer with Frances as chairman, to bring in a bill next January.

June 30, 1934
Battle Lake, Minnesota

The past two weeks have been strenuous and filled with other kinds of writing. There was first the Senate hearing on my confirmation as under Secretary which was carried through in a kind of atmosphere of high comedy much like the Wirt affair. Then there were the Des Moines speech on the 27th and the Brookings speech on the 29th. They both had to be written out rather carefully. The Des Moines speech was intended to gather up the ragged ends left from the hearing, for my strategy there was to spar and let them lead, telling as little as possible. This was satisfactory as securing confirmation, protecting my peculiar relationship with the President and all that, but not as defining as well as I should have liked what I really thought. So when I had a chance to speak at Des Moines I devoted it to defining my ideas on planning, the relation of government to business, and an attack on the middlemen who are my enemies. That speech is now in the record. And I have motored through Iowa, spending a day at Ames, a night at Moorehead with Earle Bressman's father-in-law, another at Brookings, and one here at Fred Murphy's Camp.

September 27, 1934

It would be very hard to describe adequately at all the talk I had yesterday with Street and with Elliot at the Ministry of Agriculture. I went expecting to be rather formal and stayed three hours. Both of them are men of power and force but with great flexibility and no dogma. Each has his separate charm. I believe I am right in thinking that Street is the creative agriculture. But Elliot has plenty of his own and seems to be a superb politician as well. From one or two glimpses I had I should say that he might have administrative talent as well.

Appleby and I went down to the Ministry after a somewhat formal but pleasent call on Vanier at Canada House whom Bill Herridge had set on to us. (He wanted to be helpful, though there was not much he could do.) The Ministry is a typically British fortress type of building, chilly, dark, without more comforts and conveniences than are necessary. We waited a little for Street. He came in from another meeting and introduced himself informally and we were immediately head over heels in our mutual problems on the frankest possible basis, he inquiring knowledgeably about our problems, I asking him the most searching questions I could think of. We pulled up once on something obvious, laughed about it, agreed that we saw so much eye to eye on the experimental approach that there was very little use lingering over philosophy, though we thought we might devote an evening later to finding out. Our first concern was the same about the respective methods of organization. We thought that though our great problem was preventing export surpluses and their's preventing imports which would ruin English farmers, that our central administrative problem was the same - getting a control over production. Street was especially interested in our County Associations and explored their implications thoroughly. It turned out that this was because he had an idea that agricultural commodity cartels might be worked out on an international basis. He seemed to be looking for a way to escape from government (foreign office) influence on commodity conferences. I didn't see much in that from our point of view since our control schemes function normally through the Department. For political reasons their controls here have been centered in commodity boards which are made to take the political shocks.

I didn't think much of this and said so, and asked him how about when restriction became necessary. That was embarrassing. He admitted that in one or two crops they had to dispense with Boards and go to licensing on an individual basis. I think our Federal determination of policy with county and state allotments better, though he keenly saw that our county associations might federate and become a virtual board. As to an international commodity cartel, I said I thought he was proceeding from a local difficulty with government, that I thought an international cartel was government, and that trying to escape government would create more problems than it settled.

We had a good deal more administrative talk, then he took me down to see Sir Charles So-and-So who is Permanent Undersecretary. He was a nice old career Grampus. It was funny to see Street with his brains and influence defer to him. Sir Charles in turn took us in to see Elliot who called in Lord Delaware. He is to head this delegation to Rome as I am ours - a nice young fellow who is a Socialist but is functioning nicely in the Conservative Ministry. He never had much to say: but I gather that he is very useful in the various agricultural schemes in the House of Lord.

Elliot was a surprise. The praise I had been hearing of him had steadily grown in volume. He was said to be brilliant, charming, etc. I had pictured him as dark, ascetic, slim. He actually is very blond, growing a little flabby in figure and with a great wide face, which is chased over constantly by all kinds of emotions. He talks with great force and conviction. He is very persuasive.

We talked of plans and people, of the future of events, of the functions of goverment and how to get them carried out. It was all very good talk. Street gave me the impression of great brains and ingenuity. Elliot gave me that of great persuasiveness and flashing intelligence. He has not Street's depth; but like Street he is wedded to no dogmas.

I came away at 6:30 tired out. In the evening we dined with Ray Atherton, First Secretary here. The President asked me to do what I could in sizing up the "career boys." Harry Hopkins came back last month with a highly sceptical report of the whole bunch. I've found that unjustified so far. Atherton, for instance, is a charming man, easy and ingratiating in manner, attractive in appearance. You do not realize until you have left him that he has never let you talk about anything which matters. Of course that is part of the tea-drinking technique - if you make no commitments you can't be called to account. I don't know what these fellows think they are supposed to do; what they really do is to present a pleasant face to the world and keep things going smoothly. They aren't apostles of the New Deal, of course, because they have no convictions of that sort - at least Atherton doesn't seem to have. But I suppose the economic conditions which would create war might be tightening all around them without their being at all aware.

Next to Norman Armour, Atherton is perhaps the most attractive person I've met in the service. And maybe he knows something about the fundamental forces under his feet. I couldn't find out. But there are two young 3rd Secretaries who seem to me better in these respects. Young Hi Bingham is quite a person. He and his new wife came over with us on the Manhattan. I found him not only interested in what is going on but informed and engaged in trying to penetrate way below the surface. The other lad's name I have yet to get, but he actually described the agricultural control board system and offered to get me some figures on changes in national debt - which I thought was pretty good.

September 28, 1934

Yesterday was hectic again. We drove out to St. Albans, then to Harpenden where Rothamstead is. Through some mistake no one had let them know that we were coming; but finally we turned up a nice boy by the name of Nicholls who led us around for hours and told us about everything. He went to Harpenden and had lunch with us and a poor one it was!

Except for its antiquity and continuity of purpose Rothamstead is not very impressive. Their budget is about $150,000 a year. They control or own about 500 acres; they have rather small though adequate laboratories. What was of greatest interest to me was the grass work, and indeed they don't stray far ever from problems having to do with fertility, especially forage problems of course, here. The classical fields, cropped under control and continuously since 1843 were naturally regarded as a little sacred. I was very much impressed with the affectionate regard which the institution commands even from scientists. It is, of course, not a government operation; but the government subsidizes it heavily. The director, whom we saw a few minutes before leaving, said rather self-satisfiedly that this was much better since then no scientific decision could be influenced by politics. At which I merely expressed polite interest. That kind of thing wouldn't impress anyone much who knew anything of University politics on the one hand or of the stiff stubbornness of orthodoxy in science on the other.

So we had a day, mostly spent walking in the fields on old turf. It was a lovely warm day - almost the first we've had in England. I really had a wonderful time talking of grass and old customs of cultivation and the traditions of a place like Rothamstead. I liked young Nicholls and I had the pleasantest day of the trip because of his gently, pleasant interest in two strangers who descended out of the blue and who obviously meant no more to him, in an official, way than any two people off the street who would show an interest in his work.

That night Lord De La Warr gave a dinner for me at the Marlborough Club. Elliot, Street, Enfield (whom I had known at Cornell meeting which lasted a week about four years ago) and two others, obviously important in the government, but only to be identified by me later.

We talked a good deal of the possibilities of national self-sufficiency. Elliot obviously wants to go a good ways in that direction. I had sketched out for him the central theme of my speech for Rome the day before. It had struck him enormously because he embroidered it with all kinds of pictures of his own last night. I expect that is his great quality - to seize on things and squeeze out their juice, then turn them to account. It seems to be very generally accepted that he will be the next Prime Minister.

Because Enfield was there Elliot took many amusing swipes at orthodox economists. Enfield is that all right; but no more so, say, than Ezekiel. He is more intelligent than most and his orthodoxy is greatly modified. I evidently feel into the company of gourmets. It was a dinner remarkable for food and wine as well as for company. I had a good time.

October 1, 1934

Attempts to find out something from our Ambassador Morris,

the Counsellor Ausdorf or the lady Third Secretary, Miss Willis, seem quite fruitless. The Ambassador is a nice old gentleman. He keeps up an elaborate establishment like a museum with old paintings and tapestries and a bed (which I slept in) in which the king and his brother were born. He maintains gentlemanly and friendly relations but he is somehow ineffective and unaware of the forces moving around him. He is the kindest host imaginable and he will undoubtedly do us good so far as gentle talk and consideration can do it. I tried to talk to him about trade and war and about the political movements which are stirring Europe so profoundly but found nothing there. The same for the others. Ausdorf is an athlete, interested in mountain climbing, totally incurious otherwise, didn't know whether Brussels had any public works, didn't know whether there was any unemployment, etc. The lady does odd social jobs and not much else.

We had an unusually smooth channel crossing. Somehow it always is a relief to come to France from England. I can't quite analyze it. There seems to be a lift of the spirits when escape is made from English stodginess and from ordinary English food.

England is fairly prosperous apparently. She literally seems to have rebuilt herself. There are rows and rows everywhere of new houses. They are unbelievably ugly and unimaginative of course, but better to live in than the old slums. She must have been building houses at many times the usual rate for several years. I judge that is mostly over now and that the furnishing industries are now busy. What she will do next I don't know, for fundamentallly the situation is certainly very dangerous. She can't live any more on export of finished goods; her old markets are now fitted out with factories of their own. Perhaps they can live on making machinery but I shouldn't think so.

Conditions in Belgium seem better than I had expected. There is not more unemployment than we have anyway. But then again her rural population is down to some 18% and she is geared to living on exports. What can she do? I have pretty well finished my speech and sent copies off to Early and H.A.W. from London for criticism. I think it may be pretty good. I haven't seen anyone else make this kind of statement.

Yesterday we motored over to Antwerp. It was 48 kilometers and we seemed to be in city or suburbs all the way. These dense areas of population have a problem to solve that I'm sure can't be met without a degree of social organization which no country I have yet been in visualizes at all. Especially England seems to me up against it.

October 2, 1934

Coming out of the little museum in Bruges yesterday, where so many of the Flemish primitives are collected, I sat down in the little green courtyard and was suddenly overwhelmed by one of those depressions which seem to come more often lately. I had been looking at the Virgin and the Saints, the curious pictures of torture and the bad judge being skinned alive. Some of them had been so cleverly restored that they might have been painted yesterday. Over the wall from where I sat children were evidently having recess from school. I was thinking about the odd pictures and the buildings too, in Bruges, how pathetic it is that for all man's work and sufferings, his sacrifice and boredom, only a few in any generation create anything which lasts beyond themselves. The genius may write a few pages, paint a few pictures, chisel a few stones. But it's so little. Most of the work goes just to keep us alive, and when it does last it isn't long. The winnowing of each generation sifts it out until, as in 500 years here, a building or two is left and in them a few paintings. But the children's voices reminded me that the most temporary thing of all, perhaps, has the most lasting creative effects. Love cannot project itself into the future at all, I had been thinking. Because that had been on my mind as I walked for hours and looked at a very unfriendly sea. But it does, of course, and I was hearing those children's voice with all the vigor and sweetness they ever had even while I was being made sad by the temporariness of a few pictures. Not much else is comparable to love in its creative effect on the individual. I had forgotten that its results were so incomparably significant.

October 3, 1934

Last night the Ambassador had in the Viscount Lantscheere and I sat up late with him. He had been nine years in Washington lately and could make comparisons. We covered the whole range. Belgium has been deflating. Prices here are very low; so are wages; and in spite of low costs the foreign trade by which she lives has fallen off disastrously. It is for the same reason that England's has - that the world does not want foreign finished goods and won't take them any longer. Belgium has stayed on gold too; but I think is wavering toward the English scheme. She has no duties on raw materials to speak of. But her farmers are putting on some pressure now; with world trade diminishing I don't see what this 8 million people are going to do anymore than I can see what Englands 48 million are just to exist. Certainly the 16th century greatness of Bruges won't happen again. There won't be any such solid prosperity to wash up a thin leaving of art to future generations - nor perhaps will love be able to float a creative future if the childern die of malnutrition.

We discussed quite frankly the forthcoming trade treaty. But we couldn't see much possibility in it when all was said and done that would be advantageous to either. Our domestic prices of agricultural goods are way above the world's now and Belgium is buying from Argentina. And there is little made here outside a few specialities that we really want. There aren't any resources here that we are short of.

There is a strong labor movement here and unemployment somewhat less than ours. There is no revolutionary movement apparently and no great wave toward dictatorship.

The Viscount is arranging tomorrow for me to see some agricultural officials.

October 4, 1934

Yesterday afternoon I went out to Gembloux to visit the Belgian Institute Agronomique - or rather, one of them, for there are others at Ghent and Louvain. The lot of them wouldn't make one good high-school outfit in Iowa. There are two because there are two languages in Belgium. There is a third because a lot of good catholic families have wanted the catholic University to teach agricultural subjects.

The school at Gembloux used to be an old Abbey and looks it. I met the entomologists, the forestry professor, and so on, and looked over the buildings and the farm. There were several enthusiastic people but their equipment and buildings must make work very diffucult. In spite of that they are doing some good work on wheat and on a smaller scale, that we do at home.

At noon I called on the Minister of Agriculture but the call was more or less a formality and I learned very little. There is, of course, the same tendency here as in England, to protect farmers by controlling imports. It has not been undertaken with any enthusiasm, however, and there is much more of a survival here of the old laissez faire international psychology. Belgium is in a curious situation, being organized for exporting finished products and having had the foreign markets gradually closed. Farms are small and close to factories so that many workers are part-time farmers or have relatives with farms. This has lessened the strain of unemployment but has not raised the standard of living.

The Minister of Agriculture said that the government hoped to increase small industries. He though finishing industries was the proper field for decentralization. I pointed out that Belgium has few natural resources and that if she did not export finished goods she could export nothing and would, therefore, be short of foodstuffs unless she raised all her own and also several necessary raw materials. His only answer was that high grade specialties might pay for imported foodstuffs, and raw materials, I doubt it. That is just the field that each country will want to encourage and I doubt if just now the standard of living will be high enough everywhere to support a large trade in such goods.

The Minister was a pleasant, flexible-minded politician. But he seemed to be avoiding his real issues.

October 3, 1934[2]

I find that Shakespeare has said some of the things I was trying
to express yesterday in the sonnet (II) which begins
"When forty winters shall beseige thy brow"
and has the line
"This fair child of mine
shall sum my count and make my old excuse
Proving his beauty by succession thine,"

Doubtless others have made such a theme the centre of many
beautiful knots of words. It's strange how one is struck by these things
and suddenly sees reference to them or illustration of them everywhere.
It's perhaps because I am more fully away, here, from the
American problem than I've been for several years that these ageless
themes are more in my mind than they have been for a long time -that
and a certain unsettled psychological problem which prevents even the
faintest shadow of happiness falling into my mind - or, even, I now find,
of interest in these relics of old crafts and arts, becoming strong enough
to possess my mind for even little intervals. But this has been true for a
long time. I should, by now, given the same conditions, have no grip left
on life if it had not been for the exacting and exciting events of public
service.
Yesterday I called at the Ministry of Agriculture to see a couple
of officials. And last night Morris had to dinner the man in the foreign
office who will have charge of negotiating the trade treaty. He seemed
realistic enough and the thing will probably be worked out though there
can't be much in it. A visit to Louvain in the afternoon had more interest,
sentimentally in the library and practically in the office of the Boorenbund
- the union of farms, who not only have a cooperative credit society but
who actually carry on extensive experimentation and run farmers for
stock and feed improvement and dissemination. This must be the only
one in the world which does this kind of work.

October, 1934[3]

After four days in France my ideas are beginning to jell. I have
talked to people about the Embassy, to journalists, to some American

[2]Tugwell's diary has two entries for October 3, 1934. He "mis-dated" this
entry. It should be October 5, 1934.

[3]No specific date given, but most likely it is October 9, 1934.

friends and to a number of Frenchmen of various sorts. The Minister of Agriculture is away so I can't see him.

Something is impending here. I thought that Belgium had hardly begun to take hold of her problem; but France has not made a beginning. The cost of living is very high; the problem of agriculture is acute. There is talk of change everywhere. Doumergue has a government of conciliation which has promised much but done little and I should doubt if it will be able to do much. The theory that Europe may break up in chaos through a series of feeble and futile civil or international wars does not seem so fantastic here. Spain, as I write, is having disturbances, which may result in a fascist regime. People are tired of the slowness and inefficiency of democracy; but they cannot organize and carry through revolutions. Especially I cannot see it happening in France. Education here has been universal for generations. Frenchmen are too logical and too intelligent to follow stupid leaders. And yet, smart as the politicians are, the pressures are too evenly distributed to get off center and cause revolution. Some intellectual movement, visualizing the impact of industrial technique on their civilization seems a necessary prelude to any great change. As things are there is just a vast and universal unfocussed discontent. No intellectual currents seem to run this way from Italy. It seems not impossible that Belgium might show the way to France if she undertakes something new.

This is all impressionistic and unsatisfactory. Yet I have nothing more definite now. France always seemed to me a backward and classical minded country trying to be a world power. It stills seems so. Things will not happen here first but almost last. Numerous young Frenchmen are interested in what we are doing and in England but they command no public. Nevertheless there is more hope in them than in the present politicians' machinations.

I have been staying at the Residence and working and meeting people at the new Embassy building - almost the only adequate one we have. It houses all our activities and is really something to be proud of.

It is a comment on the career service, I think, that I had to come to France to find out about a young socialist movement in Belgium. I missed it entirely there. Yet it was Pell, here, who put me in touch with the young Frenchmen. The career men here are intelligent amateurs, interested in all that goes on, but a little lackadaisical and inclined to social interests more vitally. They are likeable, good enough upper-class Americans; but they have only a little glimmer of the New Deal. None of them seem hostile, but they are less inclined to probe it than to see it as one more general move in a vast historic game.

The Ambassador must have been a good business man. He was born to wealth and accepts his as a normal attribute, but he is a Jew and a shrewd one. He is initiating a move in the war-debt tangle that may come to something. I am carrying it home in my head as I am many other comments which I feel it better not to put on paper at all.

I had hoped to see Dodd in spite of my instructions not to go to Germany. I called him this morning hoping he might meet me in Germany on my way back from Rome. He was out but will communicate with me later. A letter from him intimated rather strongly that he had some things to tell me. I should like to get them.

Paris itself shows signs of pressure. They have expelled all foreign workmen, but there is growing unemployment. Many shops are closed. The dying of the tourist trade has hit them hard. In any other country something might be predicted. There is still the struggle to cling to gold. It will be given up only in extremes but I am very sure it must come. Until it does the pressures will continue to accumulate.

Straus feels very strongly that we ought not to initiate a trade treaty soon and I agree for reasons I will note later.

October 10, 1934

I was glad to get away from the Embassy atmosphere in Paris day before yesterday - not that Straus was not as nice as he could be but that I am uncomfortable living in that kind of style. The day trip to Bordeaux was comfortable and interesting - it renewed memories of the Chateau country. The P-O goes down the Loire valley and several of the Chateaus can be seen from the train. The consul here, Findlay, met us with the news that King Peter and Barthou had been assassinated at Marseilles. I can't see yet what difference it makes except that it may hurry the decline of F. influence in the Balkans. Barthou was au courant of Straus' idea about debts also, and that will have to be begun all over.

Yesterday we visited the white wine country with the Consul and the Secretary of the Wine Association. We lingered at Chateau Climens (Barsac), Chateau Sudirirant, Chateau Yquem and Chateau Filbot. It yielded a good idea of the Sauternes methods. But the lunch at Oliver in Langon nearly killed me on top of all the irresistible food we've been having since leaving England. In the evening we went to dinner with the Consul and his assistants at the Chateau Trompette in Bordeau - another memorable one if I'd been able to eat it. We tasted all the wines and my discrimination (which is not very good) was at least improved. A long conversation last night threw a good deal of light on a Consul's problems and some on the decline of trade incident to the nationalist economic policy of all countries now.

A cable from H.A. approving the speech for Rome.

October 14, 1934

On the second day in the Bordeaux region the Consul had arranged to have M. Jean Cruse explain to us the Medoc. We went to Mouton Rothschild, Lafitte, Pontet Canet (where we had lunch) and afterward to several others, had tea at Contemerle, went back to Bordeaux and then went out to Libourne and had dinner with an American left over from the war - Sublette.

Next morning we drove to Charles Van Ripers' (Knowles Ryerson's friend) at Toneins (haut Garonne) and stayed over night. Next morning took the train at Agen for Marseilles arrived there at 6:30, had dinner at Basso - where I did not eat Bouillabaisse. Smith of Entymology met us and we drove to Hyeres where I woke this morning with the Riviera sun streaming in and was able to look out the window again at the Mediterranean, at Polius and Bougarinvillea and Pines. This morning I shall have a look at our laboratory here and go on to Cannes.

Rome, October 18, 1934

For a week I have not put down anything, partly because of rapid movement and then getting adjusted to a new Embassy, and partly because of a profound uneasiness about my personal situation and about the world which I seem wholly unable to shake off. I suppose it is because I can for a few weeks go back to watching things without responsibility and because I have more time to realize the utter impossibilty of achieving what it would be necessary to achieve in order to come close to solution of the socio-economic problem in our generation. This pessimism added to a great personal unhappiness, which never leaves me now, has almost paralysed my active faculties. Actually, from Van Riper's I have come across by train to Marseilles through a country which has always had a special appeal to me, have driven across from there to Genoa, spending nights at Hyeres, Cannes and Alassio and have been visiting at Long's since Tuesday night, the 16th. I have gone through motions in a kind of daze. I have had conversations and conferences. None of it seems worth putting down here because I seem to have grown into the conviction since I've had no daily work to do, that we cannot possibly move fast enough to stave off disaster - but perhaps this is the haze which seems to get between my mind and anything it attacks.

October 19, 1934

I have now had considerable talks with Long, with Counsellor Kirk, with Tittman and Harrison. I think I can give the President adequate character sketches of them if he seems as interested in the personnel of his service when I get back as he did when I left. I had a letter from Dodd in Berlin saying that he would meet me at Constance and I have written back fixing the 28th. We elaborately camouflaged our letters by reference to agricultural matters and to casual crossing of paths; but there was good enough understanding. I am, I understand, to meet Mussolini; but the time has not yet been fixed.

From London I sent home my proposed speech at the Institute. H.A. cabled back approval. Steve Early cabled that Hull was willing to have me make the speech if I did it as an individual and unofficially. He added that the President thought this not feasible. I don't know quite what to think but evidently Hull disapproves and the President intends to convey that he really does approve. Anyhow I have made some changes and cabled them home to H.A. asking him to check with Early and to wire me. It may precipitate conversation between Hull and H.A. which will result in my recall or in forbidding me to make the speech or something. Equally silly. Of course, Hull is not going to like what I say. His theory is, as he has said to me a number of times, that when you are going to cut off a patient's leg you shouldn't tell him about it. In other words he objects to having confidence disturbed. Well, my theory is that you have to have understanding and support for what you do in public life or you will always be prevented from doing anything. I am always therefore tempted to speak out, to present alternatives and often to argue strongly for one of them. On the other hand, concerning administrative devices I have concluded that it is best not to talk about what accomplishments are likely to be but rather to point to them after they are carried out. If you say what you are hoping to do, it puts a lot of people in position to take advantage of it and a lot of others in position to prevent it, or at least to oppose, because it forewarns them. And very little organized support can be had for anything so long as we have a privately monopolized press which is viciously and venally managed.

However, as to the speech, I have said plainly, that there is much to be said for economic isolation, that it is here to stay, and that therefore laissez-faire is dead. This poses a problem of international devices for planning and the sooner we forget tariff revision in the old sense the better, because then we can get on to the real job. This, of course, hits Hull between the eyes, but it is substantially what the President and I agreed on at Hyde Park the day before I sailed, although he had not, of course, seen a word I had written. I have been hoping to set down here the extraordinarily interesting conversation I have had with him in the first weeks in September but I have not yet found the energy.

October 20, 1934

I had some talk with R.R. Enfield and found him very pessimistic about the situation of the world economically and politically. He agreed, I found, that England's present prosperity is temporary and that nothing fundamental is being done even there.

I find Italy doing many of the things which seem to me necessary. And at any rate she is being rebuilt physically in a systematic way. The good people here too are worried about the budget, etc. Mussolini certainly has the same people opposed to him as F.D.R. has. But he has the press controlled so they cannot scream lies at him daily. And he has a compact and disciplined nation although it lacks resources. On the surface, at least, he seems to have made enormous progress. But I have some questions I want to ask about it which may or may not embarrass him. I'm told he has a sense of humor and a very direct way if you can be absolutely alone with him.

October 22, 1934

The practical certainty that anything I write and mail from here will at least be read makes it impossible to set down some notes I should like to record.

I have, in the last two days, visited the Pontine Marshes reclamation project (in which I found nothing of any significance or interest from the point of view of social arrangements) have been to two dinners and receptions, done a little sight-seeing and read thru H.A.'s new book New Frontiers which he sent on to me here.

I find in talks with Long that he agrees that the commercial and agricultural attaches ought to go to the State Dept.

There is a curious and highly important situation of which Italy happens to be the center. She is determined not to lose any more gold both because she believes in the gold standard and because when the crisis is over, she feels, the countries which emerge without having inflated will be considered strong and will have a good position to move from. Conserving gold means reducing imports and this she is apparently determined to do. On that list our cotton and tobacco come very high. There is now perfected, by a development of new machines in the rayon trade, a way of substituting cellulose (wood pulp) fibers for cotton, wool, linen or silk at least up to 75% or 80%. I have seen the resulting material and to my amateur eye it looks even better than pure cotton. It is said that this fibre made in great quantity can be spun cheaper than cotton. Italy imports some half-million bales a year. But also I am told this concern has active inquiries from practically all other European countries and, of course, we have been hearing of something like this in Germany for some time - I even mentioned it in the speech I am to make in a day or two.

I am also hearing stories of a new kind of cellulose plant which is said to produce the material more cheaply than trees - much more cheaply. I have asked that it be investigated.

Put all these stories together and project them into the future in a still unfriendly world and it seems obvious to me that we are in for years of less and less trade and more and more substitution. What this makes necessary in the way of readjustment in the cotton states is obvious. I do not believe that the structure of trade treaties can be built fast enough to stop it and anyway the disposition to self-sufficiency is strong - far stronger than I had imagined by projecting the things I saw several years ago. All Europe seems determined to live within national borders; and what modification of that there is will come through specific agreements for equality - at least it all looks that way to me. And it means that we may as well do what is necessary in the way of economic preparation.

I'm told I am to see Il Duce this afternoon. The meetings of the Institute will begin this morning and it is supposed that he will appear to open the first one. As a matter of fact I went to a review of troops the other day with Long and was directly across from him on his white horse. It was all very disconcerting, shot through with certain elements which touched American sensibilities. His force and intelligence are obvious, as is the effectiveness of administration here. It's the cleanest, neatnest, most effectively operating piece of social machinery I've ever seen. It makes me envious.

What shall I say about the Institute meetings which I came here for? My skepticism of that Institution grows. I doubt as I see it and look over its personnel and talk to those who would shape it, whether it can become a center for commodity conferences, etc, as I had thought it might, preparing the way statistically and furnishing the continuous impulse to compromise. Old H.C. Taylor, our delegate, is wordy and inconsequential. He is playing a deep game about nothing with mysterious moves and counter-moves. As my skepticism has grown I have preferred to stand aside as head of our delegation, let him as permanent delegate arrange things to suit himself and make no commitment whatever myself. There was a strong move to make me President of the Assembly. I flatly refused. It is now, I understand, to go to a Frenchman, and Lord De La Warr and myself are to be vice-presidents. There seemed no way out of this much of commitment. Taylor had a dinner the other night for the two daughters and the Secretary of David Lubin. It was one of those dreadful sloppy sentimental affairs when everyone tearfully recalls the great departed hero and no departure from worship is permitted. His daughters by now are opulent and middle-aged. My acrid dislike for the whole affair was only too obvious, I'm afraid, and I made a few enemies I didn't really need to have.

October 23, 1934
(Handwritten)

Dear Harry,

I had some time getting the speech straightened out. When I sent you a copy I sent one also to Steve Early. Evidently he took it up with Hull who was made somewhat unhappy. I hoped my changes would fix things up. Whether they did or not I don't know. I've held up the printing and translation until the last minute and only a matter of hours before I have to give it. Lacking any further word I'm going ahead.

This is an almost astonishing country and I expect will have a lot to tell you about it when we get home. There is discipline here I can tell you that. And from the looks they are pretty nearly rebuilding every living and productive facility from the ground up.

I've run into a most disconcerting situation here with respect to cotton which I'll tell you about too which I believe must have serious consequences for our program.

Paul has been sick for a couple of days but seems all right again now. In a day or two we are starting back by way of Switzerland where Dodd is coming down to meet me. Then back to London where I'm promised a real look at the pig board, milk board etc. and then sailing on the 8th.

It is a great experience to see other people doing things and feel no responsibility at all. But this whole scene is terribly disquieting and full of dangers. I've looking forward to getting home where we argue about things.

As ever,

/s/ Rex T.

October 23, 1934

The mix-up on my speech is getting embarrassing. Had another cable from H.A. saying Early out of town. Need to send it to be printed since it has to be made tomorrow but hesitate to send it without final OK.

Yesterday after opening session at which I proposed Masse, head of French delegation for President and he was elected, Lord De la Warr and myself were elected vice presidents.

In afternoon went to call on M(ussolini).

Opened by giving greetings of President. He asked about his health, then about his prestige. I said it was still good but that there would be a reaction. He asked how we got along with the Press in opposition. I said it did not seem to change the people much. He seemed interested in this. Asked where opposition centered. Said he had read an especially foolish speech on liberty by, I thought, Senator Gore and was much amused. I said opposition centered in speculators. He was delighted and implied it was the same with him.

The question of gold came up and with it trade. I gave him F.D.'s message - that we were interested in his attempt to deflate by reducing all prices, interest rates, rent, etc., but thought our method of raising them to meet the debt burden was more feasible. He said that this method was better to protect their gold. They had lost a billion lira in a year and had to stop it. I said our gold action was for domestic rather than foreign purposes, that we a believed in a dollar of continuous purchasing power rather than one representing fixed weight in gold, that our prices were rising and suggested that though we had no direct interest in it, we thought that if other countries adopted our monetary theory there would be more chance of international understanding. He jumped immediately to the question whether I thought an international arrangement could be made.

I said I thought so on the side of trade, but that if he had in mind tying each country to a fixed weight of gold there was no chance. I said trade was the real problem anyway. He was interested in this and said Italy's unfavorable balance had to be stopped. I said of course it was dangerous as long as they were afraid to lose gold because it undermined their currency but that I recognized the moral value of conserving it. In fact, I pointed out, we do it too. It is all in Treasury vaults for the security effect on people. He asked if we were really inflating now that the dollar was loose from gold. I said that if he meant by that paying current expenses with paper money, we were not and would not. He had evidently heard that we were and pressed the point. I said that he was still thinking of soundness in terms of gold and that we had an idea that gold was a poor store of value and regarded it only as an instrument and money as an exchange mechanism. But he referred again to Italy's unfavorable balance and I said that if it was necessary to conserve gold, it would undoubtedly be well to conserve the gold and to try to reach equal trade arrangements. He said I had given him much to think about and got up. I left much impressed by his grasping mind. He wants to understand and is determined to do it.

Just to visit him was something of an experience. His office is in an old Palace. I drove down in the Ambassasor's car wih a letter. There were several people in uniform but lots of them in plain clothes here and there easily recognizable as his Fascisti. My letter was read and I was put into an elevator which took me up to the second or third floor. I came out into a long, plain corridor which I walk down with saluting guards on each side. No other visitors were there; in fact, I saw no one else at all. I waited a few moments in a red-plush room with a half-dozen old masters on the wall. Then I was summoned to a great rectangular room, perfectly bare, expect for a desk in the corner. As the door opened M got up and came half way to meet me. We spoke English; but he fumbled for words a good deal and understood only when I spoke very slowly and distinctly. Yet I had a feeling that we got down to cases about real things very quickly. He was pretty non-commital, however, and more interested in quizzing me than in letting me ask any searching questions as I should have liked to do.

October 23, 1934

At noon I decided I could not wait longer to release speech so sent it to printer and cabled GEF.

Had lunch with H R Knickerbocker who was most interesting about Europe in general and dictatorships in particular. He is just leaving here for Berlin and Moscow. Has just finished a series on Fascism. He feels, I think, that M. is doing the best job of any of the dictators. Italy is certainly a remarkable study in efficiency but I get more and more certain that opposition is developing from the same people who oppose us at home and that it will gradually evolve toward government ownership of everything. Few people seem to realize that what we are up against is an administrative problem - how to run industry and distribute its goods.

More and more every nation's attentions will be forced to the consideration of this central problem regardless of whose privileges are circumscribed.

November 12, 1934
On the S.S. Washington

Head home! Left Italy on October 26. Took thru train to Schaffhausen and changed for Konstanz. Arrived on the 27th. Dodd arrived on the 28th. We spent the evening and the morning of the 29th together. Left Germany on the 29th and crossed Switzerland to Geneva. At Konstanz talked to GEF and Jerry Frank over the phone as I had from Wales before and from London - each time from a hotel. Discovered that F.D.R. had sent word for me to go to Ulster which I could not understand until I talked with Bingham in London. In Geneva talked with Prentice Gilbert, Hugh Wilson being in London with Norman Davis for the naval conversations. From Geneva went to Dijon overnight. Then to Paris overnight, talking with Straus and Marriner. In London talked with Atherton and Bingham. Found that Bingham had written to F.D.R. that Ulster would be a good place to visit. Viscount Craigavon, Prime Minister, had been in office twelve years and had much experience with recovery efforts on a small scale. Thought myself it would have been better to have stayed in London for the rest of my time for talks, with Keynes, Cole,

Clay, Elliot, Street, De la Warr and others. Considered delaying a week but thought I had been away long enough. So on Saturday made the night crossing to Belfast from Liverpool. Stayed until Tuesday, talking with Craigavon and Robertson in Agriculture. On Tuesday went to Dublin overnight, staying at the Legation with Denby (Charge since the Minister died). Went on down to Kilarney overnight then over to Cork on the 9th. All very strenuous and wearing. Got on the boat tired and with a severe cold. Spent most of two days in bed and even yet have not had ambition to make fresh notes of rather important talks with Dodd, Craigavon and Leslie Woods (Consul-General at Cork) which I must do before landing. These are also some general impressions and observations on conditions and line-ups which must be recorded. But I'm still too weary.

November 22, 1934
En route to Warm Springs

Naturally there were several busy days after getting off the boat. I came immediately down to Washington and went to work. The press interview on the boat and one after getting back to the Department were ordeals. My anomalous position as a department under secretary and yet obviously something more which I don't tell about irritates the newspaper men and that together with an unfriendly press which has spent a year doing its best to get me out creates a situation in which I am not likely to get a swelled head from public acclaim.

But people around Washington seemed genuinely glad to see me. A bunch from the Department came down to the train and met us in a way which touched me deeply. There was a note on my desk from F.D.R. saying he was sorry not to be home when I came and inviting me to Warm Springs soon. Ickes, Hopkins, Perkins, etc. all gave me a warm welcome. And went right to work.

Hopkins told me the story of further developments from our Hyde Park conversations over labor day when we plead with F.D.R. against unemployment insurance and for a guarantee of jobs on public work. Ickes, Morgenthau, H.H. and F.D.R. have been meeting often to get up a works scheme. It is not yet announced - only rumored - but H.H. says it will surely be done. There will and should be some unemployment insurance but we may be able to restrict it to twenty six weeks or so and defer its beginning for a few years while a contributory scheme is built up. This will throw present emphasis on a works scheme. H.H. says F.D.R. has avoided talking about the financing of it; but undoubtedly my proposal at Hyde Park is the essence of it. I understand Stuart Chase has hit on something of the sort and has written a pamphlet on it. I must look for it. It seems to me we were at a stalemate unless we could get out of the bankers hands. Calvin Hoover has now an additional proposal to control and force the expansion of bank deposits, taking the power to create them away from banks and making them respond to bond issues. A bank could then lend only its own money and time deposits, would have a hundred percent reserve against demand deposits.   The government could sell treasury bonds to the Federal Reserve Bank, creating a deposit for itself there which it could check out in payment for works. This would return to member banks as deposits and continue to cirulate until the bonds were retired. This will bear looking into.

I have had long conferences with several people over N.R.A. I did not note my own part in Johnson's retirement. I advised it at Hyde Park on Labor Day and the President asked me to do some negotiating when I went back to Washington. I think I helped some in the preliminary settlement but as it was then Richberg was to be out as well as Johnson. To my mind he is just as bad - muddle-headed in his economics, shifty in practice and indecisive in action. I find, however, that he got himself left in temporarily, along with Clay Williams and that Hopkins and Ickes fear he may be getting entrenched. Ickes, at a conference on the whole matter two weeks ago, suggested Hutchins as chairman; everyone, he and H.H. tell me, approved and Hutchins was called down and asked.   He accepted but has since heard nothing and now Richberg is apparently trying to discredit him. I must see what I can do. Both Ickes and Hopkins are very worried. They are afraid of Richberg and do not understand F.D.R.'s inaction.

Our gang in the Department gave Paul and myself a dinner Sunday night and we described our trip to them. It was a nice friendly occasion.

I find the report of the National Resources Board which succeeded Ickes' National Planning Board is about ready. I am working over it, especially the proposals for land planning and for setting up a new Planning Board directly under the President. It begins to look as though Planning and quarterback execution might be combined.

Long talks with Silcox and the other Bureau Chiefs have brought me up to date on department matters and settled me into harness again.

I must tell the President that Lord Craigavon's plea was largely for unemployment insurance. I put before him our doubts and our unwillingness to admit inability to guarantee everyone a job, especially when there remained so much obvious work to be done. I told him frankly, also, that the President was inclined toward a wholly contributory scheme with the government not participating. He put it to me strongly that the government had a great stake in the results - security, stability, etc. - and that it would not work otherwise. He spoke feelingly of his satisfaction in knowing that none of his people were suffering. He disparaged public works but admitted that they were better except more costly which was what governed them.

Furthermore I must talk with him about the coordination of land policy again. There are many - perhaps 20 -agencies of government which have something to do with it. My scheme of trading between Interior and Agriculture of last June was agreed to well enough by everyone but apparently F.D.R. got about equal pressures from all sides. He finally told me he would do nothing until after election. I think he still inclines to do nothing. But irritations and administrative difficulties are multiplying and it would be better to act. Of course the best thing would be to set up a new Department for Conservation including all public land management and acquisition in it. But I doubt if anything drastic will be done. Next best is to try for better coordination. Perhaps this can be brought about through the Planning Board suggested in the National Resources Board's report. But I have already written to Elliot about an agency of the Executive to look ahead in view of the past and suggest courses of action? Or shall it actually undertake to achieve coordination? If it does this it has executive duties and is not merely a Planning Board. Some one has suggested that this administration is getting government reorganization where others failed because it is following the method of coordination of existing agencies rather than their transfer to which so much objection is always made. This is true to an extent but it leaves the execution of policy in so many different hands that failure often results. There must be some compromise scheme. Some transfer seems necessary.

I am also going to have to say something about the career service and about the system of commercial and agricultural attaches.

About the career men there is only this to be said: the trouble lies at home in selection and in administration. Most of what is said about them is true enough - they are tea drinkers, they know little about economic and social movements, they are stiff, snobbish, and formal. Not all, but most. They do, however, come from the upper one percent of our intelligence. If they were differently trained, if we made it clear to them that we wanted something different, I think we should get it. It is amusing to see how different political ambassadors react to them. Dodd, who is a plain scholar, detests them; Straus and Bingham think they are wonderful - they help them socially. Long is half way between.

As to the semi-independent attaches - we made a great fuss about Hoover's salesmen, but they are still doing the same thing. There is nothing to do but take them into the State Department, use different methods of selection and training and reduce their salesmanship tendencies. Nothing but different administration at home will make a great difference in these services.

November 23, 1934

I spent nearly the whole day with F.D.R. yesterday. Went to the pool and swam, he driving his own car. Went back and had lunch with him and talked until five in the afternoon.

Talked over thoroughly the foreign trade situation. I found him in agreement that there is no prospect of increase. I told him of the European movement for self-containment and how it was being buttressed all the time by new privileged classes. Told him my feeling that the gold countries were weakening and called attention to the probable repercussions of both these on our domestic situation, especially the need for continued production control. He agreed and thought it time to begin warning the country not to be optimistic on foreign trade.

I told him my ideas on the career service and he agreed that the trouble was as I analysed it.

He told me all about the campaign and the election, his recent talks with bankers and industrialists and his enthusiasm after his recent trip thru the T.V.A. country.

I indicated my belief that the coming Congress would want some taming and that I thought there ought to be again a series of bold strokes for leadership from him, and said I suggested government reorganization as one, making the point that he was at the height of his power, that these things could not be done until '36 or '38 if not done now. He was taken by the idea and wrote out a reorganization scheme as we talked. We worked over it an hour. Then he asked me to work on it over night and have another go at it today which we will do.

I discussed with him my memorandum on the naval conversations and British policy and he suggested that as a start he might invite Herridge down to visit him here, thus causing the British to think. He said he had already told Davis to intimate in London that he might seek rapprochement with the Dominions. I pointed out the Australian and New Zealand interests in this case would probably run against us. He seemed taken with my emphasis on Ireland as an alternative.

He talked for a long time on foreign relations, opening his mind as never before to me on these questions and seemed to feel my advice worth while though I can't believe it worth much. He went on to talk about difficulties with the Cabinet, how he has to run several departments, how no one will take responsibility, etc., and indicated that he was feeling toward an enlarged cabinet of about twenty with an executive committee of about five. This is the way I have been working too but I had not hoped to find him so ready, since he had seemed to waiver so on the difficulties of jurisdiction over land policy.

We discussed the forthcoming report of his National Resources Board and he approved my suggestion for clearing up their confusion over the functions of a Planning Board. He seems greatly interested in administrative problems just now.

We talked for hours over this whole range of subjects as friends.

I felt again as I have before that my mind runs with his as with almost no one I ever knew before. What I cannot understand is why he should spend so much time explaining and justifying everything to me. I wish I had more wisdom. No one ever had a better chance to use it. I think he over-estimates my intelligence; he couldn't overestimate my loyalty and affection.

We are to spend a somewhat similar day today; except that we are going to a terracing demonstration this afternoon and dining with the Power Commission tonight.

My rough sketch for government reorganization as it stands now is as follows:

State

War

Navy

Treasury
    Customs
    Internal Revenue
    Mint
    Engraving and Printing
    Coast Guard

Budget and Planning

Justice

Post Office

Interior
    Indian Affairs
    Petroleum Administration Board
    Coal
    Tennesse Valley Authority
    Power
    Weather
    Lighthouses
    Coast and Geodetic Survey
    Mines

Labor
   Labor Statistics
   U.S. Employment
   U.S. Mediation Board
   National Labor Relations Board

Agriculture
   Animal Industry
   Dairy Industry
   Plant Industry
   Chemistry and Soils
   Entomolgy and Plant Quarantine
   Agricultural Engineering
   Agricultural Economics
   Soil Erosion Service

Commerce
   Census
   Domestic Commerce
   Shipping Board
   Navigation and Steamboat Inspection
   Lighthouses (already included under Interior)

Public Works
   Public Roads
   Reclamation
   Public Works Administration(including Housing)

Credit
   Farm Credit
   Home Owners' Loan Corporation
   Reconstruction Finance Corporation
   Housing Adminstration

Industry
   Federal Trade Commission
   National Recovery Administration
   Federal Alcohol Control Administration
   Grain Futures Administration
   Securities Board
   Commodity Exchange Board

Commercial Relations
   Foreign Commerce

Tariff Commission
Export and Import Bank
Commercial Treaties

Public Welfare
    Federal Emergency Relief Administration
    Unemployment Insurance
    Resettlement
    Veterans
    Immigration
    Education
    Fine Arts

November 24, 1934

I spent practically the entire day with the President again yesterday. We swam at the Springs in the morning, had lunch at the little White House (that grand old man George Foster Peabody was there), went to his newspaper conference and was asked to chip in several times while he went over off-the record material for an hour and a half, went with him to a terracing demonstration on his farm and for a drive afterward, and had dinner with him and his Power Policy Committee in the evening when we sat around and talked until midnight.

We had almost no time alone together; but our discussion with the newspaper men and with the power commission was fascinating. For the news men he went over the whole world trade situation, using the ideas I had brought home, and applied the lessons to our own economy, making the familiar points that self-sufficiency had worked itself into the very fabric of state organization in Europe, that it would not be modified and that our plans had to be laid in view of this. This took about half his time and was beautifully stated and rounded out; for the rest he discussed power and its uses and control, giving them the yardstick philosophy and saying that he hoped the private companies would seize their opportunity. Privately he has no notion that they will and I am sure he is moving ahead with no fear of the result.

Our long talk with the Policy Committee at night, in which we went over the whole field and discussed all issues for five hours resulted in laying down several immediate lines of actions. Lilienthal was told to move out with a new, enlarged directorate for his Electric Farm and Home Authority; the group was told to prepare for works expenditure of some two hundred million a year on rural electrification. The devise for this is to be local cooperative set-ups with a government service management company. As for regulation of holding companies as against their elimination, he came out flatly for their annihilation and directed legislation to be prepared for taxing them out of existence.

The President was in beautiful form over this whole field. He knows it like a book and his ingenuity and practical sense had a chance to show themselves. It was a privilege to be allowed to sit with him while he outlined his views.

I had considerable talk with Lilienthal and Cooke. I urged Lilienthal to make his T.V.A. more of a training school for public executives, a suggestion in which the President joined. The discussion ranged over the regulation versus government competition methods. It was agreed that both ought to be done. I would like to go with other Authorities faster than we are. The President is clearly preparing for it and has a regional set-up for the whole country in mind; how fast he will move into it, I am not clear, nor, I think, is he. The functions of such bodies are being worked out by T.V.A. but are not yet clear in all their aspects and relations. That is not the sort of thing which worries F.D.R. He has an extraordinary ability to leave things in flux and to prevent their taking concrete and final shape before the time is ripe. It is certainly one of his greatest strengths although it displeases more meticulous or interested people, and annoys some of them dreadfully.

He said rather casually, by the way, at lunch yesterday that we ought really to pass the Food and Drugs Act this session. He will send a special message and tend to the politics.

November 25, 1934

Yesterday was in many ways the most interesting day I ever spent with the President. He called for me at eleven and we went swimming together. We had lunch with Mrs. Roosevelt and Miss Cook and Miss Thompson. The lunch produced a discussion of monetary theory precipitated by Mrs. Roosevelt in which a good deal of ground was covered. I had a chance to see how far F.D.R. has gone in his thinking. He is now centering on the control of deposit currency. I put before him later Calvin Hoover's suggestion which seemed to interest him. I rather think he is inclined to see what Eccles can do with the Federal Reserve before he goes further with legislation.

He told me, later, when we went for a long ride in the country alone, that he wanted to send a special message in one of the first days of Congress on the Food and Drug Bill and asked me to clean up all the preliminaries.

On the ride we talked a good deal about country life, about the possibilities of decentralization and about common dreams for the future of the country. He has been greatly impressed by some figures I showed him concerning the heavier birth rates in the rural South compared with urban and Northern regions. In a way the South is producing the future American and future fathers and mothers of the nation in prosperity.

He gave me some definite directions in a few administrative fields which I just note for reference.

1.   Puerto Rico rehabilitation which has given so much trouble must be shifted to a Public Works grant to be earmarked by him out of forthcoming funds. I must speak to Gruening about this.

2.   We are to earmark enough of the new funds to give us our regional stations for Agriculture.

3.   We are to earmark funds also for homes and establishments for all forest supervisors so that we can begin a three year tour of duty practice throughout the service.

4.   We are to put all field service men in regulation uniform. I am directed to see to their purchase from the Marine Corps factory, consulting Harry Roosevelt about procedure. This applies especially to Forest Service and to Biological Survey.

Edsel Ford was around yesterday and came to a buffet supper at the Little White House. I had an interesting talk with him about industrial policy and expect to have more today.

When I suggested that it was about time to go back to Washington, he ridiculed the idea and expressed the desire to have me stay until he went back. I said I would go home tomorrow and come back when Hopkins comes after Thanksgiving. He didn't see why I should go home but we left it that way. He acts as though I were doing him a favor to spend my time with him. I can't say how humble it makes me feel and how I wish my wisdom were at all equal to his need. If it were only something simple I could do, such as make a physical sacrifice or some such thing, it would be easier. It is true that our minds and temperaments run together. My imagination is bold enough, and my mind tough and realistic; but not a bit more than his. He seems to think it worth while to show me how he directs this whole machine; I can't see why. But I can be profoundly grateful for the experience and I can try to contribute the utmost I can.

November 26, 1934

I decided today to go back to Washington for three or four days. F.D.R. wanted me to stay - at least he said so - but there seemed to be some reason for being back at the desk for a few days, important as it is to be with the President. I spent the entire day with him yesterday, swimming, riding, picnicing and dining at home. There were several of the Warm Springs crowd at the picnic and Miss Gay Shepperson for dinner, but we had two long talks at home, one about N.R.A. and one about World affairs, though we ranged very widely as we have come to do now. I can't believe that he completely opens his mind to many others as he has to me these past few days. It is a finely organized mind too. I have always been aware of his great purposes and his practical ingenuity. I have never been able to see so clearly as I do now a kind of dogged determination to work out dreams in practice. He is convinced that he can transform the country physically and morally in his time and do it without great changes in government structure or in democratic processes. Maybe he can. I'm willing to do my bit.

Interspersed with our long conversations concerning what we should have the country be if we could, a practical detail or two emerged for immediate consideration. I note these for reference

1. When I get back to Washington I am to try straightening out N.R.A., or at least carrying that process a step further. His strategy for the moment is to keep things as quiet on that front as possible until new legislation can be framed and passed which must come at this session. It seems that when he spoke to members of the board about appointing Hutchins they all said they would resign if the appointment were made. The question now is whether Hutchins won't come down just as another member of the Board - or as Vice Chairman - running the office and learning his job until a permanent set-up can be established at which time he will be made head of it. I am to see Ickes, Perkins and Hamilton and see what can be arranged.

2. F.D.R. is much worried about the Bankhead Act. The referendum comes on Dec. 14 and he wants to carry it with a big majority. In order to do that he thinks the regulations should be changed to exempt the smaller farmers from its provision and making some other modifications in the regulations. I am to see H.A.W. about this and call him up to say what has been done. Of course the real trouble is that H.A.W. has been pussyfooting on this issue. He thinks strict regulation is unpopular and since he is now evidently running for President, he does not want to advocate it. But with the new cotton substitutes becoming important in Europe and with the likelihood that more countries may go off gold, it becomes important for the future of the South to cut down and hold down on cotton. Of course cotton seems to me a starvation crop anyhow and I secretly hope the substitutes may come in quickly and completely and that we may turn the South to other things. This, I may say, seems also to be the President's view. But just at this time strict control is absolutely

necessary.

3. Last night we spent 2 hours again over government reorganization. I had redrafted the scheme, merely working from memory and the Congressional Record in long hand. This F.D.R. modified as we went along. We made a first attempt to visualize a Cabinet Executive Committee and talked about various personalities in that connection which it seems unnecessary to note here. After juggling around a while we succeeded in eliminating the Commerce Department which pleased us both. We have two new regulatory departments and two welfare departments. This may all be play. But F.D.R. seems serious enough about it and told me to start drafting a law in brief form. Enough attempts have been made at reorganization -all of them failures - but this might just possibly work.

Today Joe Robinson and Pat Harrison showed up. They lunched with the President and me at the little White House. I got quite chummy with them and for the first time these old Democratic wheel horses talked to me frankly and intimately about party affairs. I have no faith at all in Harrison and little enough in Robinson; but Joe at least is loyal and has a glimmer of understanding about the New Deal. The President handles them beautifully. They do what he says unaware of what he is driving at. They have to. He is kind but firm and on the whole they behave.

November 27, 1934

It is quite clear that one good method of getting things done in this Democracy is to isolate, morally, those who would oppose what it is that you want to do.

We function in such a welter of pressures and defense of privilege, and the interests concerned are so tied in with executives and legislators that the least notice sets formidable machinery of opposition in motion.

To break through this system - outside a general crisis such as existed in 1932 - it is first necessary to concoct an closely held plan, admitting as few people as possible to policy discussions, and to begin by an attack on the privileges. Congressional Committees are good media for this. The Federal Trade Commission in this way prepared for F.D.R.'s power program. It was done in Congressional committees in preparation for the Securities Act. Sensing this, and in view of the tenderness of the whole A.A.A. personnel for processors' interests, I aided and abetted Wheeler in his attempt to get a resolution for investigation through last session. The President intervened for me, but too late and it failed. It must be tried again. If I'd sensed this soon enough we might have followed this way with F. & D. It would have made things much easier.

In view of H.A.W.'s weakness on crop control and my belief that our foreign trade is threatened, and also in view of the wide-spread propaganda for unlimited production among exporters, ginners, millers, and various other interests of this sort, I have just approached Pat Harrison on the matter of investigating these gentlemen. It might work. Anyway I am sure that this is a good principle of procedure.

November 28, 1934

As I think I have noted before, the President is disposed at the earliest possible moment to get rid of direct relief and to shift over to a works program which will give employment instead of charity. He seemed to be thinking in this direction when Harry Hopkins and I were in Hyde Park on Labor Day and we both reinforced the arguments he already had in mind. While I was away in Europe Hopkins, Ickes and Morgenthau were at work on a scheme which would implement this. I was very much interested, therefore, to sit with Harry and three of his assistants last night while they put the final touches on their proposal for a works scheme. I found at Warm Springs that the only questions the President had in his mind were (1) whether sufficient works could be got under weigh so that relief might be got rid of in from six to eight months and (2) what proportion of them could be self-liquidating so that the finance scheme which we had in mind could be used. I think as a result of last night's conference that it may be possible to find enough works within, say, eight or ten months to absorb most of the unemployed and it looks to me as though fifty to sixty percent of it could be called self-liquidating with broad definition and certainly forty percent of it would be repaid.

Ickes, Hopkins and myself are to go back to Warm Springs at the end of the week when this matter will be finally talked over and the budget messages framed. I suppose Henry Morgenthau will also be present.

As soon as I got back I went to work on the N.R.A. matter. I went to see Ickes and we got hold of Charles D. Merriam who knows Hutchins very well and Harry Hopkins. We decided that the thing to do was to find out first whether Hutchins would come as a member of the Board, keeping rather quiet and learning his job for a few months until permanent legislation was passed and, second, to find out by some means whether the Board or a substantial part of it would consent to this.

The difficult part of this arrangement was to approach some members of the Board. I thought I knew Hamilton well enough to ask him how things stood but I wanted a day or two to turn around in so I asked Ickes to call Hutchins, which he did. Ickes told him very frankly that there were interests in the Board which were opposed to having him come down. We told him frankly that we thought it was the big business people and we thought he was the kind of fellow who would recognize where the opposition came from and work with us against it. Hutchins seems to see that point of view and suggested that he come down as advisor to N.R.A. This struck me as a pretty good suggestion as it would enable him to sit on both the Administrative Board and on the Policy Board and he could therefore be influential in framing the new legislation and would give nobody any excuse for resigning nor make any commitments himself which would be embarrasing to him later. We thought we might approach the President concerning this when we are at Warm Springs, meantime finding out the attitude of the Board but it looks now as though this rather difficult matter might be compromised.

November 29, 1934

Four things to be recorded about yesterday: (1) Meeting of the National Resources Board,(2) Talk with Frances Perkins, (3) Talk with Walton Hamilton, (4) Putting Jerome Frank and Fred Bartlett to work on government reorganization.

Frances has no clear ideas about N.R.A. She thinks in terms of personalities and seems to be sympathetic to Richberg. She thinks he will quit if Hutchins is brought in but why he should I don't see. The five members of the board are Williams, Whiteside, Marshall, Hamilton and Hillman. Richberg is director of the Emergency Council and as such has only an indirect connection. He seems to think Hutchins will dominate things if brought in which is probably true. Anyway I got no help from her and, in fact, felt I could not be wholly frank about the situation.

I had, however, a good talk with Hamilton. He says he wants Hutchins, and that Hillman also wants him. Marshall has an old academic quarrel with him which has no public significance. Whiteside, he says, is industry's real representative now and might quit because Hutchins would really serve the public interest. Williams is slick and devious but loquacious and thinking mostly of personal prestige. Hamilton says as things are he and Hillman can prevent obviously bad things from happening but cannot start much reconstruction. There are thirty-six codes with price maintenance provisions and three hundred others with pending provisions of a similar sort which he can prevent being ratified. He agreed that N.R.A. ought not to be brought much to public notice just now until legislation is secured. He felt, however, that threats to quit were mostly fluff and that nothing really would happen if Hutchins were made Vice Chairman with administrative control. He says he is sure that Williams and Richberg misrepresent situation to the President that clearer and quicker procedure is badly needed. He feels that Hutchins would not be on the laissez-faire side, that he, Hillman and people like Leon Henderson could work with him well both in administration and in framing legislation. He says all the codes have been hastily done and need a thorough overhauling, but that it cannot be done with present personnel which is inefficient or not social minded. Hutchins could remedy this. He says Board meetings are long and involved and apt to be indecisive. Hutchins would also remedy this. Also no progress has been made toward legislation and Hutchins would clear this up.

I outlined confidentially the general strategy of legislation for each industry of a monopoly sort and the setting up of an administrative Board in Interior as such situations jelled, leaving to N.R.A. a system of codes for industries in a midway or competitive situation. He thought this good, also the notion of a new attack by the Anti-Trust method on unauthorized price-fixing, etc., together with an extension of goverment ownership in power and similar industries.

Hamilton sees things almost wholly my way. I recall that the President took almost my whole panel for his Board in transition except the substitution of Whiteside for W.H. Davis. Who gave him this advice after I left for Europe I don't know - probably Richberg.

I went to the meeting of the National Resources Board in the morning. The Board was a little startled by the whole report and inclined to reserve commitment to some points. I wanted the report endorsed and suggested a compromise letter of transmittal which was used. The points of confusion over the recommendation for a Planning Board were cleared up in the galley proof and I had no further objection. It is really a magnificent job. Many of its suggestions would be furthered by the reorganization scheme if F.D.R. will put it through.

I am worried because H.A.W. will not accede to the expressed wish of F.D.R to be more forthright in support of the Bankhead measure. Frank found that exemption for small farmers cannot be made under the act which makes a pronouncement on that point difficult. But H.A.W. told his newpaper conference yesterday that cold neutrality was to be the Department's attitude even after I had told him of the President's wishes. There is a danger of a rift here which may be serious.

December 1, 1934
En route to Warm Springs

I have been brought up to date on Beltsville developments by Jerry Frank and Fred Bartlett and they are such as to cause some worry. Last spring HAW told me he was interested in some scientific poultry work which would require some outlays at Beltsville. I asked Bressman to see him with a view to preparing some PWA estimates and asking for funds. When I got back from my California trip late in July Bressman, after looking around - I had asked him to take a special interest in Beltsville - said he thought the work was going ahead without authorization. Sheets also came in with some new requests for money for completion of projects for which I had supposed there were sufficient funds. Bressman was instructed to find out at once what was wrong. Sheets, head of the Division of Animal Husbandry, who took chief interest in Beltsville, was very evasive. Bressman finally said he was sure Sheets was transferring funds from one project to another. I could see how that did not seem important to Sheets since he regarded the whole Beltsville development as one job. But I at once went to Ickes on the poultry matter and asked for funds to complete the laboratory whose funds had been eaten into and for a reallocation to straighten out the record. Ickes started an investigation which showed that in other instances Sheets had been similarly careless, but we had no knowledge that he was doing this and the first we heard of it was when he sent a report to the Maryland District Attorney. Meantime we had our own investigators on the job and they soon turned up the same thing. There was no evidence of dishonesty or misappropriation. Merely a carelessness about using appropriated money for specific authorized purposes. This, however, was a criminal offense. I had thought we were protected from this kind of thing by the periodical reports signed by the business manager of the Bureau which showed progress on various P.W. jobs. On these reports everything looked O.K. I felt sure irregularities must have been known to Sheets. But when investigators examined him under oath he said that Bressman and I had advised him to use funds indiscriminately - a plain lie, of course, but one that worries me. It is foolish to anyone who knows the whole situation because the Public Works Board made reallocations easy and we had never been refused a request, so far as I remember, to transfer funds. And I had asked in numerous instances.

While I was away in Europe, Sheets was demoted and sent to Chinsegut Hill station by H.A.W. This was a mistake. He should been fired for letting us down administratively. Still I have a sneaking sympathy for his impatience with red tape even if he did lie about me.

Sheets is the rather pushing promoter type who would have been a great success in business but who couldn't stand procedure and was unwilling to regularize what he wanted to do. He had a kind of passionate interest in the Beltsville project which had been a promoter's dream for years. H.A.W. and I both thought he was no scientist and had tried to think of ways to supplant him. I had been suspicious of his pushing qualities and had asked McCrory, last winter, to take charge of building operations at Beltsville. He evidently construed this as only an engineering mandate and never looked into business management at all.

At any rate the whole thing is worrisome. I doubt if anyone will believe that I told Sheets to proceed with his irregularities and yet it is only his word against Bressman's and mine and those who want to think badly of me will doubtless say that I am only making him the goat. Last year I was a Red; this winter I'm a crook. What next?

December 5, 1934

The days at Warm Springs were interesting but very little business got done. There were more people around than on the first trip and the President was less disposed to talk business. I went with him and others to four or five parties. Got the Forest Service order signed; but no chance to talk more reorganization. He made his own statement on the Bankhead Bill yesterday that he would try to see that Congress exempted two-bale farmers. H.A.W. called up yesterday and finally suggested that he make the statement. F.D.R., however, decided to do it himself. He sent me down to tell the newspaper men that he would come to see them in half an hour and he did - came into their cottage and sat and talked cotton, etc., for half an hour, asking me to check him on the figures. I don't suppose this has ever happened before. The grace with which he carries this job is superb.

Ickes, Hopkins, Morgenthau, Frank Walker and myself had a two-hour conference with him yesterday about the forthcoming works program to replace relief. Ickes presented a brief which was based on prevailing wages and cost of materials which formed the basis of discussion. It was all wrong. It showed too little direct employment per dollar and did not seem adequate to meet the problem at all. Harry had little to say though he had what I thought was a better brief based on lower than prevailing wages and cut material prices showing much more employment per dollar. Morgenthau fumbled a bit but had nothing to contribute. F.D.R. was interested in the proportion which could be made self-liquidating. My suggesting for getting around legal debt limits of cities, etc., was to provide in the bill for Federal incorporation of public bodies and I think this may be done. On non-Federal works, F.D.R. still talks of 3% interest. I did not object because I imagine he still has the financing scheme I proposed at Hyde Park in mind. On housing, of course, he looked toward about 50% subsidy for the low cost field, a thing which seems vital to me. I have the gravest doubts about fixing works wages at lower than prevailing rates but F.D.R. seems determined on it.

Ickes, Hopkins, Morgenthau and myself were told to go away and work over the thing some more, after F.D.R. worked out some 4 1/2 billions which suited him. But the talk came to nothing. Morgenthau is really opposed, I think, and finds objections but no suggestions. Ickes and Hopkins are so worried about who is to do the job that they can hardly think of the job itself. They are nice to each other but each sees the whole program as his own. The whole thing is not moving forward. The studies are inadequate. And this administrative difficulty merely emphasizes the need for reorganization. I hope he will get on with it and soon.

I played some poker and some golf, having not done either for years and years. I was better at both than I expected. It was amusing to see Betsy Roosevelt trim the Secretary of the Treasury, the Administrator of Public Works, and the Relief Administrator all at once. She took about $15 away from them. The golf was very combative and vocal and a good time was had by all. Yesterday Jim Farley and Charley Michelson showed up so a little politics was mixed in. It must be amusing if you have time for it. Had separate talks with Hopkins, Morgenthau, Ickes about fundamentals or, if you like, long-time possibilities. All very revealing.

December 6, 1934
En route to Washington from Warm Springs

Ickes and I had a talk with the President this morning about the Hutchins matter. I told him about my conversation with Hamilton and that seemed to change the whole complexion of the affair for the President. He asked us to call up Hutchins and get him to wait a few days and said that he would have a talk with Clay Williams and Leon Marshall and reiterate his first proposition to them very clearly that he wanted to appoint Hutchins a member of the Board. Ickes called up Hutchins and arranged for him to defer any action for a few days and that is the way the matter stands at the moment. I hope not to have any further part in this particular thing.

Last night I had a long talk with Ickes in which he told me the whole story of how he came to be appointed Secretary of the Interior and, talking rather confidentially, reiterated his desire that I should become Under Secretary of Interior. He said he had provided for an Under Secretary in his new budget and I said that when he got the budget thru we might talk about it again. The administrative difficulties in the Department of Agriculture have not gotten any better. It might be just as bad in the Department of the Interior but I doubt it. Ickes and I talked also about the Beltsville affair and I told him the story from our angle. He seemed already to appreciate the situation and seemed to think there was nothing further to worry about in the matter. He embarrassed me a little by going on to talk about government reorganizaton, indicating that he thought there ought to be an organization set up of some kind to include such things as Food and Drugs, Public Health, Education, and various things of that sort, as well as a rather wholesale grouping together of what are now independent commissions. The study of government reorganization seems to be very much in the air. Of course I had to be very non-responsive because of the plan which the President has had me work on. I suspect that Richberg may also be working on something of the sort but I have no idea what it can be.

Ickes also said he would like to have another talk with Wallace and myself concerning transfer of activities back and forth between Agriculture and Interior. I had nothing to say to that because of course any reorganization plan would take this into account and would settle the problem in a different way by setting up a new department to contain conservation activities.

I also had a considerable talk with Morgenthau concerning gold policy and reorganization of the banking system. I indicated that I thought the best policy for us would be to throw the gold block countries off gold instead of supporting them in their gold position at the present time, and cited the Export-Import Bank's current negotiations with Germany concerning cotton as an extra-legal form of stabilization which might come about more readily if the European countries were off gold rather than on. He seemed interested but noncommital. I also had occasion to tell him that I thought the biggest job the Treasury would have this winter was to discover some way that could escape from a growing debt service on public debt. He said he did not see how it done and I said he knew several ways in which it could be done if he wanted it done and he merely smiled. He indicated that he had been thinking about such things. I assume that the President has already broached something of the sort to him. He inquired specifically about my attitude toward long-run agricultural adjustment. He has always been opposed to certain features of the present plan.

I indicated that I thought it had drawbacks and that the best thing we could do would be to get hold of forty or fifty million acres of land and use it as a balancing mechanism. I told him I thought we ought to get rid of the processing tax which surprised him and he said he would be glad to pay for fifty million acres of land out of Treasury funds if the processing tax and current rentals for withdrawal of land could be done away with. All of which was very interesting.

December 10, 1934

I believe I have noted before that after my visit to Puerto Rico last winter and my appraisal of the necessity for rehabilitation, a Puerto Rican commission of three, headed by Chancellor Chardon of Puerto Rico University, were asked to come to Washington and work out a plan for rehabilitation, which they did. This plan involved a many-sided scheme for bettering Puerto Rican economic life but particularly it involved setting up what was to be called the Puerto Rico Corporation which was to have general charge of the economic activities. In working out the Jones-Costigan sugar bill, I used a great deal of energy in getting a clause put into that bill which allowed us to use processing taxes derived from the sale of Puerto Rican sugar for this purpose. The taxes were to be put into a special fund and the special fund turned over to the Corporation. One of the ideas was that the Corporation should purchase and operate a sugar central for yardstick purposes and another was that it should assist in the rehabilitation of coffee lands. Various adminstrative difficulties got in the way. In the first place, the home office of Puerto Rico shifted over from the War Department to Interior and a new Bureau of Overseas Territories and Possessions and a new man, Ernest Gruening, was put in charge. This delayed matters considerably because Chapman and I had been trying to work out the thing together confronted with many lawyers difficulties in setting up the Corporation. Ultimately the Comptroller General refused to let us use processing taxes for purposes of the Corporation and that held the scheme up indefinitely.

We are still, as a matter of fact, in that stage of trying to find a way around the Comptroller General's ruling but a number of us are working on it and have some hopes. The amount of processing taxes to be collected under the Jones-Connally Act on Puerto Rican sugar will be, for the three years of the operation of the Act, $8,000,000 a year or $24,000,000. This tax is, of course, being collected at the present time and it is going into a special fund to be used for general purposes of agriculture in Puerto Rico. We have the satisfaction of knowing that the tax is being collected and is lying in the Treasury awaiting the solution of administrative problems, which would not be so disagreeable if it were not for the terrible situation of Puerto Rico at the present time and our desire to get to work on it. The interest of the Sugar Section of the Department of Agriculture has always been in maintaining a balance among the quotas of the Philippines, Hawaii, Cuba and Puerto Rico and there has been a constant attempt to eat into this special fund for compensation payments to those who reduce their production of sugar cane. The beginning of the Jones-Connally Act found Puerto Rico with a current surplus of sugar which it was necessary to try to take off the market. The President instructed me several months ago to work out a plan to buy this sugar and I have had several conversations with the Sugar Section about it. The people there have been just as uncooperative as they possibly could and have put all the difficulties in the way which they could discover but we have finally today reached an agreement which the President has instructed them to accept and to put through. In order to get it, I have had to get the Secretary and Dalton, head of the Sugar Section, over there and got the President's instructions to Dalton verbally. By this agreement $2,250,000 of the special fund allotted to Puerto Rico is to be used for purposes of reducing the production of cane, but the President promised that out of forthcoming Public Works funds he will give Puerto Rico an equal amount to be used for setting up a subsistence homestead project. This will not settle the surplus problem ultimately but it will assist immediately and it does protect the fund.

I have also been mixed up in Virgin Island affairs lately. Last September at Hyde Park, the President instructed Gruening to have Lawrence Cramer, who has been Lieutenant Governor down there, brought up and placed in the Bureau in Washington on the theory that he had been too long in the tropics. While I was at Warm Springs, I had a telegram from him saying that he was sailing back to the Virgin Islands on Thursday. I reminded the President of his instructions to Gruening and he asked me to tell Gruening to delay Cramer's sailing until he could talk to him. This he did last Saturday at a conference at which Gruening, Cramer and I were all present. After looking at Cramer the President evidently decided that his three months' leave had sufficiently bettered his health so that he could go back to the Virgin Islands so that subject was not mentioned. He did, however, inquire into the Virgin Islands affairs and expressed some satisfaction that the rehabilitation program there was actually getting under weigh. Both Cramer and Gruening told him that there was considerable dissatisfaction being worked up by a small group of malcontents who hoped that they might get Governor Pearson fired and in the ensuing confusion get something for themselves. The President consequently instructed the three of us to draft a letter upholding Pearson's hand and expressing satisfaction with the present administration. As we were going out, I turned back and asked the President whether I ought not to guard against a future commitment to Pearson's continuance in office since I knew that he was somewhat dissatisfied with him. He asked me to look out for that in the framing of the letter. Today I received a draft of the proposed letter from Gruening and sure enough it had in it a sentence which would be a commitment for another long term for Pearson and I have just written a memorandum to Gruening objecting to this particular clause in the letter.

I had a considerable talk with Ernest Lindley the other night in which he, among other things, expressed greatest dissatisfaction with the tempo at which things are moving at the present time, saying he thought the President was being altogether too tender of business' feelings and that many of his reconstruction measures were being held up because of those influences inside and outside the Administration. Of course I agreed entirely with that. I think considerable forces are gathering on the left and that unless some bold strokes are forthcoming before very long, the greatest difficulties for this administration are likely to arise because it is too conservative rather than too progressive. Ernest also commented on H.A.W.'s evident turn toward the right in recent months and his fear of radical movements. He asked me what I thought had happened to him and I explained my notion that he really represents the point of view of the more prosperous farmer in the Middle West who believe first of all in property rights and individualism, who dislike radicals, and that beginning from this point of view and being ambitious he was really beginning already to run for President. Ernest replied that if he was running for President he must be doing it on the Republican ticket because all his speeches ran that way. We talked some about foreign affairs and I outlined to him my observations of foreign policies which are self-sufficiency in such countries as Italy and Germany particularly, and, of course, many other European countries. It is becoming more and more a fixed policy because of the vested interests which are being belted behind it by young and energetic men who are close to the Government. I furthermore told him that the thing as far as I could see seems to be working. They seem to be able to find or invent the resources they need and that the current propaganda in favor of free trade on the old laissez-faire lines was mistaken in its fundamental premise which is that these self-sufficiency schemes will not work. It seems to me from my observation that they will. He said that he had felt that way for a long time and we both observed that the President felt this way about it although he was not ready to say so and although many of his actions seem inconsistent with this point of view, such as for instance, having the kind of Secretary of State he has who talks continually about free trade as though it were still a practical possibility. A choice in this matter is of the greatest consequence for our future policy. If there is to be a diminution of foreign trade, as I fully believe, it makes it even more necessary for us to continue our adjustment of agriculture to a domestic market. This, of course, accounts for the recent flurry over the Bankhead endorsements, H.A.W., believing in foreign trade, determined not to endorse the Bankhead Act in the referendum which is about to occur. The President was equally determined to do something about it and was rather caught in between. It was finally settled by the President himself making a statement at Warm Springs. Temporarily everyone's face has been saved, but this difference of opinion is certain to cause difficulties later on. There is still a powerful group among the farm leaders who believe that we ought to propose the establishment of a two-price system, keeping up our domestic price and dumping farm products abroad at a lower price. This is, of course, to escape the necessity of reduction of production to a domestic basis. This seems to me both impossible and undesirable. In the first place, other countries would not stand for it and, in the second place, I see no particular reason why we should give the products of our soil away to foreign countries. There are always people who can get a following if they have some pleasant way to escape from economic realities, who always want to have their cake and eat it too. The essence of the old McNary-Haugen scheme which began the farmers' fight fifteen years ago was a division between domestic prices and foreign prices of cotton, wheat, tobacco and lard. The people who carried on that fight at that time still believe that that is the way to do it inspite of the way in which the world has changed since and they consequently attempt to shift over our program to their way of believing. My belief is that we should try to capture forty to fifty million acres of land which produce this surplus and to use that land as a balancing mechanism to be drawn in or kept out of production as the export market might warrant. I have time and again tried to persuade our people to use a portion of the processing taxes which are now simply distributed annually as rentals and benefit payments for reduction on individual farms for the purpose of leasing for a long period or buying sufficient land so that we could give up the present difficult and awkward scheme of controlling production. So far I have not been able to interest anybody very greatly.

December 12, 1934

The Secretary was away yesterday making a speech to the Farm Bureau Federation and so I attended the meeting of the Executive Council in his place. The Executive Council is, of course really an enlarged Cabinet, including as it does not only the Cabinet but heads of the emergency agencies. It was an extraordinarily interesting meeting in a number of respects: first, because the President laid down four or five rules of policy for administrative officers to follow, and second because he stated in no uncertain terms that in case of conflict of policy or of opinion among members of the administration, his was the deciding voice and he expected to have loyal cooperation in carrying out stated policy. He said a good deal about people who talk about things which he said flatly were none of their business since they affected other agencies in government than those for which they were responsible and gave them a considerable lecture on how to handle the press when the newpaper men were trying to pry into divisions of this sort. There have been a number of recent instances of this kind of thing, particularly the Ickes-Moffet row over housing and the differences between George Peek and Cordell Hull on matters affecting foreign trade. Concerning foreign trade he laid it down as a flat rule that we would not enter on a policy of free production and dumping abroad but would continue to adjust our production to a visible market at home and whatever was in sight as a result of our trade negotiations. This matter came up in connection with cotton. First a memorandum was read from the Department of Agriculture which outlined the policy of production for 1935 and then the President elaborated on it by saying that a number of people had made suggestions of another sort and had not hesitated to state them in public and that there were even bills being prepared for different kind of handling of the cotton situation than that which the Department of Agriculture had mapped out. He said all this kind of thing was hereafter to be "out the window." He said that the expansion of cotton production abroad had been going on for several years and that some of our markets were being lost to us but that this was not a result of price competition nor could price competition cure the situation. He said it was all very well to talk about the difficulties and dangers of economic nationalism abroad as it affected us but that the situation which we faced was a fact and not a theory and that we had to make our accommodation to it as a fact. He said he recognized that there were interests in the country, such as ginners, warehouse men, and large importing and exporting houses, who would prefer to have a fifteen million bale crop rather than a twelve million bale crop since they profited by handling the larger volume and that he expected we would continue to have opposition from these sources. He said, however, that limitation of production to visible demand had brought partial recovery to the South and that he intended to continue on that course. Secretary Roper spoke up and said that he was one of those who had suggested a different policy, one particularly having to do with maintaining the price for domestic supply and allowing free production for export. The President said that this was exactly the policy which had gotten us into the difficulties which we were now just climbing out of and so far as he was concerned he would not approve. This was a tremendous slap in the face not only for Roper and others who had been opposing within the Administration the Department of Agriculture policy but also for George Peek who has been making speeches and even drawing up a bill for a two-price system. I expect there will be considerable repercussions from this discussion. The Director of the Emergency Council is, of course, Richberg who sat on the President's right hand. This was evidently a source of some irritation to Secretary Ickes who called me up after the meeting and asked me how I liked the President's lecture. I said that I was amused by part of it. He said that he was amused by part of it but greatly irritated at the self-satisfied air of Richberg who sat on the President's right. While the President was laying down the law for orderly procedure, Miss Perkins leaned over to me and said "If all this is carried out, it will be the end of the dear old U.S.A." I told her that reform movement never lasted long so that I thought she need not worry, which seemed to comfort her some. Her New England resistance to rules of all kinds is incorrigible.

There was some discussion during the meeting of the arguments which had been hailed before the Supreme Court on several preceding days concerning the enforcements and the oil codes. The Justices had been very critical of the fact that executive and administrative orders carrying out the codes, particulary for N.R.A., were not in due and attested form. This led to a discussion of the necessity for an official gazette for publication of administrative decisions which affected the public and which will probably be established.

Richberg had been making a study of interdepartmental relations and made a report on the number of committees with interdepartmental status. It seemed that there were some 350. The President thought it was time to reduce the number so he asked representatives from Agriculture, Interior, Treasury, Commerce and the Emergency Council to form a committee to reduce committees. I named M.L. Wilson for Agriculture.

Yesterday Weaver approached me with the information that as he sized things up there was a very definite corner in the sugar market in New York which came about very largely because the Cubans had by degrees fixed a price for their sugar to be sold to refiners and since for assembled delivery theirs was about the only sugar available, deliveries could not be made at the open exchange. What it was necessary to do was to get the refiners, the Cubans and the president of the exchange into a meeting to get the refiners to release the Cubans and the Cubans to release some sugar so that the open contracts can be made, otherwise there might be a scandal on the exchange. I was not very much interested in the matter since correction of the situation had nothing to do so far as I could see with producers and I took an interest in it only because we had done a good deal for the Cubans under the sugar program and I disliked to see them get into a situation of which it could be said that they increased the price to American consumers and had in general taken advantage of the situation which we had prepared for them. At any rate the meeting was held and after considerable argument the refiners did agree to release the Cubans and the Cubans indicated that they would make available enough sugar so that deliveries on open contracts could be made. If this informal agreement is carried out it ought to correct the situation.

December 13, 1934

Two interesting things happened yesterday. One of them was the meeting which the President called for the preparation of legislation to go into effect on the declaration of a major emergency which, of course, means war. Baruch, who was Chairman of the War Industries during the war, called me up at about the same time that I had a call from the White House and I went over and had lunch with him, General Johnson and McGrady in Johnson's office. Baruch and Johnson had seen the President before and the President had indicated to them that he now wanted to go forward with this scheme. It is interesting to speculate on the President's strategy in the matter because of course the Senate Munitions Investigations have been going on for months and turning up a good deal of material which show relations between the munitions industry and our own Departments of governments, particularly with State, War and Navy as well as with foreign governments. Senator Nye, who is chairman of the Committee, told me the other day that he was getting very close to some individuals in our own Departments and that material would be brought out which would show definite connections between them and the munitions makers which would be very embarrassing. It is possible to think that the President may be protecting these people on their representations to him by making an administrative move to take the profit out of war and to prepare legislation to go into effect on the declaration of war rather than to let the munitions investigations run on and people in the Senate formulate legislation after their investigation is completed. Color is lent to this interpretation by the fact that Nye and Vandenberg, two Republicans, have taken most important parts in the proceedings. Ernest Lindley thinks that Baruch is up to one of his little games again as he was when we had the trouble over legal control in protecting some big interests among the munitions makers. I am inclined to doubt this at the moment but of course Baruch is subtle and the move may have come from him rather than from the President.

All I know is that we talked over the legislation and then went to the White House for this meeting at which there were representatives of State, War, and Navy as well as myself from agriculture and McGrady from Labor. One interesting point which did not come out in the papers evolved out of the discussion as to whether there should be merely a declaration of policy on the part of Congress to take the profit out of war and to do certain other things which are included in the recommendations of the War Policy Commission to Congress in 1931. The President insisted rather against the advice of Baruch and others that there should be legislation and that it should include presidential discretion to recognize an emergency before it happens and to make expenditures, gather personnel, and protect essential materials before an actual declaration of war on the part of Congress. He cited the instance of the beginning of the Great War when there were several weeks in which the War and Navy Departments were unable to make any moves to prepare even after the President knew that declaration of war was inevitable. It was decided that legislation would be framed in this way at the President insistence and the job turned over to the War and Navy Departments under the chairmanship of Baruch.

All the liberal forces in the country have been rather interested in Nye's investigation of munitions and Nye has been working toward a more stringent control of munitions industries, perhaps even government ownership of them and they will probably resent the President's move toward a milder form of control. So I think that the last has not been heard of this issue.

I had a talk with Baruch and Johnson on agricultural policy which was rather interesting. Baruch indicated that he approved of what had been done up to date but that he thought we had to move rather soon on a land retirement policy. He thought that if we could acquire control of

forty or fifty millions acres of farm land it might cost the government
less money and be a permanent instead of a temporary answer to the
problem of surplus. I have for some time been thinking the same thing
for somewhat different reasons. I am not worried about the expenditure
of money for the rental and benefit payments which are being made at the
present time but I do feel that it is strictly an emergency measure, that
it does not solve the problem at all permanently, and that a land program
ought to be worked out immediately which would be much more defensible
than the present use for processing taxes for the retirement on individual
acres. It seems to me that we are more vulnerable on this point than on
any other. I have in the past had talks with Chester Davis and H.A.W. on
this point but he did not seem to be able to get anything started. An
organization like the A.A.A. gets used to doing a thing a certain way and
resents any change in method. Then too, the farm organizations have
been taking some credit for the generous payments which are going to
farmers and would hate to see them stopped. It is difficult, however, to
get a change in policy but it seems to me necessary.

December 15, 1934

Harold Ickes asked H.A.W. and myself to come over today and
when we got there he opened up the whole subject of the trade of bureaus
between the Department of Agriculture and the Department of the
Interior which was up last spring, saying that he still was of the same
mind and wanted us to go to the President with him and suggested it
again since the President had not turned it down but merely had thought
it expedient to wait until after election. H.A.W. was not all enthusiastic
about it, saying that he thought there were many grave political questions
involved which Ickes tended to minimize and that on the whole he
thought it would be better to keep the status quo. Ickes said that if he
were not really for the change it would be a mistake to go see the
President but urged that it would be very much worth while to assure a
complete conservation set-up under one head as well as to settle the old
problems which have always tormented the relationships between the two
Departments. I said also that I thought it would be very important to
have some of these administrative questions settled and said that there
was a third alternative which would be the setting up of an individual
conservation department. But, I said, this might not be feasible at the
present time and perhaps they might not care to suggest that alternative.
Ickes said that he would be glad to suggest that to the President if that
seemed the only feasible way but that he thought that since he had an
under secretaryship provided for in his budget and since he would rather
trust me with the conservation job than anybody else he had hoped that
I might come over to the Department of the Interior and be the Under

Secretary there. H.A.W. turned away and asked me whether I would like
to do that. I said of course it would be attractive to be head of
conservation set-up but that there were many questions to be considered
besides the simple one of creating a conservation set-up and that I might
not be available in any case. I had not been known as a prominent
conservationist and doubtless it would be better for political reasons if
someone of that sort should be head of it. The conversation went on at
considerable length, talking over the possibilities involved in the question.
Finally the Secretary thought that we might at least go to see the
President and find out what his ideas were on it.

     After we came away H.A.W. and myself had a talk about the
situation. He seemed very much disturbed by my saying that I thought
it would be attractive to be the head of a conservation set-up and evidently
wondered just what I had meant by it. He evidently interpreted it to mean
that I wanted to leave the Department of Agriculture but did not ask me
directly if that was what I had in mind. He did ask me, however, if I
really felt strongly about taking over conservation work. I said well, he
knew as well as I did what the situation in the Department of Agriculture
was; that the present Administrator of Agricultural Adjustment and his
assistants took very little trouble to conceal the fact that they would feel
better if I were not Under Secretary; that I was not having the contact
with and influence on A.A.A. policy that an under secretary ought to have
and that naturally I felt sensitive about the situation. I said if he felt that
he ought to support all of Davis' policies without any consultation with
me that I ought to leave and he ought to able to appoint an under
secretary who would be persona grata to everybody. I also said I thought
it would be better if I transferred somewhere else than if I went back to
Columbia. He said that that was certainly true. He said that neither
Davis nor anyone else has suggested that they would like to have me leave
and I went on to say that it was not necessary to say so but that
everything, however, pointed to such a situation and that I was practically
ignored lately so far as policy is concerned; that it seemed to me that it
was with his consent and that if this was to continue to be the situation
I had no desire to go on as Under Secretary. He was very much disturbed
by this. He said that he did not realize that I felt that way about it and
I said that the only reason he had not realized that I felt that way about
it was because he had not let himself think about it. He then came back
with the question as to whether I really did want to leave; whether I was
really attracted enough by conservation work to leave the Department.
I told him that if I were going to leave the general problems of agriculture
I would rather do this than anything else but it seemed to me that it was
not of any importance which was at all comparable with the guidance of
the whole of agriculture policy during these critical years of transition.
He seemed genuinely relieved to have me say this and he said that that

changed the whole situation and that he would make a real effort to indicate to Davis and his assistants that I was after all the Under Secretary that I had had a great deal to do with the shaping of agricultural policy which had up to now had great success and that he would support me in every way. I said that I thought no more was necessary than that he should himself show a little firmness and a little confidence in me and have more frequent general policy discussions in which my advice was evidently valued. He said that he wanted above all else to avoid losing me and that he thought everything could be changed. I expressed some doubt and said that I was far from sure that things could be changed satisfactorily but that I was quite willing to give things a chance to develop; otherwise I was determined to leave and let the situation clear itself up that way.

December 17, 1934

The question of administrative procedure in the Department has been a troublesome one for some time. Every secretary of this Department has sooner or later left his assistants out on a limb by allowing Bureau Chiefs to come direct to him for decisions, and such a situation was developing. I spoke to H.A.W. about it on Saturday and he agreed that we ought to do something to prevent any separation of this sort, so on Saturday evening he and M.L. Wilson and myself got together over the kind of division of functions. For the time being it was decided to divide up matters in the following manner:

HAW	MLW	RGT
AAA	Exper. Sta.	BAE
BAE	Extension	BAI
Foreign Policy	Information	Beltsville
Genetics	Land Policy	Business
Grain Futures	FERA - Land	Chem. & Soils
Packers & Stockyards	Rural Rehab.	Dairy
FERA - AAA		Ent. and Pl. Quar.
		F & D
		Forest Service
		BHE
		Islands
		Labor Policy
		BPI
		Public Works
		Reg. Stations
		Roads
		Sugar
		FERA - Public Works

This will solve some problems but not all. For instance, we are all of us inevitably involved in AAA policy. He has promised to arrange for frequent policy meetings in that matter, however, so that that may be taken care of in another way. For the first time in a long time I was able to talk with him on the same old free and frank basis that we used to have and we solved a number of matters of mutual concern which were becoming embarrassing. There is always a danger of division if things are not sufficiently talked about and there are plenty of people who are glad to go to him with tails which he may or may not believe but which it is very difficult for him not to be affected by and the same, of course, is true of myself. However, I think we have a better working basis now and things ought to proceed much better.

I went to see the President this morning and warned him that there might be a great deal of discussion in the Congress just convening in the matter of land policy. I told him about the resolutions which had recently been passed by the Farm Bureau Federation demanding that all the agencies in the Government dealing with land should be turned over to the Department of Agriculture and told him that I thought that there might be a rather strong movement in Congress originating in the cattle centers to transfer everything to the Department to Interior. That led him to say that everything of this sort was involved in the reorganization plans which we had been talking about. He said that there were two ways of approaching this. One was by the piecemeal and gradual transfer of agencies which would settle one difficulty after another, and that the other way was to formulate a program of administrative change as well as it can be done now and submit it to Congress. Then again, there would be two ways of doing that: one would be to submit it without urgency and have it discussed for a long time; have committee hearings, plenty of speeches, etc. The other way would be to send it in as an emergency matter to get it through the House on a rule and to use influence to get it out to the Senate immediately. I pointed out to him that it ought to be possible to do this latter at the very beginning of the present session since there would be so many new legislators who would at least feel themselves under discipline at first. He agreed that this would be the best way to do it and went on to say that although he still had some doubts as to its expediency at the present time, they were much less than they had been just after he had considered the matter following our conversation at Warm Springs. He said he had talked with John Garner and asked him what would happen if he should send up a bill which contemplated bringing all the emergency activities into regular government departments and that Garner had said that he thought it would be very popular. He said he had talked to several other people and that they all thought it was the time for it. I told him that I had had the same experience: that numerous people had brought up the question. Of course, I had talked as little as possible and had listened to them with interest. I told him I thought none of them had as clear an idea of what should be done as we had sketched out together and that I thought it would be good judgment to it very soon. He told me that he had been talking to some more people about his career service and is still very much worried about it. He said that Bill Bullitt and other ambassadors who were coming home, all concurred in saying that the career service was inefficient. Bullitt has just come back by way of the East and he reports the same situation in Tokyo, Peking and Russia as is true of the European capitals which I know. The President said he was thinking about it very seriously and wondering how to fix the situation up. I told him that I did not think it was so much a matter of personnel, since all of these people were very intelligent, as it was of doing something which would really make Americans out of them. He then generated an interesting idea which I should like to see tried. He suggested that it might be possible to have tours of duty abroad and tours of duty at home and that in these tours of duty at home the career men be assigned to the various government departments to be used at the discretion of the Secretaries. He asked whether or not we could use half a dozen in the Department if it were put up to us. I told him we certainly could and would be glad to get them.

There followed about half an hour of discussion of unemployment insurance. The other day the Security Advisory Board, which is a Board established to study the findings of the technical committees in preparation for legislation at this session, had departed from the principle of the Wagner-Lewis Bill and had suggested Federal subsidy. I told him that on this matter he could certainly expect to get no sympathy from me since I had always believed that he was wrong and I told him that I thought anyone could really study the situation and come to a different conclusion and that the Federal Government ought to contribute about a 3rd both in order to insure that standards should be common throughout the country and to throw part of the burden on Federal taxation rather than on special taxation but I said that I would put my argument rather on the ground of the superior incidence for federal taxation than on any other. I reminded him that he had always been opposed to a sales tax and said that a payroll tax was very little different from the sales tax and said that I would even go back to the theory evolved by old Professor Patten which is that taxation in the last analysis always came from where surpluses were; that surpluses are produced by people doing productive work; that the taxable productive work is done by industry and that therefore the tax had to lie on industry. It is better that it should be of the income variety than of a uniform variety otherwise it was very little better in its incidence than a sales tax. He seemed very interested in all this argument and disposed to dispute it a good deal, although I think I shook his faith some in his contributary scheme with the complete financial burden falling on employers and employed and with the states being merely under the compulsion of being taxed if they did not have the standards indicated by Federal legislation.

I asked him if he had seen the speech that Bill Herridge, the Canadian Minister, had made in Ottawa the other day which was an excellent New Deal speech. He said that he had it in his pocket at the present time and gave me a message to give to Herridge congratulating him on it and asking him whether as a result his brother-in-law, Premier Bennett, would like him to stay in the same government with him.

We then had considerable discussion of Canadian politics and I reminded him again that he ought to see Herridge and talk the whole matter over. He asked me to tell Herridge that he had wanted to see him but was waiting until he got home from Canada.

I think nothing I have done in Washington has perhaps had more beneficial effects than the frequent conversations I have had with Herridge. He is an extremely intelligent person with a good mind and a good heart and I believe he is right in thinking that Canada could be won over to something of the sort he is proposing and that it would enable the two nations to go along together in a way in which we have never yet been able.

December 20, 1934

Yesterday Silcox and I went to see the President about certain Forest Service problems. We had intended to stay only two minutes but our talk dragged out to about an hour and a half. When we went in the President asked us a rather curious question concerning the lumber industry. It was this: Ought the lumber industry to be thought of as a natural resource such as coal or oil or ought it to be thought of as a crop like an agricultural product? I was a little puzzled as to what he was getting at when I told him that he had asked us the wrong question. I said I thought the answer to his question depended on what he wanted to do and that you could easily argue either way if it suited your purpose. He said that he had made up his mind what he wanted to do about natural resource industries and wondered whether he ought to think of lumber in the same way. I said, "Well, if you were thinking of lumber as a public utility it seemed to me that naturally the same tests applied. It is, of course, replaceable in the long time sense and is therefore a crop but it is also affected with public interest in a very real sense and ought at least to be regulated."

All this led up to a considerable conversation concerning ways and means to save timber resources and to insure better sustained yield private as well as on public forest lands. The President told us how about

1908 when he was a lawyer in New York he went to an executive
committee meeting of a certain timber company in which they discussed
the question whether they should buy enough timber so that they could
practice sustained yield with a forty year rotation. He said that was his
first introduction to these problems. Afterwards when he went to the
legislature in New York as a young Democratic assemblyman there were
an insufficient number of assemblymen to be put on all the committees
and by sheer accident he was made chairman of the Committee on Forest,
Fish and Game. He took it rather seriously and has been interested in
forestry ever since. He told us the story of the way in which he got his
top-lofting law passed in New York State. He said Gifford Pinchot at that
time had had his row with Ballinger and had been thrown out so he was
able to get him to come to Albany and make an address in the Assembly
Chamber to which he invited all the legislators and their wives. He
remembered particularly that Pinchot has some illustrated sides and
showed the contrast between a country which saves its forests and one
which allows them all to be cut. He said that he had a slide of a 15th
century Chinese valley which at that time had a town of 300,000
population with streams running forth and with wheat lands on either
side. All the mountains around were heavily forested. He then showed
a picture taken four hundred years later from the same spot which showed
all the timber cut off, the town reduced to a population of three thousand,
practically no wheat growing, the whole valley a desert and the hills
completely denuded of trees. He said that contrast has been the argument
which had enabled him to pass his top-lofting law and which had started
New York on the conservation road.

This is merely an illustration of the kind of conversation we get
into whenever we try to talk forest policy with him. What we really
wanted to talk to him about was some things in connection with the
lumber code. The code was adopted about a year ago and at his insistence.
Article 10 was included which provided in various ways for sustained yield
practices by private lumber operators and also provided that the
government should make certain expenditures, such as more protection
for private lands from fire, further assistance in forest credits and similar
things. He has been reluctant to go ahead with any of the public
expenditures because timber companies have not put into effect any
effective sustained yield practices and because he feels that they have
unwarrantedly used the code to raise lumber prices to an abnormal level
which is certainly true. He had prepared a statement which referred
specifically to the code and spoke about the public's obligations and
intimated that they would be carried out when the lumber companies had
shown that they took their obligations seriously. He said he felt there
was very little use of going further because he thought the timber
companies had had no change of heart and had no intention of doing

their part. He did, however, address a letter to governors of all states which called their attention to the need for a change in further policy with respect to timber lands which are tax delinquent, the point being that at present in most of the states there is no provision whatever for public capture. The land must immediately be put up for sale and so fall again into private hands and go through the same cycle. The letter asks the governors to make a survey of their own situation and see whether a reversal of policy cannot be brought about within the states. He said that so far as the statement was concerned he would rather make it when he had something definite to tie it to. We then suggested that it would seem desirable to codify or reincorporate all the various references to forests which had been made in various legislative acts and one new act to be submitted to Congress which would be a basic forest law. He thought that a good idea and directed us to go ahead with the preparation of such legislation and said that he might make some modified statement with respect to the code when he submitted this legislation.

By this time considerable time had passed and his secretary came in and said that Secretary Ickes and Mr. Delano were waiting outside. I said to him facetiously that I hoped that he would not give Mr. Ickes our forests when he came in and asked for them. He said, "You need not worry about that but don't think that forests belong to the Department of Agriculture, either." Just as I was going out he called me and said, I" really believe they belong in a separate department." Which leads me to think that he really is considering seriously at least a reorganization of the land agencies.

I am still rather embarrassed by the constant reference to land programs and reorganization by both Secretary Wallace and Secretary Ickes who confide in me separately. I am, of course, unable to say anything to either of them because of my knowledge of the President's desire for more complete reorganization. The Secretaries are, of course, trying to maneuver so that they can get all the land agencies into their own departments. Secretary Ickes called me again this morning and asked whether I had talked to H.A.W. any more about the things we had discussed the other day. I told him that he had talked to me a little bit but that there was no further developments. He asked whether I thought it would do any harm if he went and talked to the President himself. I did not know what to say but simply evaded the issue and said that nobody could prevent him. He said that if he did he was going to talk to him about my being in charge of the conservation set-up in the Department of the Interior. I said that I did not know what the President had in mind about all this matter and perhaps he wanted me to stick to Agriculture and that he could talk to the President about it tentatively if he wanted to since it was quite within his rights to do so.

December 28, 1934

After Silcox and myself talked with the President the other day about our difficulties in getting land titles cleared promptly through the Department of Justice, the President asked the Department of Justice to call a meeting of the various land acquisition agencies to discuss these points: first, what could be done to expedite clearing of titles; second, whether there could be a consolidation of land acquisition agencies; and, third, whether legal staffs could be consolidated. H.A.W. went to the meeting for us and he reports that everybody present found humorous reasons why nothing could be done and the result of the meeting was zero. Perhaps enough experiences of this kind will convince the President that nothing short of reorganization will solve such problems as this.

The problem of agricultural labor is one which is avoided by everyone. As a result of troubles this year in the Imperial Valley and in the onion fields in Ohio as well as various other places, AAA was forced to the extent of appointing a committee to make some preliminary investigations. Also there was the fact that child labor in the beet fields has always been a very pressing problem and that there was a provision inserted in the Sugar Act providing for some regulation of agricultural labor in sugar. The committee's investigations seem to have come to a dead stop but there had been a man appointed in the sugar section to make some investigations. In the recent division of responsibility in the Department, agricultural labor was handed over to me and I told G.E.F. to take charge of this whole matter. Her first suggestion had to do with the possibility of inserting something concerning agricultural labor in whatever labor bill Senator Wagner drafts this year. She had a conference with Senator Wagner's secretary who reported that Senator Wagner would be glad to do it with administration support. The difficulty there is that we do not know at present whether or not it will have administration support. This line must be followed up. Further than that she conceived the idea of a general amendment to the AAA which would contain same provisions as the Sugar Act permitting the Secretary of Agriculture to insert into benefit contracts, agreements or licenses certain conditions with respect to agricultural labor. This we had drafted and submitted it to the Secretary who then sent it to Chester Davis for recommendation. It will require some maneuvering to get it submitted with all the other AAA amendments but there are some hopes in this direction. Of course at this moment it seems doubtful whether any AAA amendments will be able to pass in the Senate but it is worth trying.

Day before yesterday I talked with FDR concerning the Food and Drug Bill. I had prepared a draft of a special message to Congress concerning this legislation which he went over and concerning which he made some suggestions. I have now revised the draft of this message and sent it back to him. The strategy on this is for him to send one of his short special messages concerning the Food and Drug legislation and at the same time to send for the appropriate committee chairman and give him the bill we have been drafting. There has been some trouble about this draft having mostly to do with the question of standards, but we are rapidly clearing up these problems.

After several conferences concerning conditions at Beltsville, I called in Mohler, the Chief of the Bureau of Animal Industry, and put him on notice to submit to me within a week his complete plan for a revision of the administrative set-up in his Bureau which must satisfy the general business and personnel offices as well as the Secretary and myself that business affairs in that Bureau will hereafter be conducted in such a way as to obviate future difficulties.

Yesterday Senator Wheeler came to lunch and we had an hour and a half talk concerning general problems of the progressives in this administration. The Senator was very bitter about the old Democratic organization and the way in which the progressives were being treated. We also had some talk about general policies. I told him that the difficulty with the progressives had been that they could never agree on a program, that they were all individualists, and could never submit to any discipline. Each of them has a panacea and refuses to join in any general movement unless his panacea has the most prominent place. This, of course, had a special application to Wheeler because of his silver proclivities. He agreed that this was so and protested that he was willing to go along on any program regardless of his own particular wishes. I doubt, however, whether he would do it. We had some further talk concerning the resolution which I tried to help him have passed at the last session of Congress for the investigation of the processing trades. I told him I had no reason to think the President had changed his mind about it; that he had tried to assist us in getting the resolution passed before and that it had actually passed the Senate; and advised him to go ahead with it again.

There has been lately a good deal of discussion within the administration concerning the new security legislation. The Committee of technical experts has been preparing a draft of a recommendation to the President which it is proposed that the Cabinet meeting shall adopt as its recommendation to the President. H.A.W. has been serving on this committee but he has left town today and I have to go to the committee meeting with some amendments. The chief quarrel has been between what might be called the Brandeis group and others in the administration who believe in more centralized control. The Brandeis group would like everything turned over to the states; the others would like more power left in the Federal Government. The President is pretty well committed to the Brandeis point of view and I have had several arguments with him about it, particularly with respect to the kind of tax which it is proposed to impose. The payroll tax seems to me to be very little better than a sales tax which the President has always opposed. I told him so. I also argue that without a Federal subsidy there could be very little real control by the Federal Government of standards which state administrations would impose. We argued about this for nearly two hours the other day and I doubt whether I made very much impression. I did, however, get from Lubin several relevant arguments to support the Federal subsidy point of view and sent them over to the President privately. I hope that his attitude may be somewhat changed.

The various obstacles which have been put in the way by the Comptroller and others about the Puerto Rico plan have made it necessary for us to go ahead somewhat independently on our plans for basic reduction in order to keep Puerto Rico in line with the quotas of the other regions. I have had several conferences with people in the sugar section and with Gruening and Chapman from Interior. I think we have found ways to go ahead with benefit payments to sugar growers in Puerto Rico which yet would not dissipate the funds collected from the processing tax to be used for the general benefit of agriculture in Puerto Rico. It seems necessary to all of us to hold this fund intact as nearly as possible so that it may be available for financing a plan for rehabilitation. There are many problems to be solved before the way is clear.

December 31, 1934

H.A.W. was away Friday and Saturday. As a consequence I had to go to Cabinet meeting on Friday and attend the final meeting of the Economic Security Committee. As I have noted before, the Economic Security report is very disappointing to me in several respects. In the first place, I had hoped and argued for a national system and also for a system of unemployment insurance which would be paid for preferably by income taxes and also a system of health insurance as well as old age pensions which would be adequate to meet the President's demand to Congress in his message last spring. The report as it will be made seems to me quite inadequate. The reason for it, however, is that the President himself has determined on several principles which seem to me to be mistaken. He has withdrawn from the notion of making the system contributory and has determined on the Wagner-Lewis principle which contemplates a payroll tax together with a system of punitive taxes for states which do not set up systems of their own, but the Wagner-Lewis principle seems to me to be wrong and I am afraid that some time in the future it will have to be changed over to a more directly national system. I have done all I could do to argue him and other people into seeing the situation but the Frankfurter and Brandeis influence has just been too strong. They will hold to the principle that the forty-eight states should be used as economic laboratories and they therefore want the Federal Government to do as little as possible, overlooking what seems to me to be the great difficulty, that industry does not follow state lines and that with a national spread of big business nothing but a national system would offer adequate protection and sufficient standards. The most I could do in conjunction with Harry Hopkins, who feels as I do, was to get the Economic Security Report to the President rewritten so that it minimized the part of unemployment pensions in a national security scheme and threw the emphasis upon a works program as the real effort towards security.

At the Cabinet meeting in the afternoon it had been supposed that the President would indicate to the Cabinet what his message to the forthcoming Congress was to contain. He merely told us what I already knew, that direct relief was to be withdrawn and that a works program was to be adopted, that is people were to be given jobs instead of money. There was very little else of interest at the Cabinet meeting.

The President is keeping his own counsel and putting things together in his own head. Harry Hopkins and I in the last few days have, however, had an opportunity to do some work on the appropriations bill now being drawn which is to finance the works scheme as well as all extraordinary expenditures for the next year and a half. Our interest in it was first to see that the sum was sufficiently large to finance the program and in the second place, to make its terms sufficiently broad so that we should escape many of the difficulties we have been having with limited hours. The definitions of the Comptroller General have been particularly bothersome. He has been very reluctant to permit corporations to be set up for rehabilitation purposes and to allow any flexibility in the definition of agricultural or industrial rehabilitation. Up to now this has held up our Puerto Rican reconstruction plan. Working with Bell and Treasury lawyers we have a bill drawn in such shape that these difficulties ought to be obviated in the future provided Congress passes it in the form in which it is now written.

1935

January 16, 1935

The whole question of Food and Drug legislation is very much in the air at the present time. Our people in the Department have worked on revision off and on since the bill failed in the last Congress. Copeland had his own man Salthe prepare a draft of the bill for him which, however, was done a good deal in consultation with our own people so that the bill is not wholly unsatisfactory. It does, however, fail to make sufficient provision for standards and grades and leaves out altogether any mention of an inspection service and has several other weak features. Two other bills more or less sponsored by the interests to be controlled have also been introduced and tend to confuse the situation somewhat. I understand that Copeland has been to see the President but I don't know what was said so that the situation remains at the moment somewhat confused.

The question of standards and grades is, however, just now very much to the fore and something will doubtless come of all the agitation. Riley, who has been in charge of the canners' code has worked very faithfully with the food industries in an attempt to get something into their code. He has been frustrated time after time by the canners. The situation has been somewhat changed because the A & P Company and Kroger have evinced a desire to use grade labels for retailing. They have approached us to know whether we would object to government designation being used on their labels, something to the effect that their grades were made in accordance with Department of Agriculture standards. This situation is confused by the fact that two agencies within the Department are concerned. The Food and Drug Administration has its standards for enforcement purposes and the Bureau of Agricultural Economics has certain grades which are authorized under the Clarke-McNary Act for commercial purposes. These are not altogether satisfactory from the enforcement point of view but are beginning to be accepted by the trade and for certain products have become sufficiently objective so that they could be used for consumers' grades. One problem just now is the question whether we should attempt to proceed thru these already authorized grades to provide an inspection service and permit government designation on labels or whether we shall allow them to use government designation on the label without inspection, depending on them to make a commitment that their standards are those of the government and proceeding to enforcement thru seizure when the grades vary from our own. How to secure protection for the consumer without definite and specific legislation providing for it is a very difficult question. If the Food and Drug Act, when and if it is passed, provides definitely and specifically for this the question would be settled but it seems unlikely that legislation as passed will provide for sufficient consumer protection. Copeland is very weak on this question and we can expect very little from him. Essentially he is a kind of charlatan doctor, very vain and anxious to have his name on some food and drug legislation but also consistently anxious to incur no enmity among the industry groups. He has, however, by seniority become chairmen of the Commerce Committee which handles the bill and so it is necessary to work thru him.

Some of us took a three day trip last week to Red House in West Virginia, one of the rural rehabilitation projects managed by Westbrook of FERA, and to Reedsville, the first of the subsistence homestead projects. Red House seems to me to illustrate the good points and the bad points of the whole rehabilitation work to date. It is an excellent housing venture and stands out conspicuously in the Kanawah Valley in contrast to the shabby housing which illustrates the standards of living in that valley. There is, however, so far as I can see no provision at all for a better economic basis than exists at the present time. There has been no attempt to provide new industries of any kind and I see no reason why such a project should not in the course of a short time become something of a rural slum. Reedsville, in spite of its history of mistakes and awkward administration, is rounding into a better project. Each house is set on two or three acres of its own, a barn is provided and the General Electric Company is building a small plant; all of which is just so much better than Red House but still leaves the homesteaders at the mercy of one employer and with only two or three acres to depend upon for an enterprise of their own which is independent. If the President intends to make rural rehabilitation a large part of the new works program, I am very much afraid that whoever undertakes it will merely build an extensive and widespread monument to governmental folly. This raises the whole question of my anxiety about the coming works program. The President in his message to Congress made a definite commitment to get rid of federal relief and put at least three and a half million men to work. We have the mistakes of the whole CWA experiment of last year before us and I do not see that any sufficient measures have been taken to avoid repeating them. What is needed is greater scope for employment. The theory of the thing is that employment which this present system fails to give will be given by the government. I doubt very much whether, if the government is to keep entirely out of the traditional field of private business, scope enough can be found for employment which will escape criticism on the ground that it is essentially useless. The President is avoiding the logic of the situation which would require that he take over an industry or two which would provide a lot of employment and use them for expansion and contraction purposes. However, the next few months will indicate the feasibility of what is being undertaken. The President has so far concealed from everyone his plans for administration of the works program and Ickes and Hopkins are still very much worried about what each is to do in the program. Hopkins, of course, managed CWA last year and Ickes has been head of the whole Public Works organization. Whether some new organization is to supersede both or whether there is to be merely the same kind of division there has been before is a question which is still unanswered. There are rumors that Frank Walker is to undertake coordination but I have no way of knowing whether this is true. Meanwhile the kind of planning work which ought to have been going on in an intensive way for months is not being done and I am afraid that the administration will have to start cold after the bill is passed.

We had considerable running back and forth and argument about the form that the unemployment insurance bill would take. Some of us, including Hopkins, Wallace and myself, objected strenuously to the Wisconsin plan which is essentially what I think will be suggested, but the President seemed determined on a relative state autonomy and so there is nothing to do but give in. I am, of course, very much disappointed about this and feel that it will work badly; but the Brandeis-Frankfurter influence has been sufficient to determine the President's mind on the matter. The only concession I feel that I have been able to get is the federal handling of the funds to be collected. I am afraid, however, that many states either will not adopt any bill at all, or that their standards will be insufficient; that administration will be bad and that totally unsatisfactory protection will be given to the workers. We did succeed in getting the suggested bill drafted and a report from the Cabinet to the President rewritten in such a way that standards were somewhat more protected and that it was clearly indicated that unemployment insurance was a very minor part indeed of the whole problem of worker protection in a capitalist system, throwing the emphasis on government responsibility for giving jobs and in general deflating the whole security program as it centers on unemployment insurance and old age pensions.

I have spent a great deal of time lately on sugar but no real issues have come up. The matters were purely routine administration. The gap in these notes is accounted for by the fact that I never feel like writing notes when I have speeches to prepare, and I have three coming on very soon on which I have been working along with John Carter and by the fact that I had a short siege of grippe.

January 23, 1935

For some little time M. L. Wilson, Tolley and myself have been trying to put a number of things together in a program which would round itself out effectively. In the first place, there is need for reorganization of AAA on what might be called a "regional" basis to obviate the growing probability that the commodity sections will begin to feel that they have a clientele to serve and a vested interest in the adjustment of the particular commodity on which they are working. For this reason we should like to get over to a one-contract-per-farm basis and regionalize the administration of AAA setting up what would amount to a board for the cotton region, a board for the wheat region, etc. Together with this problem there is the growing problem of the displacement of farmers, particularly tenant farmers in the South, through the reduction of acreage made necessary by the disappearance of foreign markets. There is considerable sympathetic opinion for doing something in the nature of acquiring land and restoring these tenants to ownership. This is particularly a selfish wish in the South not to be burdened with a casual and migratory population and a desire to escape the responsibility of continuing relief of displaced tenants. Along with these two there is a third situation which we should like to meet in one program if we can. This is our desire to contribute to the general reorganization of agriculture in this country. I personally have long been convinced that the outright ownership of farms ought greatly to be restricted. My observation has been that where a farm is held on long term lease it belongs to the user of the land much more than if he actually owns it because if he owns it there is constant temptation to build up mortgage responsibilities and quite a likelihood that in the first depression of farm prices that comes along he will lose his land. I also feel that for such of the farm population as is represented, for instance, in the South by the negro tenants or even by the poor whites, the bettering of farm practices and the raising of living standards requires some supervision of farm practice. There is also the problem which I feel sure will emerge in a few years of continuing adjustment without the processing taxes and benefit payment mechanism. For all these reasons we are putting our heads together to see whether a program cannot be worked out which will combine all three.

We have a conference today in which we worked out an effective plan for approaching Senator Bankhead and using his interest in settling the tenant problem for approaching the whole situation in a large way. It is our hope that we can get him to undertake the introduction of a bill which will cover the whole situation without disclosing all that we have in mind. If we can have a bill acquiring considerable of the farm land in the South which is held by the Federal Land Banks and by the insurance companies and issuing debentures guaranteed by the government on the basis of these lands as assets and at the same time providing them with adequate farm equipment and technical supervision, we may be able to meet the problem. At least it is worth trying and we are working on it.

I had a talk with the President today in which the main topic of conversation was the imminent possibility of really going to work on the so-called "Chardon Plan" for Puerto Rico, when the four billion dollar appropriation bill is passed. I got written into that bill the authorization to set up government agencies to which funds could be delegated, and also permitting the transfer of funds such as those which are got by processing taxes on sugar to such an agency as would be set up under the Chardon Plan for the general relief of agriculture in Puerto Rico. My proposal to the President was that he set up a body to be called the Carribean Authority or perhaps the West Indies Authority and that when the Act was passed we then transfer the funds collected as processing taxes on Puerto Rican sugar for capital and that he also give a generous amount from the Public Works fund for the same purpose. I also suggested that he consolidate the enterprises of the government in Puerto Rico and Virgin Islands and put Charles Taussig at the head of the whole business. I had already talked with Taussig about the thing and although he has some business plans here for expansion of his own business, he is very much attracted by the idea. I knew that he was to see the President later in the day and afterwards I called him on the telephone and he said that he and the President had had considerable talk about it and that the President had suggested in an indirect way something of the same thing which I had talked to him about. I have some hope that this long delayed Puerto Rican plan may come to some kind of fruition before very long.

I have been bothered for some time to see exactly how we were to carry on the enlarged departmental activities which would be required under the public works program, and settled it by entrusting the whole business to Lee Strong as general administrator. We have been discussing the possibility of doing something in the way of consolidating field stations by the various bureaus and providing a service business organization direct from the Secretary's office, but if the President's plan of doing all of the work under the works program with labor which is paid at less than the going rate of wages and of having all jobs done without contract is followed, there will be a considerable overhead organization required in each department to carry out the program. I also spoke to the President about this today and called his attention to the necessity for allowing such departments as our own to make this overhead set up as soon as possible so that plans can be got under weigh without delay. I have every evidence that Lee Strong will be able to handle this situation for us with efficiency and expedition.

As a result of my three day trip last week to the environs of New York to study the Dutch elm disease, I was able to explain that particular problem to the President this morning in some detail and found him very much interested. It seems doubtful at the moment whether or not our control methods will actually stop the spread of disease but it seems equally certain that we ought to make the effort. I have already got through Public Works a five hundred and sixty-six thousand dollar appropriation and there is in our regular budget next year another two hundred thousand to carry on the work. What can be done to save the elm tree will be done but nobody can say yet whether or not it will be successful.

The always bothersome problem of setting tolerances for spray residue for year is up again. There was a conference about it today and we decided to go ahead with a one-tenth of one percent reduction in tolerance, although all the work we have done in the last year in the way of trying to discover substitutes for lead arsenic as a spray and better methods of eliminating spray from fruit by washing and other methods have produced almost no results. We have made some scientific progress and have some progress in leads but there is nothing which makes the situation any better.

The Food and Drug Bill is still under discussion and I talked to the President again about sending the message I have already prepared up to Congress and he agreed to send it within the next week. He is rather afraid that Senator Copeland will behave badly and will not really fight for a law with sufficient consumer protection in it and I rather agree with him on that but I feel that, with the situation as it is at present, we really have a good chance to get a better law than we have now and I think that we had better have support to the bill which Copeland has already introduced together with any amendments which will give greater consumer protection.

The speech which I am to make at Schenectady on Friday night is now completed and mimeographed and the one for the Institute of Arts and Sciences on Monday night is also about ready. I therefore feel pretty free in those respects but still look forward with no pleasure to going to the businessman's dinner on Saturday night in New York.

Two rather peculiar things happened today in view of the difficult time I had in the Senate last year. I had a letter from Senator Bailey in which he asked me to prepare a memorandum for his investigating committee on the causes and consequences of the depression. I of course answered at once that I would be glad to prepare such a memorandum. I found subsequently that the Secretary has had a similar letter so we are going to make a joint reply. Then H.A.W. tells me that in a conference which he had with Senator Smith the Senator very definitely held out the olive branch by asking that I join a conference of his committee on the export trade in cotton, particularly with respect to cotton substitutes. The Senator is evidently having a field day, perhaps stimulated by the President's recent announcement of a plan he has in mind for cotton which is similar to the efforts which have been made for international control of wheat production. Cotton Ed evidently thinks he can take the limelight away from the President but there seems to be nothing to do but to go along and try to shape the program up and to draw the contrast very clearly between the need for extended markets or else rigid control of agriculture in this country.

January 29, 1935

I have just gotten back from a four day trip to Schenectady and New York. The occasion of the trip to Schenectady was to make an address on "The Progressive Tradition." It seemed to go very well and was, of course, recognized by everybody as something of a state paper. Union College raised a great many doubts in my mind as to the future of what is sometimes called "the country college." It seems to me that these institutions, instead of trying to be national in scope, ought to be localized as junior colleges to include the last two years of high school and the first two years of college and that the big universities ought to be reserved for genuinely advanced students beyond this point.

In New York I went to one of the so-called "Moley dinners" on Saturday night with a lot of first-rank big businessmen (listed below) and was, so to speak, put on the spot. I spoke first for about twenty minutes or half an hour respecting the administration and telling them generally what the realities of the administration's policy are as I see them in contrast with what they are generally represented to be. I took a very realistic position, putting to them the challenge which the depression presents, the necessity for assurance of work, and also the necessity for reaching such an arrangement as will produce and distribute goods and get them into consumers' hands. After I had spoken about fifteen of the businessmen spoke in turn. The general burden of their talks were rather querulous complaints about the unfriendliness of the administration and about the lack of confidence which businessmen have in the present administration. They rather indicated that until there was greater confidence, prosperity would not return because businessmen would not take a chance on further investment or on larger production. One of them complained bitterly about the adminstration's policy toward utilities, another complained that the government was badly organized to hear the views of businessmen, another that the fiscal policies of the administration were such as would not lead to any confidence in it on the part of businessmen, another complained that the administration never missed an opportunity to, as he put it, take a crack at businessmen. Throughout the evening there was not a single constructive suggestion made by any person present. One of those present, Paul Mazur, who is something of an economist, did indicate to the others present that he thought that businessmen were at least as much at fault as the government because they had never made any really constructive suggestions calculated to meet the problem. The discussion at the end degenerated into so many complaints about the attitude of the mob, as they called it, and the administration's responsiveness to it, which took the form of saying that the administration was interested only in reelection, that I took occasion, because I spoke last, to wind up the discussion by saying that it seemed to me that what they were really afraid of was not people who were directly concerned in the adminstration but that they were afraid really of the American people and the trend of their thinking. I said that it seemed to me that any administration which failed to sense the drift of a people's thinking and to keep abreast of it would fail to be reelected and that it deserved to fail, because after all we were proceeding on the democratic theory and if people cannot get a response from their government in terms which makes sense to them, they will take other means to get it. So I said that what you are really objecting to is the psychological reaction of the people to the depression which you are really responsible for through the break down of the management of your industry and that when any group charged with leadership in a community finds itself in the position of having no constructive suggestions which have to do with causes of distress and yet has bitter complaints about the attitude of the public toward them, it is in a very serious state. I said that the proceedings which had gone on seemed to me to indicate that they were not only unwilling to make any sufficient changes in the organization or operation of business but they were rapidly getting into the state of mind to try some kind of dictatorship. I said, of course, this is what we have learned to call Fascism and I indicated that perhaps, although they did not put these things in general terms, they had come awfully close to saying that what was needed was less democracy and more dictatorship. It was on this note that the meeting ended. Willkie was present and did a good deal more than his share of the complaining.

I spent two days with Ray Moley at the St. Regis Hotel and had several long talks with him. It had been some time since we had had a chance to explore matters together and I had a chance to tell him all I had been thinking about the policies which seemed to me adaptable to our present situation and I must say that I found him in rather general agreement. At any rate, we got along agreeably and came back to Washington together.

In the meantime I made another speech at Columbia on Monday night in which I used the conversation form of argument, trying in this way to put various reactions to the present situation in assumed characters' mouths. It was not particularly successful.

This morning Moley and I had a long talk with Averell Harriman, mostly about two things: first, the communications legislation which Moley is trying to line up and summarize for the President, and second about NRA. My general feeling about NRA is, first, that it should be kept fluid and flexible for some time, that is to say, be carried on partly at least as an education process and partly as a mechanism of compromise. I have felt, however, that labor questions could now be taken away from NRA and put in separate organization in the Department of Labor so that NRA might concentrate on price problems and on other phases of trade practices. I feared that this should have been done in the first place. Harriman did not agree to this last but did agree that NRA ought to be kept in a flexible and fluid state. I think he also agreed with me that as fast as industry has achieved some order and cohesion it ought to be the subject of special legislation and have administrative boards set up outside NRA. I put to him at some length my feeling that the problem of prices is the one which NRA must at all costs concentrate on and find the solution for. So long as some prices are rigid and some rather flexible, there will continue to be a disparity of purchasing power which will prevent recovery and make difficulty even after recovery comes. Gardiner Means has just completed a very significant study of this question which I recommended that Harriman read.

This afternoon Walton Hamilton came to see me saying that he was under some pressure to return to Yale for the second term. President Angell being very much out of sympathy with what is going on here and being unwilling to have any members of the Yale faculty mixed up in it. Hamilton is in a sense my man on the NRA board. That is to say that I was the one who suggested him and he is the man in whose judgment I have most confidence. I should hate very much to see him leave just in this present situation and so I volunteered to go to see the President about this case. He rather feels that since he has had many controversies with Clay Williams and with Richberg, the President may have been prejudiced against him and he would like to know whether this is true before he makes up his mind. We had a long conversation about NRA policy and seemed to agree in nearly all essentials, as I should expect we would: first, about keeping it flexible, and second, about not using NRA to enforce official AF of L labor policies and third, about special legislation for industries as fast as they achieve some integration.

The list of those attending the Saturday night dinner of "The Committee for Economic Recovery" is as follows:

T. W. Appleby	Bruce Barton	William J. Baxter
Lewis H. Brown	Ward M. Canaday	Floyd L. Carlisle
Stacy G. Carkhuff	Colby M. Chester	Howard E. Coffin
J. S. Crutchfield	T.W.D. Duke	John W. Farley
Henry J. Fuller	J. Stirling Getchell	Leslie Herman
Kenneth C. Hogate	Thomas H. Holden	Frank R. Hope
Andrew J. Maloney	Paul M. Mazur	Raymond Moley
Earle H. Rodney	Harry G. Stoddard	Charles W. Taussig
Paul J. Tochiana	George M. Verity	Theodore Weicker
Wendell L. Willkie		

February 2, 1935

I had a conversation of such interest last night that I have asked both Appleby and Carter who were present to make some notes about the issues raised and I shall append them here. It came about by W. E. Dodd calling me and asking me to dinner with him at the Cosmos Club. I had known he was in town and wondered why he had not looked me up. It seems he has had flu and been snowed in pretty continuously since December when he arrived. He has a farm down in Loudon County which he bought in 1913, according to a letter he writes me, being uncertain of a modern history professor's tenure and wanting a retreat. At any rate he bought it and now writes me many complaints of the farmers' plight. I asked him out to my house for dinner and proceeded to try to assemble a group. Walton Hamilton, Bob LaFollette and Harry Hopkins were all busy; but I got Senator Wheeler, Jerry Frank and Paul Appleby; John Carter came in after dinner. It was amusing and significant to confront Bert Wheeler, who was one of the leaders of the Progressive group in opposing the World Court resolution the other day, with Dodd who believes absolutely that this withdrawal of ours means war. His reasoning is that Germany will now feel confident that we are out of the European scene and will at once move in on Austria, the Corridor, etc. England will withdraw from the East leaving Japan a free hand in China. This is because England must have her ships in the West if Germany is again to be the great expanding power on the Continent. Italy will bitterly resent the Austrian move, Russia also will try to block the resumption of the 'drang nach östen' and France will see her hegemony in Eastern Europe crumbling.

Wheeler says he stimulated Huey Long's speeches and worked generally against the resolution because he believes Europe will have to recognize the great power of Germany and will have to permit her expansion into all Germanic territory.

The conversation went round and round this issue for some time. Dodd showed us a Nazi propaganda map which indicated the German dream. It covered most of Switzerland, part of Czechoslavakia, etc. It seemed to frighten him greatly. He told us movingly of the Nazi drive against all the old Kantian culture groups. His emotions are all against what is going on and I think his intelligence is confused in this way. Wheeler may be nearer right because of perspective. Hitler may proceed in such ways as to avoid war. But I am sure he has to proceed. Forces are moving which he cannot possibly block even if he wanted to.

I think the President feels much as Dodd does. He has been very deeply disturbed about the Hitler business from the first. The other day he showed me a letter he was thinking of sending to Joe Robinson, who had led the unsuccessful fight for the Court resolution. It congratulated Robinson on his courageous fight and conveyed thanks to the other Senators who had been in support. "As for the others", it said, "I hope they may go to heaven because there they will have so much explaining to do -- that is if God is in favor of peace, and I believe he is." I suppose he didn't send the letter in that form but it indicates grave concern and a definite feeling about the jeopardy of peace.

The other interesting thing about last night's conversation was the disillusion of a progressive like Wheeler. He has lost all faith in FDR. He complains of wobbling, of his catering to business, of unfriendly acts toward his logical supporters such as Cutting and of general administration failure to strike out boldly for economic reforms. He spoke confidently of a third party in 1936, organizing all these left-wing people: Long, Coughlin, Sinclair, Olson, etc. I'd believe it more likely if they had much in common in their programs and weren't such demagogic individualists.

(Confidential)

MEMORANDUM OF CONVERSATION AT DR. TUGWELL'S HOUSE,
Evening of February 1, 1935.

Present: Dr. Tugwell, U.S. Ambassador Dodd (To Berlin),
            Senator Wheeler of Montana, Jerome Frank,
            Paul Appleby and John Carter.

During the early part of the evening, prior to my arrival, the conversation had centered around the Senate's rejection of the World Court. Dodd said that this meant war, that Germany would take Austria, producing a crisis which would compel England to withdraw her fleet from Asiatic waters, which would in turn provide the opportunity for Japan to attack Russia, in which case we would inevitably be drawn into the Far Eastern War. The implication of this diagnosis, however, was that our function on the World Court would be to preserve the European status quo.

Wheeler--generally supported by the others present--contended that it was precisely for this reason that the World Court had been rejected, that it was <u>not</u> our function to prevent the unification of Europe under Germany or any other power and that the status quo was responsible for the very situation, including Hitlerism, which now threatened war.

Dodd said that Colonel House was much discouraged, having been in recent consultation with the secret Ambassador (unnamed) whom Japan had sent over to negotiate on the Far East. Japan wanted complete domination of China and control of the strategic points in Eastern Asia. Dodd thought that we would be dragged into war against Japan by the Standard Oil interests just as the Morgan interests dragged us into war against Germany, against our will.

To this view, the answer was made that it was not our function to prevent the unification of Eastern Asia under Japan or any other power and that the way to prevent being dragged into war in Europe or Asia was to concentrate on curbing the power of the special interests--such as Morgan's or Standard Oil--which might impel us to fight.

Dr. Dodd seemed to feel that Goering's aircraft would conquer England and that then Canada would become German. He also implied that Japan would take Mexico. On the other side, the view was expressed that such developments as he prophesied in Europe and Asia might impel Canada and Mexico to federate themselves, for defensive purposes with the United States. On the other hand, I argued that when you unify a continent you automatically create internal political tensions which cause its government to concentrate on domestic matters and ignore foreign conquests. An example of this is, of course, the United States at the close of the Civil War, which definitely ended a century of Continental expansion. I also pointed out that the balance of power and the principle of diplomatic and colonial compensation--Frank called it "keeping up with the Jones's"--had been responsible for the centrifugal character of European politics.

Dodd was much disturbed over German developments. Hitler was in the hands of Thyssen and the Ruhr industrialists and he (Dodd) showed a poster designed to encourage air-mindedness in Germany, which included the territories lost in the war and strips of territory in neighboring countries, Switzerland included. However, these latter strips were red, designed to give the optical effect of relief to the German map (which was blue) and my impression was that Dodd had been sold a pup in the argument that the red map was designed to suggest areas of German conquest. If that were the case, why did the map omit Austria? Wheeler's attitude was "What of it?" The natural thing to happen was for Germany to absorb Austria, Czechoslovakia, Hungary and the Balkans.

Dodd told of the sufferings of the old liberals, Lutherans and cultured element under Hitler, and was obviously much distressed by their predicament. In rebuttal, Frank and I pointed out that under a revolution you were killed for some assignable reason--you were a kulak, a counter-revolutionary, etc.--while in a war far more people were killed and on a perfectly indiscriminate basis.

Then Dodd left and Tugwell observed that Dodd was still suffering from a bad attack of Woodrow Wilson. The ominous thing, however, was that the President seems to be in general agreement with Dodd's thesis and regards himself as compelled to build a billion dollars worth of warships which will be obsolete in ten years.

The conversation then shifted to domestic politics. Wheeler defended Huey Long as being the best means of getting rid of the reactionary Southern Senators. He said Long would make it his personal business and pleasure to defeat Joe Robinson and Pat Harrison for reelection, that he represented the poor white trash in contradistinction to the upper crust.

Appleby seemed doubtful of Long's political integrity--it being assumed that his personal integrity was not too hot--but Wheeler asserted that Long was very much in earnest about the sharing of wealth, the elimination of big incomes and inheritances, and smashing the business privilege in the South. I expressed agreement with Wheeler if only because Long was an ideal bonfire to light under the Southern Senators. I did not mention the fact that Long's economic programme had been written by one of my free-lance political associates in New York--Leon Vanderlyn--because Vanderlyn's a shifty cuss and I should like to check on the facts before accepting his account.

Wheeler said that Roosevelt was definitely slipping throughout the country. The 1932 vote was a vote against Hoover, the 1934 was a "For God's sake do something!" vote, and now Roosevelt was playing with the conservatives because he felt that he couldn't rely on the liberals. Roosevelt had missed his chance in 1933 and could not recapture it. Wheeler said that a third party in 1936 was a definite probability, with Long, LaFollette, Olson, Father Coughlin and Upton Sinclair taking the lead, and that this party would give Roosevelt a very close run for his money. (This bears out my opinion).

Wheeler was asked why the progressives and radicals in the Senate didn't get together and do something which would make it necessary and expedient for Roosevelt to swing to the left. The Administration liberals were now out on the end of a limb and unable to move unless they got real political support. Specific suggestions were made for the character of the movement: an investigation of the processors, the nationalization of the processors, Wheeler's own bill to take over the railroads, a proposal to encourage Harry Hopkins to build up the Ohio Plan of industrial barter and self-help. Wheeler seemed a little at sea and non-committal on all these points.

Wheeler was further asked why the progressives and liberals wouldn't cooperate with each other. He said they would and that there were over twenty Senators who could be relied on for progressive action. Attempts to enumerate these Senators are not altogether successful and the subject changed.

The net impression of the evening's conversation was that there was complete irreconcilability between the Wheeler nationalistic view and the Dodd international view. Each believed that his way was the way to prevent war and that the other way would involve us in war. On the domestic front, it was apparent that Roosevelt stands to lose the support of the South and West which elected him and that the Third Party movement is growing rapidly. Whether this will produce a Republican victory in 1936 or compel the Republicans to support Roosevelt was not discussed. In conclusion, Frank remarked that we had to make up our minds to do one thing or another--go Inca or go Morgan, internally and externally--and not to continue our vain efforts to do two contradictory things at the same time.

/s/ John Franklin Carter

February 2, 1935

AMBASSADOR DODD, pointing out that immediately following the Senate vote on the World Court Hitler's purpose of effecting union with Austria was announced, himself vigorously opposed the annexation of Austria and other similar expansions of Germany and the Hitler sway; he opposed equally Japan's encroachments on China and what he saw as her projected penetration of Latin America. He seemed to adhere to the balance-of-power concept, arguing that the United States would inevitably be involved in such centralizations of power, seeing Canada deeply affected by German expansion, and thence the United States. As a passionate follower of Wilson and hater of Hitler, he falls into the situation of passionately upholding a world order, but denying the tendency to continental centralization.

JEROME FRANK, hating Hitler equally, denounced the theory of "every little language having a nation of its own", and advocated national consolidations to continental dimensions.

SENATOR WHEELER, apparently feeling unequal to this particular type of discussion, made the following observations:

Being originally pro-German, his visit to France made him anti-France; he thought if the senators had voted their own convictions, there wouldn't have been more than 8 or 9 votes for the World Court; he indicated intense resentment at not being informed by the President of such arguments for the World Court move as were presented by Ambassador Dodd, and said he was not taking orders from anybody; he took the position that whereas the world debts can not be paid, nations must admit them in principle, in order to have the good will of the American people. He said that it is ingrained deeply in the American people that debts must be paid. (No one called attention to the organized resistence to mortgage-foreclosure in Montana, and general refusal in Montana of automobile owners to buy new license plates.)

The Senator's interests quickly swung to other fields: in this company he was a little bit diffident, however, about pursuing the money thing, and apparently admitted that monetary reform is not a cure-all; he expressed deep resentment at the attitude of the Administration toward Cutting, Floyd Olsen, and Huey Long. He thought this was bad politics, and insisted that Huey Long is sincere in his championship of those things that are in the interest of the common people. His deepest feeling was expressed against the Administration timidity about business. He declared that the President feeds those who will destroy him, that "he must be with them or against them, and he is with them, but they will never be for him and will sooner or later cut his heart out". R.G.T. injected at this point that the President is neither for nor against the business people--that he is above them.

The Senator declared himself in favor of taking over many of the large basic industries, but admitted R.G.T.'s statement about the difficulty of manning them with socially-minded people. He insisted that regulation is futile, and that the necessity is continually to oppose and cut the power of centralized business.

He indicated a third party in 1936 might make Republican success a possibility. He discussed unification of the Progressive Group and thought it possible. He said that probably there are 20 Progressive senators, but a list, according to his judgment of them, showed about 14.

AMBASSADOR DODD said the vote of Progressives in the Senate against the World Court was a curious denial of the principle of majority rule, which they usually espouse. (Of course, if the Senators believe that the sentiment of the country is against the World Court, the point is not valid. The function of leadership, too, of course, would qualify this principle on occasion, as shown by Dodd in his several references to historical instances in which the President went counter to the Senate.) The Ambassador also recalled the record of debt-repudiation by our own States.

PRESS CONFERENCE
February 6, 1935.
3:30 P.M.
Office of the Secretary

Q.   Mr. Secretary, do you have any statement to make regarding the changes announced last night, the status quo?

SECRETARY WALLACE: Why, these changes have been in contemplation for some months. Chester Davis and I talked them over at some length in December; as a matter of fact, the need for reorganization of the 3 A's so we could set up what was in effect a council. When Mr. Davis came in the business was so exceedingly great that there were no regular meetings with a considerable staff. When Mr. Peek was here there were regular meetings with quite a considerable staff, and Mr. Davis in order to get things moving with the greatest possible speed, and many things were on us at the time, dispensed with that procedure and I thought it was wise at the time but now that it will be possible to survey things a little more leisurely, it seems to me advisable for him to have a staff of men with whom he will meet, and I am hoping to meet also with this particular group as often as it is possible for me to do so. I think you got in a press release the names of the men who would be acting on this council, just one name that was omitted. We mentioned the Consumers' Counsel would be on this Council but we did not name who the Consumers' Counsel would be.

Q.   Are you ready to name him now?

SECRETARY WALLACE: No, not just yet.

Q.   Mr. Secretary, what reason did you advance for asking for the resignation of Mr. Frank?

SECRETARY WALLACE: Well, I am not sure that your statement is quite correct that we have asked for his resignation.

Q.   Mr. Frank's resignation, was it asked for, or did he hand in his resignation, and what reason did he give when he handed in his resignation?

SECRETARY WALLACE: I don't know just what reason was given at that time, but it was a situation making for the greatest possible harmony; I mean the method we took seemed to make for the greatest possible harmony. I may say I believe that all of us have the very greatest faith in Mr. Frank's ability and unselfish hard work. I think we can all say that.

MR. DAVIS: Yes.

Q.   Is that an "obit"?

Q.   Have you anything to say, Mr. Secretary, as to why he couldn't fit in to make the greatest possible harmony?

SECRETARY WALLACE: Oh, it is one of those things that happens in any organization where things are driving ahead with great vigor, and necessarily in this kind of work, our objectives can not be defined with absolute clarity, and different people with the highest and best motives in the world have slightly different ideas as to just what those objectives may be, and --

Q.   There is no objection to his social or economic views, is there?

SECRETARY WALLACE: I haven't had any intimation of it, or anything particular expressed.

Q.   Was there any objection to the way he wanted to carry out any of these?

SECRETARY WALLACE: Oh, there isn't anything particular. It is just a situation which was I suppose more or less inevitable.

Q.   Could you mention --

SECRETARY WALLACE: I think, really -- what were you going to say?

Q.   Don't let me interrupt you.

SECRETARY WALLACE: I know you didn't like to interrupt me.

Q.   Mr. Secretary, you said it was more or less inevitable. Would you mind explaining that a little further?

SECRETARY WALLACE: I might say the thing I was just stopped from saying.

Q.   I wish you would.

Q.   Mr. Secretary, if I may observe, you say this was all done in the interests of harmony. Just about a year or so ago there was another, shall we say, "exodus" in the interests of harmony, and it so happens that one of the leaders of that situation a year ago was retained in the interests of harmony and now is bounced out in the interests of harmony. Now, harmony has very many sides.

SECRETARY WALLACE: Of course, music does progress in point of time.

Q.   Yes.

SECRETARY WALLACE: I mean, if you sustain the same note while other notes are changing.

Q.   I see, the notes change. You see, you may have different notes to the basic tune, is that the idea?

Q.   Does that "in the interests of harmony" apply to the others who are bounced or are going to be bounced?

SECRETARY WALLACE: I don't know. I don't know just what the present situation is with regard to any others.

Q.   Dr. Howe?

SECRETARY WALLACE: Oh, yes, Dr. Howe, yes. Dr. Howe will be shifting his activities, but in just what capacity hasn't been determined yet.

Q.   In the interests of harmony?

SECRETARY WALLACE: Well, this is a little -- in the case of Dr. Howe his capacities are not quite the capacities that are necessary for leading up this particular organization, and I think Mr. Davis perhaps would like to make a little statement on what he believes to be the functions of this organization and the type of man who should head it up.

Q.   May I ask a question before that speech comes off? How about Mr. Shea -- I think that is his name -- isn't he leaving?

SECRETARY WALLACE: Has Mr. Shea resigned, Chester?

MR. DAVIS: Yes.

SECRETARY WALLACE: Mr. Shea has resigned.

Q.   And Mr. Pressman? Mr. Rotnem?

SECRETARY WALLACE: Mr. Rotnem, has he resigned?

MR. DAVIS: That is in suspense, Mr. Secretary.

SECRETARY WALLACE: That is in suspense.

Q.   And the fellow by the name of Hiss?

SECRETARY WALLACE: I am quite sure that Mr. Hiss has not resigned.

Q.   Is that in suspense or not?

MR. DAVIS: There has been no suggestion of Mr. Hiss' resignation except in the press, as far as I know.

Q.   Who are going? How about it, may we ask for a statement as to just who is going and who is not going?

MR. DAVIS: Do you want me to discuss that, Mr. Secretary?

SECRETARY WALLACE: Yes, if you would, Mr. Davis.

MR. DAVIS: Mr. Frank, Mr. Pressman, Mr. Shea, Gardner Jackson, and as I say, the Rotnem case is in suspense, and in each of these cases, from close association, while I agree wholly with the Secretary as to the ability of the men in question, for an efficiently operating organization in the Triple-A, these changes were desirable in my judgment and I recommended them to the Secretary on Monday. Now, in the Consumer's Counsel, what we need and what we want is current up-to-the-minute reports and information on all the marketing plans and adjustment programs and their effect, and then a constructive analysis of those facts from the consumers' standpoint to help us in shaping our program and in determining changes in agreements as they develop.

Now, Mr. Howe is in entire agreement with me on this point that he is not the man -- he is not interested in that type of activity. He has enormous capacity through his public contact for educational work and promotion, but not this particular type of work which I believe we need. The Consumers Counsel stands as it is, and as constructive direction is secured for it along those lines, it will be strengthened. The one change that is made, that is, as that constructive leadership is given, instead of being part of the Information Division, it will report directly to the Administrator's Office except on matters of information and publicity, which will clear through the Information Division as it has in the past. But we want more study, analysis, and constructive criticism of the inside of the organization rather than so much stress on publicity in advance of information.

Q.   What was the matter with Gardner Jackson?

MR. DAVIS: That was a move in the interests of the Administration.

Q.   For the peace of Mr. Stedman?

Q.   Not too much publicity?

Q.   Mr. Davis, there is a report this afternoon that Mr. Jackson may resist this action. Have you heard anything of that, any intimation of that given to you?

MR. DAVIS: No, I haven't heard anything about it. In fact, I have been told his resignation is on the way to my office.

Q.   What is the foundation of the report, if any, that these people were purged from the Triple-A because they disagreed with the current milk policy; that they decided you had made a complete somersault on the milk policy, and were favoring the handlers too much.

MR. DAVIS: Of course it isn't true, this business of a somersault on the milk policy. We stand precisely where we did in January, the retail prices tending to fix margins for distributors. In the discussions leading up to this action on the milk policy, it was not even referred to. I think, in all recognition of the strong legal services these men have given, I want to make this statement, I think it is important to have in key positions in the

Triple-A, men who are possessed of some familiarity with farm problems and who have a farm background.

SECRETARY WALLACE: Chester has now made the speech I halted in the midst of making.

Q.   Mr. Davis, you know that was one of the objections raised to Mr. Tugwell in the Senate, his lack of farm background.

SECRETARY WALLACE: Mr. Tugwell has, of course, a farm background.

Q.   A farm background of some kind.

Q.   A "dirt farmer."

Q.   Can you tell us what led up to this being crystallized at this time? Any one thing that happened determining you to take this step?

MR. DAVIS: No, I wouldn't say that any one thing happened; it was just a mounting difficulty in getting things done, and after all, our job is to get things done over here.

Q.   Isn't it true, Mr. Davis, that the criticisms of persons now to be separated from the organization, namely hindering the progress, are substantially the same as those raised by the same persons against Mr. Peek?

MR. DAVIS: I don't know that I could confirm that, Felix. Of course, what we are anxious to do, and what we have been doing today is to turn faces front and speed up the tempo and devote all our energies to the outside, developing these programs and administering them instead of having to be concerned with so much of our energy to maintaining cooperative relationships within the organization.

Q.   Mr. Davis, what will be your policy on milk from now on? Do you agree with Dr. Howe that the distributors are getting too large a proportion of the amount paid by the consumers?

MR. DAVIS: As I said, our policy on milk for over a year has left the question of margins entirely to competition. We haven't attempted to fix or support the prices for distributors and while we held in November and December a series of policy conferences, and that is one of the questions we want to continue discussing until we reach a key decision or two on that, that hasn't entered into this, and no change at all in the attitude towards the milk problem is involved in this.

Q.   You say there were no fixed prices. Isn't it agreed in milk sheds what the retail price should be?

MR. DAVIS: In some cases it may be agreed on and in some cases the State Control Board may have fixed it for themselves, but in no case have the licenses which we put into a market, except for one or two unsuccessful attempts to maintain a minimum price, in no case do they fix any price which we enforce by license at all.

SECRETARY WALLACE: Any "resale" prices that we enforce by license.

MR. DAVIS: Yes. The one thing we attempt to do is establish a producers' price and require all to start from that basis and operate equally.

Q.   Wasn't it Dr. Howe's idea that some action should be taken for cutting down the amount the distributors are drawing out of that?

SECRETARY WALLACE: Mr. Howe takes a very broad, philosophical view of the ultimate objectives and I think we all realize from the ultimate objectives that there is a considerable waste in milk distribution in the great cities of the land, and Mr. Howe would like to see that waste eliminated, and I am sure that all of us in the Department would agree.

MR. DAVIS: Yes, but Mr. Secretary, Dr. Howe's attitude on the milk policy wasn't affected in this decision which we have realized was necessary for a long time.

Q.   Mr. Secretary, was this situation the last few days, the issue over the amendments going up on the Hill, was that involved?

MR. DAVIS: Not in the least.

Q.   Mr. Secretary, was the President consulted on this reorganization?

SECRETARY WALLACE: Why, I think the President was aware of it before the newspaper boys.

Q.   He said this morning he wasn't.

Q.   That is a terrible state of affairs.

Q.   Why not get together on these things?

Q.   Was Tugwell aware of it and did he approve it?

SECRETARY WALLACE: I don't know whether he approved it or not.

Q.   Was it taken up with Tugwell last December or before he went to Florida?

Q.   Is that why he went to Florida?

Q.   What is Tugwell's attitude toward it?

SECRETARY WALLACE: You might ask him.

Q.   He isn't here. Haven't you talked with him?

SECRETARY WALLACE: I don't know his exact attitude. He can answer for himself. I expect every individual's attitude is a little different.

Q.   Do you think his attitude is different from yours, say?

SECRETARY WALLACE: I expect every person in the Department has a different attitude.

Q.   Mr. Secretary, isn't the effect of his reorganization to sort of divorce Mr. Tugwell from the AAA thing?

SECRETARY WALLACE: Mr. Tugwell hasn't had anything to do with the Agricultural Adjustment Administration. I suppose for -- I don't know how long, except on the sugar phase of it -- for nine months.

Q.   Eight months.

SECRETARY WALLACE: Is that right? Eight months? What is the date?

Q.   January 19, 1934.

Q.   Just what does he do here?

Q.   Travels.

Q.   And writes books.

SECRETARY WALLACE: No, Professor Tugwell really has a great deal
to do. You may not realize it, and some apparently do not, insisting on
creating a mythical man. Professor Tugwell does have an excellent
scientific and agricultural background, and he is interested and has
worked very closely with the bureau chiefs and representatives.

Q.   I thought that was Secretary Wilson's function; he is a scientist
too.

SECRETARY WALLACE: Mr. Wilson is interested in slightly different
aspects. As a matter of fact, there is plenty around this Department for
a good many people to do.

Q.   Lots of them are being thrown out.

SECRETARY WALLACE: Mr. Wilson is especially concerned -- you see,
the Extension Service is really quite an affair here.

Q.   Did you say "extension"?

SECRETARY WALLACE: Yes, we have an Extension Service. Have you
ever heard of it?

Q.   I have heard of extension. You have been doing a lot of extending.

SECRETARY WALLACE: The Extension Service has been in existence
under the Smith-Lever Act and other Acts of Congress for a good many
years, and Mr. Wilson has been concerned with a good many of their
activities.

Q.   Don't you even consult Mr. Tugwell any more on AAA policies?

SECRETARY WALLACE: Mr. Tugwell, I should say, if you didn't get it
before, is very much interested in the sugar part of the AAA program, and
we consult him with regard to that.

Q.   But not with regard to wheat and corn and hogs?

SECRETARY WALLACE: Just like we consult -- we pass the time of day;
we are all members of one big family here.

Q.   All brothers.

Q.   Just one big happy family.

SECRETARY WALLACE: Yes, I think as these families go, I think we are an exceptionally happy family.

Q.   How about Mr. Stedman?

MR STEDMAN: By the way, I have a remark to make.

Q.   Wait a minute; we will get around to you. If I may observe, Mr. Secretary, from what you said, seriously, is it fair to assume that Mr. Tugwell has been very largely, shall we say, put out or eliminated from the AAA picture?

SECRETARY WALLACE: Why, that goes back quite a long time.

Q.   Then that is something we have missed.

Q.   Oh, no, you missed it, we didn't miss it.

SECRETARY WALLACE: I tell you, you haven't been doing right by us. You haven't been attending these conferences.

Q.   Mr. Secretary, a year ago --

SECRETARY WALLACE: Ted Alfred brought that out a long time ago.

Q.   A year ago, Mr. Secretary, when the Peek situation was up here, Tugwell went to bat for Mr. Frank and fought the fight. Now, did he go to bat for him this time?

SECRETARY WALLACE: I am not sure Mr. Tugwell was involved in that situation particularly.

Q.   How about the second part of the question? Did he got to bat this time?

SECRETARY WALLACE: No, he didn't go to bat this time.

Q.   Did he know about it?

SECRETARY WALLACE: I don't know that he knew about it.

Q.   He wasn't ever consulted?

SECRETARY WALLACE: I don't know. As I said, he hasn't been concerned with the Three-A matters.

Q.   Isn't it true that shortly after the Peek episode, Mr. Tugwell devoted more of his time to the reorganization and coordinating of bureaus within the Department of Agriculture?

SECRETARY WALLACE: He has been working especially on the scientific side, in the coordination of scientific work.

Q.   Mr. Secretary, isn't this something along the lines of what actually happened? In the situation of Peek, the issue was between you and Mr. Peek and Mr. Peek walked the plank, and this is a question between Mr. Davis and Mr. Frank, and Mr. Frank walks the plank?

SECRETARY WALLACE: Mr. Frank is a part of Mr. Davis' organization.

Q.   And this was an issue between them, and Mr. Davis stays and at that time it was an issue between you and Mr. Peek, is that right?

SECRETARY WALLACE: Yes, that is substantially accurate.

Q.   Now, does this shift in personnel or change in personnel mean that the AAA from now on is going to take, shall we say, a more stable policy --

SECRETARY WALLACE: Go ahead and say it.

Q.   -- Stable and right policy, or "old guard", whatever you want to call it?

SECRETARY WALLACE: I don't think it means that at all.   I don't think it is that kind of a situation.

Q.   Pursue the middle course, Mr. Secretary?

SECRETARY WALLACE: Well, you see we don't like to have a ship that lists stronger to the left or the right, but one that goes straight ahead.

Q.   You were going to the right when Peek was in and you got rid of the right, and now you are rid of the left and are going down the middle course.

SECRETARY WALLACE: Now we are going right ahead.

Q.   Here is a suggestion, that you have thrown out all the left-hand ballast and you don't want to shift too much to one side.

SECRETARY WALLACE: We might have to take on some more left-side ballast so we can go straight ahead.

Q.   Are there any more retirements coming?'

SECRETARY WALLACE: I don't know of any.

MR. DAVIS: I would say, Mr. Secretary, that the Solicitor taking charge of the legal division will, of course, have charge of that. I don't know what may result in the reorganization of the legal division, but I am confident that the reorganization will result -- by having common legal counsel will result in bringing this branch of the Agricultural Department into closer contact with the other brances of the Department and the Secretary's Office.

Q.   What did Victor Christgau do? What is his situation?

MR. DAVIS: Christgau has been devoting practically all his attention to the drought and a number of these emergency activities that come up from week to week and day to day, which if someone didn't get his back under them, would swamp my office. Then, in the development of that, it became impossible for him and the organization in his office to give the time to the commodity program that ordinarily would be expected. As a result of that, they came to mine, and this grouping into smaller units with a Council, whereby a representative of my office in each case will work closely with the unit heads, more or less formally puts into effect the situation we have actually been working under for some time.

Q.   This isn't exactly a promotion for Mr. Christgau, is it?

MR. DAVIS: Mr. Christgau will have plenty to do in this outline of work laid down before him.

Q.   Do you intend to stay on yourself? There are some reports that you may retire.

MR. DAVIS: I have never made any plans looking toward the date of resignation here, and furthermore, for the sake of some of you who have printed such stories, I have never been approached by any representative of business or industry looking toward employment.

Q.   Would you mention some specific differences which brought about this shake-up?

MR. DAVIS: I would prefer not to. As I said, I want to look forward and we want to go with faces out and work constructively.

Q.   Isn't the idea that some time in the future you will consolidate the AAA with the Department of Agriculture, and perhaps make it a bureau or in words a merger of the two?

SECRETARY WALLACE: That is what it is now.

Q.   I know it, but nevertheless you have the different --

SECRETARY WALLACE: It is such an enormously important thing that it occupies more of my time than any other bureau.

Q.   It is now really --

SECRETARY WALLACE: It always has been. That is the way it is set up in the law.

Q.   I thought that since you had an Administrator --

SECRETARY WALLACE: No, it is no different from the other parts of the Department in that respect.

Q.   I thought it was separate.

SECRETARY WALLACE: No, it is no different from the other parts of the Department in that respect.

Q.   I thought it was separate.

SECRETARY WALLACE: No, except it is so exceedingly important that we have paid more attention to it than any other bureau. It has more employees engaged in more significant activities.

Q.   Mr. Secretary, in regard to the Consumers' Counsel, is there a plan under way to coordinate the activities of the Consumers' Counsel of the AAA and the NRA under Mr. Blaisdell?

SECRETARY WALLACE: I don't know. What do you care to say on that, Chester? Is that all cleared and ready to make a statement?

MR. DAVIS: I think I can go some distance with it. Before Mrs. Rumsey's death, plans were drawn up for a Consumers' Division of the Emergency Council, coordinating the consumer activities. Mr. Blaisdell has been asked by the Industrial Emergency Committee of the Emergency Council to proceed to draw up the plans for that organization, and he is working on that now.

Q.   Will you have this consumers' bureau within your Administration to advise you as you outlined a few minutes ago?

MR. DAVIS: Absolutely.

SECRETARY WALLACE: We are planning, also, is it proper to say this that we are planning to continue the "Consumers' Guide"?

MR. DAVIS: Yes, it stays in status quo, but at the time that plans for a consumers' division are worked out, the question will arise (and it is one on which I have an open mind) as to whether each of these agencies should have a publication or whether there is some possibility of a merger. That will probably be raised at that time.

Q.   You will still have a consumers' division even though it is unified centrally?

SECRETARY WALLACE: We would have to under the law.

MR. DAVIS: And it is important even if it weren't in the law to have that continual gathering of information on programs.

Q.   As I understand it, this new setup instead of being a crusading agency in the interests of the consumers, it is going to be a statistical agency in the interests of the Administrator.

MR. DAVIS: It won't be a statistical agency at all, and won't be operating in the interests of the Administrator.

Q.   That is the way it was explained.

SECRETARY WALLACE: That's a good question.

MR. DAVIS: That is a misrepresentation, the way it was explained. What we have in mind, what we have as a matter of fact now, although it has not been as active as I would like, is a group of men whose job it is to analyze these programs as they are developed, from the consumers' standpoint. In every marketing agreement or license issued, we have had full provision for securing reports and backing them up with books and records and examination of them. I want to see that made effective and brought up to date so that there is ready at hand records for our information at any time on any agreements to guide us in administration and in making new ones.

Q.   That is what they have in NRA but it has never done any good.

MR. DAVIS: We are going to have it so that it will do some good.

SECRETARY WALLACE: In the law, the chief part of the consumer activities -- this part provides that "the Secretary of Agriculture in order to prevent pyramiding of the processsing tax and profiteering in the sale of the products derived from the commodity, shall make public such information as he deems necessary regarding (1) the relationship between the processing tax and the price paid to producers of the commodity, (2) the effect of the processing tax upon prices to consumers of products of the commodity, (3) the relationship, in previous periods, between prices paid to the producers of the commodity and prices to consumers of the products thereof, and (4) the situation in foreign countries relating to prices paid to producers of the commodity and prices to consumers of the products thereof."

Now, that is what we are authorized in the law to get, and as a matter of fact, we haven't filled in all those holes.

Q.   You have been doing some good work.

SECRETARY WALLACE: Well, you might say in a broad, general way that we have done some good work in fighting the consumers' battles, but in a precise statistical way, if anyone in Congress should say, "What have you done in this matter of foreign countries?" Of course, we don't have to; it is just when the Secretary deems it necessary, but there are still some holes that we haven't filled in.

Q.   Why didn't you fill up the holes without abolishing the holes you had already filled in?

SECRETARY WALLACE: I think Dr. Howe is not interested in a precise careful study along that line. His genius runs in other directions, and a very remarkable genius it is.

MR. DAVIS: We are continuing the Consumers' Guide and the educational activities, but we want more emphasis thrown on the collection of current information and on the books and records provision so that we can have the information before us to act on.

Q. Will the Council retain its connection with the local consumer groups?

MR. DAVIS: That is under the National Emergency Council.

Q. Under this new machinery, what will be done with the Grain Exchange and Millers' codes? How will they be handled now? Mr. Weaver is handling them?

MR. DAVIS: That's right, and reporting to Mr. Tapp. That will remain practically the same.

Q. Are we to understand that all separations that will take place have been effected?

MR. DAVIS: I said except in the reorganization of the Legal Division; I don't want to answer for the Solicitor on that.

Q. Will the reorganization be confined as far as separations are concerned to the two divisions, Legal and Consumers' Counsel?

MR. DAVIS: As far as I am concerned, yes.

Q. If the AAA is just merely a branch of the Department of Agriculture, then Secretary Wallace is really the head of the AAA and in his absence of course, Mr. Tugwell, the Undersecretary?

Q. How do you work that out, Mr. Secretary?

MR. STEDMAN: I would like to ask that the remarks of the Secretary with regard to the President be off the record.

Q. He didn't say anything about that.

SECRETARY WALLACE: Yes, I guess all the statements regarding the President, by common consent, should be considered off the record in my press conference.

Q.   We don't quote you as saying them.

SECRETARY WALLACE: As a matter of fact, to be absolutely square on that, just one phase of the matter was very hastily presented to the President just before his Emergency Council, and I don't think he got any of the matter except that Jerome Frank was going out. I think that was about all we had time to get across to him. Due to the limitation of time it is so easy to have statements that appear to be conflicting. My observation of this work is that possibly three-fourths of misunderstandings are due to things that start that way.

Q.   Getting back for a moment to the Consumers' Guide, can it be categorically stated that it is definitely the intention of the AAA to continue that or some other presentation of the factors for public consumption?

MR. DAVIS: Yes, as I say, the question of whether we use that for a joint publication or not is one for future determination. In the meantime the Consumers' Guide and related activities will continue.

Q.   But if that is discontinued, there will be something else to take its place?

MR. DAVIS: That is way down the gun barrel, but if that time comes it is necessary that we have some provision.

Q.   I would like to ask a pertinent question. What happens when you are out of town and the Undersecretary is acting, as to the AAA?

SECRETARY WALLACE: Of course he is head of it when I am out of town.

Q.   Then he does give Mr. Davis orders and he does participate in the AAA?

SECRETARY WALLACE: I think Mr. Davis and Mr. Tugwell are the best of friends, and there is no trouble from that source.

Q.   You referred to his supervision of sugar. Is that continuing in the drafting of the control plan?

SECRETARY WALLACE: It happened he was in on the sugar thing. You see he had visited Puerto Rico and as a result of his visit to Puerto Rico he had knowledge early in the game which made it advisable to keep in close touch with sugar and he has continued to do so, but not an intimate executive supervision at all, but when anything comes along and the whole sugar thing quivers from stem to stern, he is aware of what is going on.

MR. DAVIS: I think that he has been interested more in the insular angles of it.

SECRETARY WALLACE: I don't think he has paid any attention to the sugar beet allocation.

Q. Can you give us any information on the matter asked for in the Vandenburg resolution which will be presented to the Senate?

SECRETARY WALLACE: No, I put in a call just two or three days ago to see if the boys wouldn't get a move on, and I happened to meet Senator Vandenburg in the hall of the hotel and he asked what is the trouble with the boys over here that there is so little activity.

Q. Did you say that Mr. Frank agreed, as Mr. Howe did, that his resignation would be in the interests of harmony?

MR. DAVIS: That question was not raised.

Q. Was he given a chance to raise it?

Q. Apart from what you told us, I have been informed with regard to the President that Mr. Davis talked with the President a few days ago about this reorganization in general terms, and the President told him to go ahead, is that correct?

SECRETARY WALLACE: How long has it been since you saw the President, with the Emergency Council?

MR. DAVIS: I have never discussed this matter with the President.

Q. Have you, Mr. Secretary, discussed it with the President?

SECRETARY WALLACE: You mean the general reorganization?

Q. Yes.

SECRETARY WALLACE: No.

Q.   I wonder if you have any comment to make on the rise in food prices last month; there has been quite a rise.

SECRETARY WALLACE: Retail food prices?

Q.   Yes.

SECRETARY WALLACE: Just in certain commodities, isn't it? The general level doesn't show much rise.

Q.   In livestock --

SECRETARY WALLACE: You have it in meat and butter and eggs -- more recently have butter and eggs?

Q.   They have been maintained.

SECRETARY WALLACE: But when you take the whole Bureau of Labor figures on retail prices, they are not quite as high as they were last September, are they?

Q.   Food prices certainly are.

SECRETARY WALLACE: Taking the figures as a whole, will you find that the Bureau of Labor index of retail prices as high as they were?

Q.   I would like to raise a question, just as newspaper men among newspaper men, there was a release gotten out last night about seven o'clock on this situation. I want to raise it right here in the presence of Sted -- A. I think that statement is misleading.

SECRETARY WALLACE: In what way?

Q.   The statement said about these changes and in a more or less insignificant from a news point of these various commodity divisions and said nothing of the fact that there was this very important upheaval within the organization except this very innocent or innocuous statement that the Office of the General Counsel of the AAA was being consolidated with the Solicitor of the Department of Agriculture, and that was the tip-off on the story, and I don't know how that got in.

MR. DAVIS: The resignation hadn't been received at that time.

Q.   All resignations had been received at that time?

MR. DAVIS: Not at that time.

Q.   Certainly Mr. Frank's was received yesterday afternoon.

MR. DAVIS: It wasn't received until this morning at 10 o'clock.

Q.   There were no means in there on any of these changes and it seems to me in view of the fact it was known these things were going to happen, the issuing of a statement about these --

SECRETARY WALLACE: The precise nature of it was not then fully known. As a matter of fact, with regard to Mr. Rotnem it is not yet fully known.

(Conference adjourned at 4:15 p.m.)

February 10, 1935

A week full of grave disappointments which has left me disillusioned and cynical.

1. On Saturday, the second, I took the night plane for Miami and spent Sunday going over the Plant Introduction Garden at Cocoanut Grove. Earl Bressman went with me and Richey, Ryerson and Strong met us.

2. On Monday took the Pan American plane to Key West to stay a day or two with Julius Stone and see his experiment in rehabilitating this old city. Looked over the town, met a number of artists and writers who winter there or are on the F.E.R.A. payroll, spent two hours on the beach and dined at Stones' with Ned Bruce and his wife.

3. On Tuesday sent a wire home telling GEF where I was and took a plane out to Tortugas, Julius, Bressman and T. S. Stribling in the party with several others. Got back at 2:30 with the telephone ringing and GEF at the other end to tell me that Jerry Frank had been forced out suddenly. I afterward talked with Harry Hopkins, to Jerry and to Calvin Hoover. It seems that Chester Davis and HAW after a long conference decided to fire Jerry and several of his assistants, the particular excuse being a legal opinion written by Alger Hiss and O.K.'d by Jerome interpreting the cotton contract to mean that landlords had to keep the

same tenants for the life of the contract. But the incident had little significance. I could see that it was part of Davis' studied plan to rid the Department of all liberals and to give the reactionary farm leaders full control of policy, this meaning, of course, full satisfaction to all the processors with whom we have dealings since most of the farm leaders are owned body and soul by the processors. There was nothing I could do immediately. I found I could not get the plane home until the next night.

4. On Thursday morning I got home and Jerry came to breakfast and told me his story. The whole thing seemed to him planned to take advantage of my absence and the papers were full of stories about a radical purge in the Department.

5. I went and talked to Harry Hopkins who was outraged, to Louis Howe who was sympathetic, to HAW who was red-faced and ashamed, and to the President. My first impulse was to resign at once. I was mad all through. I had been aware of JF's situation and had for weeks been trying to work out something for him. The Solicitor, Seth Thomas, was to resign shortly to take a Judgeship and my idea was to move Jerome into that job and get another general counsel for AAA. This would have worked out in a few weeks. But HAW's cave-in to Davis had spoiled all this. Besides he had had a press conference the day before in which he had told the whole world that I had nothing to do with AAA policy and had formed a new council which excluded me. How could I stay as Under Secretary of the Department with the Secretary deliberately removing me from authority?

6. I made up my mind that (1) Jerome must have justice (2) that my position must be recognized and (3) that the ownership of the Department by the processors must be prevented. The Secretary had no excuse for having acted as he did and made the gesture of adding me to the Council. The President called up Justice and asked that Jerome be given a job of requisite importance; he also wrote a note directing that all marketing agreements hereafter be submitted before approval to the Attorney General and to the Federal Trade Commission and also said he would call a conference defining the government's attitude toward processors. In consequence of all this I decided to let things rest for the time being and advised Calvin Hoover to take the post of Consumers' Counsel.

February 13, 1935

Several days of suspense have resulted in no developments of any consequence. H.A.W. suggested that Jerome might be made Assistant Solicitor and they spent Monday evening talking at my house. Yesterday, however, H.A.W. talked with Davis who refused to go with Jerome in the department. That was final with H.A.W. I told him that outlined my own position too. He said that Chester felt friendly toward me and wanted me on the operating council. I told him our economic views diverged sharply, that there was certain to be a clash and that when it happened I knew he would certainly support Davis. I said that after all I was Under Secretary and if I did not enjoy his confidence I ought to get out. He said he thought the thing for me to do was to observe quietly for a few months and see what happened. I said that I would think things over for a few days and talk with him again. Meanwhile he has gone away on a trip for several days and I am trying to figure out the wise thing to do.

The situation would be better if the President had done any of the things he promised to do. I am to see him again today. After that things may be clearer.

I had a talk with the President this afternoon which lasted about an hour and a half and covered many subjects besides the one which has been uppermost in my mind for the past few days - my own situation in the Administration and in the Department of Agriculture.

The President opened the conversation by asking me if Homer Cummings had done anything for Jerome Frank as yet. I said no. The President seemed very much surprised and asked me why not. I said that I did not know why but that he had been rather firm in his refusal. He indicated some displeasure about this and said he had assumed that it had been done. I said I thought I had a better suggestion. I said I understood that in the RFC there was about to be a good deal of railroad reorganization which would require skillful legal handling and that I understood the General Counsel, Stanley F. Reed, was favorably disposed toward Jerome and that that might be an opportunity for using his talents in perhaps the best way. The President called Stanley Reed on the telephone and told him about the situation. He said that he regarded Jerome as an exceptionally able lawyer and was particularly interested in keeping his services in the government. Reed said he was glad the President had called, that he only needed some such indication to appoint him at once. I thanked him for this particular intervention because that takes care of the past. "But", I said, "that doesn't solve my own situation. This is apparently a wider problem and I talked with the Secretary yesterday when he indicated a certain lack of confidence in me; or rather that he expected to follow Chester Davis' advice and not mine." I said that this indicated a situation in which no self-respecting Undersecretary can go on functioning. I said, of course, that I saw no particular reason why I should not resign and that all things considered that perhaps that might be the best thing to do and asked him directly whether he would feel that my immediate resignation would be embarrassing to him. He said it would not only be embarrassing to him politically because he regarded me as a distinct political asset but that he had no intention of letting me go at all. I said that the situation in the Department of Agriculture is rather bad. "I don't know whose fault it is but administratively it is difficult. The Secretary makes no decisions and when I make decisions he is quite as likely to back up the person decided against as he is to back up me. I have been told that I am to have nothing to do with AAA policies and I do not feel that I can function properly as things are; that if you really feel that you want to keep my services in some capacity, I think it would be much better to move me." He said that he was aware that Henry Wallace was a poor administrator and said he had always spoken of me in the highest terms and did not believe that Henry had intended to hurt my feelings or to interfere with my administration of all the rest of the Department. He said, "After all, you have one of the biggest jobs in the government if you are running all the rest of the Department besides AAA and that ought to be a big enough job to suit anybody." "Of course" I said, "the difficulty is that I am not allowed to run it and I never feel free to make administrative decisions even when I know that they ought to be made." He said he thought that could be fixed but he did not insist on my staying in the Department of Agriculture if I thought the situation was impossible. He wanted, first however, to have a talk with Henry and explore his feelings in the matter. Then I suggested that there would be an Under Secretaryship in the Department of Interior which perhaps I could fill. He said that he thought I might have more difficulties there than I had in the Department of Agriculture and said, with a twinkle in his eye, you know Harold Ickes. I said "there are going to be plenty of jobs in the new works set up; perhaps you would like to have me do one of those." I said I thought I was well fitted to handle the job concerned with land and land uses, conservation, forests and parks, etc., and he said, well, he was not yet ready to tackle the problem of reorganization and had given no thought to personnel even in the new works set up. So, he said, for the time being he would take it as a personal favor if I would simply sit tight and wait until he could work the situation out. I said of course I would do that and then we went on to talk of other matters having to do with sugar, food and drugs, public roads, forests and other departmental matters I had to take up with him.

As I was leaving I said "You remember Mr. President you told me that you were sending over a memorandum requiring marketing agreements to be submitted to the Attorney General. That memorandum has never arrived and I thought that was one of the things which were needed to correct the situation in the Department." He said he had already dictated the memorandum and it must be on its way somewhere. He immediately told one of his secretaries to find it and see that it got here at once.

February 16, 1935

After talking with the President the other day I saw Harry

Hopkins in the evening and he said he had discussed my situation with the President somewhat at length. The President had told him that I was rather unhappy in the Department and Harry said that he did not blame me. Then the President and he discussed several things that I might do, the most prominent of which was undertaking to manage the whole housing program under the new Public Works bill. The matter is in suspense at the moment but this morning I had another talk with HAW in which he appeared to be rather disconcerted at the thought of my leaving the Department, but I simply told him that I had asked the President to have a talk with him about it and that I felt very strongly that if his confidence in Chester Davis was greater than in me in matters of agriculture policy, he ought to be Under Secretary rather than me. He said that was not the situation at all; that he did not regard Davis as at all important in policy matters but that he was needed to carry on the detailed administration of AAA very badly. I simply repeated that I preferred to leave the matter in suspense until after he had talked with the President.

Yesterday afternoon, HAW being away, I attended another Cabinet meeting. I think the mediocrity of the present Cabinet can hardly have been equalled in recent history. The President treats them like children and almost nothing of any importance was discussed. I believe it is true to say that there has never been a vote taken in Cabinet during this administration; but perhaps that would be proper in any cabinet.

The progress of the Social Security bill in its House hearings is rather interesting, perhaps as a comment on democracy, for up to the present practically all the progress which has been made is the removal from the bill of federal power to make standards so that it would amount merely to a federal hand-out to the states.

Yesterday there was a long meeting of the Committee on Economic Security to discuss the forthcoming report on health insurance. I was very much surprised at the indication of general support among the health professions for some kind of insurance but I am still skeptical and believe that medical opposition will be strong enough to prevent any immediate action.

Senator Bankhead has now introduced the bill for land reorganization of which I have spoken before. It has been thrown into the form of a Farm Tenants Home Corporation with assignment to the Department of Agriculture. The Secretary of the Treasury would buy a hundred million dollars of capital stock and the bill would authorize the issuance of a billion dollars of debentures. Senator Bankhead obviously thinks of the measure as merely loans to tenants which would enable them to buy the lands they operate. We are, of course, thinking of it in a much broader sense. After discussing it with M. L. Wilson the other day, we decided that I had better talk with the President about it, which I did.

He was very much interested in it as a move to attack the tenancy problem of the South, which is giving so much trouble, in a really constructive way. He asked a practical question immediately which I was not prepared to answer; i.e., how this device would affect the rural rehabilitation work which has been developed in various places, notably by FERA. I put him off for the moment and we have been having discussions of that in the Department.

My own feeling at the moment is that we might, if we were certain enough of sufficient administration, substitute this for the whole rehabilitation and resettlement program.

An interesting comment on the operation of AAA came up yesterday at the first meeting of Davis' new council to which I went. It seems that the flue-cured tobacco raisers last year received forty percent more than parity and that they expect the program for next year to be based on their returns for this year rather than on a planting which would be expected to yield only parity. They are bringing all kinds of political pressure to bear to sustain this point. It will be interesting to see whether consumers' interests play any part in the settlement of this particular problem. The constitutional problem also arises, of course, for it we keep processing taxes to pay benefit to farmers we keep higher than parity price which constitutes almost a complete delegation of constitutional taxing power by the Congress. Our position, of course, would be wholly indefensible, legally as well as economically, but there will be a tendency of course to give in to this particular pressure.

February 19, 1935

I found FDR feeling particularly good yesterday afternoon - the Supreme Court had just handed down its gold decision. There hasn't been time to assimilate it yet but it's clear that it makes a dollar of constant purchasing power possible.

FDR said nothing could make him mad but when I told him the House Judiciary Committee was about to report the bill for Justices' retirement unfavorably, he showed some signs of irritation. Karl Llewellyn had called me to tell me of it Saturday. Ray Moley came in - he had been working on the forthcoming short messages on NRA, Communications, etc., and the President read us several passages from the orders and proclamations he had ready in case of an adverse decision. Ray said he might have some of his language for the time when NRA was declared unconstitutional. Ray went out and I protested at the projected moving of Walton Hamilton to the Labor Board in Willis' place to make way for an A F of L man on NRA. FDR said "Perky wants it" and I told him she ought not to have it. She's playing for A F of L support. He said he wouldn't do anything without talking to me again. I seem to have a bad time keeping Hammie on NRA in spite of - or maybe because of - his value to the cause.

Speaking of the Supreme Court he said he especially hoped one case would get by - that having to do with land condemnation. I told him that unless it did it seemed to me little could be done with a real housing program. Then we got to talking about housing and he indicated that he wanted me to work with him on it. I asked him if that meant my leaving the Department and he said "No, you and I agree too well on agricultural policy and others aren't really in accord." He referred to HAW's constant wish for vanished foreign markets and his unwillingness to go straight through on the course marked out. He told me of a conversation with HAW and Phillips in which they wanted drastic reductions in tariffs on textiles, steel and cement in the Belgium treaty and said he had indicated how that really favored others more than Belgium on account of the generalization the State Department clings to. Consequently it was greatly modified to meet his wishes. I presume it won't amount to much. But he said he asked Hull which he wanted and Hull said only moderate reductions "because he had some political sense left." Still Hull appears in public as the great champion of reductions. It must have been hard for the old gentleman to really face the choice.

In talking again about housing, FDR explained his idea about a board of twelve and one in it for housing of all sorts. I said that farmers' resettlement and his city-to-country settlements were different problems but both had agricultural implications. He asked me if I would take them into the Department and also act as supervisor or coordinator for urban housing. He then drew a little chart as a beginning and said think over it a few days and try to work something out. So today on the train to Chicago to make a speech tonight on economic security I have been all day drawing charts, projecting organization, thinking of personnel and relationships. What will come of it I don't know but I expect I may talk to Ogburn and Hutchins in Chicago.

February 20, 1935
Pittsburgh

Made my speech to the Dentists in Chicago last night; stayed with Will Ogburn and talked with Hutchins this morning. I talked with them confidentially about my resettlement scheme and found them interested. I believe both could be enlisted. Very interesting talk with W.O. about the kind of planning necessary. Asked him to put his mind on it. Nice smooth flight here thru heavy weather. Waiting now to go on to Washington.

February 24, 1935

We flew home in good time from Pittsburgh on Wednesday - 13,000 feet over blizzards all the way but up in the sunshine.

I fell into another Departmental mess. Victor Christgau had been deprived of most of his duties by Davis and had resigned, causing a lot more newspaper talk and more rumors of my resignation. Next day I had a talk with FDR covering a good deal of ground. I asked him to appoint Christgau to the Federal Trade Commission in Matthews' place which belongs traditionally to a Western Progressive. He said he would if I would arrange to have Ryan Duffy (Democratic Senator from Wisconsin) ask him. I got hold of Christgau and he went to a Minnesota Democratic Congressman (Ryan) and got him to get Duffy to ask FDR. The President was leaving for New England for five days so there the thing rests now.

Jerome Frank is fixed in RFC in charge of railroad reorganization, Lee Pressman is in FERA, Shea in SEC, etc. So all those cleared out of AAA in what the papers called a "purge" are now as well fixed as ever. But it leaves AAA committed to the farm leaders' policy of cooperation with the processors and so makes my position pretty impossible.

I submitted my charts and plans to FDR and he approved completely giving me permission to try to get Hutchins as executive and to discuss the thing with Harry Hopkins (which I had already done in a preliminary way, wanting to keep everything straight since I knew he was to be executive secretary of the President's Board. I had had Fred Bartlett make me a chart....

This makes "Resettlement" the generalizing word and draws all these activities into that category. I should plan a council of seven or nine made up of myself, chairman, an executive and the heads of the Corporations.

The President has however been having a bad time with the appropriation bill for all this. There has been a bad fight over the prevailing wage provision vs. a "security wage" to be less than going rates but steady. The AF of L succeeded in combining the reactionary Republicans and the progressives and the President was defeated by one vote in the Senate. The bill has now been recommitted to Committee for strategic reasons and what will happen no one knows exactly. I sat with him in his office as a good deal of the fight went on.

The political situation is interesting just now. Huey Long and Father Coughlin are demagoguing at a great rate and are said to be getting a considerable following. Unfortunately the only support for legislation the President can really count on comes from the reactionary democrats who are held in line as party men; but of course none of them believes in the New Deal program. The Progressives disperse and go off on tangents on every issue. They cannot be counted on for anything. The question is whether this situation will not now stop progress. At dinner last night at Bob LaFollette's I was sharp with him about this Progressive refusal to accept any discipline or leadership - unwillingness to give up any minor point and the consequent appearance of sabotaging the program. I thought he had no good defense. I warned him that it jeopardized everything and might result in a closer association of FDR with the reactionary party men he can count on. This would be tragic for it would mean that all measures would have to be tempered to the reactionary swallowing capacity.

In a long talk with Harold Ickes, yesterday, I found him discouraged and bitter. He has been pretty much left out of all planning for the new works program, has had a fight with Morgenthau who has been trying to capture all government building for his Procurement Division, and has a feeling that several major political mistakes have been made:

1. Farley has been allowed to cut under the Progressives - notably, although this is only an incident - in opposing Cutting for reelection.

2. In keeping Richberg as coordinator resulting in a wrong action against the newspaper guild and in another on the automobile code which went against labor.

3. In letting agriculture be handed over to the processors.

4. In handling the works bill so ineptly.

5. In bringing up the World Court issue at the instance of Hull and Joe Robinson and being badly defeated on it.

These are hard to deny. FDR will have to recoup somehow - but the way is far from clear.

February 27, 1935

With FDR at Hyde Park for five days and with the works bill in cold storage with a deadlock over the prevailing wage amendment, not much has been going on.

I am still concerned by the compact between the Republicans and the left wingers and besides talking to LaFollette have talked to Homer Bone without much result. I should like to suggest to FDR that he try talking turkey to the Progressive group and trying to get a little discipline into the situation but he is not available.

I have been thinking and planning the Resettlement set-up. It now seems clear to me that I had better try to get City Housing out of it on the ground that Ickes' Housing Corporation is progressing and that the others can be logically assimilated to the Department of Agriculture and set up within it.

Hutchins never communicated with me after my phone call so I assume he is turning me down. Paul A. suggests Tom Beck - which is not a bad idea.

Spent the evening with two Western regional land retirement directors last night at Lansill's where I am living for the moment - his family and mine having gone to Florida together.

Rather quiet here. GEF is in Puerto Rico; Bartlett and Baldwin have gone South and West to investigate locations for consolidated federal agriculture stations.

The Christgau affair is progressing. Senator Duffy has written his letter to the President. If nothing happens we may have him on the FTC.

The Wheeler resolution passed the Senate yesterday but I find the Budget Director has written a stiff letter to the House Committee against it. He says he consulted with FDR. This lets me down since FDR helped me support it last year. I must try to fix it up. I certainly would like to see a lively investigation of processors just now.

A letter from Hutchins refuses service. Can't say I blame him.

March 3, 1935

1. I spoke to FDR about the Wheeler resolution. He had forgot what it was about. He had me call Bell to bring it up again and promised to withdraw objection.

2. HAW and I had lunch with the President Friday. We talked over at some length (1) the position of the Progressives and the need for consultation constantly. FDR promised to do something. (2) My Resettlement job. FDR let me off city housing, though he laughed at me for not wanting to do it. I talked to him about satellite cities as an alternative and interested him greatly. My idea is to go just outside centers of population, pick up cheap land, build a whole community and entice people into it. Then go back into cities and tear down slums and make parks of them. I could do this with good heart and he now wants me to.

Yesterday he and I drove to Beltsville and went over the whole property. He was much surprised at its scale and took a great interest in everything. One of his saving qualities is an enormous interest in physical construction and growth.

After thinking over my problem in setting up the Resettlement scheme, I thought (1) of the need for conciliating the agricultural interest (2) of securing continuity with past land and agricultural planning (3) of the need for assimilation to the going Department (4) of the need for an effective executive assistant familiar with settlement problems as well as with government procedure. I then asked Howard Tolley if he would be that executive assistant. It may be a mistake. Some of my friends say he has worked against me in the Department. I think he has been on the other side of all arguments about marketing agreements and has consistently favored processors but we have always worked together amicably on land problems. He is smart, an able executive and has grown up in an agricultural economics atmosphere. Even if he has worked against me it may be well to take him immediately into this work and make use of his abilities in ways I can control. At least I think so. He is thinking it over.

I talked to FDR about actual procedure yesterday and found him ready with an excellent practical suggestion which I outline as follows:

Make contract with firms as follows:

1. We pay all unskilled labor furnished from relief rolls.
2. We meet, once a week, a certified pay roll of necessary skilled men and foremen.
3. All materials must be bought on certification of the Procurement Division which will make general bargains with industries for yearly prices.
4. Figure out a reasonable profit on the job and give it to the firm as a fee.

Approval procedure will be to take projects to board for approval with schedule of costs and expected employment. On approval will be returned for execution. Weekly reports must be furnished showing employment given and general progress made.

Architectural and inspection service must be done by government agencies.

One thing I wanted him to see at Beltsville was the hill to the South of the farm where I would like to build a city for the Resettlement job. He liked it and approved the scheme.

He asked me why we didn't find a better name than Beltsville. I had thought before of naming it the Theobald Smith Research Center. I must attend to this.

Had Chapman and Chardon to dinner at the Cosmos Club and talked Puerto Rican problems. But nothing can be done until the

Appropriation Bill is passed.

March 14, 1935

I gave the President a certain amount of amusement this morning by breaking into a busy day and asking him to read a few pages of Demosthenes. They were from the third Olynthiac and had to do with the uncomplimentary remarks Demosthenes made to the Athenians about accepting doles and listening to demagogues.

I also asked him to repeat to me the story of how he became interested in conservation, telling him that I wanted to use it as part of a speech which I am to make before the American Forestry Association before long; so he told me the whole thing in some detail. He was apparently pleased to have it used in that way.

Yesterday afternoon I talked to Tom Beck about handling the rural industrial community phase of the resettlement program and, rather to my surprise, he indicated that he would do so but said that in order to make his peace with Joe Knapp the President would have to write a letter. So today I prepared such a letter and the President is signing it. This ought to strengthen that part of the work considerably.

The Senate is still dawdling over the works bill but apparently when all the talking is done they will come around to somewhat the same provisions as the bill which we gave them in the first place. The delay is useful for one thing at least: it is giving me time to talk to a great many people about the problems involved and to settle the type of organization which seems best and to assemble at least some of the top personnel. These are, in fact, about the only activities I have been engaged in in the last week except for some conferences with Wallace and Davis on the cotton situation and the wheat program for next year.

I am not yet sure whether Tolley is going to join this enterprise of mine. It is my impression that he has been jockeying to get more control of it than I want him to have and I have told him rather frankly just what his position would be. I think in the end he may not come in which will probably be all right too, except that it may lose me the advantage of some confidence among the farm leaders who view all this kind of thing with some suspicion and perhaps some future trouble with the AAA organization. But I would rather have those problems than disloyalty or withdrawing in an organization for which I am directly responsible.

After thinking it over, it seemed desirable to me to put Lansill in charge of the satellite city phase of the problem and he is already at work on plans for one outside Washington, near Beltsville.

The President has been very dilatory about moving the Soil Erosion Service from the Interior Department to Agriculture, although he knows he has to do it. I know that he had a talk with Bennett and that he has settled in his own mind that it is the thing to do. I told him this morning that I thought he ought to do it very quickly and he promised he would write the letter to Ickes this afternoon. My conception is that nothing more is necessary than a resolution of the Public Works Board, since the Service was set up to use Public Works funds and this is the way the President is planning to handle it.

Among other things I told the President this morning I thought, I said, that he was handling one general situation in the wrong way. I said what we have discussed several times before, that it seemed to me that all human history illustrated the attempt of man to get out of work and that now that we have eight or ten million unemployed we don't seem to know what to do about it; that there is still a morality abroad that people who are unemployed are in a sense bad. I told him that I thought his attitude on this had always been wrong and that his insistence upon putting men to work ought not to be so great but that he ought rather to turn it into the channel of advocating public work of a sort in which the profit motive and individual incentive would play no part. Call it the "Decoration of Civilization" if you like, but it is the only field that is still open because technology has carried us to a point where we can reestablish the production which gave us a high standard of living a few years ago and we should still have perhaps five millions of unemployed. The problem is to divert sufficient income to their support or to the support of useful civilizing works which will give us some more amenities of life but in which nobody could see any profit. I said that the attitude toward our increased productive activities ought to be not that we should restrict production because our efficiency was greater but that we should use our efficiency to its utmost extent and see that the goods got distributed around the community. I said I thought this would call for several changes in general policy and that I wanted him to think about it. He objected strenuously to my implied aspersion on his attempts to put men to work. He said he thought we ought to do a lot of this public work by hand methods. He had just been talking to Mayor LaGuardia about using more hand labor and less machinery. I told him that that reminded me of a story I had heard of two unemployed men who were watching a steam shovel. One said to the other, "If they did not have those damn machines, we would have a job." The other said, "Yes, and if they did it with spoons a lot more people would have jobs." The President said I was just trying to be clever and reduce the thing to an absurdity, but I had evidently made my point, because he was very much disturbed by it.

I said in reply to his criticisms that I was reducing it to an absurdity; but that he evidently shared the same theory as the A F of L whose conception has always been that there is only so much work to be done and that their members ought to have it. I said there is no limit to the amount of work which may be done to improve the community. There is only a limit to the amount which may be done in making suitable goods which people will buy or can buy. Therefore it is entirely legitimate to create work in the sense that you do public improvements which the business system would not undertake; but we ought not to limit the efficiency of work on public works any more than we would limit the efficiency of the work of a factory. There is plenty of work to be done and we ought to use all our contrivance to do it.

We then went on to talk about the farm tenancy bill which has aroused unexpected opposition among the farm leaders, apparently because their clientele consists of prosperous farmers and they object to doing anything for anyone else. Also I presume because they think that their labor supply may be limited or increased in price. I asked him whether he would not have some general conversations with such farm leaders as come in to see him about other matters, and try to win them over to support which he said he would do. There is real hardship in the South among the share croppers, partly as a result of our cotton reduction program and we are in a wholly indefensible position unless we do something such as is contemplated under the Bankhead bill to repair the damage.

March 31, 1935

Several weeks of hectic preparation for the resettlement task have gone by unsatisfactorily with constant uncertainty as to just what the task is to be and therefore how it ought to be done. The Senate cut the bill up unmercifully. It is still in conference with several ambiguous provisions remaining. It was in my interests that the worst bungling was done. The whole submarginal land scheme seems doubtfully included at the moment with question as to land buying, the power really to make rural-industrial communities, etc. I wired to McIntyre yesterday in Miami describing the situation, the President being on the Nourmahal somewhere in Cuban waters.

After much thinking and consultation I know how to set up the organization for what I want to do, considerably modified from my original scheme but still retaining its main features. Tolley is to stay with AAA. I tried to get Tom Beck and got FDR to request his services from Joe Knapp but was refused. I am falling back on L. C. Gray who has been running the submarginal land program. I think we can proceed successfully given a clear law.

Last week I went to Key West and flew back to Clearwater chiefly to see my father whose condition is serious.

Night before last I had dinner at LaFollette's with several Progressive senators and later had a long talk with Byrnes, Rayburn,

Pittman, Moley and Harriman. We talked cotton a good deal. Cotton is very much to the fore with everyone failing to meet the real issues. They want high prices and foreign markets at the same time and refuse to meet the social issue restriction created in the South.

The Bankhead Tenant bill has fallen into a bad state with the Southerners wanting merely to make land loans which are as bad as nothing without planning for economic independence and for supervision of farm management to secure some kind of success.

April 14, 1935

The past two weeks have resulted at least in the passage of what has become familiar to me as Joint Resolution 117. But it was passed in form unsatisfactory for my purposes so that it will necessarily involve considerable interpretation by McCarl and a good deal of legal skullduggery. It turned out that even after most of the emasculating amendments were killed a conference committee really hostile to the bill held things up and refused to make the changes I requested. The President went off on a fishing trip. I wired him and he communicated with Senate leaders but it did no good.

The submarginal land retirement program on which we had a good start with emergency funds will have to be turned around and worked so that each land purchase is done for a specific purpose.

The President signed 117 on the train from Jacksonville and sent me a note to discuss the issues I had informed him of with McCarl, which I have done. It seems to be a question of winning him over to the policies I have in mind - which is a comment on the Comptrollers' function. I have been very full and as persuasive with him as I could. It looks favorable now. I saw the President Friday and talked it all over. We seem about ready to start business as soon as F.D.R. settles on his executive order setting up the general machinery. That is complicated by the jockeying for position between Hopkins and Ickes. Hopkins has been told by FDR that he is to have a central position in the works scheme but Ickes has had control of works funds up to now and is exerting every influence and energy he can command to prevent it. It's no skin off my nose either way so I have kept out.

Soil Erosion Service has now been transferred to Agriculture and I have been busy with its reorganization. It is in bad shape administratively and has a confusion of policy to straighten out. In preparation for this and for my new set-up I have had a land policy committee set up in the Department with M.L. as chairman to coordinate land purchases and policies with respect to all our land treatment which promises to be useful.

The processors have been making another drive on processing

taxes and Davis and Wallace are finding out too late that they will have to fight them. They should have followed the lead I furnished in the Des Moines speech last summer but they lacked the courage then and now they are vulnerable. Davis thought he could use them but they have turned on him as they were bound to do. There is probably a nasty fight over our requested amendments to AAA in which we shall probably be licked.

I have been working a good deal on the Bankhead Tenant bill which, if it were right, could be one of the Administration's greatest achievements. But Bankhead can't see much but a contented and scattered peasantry and is scared of any community reorganization. I should like to foster cooperatives and community enterprises of all sorts. The President supports me mildly but I'm afraid it will be a bad bill when it passes.

April 27, 1935

After several days of uncertainty about just what the President was going to do concerning the Works Program, there was a meeting last night at the White House. There were present Frank Walker, Harry Hopkins, Secretary Ickes, Charles West, Joe Kennedy, Dan Bell, Henry Morgenthau and myself. The meeting lasted from about 8:30 until about midnight. First the President ran over for us the situation which had been developing thru the press releases during the last four days in which he had set up the machinery for works relief. Essentially the machinery he has in mind consists of three parts: first, the Application and Information Division, as he calls it, in charge of Frank Walker; second, there is what he calls the Allotment Board of which Ickes will be the Chairman; and third, what he calls the Progress Division of which Harry Hopkins will be in charge. This means that projects will flow in thru Walker to be turned over to the Allotment Board and then be executed by the Progress Division. Really I should say that the Allotment Division will be more or less formal and that the real work will be done by Harry Hopkins and his outfit.

The President announced simultaneously that about sixty governmental agencies would form the operating divisions for the works set-up. Of these only three were new, one of them being my Resettlement endeavor. He told us all this at the beginning of the meeting as though we had not read the papers and we then went on to discuss various questions which would be raised concerning it. He first gave us a long lecture on how important it was that this thing should be a success. He said that he had committed himself to the thing, that it meant a great deal to all of us, politically, and that it meant a great deal to the American people as well. The success of the thing, he said, would depend on execution and he expected to be extremely hard-boiled about that. By that he meant there would be a regular check-up of success in operations, and that we were to be expected to say when we estimated for a project how much money would be spent and how much employment would be given, and what the rate of progress would be from month to month. For this, he said, we would be held accountable and he would be extremely rigorous in his follow up of the whole thing. In general, he said, he would demand that all projects should be finished by July 1st, 1936 but he indicated that a great many would have to be undertaken which could not be of that sort. There was more flexibility about that, he indicated, than about many other things. He then said that the labor regulations and all things having to do with operations would be determined by Harry Hopkins' Progress Division. There was then a consideration discussion of the relations of projects to actual employment. One of the difficulties he sees here is that we should have to spend about half the funds available within a short distance of three or four large cities if we were to completely relieve unemployment. Those cities are, of course, New York, Detroit, Chicago and Los Angeles but we cannot afford to say that for political effect and, as a matter of fact, it is probable that some labor will be drained away to other districts by projects being started there. This matter of making the progress of projects undertaken run with unemployment will make great difficulty for all of us who are administrators, because it is necessary to look ahead in planning for considerable length of time, and if we undertake a project which then has to be stopped because labor is exhausted or for some other reason, it will make it very awkward and inconvenient. All such things as this remain to be worked out, apparently just as they did at the beginning of the other Public Works program. Many of these difficulties we went over at that time but we seem to have learned very little by the experience.

I rode home with Harold Ickes and we were talking all this over. We both remarked that the experience we had had on the Public Works Board seemed to be in process of being completely repeated here.

There was a good deal of discussion of the problem of establishing self-liquidation but without much result. That remains still to be settled in the future.

Nothing was touched directly on the two problems which are bothering me most. The first of these problems has to do with whether or not the Rural Rehabilitation work is to be carried forward as a project or whether it is to be given funds which are to be flexible as they are in the Relief Administration. I do not see how this Rural Rehabilitation work, which apparently I am expected to take over, can be carried on by the project method altogether. The other problem which concerns me most is the extent to which the President expects us to develop our housing projects. I have never got clearly in mind just how much emphasis he expects to put on them but I suppose that, along with other things, will be revealed during the next week.

The way in which the Bill was passed makes it difficult for all of us to operate. The reactionary Democratic Senators intended, apparently, to make it difficult for us and they certainly did. Of course, the worst handicap under this program will be old difficulty of finding work to do which does not compete with private industries in ways which will bring terrible pressures and reactions against us as we try to work. There was a little discussion of this last night but it did not go far. I raised the question of whether it would not be better to pick out certain fields in which we would operate and concentrate on those, letting it be known that we would not interfere in others. Joe Kennedy chipped in and said a good word for the public utility industries. I said, yes, but this was negative and perhaps we ought not go too far in building power plants but what ought we to do? I asked whether he would consider housing an appropriate field and he, being rather at a loss at the moment, said yes, he thought it would but I am sure Kennedy feels that way. The President stepped in to defend his power policy and indicated that he rather thought that we ought to go ahead with a good many power projects. We told him that this did not seem to fit with his notion of getting projects completed by July 1st, 1936 and this caused him to back up on that principle. I talked with him a little bit privately about what I was to do with rural rehabilitation and how difficult it would be to make that conform to his project system. He said he would talk with me about that later, so that it remains at the present time in a rather unsettled state. Of course part of this difficulty is also due to the fact that Harry Hopkins and I have been talking over the matter for some time past, and we have been uncertain whether I ought to take over all of rural rehabilitation or only that part of it which has to do with the building of communities. I came to the conclusion some time ago that the only satisfactory way to do it, although I would prefer to have it another way perhaps, is to take over the whole business and to reorganize it but to go on using his rural rehabilitation corporations which are of course organized and in being, though many of them I am inclined to think are rather inefficient. They are organized under state laws, having on the Board of Directors as the relief administrator usually somebody from the agricultural college, and several prominent citizens. Their stock is pledged with Harry Hopkins which he has felt kept them sufficiently under his control. They have served to do a number of things in the rural areas of the state, all the way from building communities down to furnishing a mule for an individual farmer or fixing up his barn, or something which would put him on his feet. This whole problem still remains to be settled.

There is also the problem coming along of drought relief because it begins to look as though the year of 1935 will be a great deal like the year 1934. There have been dust storms all spring; the winter wheat crop in Oklahoma and in eastern Colorado is already ruined, and it looks as though the drought might extend up into the Dakotas. If it does we shall have to undertake another emergency program similar to that of last year. The AAA has already released its restrictions on spring wheat planting, and we are considering releasing also the farmers who are under contract for corn acreage. What effect this will have on the whole agricultural adjustment program still remains to be seen.

The problem of cotton continues to be the most acute one. It has a number of phases. The South simply cannot bring itself to realize that it faces either low priced cotton which can sell in the world market, or high priced cotton which will be confined to the domestic market. This makes a difference of some five to six million bales in the production and if we permanently reduce the production to only the domestic requirements, it means that about half the people in the South will have to change their occupation to something else, and no one so far has had any foresight about this. This situation is also complicated by the fact that mechanical cotton pickers seem to be immediately in the offing. This will throw more people out of work. My rural rehabilitation program if conceived in the right way, in the long run we should step into this situation and reorganize the agriculture of the South so that there could be something to do for the people who will be thrown out of employment by the reduction in cotton and by the new efficiencies in agriculture. But I am not sure that anybody else sees the program in the same way or with the appropriate foresight. It remains to be seen what can be done. I still have to have a considerable talk with the President about this, although I am inclined to think from my conversations with him in the past, that he sees it much the same way that I do.

There has been a vigorous attack on the whole adjustment program in recent weeks by the New England and Southern mill operators in an attempt to get the processing tax removed. This happens every year at about this time because the industry is overequipped and over capitalized and the attempt is made to blame somebody whenever a stoppage occurs. The attack seems to have reached its worst point at the present time. All of us, including the Secretary and myself, are being denounced by New England mill operators and by Southern reactionary Senators. It will probably blow over this time but I am not sure whether the processing tax can be saved in the long run or not.

I have gone ahead in the last few days planning for my organization. My executive order setting up my resettlement organization has been prepared and the President has told me to clear it with Dan Bell, the Director of the Budget and with McCarl the Comptroller. I cleared it with Bell and it is now in the Comptroller's office in process of being cleared there. I had hoped to have it cleared up today but so far nothing has happened. I am anxious to get the executive order settled so that I can actually put people on the payroll and go to work. I think I am fortunate in having Gene Agger agree to come down Monday and go to work.and take some of the burden off my shoulders. I think I shall make him head of what I shall call the Management Division which will take over the management of communities after they have been built by the two operating divisions with Gray on the rural side and Lansill on the satellite city side.

April 29, 1935

I had a talk with the President this morning. I made the appointment in the expectation that the executive order setting up the Resettlement Administration would be ready to be signed. It had to be cleared with Justice, however, and consequently it did not get there in time. We did talk over a number of things. For instance, the President made it perfectly clear that he expected me to take over Subsistence Homesteads from the Interior Department and we talked some about how it might be worked into my organization. I told him that my plan would be to merge it with my organization almost completely and to put everybody on notice when they came over here that they would need to be reengaged. This will be a headache but my objections went for nothing.

We also talked with Rural Rehabilitation and the President agreed that it ought all to be turned over to me instead of dividing it as Harry and I had intended to do a little earlier, he keeping the relief phases and I taking what might be called the community phases. Harry and I have talked this over in recent days and Harry seems to agree that this is the thing to be done. I feel rather pleased about it because I think that it will save a great deal of administrative confusion in the field and that if I can get Will Alexander to administer it we can have a set-up with which we can go ahead to do a great number of things.

Into this set-up the Bankhead Bill, if it is passed, will also fit and we can go ahead with the rehabilitation of a great many communities, and operate in a great many situations that we could not otherwise do. We have had considerable trouble about space and I have finally come to the conclusion that it will be necessary to build a temporary building, either at Beltsville or at Arlington Farms of the Department. I talked this over with the President this morning and he agreed that perhaps I had better go ahead and build a temporary building. I also talked to him about politics and appointments and told him that frankly I expected to make all my most important people myself without any outside interference. He agreed to this. I then said that so far as politics was concerned, we could afford to let political consideration enter the lower classes of jobs and told him that I would handle it through Julian Friant as we had handled

similar departmental matters in the past. To this he agreed completely.
We talked at great length about the problem of working my
particular organization into the project system which he has outlined for
the general work of the Works Board. I explained that rural rehabilitation
was a continuing thing, that it would be difficult to make a project of
every little rehabilitation effort, and he agreed that the thing to do was
to estimate the number of people and the kind of work and the cost for
several months ahead and present that as a project.

We also talked at considerable length about the problem of buying
sites for our satellite cities. I told him that if I had to send the projects
through for preliminary approval with the sites known and without any
options or without owning the land, that it might be very difficult to get
the land after that because everybody would be on notice and real estate
speculators might prevent us from doing the thing that we want to do.
He agreed to give me enough money as administrative expenses so that
we could go ahead and either buy the site or option it verbally so that
when a project is presented to the project board it can be with the option
attached and therefore no real estate speculation will be possible and the
chief problem, which is one of land buying, will be solved in advance.

We talked also about the problem of Chapman Field which has
been a subject of controversy between the Department of Agriculture and
the War Department for some time. The President wants to give us
Chapman Field for tropical plant development but the War Department
is objecting. We agreed to let it go until after Congress is adjourned and
then take the matter up.

The legal work involved in settling our executive order is going
forward as fast as can be expected. Pressman is doing a wonderful job in
clearing all these legal matters. Our executive orders have to be cleared
thru three agencies: the Comptroller General, the Attorney General, and
the Director of the Budget. But this is not so difficult as it seemed to me
when we first entered on the task.

On Saturday night I went to the White House press
correspondents' dinner. It was rather amusing. Perhaps the most
amusing feature from my point of view was that Ray Moley and I sat on
either side of old Bert Snell, the Republican leader from New York, and
we had a rather hilarious time all evening with him.

I had breakfast with Ray Moley yesterday morning, it being
Sunday, and then we came over to my office and worked for several hours
on the President's radio speech which he made last night. We didn't
succeed in changing the speech as much as we would have liked and I
thought it was one of his poorest speeches but it did bring out certain
things which was necessary at the present time and perhaps it will have
a good public effect.

A considerable change seems to be coming over Washington after the confusion and hesitancy of the last few weeks. Everyone seems to have taken new courage now that the works relief set-up has been determined. Congress seems to be going along a little faster and I think that things are going to straighten out very rapidly from now on. The general talk about the country that the administration has been loose and that the President has been losing the confidence of the people seems to have stopped to a great extent. I think this current depression politically is very much like that which happened in October a year ago and that the President is bound to be stronger than ever once it is over.

This noon I had lunch with John Coss and Tommy Blaisdell and Frank Tannenbaum. We talked over the Bankhead Bill and the possibilities under the resettlement program. This is the first thing I have found John Coss enthusiastic about what I have done since I came to Washington. I asked Tannenbaum to call up Will Alexander and find that he will be here on Wednesday. Agger went to work this morning so that the four heads of my organization are now settled and will be at work before the end of the week. I hope that things are going forward adminstratively from now on in a much better way. The past few weeks have been pretty trying, what with all the waiting and uncertainty, but it looks now as though we might get to work soon.

May 2, 1935

There continues to be a good deal of confusion surrounding the set-up for the administration of the Public Works Bill. The chief difficulty is that everyone at the present time to be jockeying for position and to have a desire to control the whole works so far as possible. This is particularly true of Harry Hopkins and Ickes and Henry Morgenthau in the Treasury. So far as my own set-up is concerned I have wanted to avoid all this, and so was anxious to have the President set up my Resettlement Administration as an independent agency, in advance of the beginning of the allocation of funds. Yesterday morning I got him to sign an executive order which set up my agency to be called the Resettlement Administration. Yesterday afternoon there was a meeting of the same group which met at the White House the other evening and I found that Henry Morgenthau had been to the President apparently and protested against my having been set up in advance. The President did not raise that question but he did raise the question of giving me ten million dollars for administrative expenses and after a great deal of argument cut it down to two hundred and fifty thousand dollars which somebody had told him would be sufficient for a month. Of course it will not and I was stopped from saying very much in the meeting because I could not tell how much the President intended to turn over to me and could not say anything in the presence of Ickes about Subsistence Homesteads nor in the presence

of Hopkins about Rural Rehabilitation, neither of which questions have
been finally settled as yet. So I was caught in a perfectly impossible
situation and am still in that situation. My contention is that my agency
should be thought of as an independent agency just like any department
of the government and that I should not have to go to an allotment board
or anything of the sort for administrative funds. There is no objection to
justified projects, but so far as administrative expenses are concerned, I
think that is another question and a matter which ought to be settled
between the President and myself and not through the submission of a
budget to any administrative board. How this matter may be settled I do
not know but unless I can operate independently so far as the control of
my administration is concerned I am not interested in going on.

There is still a great deal of confusion; nobody seems to know just
exactly what his duties are and we are unable to get started, although the
public thinks that everything is going on. This is later in the day on May
2nd. I have just had a long conversation both with Alexander and with
Lawrence Westbrook. My first idea was in taking over Rural
Rehabilitation that Alexander should head this organization and replace
Westbrook. On thinking over the delicate relations which have been
established by the state corporations to carry out the rehabilitation policy,
it seems to me best to keep Westbrook at this work for some time to come
at least. Then came the problem of using Alexander whom I am anxious
to have in my organization. He is a strong man and knows the South
particularly well and is used to large plans. It has occurred to me that I
might use him as Assistant Administrator. I talked to Alexander on this
tentative basis. I told him that I had not yet talked to Hopkins or
Westbrook about taking over Rural Rehabilitation but that it seemed to
me that perhaps we might use Westbrook and that he might be my alter
ego so to speak and administrator here and help me with the large
problems of diplomatic relationships and in the general administration of
the set-up, if that was agreeable. My conversation with Westbrook ran
along these lines. He said that he had been told by Hopkins that Rural
Rehabilitation was to be handed over to me and that he was over here to
make whatever adjustments necessary. I said he had been so involved in
the organization that he really almost belonged to him personally and that
it was too bad to separate him from it violently. He said that Hopkins
intended to use him in some other capacity and he felt that the intention
was to separate him completely. I said then that I would have a talk with
Hopkins which I am to do later on in the day. Westbrook's attitude was
very good. We talked over various administrative problems involved.

I find another problem arising in that the Secretary is apparently
still worried about the relationship of this Resettlement Administration
with the Department of Agriculture. He has said nothing to me about it
but apparently has talked to LeCron and Baldwin and is rather upset. He

seems to think that there are chances of great difference of opinion in the future and that they might become abrasive between him and myself over this new set-up. I had thought that all those problems were ironed out a month ago and he has seemed to be quite resigned to the situation since but somebody seems to have excited him again - Tolley and Davis probably. This simply makes another diplomatic situation to be straightened up as fast as possible.

This has been a very full day with many happenings which have had to do with the future both of the Resettlement Administration and with the Department of Agriculture, and I hope, with the welfare of the whole rural population of the United States.

I lunched with Frank Walker and we talked at some length over the various problems. I told him that I was very much disconcerted by the prospect that I might have to go to a board to ask for administrative expenses for what was really a continuing organization and explained to him my thought that what happened was that I had got caught in a kind of a struggle for power among Hopkins, Ickes, Secretary Morgenthau and the Comptroller General and it just happened that the various cases with which I was concerned had come up first. He said he realized that and that he would be willing to help me out and see to it that my administrative expenses did not have to come before a whole board for allotment every time.

I sent Baldwin over to have a talk with Bell and Bell evidently was very much surprised by the specific way in which we could present the job we have to do. In fact, I think our organization is better prepared to go to work than any of the others now undertaking this public work stuff. Walker himself is very confused about his duties as is Hopkins.

I had another talk with Gray and Alexander this afternoon and it seemed to be their impression that it would be better if we did not have Westbrook go on with the rural rehabilitation work. I said that it looked as though we should not be able to get him anyway and had thought for some time about who I should get. I understand that the Secretary has been rather concerned for fear that the Eastern viewpoint would dominate the work of this administration as well as being concerned about its relations to the Department in general. Of course it is true that it is unusual for the Under Secretary of the Department to be given an administration of his own and still to remain Under Secretary. It is a very peculiar relationship and I can understand how a Secretary might feel that he has been rather overlooked in the matter. Still I have talked with him this afternoon to try to smooth things over and try to get him to suggest someone to me from the Middle West to take Westbrook's place, if Westbrook should not come into the new administration as I feel now he probably will not. A few weeks ago it happened I was visited by a very pleasant and liberal gentleman from the state of Arkansas. His name was

Brooks Hayes. He was very much interested in the share-cropper situation which I hope the Resettlement Administration will go pretty far to help solve. He talked to me in a way no one from that state and that region has talked to me yet, calling attention to the way in which the landlords exploited the share-croppers, how there was very little liberal sentiment in those states but that there was some which might be mobilized. I had a long talk with him at that time and I was very much interested in him as a person and in his point of view. It occurs to me now that he might be the person to send for to take Westbrook's place. I had a confirmation from another source about him. Francis Miller was in today asking me to make a speech in Atlanta in the middle of June and said that he had just been at a meeting in Atlanta at which he had met Brooks Hayes and spoke of him as a very liberal person and an unusual person to find coming from Arkansas. I think if everything goes well and if I find that Westbrook is satisfied in staying outside the administration and staying with Hopkins that I may send for Brooks Hayes. In case I do find someone who is capable and willing to take up the rural rehabilitation work and I should make a successful division between the work Gray has been doing and the work which would be done by the rural rehabilitation section of a personal sort, I shall communicate with Hayes as to what his situation is.

I talked this afternoon with a delegation of Farmer Union people from northern Wisconsin. I had Gray and Alexander in to listen to their story. It was the familiar story of heavy debt and of overburdened farmers, about fifty percent of whom in a number of Wisconsin counties are on relief, and of ways in which the situation might be met. I was very much impressed by their story and by their personalities. It seemed to me that rural rehabilitation would be in safe hands if it were in hands like theirs, but their report is that rural rehabilitation is carried on by people who are more sympathetic with the gentleman farmers than they are with the dirt farmers or with people who are under disadvantage and really need help. I suspect that this is true in more cases than Wisconsin and this is one of the things which I hope our administration will be able to fix up. I asked them to send me in some recommendations and I very much hope that they will.

I also had a talk with several congressmen from Oklahoma including a delegation of other people from that State. The drought situation there is very bad, and it is difficult to see what can be done. I explained to them that under the bill which we are operating it will be difficult for us to allocate more than a proportionate amount to the State of Oklahoma even though there are a great many farmers who are suffering from disadvantages for the reason that our allocation from this appropriation will have to be apportioned according to the unemployment. Now a great many farmers in Oklahoma may not be in the classification of unemployment but there is a great emergency there because of the dust storms and because of the serious situation the farmers will be in for more than a year. I pointed out that last year Congress gave a specific appropriation; in fact they passed a five hundred million dollar drought relief bill, and said that rather than expect an apportionment board to be sympathetic to Oklahoma farmers, it would be safer for them to have a special legislation of a drought relief sort. They seemed to be satisfied with this and went away, I thought, with the notion of starting something in Congress. I very much hope that they will because the situation there is really terrible and there is very little that an administrative agency can do, especially the Department of Agriculture because we have no funds to call on and the situation is such that we are going to go before an allocation board and ask for everything that we get. And there we shall always be confronted by the necessity in sight, and it will always be more difficult to get something for farmers off relief than for those on relief.

May 5, 1935

Governor Phil LaFollette and his brother Bob called on me yesterday concerning a plan which they have cooked up to use all Public Works funds under the direction of the state of Wisconsin. The plan is interesting from a number of points of view and has a lot of complications. Whether the Federal Government ought to turn over all its powers in these respects to the states is a grave governmental question which I think ought to be considered at considerable length. They had talked to the President about it the day before and the President had expressed great interest. In fact he had practically directed Frank Walker to have an allotment ready on this basis to be acted on by next Tuesday. It seems that the plan may go thru. One of the difficulties, of course, is that if all Public Works funds were handed over to be expended under state direction the Federal interest there might not be protected and also it would upset all our plans for Federal management of these funds thru such national services as the Forest Service, and the Soil Conservation Service. Still these things do not worry me so much as general governmental question which is involved. Politically it is good to hand over to the LaFollette's this sum to spend; but suppose Huey Long asked to do it in Louisiana or Gene Talmadge in Georgia. That might be a different matter. It is clear that there will be similar attempts of this kind to get in on the works funds by many localities. LaGuardia, speaking for the Conference of Mayors, for instance, has asked the President that all funds be given to the cities as grants rather than as loans spent under city direction. Also Alexander Fleisher, whom I have not seen for years, called on me yesterday, coming as a representative of the State Planning Board of Pennsylvania. They had a similar plan although it did not go so far as that of LaFollette. All they asked was that all federal funds allocated in the state of Pennsylvania be spent only when approved by the State Planning Board. The LaFollette scheme is simply to set up a state finance corporation which would be made up of directors selected largely by the Governor. This state finance corporation would take the responsibility of spending first, a grant of a hundred million dollars which would be the approximate state quota if Public Works funds were divided up on a state basis, plus another hundred million which would be loaned to the state and for which the government would take obligations and that these obligations would be paid off thru taxes raised in the state of Wisconsin, half by localities and half by the state direct. The thing has so many governmental and political complications I expect we shall hear a great deal more about it later.

Yesterday I also had a talk with Berle and he stayed to lunch with me. We discussed the state of the world and of the nation at considerable length. I am always glad to talk to him. He has made a very successful job of New York and his mind ranges over a great variety of subjects in a most fertile way.

Respecting the administrative set-up which we are trying to complete for the Resettlement Administration, I had another long talk with Westbrook and found that he would be amenable to joining our organization with some modification in his duties. I had thought that he would be very resistant to dividing up the kind of work he is doing now, which includes not only rural rehabilitation in the individual sense, but also the construction of a great many communities. This community work it is my desire to hand over to Gray's division along with all land planning and all activities which have to do with the supervision of farm management. There are, however, at the present time a hundred and fifty thousand families being taken care of by the Rural Rehabilitation organization practically on an individual basis and this work has to go on. This I think Westbrook could undertake successfully because he is so sympathetic and so familiar with the situation. I went further with him asking whether he would not prepare an estimate for me based on the number of families actually in need in rural areas and represented by relief rolls as indicating the job really needing to be done during the next year; that is, it would be a provisional budget for rural rehabilitation. He said that he would have this prepared. It is my intention then to take this to the President and say to him: "Here is the job which needs to be done in this particular field. I hesitate to take the responsibility for deciding what percentage of this actually shall be done and what percentage shall be put off. It seems to me that you must give me an answer concerning this." Having got such an answer I can then set up projects to be sent thru in the regular fashion which will conform with the general standards the President has in mind.

May 7, 1935

There are a few notes to record yesterday's happenings. In the first place, yesterday was the day Senator Cutting was killed in an air plane accident. I did not know Jim Cutting so well as Bob Lafollette. He had been very friendly to me, however, and was one of the people who came up to me after the hearing in the Senate last spring and expressed his confidence and belief in me, and we had numerous talks. I have also had occasion to bring him and Eccles together recently, spending a delightful evening and we got rather well acquainted. Although I did not know him ultimately I feel as though I had lost a good friend and I am sure the country has lost a really great statesman, one of very few in the Senate. I heard of his death just after I had put his name down as one of the people I should like to have on my Advisory Council for Resettlement.

The administrative problems are gradually being cleared up. This morning there was published the Executive Order covering the Application and Information Division, the Allotment Division, and the Works Progress Administration. It finally appears to the public, I think, that Hopkins is really to direct most of the work.

For my own Administration I have set up a departmental advisory committee to keep relations straight with the Department of Agriculture which is always going to be a rather difficult problem. For an Under secretary to be head of an independent administration which is yet closely related to the Department is a very unusual governmental proceeding and it will require a great deal of diplomatic effort on my part to keep all our relations straight with the Department. In order to further this I have appointed a committee with Milton Eisenhower as chairman and including Tolley, Warburton, Strong, and Ezekiel to give advice on administrative matters and on departmental relationships. I have also in mind to request the President to appoint what might be called a Resettlement Council which will include several Senators, several Representatives, several prominent citizens and some farm leaders, to act somewhat in the way in which the Forest Reservation Commission acts for the Forest Service and to give us a body of informed legislative opinion which may be a source of strength as we go on.

As a matter of fact it seems to me that the work we are supposed to do is almost bound to be unpopular in the long run. What we shall have to do is to help out the poorest class of citizens and to do this we shall always be helping the shiftless and unfortunate in all local communities. It has been my experience that for these people, especially in small town rural areas, there is very little public sympathy. They are regarded as lazy and shiftless; their children are not well dressed and are rather looked down on by the community. I am afraid that what might be called a good citizen will always be against these efforts we are making. It must be one of our first considerations to try always to conciliate public opinion so that we may go ahead in the effort to lift the level of living of these people.

I was supposed to have had lunch with the Secretary yesterday and the two LaFollette's. Bob did not come because he was busy with arrangements made necessary by Cutting's death, but M. L. Wilson came in and he, the Secretary, Phil LaFollette, and I all had lunch together.

I have had some very interesting conversations with Phil LaFollette. I find him a really brilliant mind and I should be surprised if he is not an equally brilliant administrator. He comprehends all the problems in government and understands economic questions very well. He has a feeling that the main policies of the New Deal have led to a kind of economic contraction, when expansion was really necessary, and his defense of carrying the matter back to the states in the way I have suggested he wants to, is that if we go back there the procession of expansion will start there, whereas special interests will always prevent it here in Washington. I am not so sure about this but it is a thought well worth considering.

Yesterday Senator Bankhead came down to see me. The Bankhead Bill, so-called, or the Farmers Home Corporation, is still on the Senate calendar and is being considered by an executive session of his committee today. Senator Bankhead has been seeing that all this resettlement work has been turned over to me and he comes with a proposition to revise his bill so that all the activities which are now in the Resettlement Administration may be included. The argument in favor of letting him do this is that it furnishes a permanent set-up whereas this Administration is only set up under emergency law and will presumably disappear when the law runs out. The argument against it is that the bill will probably not be an awfully good one if passed this session and also that the administrative set-up is a board which includes the Secretary of Agriculture and the Governor of the Farm Credit Administration, ex officio, together with three members to be appointed by the President, which would not be so good an administrative device as we have in the Resettlement Administration with me responsible only to the President. However, I am in the dilemma that the Bill may pass anyway and if it does there would be a duplication of the activities which I intend to carry on. I think I must make a compromise with him and in order to do that I have asked Lee Pressman to draft suggested changes to the Bankhead Bill which would make it satisfactory from the point of view of the things which this Administration intends to do. Bankhead was very conciliatory and offered to try to get in almost anything we wanted. Whether he can or not remains to be seen. Legislative history of the Bankhead bill up to now is not very good. There is an expressed desire to resettle farmers only on individual farms and only individual ownership. The problem of building up communities is a very difficult one under any legislation which may be passed at this time. There is also the matter of marginal land retirement in which many of us are very much interested. It was completely left out of the works bill and seems to have no sentiment behind it in the Congress. So I think we might have great difficulty in getting an amendment to the Bankhead bill which would include this activity. But Bankhead offered to try and I think in good faith, and perhaps we can work together.

May 9, 1935

Day before yesterday the first meeting of the Allotment Advisory Committee was held in the Cabinet Room with the President present and with Ickes presiding. It was a long meeting with the President making an introductory speech and many general policies discussed but with very little concrete result. The reason for lack of results up to now is the political cross-currents and the general struggle for power which is going on. The announcements up to now make it fairly clear that Harry Hopkins and Frank Walker are really charged with making the Works Program work. With Ickes presiding, he was, of course, anxious to put across a number of his Public Works projects but they were very generally smothered. Harry's obvious effort is to think in terms of three and a half million men off the relief roll going to work with four billion dollars to do the job with. This, of course, means roughly a little over a thousand dollars a man which is very little, which makes it very difficult to think in terms of any large construction projects. Those of us who have jobs to do naturally want to get our construction jobs done but there does remain the problem of putting three and a half million men to work which we cannot dodge. I myself have been impressed with the necessity of determining some large issues before the Works Program is undertaken, such as really dividing up the funds in an earmarking way and discovering what the function of each agency will be actually in putting people to work. Our own job in the Resettlement Administration divides itself into three parts very nicely. The first is the suburban towns with which Jack Lansill is charge, the second is the rural rehabilitation program with Westbrook in charge, and the third is the general land and resettlement program for rural people with Gray in charge. The one likely to suffer most from the test of number of dollars per man is Gray's program because there is so much land buying involved.

One of the unsettled problems which has been bothering me a great deal also is the expense of the rural rehabilitation program. There are actually some nine hundred thousand families of a rural nature who are not on relief. The question is how much responsibility we have for these nine hundred thousand families. The President seemed quite settled in his determination to get rid of relief so that these nine hundred thousand families would presumably go on work-relief and this means the devising of a works program in country districts with very low material costs which will put them to work. The dilemma here is that not very much work of a worthwhile sort can be thought of in those terms.

In an attempt to get some answer to these questions I asked for an appointment with the President yesterday and he asked me to lunch. It was a very interesting conversation. We lunched on the porch and talked over a great many general problems as well as my own specific problems. He seems to feel that I ought to have the responsibility for all the rural people and, if so, this means a great job, much bigger than I had expected to do.

Walker and Hopkins have been going around gathering up the expectations of the various agencies who would do the spending of this money and devise the projects and adding them up to find what their expectations are and what the ratio of dollars to work would be. The army engineers want two hundred and fifty million dollars and other agencies similar amounts, which would put very few people to work. When it is all added up it is clear that with about three quarters of the money spent not half the people would be put to work. This kind of thing will not, of course, answer the problem.

Last night we had a dinner at which I had all my chiefs together with Frank Walker, Harry Hopkins, and General Wood, and we attempted to see where our program lay in these terms. It lies part way between the war engineers large construction job, Ickes' large Public Works, and the C.W.A. of Hopkins. It is better by the test of putting people to work for few dollars than most of the other projects, but it is not so good as it might have been. Of course, one of the problems here is the buying of land which substantially raises the material costs to a very high level. We are committed to go on with the land program which Hopkins recognizes and I think some concession will be made for that. There is also the fact that the rural rehabilitation program keeps people off relief, which is an argument in its favor although it does not actually take people now on the relief rolls off them. The upshot of our conversation was that we agreed this morning to take hypothetical programs at three levels, seven hundred, six hundred, five hundred million dollars, and try to manipulate it so that we will have the general kinds of projects which will put people to work for the least number of dollars. That effort we shall undertake today.

I found yesterday that the President feels about as I do that European war is likely to happen within a few years and that this complicates our international situation very greatly. We also talked about the results of the Supreme Court decision the other day on the railway pension act which was declared unconstitutional on the grounds of too large delegation of power and which we both agreed will probably mean that the Courts will declare the NRA Act unconstitutional in the pending case. If this is so I pointed out that we have a campaign issue for the President's campaign which is really ready-made. We shall have to ask for a constitutional amendment and get a mandate on it and it seems to me that a better campaign issue could not be devised. I thought, however, that this would immediately separate the sheeps from the goats; that is to say, the conservative Democrats would certainly join up with conservative Republicans. Still if we are to extend what we have called the New Deal, there seems to be no way out of a constitutional amendment which would prevent a reactionary Court from stopping our further progress.

May 19, 1935

On Sunday, May 12th, I worked all morning on the speech to be made in Albany on Wednesday. I have been working on this speech for some time. The anniversary of the founding of the Adirondack State Park was the occasion for the speech and what I wanted to do was to put conservation in something of a new light. As I worked Sunday morning what I was trying to do suddenly became clear and I knew that I was trying to redefine conservation so as to include conservation of people as well as of forests, wild life and water.

On Thursday afternoon I left and went up to New York, Lansill going with me. We spent the evening with Ray Moley at the St. Regis and I had a long talk with him about the confused situation of public works and the difficulties of getting it started, urging him to do what he could to get an executive committee appointed which would make it easier to work. We also talked at breakfast the next morning and I outlined to him my notion that the campaign in 1936 ought to be run on the issue of a constitutional amendment, making it possible for the federal government to enter onto the determination of standards for social security as well as control of commerce which the Supreme Court with Judge Roberts sitting in the middle between our right and left wings seems determined to construe literally, making it impossible for intrastate commerce to be interfered with. Moley was very much interested and I noticed that he had pointed out the issue in an editorial in "Today" the week before. I urged on him, however, that some of the difficulties would be very great. For instance, the Frankfurter-Brandeis group will not want any extension of federal power and will oppose an amendment which permits it. I outlined again my favorite theory that the technique of large-scale industry makes it necessary for us to have social institutions which will enclose and implement it. The Brandeis people believe in small-scale enterprise and the use of taxation to force it. I think this is derived from that and that it would be very dangerous for the government to assent to such a theory.

Lansill and I subsequently went to Rockefeller Center to see Frank Lloyd Wright's exhibition of his model city called "Broadacres." We found it very interesting. That afternoon we went to Albany and that evening made my speech. It was a very tiring occasion. The room was small and the crowd was big; I did not speak until last, after Graves, Pinchot and Moses had spoken, but the speech went pretty well although I was very tired. Took the sleeper to New York; got up very early and took the plane back to Washington, arriving here at about nine-thirty.

In the succeeding days there has been a great deal of work setting up the administration of the Resettlement Administration. Most of the problems which are immediate for me are, I think, on the way to solution. For instance, I have Karl Taylor to take Westbrook's place in Rehabilitation, and have an agreement between all the heads of my divisions as to where the lines of their operations fall. This has taken many conferences and a great deal of work and I am feeling rather satisfied just at the moment.

On Thursday at a meeting of the Advisory Allotment Committee a hundred million dollars was set aside for the work of the Resettlement Administration, although projects have to be submitted to a sub-committee for approval. I have been urging Hopkins, Walker and others to do more of this earmarking. The problem which Hopkins faces, which I think I have outlined before, is that of putting three and a half million people to work with four billion dollars which is an average of eleven hundred and forty dollars apiece. The earmarkings on Thursday were for about a billion dollars for large projects all of them costing a great deal per man, leaving very little for the rest of us and added pressure for kinds of projects cost very little per man per year. I am faced with the necessity of finding two hundred million dollars to care for rural rehabilitation for the year before any projects are undertaken of a very constructive sort. I also am trying to show that the Forest Service, Soil Conservation Service, Land Development and Resettlement work are good projects which ought to be supported with these funds. I find Hopkins sympathetic and Walker becoming educated but Ickes pays very little attention. I have hopes that these earmarkings will be completed in a few days.

The business operations in our administration are being set up very rapidly. We are putting on personnel and I hope to be ready to operate by the time the situation with respect to the funds to be allotted is cleared. The chiefs of my operations divisions now include: Lansill, for Suburban Towns, Agger for the Management Division, Taylor for Rural Rehabilitation and Resettlement, and Gray for Land Development and

Resettlement from submarginal areas. Besides this, Lee Pressman is General Counsel and Baldwin is my Business Manager. Alexander has turned up the first of the week and is now Assistant Administrator. I hope to get a great deal of help from him. But all this has taken many conferences and a great deal of tiring work and I find myself pretty well exhausted by now.

The Subsistence Homesteads Division was transferred to me along about the first of the week. I have put Straus in charge for liquidation purposes with the intention of transferring the activities as rapidly as possible to one of my own operating divisions and am also asking them to take over such of the personnel as the job analyses which Straus will carry out show are able to do the kind of work which we want to do. McCarl has said that Subsistence Homesteads must be liquidated but our conversations with him indicate that merely means that the agency is not authorized under the new Joint Resolution but that the activities may go on. We are not sure about the use of the unexpended in the Subsistence Homesteads balances. McCarl has said that in any case if they are not made available he will put such an amount in the deficiency bill and will see the projects through. Most of these activities will go to Lansill's Division although a few of them should be taken over by Gray and a few, I think, are far enough along to be taken over by the Management Division.

I have met this week with the policy committee of the Extension Directors with the hope of working out with them some kind of relationships to the rehabilitation and resettlement program which will cause them to support it rather than to oppose it and I have some hope that this may be done. I am, of course, very suspicious of all the Extension people. I think Taylor shares this suspicion but feels much as I do that this program, if properly run, can do Extension a lot of good as well as throwing them into our service. This is a diplomatic game which I am anxious to handle as delicately as possible. I am rather of the opinion that the success of the whole program depends on the extent to which Extension can be brought into it and yet made to serve the purpose which we want it to serve. The committee came in twice and we talked about the relations in the states of the Extension Directors to our program. They professed sympathy and, a desire to be active in the supervisory work which will be necessary when we rehabilitate farmers either on a community basis or on an in-place basis. Taylor feels, as I believe I do, that Extension can be useful in this if we can manage the thing so that they are placated and yet very definitely do the things that we want to do. The problem of keeping it in our control and yet having them active in it will be one which we will have to work out as we go along. The general political picture has been cleared up some, I think. The Chamber of Commerce recently meeting here in Washington, was actively against the New Deal which is perhaps one of the best things which has happened politically. The President must begin to consolidate the support which is natural to him among the workers and the farmers and I am anxious to see him step out more boldly than he has done in the past. He has this week to get over the bonus issue which has been put up to him again by Congress to give it in person. I think it is a very good message, one of the best he has ever done, and I am hoping that this too will set up forward politically. Everybody has been very much worried lately about an assumed reaction against the Administration. I think the President's speech last Sunday night was not a great success. I did my best to get it rewritten, working over it with Moley, but the President adopted none of my suggestions. I think they would have made the speech a great deal better; as it was it was certainly not a success. He said nothing new and he said nothing which would draw to his support those who would naturally come if given a chance. I think he must define the issues more clearly and consolidate the supports which he ought to have and I imagine that by now he sees that.

There was a great deal of talk about politics at the last Cabinet meeting which I attended a week ago Friday, the Secretary being away, and a good deal of talk about loyalty in the Administration being one of the causes of political uncertainly. This is certainly true. I hope it will lead to a dividing of the sheep from the goats before very long. The reactionary Democrats are giving a great deal of trouble. They cannot be counted on to support the New Deal and I wish they were well outside the ranks so that they could be counted there. People like Bailey, Gore, Byrd, Smith and others of that sort, will never be for us and they are more dangerous inside than they would be outside. There is some little political talk of the Republicans nominating a conservative Democrat for next time candidate. This idea is proposed by Mark Sullivan. I wish it could be followed up so that we can have a liberal as against a conservative candidate. Then the President would surely step out, consolidate his support, and go forward in the direction which we ought to follow. Then, if the issue could be made, the constitutional amendments, I should feel that we were making real progress.

One of the things which contribute to my difficulties, these days, is more trouble with Tolley. He seems to be determined to make difficulties between the Secretary and me if he can. He talked to Paul Porter last week and said that he thought I was likely to ruin the Secretary with this Resettlement Administration. Well I hope not to do that, yet I am determined to keep it independent of the Department of Agriculture of the moment so that I can move forward and do what I please. He is so unstable an administrator and so temperamental about the things he demands that it would be ruinous to be brought under his control. I have not succeeded in doing the things in the Department which I knew ought to be done and I should have no more luck with the Resettlement Administration if we were under him. And yet Tolley gives me a great deal of worry; he is very influential with Davis and others and I am sure to have opposition from them from that whole crowd.

- *May 30, 1935*

This is Decoration Day. It is quite appropriately being celebrated as a kind of memorial day of a good part of the New Deal. The Supreme Court decision was about what I anticipated only a good deal worse. They looked askance not only, as we anticipated, on the delegation of powers, but also on the interstate commerce clause; and in the simultaneous decision on the Humphrey case seriously limited the powers of the Executive. There was a kind of a calm after the storm for a couple of days but yesterday I saw the President and I was all steamed up about the situation and found him much in the same mood. He commented on that and said I was the first person who had been to see him who felt exactly as he did that we faced a great crisis which must be met head on. He said, "I suppose you and I are rather dumb because all the smart people think that what we should do is compromise and temporize with the situation but I am inclined to fight. "He had been seeing a great many people about the situation including, of course, Felix Frankfurter, Bill Green, Richberg and many others. All of them are apparently trying to find a way to rewrite NRA and satisfy the Supreme Court. I myself think it is impossible and think we are up against a constitutional amendment. I told the President so very clearly. He seemed to be feeling in that mood himself, not that he was influenced by me, but that he had arrived at the same conclusions. I gather from what he said that he intended first to make it clear to the country. By that I suppose he meant that he would make a radio talk in which he would explain the issues to the country. I told him I thought it was very necessary to separate the issue from the specific NRA case. I told him I thought NRA was very popular. He seemed to agree to that so I think he may make a radio speech immediately in which he will draw the issues rather clearly.

I have been busy the last week with a great many details of setting up my administration of the Resettlement Administration. I think we are making progress and that we have a working organization which may develop into something pretty good. We have been very successful so far in keeping publicity down and I am anxious to go on with that policy as far as we can. This is of course assisted by the NRA case which is filling the press and enables us to go ahead with our organization without being noticed too much. I found time, however, after the Supreme Court decision to get a few fellows together and talk over the issues. Jim Landis is in favor of a constitutional amendment which will limit the powers of the Supreme Court to defense of federal powers but the question is Machiavellian in its intent and would go too far. I suppose nothing like that will be done. I imagine the country is too tied up to the constitution and the Supreme Court to stand for such a thing. It seems to me that what we will have to come to is an amendment which will give the Federal government greater right to control commerce, redefining interstate commerce and anything which affects the stream of commerce because this is really the issue in the Supreme Court decision. They talk as though they had never heard of economics; they indicate that goods come direct at a certain point in interstate commerce, then that their control becomes intrastate. This is a principle which must be fought. I have a feeling, however, that something can be done by passing an immediate bill which would not be declared unconstitutional until next year anyway and might meet the issues of delegation of power. I should proceed through the tax powers and through the same general principle which we have used in the AAA Act which of course has not yet been tested in the courts but which we feel is somewhat safer than the NRA. In fact when I went over to see the President yesterday I had a memorandum prepared by Ezekiel and myself which outlined what we called an industrial adjustment, corollary to the Agricultural Adjustment Act. This would levy a tax on all industry, which would sign voluntary adjustment contracts which specified certain conditions of type and volume as well as conditions of labor and hours and the like. The voluntary nature of this might get around the problems of control of interstate commerce, and the use of the tax power, if clearly specified, might get around the problem of the delegation of powers. I have no great confidence in it but it seems to me the only thing we can do at the present time

The President is being besieged by all the people who were fighting NRA before to save them from industrial chaos. The markets all went down yesterday and I think it is clear to the country by now that something terrible has been done to the economic system, although they were inclined to be jubilant the day before, just after the decision. If the President could draw the issue rather clearly now and patch up something which would get us over the next year, the issue might be carried into the campaign in such a way as to insure a constitutional amendment which would settle this question, once for all. Certain it is that the wings of the Supreme Court must definitely be clipped. They cannot tell the Executive how to manage the country in crisis of this kind. What I am afraid of is that powers will be so dispersed that no crisis can be met and we will fall into a kind of chaos. If we followed out the logic of the Supreme Court of course we should break up into forty-eight principalities. The country economically cannot be run on that basis and it ought to be apparent to everyone now except perhaps to legalists like the Supreme Court Justices. We are all of course disappointed at the unanimity of the decision. We thought that people like Cardozo and Brandeis, or perhaps not Brandeis but at least Cardozo and Stone would go along with us, making economic rather than legal tests of the situation: but it proved not to be so, and the issue is drawn very clearly, it seems to me, between lawyers and those who take an economic view of the situation.

May 31, 1935

Yesterday I spent the greater part of the day with Harry Hopkins. I found him in a frame of mind to go back to the issues which we were discussing about a month ago and tried to start over again in that way. Along about that time we were considering the use of the four billion dollar fund and were trying to arrive at a general earmarking which should enable us to put a million and a half men to work for four billion dollars. We had numerous conversations of this kind but somehow this kind of approach seemed to be dropped for a while and attention was centered on setting up of specific administrative agencies and on the preparation of special projects. Also the Allotment Board was organized and all the administration people seemed to center their attention on ways to prepare their projects so as to get by this Board. Numerous projects of course have been approved by the Board which cost a great deal per man per year so that going back and figuring on the commitments which have already been made the situation appears about as follows: About one billion, four hundred million dollars have already been allocated and this money has gone mostly to high cost projects. There are probably some three hundred million more of such projects which leaves about two billion, three hundred million dollars. The projects already approved are so high in cost that the billion, four hundred million will scarcely put to work more than nine hundred thousand or a million people. This leaves at least two and a half million people to put to work with only two billion, three hundred million dollars. This is only four hundred million dollars more than relief cost last year so that the problem remains of putting people to work at about the cost of relief, a task which seems to me to be extremely difficult in view of the fact that the CWA campaign of last year used up a great many of the low cost jobs. The situation is complicated by the fact that we have six hundred thousand farm operators on relief who were not counted in the three million and a half which the President promised to put back to work. Dividing all this up it would only leave about eight hundred dollars per person per year to be spent for both wages and materials, a situation which makes it practically impossible to do the job which the President promised in his public statement to do.

Assessing this situation Hopkins and myself felt that if we were to make any kind of a try to do the thing which the President has wanted to do , all the rest of the money must be saved for the kind of works projects which we can invent and for the rural rehabilitation work which is now my responsibility to do. We talked this over forwards and back yesterday for a number of hours. We then decided to see whether we could go to see the President about it. We called the White House and in the afternoon we went to see him. We found him in his upstairs study pondering over the NRA situation. We talked about that for about an hour and a half and finally got down to talking about the relief situation. We found him sympathetic with the task which was before us but somehow unwilling to meet it head on. He has a great many conciliation jobs to do, particularly with Ickes whose heavy Public Works jobs are pretty much left out of the program which we must follow now if all the people are to be put to work as the President would do. There are also some other heavy projects which are desirable but which it is difficult to undertake under these circumstances. Among these are the housing work and the kind of work which cities normally do with their borrowed funds. The President suggested that we have a resolution prepared for the next meeting of the Allotment Advisory Committee which should make a definite commitment not to make any more allotments for any project which costs more than eight hundred dollars per man per year. I thought that sounded pretty good at the time but since thinking it over I am not sure it is wise to do this because what we want to do is merely to come out with an average of that kind and not necessarily turn down specific projects because they cost somewhat more. I am particularly worried about it because this would not enable us to build any of the suburban towns which I have been counting on doing; but perhaps there may be a way to work that out. We also suggested to the President that some money might be saved by continuing with relief beyond July 1st , which is of course cheaper than works projects and that we might gradually get all people on work relief rather than direct relief working up to a climax about the first of November. He seemed to think this was also a good scheme. I went on then to talk to him about the problem of drought relief. Under the particular provision of this bill it is very difficult to do the job which ought to be done in the drought states in view of all soil - blowing which has been going on this last winter and in view of the really catastrophic condition of that whole section of the country. After talking it over at some length he agreed to sponsor a hundred and fifty million dollar drought relief bill which I am to prepare and submit to him within a few days. I anticipate we may have some trouble with Morgenthau and Bell but I think the President really meant what he said and I shall proceed therefore to prepare the bill, getting into it not only this but provision for buying land which will enable us to go on a reduced basis with our land program as well as providing for the purchase and distribution of surplus commodities which I think is a valuable adjunct to AAA program.

The President explained to us at some length the kind of telegrams which were coming in and the general tenor of them seems to be wanting protection, not so much against cutting wages and hours, as against destructive price cutting. Well, this is a situation which worries me a great deal because that has been the difference of opinion between the President and myself which has been the most irreconcilable of any we ever had. I feel that the Constitution ought to be amended to prevent the fixing of prices in every situation in which monopoly is not controlled by the Government. The President has never taken price control seriously and he has never been worried by restrictions on production which trade associations authorized under the NRA Act really made possible. He is talking now in terms of a substitute NRA Act which will limit hours and set a minimum on wages and authorize trade associations to make certain rules and regulation with respect to standards of competition. My own feeling is that this procedure ought to be followed, but that he ought to tackle the constitutional question directly. He takes a political view of this and says an amendment to the constitution ought not even be suggested at the present time but that we ought to wait until we get some more decisions next year and get closer to an election issue. I explained to him my own feeling that our great difficulty was the restriction of production among industrialists, the putting bottoms on prices rather than tops on prices, and the general diminution in purchasing power which resulted from this particular policy of NRA. I said it wholly favors the big people and enables them to do the things which they have wanted to do for twenty years but were prevented from doing by the Anti-Trust Act and really provided no effective control over them. The President seems not to understand these issues in the same terms that I do and feels that destructive price-cutting is much more important than it seems to me. My own feeling is that if this temporizing view, this waiting policy, is adopted, the Supreme Court will have given the New Deal a very bad licking and that he shall have taken it lying down.

I talked to the President about our scheme for an Industrial Adjustment Act and explained to him that this put a premium on the expansion of production on large volume and low price and at the same time protected competition where it is appropriate. He said it sounded interesting to him and that he thought it was the kind of thing we should do but that we were a long time ahead of it. I explained that his particular attack on the present situation of a temporizing sort would do no good except that it might perhaps stop a few strikes and that we should be no further forward because of it and that we might have lost the opportunity for a constitutional revision. He was thinking so definitely, however, in terms of a reform that he could not see my point of view. He thought the Industrial Adjustment Act would sound queer to the country, that it was not ready for it, and that it was much safer to take up specific reform measures and get them across. He seems to think that we can tackle the whole question by way of labor and conditions of work which seems to me to be starting at entirely the wrong end. I stated my views rather specifically but found that he was in entire disagreement with me, as was Harry Hopkins, I might say. I came away with the feeling that it was a very good thing that NRA had been terminated with this whole philosophy of price stabilization dominating it, but still feeling that it was a mistake not to fight back at the obviously political decision which the Supreme Court had handed down and not taking up the issues of delegation of powers and the restricted definition of interstate commerce as well as the Humphrey decision which so seriously encroaches on the Executive powers. I think that in our long-run policy what will have to happen is that one commodity after another will have to be tackled as needing control and regularization. I also talked to the President about this a little bit. He suggested that they might one after the other be put into the category of public utilities. We had some discussion of whether or not a public utility could be a Federal designation. I said I thought not, in view of the Supreme Court decision, that being a thing which belongs very definitely to the States' police powers, but he seemed to disagree and feel that we could set up legislation for one basic industry after another on this basis and control them in that way. I have grave doubts as to whether the Supreme Court will allow it.

While we were talking Felix Frankfurter came in and I had some little private talk with him. He admitted that we needed a constitutional amendment but thought that we had to have some more adverse Supreme Court decisions before we got to it, on very much more popular issues. I pointed out to him how fundamental the decisions were and he admitted all that, but felt that this was not the time to tackle or to begin discussion of a constitutional amendment. The opinion of everyone seems to be against me on this and I am afraid the New Deal is going to lie down and take this political decision of the Supreme Court as the final direction in which we must go for the next year until we get some more decisions which make a constitutional amendment seem obvious to the whole country, and I am afraid that we are in for passing new legislation which will be of just as bad a sort as the NRA policy turned out to be. On the whole, I am very discouraged with the situation as it stands at present. I think that we have lost many of our gains and that nobody is in a position to get any of them back.

June 5, 1935

It has been a very exciting week. I still have the feeling that we are facing the greatest crisis of not only the New Deal but of many, many years. Last Saturday Harry and I went to see the President to see whether or not we could get some more order out of the allocations for the recovery fund, both of us feeling that what was needed was to work out a general plan by which allocations could be made in each of the regions in the country, comparing unemployment with the number of dollars available and working it out on that basis. We are about ready to start on something of that sort. This of course should have been done long ago but, because there was so much machinery set up, and because there was so much confusion about organization, it just did not get done. Then individual projects began to come in and everybody was suspicious of them because they could not see where they fitted into any particular plan. That has caused delay and many difficulties but I think now we are in a position where in a week or two we can get it straightened out.

I am going down to Albuquerque to make a speech, a commencement address, and expect to be away for about a week and Harry is going away for a week too, to Canada and down to Mississippi. We are planning how to put some people to work on this general scheme and have a report ready for us when we get back which may help settle the whole business.

On the NRA decision the President has been confusing everybody on the issues - which is exactly what he wanted to do: Playing for time and setting things up so that people have a chance to realize the real situation, which is of course that ultimately we must have a constitutional amendment which will give the Federal Government greater power. I suppose the amendment will have to be aimed particularly at the Interstate Commerce clause, although I think the delegation of powers ought to be taken care of too. There has been considerable argument around Washington as to what ought to be done under the circumstances, a great many people advocating proceeding by restricting controls to obvious interstate commerce and letting the rest go. General Johnson has got himself out on a limb on this theory and Frances Perkins feels that way too, as do a good many other people, including Hull and Homer Cummings. But the President has staved them all off. I went to a Cabinet meeting yesterday, Henry Wallace being up at Columbia getting an honorary degree - which was very interesting! The President said that there were several suggestions. The first of these was to continue NRA for record purposes and for making a survey of conditions brought about by the Supreme Court decision. This would keep an organization of about two thousand, with a skeleton field force, to check on the abolition of codes. He favored this because there has been a joint resolution which is passing the Senate already and is now before the House; and if this scheme could fit into that without having to go back to the Senate for debate it would have controversy again.

I suggested that it might be better for his future purposes not to do this but to get rid entirely of the name NRA and perhaps put the skeleton organization which he spoke of under the Federal Trade Commission or some other place. He said that he would do that if it were not for the Congressional situation but that things being as they were it was better to do it this way and that he would make it extremely clear in the newspaper statements that the codes were not to be enforced and there was to be no attempt at voluntary enforcement. This was the point of which I was most afraid, that people would think that something was being done when it really was not and it would have hurt the long-run issue of constitutional amendment. The President avoided very carefully in Cabinet meeting talking about the Constitution at all and he really let nobody know where he was going and I don't suppose there are three of us in Washington who do know. I know because of my rather intimate talks with him that what he is hoping is that the true situation will sink into the consciousness of the country so he will be able to get a constitutional amendment within a few years. Some of the other suggestions were that the Federal Trade Commission be given some of the powers which NRA had; and that the Wagner Act supplement it. This suggestion was made by the Vice President. Still another suggestion was that standards of competition be rather carefully written by Congress and that the Federal Trade Commission be given power to issue cease and desist orders. The President objected to these on the grounds that they would confuse the public mind; they would confuse immediate with long-run issues. He said that what we must not do is to give people unfounded hopes. We cannot afford, he said, to give people the idea that the thing can be worked out as the Supreme Court has dictated, because it cannot. Hull and Cummings argued for the adoption of substitute measures; they said the thing to do was to say that we were going forward with our policies unchanged but with different titles. The President vetoed that. He also vetoed Frances Perkins' suggestion that voluntary agreements would be sufficient. He said, "They won't; and there is no use of temporizing with this issue; the thing to do is to pass these temporary measures without saying that we expect to do very much . The skeleton NRA will be there for record purposes and we can check what happens when there are no codes and make the record clear to the public as we go along. What he did not say, but what I know is in his mind, is that he hopes there will be a public uprising: but I still feel that the only way to solve this issue is to have a constitutional amendment.

Milo Perkins, who is the new Assistant to the Secretary, in Baldwin's place, had an interesting conversation with Justice Brandeis which shows where he stands on this thing. He is determined to break up federal power. Milo Perkins' notes of his conversation are attached.

UNITED STATES DEPARTMENT OF AGRICULTURE
OFFICE OF THE SECRETARY
WASHINGTON

June 5, 1935

MEMORANDUM FOR DR. R.G. TUGWELL
UNDER SECRETARY

Dear Dr. Tugwell:

The justice received us very informally in his study. All that he knew about me was that I had resigned as sales manager of a large corporation several years ago to start my own business, and that I had been fighting stiff competition from the "big boys" ever since. The simple fact of my being in Washington showed my interest in Government. His whole attitude toward me was a fatherly one; at times it became full of feeling, such as old men have when they are seeking zealots among younger men to carry forward the things for which they have fought. I listened intently and with a sympathetic desire to understand him. My questions carefully avoided anything which might seem to challenge his position.

For fifteen minutes he "held forth" philosophically on the horrors of bigness and the sanctity of littleness in all fields of human activity. These views of his are well known; what seemed significant to me was the fervor with which he made these sweeping statements.

Then he took out some charts on insurance companies, showing among other things the cost of doing business in the last three years. That of the major companies showed an increase. With considerable pride, he pointed to the small one in which he had long been interested, and remarked, good naturedly:

"While some of you have been raising costs through N.R.A., A.A.A., and all the rest of it, we have cut ours. Not a man in our organization has ever made over $5000 a year. The business is run by little men whose jobs are not too big for them."

Here there followed a tirade against the present tendency to place men in jobs calling for superhuman abilities. He feels it makes tyrants of men who might be useful in smaller positions. His conclusion was that we have ruined our people and killed their power to think creatively by encouraging the structure of bigness. He added that it would take time to reverse the process, but that it must be done no matter what it cost. I gained the definite impression that his aversion to bigness was not limited to industrial corporation! He made the definite statement that the present could well afford any suffering which came with such a transition back to littleness, for the sake of a sound future. Here he reached his emotional peak, and it was shot through with the typical outlook of martyrs.

There followed his reference to a clipping from a Wichita, Kansas, paper, showing voluntary public reaction against chainstores. It was interpreted as one of the signs of a great public awakening.

Then we asked him if, on paper at least, the theory of AAA might not be a perfect pattern, with a minimum of centralization in Washington, and a decentralization of administration through county associations. He replied emphatically that it was not; that there was no trace of economic democracy in such things as a rural referendum on the cotton program, for example. His reasoning was that the program was imposed from above, and did not arise locally out of understanding from below. By way of illustrating how such a referendum might be truly democratic, he added that the thing hung on the _nature_ of what men were asked to consider. A local vote on a five cent car-fare, or on lower utility rates, was held to be within the range of local capacity for intelligent determination. On the other hand, a referendum on things involving complicated problems, especially when originating from above, was held to be sham democracy.

As a last question, we asked if decentralization of industry along advanced social lines might not solve the problem. The reply indicated that it depended on _where_ such schemes originated. If they were imposed from above by large units, no hope was held out, whereas if they had their origin in local communities, as co-operative undertakings of small individuals, then it was felt that there was promise in such a movement. The country lass of Denmark, who takes her whole milk to a co-operative dairy and waits for the cream to be skimmed, returning with skimmed milk for her hogs, was held up as a sort of emblem of what rural femininity might ultimately reach in this country.

We got up to leave; he told me in all sincerity to go back to Texas, to the country, where the real movement to reshape America would originate. By way of encouragement, he indicated his feeling that our people would change their structure of things, (mention of laws was carefully avoided), in such a way as to _encourage_ littleness, the disintegration of bigness being therefore but a matter of time.

Here is a grand old man who really feels that he is helping people. His mind widens when he talks about a greater happiness for the average man. It begins to narrow when he considers just what constitutes well-being for ordinary people. But when he turns to the _means_ of bringing it about, strong emotions surge through him, and his reason seems to abdicate in favor of his feelings. I cannot imagine a person less open to change on the subject of his pet conviction. What irony, for a man who abhors the imposition of programs from above!

Sincerely,

Milo Perkins
Assistant to the Secretary

July 17
Idaho

Hon. Rexford G. Tugwell
   UnderSecretary of Agri.
   Washington. D.C.

Dear Rex,
        Had a nice visit and trip with the Colorado Forestry people with whom you visited earlier in the year. Saw their nursery at Monument. Always like to see big nurseries well managed.
        Enclosed a Denver Post crack on Rural Resettlement and Costigan. The hatred of the Post for Costigan is incredible. My ref to Costigan at Greeley got a good hand, however.
        How long will it be before you can know which if any Self Subsistence Homesteads or Resettlement communities can be used on a contractual basis for increasing members of Danish swine or Danish Red Cattle? I like the idea of having several thousand head of these under government contract before they are made available to the general farming public. Perhaps the same thing might also be done with chickens of superior heredity. But of course you must be able to make a contract which will hold for several years or which in the breach can be satisfactorily liquidated.
        This sage brush country of Idaho is certainly full of wide open spaces. I understand now how a certain senator got that way.
        Please keep an eye on the efforts of the Interior Dept. to dismember the Dept. of Agri. Secy. Ickes cannot in any way be trusted in this matter no matter how pleasant or plausible he may seem.

Yours,
/s/ H.A.W.

August 15, 1935

Attempts to say exactly how and why Americans are different from other people in the world are always unsatisfactory. They break down into vague generalizations mostly unusable for practical purposes. And, of course, the reason for it is easy enough to see. We are those other people. So far as I know not many of us are sorry about this. There are some few whose pride of race exceeds their knowledge of it who become disturbed from time to time. But mostly we accept our polyglot character with a kind of pride.

Being American or doing things in American ways -- These are not racial characteristics. They are social or institutional or something of the sort. Yet anyone who has traveled widely, especially among the humble folk of other lands, must have been impressed as I have been with the likeness rather than the difference in attitudes everywhere. The cowboy of the Camergne or of the Hungarian plains is much the same sort of fellow as the Wyoming variety. He loves horses, knows cows, has an independent relationship to authority and acts the same in town on a Saturday night. Farmers everywhere have crops and the weather on their minds, live in a perpetual feud with townspeople, and think themselves exploited whether they are or not. And it is the same with workers of every other sort with whom I have ever had dealings. The affairs of government are remote to such people. They dislike bureaucrats and so have a tendency always to turn out the crowd which happens to be in. They have a similar feeling about higher-ups of all sorts whether it be big business men, Bishops or Secretaries. They see no connection between the functions performed by higher-ups and the getting of the things and services they want. And they have a tendency to want everything kept small because when it is small they feel themselves able to cope with it. I suppose this is why it is universally true that the favorite theme of every ambitious politician is a double belittling of bureaucracy and big business. Every man responds to the proposal that the people he must deal with ought not to be allowed to grow stronger than he is. I have watched hot political campaigns in four countries and they were all alike in these respects. And none of them resulted in any change in the institutional structure of the country.

What it takes to get elected is often what it takes to disqualify a person for doing what he has had to promise. This is the reason bureaucrats are strong in spite of attacks. Politicians are almost always defeated in the long run by people who know how to do the job of work which has to be done. So campaigns come and go, one politician is displaced by another, but things go on pretty much as they did before.

These observations are fairly applicable to America and to this Department. Our people like oratory as well as any other people. They enjoy the squirming of the ins when they are threatened by the outs. And periodically they change their majority voting. But things go on. The Treasury survives, the minor administrators do as they please, taxes are collected, jobs which do not matter are judiciously distributed.

When there is a variation from this pattern so violent that it really changes the course of the bureaucracy we call it a revolution. In that sense we had a revolution in 1932. There was hardly a bureau in the government which was not up against it in March of 1933. A singularly determined set of new people, many of whom turned out to have administrative ability enough to enforce their wills, took hold of the government. And new bureaus were created to do new things. Humble folk regard it as a circus for a while until the disgruntled outs began to talk about the cost of it and until the redistribution of favors began really to be felt by the formerly favored. There then began a vicious attack on the present ins which continues still. It takes courage and skill to initiate a change of this sort; but it takes infinitely more of them to persist in the face of calumny and with the tremendous disadvantage of being in office. This is why reform movements usually bog down. To stop being attacked it is necessary to stop offending powerful people and powerful people have to be offended if there are to be any reforms. The problem is to prevent the powerful from convincing the beneficiaries of the new policy that they are being injured rather than helped; and there is the difficult handicap of having built up a new bureaucracy and of having raised up new leaders to be attacked.

Since 1933 the classic course has been followed. The new people have been pictured as wild and dangerous fellows, strangely un-American in their derivation; the cost of new services and of redistributing income has been pictured as falling on workers and farmers, so that they are really worse off than before; precious institutions, for which our forefathers sacrificed much, have been said to be in immediate jeopardy; liberty is said to be lost and its place usurped by dictatorial officials who tell farmers what to plant, workers where to work, and businessmen how to manage their affairs. Not very imaginative, all of this, but perhaps more effective because of its dullness and predictability. The problem faced by the present administration is how to save the work it has begun. And I, for one, regard this as a formidable task.

August 20, 1935

It is true, as I think it is, that common folk the world over deal with the same problems and have most attitudes in common, why is it that we can and do speak of American roads to progress? It is perhaps, because we live in a unique institutional structure, and because we have resources which are so great. Experts say that our government is clumsy and antiquated but we have got used to it and we resent being told that there is a better way of getting those things done which government customarily does. It is only when we put unaccustomed burdens on it that the old machine creaks so audibly that it cannot be ignored. The burdens have grown without our willing them to do so, in practical fashion; and to carry them we have simply added appendages until the friction of movement became unbearable. Instead of anticipating changes in the future and preparing administrative machinery for the task we always improvise it as an incident to a pressing job. Being pressed, of course, and not allowing ourselves to think in general terms, we have not paid attention to corollary strains or to inescapable accommodations elsewhere. I speak feelingly about this because I have just been setting up an administration larger than most departments of government. It has had to be done in two months, on a problematical budget which could be foreseen only for a month or two, and with work to do which was partly dependent on the digestion of hostile colleagues and partly on the crowd psychology of a board of allotment.

That this is not the best way to undertake a serious nation-wide task I do not have to be told; and no one knows better than I the unlikelihood of success under such circumstances. But I, no more than anyone else, could refuse to begin the repair of fifty years of neglect in the field of land use and resettlement, just because emergency funds were to be used or because an organization had to be thrown together hastily.

There should have been an organization planning and working in this field for at least thirty years past. Every sensible person knew that it ought to be done and that the social gains would far outweigh the costs to individuals. But the weight of neglect had to accumulate until there was no denying the need for the function. Only then could a start be made. It has been this way with all the new tasks undertaken by the Roosevelt administration, whether in the field of public credit, of relief for the farmer, or the regulation of industry. Everything undertaken so hastily and with such necessity for doing much quickly should have been under way many years ago - and would have been, perhaps if we had not been Americans. For certainly all these tasks were undertaken by European government many decades in the past. And certainly the need has been sufficiently obvious.

We may do them just as well this way. For Americans work pretty well under pressure. They love to do a job quickly and dramatically, with excitement and public attention. The ruin has not gone to irreparable lengths. There is still much to build on. But I am still not convinced that preparation and careful budgeting are not better than haste and improvisation. These will come later now. But not until after a good deal of unnecessary waste and lost motion. Yet there is this clear challenging fact: the President has dared to take chances in catching up with civilization. He has risked his political future in doing so; but that ought to be a credit rather than a debit, though I am not sure that any allowance will be made for the special difficulties forced by delay and the accumulation of grievances. One administrative mistake counts more than a hundred successes; and every man is regarded not as a sacrificing executive but as a selfish job-holder. He is a waster of tax-payers' money always; never a public servant laboring for the general good.

What is being done corresponds, in my experience, to what common folk expect, though it has not always been necessary for government to do it. They want to live better, have more security, and still not be interfered with more than necessary. And they have been given employment, or lacking that, relief; farmers have had their incomes raised and insured; workers have been given protection and at least more security than they have had before; some families have been resettled and more have been relieved of unproductive farms; homes have been saved from foreclosure; public recreation facilities have been widely expanded; conservation of national resources has been rigorously undertaken; financial swindling has been largely stopped. All these activities are so good that any administration which follows this one will have to go on with all of them. If the Republicans should return to power in 1936 there is not one of these activities they would dare to stop. They might even be enlarged. But while they are not in power they will not say so.

In all of this too, in spite of howls of rage, there has been interference with the lives of common folk.

August 21, 1935

Mr. Thomas Beck called on me this morning with an idea which grew out of some of the same considerations which led me to write these observations. "It's got so," he said, "that I am lonely. There's this organization, and that league, and so on, all with a lot of money and highpowered publicity staffs, all trying to ruin the administration. And if you or Secretary Wallace or others make speeches or write articles you are prejudiced witnesses. But poison is being spread very cleverly everywhere. At every convention of a national sort, the professional poisoners are put on the program and their remarks are spread all over the newspapers. Now what I want to see is a League of Grateful Americans. I'm grateful that ten million Americans were prevented from going hungry; I'm grateful that several million homes were saved; I'm grateful that the forests and parks and the wild life of America are being restored; I'm grateful that the farmers have been given a break; I'm grateful that I am less likely to be caught in some swindle soon. I'm really grateful and I want to tell the world about it. I don't want to sit and say "that's so' when you fellows claim credit for it."

This is one of the most interesting ideas I've heard in a long time. I shall be amazed, however, if anything comes of it, because it takes money to do these stunts and unless little contributions could be gathered up here and there it could scarcely be financed. For the benefits of this Administration have gone to those who never had any before. And most of the wealthier group have made an enforced sacrifice for it. Of course this sacrifice has been largely imaginary, as Mr. Beck went on to point out. For, as he said, on a descending scale of income we have been paying 13 1/2% for our company; and now that income is going up we have to pay 16 1/12%. "I'd pay 3% for that any time; in fact I'll make bids on further increases."

But people object to paying for their prosperity. And I doubt if they will finance Mr. Beck's league. I'd like to think they would, however, for like others I want to believe that some people, at least, are like that. I think it is useless to disguise that hurt that any public man feels -- and feels more for his leader than for himself - when there is loosed upon him the kind of cynical torrent of abuse which has rushed upon the President in recent months. It hurts particularly when people of the sort we have been taught to respect lend themselves to it and when the shibboleths of honor are used to cloak the defense of crookedness and profit. It raises doubt in the mind concerning all the common reliance of mankind in dealings with each other. It is the kind of thing gentlemen don't do -- it is worse; it is the kind of thing thugs don't do to each other. It makes one feel that the world is full of monkeys rather than men and that conduct had become as unpredictable as it would be if simians were suddenly substituted for leaders in all the positions of influence. The kind of feeling I have about this isn't mitigated, I find, or made any the less a source of grief, for having anticipated it. It was bound to happen and yet somehow it ought not to have. I got used very early to personal attacks. I understood their source, and having had a very low opinion anyway of the people who considered me temporarily dangerous enough to be worth discrediting, I had no reason to be other than amused at my own notoriety. But I found it very different when the President was treated in the same way. The cruelty and injustice to which I had been indifferent so long on my own account suddenly got terribly under my skin. It did me a lot of good, therefore, when Mr. Beck even suggested his league of gratitude.

I am sustained, and all of us are who are in this fight, by the faith we have in a different kind of American. There is nothing the matter with these other Americans except that they are not vocal. Of course they can be fooled; we all can; but they are not the sort who, if they have a quarrel to settle, do it from ambush or with instruments of torture.

It is a wise old saying that often things have to become worse before they can be better. I think we should not have had any new Food and Drug legislation if the fakers had not taken to the radio and begun to pour their slush into the ears of the family at the fireside. Sensible men are only amused at advertisers' extravagances; but they become enraged at the same phenomena when their children are exposed to it. The hand was overplayed. The credulity and patience of people were asked to stretch too far. And I think they are being asked to stretch too far in number of directions. All the nasty things being said about the President can't be true, even in the opinion of the credulous. And the sayers of them are likely to suffer more than he.

August 23, 1935

The sense in which President Roosevelt has given us a revolution is to be measured, it seems to me, by the feeling among the underprivileged that he is their friend as well as by the corollary feeling among the overprivileged that he is their enemy. Both of these sensibilities certainly exist at the present time. They have been growing and deepening as the months have passed since March 1933. The first of these -- the apprehension of a new deal among farmers and workers - - is inchoate and, for the most part, unexpressed; the second - rage among the privileged - quickly becomes organized and expressive. It is the latter group which controls the larger part of the organs of opinion and which is able to travel and to meet in national forums. The convention has become a significant American institution and it is a convenient means for passing the opinions of big fellows on to the smaller ones. In practically all kinds of industries too there are trade journals which serve a similar purpose. Take it altogether, any rising apprehension among the leaders of business reflects itself very quickly in a spreading uneasiness among their followers. It does not matter, apparently, that the policies are unlikely to have any really adverse effect upon the majority who have been conducting their affairs with ordinary integrity and with a minimum of exploitation. An unease of this kind has little relation to reality. Small business men, as well as workers and farmers, have been caught in the net of our modern insecurity and they long, with the rest of us, for peace and certainty. They remember a time, not so long ago, when they appeared to have it; and they forget that they lost it before President Roosevelt began to try to win it back for all Americans. The means for getting it back are confused with its causes and so, the process not being of the nature of instantaneous magic, they are inclined to blame whomever happens to be operating the social machinery. This is perhaps why Mr. Walter Lippmann's specious distinction between "recovery" and "reform" fell on such grateful ears, crystallizing a wish and at the same time furnishing a convenient devil.

Those people are very few, even among business men, who really want a recovery in the sense of restoring those conditions which led to 1929. The difficulty is that in their apprehension they believe they can have 1928 back again without precipitating another 1929. They know in their hearts that it can't be done but the impossibility of a dream has never prevented people from hoping or even working to make it come true. There were those who felt that our sufferings were deep enough in those dark years so that for once we should be willing to face reality and its drastic necessities. But that has not proved to be the case. I suppose the President might be blamed for this. The very fact that he claimed nothing and predicted nothing but proceeded to act with a kind of glorious certainty gave the whole nation a renewed confidence in itself. What he did not say himself about confidence in a future without change and sacrifice, plenty of people said for him. There were almost two years when no voice of criticism was raised against him and when the discharge of venom against his conception of institutions spent itself futilely against lesser officials. The rising rage of those who hated him finally found direct expression, but only after sufficient restoration of normal life so that the immediate crisis could be said to have been passed.

The confidence of business leaders restored itself rapidly. Financiers, speculators, captains of industry, had undergone an ordeal. Characteristically, they had been used in the old days to a role of infallibility. They really believed that they had made us great. Suddenly they were discredited. No one was poor and humble enough to do them honor. All of their prestige transferred itself to one man. He had not asked for or encouraged it; he knew its dangers. But the need of the people for hope and for rescue was so great that there was no denying their grateful adulation. The result of his thought and labor was paradoxically the restoration of independence and confidence among those few who had least claim to it and who would be sure to lose it again as they had before if his policies should be discarded. The battle now is on a different front. It is not to raise ourselves from despair but to prevent the recurrence of conditions which would plunge us into it again.

I have felt from the first that what we could gain would probably be safe, that no political change is likely to cause its abandonment. But what has been done is not enough; the work is not complete if it should stop now. We should find ourselves sharing poverty rather than wealth and perhaps putting an end to the progress we ought to make in the future. Those who are asking us to stop where we are do not come into court with clean hands. They ask us to stop because going further may hurt them, not the American people. And we shall not stop. The only question we face is whether we shall have another of those reactionary interludes such as we went through in the twenties, leading to another crisis and unpredictable change. If that is what we choose, we may not find at the end of the reaction when the crisis is upon us another Roosevelt who understands the genius of our institutions and who moves toward practical change rather than doctrinaire revolution. That is what this present issue consists in -- Commitment to uncertainty on the one hand with years of intervening reaction or, on the other, to consistent change and clearance for progress, with year after year of rising standards.

August 30, 1935

No one can say of Americans that they are not inventive. I refer anyone who thinks so, and who prefers to think that their contriving genius is only mechanical and so rejects the evidence of the patent office, to Raymond Moley. It was President Roosevelt's habit, during the campaign of 1932, to refer to Mr. Moley, the various plans and schemes for social change which came to him. And they came by scores and hundreds from people of all sorts. Some were well considered; many were half-baked; some reflected an engineering turn of mind which was impatient with the fluidity of social forces and which sought to impose a pattern upon them; some came from doctrinaries whose knowledge of life was largely literary and who had been won over to some system or some panacea which it was suggested Mr. Roosevelt might enforce; others came from lawyers, who attributed our ills to lack of legal reform or to non-enforcement of the law; still others from amateur economists who had a theory of money or credit which, if used, would make other reforms unnecessary; and there were a scattering from people of other sorts. But there were surprisingly few which seemed to reflect any thoughtful care for what I had supposed to be the conditions of change in our life. I wondered whether this lawyer or that economist could really be serious. Those of us in this administration who have assisted in working out the various measures which collectively constitute the New Deal have often enough been called amateurs, theoreticians and academic impracticals; but if any of the thousands of plans which came to the presidential candidate from authentic business men had been taken literally as a basis for policy making, I am sure that the epithets would have been much worse - and justifiably so.

It has long been a favorite generalization of mine that the true doctrinaire theoretician of our society is the business leader. The experience of examining most of the plans which passed through Mr. Moley's hands raised this feeling to a conviction.

September 1, 1935

If I should succeed in getting out of office soon, as I hope, I should like to write something to be called, "The Consent of the Governed".

One of the difficulties in gaining and keeping consent is the very practical one that exposure of a program gains enemies as well as friends. The easiest way to prevent any progressive measure from becoming law, for instance, is to disclose it prematurely. By definition such a change affects some powerful interests; and those interests are quick to rally lobbyists, lawyers and all the horde of kept hangers-on who rush to the defense. Time is often of the essence in such cases. The public will seldom rise quickly in its own defense. An outburst of popular approval seldom supports any attempt to guard the public interest; but one who touches a private interest anywhere is instantly pilloried as a dangerous fellow. And so long as the avenues to the popular mind are monopolized by special interests there is little chance to put the case for reform clearly before the public. The problem of consent is thus confused. It takes a great deal of very smart work to get anything done under these circumstances. So far as what we call the New Deal is concerned, the power to accomplish anything legislatively has depended upon public trust in the President. This was not a belief in any specific part of the program, because the program has been deliberately and successfully misinterpreted; it was not even a belief that the President had any assistants who might be trusted because the cabinet has been ridiculed as weak and ineffective and all the rest of us have been lumped as academic busybodies. Only a few have had any praise and those few were conspicuously antagonistic to what was being done and therefore persona grata to the special interests. It has been because of a kind of faith in the office of the President, together with a warm and kindly feeling for its present occupant which no villification has been able to eradicate.

It is amazing to observe how close a net these special interests form to screen the government from the people. They touch shoulders everywhere. From patent medicines to electric power, from the stock exchange to the packing plants, from sugar refiners to steel manufacturers, the league against government has articulated itself more and more effectively as it came to be understood that the President was genuinely interested in the common welfare and that his pleading was not a political trick.

September 8, 1935

How deep are the sources of our indignation? Sometimes I have a feeling that they are inaccessible to most righteous causes and only open themselves to specious appeal. Indignation opens the way to progress only if it is righteous. Palpitating with the wrong emotions only leads to confusion. We had a moment when the worst elements in American life were completely exposed, when anyone could cast a stone with impunity. This was a strange experience, for the business classes had built for themselves an extraordinary structure of specious respect. We were perhaps willing to have them do it because they represented our ambitions too; but they were clever, also, in hiring those modern intellectual prostitutes who specialize in the creation of respectability and in having at their command the greater part of the press in a time when every man and woman could read.

It crumpled so completely and so quickly that for a time all defenses were down. And the way lay open for reform. But reforms take time to think out and before they could be formulated and made into law, business was again prosperous and assertive. It is perhaps, astounding that within two years of complete demoralization they should again be shouting their own virtues in press, pulpit and over the air; it is, perhaps, more astounding that anyone should take it seriously. But there it is - something for the student to record and for the statesman to reckon with. I am willing to say that it is the most surprising social phenomenon I have ever watched and the most discouraging. This alone is enough to make one doubt whether our genius is sufficient to cope with our problems. Those critics may be right who ridicule the liberal approach and advocate the revolutionary.

September 10, 1935

As time wears on it becomes clearer that the progressives in the Administration can depend very little on intelligent support from progressives in Congress. We are increasingly isolated and exposed to reactionary villification and when we turn to our legislative friends for support we find that they, like Baal, have gone upon a journey or are asleep. It is true that they vociferously complain that the administration is moving onto the conservative camp but they do absolutely nothing to keep it from going there and absolutely nothing to help those of us who, inside the Administration, are striving to keep its policies sane.

Today, as a result of this inadequacy on the part of the progressive mind, the Administration has become defensive after an election which has given it overwhelming endorsement and majorities in both houses of Congress which are certain to survive the election of '36. I do not complain of the incident which led to the rejection of the World Court or even of the recent deadlock on the Relief Bill, so much as of the fact that on both of these measures - which are neither illiberal or unprogressive - we found the liberals and the progressives in the Senate voting side by side with the most avowed conservative opponents of the Administration. Moreover, this weakening came at the precise juncture when a series of judicial decisions struck at the very root of the progressive program. The functioning of the Tennessee Valley Authority as a "Yard-stick" for public utilities has been impeded by order of a Federal Court, and this - the Muscle Shoals question - has been a test of the Senate Progressives since the War. They have favored public ownership, operation and distribution but when they find an Administration which is willing to execute this policy, the progressives turn and weaken the Administration so seriously as to jeopardize the policy itself. Other Federal Courts have ruled against the N.R.A., with respect to the coal and steel industry, and have in particular challenged the constitutionality of "Section 7A", by which the Government, with progressive support, had sought to buttress the rights of organized labor to form unions of their own choosing and to maintain wages. The outlook for a constitutional struggle, which must come, is dark. Both the Federation of Labor and the Progressives found an Administration which was anxious to win rights for labor, but they hastened to attack the Administration when it proposed the most generous relief bill in American history, in order to get still more for labor, and at the very time when these Court decision required a united front between organized labor, the Progressives and the Administration.

It is evidence of a fundamental indiscipline which, unless checked, will undermine the whole progressive cause and with it self-government as we know it. At the moment, since the Administration is pledged to a progressive policy, the effect of this attitude is to enact governmental paralysis. None of the Administration's major measures had been enacted after two months of Congressional debate, not because the Administration's policies were unprogressive or because the Progressive votes were in the minority, but because certain Liberals and Progressives announced that the Administration did not go far enough and preferred to wreck its measures for the benefit and with the support of the reactionaries, rather than follow the rule of politics, which is to obtain as much of the desirable as is possible, and to remember that half a loaf - in this case, three quarters of a loaf, - is better than no bread at all.

As I say, the first-fruits of this Progressive revolt are inaction and paralysis. But it is impossible permanently to commit a great government at a critical time like this to a policy of inaction. The oldest rule of war is that any action - even a mistaken one - in an emergency is better than no action at all. The same is true of politics. So the real danger, to my mind, is not that to being driven into a paralysis of the sort which tortured us through the last two dreary years of the last Republican Administration. The danger is that when the Roosevelt Administration acts, it will find itself forced by the non-cooperative attitude of the progressives to become more conservative than is either wise or safe. For conservative votes are always to be had in Congress at the price of conservative policies. If the President cannot obtain progressive support, after it has paid the price of progressive policies, it will have no alternative.

I speak strongly, for I feel a sense of personal responsibility in these matters. I am, myself, a progressive and have even been termed a radical. I enjoy warm personal friendships with such progressive leaders as Ned Costigan, Bob LaFollette, Homer Bone, Burt Wheeler, Maury Maverick and others. I feel that we share the same aspirations. If then I point out the Ned Costigan voted for the World Court, which I favored, and Bob Lafollette against it; and that both of them voted for the paralysing "prevailing wages" amendment to the Relief Bill, which bill I also favor; it is because such differences of opinion of simple issues between men of the same political stripe suggest that there must be something fundamentally wrong with the progressive mind and character.

I have striven to analyze, in my own character and in the conduct of other progressives, as they have revealed themselves to my mind, the defects which inhibit rational cooperation among progressives and which threaten to undo all of their best work. In general, I think it can fairly be said that they cannot lead, they will not follow and they refuse to cooperate. This statement deserves some elaboration. They cannot lead because they will not accept leadership and are unwilling to pay the substantial accomplishment of their dreams by the small change of petty compromise. Twice within the last generation, they have attempted to form a political party, independent of the two traditional parties. Each time, a single defeat has sufficed to deject their followers and to divide their leaders. Theodore Roosevelt led the Progressives against Wilson and Taft in 1912. Four years later, the Progressives were back in the party of Boies Penrose and Henry Cabot Lodge. In 1924, the late Senator LaFollette and Senator Wheeler led the Progressives against Coolidge and Davis. Four years later, LaFollette was back in the party which nominated Herbert Hoover and precipitated the most disastrous economic and social crisis in our history. And Burt Wheeler seems cold to most issues this Administration has pushed.

The progressive reforms of Woodrow Wilson's first Administration were accepted in the same spirit of critical bitterness with which the do-nothing Big Business measures of the Coolidge-Hoover period were accepted. They have regarded the New Deal reforms, not as a common enterprise created by forward-thinking men but as things to be tolerated only in default of something better of their own. I sometimes catch myself thinking in these terms and becoming depressed and discouraged by every concession that must be made to the forces and the inertia of the conservative spirit. Instead of frankly recognizing that the mass of Americans moves slowly and that every step ahead must be paid for by concessions to this lag in national psychology, we progressives tend to slip into the same intransigence which has characterized our foreign trade as a nation, and to believe that we can export indefinitely without importing goods in payment. So we tend to regard all advances in our direction as clear national gain and all concessions to the conservative forces as an outrageous perversion of policy. This attitude, I feel, militates strongly against our effectiveness as national leaders.

Our fault in this connection is increased by our tendency to shrink from executive and administrative responsibility. We are fine people to offer advice, especially the counsels of perfection, and we are equally fine people to say, "I told you so!" when things go badly. We seem to fail to realize that a policy and especially a reform must be administered and that many things can happen to it in the course of that administrative process, if the men who take the responsibility are inexpert or unintelligent. Yet the government's work must be done and it must be done by men. Laws are not automatically self-enforcing. Not even the Ten Commandments are that way. Such a measure as the Agricultural Adjustment Act calls for pains-taking, unromantic, day in and day out, cooperation by thousands of men, at Washington and throughout the country. It is not enough for liberals to demand justice for agriculture, cooperate in drafting a law for that purpose and then stand back and complain bitterly if the result fails to bring the Millennium. If we refuse to accept responsibility we cannot rationally blame those men who do accept it and who, despite what we may regard as their failure to share the Inner Light which we assume to monopolize, have both the patience, the industry and the self-control to do the job which needs to be done, and to deal with men and women as they actually are and human nature as it actually exists.

Not only do American Progressives shrink from responsibility, they are actively irresponsible. They will follow any demagogue who makes a loud enough noise, without raising the uncomfortable issues of either his sincerity or his ability to perform his promises. They automatically assign themselves the position of tail to any kite which is raised by a sufficiently powerful wind but prepare to jump off the moment the wind shows any signs of failing or they see another kite soaring a little higher. Progressives pose as men of rigid principles and the strictest intellectual integrity; but there is a pathetic propensity to fall for anything and everything which sounds plausible and to judge a man, not by his mass but by his velocity. I confess that I have more than sneaking admiration for the demagogue who has mastered the art of filling the public's eyes and ears, in the face of the holier-than-thou opposition of the ultra-conventional, but very little respect for those who, professing themselves to be independent, follow such rambunctious opportunists. All of us have far more liking for the knave than for the fool, and I sometimes blush to think of the follies of the liberal mind when confronted with any impressive political windmill.

This peculiar emotional instability is even more incomprehensible when I consider that the progressive mind is stratified with dogmatism of the most appalling kind. The Catholic Church, in matters of dogma, recognizes but one infallible authority. We progressives tend to set ourselves up, every man a Pope, announcing our own individual infallibility in matters of political dogma. I probably share this defect as much as anyone still could who has been disciplined by Administrative responsibility. Certainly I have detected traces of polite boredom and mild impatience when I have continued to urge my own view, that under intelligent State control it should be possible to introduce a planned flexibility into the congestion and rigidity of our out-dated economic system. Yet this polite, shall I call it sales-resistance, on the part of some of my colleagues is nothing compared to the water-tight mentality of some of the progressives I know. The Progressive theme-song is, "I'll tell you about my panacea but you won't tell me about your panacea." We all, conservative and liberal alike, are inclined to be that way. But politics is the art of human association in collaboration and such an attitude cannot fit into any form of association or collaboration which is free and equal.

Yet this is the very factor which makes the progressives so undependable and so undisciplined. So far as political action is concerned, many of them are perennial skirmishers, gentlemen adventurers on the outskirts of politics, free, like feudal chieftains, to change sides whenever the ideas to which each holds allegiance prompt them to do so. They are like Chinese warriors who decide battles, not by fighting, but by desertion, and they bitterly resent the idea that there can be any superior control of their actions. Progressives are, therefore, untrustworthy allies. Their loyalty is a matter of day-to-day renewals and their cooperation is withheld at the moment when it is most needed. They rush to the aid of any liberal victor, and then proceed to stab him in the back when he fails to perform the mental impossibility of subscribing unconditionally to their dozen or more conflicting principles.

In short, to bring this act of self-accusation to a conclusion, I must reluctantly admit that, judging by our actions, we progressives belong with the lunatic fringe of national politics. This lunatic fringe is not, as the conservatives contend, crazy because its ideas are wrong, radical or unsound. Frequently its ideas are right as rain and the only conceivable way of dealing with the situation, as is shown by the unanswerable fact that the conservatives are compelled eventually to enact them into law. The lunatic fringe has earned its derisory adjective mainly because its methods are automatically self-defeating. I think the same can fairly be charged against those progressives who have blocked and jeopardized the Administration's program, not because it was unprogressive but because some of them wanted to make it progressive in their particular way. When as I say, I see our progressive politicians voting side by side with the most conservative Republican against the social policies of the most progressive Administration and the most liberal measures this country has ever had, then it is time for us all to take counsel together. Otherwise, the consequences will be disastrous, not only to the progressive cause but to the country, itself. Think what may happen when the constitutional issue sharpens!

First of all, that would force the Administration to accept the Southern conservative as the only dependable body of men who can be counted on to stick by their bargains and pass legislation. This means, in turn, that the policies of the Administration must become more conservative at the very moment when the mass of our people are requiring more fundamental action to adjust abuse and alleviate suffering.

In the second place, by forcing the Administration toward the right, it would render inevitable a more rabid movement towards the radical left. The creation of two parties - one radical and one conservative - may or may not be a desirable development. I am inclined to believe that it is most desirable that men should divide on the basis of their political opinions rather than their geographical residence. Nevertheless, such a development will end the social truce under which by a process of common consent and mutual forbearance, the New Deal has striven to reform our institutions where they have developed serious faults. Moreover, this process is impossible without splitting both of the major political parties - the Democratic as well as the Republican - with the result that, at a time when action is needed, neither the Executive nor the Opposition can count on any dependable body of men, and we shall have Congressional confusion leading to political deadlock.

Third - and this is the most important consequence of the limitations of the Progressive mind - such a deadlock has in every other country been the precursor of either a Fascist or a Communist seizure of power. At the very best, it would provide real opportunity and justification for such movement in America. The Mass of our people want action, want results. They did not vote for a squabble between Congress and the President. They have no patience with the old tradition of burning while Rome fiddles. If the Government is deadlocked over non-essentials, they will seek other leaders who will promise them more drastic action and more rapid results -and they will find such leaders.

In our zeal to promulgate our own True Gospel, we are forgetting the forgotten man again, two short years from the time when we sought his vote and promised him relief. Like the dog in the fable, we are dropping the bone we already have to snatch at its reflection in the stream of events. Now, as the forces of reaction gather force against what we have already accomplished, we should close our ranks and stand shoulder to shoulder in defense of the New Deal, and should sink individual differences of opinion and even of doctrine for the common cause. Instead, it is quite possible that we shall lose in the next few years of inconsequential bickering, back-biting and confusion, all that we have gained by a generation of agitation for reform.

I know of only one way in which those of us who call ourselves progressives can avert these consequences. It is to cooperate under the leadership of the President. We supported him for election to his present office and we know that he is on the side of progress and reform. We must learn to work with him, for he will assuredly remain in office for some time to come, and cannot be displaced by the emergence of an adverse majority in Congress. In supporting him, there is no need for us to surrender our independence of thought. We can advise and, if necessary, criticize his measures, but where he has taken a position, which substantially embodies the liberal position in politics, I can see no other course for us liberals to follow except to support it, only as the lesser of two evils. Otherwise we shall deserve the fate which history has always reserved for those loquacious minorities who have sought for perfection in a necessarily imperfect world. What happens to us as individuals is of little monument to the people of this country, but if our own unreasonableness should thwart a program for substantial progress it may well prove fatal to the cause of orderly self-government in the United States. We must let the President play out his hand.

Rexford G. Tugwell, U.S. Department of Agriculture. Courtesy of
Franklin D. Roosevelt Library.

Raymond Moley (left) and Stephen Early.
Courtesy of Franklin D. Roosevelt Library.

Rexford G. Tugwell (third from left, top row) and Charles Taussig (second from right, bottom row). Courtesy of Franklin D. Roosevelt Library.

Franklin D. Roosevelt, December 1932. Courtesy of Franklin D. Roosevelt Library.

Rexford G. Tugwell. Courtesy of Franklin
D. Roosevelt Library.

Adolf Berle. Courtesy of Franklin D. Roosevelt Library.

Rexford G. Tugwell (center), western trip. Courtesy of Franklin D. Roosevelt Library.

Rexford G. Tugwell and his wife Grace Falke Tugwell, 1943. Courtesy of Franklin D. Roosevelt Library.

Franklin D. Roosevelt and Harry Hopkins. Courtesy of Franklin D. Roosevelt Library.

(Left to right) General Malone, Louis Howe, Harold Ickes, Robert Fechner, Franklin D. Roosevelt, Henry Wallace, and Rexford G. Tugwell, 1933. Courtesy of Franklin D. Roosevelt Library.

REVISED DIARY

Introduction

In the spring of 1932 it became apparent that Franklin Delano Roosevelt, who had been Governor of New York since 1928[1], might very well be the nominee of the Democratic Party for the Presidency in the election of that year. It was not yet certain; there were other contenders, some of them formidable; and there was still to be felt the strength of a stop-Roosevelt movement among all of them. But there was no doubt that he was the leading and logical candidate. The situation was one of growing tension because, as the depression, which had spread and deepened month by month since 1929, made itself felt politically, it became more and more likely that the Democrats might win. The Democratic nomination had not been so valuable in a long time or so worth contending for. Alfred E. Smith, who had run and lost in 1928, seemed to feel that the party owed him this better opportunity. And, egged on by a coterie of close associates, he not only offered himself as the candidate but actively organized the stop-Roosevelt movement.

For this reason, particularly, as well as for others, it was by no means a foregone conclusion to the dispassionate observer that the

[1]And before that, of course, a Vice Presidential candidate on the ticket with James M. Cox of Ohio in 1920, following eight years as Assistant Secretary of the Navy in the Wilson Administration, and a term as State Senator from Dutchess County in New York. These political experiences began in 1910 when he was 28. Until then he had been a young practicing lawyer in the firm of Ledyard, Carter and Milburn in New York City. His schooling had included Groton, Harvard and the Columbia University Law School. All this and much more is told in many accounts of his life and his associations; these will be referred to in appropriate places later, and a bibliography will be found at the end of this book.

nomination would actually go to the New York Governor. What could be said was that it was likely. There were those about the Governor who were not dispassionate observers. They were in fact passionately partisan. And if they had any doubts they were drowned in the flood of political activity now engulfing Albany.

Samuel I. Rosenman was as partisan as any of the others. He was, however, less overwhelmed with day to day occurrences than some of the rest. It came to him, at first as a kind of uneasiness, but presently as a matter of urgency, that beyond the nomination there lay a campaign; and even beyond that a Presidency. What he remembers of what was said between himself and the Governor about the need for preparation is recalled in his Working With Roosevelt.[2] But Raymond Moley, whose After Seven Years was published twelve years earlier, had already, as it were, put in a previous claim.[3] Ray did not doubt that a conversation might have taken place. But it did seem "very queer indeed that a man who had been closely associated with Roosevelt for two years should say 'Why don't you try the Universities for a change?' to a governor who had habitually consulted with Professors Robert Murray Haig, James Bonbright, Frank A. Pearson, William T. Meyers, former Professor Milo R. Maltbie, and, I may add, with me, in constructing his state policies." And Ray had a real question in his mind concerning "the implication that such a conversation was anything more than an incident in a development wholly unrelated to Sam Rosenman's planning or imagination. Sometimes the lady who smacks the champagne bottle against the ship's prow has the illusion that she is causing the ship to slide down the ways."

There is, it will be seen, some controversy for the historians to play with about the origin of the Brains Trust. If you ask me, Ray Moley has the more reasonable explanation. Sam Rosenman's story excludes too much. It far oversimplifies the situation which had to be met, a situation which is brilliantly summarized in a few pages of After Seven Years[4] There is no doubt that Ray was as close to the Governor, and understood him as well, as anyone. There is no doubt, also, that Ray, having at least the detachment of his professional status, was likely to see as early as anyone the upcoming problem, in that year of crisis, for a candidate. It was not possible to go through the ordeal with only the equipment of gubernatorial experience added to that of an Assistant Secretary of the

[2]New York, 1951. The remarks I refer to begin on p. 56.

[3]He was apprised of the "popular story" by Men Around the President, New York, 1939, by Joseph Alsop and Robert Kintner. The relevant reference will be found on pp. 19-20.

[4]Pp. 6-9.

Navy. It was not possible even for a man talented as an observer and gifted with insight. There simply had to be exhibited an understanding of the malign forces which were destroying the American economy. There had, moreover, to be offered plausible alternatives to the policies now so discredited. This was no job for professional politicians. It called for knowledge and imagination.

Whether it was Sam or Ray who suggested the organization of our group endeavor the reader is at liberty to choose. At any rate it was done. And I was the first of several to undergo the ordeal of selection. It was not, by academic standards, very rigorously done. Ray had already made up his mind that he wanted me. Sam or Doc (Basil O'Connor, the Governor's rather nominal law partner) could have entered a veto; but neither did. After a few minutes it was obvious that I had engaged their interest; after a few more they were asking questions; and after half an hour we were discussing the uses of my ideas in the present political circumstances.

I might just say a word about those ideas, asking the reader to remember what the setting was. The spring of 1932 was one of deepening misery for millions of Americans. The warming season might release them from chill; but there was no prospect of release from hunger and from the enlarging losses of everything they valued. The depression was reaching a paralyzing hand into one activity after another, damping the fires of industry, stopping machines, and turning men into the streets. There seemed to be no way of arresting the spreading disease. Certainly nothing was being tried in which anyone had much confidence; and it was becoming clearer that the limitations in the minds of those with authority would prevent anything remediable from being tried.

The movement of public discussion within rigidly circumscribed areas lent a fatal cast to the developing crisis. It began actually to seem that there was no stopping place short of complete paralysis. The economy was seized with an incurable illness such as an individual is. And the economic doctors had no more helpful advice than medical doctors have when faced with approaching death. In these circumstances cheerfulness and optimism can easily become an affront to the intelligence. By 1932 Hoover's early attitude--that what was happening could not happen, and if it did would soon stop happening--was returning to haunt him. We can recall now, with more sympathy than any of us felt for him then, that he had been elected in 1928, the third in a Republican succession which had ridden the boom of the twenties, when the "new era" had reached its apogee. There was a nearly universal conviction that prosperity had become permanent. To have had events of 1929 follow so close on the beginning of the new administration was cruel. And the members of Hoover's official family had not been able to believe that anything fatal had occurred. It was thought that readjustments would occur and that presently things would be as they had been before the crash of 1929.

It would not be true to say that nothing had been done. The Farm Board had been established; so had the Reconstruction Finance Corporation; and there were attempts to organize relief for the unemployed. But the Farm Board could only buy up surplus farm products; it could not sell them. The Reconstruction Finance Corporation could make loans to stave off bankruptcy; it could not affect the causes of failure. And the relief efforts were, by the strange barriers in the Hoover mind, limited to private agencies or to local government. None of these had an appreciable effect. They might as well not have been undertaken so far as public credit was concerned. They were drowned in the advancing tide of disaster, pitiful dissolving monuments to the Great Engineer in the White House. He was a figure of tragedy by now: a Canute. His dignity was lost in a spate of ridicule. Stories, supposedly funny, actually venomous, ran from mouth to mouth all over the country. Louis Howe was heard to say that he could be beaten by a Chinaman in the approaching election.

2

There was more competition for the role of Chinaman, more competition than Louis liked to see. But neither he nor Jim Farley thought it necessary to elaborate an alternative to the Republican conception beyond that already in the Democratic book. That was the inheritance from Wilson and beyond him from an honorable line of liberals. Ray felt the inadequacy of this. Perhaps Sam did too, and maybe Doc had some intimation of it; but I think that mostly they had a practical view of the political situation, and the old stuff seemed inadequate. Desperate illness calls for something more than a pleasant bedside manner. It calls for something more even if you are thinking just about appearances and not really about the prospect of recovery.

It seemed to them practical to talk about cause and cure even if the talk got far more drastic than current political tolerances allowed. And before long we were hard at it.

What I had to say seems at this distance not very profound or dramatic. This in itself is some indication of the distance we have travelled in the intervening years, I suppose. As things were--contrasted with the mush in so many mouths--my exposition was stark and shocking. I said that our troubles were made by business and could only be corrected by disciplining business. Businessmen had been able to take advantage of an unusual situation, arising out of the advances in productivity during the war. Costs had fallen. But prices had not. Nor had wages risen. Therefore what consumers had to buy with had become disproportionate to the goods being produced. Some of them could not be sold. This caused unemployment. The unemployed, of course, reduced their buying to a minimum. And thus a spiral of decline set in.

Presently the banks had become involved because borrowings could not be paid back and everyone had tried at once to collect what was owed to him, a process which squeezed the life out of commercial credit. With loaning stopped, production restricted, unemployment growing, there was only one possible means of relief--to re-establish consumers' buying power. Even that would give only temporary stimulus when the disparity between total consumers' incomes and total prices for goods were somehow equalized. Only the Federal government could give relief because it had the exclusive power to issue money; only the Federal government could administer discipline because no other jurisdiction was wide enough. All businesses had to be thought of as "affected with the public interest." Their prices had to be brought under supervision and made to have a relation to each other which would enable each to buy the others' products--and keep on buying them.

This--with elaboration--was the story. It will be recognized that it was original. It will probably be identified by most readers as owed to John Maynard Keynes. That would be mistaken. I was, of course, familiar with Keynes. But I knew him as the author of The Economic Consequences of the Peace, not as the monetary theorist. My views in this matter had been influenced by J. A. Hobson more than any one other individual. But of course that was a time when intensive work on the business cycle was going on all around me at Columbia, with Wesley C. Mitchell as its center. I was not directly involved in any of these studies; but I was a teacher of economics and I could not help but know all about them. Also I had some special knowledge in two fields that many of my colleagues did not have. I had made some effort to understand scientific management; and I had studied agricultural policy. Both these were involved. It was scientific management which had reduced industrial costs. And it was agriculture which was hardest hit by the depression.

As a matter of fact Ray took me to see Sam Rosenman and Doc O'Connor not because I had a general theory of the depression and a suggestion for remedy but because I was supposed to be something of an agricultural expert. This requires some explanation. For the Governor had rather close relations with Cornell, and presumably his advice would come from there. The College of Agriculture at Cornell was a leading one and it was a great power in the state. Its contributions to the farming arts had been innumerable and the extension agents spread its influence everywhere in rural New York. It was nevertheless true that the depression which was now eating into industrial vitals, had struck the farmers nearly a decade before--in 1921--and had held them in its grip ever since. It was also true that advancing productivity--in agriculture as in industry increasing efficiency in production was the characteristic of the 'twenties--was not likely to get them out of it.

There had been going on in Washington a good deal of agitation. There was a farm-bloc; and it had put forward remedies. These had gradually become embodied in the successive McNary-Haugen acts only to be vetoed first by Coolidge and then by Hoover. I had watched, studied, and written about this movement. Ray knew this and had talked with me about it a good deal. He thought I would be worth listening to. And it was the farm problem that I was supposed to discuss with Sam and Doc.

That we presently developed a more general discussion was owed to my intense feeling that what was needed was balance and direction and that these could be supplied only through Federal intervention. The farmers' ills were special in the sense of being older and deeper; but they were part of a whole trouble and not to be solved by themselves.

This approach appealed to Sam and Doc as sensible. Even when I suggested that there were some gross disparities which government must correct, they followed the argument without the revulsion politics usually exhibited. This was really striking because the cost of living was involved. If farmers were to get higher prices consumers would have to pay more. Louis Howe was to contend that it could come out of the middlemen, but even he would eventually give up on that. The margins, inequitable though they were, were not that big. But to suggest higher prices for food in the midst of depression and universal restricted diets seemed on the face of it politically inexpedient. It had even seemed inexpedient in 1928 when I had made a similar suggestion to Belle Moskowitz, Smith's campaign manager. It was a question of having incomes to buy with. We had to think of farmer's products being bought by the farmers. When both could buy each other's products both were kept employed. No one was hungry who had an income even if he had to pay well for his food.

There are--as I had discovered during that year--many different ways to approach and expound the idea of balance or equality. I had been devising them industriously. My friends were probably pretty sick of hearing about it. But I was too full of indignation to care. And to anyone who would listen I held forth on the causes and cures for our troubles.

That Hoover was incapable of reaching an effective policy I was certain, because his analysis excluded so many facts and because his preconceptions so limited his range of remedies. I had been so impressed with this that I had written a pamphlet called Mr. Hoover's Economic Policy which had been published and had had a considerable distribution. When Ray and I, early in the spring, began to have conversations, I was a fairly practiced expositor. At any rate, I had my material so pat that Ray was impressed not only with its appositeness in the circumstances, but with the economy and force of my explanation. It had somewhat the same effect on Sam and Doc. After one evening together I was passed for exhibit in Albany.

3

Ray, in <u>After Seven Years</u>, had told the story of our association. We were unnamed at first, and quite unnoticed. But in April Ray was told that he was to be chairman--Chairman, the Governor hesitated. . . of my "Privy Council." Ray thought, he says, of what an enterprising reporter could have done with that phrase. To me, he said, for God's sake not to whisper it out loud. But that was what our principal called us to our faces until September when Jimmy Kieran of <u>The New York Times</u> gave us our permanent label. We were thenceforth the "brains trust."

By then the Governor was the official candidate and going strong with a steady supply of our speeches at hand and with Ray constantly at his side to tailor them to last instant requirements. But a lot had been done before that. I have said something about it in "The Preparation of a President"[5] and I will not repeat it here. I doubt whether his mind was changed by his association with us on any single issue. His knowledge was beefed up by what we brought him; and perhaps his intellectual muscle improved. But before we began he was a progressive of the old-type; and in spite of earnest efforts on our part he remained that. This I regard as our worst failure. All of us could be described as believers in the efficacy--indeed, the inevitably--of large-scale social organization and particularly for industry. And we wanted to depart altogether from the notions of our progressive elders in this respect. This went to the giving up of anti-trust procedures as the only reliance for industrial discipline. N.R.A.--or something like it--was our idea of inter-industry relationships and of the way governmental influences on industry ought to be arranged.

We had not yet arranged our ideas in mechanism form; but anyone who cares to can see how close we were by reading the last chapter of a book called <u>The Industrial Discipline and the Governmental Arts</u> which I had already written and which would be published (by the Columbia University Press) in 1933. It is also obvious that if our mental preparations had not already been made we could not have produced the National Recovery Act in the short time we had for its writing in the spring of 1933. None of the Brandeis crowd, needless to say, participated in that activity. They were busy with legislation for reforming the stock market and investment banking--something that needed to be done, Lord knows; but something, also, whose doing had nothing to do with recovery or with prevention of future crises. The task was left over from an earlier

---

[5]<u>The Western Political Quarterly</u>, June, 1948.

day. In a sense--a real sense--N.R.A. was sacrificed to Securities and Exchange legislation.

We had powerful opposition. We did not know, at first, how effective it was. We thought for a long time that, in this matter, as in so many others, the Governor agreed with us. As I look back I realize that this was one of those instances of theoretical schizophrenia which are more common than is usually realized. He talked about planning; he seemed to have a concept of wholes; he apparently believed in concentration and control (to use a phrase made familiar to an earlier generation by one of Ray Moley's teachers, Van Hise). He did not, however, accept the inevitable concomitant. When it came to using all the political credit he possessed to get a program out of the Congress, practically the whole expenditure went for such items of an old-fashioned progressivism as I have mentioned. When N.R.A. was thrown out by Brandeis-dominated Supreme Court, he talked of horse-and-buggy thinking. But what actually followed was an enlargement of the anti-trust division of the Department of Justice. It was entrusted to the spectacular management of Thurman Arnold, one of the Administration's most picturesque operators. This was an indication of its imputed importance.

There were none of us in the brains trust who could stand in the father relationship to the candidate. And that was what he really longed for. This requires more substantiation than I can give it here; but I am confident that it is true. It had a significance much wider than this one issue; but it is in this issue that the results can be most clearly seen. Moley, Berle and I--as well as others who were more temporary--came distinctly in the category of aides and assistants. We took orders. Of course, we had ideas and put them forward; we made patterns for his inspection; we even argued with him. We often saw them used; but often too we saw them cut up, transposed, sacrificed, even ignored. It was he who was putting things together, making a philosophy, rounding himself.

There were those about who might have been treated with more respect. There was Colonel House, left over from Wilsonian times, for whom the Governor had an obviously weighty respect. We heard of him. There were communications. But Colonel House was not a man with a philosophy. Judge Mack was respected too; but that respect had no relationship to the development of a Presidential pattern. So was Uncle Fred Delano, and so far as his influence went it was good; but it was not a considerable one. Nor, in fact, was that of Judge Mack, although he too was greatly respected. The first time I ever talked with Homer Cummings on the porch of the Albany house, I sensed a tough and able mind, shaped in the modern mold. I thought momentarily that the fondness of the Governor for the older Connecticut politician was more than was warranted by convenience. It turned out to be so. Homer

Cummings, I thought then, and still think, as a good influence as ever was brought to bear on our man.

There were others he respected. There was Charles E. Merriam, who, along with Uncle Fred Delano, and Wesley C. Mitchell, made up the first Planning Board. It was Merriam, probably assisted by Louis Brownlow, who argued it into the Presidential office after its beginnings in Ickes' Public Works Board. Merriam, also, was owed respect as a politician as well as a political scientist. And the President may well have wanted to earn his good opinion. But Merriam's conception of the role of planning did not go much beyond research. The organization of which he was chairman did present the government with badly-needed fundamental studies; and he himself did give confidential advice at times. But his role, like that of so many others, was a far lesser one than Brandeis' shaping policy. There is a temptation to oppose these two--Merriam and Brandeis--with respect to Presidential influence. And in some ways the arrangement is realistic. But what happened, really, was that the President went the Brandeis way, pretending even to himself that he was also being a planner.

What I did not know in 1932, and never gave enough weight to when I did know, was that there was one old man in the shadows to whom the awe and reverence of sonship went without reserve. This, of course, was Brandeis. And Frankfurter was his prophet. Frankfurter came sometimes to Albany and occasionally we saw him. He never joined in our discussions; but we heard of him and sensed his influence. Because he sometimes gave contrary advice--not about important matters--Ray was sometimes annoyed by him. I remember some furious denunciations of his "interference". Berle and I were not so innocent that we did not recognize our great opponent. But we thought time was against him. All this liberal atomism seemed so completely inconsistent with the reality of our high-energy, large-scale economy that we could not take it seriously. That was our mistake. It was to have another run. And the Roosevelt administrations were not to be known for advancing into new economic ground except in the matter of accepting responsibility for a social welfare which extended to the prevention and relief of unemployment and even to the adoption of the principle of minima, in making some tentatives toward compensatory spending, in experimentation with monetary devices to achieve stability, and in correcting gross tendencies to unbalance the economy. This may seem a not unimpressive list. Actually, examination of it shows that it did not go beyond Hoover. To me it seems strangely inadequate. It so clearly indicates the necessity for finding direction and for setting up mechanisms to maintain balance; yet it stops short of establishing these. The devices which were adopted really make sense only in the framework of a plan for their use. That the executive should attempt to manage them with no more materials for judgment at his command than he is able to muster and with all the disabilities inherent in his other duties as head of a political party, national leader, commander in chief and head of state, seems to me absurd.

That even President Roosevelt could not do the impossible ought not to be held against him. That he did not attempt to escape from his dilemma may be held against him. It will be said that N.R.A. was such an attempt. It was certainly intended to be that by some of us who participated in its devising. But if the President at first conceived it as we did he soon found it inexpedient to press this aspect of its potentialities. It became the medium of a back-to-work movement--the Blue Eagle campaign; it was used to spread the eight-hour day, to abolish child labor, to fix minimum wages--these were "fair trade practices". But its use as the central balancing mechanism of the economy was never developed. Indeed no attempt was made to develop it.

Everything else done by N.R.A. could be done better by other agencies--and would be done by them. The only real reason for going on with a rewritten law to perform the function of adjustment among industries, after the Supreme Court outlawed the original Act as a delegation of powers beyond the constitutional competence of the Congress, would have been to bring to life its adjusting and balancing potentialities. It could have been done. But it was not done. It was not done because the old gentleman in the fatherly robes did not approve.

There is no one who can say whether the Roosevelt mind changed or whether it was never made up. And there is no one who can say, if it did change, what made it change. I think it did; and I think the evidence is quite conclusive, if I am allowed to distinguish between a conviction of the mind and one of the heart. There are the early campaign speeches in contrast with the late ones. The difference is a very striking one, and to me significant. About this I have no doubt. But as to the reasons for it I have some question; and weighing all I know and have been able to learn I think the Brandeis disapproval was important. But it has also to be recalled that the old progressivism was comfortably orthodox with many others who together composed the President's higher audience. They wanted to believe that big business was bad and that the kind of regulation represented by the breaking-up of efforts of the Department of Justice, together with the enforcement of fair-trade practices by the Federal Trade Commission, were sufficient punishments.

That this had nothing to do with the formulation of an industrial policy and its carrying out was admitted. But this was not government's function. It was to be a policeman merely. This was the attitude--even after the events of the depression and the forced change of attitude necessary to escape from it. There was not a limited but a general acknowledgement, when the troubles of 1933 were upon the nation, that responsibility for recovery must be assumed by government. It was a short jump to the inference that government had the responsibility of preventing more depressions. That meant, as candidate Roosevelt had repeatedly said, the maintenance of a concert of interests. N.R.A. was the concert of interests in action--or was so intended by those of us who thought that way.

Inflationary spending was a gross and violent medicine for recovery--necessary perhaps, but only necessary because the surgery necessary to both cure and future prevention could not be resorted to. It could not because orthodoxy forbade. And the high priest of the orthodox sanctuary was Brandeis. Presently, however, the vestal virgins--Frankfurter, Corcoran and Cohen--were busily at work and much more effective than Merriam. It was they who prevented N.R.A. from becoming a mechanism for adjustment or from being revived after the blow of court disapproval. Brandeis had done his part; now the others did theirs.

I dwell on this as a crucial matter. It was a crucial matter for the shape of the New Deal. But whether the President accepted atomism because Brandeis' disapproval was intolerable or whether he made up his mind that progress toward social integration would be impossible in his time, I cannot say conclusively. It is possible that he fell back on Brandeisism because he became convinced that integration was a political impossibility--and perhaps it was. Yet there is this to be considered: the one real rival of Brandeis for the father role in Franklin's life was Theodore Roosevelt. Theodore had been dead for nearly two decades and so could not exert the kind of living influence which judges men and events--including proposals--by a criterion and makes known its conclusion. If Franklin wanted to ask--or even if he did not want to ask--it was made known to him what the Brandeis judgment was about everything he intended to do or be. The influence was all around him, giving comfort and certainty as well as daily advice. The comfort came from remote Olympus as a kind of emanation which could turn baleful if the god was displeased. But there were disciples who would carry an enormous part of the Presidency's burden and would see to it that every task was carried out within the rules. The network of approved appointees grew with great rapidity. The time came when everyone else, even those who had been loyal and sacrificing, could be ruthlessly excluded. I was one of those.[6]

If you happened to have an interest in Franklin's development, and if you went back to his youth and young manhood, you would find that "Uncle Ted" had always played a significant role. It had by no means ended with Theodore's death; but it was necessarily reduced then mostly to emulation, or to asking himself what Uncle Ted would have thought;

[6]Moley deals with this also in After Seven Years.

and what one who is gone would have thought can become significantly subject to wishful shaping. Still Uncle Ted, if he learned any one thing from his long experience in public life, had learned that public policy had to move with the cultural drift. His loud talk about "malefactors of great wealth," like the rest of his sloganeering, was strictly for its appeal to the backward. Actually his distinction between good and bad trusts was a selective beginning which might have led to a positive program. But the progressives would not tolerate such tentatives and they were eliminated from the Bull Moose platform in 1912. But Franklin must have known well enough that Theodore had been groping for something more satisfactory than trust-busting. There is every evidence that he thought at first that the twenty years between 1912 and 1932 had been long enough for the progressives to catch up. In fact, there was a distinct air of relief in his discovery that Berle and I had got beyond the Wilsonian concepts. And all our spring conversations proceeded on this basis.

Imagine our surprise--and chagrin--when the turn came.[7] We were enlisted and we did not secede. But we were dismayed. Ray cursed Frankfurter, the chief architect of that speech, but probably not within the candidate's hearing. And then, of course, we could not know that this swallow did actually presage summer. Things by then were pretty hectic. There seemed to be very little order in our business in spite of our careful laying out, earlier, of a program. We knew as well as the professionals did that things had changed. But that change meant something to us it did not mean to them. It was clear that the campaign was won. This, to Farley, Howe and others of their sort, meant that no more remained to be done except to avoid mistakes. They pressed for innocuousness. It seemed to us of the brains trust, on the other hand, that if the election was certain some few chances could be taken in the interest of the future. The party was an awfully loose coalition of diverse-minded groups. If any program was to be got into legislation it was necessary to force commitment to it. This was possible for a candidate whose election was beyond much question. We would have had him play for an unmistakable mandate which party dissidents could not run out on without extreme embarrassment.

It was not done our way. The latter part of the campaign was cloudy, discursive and no more than mildly progressive even in the old fashioned sense. The word planning was dropped. The familiar atomism was adopted. The small businessman, the little enterpriser, the fellow who would wreck N.R.A. and consistently oppose change, became the

---

[7] It came, as I see it, in his speech on 20 August 1932 in Columbus, to be found at p. 669 of Vol. II of The Public Papers and Addresses of <u>Franklin D. Roosevelt</u> edited by Samuel I. Rosenman, New York, 1938.

campaign pet, as he had been the pet in campaigns since representative democracy had begun. There was no mandate. And, when it was needed, there was no party principle.

4

It would be difficult for me to explain satisfactorily why I kept no notes of my various activities from the time I was coopted into the brains trust in spring until some time after our candidate had been elected. Those notes, if I had them, would be of use to me if to no one else. There are things I cannot now explain; and they might be explainable if my impressions at the time had been put down. I can recall well enough the more dramatic incidents. But even these I have a tendency to displace in time unless I take the trouble to check them with some reference to others' notes or to concurrent printed material. And if I cannot be certain of events, I can be even less certain of conversations, of discussions and disputes, and of changes in policy or direction. It is sometimes important to recall such matters because they are clues to what happened later. When policies or attitudes are far enough developed to be announced they have probably been developing for some time. It would be interesting to know not only their origins but something about the course of development.

I was more dense, I think, about the development of the President's monetary and fiscal policy than about most other matters, and it illustrates why some Roosevelt policies are still mysteries. I had something to do with it and certainly assisted in its evolution; but I am not prepared, as I ought to be, to say how it originated and what its evolution was. I was spoken to about the matter very early and so alerted to it. I told what I knew and thought which was little enough, except that I was prepared with a satisfactory precis, having written an elementary economics text whose relevant passages I could display.[8]

The Federal Reserve System was one of the disappointments of those days. It had been thought capable of preventing the kind of occurrences we had been passing through. Perhaps it was capable of checking them. President Hoover thought so. But he entered such conditions as: if it had been effectively managed; and if it had not given way to unwise European appeals for management in the interest of their

---

[8]This was American Economic Life and the Means of its Improvement. Co-authors with me were Thomas Munro and LeRoy Stryker. But I wrote the financial and monetary passages, having them checked by my friend and senior colleague at Columbia, E. E. Agger, whose field it was.

banking systems.[9] But anyway its existence had not prevented disaster and so it was to an extent discredited. Something more had to be looked for. Both Berle and I had thorough talks--and repeated ones--with the Governor. I had some ideas about the managed currency. I was inclined to believe that a weighted commodity index ought to be substituted for gold as the basis of the dollar. So far as I could see the most sensible and informed expert in this matter was James Harvey Rogers of Yale. And one of my first concerns was to see that the Governor had direct contact with him. This I did by getting from Rogers a memorandum and then seeing to it that an interview was arranged. I participated in the discussions, and they went satisfactorily.

But it was not possible for a Democratic candidate to proceed without the benefit of Carter Glass' advice. The old Senator from Virginia had been so integral a part of the Wilsonian scene that, as a survivor from it, he could not be ignored (and, in fact, when the time came, he was offered the Secretaryship of the Treasury, perhaps the most extreme instance of party, sectional and traditional influence on cabinet formation). But if his position was not well enough known, he made it perfectly clear to the newcomer. He thought the Federal Reserve ought not to be touched; he also thought that recovery ought to be sought only in the processes of liquidation. This too was the position of Willis of Columbia and Kemmerer of Princeton, the two weightiest pundits in the monetary field. And although they were by now squirming themselves, after watching lesser institutions than their own crumble in the storm, the big New York bankers had no more constructive suggestions to offer. Many of them were talked to. I had great admiration for Walter Wheeler Stewart who had left academic life for banking; but he too had no assistance to give.

Irving Fisher was certain that he knew all the answers. He had been all his life an earnest advocate of a managed currency. And I arranged for him to see the Governor. But he was not one to share his wisdom and then retire. He was inclined to be something of a nuisance. During the spring before the nomination there was time for more of this than could be managed from July to November. But there was a resumption of it after that. During the winter the crisis deepened; moreover it was complicated by European troubles to whose solution we were related, if in no other way, through a forthcoming World Economic Conference. When this phase was reached in December I found myself caught in such consequential negotiations that I did begin to make notes for my own guidance. These have survived; and they are where the Diary part of this miscellany begins.

[9]Cf. various passages in Vol. III of his Memoirs, New York, 1952.

One of the most criticized phases of the early Roosevelt regime are these monetary and financial affairs. I was in or close to all of them. Yet there are matters about which I am still puzzled--perhaps more puzzled than those who had nothing to do with them. I was an ardent believer in a stable currency and I was therefore violently opposed to inflation as a continuing policy. I did not argue against reflation. That was merely getting back to a situation in which debts might be discharged in dollars roughly equal to those of the time of their contraction. Nor was I opposed to the gold revaluation. I though the business of buying and selling it as a means of managing the currency would not work, and it did not.

Most of what I felt and thought I had a chance to express right down to the time of inauguration. After that I might as well have been removed to the moon so far as this range of problems was concerned. The exception to this was that I had a good deal to do with the preparations for the Economic Conference. I was party to the conversations with all the visitors who came to Washington for preliminary conversations. I was even supposed to follow Moley as the next Presidential envoy at about the time the Conference blew up. I approved the President's action if not the manner of it but it was taken without my knowledge. I should have argued for a different course--did argue, but too late. We should have tried harder for an international New Deal with revaluation, large expenditures on unemployment relief, and the undertaking of public works on a grand scale. This would have been difficult politically, because of the general irritation about the war debts. But it could have been done.

If this was not to be done, we had to seal ourselves off and proceed with our own program. This we pretty much did. But Hull and his group--including, for instance, Herbert Feis and others in the Department of State--remained convinced free traders. They entered on a long campaign for the freeing and enlargement of world trade at the very time when most of us were working intensively on a program of domestic recovery which depended utterly on non-interference from outside. We were temporary isolationists. The President allowed both to go on concurrently. Why did he do this? And why did he believe that the dollar of stable purchasing power "from one generation to another" about which he spoke could be reached by mere manipulation of the price of gold? He allowed the budget to go on unbalanced from year to year without apparent worry over the consequences. There are inconsistencies here which I cannot explain. I might be able to understand them better if I had made more notes of our very intimate conversations on many occasions before he had the responsibilities of the Presidency. He was not then defending any policy; he was trying to arrive at one. Obviously he still had to improvise when he assumed office. He had not arrived at any clear pattern to be worked out. I wish I could say why.

This is roughly true about other matters, most of them less

consequential; but some of them just as significant. There was, for instance, the matter of policy toward Japan.

5

The two most consequential events about which all the others of the Roosevelt years group themselves, were the great depression and the second world war. The attempts to struggle out of the paralysis and despair of the years 1929-33 are the efforts with which I was most closely associated and about which I ought to know a good deal. It is true that these were for me very full years, and my memory is crowded with the important events in which I had some part. But even about these I have some difficulty, as I have tried to say, in explaining why occurrences assumed the order they did, and sometimes also why they happened at all. With the great war, which as we can now see was made inevitable by the election of Roosevelt in 1932, explanations are even more difficult. So far as I myself am concerned, also, I was removed from participation in any of the contributing developments after 1936. I was in an exceptional watching position and was anguished by the march toward disaster but I was not part of what was going on. The spectator role irked me and I tried to get back to participation of some sort. But all the time we were progressing toward conflict. I was trying to look back to the years of my intimacy with events for some clue to causation, some explanation--which must lie in the years 1932-36--of the approaching denouement. I knew war was coming a long time ahead and I therefore had a long time to think about it. But there is much that I cannot explain.

There are some things, however, about which I am clear enough. The Stimson policy toward Japan was approved and adopted by the President-elect in the early spring of 1932. This took me by surprise. It was at a time when Moley and I, almost alone, were acting as confidential aides in matters having to do with economic and social policy. This matter came up at a time when I was happily plotting with the Forest Service for what afterward became the Civilian Conservation Corps. I was also engaged in trying to shape and push along legislation about agriculture we had thought might possibly be got through in the last weeks of the regular session of the Congress. There were going on too almost incredibly difficult arrangements concerning the London Conference which fell mostly on me.

Moley, in a few succinct pages of After Seven Years[10] describes the complex situation into which we--a couple of amateurs--had been drawn. We thought it had been clearly enough established that for many reasons the policy was to be one of no more than distant collaboration with other nations whose economic troubles their statesmen were trying to make us responsible for. We were to recover first; then we would see what we could do to help them--unless, of course, they cared to collaborate, as they evidently did not, in a general recovery effort. The instructions for our delegates to meetings in Geneva preliminary to the economic conference were being discussed. We were determined to keep war debts, tariffs and currency stabilization apart. European politicians had staked a good deal on getting us to forgive their debts. They wanted to trade this forgiveness for a reduction in tariffs which we might think an advantage. They were inclined also to include disarmament in the package.

Two of Hoover's people were involved in all this: Secretary Stimson and Norman Davis. Stimson, Hoover's Secretary of State, had repeated in January his non-recognition doctrine with respect to Manchukuo, thus giving notice to Japan that the United States was opposed to her activities on the continent. But in his statement there was a broad hint that the new administration would support the same policy. On the next day, Governor Roosevelt without giving us any intimation or asking us to participate in drafting the statement, said that "American foreign policy must uphold the sanctity of treaties." This meant to us that the policy we had been pursuing was to be reversed in the case of Japan. It was inconsistent with all we had been planning. It was inconsistent with American tradition. Furthermore it accepted responsibility for China's integrity as against both Japanese and Russian encroachments--even in the doubtful northern area of Manchuria.

It seemed to me quite clear that this was not only a mistaken general policy for that time but that in the particular instance it involved a bottling up of the Japanese which would issue in explosion. The Japanese could not stop. They might be influenced to find other than military ways to expand; but they could not reverse their economic dependence on the mainland.

Ray and I were so certain that a grave mistake was being made that we insisted on talking the matter out with the Governor. We got no satisfaction. Both of us said what we had to say, I almost too sharply, as Moley implies. What I finally said was that the Stimson doctrine meant war and that not too long delayed. Whereupon I was interrupted by the incredible remark that war with Japan had to come sometime and it might as well be soon. Ray, in After Seven Years, did not repeat this, but only

---

[10]Beginning on page 90.

what came after. This was to the effect that the Roosevelts had a traditional sympathy for the Chinese and that Stimson's Japanese policy was one with which they must agree.

That the Stimson non-recognition doctrine was not the way to approach the Japanese question I was convinced. I also thought it dangerous doctrine at any time. For what reason did the President-elect choose this particular issue to establish a collaboration with the outgoing administration which he had refused in every other instance? This is a puzzle to me still. Was Stimson another elder for whom Roosevelt felt the same kind of uncritical loyalty that he had for Brandeis? There is an argument here which could, and doubtless will, go on and on. Two whole administrations later, when the consequences of the doctrine were being consummated in war, he chose Stimson to be his Secretary of War. Was that only because he was a respected Republican who would stop the mouths of some partisan critics?

The Davis matter I am able to explain to my own satisfaction. His maneuvers in the spring of 1932 annoyed Ray and myself to no end. There was also a strangely appeasing attitude toward him. But it has to be remembered that he was a life-long Democrat, even if a reactionary one, and that disarmament, although it is now forgot, was very hopefully looked at then. The conferences had been going on for some time but had got nowhere. The governor had some hope that he might break the inertia by a few startling suggestions. Davis was a practiced diplomat and he did not want to let him go. What Davis had not been able to accomplish for Hoover, he might succeed in doing for Roosevelt. It would be a triumph.

But that this was completely inconsistent with the provocation involved in the Stimson doctrine was all too obvious. I did not fail to point it out. And I continued to be so worried about our situation vis-á-vis Japan that I mentioned the matter occasionally. But I had nothing to do with the conduct of foreign affairs; and after our move to Washington, when the President had the whole Department of State at his disposal, already committed to non-recognition, I only heard of such matters incidentally. I have often speculated on the course events might have taken if the policy had been a different one. Suppose, for instance, we had set out deliberately to assist Japan in finding resources and markets; suppose we had tried to encourage her liberal forces and discourage the militarists; suppose we had encouraged the development of relations with China which would have given her a privileged position such as we have in Central and South America.

Such an alternative was reasonable in 1933. Perhaps the military had too much power to have been turned aside from their aggressions at any time after that. But nothing could be more ridiculous than the reversal of policy toward Japan after her defeat. Having destroyed the only effective check to Russian imperialism in the East, we had not only lost our position in China, for which the Japanese affair was undertaken, but have been forced to meet a now-combined Chino-Russian force with force of our own. The Japanese might have prevented all this if our statesmanship had been different.

This was a choice of no one but the President. He allowed himself to be guided into it by Stimson. Whether, if Stimson had not begun it, he himself would have invented it, no one can say. The British would not follow. It was a purely American policy. Before long it had taken on moral aspects: that is to say Japan was an aggressor, China was oppressed and so on. All of the allegations of this sort were true enough. The question is whether they would have happened if we had acted as a restraining friend of the Japanese instead of as a rather muddled friend of China.

As to the onrush of war in Europe the situation was different. In the beginning there were mistakes of the Versailles treaty repeated ad nauseam in the successive compromises. These ruined the democratic government of Germany and gave Hitler his chance. There was not much chance of escaping the logic of these events after 1933, even if the President had devoted himself to the task. Something might have been done for Mussolini if he had been no more than a little more reasonable; but Hitler's megalomania, so efficiently implanted by the thorough Germans, and the awful cruelties of the long pogrom, made it impossible for any Western politician even to be neutral. And, of course, the President did not try. Brandeis was not exactly a pacifist in these circumstances; he could not have been. And it was his lead more than any other which was followed. These were not matters in which I had any active concern. I was elsewhere.

6

During 1933 and 1934 and into 1935 it seemed to be the general opinion that my star was rising. I knew better. I dissented from the developing foreign policy; I did not agree with Hull and the state department that we had to stake everything on international laissez faire. I was opposed to American business interests in several important fields: notably that covered by the Food and Drugs legislation and that affected by the marketing agreements under the Agricultural Adjustment Act. I had had a quarrel with Douglas about the use of emergency funds to further recovery. I had an even worse quarrel first with George Peek and then with Chester Davis about the incidence of agricultural benefits. So it had gone. I always seemed to be throwing myself across the path of aggressive interests who were intent on getting something and were intolerant of any opposition. To make matters worse I had annoyed the newspaper and magazine owners who were afraid of any injury to their lucrative food and drug advertising. They had carried on something of almost the proportions of a crusade to get rid of me.

All this resulted in a build-up I did not seek and would have avoided if I could. To the outside observer it seemed that I was getting more and more attention and therefore reaching a more and more strategic position. There was a certain amount of truth in this. But it did not take account of the consolidation of the Brandeis forces and their implacable hostility to me. They were determined to check me everywhere, to discredit and eject me from government. They succeeded. They succeeded, however, not because their manipulations made my situation impossible, but because N.R.A. and A.A.A. had been declared unconstitutional and because the turn to atomism as against concentration and control became administration policy.[11]

[11]For some three years before my resignation I had been made aware of hostility in the Brandeis coterie. It became serious when Corcoran, for all practical uses, moved into the White House. Very cautiously, because I rated as a fairly old and loyal aide, the maneuvers to shut me off, to discredit my projects and to displace my friends in the administration began. Events, of course, helped. It was a discredit to me that N.R.A. was outlawed. This was a serious blow to what slight hope remained that national unity rather than atomism might win out as a policy. And I was more or less the symbol of the one and certainly the avowed enemy of the other.

That I was excluded from any part in the campaign of 1936, even as a Presidential helper, made my position impossible. It was after I had told the President that I would stay no longer that Moley had the talk with Corcoran in which his animus was revealed. He had won; but he did not yet know it.

Corcoran broke a rather embarrassing silence in their conversation by asking Ray if he knew when "Tugwell was getting out." Ray was, he says, about to answer noncommittally when Corcoran went on, speaking of me:

"I've never seen anything like him for arrogance. He picked up the draft of a speech the skipper was to make, laid it down in front of me, pointed to the word 'competition,' and said, 'That ought to come out.' When I paid no attention to him he turned to the President and said, 'You know you don't believe that.' The President ignored him. Can you imagine the nerve? Well. . . we'll take care of him. Not that he doesn't serve a useful function. He is a sort of catfish to keep the herrings from getting sluggish when the fishermen take them back in tanks to port. But the skipper shouldn't get the idea that he is an edible fish."

That seemed to dispose of Rex.

I do not recall the incident concerning the speech, so I cannot say

Some of the more interesting episodes of my New Deal years are mentioned in the Diary which follows; some are not. I knew that I ought to be keeping some record and periodically I did. But the truth is that I was faithful about it during the less crowded intervals. When a crisis was boiling up and I was working early and late with an exhausting schedule of conferences, discussions, meetings, committees, boards, drafting groups and the like, in addition to my regular work, I neglected record making. Such moments or hours as I could steal were devoted to what I am still convinced was a better business. I tried to stay creative. I tried to remain what I had been before, one of the President's idea men. Whatever situation we were in I tried to think of ways out. I took literally dozens of these to the President, sometimes after consultation with others, sometimes after going to the length of drafting a memorandum, but sometimes just as suggestions to catch his mind as it worked on a problem.

For a long time I was quite free to do this. But the relationship grew less intimate in 1935 when I became an administrator on my own and also when the Corcoran influence at the White House became really possessive. There were many occasions even after that when I went to the President in the old way. He never refused to see me when I asked; and occasionally he showed me favor in the only way he ever did: by asking me to lunch with him at his desk, or seeing to it that I was asked to join the more intimate occasions in the evening. After I left the government my contacts with him naturally were much less frequent. But we never had such a break in friendship as happened--to my sorrow--with Ray Moley. At one time he was determined that I should become Chief of the Forest Service. This was approaching me on a very weak side. I was an inveterate conservationist. I countered by telling him again, as I had done before, that he ought to get along with the necessary reorganization of all the agencies having to do with public land. They were scattered about and

whether Corcoran reported it accurately. But I am sure that Ray's report of Corcoran's little speech was verbatim. At any rate Corcoran was obviously not so sure as he tried to make it appear. After three years of effort he still did not know whether the President thought me "edible."

In the talk we had had when I had insisted on resigning the President had apologized handsomely for having allowed me to be boxed during the campaign. He spoke about my having been just as much an issue, perhaps more, than if I had still been an administration favorite. It was, he said, Farley's mistake. He then pointed to the unprecedented victory, a very great one--the greatest in all his long career. What "we" have stood for, he said, is what they voted for. I was too weary then, and too discouraged to reply, as I should, that we ought then to go on. When I got around to it a month later, after a rest, and after my resignation had been announced, he listened and discussed the main issue with me at length. I thought we might resume. But the court fight went so <u>badly that</u> nothing else was every really attempted.

to a certain extent competing. There was no general policy and very little coordination. He promised; and we worked on it for a while. But the jealousies were too bitter and had penetrated too far into the Congress. He put it off and it never did get done.

Ultimately I left my congenial work as Chairman of the Planning Commission in New York City--where Fiorello LaGuardia was Mayor-- to go to Puerto Rico. I have told about that adventure in The Striken Land. And the account here ends as that begins. When I went to Puerto Rico, however, it was with the understanding that when (not if) the consolidation of the public land agencies took place I was to have charge from the first. This was in 1941. All of us should perhaps have anticipated Pearl Harbor, or, if not such an attack, at least war with Japan. I, like others, had been regarding the squeeze on the Japanese so long by then that the climax took me by surprise. And even the President was evidently surprised by the violence of the reaction. At any rate the concentration of attention on the conflict and the interest I developed in the struggle I got into in Puerto Rico prevented any further progress in the land matter until the President died, after which presently I returned to academic life at the University of Chicago.

When I went into the Department of Agriculture as an Assistant Secretary in 1932 it was with the expectation of staying no more than a few months. In fact I never expected to stay more than a few months longer. My situation, almost from the first, was an impossible one; and it grew worse as time went on and I accumulated opposition. I was no doubt more careless because of this expectation that I should otherwise have been about the enmities I incurred. There is no virtue, and there is a good deal of unreality, about the way I conducted myself in the Washington milieu. I walked head on into and through what had to be done. I conciliated no one, made no compromises, and I am afraid I made myself a nuisance to many of those around me, especially the Secretary, Henry Wallace. For this I was called arrogant in a vast variety of ways and by many skilled practitioners. I had for a while a notoriety as a result of my ability as a nuisance-maker which was equalled by very few of my generation.

My intention to leave the Department was frustrated again and again. There seemed to be some reason why I should not go whenever there was a good opportunity. Jesse Straus, our Ambassador to France, tried to get me to go with him when he took up his post and the President widened the idea into a general Ministership in Europe with an economic frame of reference. But when it came down to it, the President did not want me to go just then. This was in the summer of 1933. A number of times Harold Ickes asked me to move to Interior and be Undersecretary there. He was especially insistent in 1934. This would have been a logical and useful place for me. But Henry did not want me to leave. And by then I was fond of the Department and caught up in several projects it seemed important to complete. Then in 1935 the President and I between us invented the Resettlement Administration and, in addition to remaining Undersecretary of Agriculture, I became its first Administrator.

The intention of Resettlement was to do something for a group of rural people who had been neglected for too long and who were untouched by the benefits of the A.A.A., and at the same time to carry out a vast conservation scheme. Poor land made poor people. The idea was to find the people better land, teach them to work it successfully and return the poor land to forests or other similar uses. This kind of work had been going on partly under Harry Hopkins' relief organization and partly under a special set-up in the Department. It had not been coordinated, however, and tackled with real earnestness.

This was again one of those matters which I thought I could start and then turn over to someone else. To escape the inertia and hostility of the Department toward this kind of thing, I thought it ought to be a separate administration at first; then, when everyone had got used to the idea, it could be returned to the Department. I had done the same thing with the Soil Conservation Service, except that Ickes had tried to steal it, and, when the time came, I had a hard time getting it back into Agriculture. But this was the reason for keeping the title of Undersecretary while I undertook the new job.

There were many vicissitudes; and about all we really accomplished was the shaking up of the agricultural hierarchy. The unfortunate among rural folk had been shamefully neglected. They never would be quite so neglected again. But the fraternity closed in on us in a remarkably short space of time, changed the direction of the effort and finally liquidated most of our work. My maneuver was successful. I did get the job started, and I did get the Administration back into Agriculture. But there it was quietly strangled. And the coup-de-grace was administered by a Congress acting under the orders of the Grange, the Farm Bureau Federation and the processors of agricultural products.

It did not help any that I had by then (1936) become such a notorious character. Resettlement had to carry a heavy burden of disreputability into its future because I had started it. What was a genuinely conservative effort was pictured--with fair success--as an attempt to Sovietize rural America. The poor seldom have any real defenders in legislatures. They contribute very little to campaign funds; and they cannot be trusted even to vote in their own interest. No one paid any penalty for killing Resettlement. But I still believe that something like it must be done both for the sake of the people and the land. I hope in its next incarnation it will have a more orthodox sponsor.

7

I am, after all these years, still bitter about the disappearance of the Resettlement Administration and still harbor, in spite of myself, a good deal of resentment. This is made worse by an inability to see how I could have done much other or managed things very differently. I ought perhaps to have persuaded someone else to father it. But that would not have been so easy at the time. The President wanted me to do it and the allocation of emergency funds to the work was conditioned on my agreement to undertake it. I might have persuaded him to start someone else as Administrator. My effort to do so was probably quite feeble. At any rate it was not successful.

The truth was that I wanted to do this one thing myself. There came together in it my closest interests, ones I had discussed many times with the President, for they were his closest interests too. Resettlement was organized in May, 1935. It was set up by executive order. It brought together all the rural relief and land retirement work in the government. And I thought that with this enormous task to do I could pretty well retreat from my position as whipping boy for the President--a post I still occupied, although it ought long ago to have gone to Corcoran--and become a respectable administrator.

I had already been squeezed out of any control over A.A.A., and my position in the Department was becoming more and more nominal as my respectability declined. There was less and less scope for activity. If I had not begun the Resettlement adventure in 1935 I should have left the Department. Resettlement delayed my going for a year and a half. This seems a short time. But when I had suffered the humiliation of being a considerable issue in the election of 1936 without any defense from my colleagues or even permission to defend myself, I had had enough. The President had repeatedly refused to let me go, saying in a variety of ways, that he understood my position, that it saved him from direct attack and so on. But when Farley asked him to keep me quiet during the campaign and he acquiesced, I rebelled. On the day after the great victory of 1936, when if I had been an issue, it had been one we had won on, I told him that under no circumstances would I go on. I was through.

By then it was no longer possible for me to go back to Columbia although I was still on leave. The fact is that I was no very reputable person. We had just finished a campaign of much bitterness in which businessmen and most of the other respectables had extended themselves in an effort to convince the electorate that we were untrustworthy. If there was one word used more than any other it was "crackpot." We were ruining the country, undermining American character, and undermining all the traditional institutions. I was the chief "crackpot." This was largely because I had been a professor, a theoretical and doctrinaire pedagogue, who had "never met a payroll" and had no sense of responsibility.

I could understand that the Columbia trustees were probably taken in by all this. In fact most of them were probably part of it. To an extraordinary degree the Liberty Leaguers and their sympathizers believed the fictions they created. But that it had affected my colleagues I would not have believed. Nevertheless my old Dean at the Wharton School, now head of the Department of Economics at Columbia, was deputized by the other professors to tell me that they did not want me back. Since I had already announced that I was going to join Charles Taussig's business organization, and, as a matter of fact, had my resignation written, this came as an added humiliation, perhaps the hardest to bear of any in the whole episode of my retreat from Washington.

Nevertheless, I meekly sent in my resignation and Columbia's hands were washed of me permanently. My business interlude was a short one. There was no real place for me and no real work to do. The opportunity, after a year, to become chairman of the Planning Commission for the City of New York, was one I welcomed. And of all the public work I ever did, this proved to be the most congenial. Not that much was accomplished. When I left in 1941 we had done something toward seating the planning function in the government as the foresighted drafters of the new charter had expected. But there had been and still were formidable obstacles. I was entitled to think, of this job, that I had done as well in it as perhaps I could, even if much remained to be done. If I had stayed much longer I should probably have been in the same kind of trouble I always seemed to find myself in.

The real estate interests in New York were as self-centered and as effectively obstinate a group of reactionaries as can ever have existed anywhere. They had no intention of allowing the Planning Commission to assume the functions plainly allocated to it in the Charter. It was my duty to subdue them. In the process I very rapidly built up the same kind of violent opposition I had had in Washington. Also it suited Bob Moses' intentions--although we had got along very well as we worked for the city's improvement--to attack me in the same old terms. I was a "long-haired planner," wholly impractical and so on. He thus took advantage, of the elaborate campaign behind the stereotype, and he became a kind of hero to the exploitative interests. Few of New York's citizens have done so much for her as Bob Moses. And no one admires him more for it than I. All great men have their weaknesses, however, and his is a weakness for approval. It was easy to get it at my expense.

Everything was not happy in New York. But the problems of the city were not only dwarfed by those into which the nation was drifting, they were also conditioned by them. For New York was an international

center of trade, of finance, and even of culture. It could be abstracted
from the world. As a planner for the city I felt the impact of the repeated
shocks of those years. By 1940 the war was going on in Europe; and our
relations were disturbed to the depths. I would have been insensitive
indeed if I had not felt the impulse to play as a city official.

There seemed to be no place in the Federal Government where I
could be effective, considering my accumulation of enmities. But the
Puerto Rican situation seemed to be one of those fortunate opportunities
which sometimes join personal desires with convenient circumstances.
I could bring the New Deal to an island where its coming had been
delayed for a decade. I could also have a part in the great events now
shaping up. So I responded to the suggestion of Harold Ickes and became
Puerto Rico's war-time Governor. I also became her last appointed
outside Governor. It was my last public post. I still held it when
President Roosevelt died. And I was not the type preferred by the
Truman administration. We soon parted company.

8

As I went along I did sometimes comment on the events occurring
about me and on the people who were involved in them. If those
comments were not so systematically undertaken or persistently pursued
as they should have been, this was not because I did not have a sense of
history, of participating in fateful events. It was because I was usually
exhausted by the pressures upon me. And there was literally a choice to
be made between record-making and doing something about what was
coming up next. The future usually won over the past.

But I was sometimes convicted of neglect; and at such times I tried
to catch up and promised myself that I would go on. But I never was able
to persist. So that my journal is spasmodic and my comments partial.
The interest in that period has been so great, however, that from all of us
who had any part in what went on, there is expected, even demanded, an
accounting. The times are almost innumerable on which I have been
asked in one way or another to yield up such knowledge as I have. I have
always responded when I could. But for years now I could have spent
most of my time answering the demands of those who want to know
something they think I must be able to tell them.

I am hoping, later on, to write another kind of book than this--
an account of what went on when I was younger from the viewpoint of
age. For it shall use my own records as well as those of others. But I have
seen no reason why others should not have such raw material as I can
furnish now. Hitherto I have had to send typescript copies, photostats
and so on to inquirers. They can now find it more conveniently between
covers.

What most of them understandably want it to enlarge their knowledge of the President. In recent history, at least, there has been no more glittering character. As the historians take over from those of us who have recollections, the refulgence seems to brighten rather than to dim. Younger people feel that we ought to be able to tell them more than we can; and they are apt to be somewhat impatient at our inability to clear up what seem to them mysteries. They do not know why this Roosevelt turned out to be a progressive, why he so single-mindedly pursued a central ambition, or why he made the uses he did of the great power centered in him.

They tend to see the period he lived in as a kind of play in which the protagonists were Roosevelt and Hitler. Because of this they are inclined to dispose in an order of their own the events before and after the climax of 1945 when the villain was consumed in the fires of retribution and the hero moved off the stage just as the decisive blows were delivered. It is certainly possible to go back and arrange matters so that this sequence is quite clear. If I had been paying the attention hind-sight would seem to call for, I should have written my notes as stage-directions and comments on the effectiveness of this central drama. The trouble was about to happen, and then what was happening, I did not have the wit to accept it. Like so many others of my time, I saw, and tried to enlarge, the alternatives. What seems, looking back, to have been inevitable did not seem so to us. We always thought something meliorative could be done.

The President said to me in January of 1933 in a conversation I shall not forget, but which I cannot reproduce because I did not write it down, that the accession of Hitler was a portent of evil for the United States. He would in the end challenge us because his black sorcery appealed to the worst in men; it supported their hates and ridiculed their tolerances; and it could not exist permanently in the same world with a system whose reliance on reason and justice was fundamental.

I can see too, now, that what he was intending to say was that he would have no fear of a military trial of strength. What he would fear was the latent Nazism in Americans. How considerable this was he obviously did not know, but it can be seen that during the next few years he took some pains to find out. It is my belief that what wore him down as time passed was the successive retreats he had to make from the forthright policy he would preferably have followed. He had to compromise with Hitlerites in our own electorate.

There is no way of knowing whether the President thought that if Hitler had from the first been put on notice that any aggression would be met by force from the combined democracies, he would have held back. It is my belief that this is what he did think. Later on, matters went beyond any reasonable possibility of such a check. Preponderant opinion in the United States had not supported the necessary hard policy. There was nothing to do after a certain point but build up strength and wait for the show-down.

Japan was always out of the center of consideration. Japan was moving because the West was engaged in a quarrel; the outcome of that quarrel would determine Japan's fate. Meanwhile nothing was to be gained from compromise. Any weakness would cause the Japanese to move faster.

This, it now seems to me, must have been the fundamental orientation of his mind. It is exasperating to realize that he gave me all the materials for understanding and that I did not grasp them. I did not accept what now seems to have been inevitable; I was hotly and almost totally engaged in the New Deal development. I should have known that when it was being allowed to attenuate, there was a greater interest being served. The President was gathering up and hoarding support. He wanted it to be shaped and ready when it would be needed. For this he would sacrifice what he had to. He would not try the great experiment of concentration and control; he would retreat to orthodoxy. Thus he would gather behind him the traditional strength of a minority which had now swollen into a majority. He would manipulate and pamper it. He would have a sufficient national unity, when it had to be fallen back on in the coming trial.

In the years when I knew the President best and shared such of his responsibilities as I could, these movements were just beginning. What was much more obvious was a need to recover from depression and to reshape our economic system. This was what I had an interest in. When it became obvious that the recovery method was determined and that the economic system was not to be reshaped, my motivation was weakened. But I turned with satisfaction to the developing of an organization for the relief of distresses, the correction of some old injustices, and the furthering of conservation.

I like to think now that I did at least dimly know what was going on; but I suppose the most I can really claim is that my loyalty was equal to the strains put upon it. This was not true of many of my contemporaries. People like Jesse Jones, Jim Farley, Jim Byrnes, Ray Moley, Jim Warburg, Hugh Johnson--to name only a few--could not understand that they were minor actors supporting the hero about whom the play revolved. They were discarded, gesturing and sputtering violently--as they still do, such of them as still survive, still not understanding why they were utterly unimportant and why the President owed them no consideration.

He owed his consideration to history. He would not be forgiven if cruelty, hate, intolerance and fear were allowed to take the world when he had been appointed to prevent it. I thought he compromised too much. I often entered objection. Quite often he gave me reasons; but of course

I could not give them the weight I should if I had known what the denouement was to be. Even now, knowing what I do, I think he overdid it. He gave up too much, far too much; but that he was simply taking no chances I can see. One thing I never learned very thoroughly, I am afraid, was the art of compromise. I thought I had learned it; I was kept awake by a troubled conscience sometimes, wondering whether I had not compromised too much--given more than was absolutely necessary to secure what must be secured. But I was working with a great master who did not worry about this. He only worried about the great objective. I ought to have learned a lot more than I did in his school.

It sometimes seemed to me that I had bad luck. I tried to withdraw from the Food and Drug controversy for the good of the bill. But just at that time it suited a good many people to create a horrendous picture of me as a radical and the effort was unsuccessful. Likewise when the Resettlement Administration was set up, I did my best to conciliate, and even to enlist, the Farm Bureau Federation. But all the concessions I could make were not enough to smother the fundamental unwillingness of the more prosperous farmers to allow their poorer neighbors an opportunity to better themselves. That failed too. These are illustrations of my willingness to compromise. Sometimes, in despair, it seemed to me that I did nothing else. Perhaps I did not do it properly; perhaps my timing was wrong; perhaps it was just my luck to be caught in the gears and ground up.

Something of that experience must be caught in the notes I made at the time. Some of them are less notes than short essays on contemporary situations. Some of them--such as the syndicated pieces-- were for publication. Whatever they are I turn them over to those who are so eternally curious about what was going on when Roosevelt presided over Washington.

The Hundred Days

March 31, 1933 to May 30, 1933

I have fallen so far behind in this record of events that it seems almost impossible to catch up. Yet we are doubtless in the midst of one of the most interesting periods in the history of the country and my recording ought to be kept up. It is the sheer pressure of decisions and responsibilities which prevents.

"Word has been received that President Franklin Roosevelt has appointed Professor Rexford G. Tugwell, of New York City, a teacher in Columbia University, as Assistant Secretary of Agriculture. Professor Tugwell is a son of Mr. and Mrs. Charles H. Tugwell, of Wilson. He was educated in the Wilson High School and later obtained three degrees from the University of Pennsylvania. He and his wife and two children have moved to Washington. We consider this appointment an honor to Wilson and congratulate the Tugwell family."
-- The Wilson Star

After the inaugural events we were plunged immediately into the banking crisis in which the presidential proclamation was based on the Trading with the Enemy Act of 1917 (Act of 6 October 1917 -- Stat. L. 411, as amended, Section 5 (0).) which I worked over for some time, consulting various people and discovering that Hoover and Mills had inspected the Act and rejected the suggestion of acting on its authority. This rather doubtful executive act was validated in a few days by a scared

Congress called into special session.[1]

[1]My connection with this was that I was asked by FDR, after the suggestion
had been made to him by Rene Leon, to find out whether the relevant section
of the Act had or had not been repealed. I have mentioned this earlier and said
that the repealer applied before but not after the semi-colon; but that it was a
doubtful matter everyone agreed.

It appeared afterward as I noted--Hoover tells about it in his
Memoirs--that Ogden Mills and Hoover had considered its availability and,
after consulting Senator Glass, had decided against it. At least Hoover says so.
But that he would have used the authority at all, I doubt. When he heard, as
soon as he did, that we were making inquiries, he was reported to have
exclaimed in horror, "My God, they're going off gold!"

My inquiries in February were discreet enough; the search for a copy
of the Act after I had asked for it confidentially, turned up one in Dan Bell's
desk. And the passage on which we intended to rely if we could was
underlined in red ink. Some one had been studying it; and we were told that
this was the copy Mills had taken to the White House for consultation.

At any rate, after I had talked with Pittman, and finally Byrnes, the
President decided to take the chance. His proclamation and comment on it is
to be found in the Public Papers, Vol. II, pp 24 ff. what the President says
there is that after consulting with Senator Thomas P. Walsh, who was slated
to be Attorney General until his death on 2 March 1933, he had come to the
conclusion that the Act was still in effect. I doubt whether this was fact unless
he talked with Walsh over the phone. I think he came to his conclusion after
being assured by Pittman and Byrnes that there would be no delay about a
ratifying resolution. And, of course, there was none.

The Proclamation was issued at one o'clock in the morning of 6
. March. It declared a bank holiday to be continued through the four days
ending 9 March, the date set for convening the Congress, in Special Session
(pursuant to the proclamation of 5 March).

Besides declaring a bank holiday, the Federal Reserve Board (on 8
March) asked the Federal Reserve Banks to prepare lists of "hoarders" -- those
who had withdrawn gold or gold certificates and had not returned them by 13
March. This was to get gold back into the banks. It worked. The threat of
publicity caused the return of quantities of the precious metal and restored the
country's gold reserves.

Also under the proclamation the Treasury officials (Mills' assistants
Ballantine and Awalt stayed on temporarily for this purpose) issued
regulations permitting certain kinds of transactions even during the holiday:
such as completing settlements not involving currency, making change,
transacting fiduciary business, etc. But withdrawals were prohibited.

On 9 March a message was sent to the Congress asking for validation.
The Emergency Banking Act, as it was called had kept a lot of people in almost
continuous session from the eve of inauguration day. It was in this period, and
under these pressures, that future policy was really decided. And what was
decided was merely to restore confidence, get the banks going again, make
some future changes of a minor sort -- but not to make any basic revision of

Such a wave of approval for F.D.R. after the vigorous inaugural swept the country -- so long disgusted with governmental inaction -- that it seemed best to Henry Wallace and myself to press for immediate farm legislation. To this F.D.R. agreed. It was the kind of notion he appreciated.

It happened this way. On the first Sunday night after inauguration it occurred to us that something like the broad powers assumed by the President for banking might also be assumed by him for agriculture. But we rather gave this notion up, since so much must in any case depend upon consent. We did, however, determine to call in the farm leaders for a conference. Henry talked with each of them in turn by phone, telling them what we had been thinking of but not really suggesting a conspiracy. When the first leaders arrived they proposed broad general powers too, having reached this decision at a midnight conference on the train. We accepted the idea immediately, provided they could get general agreement, glad to have the initiative passed to them. At the conference next day, held in the Department, myself presiding, they secured this unanimous agreement.

the Federal Reserve System.

The Emergency Banking Act validated all the actions taken under the Proclamation and also gave the President further emergency powers to control foreign exchange transactions, gold and currency movements and banking transactions in general. In addition, of course, it provided a procedure for the gradual resumption of banking business.

It was not until 5 April that the President used his new powers to prohibit the hoarding of gold; and on 19 April the Secretary of the Treasury announced that no further licenses for gold export would be issued. It was this which began the process of dollar devaluation which caused such a sensation. From then on a progressive decline of the dollar in terms of foreign currency took place. But it was not until 30 January 1934 that a law was passed making devaluation a Congressional policy (The Gold Reserve Act of 1934). On 31 January a proclamation under the Act fixed the weight of the gold dollar; (see Public Papers, Vol. III (1934) pp 64 ff.)

Currency management was then underway. I had to do almost altogether with the preliminaries at the time when I was assisting to get things in order for the President-elect's move to Washington in the midst of crisis. After inauguration these matters were taken over by the Treasury people.

Report of a special Committee of
farm organization leaders authorized
at a general conference called by
Secretary of Agriculture Wallace,
Friday, March 10, 1933.

Your Committee recommends the enactment of an
emergency law, as hereinafter outlined:

That following the preamble setting forth the
condition that exists in Agriculture, the measure shall
declare that an emergency exists and that the powers
granted to the President under the Act shall continue for
such period of time as in the judgement of the President
the emergency continues.

It shall be the purpose of this legislation to
establish the principle of parity of prices between
agricultural and industrial commodities on the basis of
their pre-war relationship and to approach this parity of
prices by stages at as rapid a rate as seems feasible in the
circumstances.

POWERS TO BE CONFERRED UPON THE
PRESIDENT AND THE SECRETARY OF
AGRICULTURE, as follows:

One: To lease agricultural land and/or enter into contractual
agreements for the control of agricultural production.

Two: To take such action and to make such settlements
as are necessary in order to acquire full legal title to all
cotton or other farm commodities on which the
government has made loans or advances, upon such terms
as may seem fair and just, and to exchange such cotton or
other products with growers for acreage reduction.

<u>Three</u>: To regulate and supervise the marketing and processing of agricultural and competing products in domestic and foreign commerce.

<u>Four</u>: To levy such charges on agricultural products or products manufactured from them as seems necessary to accomplish the purpose of the Act.

<u>Five</u>: In the drafting of a bill to carry out these recommendations, all powers necessary to the successful carrying out of the purpose to be achieved shall be included.

****

The Secretary of Agriculture shall in his discretion apply the provisions of this act to the following farm commodities: Wheat, Cotton, Corn, Hogs, Cattle, Sheep, Rice, Tobacco, Milk and its products.

———————

Chairman, Mr. W. R. Ronald
Chas. Ewing
U. B. Blalock
Clifford Gregory
L. J. Tabor
Chas. Holman
C. E. Huff
E. A. O'Neal
Ralph Snyder
W. P. Lambertson
M. S. Winder, Sec.
Fred Lee, Legal Adviser
M. Ezekiel, Economic
Adviser

Next day we conducted a committee to the President; and he told us to frame legislation on this basis. We engaged Fred Lee and set about drafting a bill. In a few days it was done and sent to Congress with a message (which I now have in original draft, F.D.R. having sent it to me).

My thanks (on 17 March) for the pencilled draft read as follows:

*I offered to bet Henry Wallace on the way home
yesterday that you would remember to send me a draft of
your message. He counselled me not to be silly and so was
properly set back when it came. I shall value it as a
momento of your leadership in good cause. I believe our
bill may be something of a new charter for an oppressed
people. Now if we can do as much for consumers with a
new Food and Drugs act I can return happily to academic
life!*

We had hoped to get the thing through before lobbyists of the processors
could descend on Washington; but we immediately met with strong
opposition. The packers, millers, and spinners are quite adequately
represented in Congress. It seems impossible, in that group of small-town
lawyers, to find anyone with the slightest interest in farmers or workers.
They represent business interest for the most part. Our great difficulty
was that the Chairmen of the agricultural committees in both House and
Senate were also very sensitive to processors' interests rather than
farmers'. We were able to bring enough pressure to bear to force the bill
through the House in about four days. But as I write it is still in a Senate
committee and we are busy night and day trying to save it.

It is unique in a number of respects.   It declares the policy of
restoring farm prices to parity but it allows us to approach this end
gradually. It provides for a reduction of production but allows to choose
the method.   It provides the funds necessary to persuade land out of
production but leaves us wide discretion in acquiring it. The processors'
tax is used; but it can be applied gradually and with caution. But most
interestingly, the section which was written to provide for licensing of
processors (so that we might control them) turned, as we wrote it, into
something with vast possibilities. It allows the Secretary to enter into
agreements with associations of producers and processors on such terms
as may be necessary to "eliminate unfair practices or charges that . . .
prevent the effectuation of the declared policy" and the restoration of
economic balance. This amounts, of course, to the suspension of the anti-
trust acts for the food industries with broad regulatory powers lodged in
the Department of Agriculture.

Our enemies read this with care. Some of them saw that they
had more to gain from the power to agree than they had to lose from
being controlled. The opposition was, consequently, split. It is a bitter
fight but not so hopeless as it might otherwise have been. From the first
H.A. and I have felt that it would eventually pass and it is true that the
opposition has grown weaker as time has gone on and had come finally

to obstructionist and sniping tactics. The greatest handicap has been in not having any real push in Congress. For real radicals such as Wheeler, Frazier, etc., it is not enough; for conservatives it is too much; for Jeffersonian Democrats it is a new control which they distrust. For the economic philosophy which it represents there are no defenders at all. Nevertheless, in spite of everything, it will probably become law because something has to be done. And there had been nominal agreement to this among diverse groups. Also there is no alternative.

While this rough-and-tumble fight has been going on I have been working on two other major problems--besides, of course, getting acquainted with my administrative duties. One of these has had to do with the forestry bill and the other with departmental reorganization.

The forestry bill was conceived by the President himself. He proposed to have 250,000 of the unemployed taken into what he called a 'Civilian Conservation Army' who were to be organized in groups and were to work in the forests and national parks at a nominal wage. I had discussed it frequently with Roosevelt the candidate and Roosevelt the President-elect, and had taken part in the preliminaries beginning last December. Opposition to it developed as it reached the legislation stage from organized labor. It was said to threaten wage standards. But the unemployment problem is so tremendous that the opposition was not sufficiently effective to prevent its becoming a law. It is being signed today and the Department of Agriculture, of course, will have major administrative responsibility for its operation. The Forestry Service I have found to be a very efficient organization, and there is no doubt that they will be able to carry out their part of this plan successfully. I have worked on it a good deal in conferences with the Forestry people and they are now at work on regulations to put it into effect. I have been attracted to it because of my interest in long-run management of public property and because of promises to do something almost immediately at least to relieve the problem of unemployment. We expect to care for at least 250,000 men in this way.

The other problem -- departmental reorganization -- is really difficult. The Department is a good deal like a big university. Many of its activities are of a research sort but intermixed with these everywhere are more than forty regulatory acts which bring us into contact, in mostly unpleasant ways, with the business community. Many of the activities of the Department have been set up by statute from time to time and the organization has become rather unwieldy and needs recasting. The problem of mastering the great mass of detail involved in coming to definite functions and reducing them to some kind of order has been tremendous, but progress is being made and I have great hopes of being able to simplify the administrative structure and putting the Department on a better functional basis. The details of this I suppose no one will be interested in later years. It is one of those immense and thankless tasks which necessarily fall to anyone who accepts administrative responsibility in times like these.[2]

It has been greatly complicated by difficulties with the budget. The President has pledged himself to make reduction in governmental expenditures; and Lewis Douglas has been appointed Director of the Budget. It is a theory of his that research ought to bear the brunt of what he conceives to be necessary reductions; and very shortly after his appointment he presented us with an ultimatum which required the reduction of our activities by some sixty percent. This, of course, caused a rebellion and we in the midst of a running fight with Douglas to see how much we can save of the Department's fundamental work. We refused to accept his first proposition and we are in process of making a new one to him on the basis of our reorganization plans which will reduce expenditures but yet, we hope, save the best of our activities. There is an immense amount of detail in working over these budgets. Unfortunately the President originally agreed with Douglas and modifies his agreement only gradually and about individual matters of interest to him.

April 2, 1933

The great battle over the farm bill still goes on, with the opposition slowly crumbling under persistent effort. It is to be reported to the Senate tomorrow and tonight we must work again on last-minute amendments.

Yesterday Jesse Straus, the new Ambassador to France, suggested that I go along with him as economic adviser to the Embassy. I thought that I might when my creative job was done here, but insisted that Moley and F.D. must agree. We talked to Moley who liked the idea and agreed to ask F.D. There are reasons both for and against. I shall be under continual pressure here with all the regulatory acts making friction. I have felt it considerably already, having been denounced on the floor of the House, etc., but have not minded greatly except to accuse myself for somehow lacking tact. I shall doubtless be unpopular in the Department also when my reorganization plan comes out and disturbs old bureaucratic customs. This, combined with the necessity for economy, will make my position difficult, perhaps destroy my usefulness. Or so I

[2](Picture here of RGT with Lee Strong) A photograph (taken a year later in Mexico) with Lee Strong, my favorite among Bureau Chiefs. He was made Chairman of the Departmental Reorganization Committee and brought about great administrative improvements. One of these was the combining of the Bureaus of Entymology and Plant Quarantine of which Strong was thenceforth Chief until his untimely death in....

foresee. But, then again, we are all needed here at home. I shall be a soldier and do what seems best to F.D.R.

Bob LaFollette is much worried for fear our expansionist program will not follow quickly enough the conservatory steps which have been, or are about to be undertaken -- closing the weak banks, consolidating railways, exposing crooked bankers and the like. I am of that feeling myself. Moley and I talked about it yesterday and he said he thought Woodin would finally see a way. I hope so, though I think the way is clear enough -- government expenditure, and we must do it. We remarked that it seems a thousand years ago we were arguing with Stewart and Warburg -- they contending we must not jeopardize gold, etc., and I, who am no financial expert at all, proving at least somewhat wiser than they. It seems unbelievable now that they should have been so blind.

Tomorrow we start meeting again to discuss matters concerning the World Economic Conference. Moley in his capacity as Assistant Secretary of State has been talking to Lindsay and Herridge[3] and has finally settled with the President that he is to have charge of preparations. He says Hull has a mush mind and that Phillips[4] is a "stuffed shirt." His remarks must get around and his informal ways must scandalize the over-formal State Department. He told someone the other day, who objected to a conversation with Lindsay which had not been too carefully prepared for, that "his Irish Grandmother would turn over in her grave if she thought he had to prepare for a conference with an Englishman."

April 3, 1933

It is hard to foresee how long the general public's approval we have had so far will last. Not very long, I think. Governmental economies, reductions of pensions, etc., please the "fat boys" as Bob LaFollette calls them (the President uses the term "fat cats" but means the same thing). But the financial pages already reflect uneasiness concerning the other side of the picture. To refinance farm and home mortgages -- government guaranteeing interest -- and to expand public

---

[3]Wm. D. Herridge, Canadian Ambassador. He was a brother-in-law of Prime Minister Bennett, a lawyer, and one of the finest minds among my new acquaintances. We became fast friends, an association which was a great comfort to me throughout my years of service.

[4]Phillips, William, Under Secretary of State. Phillips was a career officer but owed his prominence in these years to an old acquaintance with F.D.R. back in the Wilson administration.

works, will necessitate really huge bond issues. There seems to be no faith that any of these will really be "self-liquidating", or else the fear is that the bond market will have a sinking spell. It probably will. But something must be done about unemployment and, whatever it is, taxpayers will not like it. Or if it is not paid for by taxes, inflation will impair the dollar still further. This will alienate all creditors.

One of the paradoxes of the situation here is interesting. It has to do with reduction of the budget. We seem to have a policy of reducing expenses in government services and of expanding them in making work, though the latter policy had not yet become clear. We have been having an argument with Lewis Douglas, Director of the Budget. He has presented the Budget Bureau's estimates to the Departments and they call for severe reduction in which Agriculture suffers worst. His proposal would have meant the dismemberment of several of our research bureaus. We are, of course, resisting. We argue that research is a long-time need; we also point to the foolishness of creating unemployment and then relieving it by government aid. I have no doubt that we can reduce with benefit to the service if it is skillfully done, and I am willing to use my best efforts at that. But it must be done reasonably, not slashingly, for everyone's sake.

Douglas argued the other day that the nation had never come out of a depression with an unbalanced budget. This stirred up H.A., who believes in inflation anyway, and he put Louis Bean[5] to work. Bean was able to show, in a neat memorandum, that we have never maintained balance but have always recovered it by expansion. Of course, H.A. tells me little of what goes on in Cabinet[6] -- he is not supposed to discuss it at all -- but I gather there are warm discussions there for and against expansion of government operations. The progressives -- Wallace,

[5]Bean, Louis H., economist, on research staff of Bureau of Agricultural Economics U.S.D.A.

[6]The President had instructed him not to, saying "Daniels never told *me* what went on." This exclusion was maintained only a few weeks. F.D.R. conveniently forgot what he had said the first time Henry was away on Cabinet day and blandly sent for all to sit in Henry's place, which I did from then on without further discussion about it. I presume I attended from 20 to 25 percent of the Cabinet meetings during the next two years since Henry had to be away so frequently. He was depended on to convince farmers that they had to cooperate with our program. To carry out this responsibility he had to appear on many occasions in many different places. Presently we found ourselves needing to correlate schedules so that both of us would not be away at the same time. He made it a point, however, to be present if any issue in which we in agriculture had an interest was particularly lively.

Perkins, Ickes -- line up against Roper, Swanson and Cummings. Farley leans toward Wallace, and so, I think, does Dern, but Garner[7] is a rabid conservative. It will be interesting to see what happens finally.[8]

We worked late last night on modifications of the farm bill which we hope the Senate Committee may adopt today without much argument.

We have puzzled a good deal -- H.A. and I -- about the administration of the farm act, the Agricultural Adjustment Administration. I think we have pretty well settled on George Peek. There are reasons for and against. But he carries much weight and will enlist with himself the whole Baruch faction. We do not like this crowd particularly and would rather have a hard-boiled progressive. But this is a new thing and much depends upon cooperation amongst the processors who are affected. If we do this we shall advance in our chosen direction more slowly, no doubt, but perhaps more surely.

Peek is a wealthy man and perhaps would have been Secretary if H.A. had been eliminated. He was an implement manufacturer and worked with Baruch on the War Industries Board. There is no doubt of his fidelity to the agricultural cause; he has worked at it long and earnestly for years. He and Hugh Johnson[9] were proponents of the first

---

[7]Garner, John Nance, Vice President

[8]These, of course, were the members of the first cabinet. I see I have not mentioned in this either Hull or Woodin. This was probably because they were silent except when the affairs of their own Departments came under discussions. This, of course, was infrequent. Such discussion would be likely to arise only if they raised some question.

The President, after some opening remarks, customarily went round the table, beginning with Hull. At first, apparently, some questions of importance were raised; but very soon the Cabinet members learned better. They were cagy about taking any position except an obvious one on policy, and they much preferred to discuss Departmental matters alone with the President. Exceptions to this were Wallace and Frances Perkins who persisted in opening up issues of importance; but it was discouraging.

I think I do injustice here to Homer Cummings, who, it was true, was not classifiable as a progressive, but was a wise counsellor with genuine concern for human distress. I came to know all these men much better during the next three years.

[9]General Hugh S. Johnson was destined, during the next two years, to have the kind of governmental career usually described as "meteoric." He certainly rose rapidly and fell as rapidly as he had risen. At this time we had known him since he had been attached to the brains trust group after Mr. Roosevelt's nomination. He came to us as a gift of Bernard Baruch for whom he worked and who assigned him to us. He was accepted by Mr. Roosevelt because he was

McNary-Haugen measures, and are, in fact, old-timers in the farm relief
agitation. He is forceful and intelligent. He is, of course, conservative in
philosophy and more internationally-minded than we think practical at
the moment -- that is, he overestimates the possibilities of foreign
markets for our agriculture. He is consequently rather opposed to crop
control. But he has the best grasp of anyone on the possibilities in the
sections of the act which modify the anti-trust laws in favor of "marketing
agreements". Altogether he seems the logical choice. He may run away
with the show since he is older and wealthier than H.A. or I, and since he
is close to a crowd of powerful people. He will not want to look to us for
advice, probably, but we shall have to make out as best we can in that
way. I have never found it necessary to try to surround myself with
smaller men, anyway; and when I do I shall hope to be wise enough to
defer. The administration of this farm bill, we are perfectly well aware,
can make or break this whole Democratic venture. It would be foolish to
take any avoidable risk with it. The chances of success are not too great
in any case; and we must be assured of skillful administration. The only
danger is that he will oppose production control and want to urge too

Baruch's man and because Baruch had a good deal of political power, got from
his influence on Congressmen (through campaign contributions) and because
he was one of the inheritors of the Wilson tradition (from having served as
Chairman of the War Industries Board). It is only fair to say, however, that
Hugh had imagination, picturesqueness, and a most unusual gift for invective.
These were useful in campaign speeches. What was less useful were his
ventures into policy. He, with Baruch behind him, persuaded Mr. Roosevelt as
candidate to adopt the policy of "restoring confidence" -- that is of assuring
businessmen that they had nothing to fear. The idea was that this would
persuade them to renew their activity and so produce recovery. This was a
kind of fancy to which the President would be persuaded over and over. It is
doubtful if he ever had the least belief that any result would come from it. On
the other hand he probably felt that he had little to lose from reassuring
speeches and statements. When, however, "restoring confidence" resulted in
the famous Pittsburgh speech of the campaign which promised a budget cut of
25 percent, he got into something which would return to haunt him. Johnson
wrote that speech.
    At the time at which we have now arrived -- April, 1933 -- Johnson
was again in Washington. He was, as a matter of fact, busily working in an
office in the old State, War and Navy building on a version of what, after
various compromises with those of us who were also at work on other versions,
would become the National Recovery Act.
    The President would take us by surprise, in due time, by appointing
Hugh Administrator under the Act. Baruch men would then be in charge of
both agricultural and industrial recovery.

much on marketing agreements and dumping abroad.[10]

April 5, 1933

Reading THE TIMES this morning I discover that the Henderson case is being aired....

Henderson is a psychological case. He was a student of mine and I have helped him all I could for years -- got him a job with Agger at Rutgers, took him back to teach at Columbia, protected him from his enemies. He used to be a serious student and I thought he might develop into a good scholar. I took him at Columbia five years ago so that he might finish his doctorate and so find a fixed place in the teaching profession. He was to leave in two years and find that place. I let him stay. From then on he began to be an agitator. He turned from Socialist to Communist, mostly, I think, because his pride was hurt. He made a vigorous speaking campaign as a Socialist candidate and discovered toward the end of it that his name had been left off the ballot.

He began to neglect his work as a teacher and there were more and more complaints about him. I should have let him go last year, but I hated to let him go without a job in prospect. The situation was complicated by the fact of his radicalism. I knew when I told him he might go on a fellowship next year that there was danger in it but I wanted him to have a year to turn around in. Besides, I thought I might prevent him from creating an unpleasant situation for the University. There was a "strike" last spring over another student radical (Reed Harris) and we didn't want another. The young radicals have evidently decided to make an issue of it and no doubt there will be much unpleasantness.

I shall have to make a statement. I think it should be as follows:

> The reasons which led to our decision not to reappoint Donald Henderson as Instructor in Economics for the coming academic year are ones of manners rather than of

---

[10]What is said here seems to me, looking back, to be both perceptive and naive. I ought not only to have had a vague uneasiness about Peek. I should have been certain that his appointment would not work. I was obviously not yet tough enough. One of my weaknesses has always been an inclination to believe the best of people and to ignore jealousies and intrigues. It works sometimes. But the stakes in Washington are very large and the struggle for power becomes ruthless to a degree which seems incredible to an outsider. I learned. I learned as much from the Peek case as from any other. But it was not a lesson I accepted willingly.

morals. Karl Marx could have taught at Columbia all his life without disturbance because a university is the place for the fostering and development of ideas no matter what their implications may be. Anyone who associates himself with a university, however, has a kind of obligation to work within the traditions of scholarship and tolerance. It is this obligation which Donald Henderson, in spite of my hopes for him, failed to recognize. It is not that he differs from me or from his other colleagues in social philosophy which causes us to feel that he has failed in his duties to the University community; it is rather that he has refused to extend the tolerance to us which we were willing to extend to him. The ideas generated in a university are expected to find their realization by reason and argument. Scholars proceed by persuasion, not by force. Again and again Mr. Henderson has shown his contempt for the opinions and methods of his colleagues and has preferred to turn to methods of force in furthering his own philosophy.

I prefer to leave the matter on this ground rather than to call attention to any deficiencies he may have shown as a teacher or as a scholar. I would not plead poverty, either, on the part of the University, although that was a real factor in the decision not to reappoint Mr. Henderson. He is not the only individual who is suffering from the exigencies of these times. It is much better to have it understood that the real issue is that of freedom from compulsion and of loyalty to the traditions of scholarship.

I feel free to say that Mr. Henderson had been kept at Columbia University for several years longer than he otherwise would, simply because his opinions contrasted sharply with those of his colleagues and because we wished to avoid the slightest excuse for criticism on the grounds of differences. I happen to be the Executive Officer with the immediate responsibility. I feel this responsibility very strongly because Columbia University has always protected my own departures from accepted doctrine. Never once have I had the slightest reason to believe that, so long as I retained my own tolerance and met the requirements of decently methodical work, would the University fail to support my efforts. It is because I have had this experience at Columbia that I resent the implication that anyone could fall under criticism there because of any opinion he might hold. My situation is complicated by having tried to protect Mr. Henderson in his position at the University longer than I should. If I am subject to criticism in this matter, it is for that reason alone.

April 14, 1933

The great farm bill debate still progresses slowly in the Senate. The change toward the assumption of powers by the executive in these emergency times comes very hard to the debating body. But they will have to give way. The maneuverings by the conservative Democrats and the Republicans have been amusing even if irritating. They know that we have a new conception of the role of government in economic life and they hate and fear it quite aside from the fact that they represent, really, interests which are not the common ones.

We are working on a new draft of the Food and Drugs Act and are arguing with Douglas of the Budget Bureau over the departmental appropriation. The real danger is that our research activities may be cut to pieces and all my strategy is directed toward saving as much as is possible.[11]

What this administration must concentrate on is a grand effort for the resumption of industrial activity in normal ways. A number of schemes are on foot to accomplish this and it must be worked on along with the expansive fiscal policy which needs to accompany it.[12]

There are intimations that I may be expected to take a part in the coming World Wheat Conference. The scheme for me to go to France seems less likely to come off. More people than I thought seem to want me here. While I am in this I suppose I may as well see it through as best I can.

H.A. is away today and for the first time I shall be Acting Secretary though that doesn't involve much difference in routine -- more papers to sign, more meetings to attend; also I am to attend a cabinet meeting. This is in spite of the President's remark that Daniels did not allow him to know what went on.

I have written an article on the prospects for the World Economic Conference which expresses our present hopes and fears. Perhaps it is

[11]See the N.Y. Times, April 9, II, 15:5 - Advertisers disturbed by advertising censorship provision of Tugwell bill.
  N.Y. Times, April 16, II, 15.1 - Asso. Grocery Mfrs of Amer. Inc. volunteers aid in strengthening law.

[12]This effort resulted presently in the National Recovery Act.

optimistic about tariffs and monetary agreement. Privately we have no hope, or hardly any, that anything will come of it:[13]

WHAT THE WORLD ECONOMIC CONFERENCE CAN DO

By R. G. Tugwell
Assistant Secretary of Agriculture

There never was a time when an economic conference looked less hopeful or was more needed. The urgency of the need may just furnish the lacking element for success. The history of the conferences which have gone before is certainly not happy. Nations devoted to small and selfish concerns did not discover the mechanisms by which the interest of each could be merged in the interests of all, which is a condition of any social improvement, defining, as it does, the relations of individual and group, of group and nation, and nation and world. It is a time for some inventor, gifted with ingenuity and possessing the qualities of dominance and persuasion; if, among the statesmen, such a man exists, he can have immortality now.

The descending spiral of depression has carried the fortunes of the human race downward until there seems no logical stopping place short of universal destitution. Our marvelous mechanisms are paralysed; fear of the ultimate possesses all mankind. It is still going on, this decline and panic. No one believes anymore that action on the international field possesses the power to reverse this process; many do hope, however, that its momentum may be checked there and that internal forces may so realign themselves in consequence as to provide the materials for recovery.

The statesmen will have to work in an atmosphere of extreme exigency; their decisions will be watched by fear-ridden people. It is difficult in such circumstances to come at judgments which are coldly considered. And this is, perhaps, just as well. For, instead of petty horse-trading tactics, the urgency of the situation may dictate a grander strategy of the common purposes of mankind. The people of the world have, it is true, only an inchoate idea of the elements of this strategy; they are likely to be intolerant of the technique involved and to be insistent only on results. Peace and prosperity are the simple desiderata which democracies cling to. But nothing less than the insurance of these is likely to bring credit to public leaders now.

Yet there is a poor tradition to work from in achieving these results, and the difficulties of working out from it will be immense. The

[13]This was published in the N.Y. Herald Tribune on April 12, 1933.

first great test will come in this field. If each nation comes to this meeting determined to hold other heads under water so that it may breathe -- and this is the traditional way these things are done -- the possible achievements may as well be discounted by half before a beginning has been made. But if the urgencies of human suffering have penetrated statesmen's minds so that they have come really to understand the need for common defenses against the threatening political debacle, everything is possible.

The choice is fundamental in its implications. During the years of the depression the world has been breaking up slowly into national economic units. Measures taken by nations individually with the hope of protecting themselves from the impact of the depression have further restricted the exchange of goods and thus aggravated the distress. The world therefore finds itself confronted with the alternative of sharply reversing this trend or of carrying economic nationalism to an ultimate conclusion, which would require more painful adjustments than have yet been made.

"In stressing the necessity for concerted action, we do not wish to suggest that nothing can be accomplished before the Conference meets. On the contrary, the success of the Conference will depend in great measure upon the vigour with which the participating Governments enter upon preliminary negotiations in the meantime. The prospects of substantial all-around success in the necessarily complex and multilateral conference discussions will be greatly enhanced if, in the intervening months, preliminary negotiations have cleared the way for the reciprocal concessions."

In inviting leading nations to send representatives for preliminary discussions of world economic problems, the Administration is therefore taking a step vigorously urged by the Preparatory Commission and recognized as indispensable to the achievement of concrete results at the Conference itself.

The Administration has set as its first objective the reopening of the channels of world trade. In this connection, it is important to note a change in the conception of the World Economic Conference during the last six months. The policy of the preceding Administration was to prevent the inclusion of tariffs on the conference agenda. But the results of the November election required that the views of the incoming administration guide the work of the American experts. Shortly before they returned to Europe early in January for the second meeting of the agenda committee, Dr. Day and Professor Williams, the American representatives, conferred with Mr. Roosevelt at Hyde Park. They left with the request from him to make the agenda inclusive and, particularly, to include tariffs and the question of regularizing the production of commodities, such as wheat and silver.

As the Secretary of State has recently indicated, tariffs, instead of being ignored, are the very point at which the new Administration believes that the attack on the international depression can most effectively be begun. In reversing the trend toward the ever higher national barriers which are constricting trade, the United States should be in a particularly strong position to assert leadership. Although during the depression years we have not reached the extremes of some other nations in the imposition of embargoes, quotas and restrictions on importation and exportation, we were among the worst offenders during the post-war decade in the general movement toward economic isolation. The worst of it was that we were inconsistent. We tried to export capital without importing goods. Many of the restrictive measures undertaken by other nations were consequent on this policy of ours. We now find ourselves among the heaviest losers in the decline of world trade. We therefore have an interest in a new policy; but also we have a responsibility to reverse a disastrous policy which we fostered.

In 1928 our exports were approximately ten percent of our total production. They were roughly equivalent to the entire output of our automobile industry. So our lost export market is worth recovering. We have large surpluses of wheat, cotton, lard, and other agricultural commodities of which we would like to dispose. Our manufacturers, too, would like to find markets for our surplus and to keep them unless we are willing to accept payment for the goods which we have to sell. Ultimately those payments must be in the form of goods or services. The method by which we preserved a foreign market for our surplus while surrounding our own domestic market with a high tariff wall was to lend the money with which the surplus was bought. That is, we arranged for the buyers of our goods to defer payments, without giving very much thought to the question of payment. The international debt structure grew top-heavy, just as the domestic debt structure did.

If we are to free the channels of trade, we must be prepared to receive other goods or services in payment or we must revert to the system of lending the money with which our goods can be bought. A realistic handling of the problem must be based on the realization that if we are ever to be repaid for the goods we sell abroad it must be with other goods and services and that the sensible solution is to make it possible for us to receive payments as we go along in goods which we lack or which other nations can produce more efficiently than we can.

No nation alone can afford to lower its own tariff barriers at the present time, for if it did it would immediately become the dumping ground for the surpluses of other nations. This is a part of the general international dilemma. But all nations, or several leading nations, can profitably cooperate to reverse the trend toward economic separatism and reopen channels for international trade. Meanwhile, whatever the results of these general attacks may be, it may be wise to begin as soon as possible the penetration of mutually restrictive walls by reciprocal arrangements for exchange. This policy rests on the simple belief that, in the end, revival of trade will result from selective processes, whereby one nation will agree to take goods which it wants in return for a market for the goods which it wants most to sell.

If nations are to engage in trade they must have a definite standard of measurement for the value of the products which they exchange. The restoration of stable currency relationships is therefore necessary to revival and maintenance of international trade. The departure of most of the nations of the world from the gold standard, exchange restrictions and other interferences with normal currency relationships, have had an unsettling and depressing effect upon commerce. It must not be forgotten, however, that they were caused originally by the unbalancing of commerce. Exchange restrictions and "standstill" agreements became necessary as emergency measures to keep this country or that from being drained of all its reserves and being thrown into complete collapse.

One of the fundamental objectives of the coming Conference must be to restore the currencies of the world to a stable relationship. That achievement must rest on an understanding of the means by which such a stable relationship is to be preserved. If the international monetary standard is to be gold, as the Preparatory Commission has suggested, it will be necessary for the leading nations through their central banks to cooperate in making this standard work.

The increasing weight of the structure of debts, as prices have fallen, has engendered a desire everywhere to arrest deflation and to achieve such an increase in prices as would lighten the burden. Only by raising prices can the deflationary spiral of the last few years be stopped and debts and commodities be brought into supportable relationship to each other. The reopening of trade channels, the removal of exchange restrictions, and the stabilization of currencies would furnish certain elements for economic recovery which might have this desired effect. As the Preparatory Commission observed in its report, "The very fact that exchanges continue to fluctuate is not without its effect on the level of gold prices and may hamper a monetary and economic policy designed to promote a recovery of prices in gold countries." Furthermore, the thawing out of frozen debts will release purchasing power. Credit locked behind exchange restrictions and standstill agreements in the countries of central Europe is no less frozen purchasing power than credit locked in closed banks in this country.

By coordination in the management of rediscount rates, in the provision of easy credit, and in their reserve policies, the central banks of the leading nations can make an additional contribution to the lifting of prices. A conference of central banks is therefore an important adjunct of the World Monetary and Economic Conference.

Another method which could effectively be employed to lift prices and stabilize the world's economy, is the restriction of production or export of certain basic commodities by agreement among the principal producing nations. The organization of production and trade is one of the subjects on the agenda for the Conference. Discussions of means of regulating the production and export of wheat, copper, sugar, coal, timber, and other commodities have been held among various governments during recent years. It may be recalled that our own country was largely responsible for the failure to reach an agreement on control for wheat in London in 1931. Argentina, Canada, Australia, and other wheat-exporting nations at that time were favorable to the idea. We did not then have any domestic mechanism for controlling the production or export of wheat or other agricultural commodities. We are in the process of perfecting such machinery under the emergency agricultural adjustment bill. We are now in a position to approach other nations with a view of bringing the world production of various agricultural commodities into line with the world's consumption capacity. Similar agreements should for copper, silver, oil, and other raw commodities.

International debts, particularly the war debts, are not on the conference agenda. There is a long history of controversy behind this omission. Our debtors have felt and said that these ought to be written off as a preliminary to world recovery. It has been the American position that the necessary writing down of these took place when the permanent payments were arranged for, that this reduction is already as great as is justified by the decrease in price levels, and that anything more would be an imposition on American taxpayers. There has been no disposition to be dogmatic about this; the President has again and again intimated that any debtor would be heard with courtesy and consideration. He has made it very clear, nevertheless, that our position is considered morally and economically impregnable. He has been unwilling to go further without some intimation that those upon whom the burden would necessarily fall are willing. Our debtors are doubtless unsatisfied with this. There will be much discussion of it but with what result no one can say.

The nations of the world cannot hope to escape quickly from the prisons within which they have confined themselves for so long. The most that can be hoped from the Conference, perhaps, is that a real beginning may be made toward the resumption of freedom. That in itself would be enough, since it would reverse the incidence of all our hopes and fears. We, who are experienced in the game of economic nationalism, are willingly taking a leading part in the attempt to revive international economic life, believing that it will be to the advantage of ourselves as well as of others. Yet we remain assured that if the attempt fails, we, with our great range of productive resources, are better situated than almost any other nations to fall back and carry economic nationalism to its logical conclusion. If that must be the result, the burden for us will be less heavy than for others. But it is the challenge of the Conference to the statesmanship of the world that these burdens may be lifted from all people. Peace and prosperity are not easily achieved. But they must be tried for now before they become impossible of attainment.

April 15, 1933

H. A. and I, the other day, went to see Justice Brandeis.[14] Most

[14]Justice Louis D. Brandeis was a far more important figure in the affairs of the New Deal than would be gathered from this short reference. This meeting at which I had introduced Wallace to the Justice was only one of many. Others I had with him were attended by Jerome Frank and others. There will be other reference to him later; but here I should not a certain concern not evident from the short sentence in the diary.(sic)

It was natural that I should have been worried by him and anxious to keep track of his activities. I had no need to make note of this. I was not likely to forget. Frankfurter, Corcoran and Cohen were out-and-out disciples and they had to be dealt with in important ways. Frankfurter was still at Harvard but he was beginning to fill numerous posts in the new administration with like-minded students. Most of Jerome Frank's lawyers -- and indeed Jerome himself -- were thus recommended. And Corcoran and Cohen were already at work, along with Jim Landis, on the preliminaries to the controls over stock selling and company financing.

But what concerned me most was his philosophy of littleness. He believed that nothing big could be good because it was beyond human capability to manage it. At the same time he had a kind of plain integrity which was very attractive. He was very well known. The fight over confirmation after his appointment by Wilson had become a liberal cause; and he had consistently stood for many things in which all serious progressives believed.

It was very important because of his position as a social philosopher and influential guide to public men, that he should approve what we were about. I was sparing no pains to gain his approval. At the same time I was aware that we were not likely to get it. He was suspicious of Federal action; he was against any kind of planning; he abhorred the idea of condoning industrial integration. I did, however, hope we might have his approval for the AAA on the ground that it would restore individual farmers to prosperity. This was why I took Henry Wallace to reinforce my pleas.

I think we were not doing badly with the old gentleman until we unveiled the N.R.A. From then on he was an enemy.

His way of working was devious. It had to be. He was, after all, a Supreme Court Justice. But he talked freely to Sunday afternoon groups who came to tea -- perhaps generally, but still with clear enough implications.

of our talk concerned industrial philosophy: he arguing that bigness is always badness, I maintaining that bigness needed only direction and submission to discipline.

I have had entangled in my mind ever since an analogy he used. He spoke of his age and said that after seventy life was like living in Poe's room, the walls of which continually converged.

Being in the forties instead of the seventies that feeling has not yet come to me. Indeed Washington stimulates quite the opposite emotion, just now. We may be on the verge of great things. The way, it seems to me, is cleared for a great constructive effort. But perhaps after seventy great constructive efforts are regarded with skepticism.

April 21, 1933

All the President's steps up to now in financial matters seem to me to have been right. He has now definitely banned the export of gold. This allows the dollar to depreciate in foreign currencies and pulls us down off the high plateau we have inhabited too long.[15] It is especially

What I was most afraid of -- and, as it turned out justifiably so -- was the influence he might have on the President. I should have worried about his veto power as a justice, I suppose; but at this time I was much more concerned about the President.

Mr. Roosevelt was not yet certain, as was very evident, whether he was to be an atomizer, with all that implied, or whether he was to sponsor the development of "concentration and control." Sometimes it seemed to be the one and sometimes the other. We were just working into the formulation of N.R.A. and so we were currently very acutely concerned. It did not seem impossible to convince the Justice, even about N.R.A., that it was well within his philosophy (we thought we had succeeded with AAA); and if we could we should not have to worry about the erosion of Presidential resolution under his pressure.

Brandeis had, as his biographer, Alpheus T. Mason, (Brandeis: A Free Man's Life, N.Y., 1946) remarks, (p. 615) "long favored 'regulated competition' as against 'regulated monopoly'. Having exposed the evils of anarchic competition, he urged cooperation among those engaged in a particular industry. . ." But I think we always knew we should lose his approval and be forced to move in dread of his influence on the President. And, of course, that time would come.

[15]It is interesting, I think, that in a famous pamphlet by William A. Wirt (with a foreward by James A. Rand) it was said in an introductory paragraph: "We should celebrate April 19 as a Second Independence Day because it is one of the few really important dates in our history. . ." This referred of course, to "going off gold." This was the day on which the Secretary of the Treasury announced that no further licenses to export gold for foreign account would be

opportune with the conversations just coming on preliminary to the Economic Conference. McDonald and Herriot[16] are now on the water. F.D.R. is now in a position to say to McDonald "You can see the mess the continent has got into. It means war unless we block it. Will you stand with us or with them?" And our going off gold, as England did a long

granted. (of. Public Papers, Vol II, p. 111, and the press conference account on p. 137).

It was curious that the propaganda on this matter should have taken the turn it did and that I quite fortuitously, should have become the center of still another celebrated controversy. More will be said about it later, as the incident develops; but it should be noted here that there was a very active group of inflationists, called The Committee for the Nation, of which James A. Rand was Chairman. Some very important persons were associated with this group (Frank A. Vanderlip, F. H. Frazier, Fred H. Sexauer and L. P. Rosenwald, for instance). It was their idea that recovery would result from inflation and that inflation would come from manipulating the price of gold and so the value of the dollar.

George Warren and others of his school had written numerous pamphlets for the Committee. This, of course, was the Cornell group.

They thought that all our recovery efforts were unnecessary and, in fact, dangerous to "the American system." They were inclined to picture the rest of us as a menace to our institutions, and, I suppose, it was not too strange that eventually I should be centered on. I did not believe in their panacea; I did believe in the other measures we were adopting. They wanted business and farming let completely alone while they resorted to inflation as a sure means to recovery.

One of their pamphleteers was Dr. Wirt of Gary. In one of his effusions he would make some "revelations" which bring on a Congressional investigation. This would be one of the blown-up cause celebres of the following year. But the ferment of antagonism was working now, still largely unknown to me.

It still seems to me ironic that I should have been attacked by this crowd so immoderately for being against inflation, but that I should presently lose face with my economic colleagues as presumably associated with the fiscal vagaries of these same people. After the Wirt affair which should have rehabilitated me with the more orthodox economists, I was regarded with more suspicion than ever.

What happened, of course, was that my reputation developed to the stage of being bad in any case; even if I had been right, I could not really have meant it. There was something sinister.

[16]Herriot, Edward, special representative of French Government to these preliminary conferences. He was not a member of the current government but was sent because of his reputation for sympathy with America and a former acquaintance of F.D.R.

time ago, leaves us in a position to say "We are ready to establish a relationship between the pound and the dollar which will make friendship possible. We can both support it by central bank policy."

Douglas seems to have been taken into F.D.R.'s confidence in financial matters. Although we are having a fight with him about the foolish lengths to which he wants us to carry Departmental economy, I know from talking to him that he has a real knowledge of the function of central bank policy. So his being consulted is good. Moley is very busy with the impending visits of diplomats; Berle is special counsel to the Reconstruction Finance Corporation; another professor, John Dickinson[17] is Assistant Secretary of Commerce. Scattered throughout the service there are numbers of us in important places to influence policy.

I have been worried, (in spite of some confidence in Douglas) about the further development of fiscal policy. We are just at the turn of events. We can be wise or foolish now. And the whole fiscal administration is in reactionary control. We missed a trick during the banking crisis by not setting up a national bank. That is now a settled matter. But we can miss another trick now by going in for currency inflation instead of expansion. This is curiously radical and reactionary at the same time. The government really ought to take over immediately large blocks of paralyzed industries, in my opinion, to make certain that production is set going, especially in the heavy industries. At the very least it ought to take them on lease. There is a feeling of confidence in the country and great affection for F.D.R. but this is ephemeral and unemployment is still increasing. Activity must be revived and expanded and fiscal policy must support and further the movement. The danger of currency inflation is now being shown. In the stock and commodity markets there has for several days been feverish speculation for a rise. Prices have increased some 10%. But the bottom will drop out of this unless something solid is furnished in the way of support. This ought to be a public works program and the leasing or taking over of the industries now working at 15 to 25% capacity.

Bobby Straus, Louis Bean, and Jerome Frank[18] are working with

[17]Dickinson, John, Professor of Law, University of Pennsylvania. Assistant Secretary of Commerce.

[18]Jerome Frank, at this time a briefless lawyer, acting as my counselor and friend. At Frankfurter's suggestion we (Henry and I) had offered him the solicitorship of the Department. Farley, for a mistaken reason, had objected. At F.D.R.'s suggestion we were waiting for the AAA to be organized so that he could become its General Counsel. Meanwhile he was busying himself with my numerous affairs, notably just now, in the discussions which led presently to the drafting of the NRA Act.

me on a round-up of the various schemes put forward by Kent[19] and others for stimulating private industry. Hugh Johnson is also working on something. When that is done we will see whether something of a scheme can be fitted together to submit to F.D.R. It will not involve government ownership or operation, but will be something of the sort I have suggested before. F.D.R. seems not to have in view as large a conception of public works as I should like to see; but he has been very wise so far - - remarkably so for a person of his temperament. But we come now to critical moment.

For two weeks I have been keeping at the Food and Drugs Act revision. I took Campbell,[20] the Director, to see the President. He agreed to our reworking the Act and to its being introduced at this Session as an administrative measure. I called in Handler[21] of Columbia and Cavers[22] of Duke and they have been working out a new draft. To see this through Congress will be an immense task for which I am badly fitted and for which I shall have no support from H.A. who has no sympathy with the Act. I am trying to find a way to get Fred Lee to handle it with Congress. He has great ability and the necessary tact to handle it with Congress. I can see that we shall, as we did in the Farm Act, have to try to divide the enemy. Many good firms of manufacturers will support us. Many of the better newspapers and radio broadcasters will, also. We must get them on our side. If we can, and if we have the support of the President, something may be done. In this matter, I talked this morning to Father Coughlin in Detroit to enlist his support.[23] He was about to start on a

[19]Kent, Fred I. This plan is reproduced herewith; from the N.Y. Times, February 12, 1933.

[20]Campbell, Walter G., Director, Food and Drugs Admin. U.S.D.A., devoted public servant, just now becoming my close colleague in the Food and Drug fight.

[21]Handler, Milton, lawyer, formerly editor Columbia Law Review, specialist in trade-marks and anti-trust and labor law, a colleague at Columbia.

[22]Cavers, David F., professor of Law, Duke University, the son of an old friend in Buffalo of whose progress I had been very proud. He was to go on to a very distinguished academic career at Harvard.

[23]The whole incident about Father Coughlin had its humorous aspects. As I have indicated, I hoped, when this fight began, to divide the enemy. Indeed I hoped that most manufacturers would turn out not to be enemies at all, but rather allies, interested in the suppression of fakers and quacks, and conscious of their gains from ethical standards. This turned out to be so in a few

month's vacation but promised to come to Washington next week to talk the whole matter over.   Campbell is preparing lists of (1) good manufacturers, (2) newspapers and radio people, (3) consumers' organizations, and (4) advertising people to whom we must talk in the attempt to get general support. Then Congressman and Senators must be enlisted (this will be a tough job). There seems to be work ahead.

April 26, 1933

Day before yesterday seemed to me one of the hardest days I ever went through. It was an enforcement day -- one of those on which many people whose toes have been stepped on by one of the numerous regulatory acts of the Department (there are forty-three) bring pressure to bear to get some modification of the incidence of the rules. It is a nice question to know when to bear down and when to ease up. The Food and Drugs Act gives the most trouble; and it is the one which my conscience gives me least leeway about. The current trouble centers in the spray residue of fruit. Metallic poisons are peculiarly subtle in their effects. It is hard to trace direct connections. Besides the enforcement enrages some farm groups whose support we hate to lose. So far I have made no concessions at all in this matter.

The rest of this week was to have been taken up in pursuing the strategy involved in the rewriting of the old Statute on Food and Drugs. The enemy has to be divided and support, wherever any exists, marshalled and made effective. Handler and Cavers whom I called in

instances; but it was unimportant because the press fearful of its advertising revenue deliberately worked up a crusade against the bill with an energy worthy of a better cause.

In a moment of inspiration the "boiler plate" producers in Chicago, suppliers of inside pages to thousands of small newspapers, determined on the deliberate policy of discrediting the Act by (1) calling it the Tugwell bill, and (2) by establishing it firmly in every mind that Tugwell was a "red". Enormous efforts and expenditures would go into this campaign. It would succeed. The Act would not be passed. There would be an Act several years later; but that would be an innocuous regulatory bill largely written by those it would regulate.

This was one of my worst defeats; and it was responsible for the creation of the stereotype which passed for me from then on.

Father Coughlin, of course, did not see his way clear to cooperate. Presently he would be denouncing me in the most unrestrained language he could command.

Another idea I had was to persuade Colliers to make a cause of this bill as it had of the original one in 1906 -- a crusade which had "made" both Dr. Wiley and Colliers. But the Colliers of 1936 was not having any.

have shaped up a new draft of the Act; and now the interests affected must be called in and asked for cooperation. It must be made to seem to the better businesses that they shaped the legislation. There is besides the problem of enlisting Congressional support -- particularly of the Committees which will hold hearings on the Bill. There was a whole schedule arranged of such meetings when I was suddenly called in to the conversations with the foreign diplomats and experts who are here to explore the ground for the coming Economic Conference. My whole day yesterday was spent at the White House.

There follows a summary of the provisions to be included in the new draft, as we have prepared it, of the Food and Drugs Act.

Summary of Proposed Bill

Section 2.   The scope of the statute has been extended to include cosmetics. The definition of foods has been broadened to include substances entering into the composition of food. The definition of drugs has been broadened to include therapeutic devices, surgical dressings, obesity cures, etc.

Section 3.   Defines labeling and draws a distinction between the principal label upon which all compulsory declarations must appear and printed matter which is placed upon or in the package or otherwise accompanies the article in commerce.

Section 4.   Defines adulteration of food, distinguishing between hygienic and economic adulteration. The former covers foods in such condition as to prejudice health. The latter covers foods so prepared as to deceive the public. Hygienic adulteration, as defined, embraces foods containing poisons in their natural state. The act now in force is believed to cover the addition of poisonous ingredients and not the presence of poisons in the natural article. The secretary is given the power to forbid the addition of technical poisons or to establish tolerances limiting their use. Sanitary conditions of transportation required; contaminating containers forbidden.

Section 5.   Defines adulteration of drugs. All U.S.P. and N.F. preparations must comply not only with standards of strength, purity and quality but also with the definitions, formulae, description and methods of packing of the U.S.P. and N.F. tests are insufficient, Secretary may

prescribe new tests. Informative labeling of non-U.S.P.
and N.F. preparations is required and substandard
preparations which are dangerous to health are
forbidden.

Section 6.   Deals with adulteration of cosmetics. Preparations which
may be harmful to health are deemed adulterated.

Section 7.   Defines misbranding of foods to cover
A. Labeling which is false and misleading or which
creates misleading impression.
B. Imitations unless labels are informative. Contents of
such label prescribed.
C. Deceptive packing.
There are several provisions as to informative labeling.
Weights, measure, or numerical count, the name and
address of manufacturer, processor, or distributor, and
the location of the factory where article was prepared
must be disclosed upon label. The ingredients of articles
sold under arbitrary and fanciful names must be disclosed
upon label. Labels of foods differing from definitions and
standards promulgated by Secretary must indicate that
they differ from such standards. Secretary may prescribe
form of labeling for substandard products.

Section 8.   Defines misbranding of drugs
A. Prevents false and misleading statements or
statements which create false impressions.
B. Forbids therapeutic, curative and preventative claims
which are opposed to consensus of medical opinion.
C. Prescribes method of labeling narcotics, hypnotic, and
certain highly dangerous drugs.
D. Requires dosages and directions and various
precautions to be states as e.g. necessity for medical
supervision.
E. Requires full disclosure of all ingredients of every drug
product to Secretary under oath and gives Secretary
power to prescribe form and contents of label.
F. Requires informative labeling of name and address of
manufacturer and compounder, date of preparation,
weights, measures, and numerical count.

Section 9.   Defines false advertising as dissemination of false and
misleading statements or creation of false impressions

through innuendo. Statements of opinion must not be asserted as proven facts and must have scientific support. Certain types of medical advertisements are forbidden. Advisory service to be established by Secretary to advise manufacturers and agencies of truth or falsity of advertisements.

Section 11.   Secretary authorized to establish standards, grades and definitions of identity and to forbid use of added poisonous ingredients and to establish tolerances limiting their use.

Section 12.   Establishes permit system to be invoked when other methods of control are ineffectual.

Section 13.   Provides for criminal penalties, graded in accordance with seriousness of offense.

Section 14.   Provides for injunctions by government and consumer and trade groups to restrain violations of act. Publisher and advertising agencies may be enjoined as well as advertiser in cases of false advertising. Courts may, for a period of a year, require violator to submit goods and advertisements to Department for inspection.

Section 15.   Provides for action for damages by persons injured by violations.

Section 16.   Publicity of all judgments and radio broadcasts by Department.

Section 17.   Revocation of mail privileges and radio licenses in cases of repeated violations.

Section 18.   Trade practice conferences to raise standards. Rulings of conference enforceable against signatories.

Section 19.   Voluntary inspection service at cost of manufacturer.

Section 20.   Guarantees to retailer.

Section 21.   Relates to libel proceedings.

Section 22.   Establishes system of statutory costs to be imposed against violators to cover cost of inspection, seizure, analysis, etc.

Section 24.   Import provisions.

Section 26.   Secretary of Agriculture given sole authority to make rules and regulations except in case of imports where he is jointly responsible with Secretary of Treasury. Secretary of Agriculture given powers of subpoena.

Section 27.   Liability of corporate officers and agents.

Section 28.   Separability clause.

We talked to the British and French separately yesterday. Moley, Taussig, Bullitt[24], Warburg, Douglas, Feis and myself talking to the experts while F.D.R talked to McDonald and Herriot. We talk separately for a couple of hours and then are called in to talk things over with the two principals. Everything is very friendly. There is more attempt to arrive at concrete understandings than appears on the surface. The talk so far has centered on exchange and trade. We being now off gold, can agree with the British on tentativeness for a few months. The French, being still on gold, are anxious for both of us to return to it quickly. We offer more willingness to modify tariffs than either. The British, having only recently adopted protection are trying to protect their own and to get us and the French to reduce the highest rates. After listening for a while yesterday I offered the idea of progressive percentage reduction. It seemed to take hold and will be further explored. It seems to me that we, having been among the worst offenders in maintaining barriers, and worse than that, being all the time insistent creditors, can afford now to make generous concessions. It would be to our interest to do so. And, perhaps, at this moment, it could be done.

May 3, 1933

The days are very full of rather confused activity in which there stands out the effort I am making to save as much of the Department's research program as can be salvaged in the present drive for economy.

[24]Bullitt, William C., formerly asso. ed., foreign correspondent, and Wash. Corresp. Philadelphia Public Ledger, attache to Amer. Commission to Negotiate Peace 1918-19; special minister to Russia 1919.

This involves a long and difficult correspondence with Douglas, the Director of the Budget. With so many other things to be attended to, it is difficult to master the details of departmental operations. But the essential must be distinguished from the merely important. We must guard against the dissipation of intellectual resources which ought to be conserved. Stopping research projects and dismissing scientists seems to me a good deal like cutting down a natural orchard. It will require many years to grow the trees again. And they will have to be grown.

Besides this, there are a number of other activities in which I necessarily have to take part. Foremost of them and the one which requires the most time, is of course, the international conversations which are going on. The French and the British have departed; the Argentines and the Italians are now here. We meet with them twice and sometimes three times a day. Out of the French and British conversations there came very little in the way of concrete results. It was determined, however, that the Economic Conference is to meet in London on 12 June and, as a preliminary to that, we did succeed in establishing the principle of a tariff truce running for the period of the Conference; also there is still in abeyance the possibility of an agreement for a truce beginning immediately and running until the opening of the Conference. This will at least prevent them from erecting barriers to trade for a period of perhaps a year.

Into our proposals for a tariff truce the French very early injected the demur that a tariff truce would be unsatisfactory if it were not also a truce on fluctuations of international exchange. Their objection, of course, was to the present unsettled state of the dollar, France being still on gold. We surprised them very much by accepting this challenge and offering to go further than they had expected. In fact, we offered them a three party stabilization fund which would act to keep the three currencies -- the dollar, the franc and the pound -- in some kind of understood relationship to each other. They were not prepared to accept this, nor were the British, but something may come of it in the near future.

There were dangers and difficulties in our making this offer, principally because we do not know what may happen to the dollar in the coming few months. Our preference would be to let it find its own level as our internal program of expansion develops and not move for any stabilization until the relationships have found a level. We were, however, willing to make a guess as to the devaluation of the dollar in international exchange on the basis of the expectation that our internal program of expansion would carry it from par to 80 to 85 cents. This is sheer guess, of course, but we were willing to try to manage our internal program in such a way that we would not exceed these limits.

The British and the French contend, of course, that the dollar will not go down. We have ample reserves in gold; and in order to adjust debtor and creditor relationships here we should have to make a kind of tour de force to keep the dollar down. We realize the difficulties, but feel that our internal program is so necessary and must be so large in order to absorb the great number of unemployed, and to create activity which does not now exist, that the devaluation would be at least this amount when the program gets under way.

Up to now nothing has come of this suggested international arrangement; but we rather believe that something might in the near future. Warburg has conducted most of the conversations on the monetary program with Senator Pittman joining in on silver, and he has done very well. He is still unable to think clearly about a world in which gold is not a medium of exchange. The same kind of disagreements which I had with him when we were talking about these things in a preliminary way some months ago keep cropping up. He tends to think of the program in classical terms; but I was right in the matter before, and I believe, in spite of his superior knowledge of mechanisms, that I am right this time; and the one thing I am perfectly sure of is that I see eye to eye with the President.

We had a long conference with the President yesterday following our preliminary joint talks with the Argentine delegation in which we went over the whole matter of exchanges and the President very clearly outlined the necessities of the immediate future. I believe he understands the situation better than any of the experts. He ran back over two months of history and showed how the banking crisis in the United States made it possible for us to do things in the way of change in the structure that could not have been done otherwise; and foreshadowed a similar international crisis in which we should be able to take a further step in international cooperation than had ever been taken before.

This was put very tentatively, of course, but I sense a firmness of his and I must say I agree with him, for the French and British are still in a frame of mind in which a long step in international cooperation seems to them undesirable.

In view of the fact that they may think they can force single action on our part and stabilize the dollar, we are in a good position to wait for an international crisis and then make our moves quickly and surely.

May 6, 1933

It seems to me that I have lived in formal clothes for two weeks. We Americans do not wear them at our conferences as the foreigners do; but there are almost daily luncheons and dinners. The Germans and Mexicans arrive today so there will be no relief for a while.

Yesterday I went to Hull's luncheon at the Carlton. Last night I dined at the White House and I lunch there again today. But the occasions are different. Today's is a state luncheon for the Germans. Last night's was a family party. Sam and Mrs. Rosenman were there. Mrs. Jimmie and her sister, and Mr. and Mrs. Breckinridge Long. Long[25] is about to sail for his post in Italy.

The President told us several interesting stories. For instance, the recent dramatic leaving of the gold standard was precipitated by the information that the Fritz Mannheimer group in Amsterdam were going to start a drive to depress the dollar. The question was whether we should defend it or not. The President asked Woodin and they disagreed about it. He then thought about it all Sunday and Monday (which happened to be a holiday abroad) and simply told the newspaper men at a press conference the next day that the exportation of gold would not be permitted. Woodin now agrees that he was right.

He told a very amusing story, too, about McDonald's visit here. As he and McDonald talked they wanted to get in touch often with Tyrell, the British Ambassador in Paris. They telephoned code words which were to be identified by the previous giving of two numbers, 162 and 84, for instance. On one occasion, McDonald got Tyrell on the phone, gave the number and several words, and got the reply that it didn't make sense. He tried again with the same result. Finally a voice strongly flavored with French broke in and between malicious giggles informed the Monsieurs that a slight mistake had been made. The number was 164, not 162, it said, and then clicked off. He swears it happened, but it seems incredible that any sense of humor could run quite to that.

I think he told the story to preface his telling Long that pouches, telephones, codes -- none were safe. There must be courier service. The truth is that F.D.R. really loves the appurtenances of the job. He savors the romance and significance of each experience. He works hard and honestly though, and am I glad he does get such a kick out of it. The White House has been made liveable again, too, and he seems quite as much at home there now as he did in Albany. His health is good. He seems not to worry - and he knows people will not always love him as they happen to this minute -- which prepares him for the inevitable.

In taking stock of what has happened so far in the international conversations preliminary to the Economic Conference -- France, Britain, Italy, Argentina have now come and gone -- I have a strong feeling of defeat. At first we thought we made real progress with the British and

---

[25]Long, Breckinridge, (international) lawyer, St. Louis, Mo., 3rd Asst. sec. of State under President Wilson, just appointed Ambassador to Italy. During a meeting of the International Institute of Agriculture in 1934 I would stay with him.

French. It seems clear now that nothing was gained and it was my present feeling that the Conference will be a failure. Neither currency stabilization, a general recovery program, nor lowering of tariffs seems likely. McDonald is in trouble with his die-hards since he has got back home; and Herriot is arriving in a France enraged because he did not get the intergovernmental debts forgiven. If we could do so, I would be glad to see us withdraw now.

This administration is at a crossroads in more than one sense. This matter of international affairs will see us on the nationalistic road within two months, I should say, unless there are some wholly unforeseen developments. But we probably will not accept the logic of that position. The matter of monetary policy is hanging fire. The President is improvising as he goes along in this field which I am glad to see him do, feeling that this policy should follow expansion, not attempt to cause it. Then there is the big question whether we are to expand, how much, and what way? I am terribly afraid that what we do will be too slow and insufficient.

Meanwhile it is interesting to talk to the foreign experts, to see the President handle them and to feel for the real motives beneath the ostensible ones.

May 30, 1933

The most interesting, in a way, of all the legislation of this period to later observers, will probably be the National Recovery Act. It did not fix the design -- the AAA bill did that -- but it carried it out even more perfectly. It provides for executive recognition of associations, exemption from anti-trust compulsions, and enforcement of cooperation. It had an interesting history in which I had some part.

For weeks I had been uneasy for more footing under the optimism spreading through the country. I had seen many people and groups who were working on various schemes for putting government credit behind industry for programs of public works, etc. I found Moley had been doing something similar in a desultory way and had put Bobby Straus to work at it. He and I got Louis Bean -- who had been working with Meyer Jacobstein[26] -- and Jerry Frank to work on it. They made contact with John Dickinson -- now Assistant Secretary of Commerce -- and together threshed out the various schemes and proposals. This group then made contact with the Wagner-LaFollette group and reconciled their views.

[26]Jacobstein, Meyer, economic counsel, formerly labor manager for Stein-Block Co. Rochester, member of Congress from N.Y. 1923-29; member research staff Brookings Institution, Wash., D.C.

Meanwhile Hugh Johnson had been working at something of his own and acting cagy about it. He gets that way: is extremely sensitive and doesn't like to cooperate too well in working out ideas. He had a draft of his own based on the War Industries Board experience.

Of course nothing could be settled really without the President. I liked the draft worked out by Frank and Dickinson which I had constantly talked over with them and which, in fact, embodies my ideas. But Johnson had more power in his bill -- with clearer compulsions -- and I like this part of his if we cannot have my own method of making compliance profitable. But Johnson and Dickinson came to loggerheads and we finally took it to F.D.R. Each side told a story and he too leaned toward shorter and quicker action but his mandate was to go away and agree.

Wagner, Dickinson, Frances Perkins, Johnson and I fought over the thing in Lew Douglas' office for some time. I failed to get them to adopt my tax and reserve-fund scheme[27]. I argued for it strongly but dropped it for the sake of harmony. But I sided with Johnson in his demand for more teeth in the penalty provisions if we could not have the tax. Dickinson was compelled to give way after really being unpleasant and arrogant -- which surprised me very much since, though he is a keen thinker, he is rather slow and lethargic in manner. He was downright nasty to Johnson.

But the General had his revenge when, a few days later, it leaked out that he was to run the show. To tell the truth, this rather surprised me. I had got used to thinking of him as Baruch's man rather than an independent personality, not doubting, of course, the strength of character and real brilliance, which are obvious. I think his tendency to be gruff in personal relations will be a handicap and his occasional drunken sprees will not help any; but on the whole I am quite happy about it. It was a hard job to fill. Hugh is sincere, honest, believes in many social changes which seem to me right, and will, I think do a good job. It would doubtless be better if he had been further from the Baruch speculative influence and if he believed more in social planning, but the

---

[27]This refers to an idea I argued for very strenuously. I wanted to levy a processing tax the proceeds of which would go into a reserve fund. This fund would be distributed periodically to those who had complied with the code provisions.

Johnson wanted merely to put all industries under license and withdraw licenses from those who did not comply. This had obvious difficulties, it seemed to me; and probably would cause vigorous protest.

As it turned out compliance was the weakest phase of NRA and general disregard for code provisions brought the ill-repute into which it soon fell.

one gives him an inside knowledge which will be useful in his dealings
with business and the other is something which comes out as it is done.
I doubt if one is a much better planner for believing in it as a principle.

Of course the Act hasn't yet passed. The National Manufacturers
Association has gone off the reservation and are calling their whole
membership to Washington to fight it -- because of the labor provisions -
- but I believe it will pass in substantially its present form with the
President's prestige behind it.

May 31, 1933

The argonauts leave this morning. Moley pronounces this word
sardonically and I think we feel alike that the results of the Conference
are sure to be pretty slim -- in the vague, hazy sense that Hull means.
His rambling, lisping speeches on the evils of protection, and his extolling
of the old laissez-faire liberal internationalism have become harder and
harder to bear. The reporters have begun to see the split between those
of us who are bent on pursuing a domestic policy which will put our house
in order and take us out of this crisis, and those like Hull (and most of
the rest of the State Department) who are apparently little concerned
about the domestic policy but who want to keep the rest of the world
sweet-tempered.

PROFESSORS' PROGRESS

Always latent in American opinion -- in some contrast with other
nations -- is an anti-intellectualism which any politician has to deal with.
The President's reliance on a group of academicians made him peculiarly
liable to criticism of this sort. It was implied in the tag "brains trust" and
had, by now, been exploited mercilessly by cartoonists for many months.
The Chicago Tribune, The New York Herald-Tribune, the Hearst Press
and the boiler plate material sent out from Chicago to the smaller
newspapers, played daily on this weakness. These had been invented a
thin and bloodless, but swell-headed stereotype, fitted out with academic
gown and cap; and he was represented as forever interfering in practical
affairs. No senseless suggestion was too fantastic for him to put forward.
And he was always at the President's side offering foolish counsel which
was fatuously accepted.

It was extraordinary to what lengths the press was willing to go
to impress this stereotype on the public mind. And, of course, it had some
effect. The first to accept it were naturally those to whom it was
agreeable for some reason. These included those who dissented most
violently from the Administration's policies as well as those whose
partnership matched that of the newspaper publishers.

The following exchange is typical of the kind of criticism which came to the President. His soft reply indicates, also, his healthy respect for it and his desire to turn it aside. He had never recognized the "brains trust" publicly. He never would. And he counselled those of us who were included in its putative membership to escape the labelling if we could.

(President's Private File, Hyde Park)

(COPY)
United States Senate
Washington, D.C.

May 6, 1933

Dear Mr. President:

I have no desire to bother you with letters or comments, but Mr. Edward J. Dempsey who wrote the enclosed letter is probably the most able lawyer in Wisconsin, and has been a genuine Democrat for his entire adult life. The comment of the Chicago Tribune, a very influential newspaper, as you know, I believe is very interesting. I do not expect a reply to this letter, but hope that you can take five minutes to read it.

Very sincerely

F. Ryan Duffy

Honorable Franklin D. Roosevelt,
President
Washington, D.C.
                                        ****

May 16, 1933

Dear Ryan:

Some day I hope that your friend Dempsey will come down here and have a talk with me. He evidently thinks that the government is being run by Professors.

Very sincerely yours

F.D.R.

Hon. F. Ryan Duffy
United States Senate
Washington, D.C.

(COPY)

Bouck, Hilton, Kluwin & Dempsey
Oshkosh, Wisconsin

May 3, 1933

Hon. F. Ryan Duffy
Senate Office Building
Washington, D.c.

My dear Senator Duffy:

. . .There is general distrust of the academic group that seems to
have the last say with the president. Personally, I have had a long and
extended contact with the men from the schools and colleges. Up to a
certain point they serve a useful purpose but on the whole I have found
them entirely lacking in common sense and sound judgment. They have
a lust for jurisdiction and an uncontrollable appetite for power. It was
the advice that Phil LaFollette received from men and women of this type
that caused his downfall here in Wisconsin. Schmedeman has succeeded
because he has pursued a rational course that has appealed to the
common sense of the great mass of our people. The Democratic victory
in Rock County shows conclusively how the people have appraised the
governor's official acts. He has been successful up to this time because he
has turned down all of the visionary theoretical and impractical schemes
that have been seriously presented for his consideration . . . .

Sincerely

Edward J. Dempsey

The later conversations with visiting delegates have been about
like the earlier ones with Jimmy Warburg presenting the fiscal picture
and Feis or myself talking about the trade. We haven't accomplished
much. What has come out clearly for ourselves is the offer we are really
making to guide our domestic policy a good deal by international
requirements provided we can persuade Great Britain and France to do

something real toward ending the crisis. To that extent we are willing to be international. But we cannot go too far that way and sacrifice the chance of recovery for ourselves.

F.D.R. carries on all the conversations concerning debts and disarmament himself. He has centered more in his own hands than any President ever did -- and I do not mean just powers to delegate but actual operations. For the last month, with everything else going on, he has been his own foreign minister. I'm sure Hull doesn't know half of what goes on.

The new man at the Treasury -- Sprague -- looks good to me. I think he will be a source of strength. He seems to me right in most things. We badly needed some one there. He is a curious dumpy little man, quite wall-eyed, but I like him so far. F.D.R. seems to trust him too, which is good.[28] He had got far too dependent on Douglas. It is so easy to like Douglas that his biasses tend to be forgotten. But he has them -- he is not too liberal. He had taken this budget balancing business too seriously and literally. He has been much under Stewart's influence and talks like Wall Street. But he has beautiful brown eyes and everyone says he is a lovely fellow -- if only . . .

---

[28]Sprague, Oliver M.W., Edmund Cogswell Converse professor of banking and finance Harvard, 1913- economic adviser to Bank of England 1930-33, financial and exec. assistant to Secretary of Treasury since June 1933.

Addendum to the Diary
for The Hundred Days

There were some additional events and activities during the Hundred Days, not mentioned in the diary, or not made much of, which ought to be noted.

They are listed here and letters and memoranda referring to them will be saved in files to be made available at the Roosevelt Library. Some of these are more interesting and more comprehensive than others as would be expected. My files have gaps which are unexplainable -- as I suppose is true of most such collections.

1.   Departmental reorganization.
        Numerous meetings about this matter were held. I relied on Lee Strong, Chief, Bureau of Plant Quarantine, Wm Jump, Budget Officer for the Department, and F. P. Bartlett, my own administrative assistant. There is some correspondence in my file about these difficult, but now uninteresting events.

2.   Difficulties with Douglas.
        As time passed Douglas' attitude concerning Departmental economics seemed more unreasonable and my resistance increased. I was better able to combat his insistence as I became better acquainted with the Department.

3.   Henry Wallace and I began an active exploration for assistants when it became obvious that rapid expansion would take place in the Department. Concerning the solicitorship we were especially anxious and wrote to Felix Frankfurter for suggestions. This resulted in our getting Jerome Frank who became General Counsel for A.A.A. This was an embarrassing

affair, because after we had asked him to be solicitor, the President had stopped the appointment because of Farley's objection. This proved to be a case of mistaken identity, but by the time it was straightened out Seth Thomas of Iowa had become Solicitor and Jerome General Counsel for A.A.A. Pending the passage of the authorizing and the organizing of AAA, Jerome acted as an assistant to me. At this time we were discussing what became of NRA and he was very active in this -- in fact, he perhaps more than anyone else was responsible for its drafting. The Frankfurter letters concerning appointments show his interest in the staffing of the New Deal Agencies.

4.   When I sacrificed my scheme for a processing tax and reserve fund in the drafting of N.R.A., I turned to another device. I tried to persuade various of my New Deal colleagues that there was needed a Bank for Corporate Surpluses. I remember numerous conversations about it; but in my file I find only a rough note which indicated what I had in mind.

The BCS was conceived as an alternative to the undistributed profits tax then being much talked of as a way of forcing corporate surplus into use. One of the troubles of 1929 had been the lavish use of these for money-market loans.

My suggestion was that undistributed surpluses might be required to be deposited in a special bank -- the BCS. These might be withdrawn by the depositing industry at 60 days notice by paying an alternative tax. Since this tax would be perhaps 25% most deposits would be left.

But business enterprises might borrow from the fund so created to increase working capital or for expansion purposes at the discretion of its director.

Directors would be chosen by election from among depositing industries. Interest rates would be fixed at the Federal Reserve Board's current rediscount rate.

This still seems to me an ingenious suggestion. F.D.R. liked the idea. But nothing came of it, largely, I suppose, because of the press of other matters. I do not exactly recall.

5.   It is pleasant to recall that in moving to Washington I was able to renew an old association with R. C. Rowe who had been my professor of constitutional law at the University of Pennsylvania. He had had a distinguished career, now, climaxed by the Secretary Generalship of the Pan American Union. He included me in invitations to social events at the Union, offered to sponsor membership in the Cosmus Club (I was already a

member), and frequently wrote comments on my articles or addresses.

6.   It presently became obvious that Lewis Douglas was using his office as Director of the Budget for some purposes not strictly within his competence. One of these -- not to speak of others -- was to excise from the government all the research projects he could reach. That this would be fatal to agriculture was obvious. And Henry Wallace and I took on ourselves -- as in the circumstances we were forced to do -- the burden of proof in support of these activities.

To a certain extent the President shared this prejudice. And I argued with him frequently. The outcome of these arguments was usually that I won in the instance at hand; but that it did not seem to affect his general attitude. He could always be interested in specific problems and their solution. It was not possible to talk to him, however, about the hundreds of them we had within our responsibility. So far as Douglas was concerned, he was stubbornly uninterested. Also he tended to be incensed (by) any ability to persuade the President contrary to his advice. This made him vindictive; and before many months had passed we were pretty much at war.

This continuing state of affairs took a lot of time and energy, at a time when they could ill be spared, for purely defensive operations.

Douglas was defeated when our appropriations were made in the Congress. We lost nothing essential. But this was a way of doing it that I deplored. I would much rather have had a satisfactory executive budget to submit. When Douglas's really absurd estimates went to the Committees, they mostly ignored them. We were then in a very delicate situation. We could not advocate the restoration of cuts and display a complete division in the executive family. On the other hand we could not see our Department wrecked. This dilemma was met by having that remarkable public servant, Bill Jump, our finance officer, advise the Committee members in private what we regarded as essential. As I say, a deplorable method; but one that worked.

7.   My approach to the problem of depression and recovery from it had been one of encouraging price rises in some instances and trying to affect reductions in some others. There were several thoughtful members of the administration who agreed with this. But it was an attitude which infuriated me particularly; and we were subjected to one group: great pressure

from it. This was the sheer inflationist <u>Committee for the Nation</u>. These people pictured those of us who thought regulation and the encouragement of expansion necessary, as being hardly less than Russian emissaries. We wanted regimentation for its own sake, they said. Also they pictured us as running the nation through an unbalanced budget.   To inflate by this method was Communistic or something equally radical; to inflate by monetary methods was, however, quite all right.

There were other orthodox academicians and financial people who regarded both programs with equal horror. These, of course, were either creditors or those who instinctively assumed the creditor psychology.

In spite of my best efforts, I was represented by each of these groups as belonging to the other and lost equally my reputation with all of them.

The fact was that I never stopped trying to convince the President that our attack ought to be selective. I had pursued this theme all through our various pre-campaign, campaign and post-campaign conferences. He was never convinced. As a last effort, when I saw him embracing inflation but still unwilling to undertake regulation of those industries whose prices ought to be decreased, I tried to get him to have a study made. I framed the following letter and urged him to send it. He never did.

Draft of letter to be sent by F.D.R.

Social Science Research Council
        Washington, D.C.

Gentlemen

There is a suggestion in the recent report of the President's Research Committee on Social Trends which seems to me to have possibilities of fruitful development.   The problem of coordinating research and of finding an adequate consensus of view on pressing economic and social questions is one which no satisfactory method of approach has ever been worked out. The Social Science Research Council, representing, as it does, seven great scientific societies and devoted to research in the social field, might cooperate with the Executive to determine what seems best to be done in some, at least, of the exigencies of policy-making.

I can think of many ways in which such a scientific body might be of great assistance in these matters and this letter is merely a suggestion concerning one problem which is especially puzzling at the present time and around which there are sure to converge many dissenting opinions and much disagreement. I refer to the problem of price disparities. There seems to be no clear consensus of judgment at the present time as to whether we ought to enter on a policy looking toward a generally higher or lower level of prices or whether policy ought to be directed toward the raising of some prices and the lowering of others in order that the normality of exchange might be substituted for the present inability of many groups to acquire the commodities of other groups.

It would be of the greatest assistance if the Social Science Research Council could undertake an investigation, it might, it seems to me, be the beginning of a new approach to this general range of problems.

Later on I should engage Gardiner Means as one of my own assistants. He made such a study. It was widely circulated in the Administration and had a good deal of effect. But this did not occur until the embarrassing incident of gold-buying to influence the dollar had run its course, and NRA, as it was administered, had proved to be wholly futile in the price field.

The letter above has some added interest as representing an attempt on my part to establish continuity with the research work Hoover had sponsored and which had resulted in the influential reports on Recent Economic Changes in 1929 and on Recent Social Trends in 1932. These reports had great influence; but not so much as they ought to have had in the Roosevelt circle.

Although this tentative effort came to nothing, research into American resources and capabilities would be enormously expanded by the successive planning agencies, the first of which would be set up by Harold Ickes as an adjunct to the Public Works Administration.

8.   The Tennessee Valley Authority was in the making during the months of March and April; in fact a good deal of preliminary work had been done on it before inauguration. On 6 March, however, I sent a memorandum to the President suggesting that a considerable contribution could be made to the preliminary studies by various members of the Department. An informal committee was set up and contributed significantly to the drafting and passage of the bill as well as to the subsequent organization of the administration.

9.   Work on the revision of the Food and Drug Act began almost at once after inauguration under my auspices. After

preliminary talks with Dr. Walter G. Campbell and his assistants
in the Food and Drug Administration I was very quickly
disabused of the preconceptions I had had concerning the work.
These had mostly come from the violent criticism made by self-
styled "consumer's research" group, who pictured the
Administration as being so favorable to those it was supposed to
regulate as to cast doubt on its integrity. What I discovered was
an extremely able and devoted administration whose efforts were
frustrated (1) by a law which had not been revised since 1906, (2)
by the downright hostility of successive Secretaries of Agriculture
who had not wanted food processors harassed, and (3) by a public
indifference which enabled these conditions to persist.

I was, in effect, challenged by Dr. Campbell to do
something about all this. My first step was to enlist two
appropriate professors in a revision of the bill. These were Milton
Handler of Columbia and David Cavers, then at Duke University,
later of Harvard. This work was going on all during the Spring.
I evidently had had some hope that we might secure the passage
of the revision during the Special Session. This was a grossly
optimistic estimate.

In my papers there will be found some of the
correspondence with Handler and Cavers, together with other
notes.

During the next few months some really good propaganda
work would issue from our side of the controversy that very
rapidly grew up. It would never be sufficient to overcome the
opposition, however, which was generously financed and well
managed, and which, moreover, enlisted the entire press of the
country on the representation that advertising was threatened -
- which, in fact, it was, in so far as it was misrepresentational --
and this was most of it.

I learned a good deal from this incident, but to say that
is to risk reference to the old story of the man who was being
hanged and who, when asked if he had any last words, said he
supposed what was about to happen would be a good lesson for
him.

The forces massed against the kind of thing I represented
had a hanging in mind for me.

10.   Several of us spent an unconscionable amount of time
during this period on international economic matters. This is
indicated in my notes. From time to time we made suggestions
which I suppose deserve no better label than brash. Yet what we
had in mind was laudable enough. We wanted to increase trade

and so make a contribution to recovery.

If we were to be forced to develop an economic nationalism of our own to match those in Europe -- as seemed likely to me, but not to Hull and his advisers -- we could still make some progress by a system of bi-lateral agreements. Hull, of course, was a free-trader, made circumspect by circumstances. And all our efforts to devise ways and means for implementing a nationalistic system were met by a bland but determined opposition which infuriated Moley. It annoyed me too; but I kept on working at this kind of thing, partly because of the President's interest. As everyone knows, he seemed one day to be convinced that we must shut ourselves up and go it alone, and on the next to agree with Hull that free trade was the only objective worth consideration.

Moley and I would have been free traders in an ideal world -- that is a world in which wages were roughly equal etc. But the reality was very different. There existed, in fact, such a complex and formidable system of tariffs, quotas, blocked currencies, and all the other paraphernalia by which each nation tried to improve its situation vis-á-vis all the others that the large idealism of old-fashioned laissez faire was simply not open to choice. We should have been mercilessly exploited by all the other trading nations if we had adopted it.

What we wanted was a way of persuading the nations toward modifications by holding out rewards. The reward was a sharing in our consumer market. But the quid-pro-quo was an acceptance of those commodities we had for export.

Our approaches to this were many and various. The President himself began the elaboration of one approach as several of us sat talking one evening. It appealed to him so much that he then and there elaborated a considerable structure on his original foundation. I, among others, took notes; so did Charles Taussig. And we began a process, which went on for weeks, of trying to reduce the scheme to workable specificity. We called it, among us, "the wooly lamb" -- a name given it by F.D.R. himself. He came back to it again and again.

I find among my papers several drafts which I recognize as relevant to this. And evidently I enlisted Jerome Frank in the drafting. I also elicited criticisms from the economic advisers -- Feis and Livsey. They, of course, were made very unhappy by these activities, an unhappiness reflected in their memoranda.

I shall not refer to this at any length. Nothing really came of it. But the study of it did carry me further in considerations of this kind than I had gone before. The curious thing was that the President again and again pressed us to develop a practical program of "trading" as he called it. And it was the feeling that we must cultivate our own economy without "foreign complications" which governed his policy for some time--for instance, his rejection of the arrangements at the London Economic Conference. But in the end he could not be classified as a nationalist. The Trade Agreements Act (of 12 June 1934) would be a fairly even compromise. It would center on "agreements"; but each of them would contain a "most favored nation" clause, and so look toward free trade.

One of my duties throughout my years in Washington would be to sit on successive interdepartmental committees dealing with trade. It was always difficult. The fact is that this is a field in which it is peculiarly difficult to persuade special interest that their prosperity is to be sought in the prosperity of the whole. They do not believe it; they will not yield to the public interest; and they seek ruthlessly for every advantage. Their power can be brought to bear on Congressmen, also, under peculiar conditions. There is no countervailing power. Foreigners who are discriminated against cannot retaliate with notes; and if they retaliate at all, the injury will be done to another group.

If we succeeded in modifying the Smoot-Hawley spirit somewhat in our time it was not a permanent gain. In the two decades since a majority of the Republicans in the Congress have consistently opposed the Trade Agreements Act; and they have written in it emasculating amendments whenever they have had the opportunity -- the "peril-point" provision, the "escape" clause, and the disclaimer of the General Agreement on Tariffs and Trade (written into the 1951 Act).

As Mr. Clair Wilcox recently remarked (in a letter to The New York Times, 23 November 1952):

... The Congress voted in 1947 to increase the duty on wool ... the Senate cast a tie vote in 1949 on a bill to curtail the imports of petroleum; the House voted in 1951 to impose a duty on tuna fish; and the Congress attached a rider to the Defense Production Act in 1951, and continued it in 1952, imposing quotas on cheese and other dairy products on the ground that imports, amounting to a tiny fraction of domestic consumption, would imperil national security.

Nothing is more difficult in a representative democracy than the management of policy in the general interest. But we were optimists in 1932. We thought we could make bargains and see them through. We even thought that we could manage to increase industrial imports which would enable others to buy more of our farm products. We accomplished a little but not much.

11.   Another activity in which I was engaged at this time was the preliminary planning for what became the National Agricultural Research Center at Beltsville, Md., just outside Washington.

The possibilities in such an institution were called to my attention by various Bureau Chiefs; but I think I can claim to be responsible for the subsequent embodiment of our combined thinking in a going institution.

What occurred during the next few years would not have been possible in ordinary circumstances. Only because emergency funds were available to be processed outside the usual budget procedures were we able to purchase the large tracts of land, improve them, and build the many necessary facilities. If these sums had been submitted in a budget to the Congress they would have met the determined opposition of the extremely powerful land-grant-College lobby and Congressman, always anxious for funds to be spent in their own localities, and always reluctant to authorize spending elsewhere, would have rejected the proposal. The truth is that nothing is so easy as to get approval for local spending; and nothing is so hard as to get approval for national spending. And this project had the added handicap of seeming to compete with the research stations attached to each of the colleges.

That these colleges and research centers were in fact not meeting the need for fundamental research would not be weighted very heavily. That, of course, was why I -- and others in the Department -- were so glad to seize this unusual opportunity. It would not be long before emergency funds would no longer be available; why they were not, all progress at Beltsville would be abruptly halted. Practically everything at the modern Beltsville dates from the years 1933-36.

12.   I might note, also, that I began at this time to write and speak in explanation and defense of administration policy. This I was encouraged to do both by the President and Secretary Wallace. These efforts grew as time passed, to a considerable volume and took much time and effort. In fact, this kind of thing was accountable for my delinquency in keeping a diary.

Monetary Preliminaries

Among numerous other activities in behalf of the President-elect, Moley, Berle, and I undertook to bring to him in person those people, of whatever persuasion, who had something of importance to say about the issues he would have to deal with. One of these was finance. It happened to be me who arranged, so soon after the election as 17 November 1932, for such a briefing session with H. Parker Willis and James Harvey Rogers.

Willis was a Professor in the School of Business at Columbia; Rogers was at Yale. Willis was generally spoken of as the unseen author of the Federal Reserve Act whose authorship was usually credited to Senator Carter Glass. In some respects even Willis and Glass admitted that further legislation was needed. There was in fact a "Glass bill" before the Congress. The Federal Reserve Act had been passed in 1913 and far from establishing the hampering agency the bankers had uniformly predicted it would, it had allowed numerous abuses now sought to be corrected.

The new bill would not modify in any important respect the Federal Reserve structure and it would not change the method of creating the medium of exchange. The President did not think this bill went far enough. And he had some changes in mind that it did not suggest at all. Also he evidently had some thoughts, got from his Cornell correspondents, which he was not yet prepared to discuss. At any rate he seems not to have discussed them at this interview. I have in my file, and herewith reproduce, the memoranda written by both Willis and Rogers after that November interview. The Willis paper is in the form of a letter to Glass, copy of which was sent to me. The Rogers paper is an original sent to me.

November 19, 1932

Honorable Carter Glass
Lynchburg, Virginia

My Dear Mr. Glass:

I do not know whether you are at Lynchburg or Washington and, therefore, I am writing this letter addressed to you at Lynchburg and sending a copy of it addressed at Washington. It relates to the interview that I had on Thursday, November 17 with the President-elect Roosevelt at Albany.

Some weeks ago I had asked Professor Tugwell of this University whether he could tell me in a general way the views of the President-elect with reference to certain foreign policies and his answer was that he thought that this might be best learned from Mr. Roosevelt and that he thought it likely that the latter would be willing to see me. My purpose in asking the question was to get some material for some articles I was writing. Incidentally Professor Tugwell expressed the thought that Mr. Roosevelt was keenly interested in the whole problem of what should be done on banking and that he might be disposed to discuss the provisions of the Glass Bill with me. This matter Professor Tugwell thought had better be deferred until after election.

Meantime as you will recall I had a conversation with you on the whole subject when I had the pleasure of seeing you in Washington at the time when you were preparing your campaign speech. As you will recall I outlined to you then the conversation I had had with Professor Tugwell.

When the election was over Professor Tugwell undertook to ascertain whether such a conversation would be of interest to the President-elect and on Wednesday last, November 16 he advised me that he thought it would be and he suggested that I should telephone you and see whether you would be inclined to be present at a general discussion of the general banking situation in which several persons would participate. Accordingly, as you will remember, I called you on the telephone and found that you did not feel strong enough to make the journey.

On Thursday, November 17, I went with Professor Tugwell to Albany and there we met Professor Rogers of Yale. The President-elect was kind enough to invite us to have luncheon at the Executive Mansion and after luncheon was over we had a conversation in which the major subject, I should say, was banking, while incidentally some references were made to agricultural credit, foreign debts and the proposed World Economics Conference. This conversation lasted the better part of an hour.

The first topic taken up was banking and I was requested to state the present situation of the Glass Bill. This I did following the lines that I had spoken of in our telephone conversation. Mr. Roosevelt was very desirous to know whether there was a good chance of passing it at the coming session of Congress. I answered that such possibilities were always subject to doubt owing to the crowded condition of the Session, but that you thought it very likely that it would go through the Senate with the possibility of going through the House, doubtless with some amendment. Mr. Roosevelt expressed the opinion that it was very desirable to have it passed at the short session of Congress, if possible. He was fairly familiar with the Glass Bill and in sympathy with most of its provisions, especially as presented in the earlier draft. He thought that if it could be passed at the short session it would save time after the opening of his administration. There were various things that he wished to do that had a bearing upon banking or were incidentally connected with it. They embodied a very large program. It would help these projects greatly to have the underlying measure of correction (the Glass Bill) disposed of. When I ventured to suggest that perhaps it would be better to take the whole thing up afresh in the new administration, have an investigation, and thorough revision of the Glass Bill, etc., he said that he thought that the greatest thing to do was to get what was to be had now and if the bill did not turn out when passed, to include all that was desired, to go on then with further amendment and legislation designed to complete and perfect a program of banking reform.

Mr. Roosevelt then proceeded to express strong interest in the following topics:

1.   He was very desirous that there should be somewhere in the form of early legislation provisions designed to protect the investor against the offering of fictitious or bad securities. I replied that this was not dealt with in the Glass Bill except in so far as related to banks but that the committee had endeavored in the original Glass Bill to keep the banks out of the underwriting business and to regulate their portfolios. This had been very distasteful to the bankers I pointed out, with the result that the provisions had been greatly weakened and many of them eliminated in the final edition of the bill.

2.   Mr. Roosevelt was anxious to have segregation of savings deposits and (as I understood him) better reserve protection for them. I told him that these had been in the Glass Bill originally and had fallen out under pressure.

3.   Mr. Roosevelt was greatly interested in the Liquidating
        Corporation but was desirous that a change should be
        made, such as to permit the re-opening of a failed bank
        immediately after it had been closed, the name being
        changed and the capitalization altered while the bank was
        given as a working fund the proceeds derived from the
        Liquidating Corporation through the sale of its old assets.
        The institution would then go on providing services to its
        customers on the new basis, as before. I explained to him
        the liquidating provisions of the Glass Bill and contrasted
        it with those of the bill proposed by the Comptroller of the
        Currency and he said that he preferred greatly the Glass
        provisions because they eliminated the costly, long-drawn
        receiverships, to which he said he had always felt a strong
        opposition.

4.   Mr. Roosevelt thought that the present branch banking
        provision was politically unwise and if it were to be
        included at all it should be limited to county-wide branch
        banking -- this because of the strenuous opposition of
        large sections of the country to the branch idea.

The conversation then took a wider range, dealing with the question of agricultural credit and, on request, I outlined the plans in vogue in Ireland and attempted in Rumania for relieving the mortgage-burdened farmer, and I indicated how I thought they might be applied in a modified form here.

The President-elect then discussed with Professor Rogers at some length various problems concerning international relations and the method of settling indebtedness, but he expressed very little definite opinion of his own on these scores, merely outlining some of the problems he had to deal with and the points on which he wished information. In later conversation with Professor Tugwell the question came up of how far the government should intervene to protect the public against bad flotations of foreign bonds, and I suggested that if anything of the kind were to be undertaken it would have to be done on the basis of actual knowledge obtained from abroad through the efforts of financial attaches attached to foreign embassies and devoting their time to ascertainment of facts. Such work would enable the government to state in an objective non-partisan way what it thought of different issues--whether they were as represented or not. Of course, the question was seriously raised how far the government had any right or duty in this field as so far as I remember there was no expression of opinion anywhere except as to the fact that the public had been greatly befooled with the foreign issues and needed protection in some way.

The President-elect spoke most cordially of his interview with you in New York, asked to be remembered, directed me to convey to you the substance of the conversation with him, and asked me whether I thought that you were strong enough in health to go to Washington to be present at his interview with Mr. Hoover. Of course I told him that I had no knowledge on that point but I thought it would be a most excellent thing if you had the strength to be present, but that I knew you were conserving your physical resources as much as possible. He expressed a strong desire that you should be there and then added that he felt great hesitation about asking anything that would impose additional burdens upon you.

I have written thus fully in order that you may know as nearly as I can repeat, and exactly what was said at this interview.

With regards, believe me

Yours sincerely,

H. Parker Willis

HPW:S

Memorandum for Governor Franklin D. Roosevelt relating to subjects discussed in conversation of November 17, 1932 by way of Professor Tugwell.

1.   War Debts
2.   International Economic Conference
3.   French Monetary Situation
4.   Security Investment Provisions of Glass Bill

1.   War Debts

Apparently, the only value still retained by the War Debts is as bargaining points in the forthcoming Economic Conference. Defaults would greatly diminish this value. Hence the desirability of avoiding defaults prior to the Conference discussions.

2.   International Economic Conference

International Conferences rarely solve any problems. Very frequently however, they may ratify solutions already found. Hence, the desirability of advance understandings with the British, tying debt revision with gradual removal of trade restrictions.

3.   French Monetary Situation

France is destined soon to lose gold, and with it, much of her financial power.

Reasons:

(a)   The great inflow of gold to France prior to the financial crises of the Summer and Fall of 1931 were chiefly a result of the low rate at which the franc was stabilized and of the sluggishness with which French prices adjusted themselves to its new gold value.

(b)   The recent great gold inflows (since the Summer of 1931) have resulted very largely from the withdrawals of French balances abroad and from the flight of capital to Paris from the other money and investment centers.

The first set of influences have completely spent their force.   French prices are now somewhat above the world level.

The second set have not only spent themselves but have given rise to two powerful influences operating in the reverse direction.

(1)   The foreign balances of French banks and business firms have apparently been drawn down to uncomfortably low levels.

(2)   The refugee funds in Paris draw very little interest. Hence, as soon as stable money and investment conditions are re-established in New York and London, funds may be expected to flow from Paris to those centers.

4.   Security Investment Provisions of the Glass Bill

Severe restrictions placed upon the types of securities purchaseable by commercial banks is apt to lead to a sale of portions of their security portfolios. The fact that the provision is made applicable to future purchases only is unlikely to prevent such sales. Conservatively managed banks would no doubt find considerable pressure to rid themselves of the tabooed holdings. There is danger that such action might retard business recovery through a disturbance of the securities' markets.

/s/ James Harvey Rogers

The World Economic Conference

The World Economic Conference in London opened on 12 June and ended--virtually--on 8 July, five days after receiving the "bombshell" message of President Roosevelt.

That message read as follows:

I would regard it as a catastrophe amounting to a world tragedy if the great Conference of Nations, called to bring a more real and permanent financial stability and a greater prosperity to the masses of all Nations, should, in advance of any serious effort to consider these broader problems, allow itself to be diverted by the proposal of a purely artificial and temporary experiment affecting the monetary exchange of a few nations only. Such action, such diversion, shows a singular lack of proportion and a failure to remember the larger purposes for which the Economic Conference originally was called together.

I do not relish the thought that insistence on such action should be made an excuse for the continuance of the basic economic errors that underlie so much of the present world-wide depression.

The world will not long be lulled by the specious fallacy of achieving a temporary and probably an artificial stability in foreign exchange on the part of the few large countries only.

The sound internal economic system of a nation is a greater factor in its well-being than the price of its currency in changing terms of the currencies of other Nations.

It is for this reason that reduced cost of Government, adequate Government income, and ability to service Government debts are all so important to ultimate stability. So too, old fetishes of so-called international bankers are being replaced by efforts to plan national currencies with the objective of giving to those currencies a continuing purchasing power which does not greatly vary in terms of the commodities and need of modern civilization. Let me be frank in saying that the United States seeks the kind of dollar which a generation hence will have the same purchasing and debt-paying power as the dollar value we hope to attain in the near future. That objective means more to the good of other nations than a fixed ratio for a month or two in terms of the pound or franc.

Our broad purpose is the permanent stabilization of every nation's currency. Gold or gold and silver can well continue to be a metallic reserve behind currencies, but this is not the time to dissipate gold reserves. When the world works out concerted policies in the majority of Nations to produce balanced budgets and living within their means, then we can properly discuss a better distribution of the world's gold and silver supply to act as a reserve base of national currencies. Restoration of world trade is an important factor, both in the means and in the result. Here also temporary exchange fixing is not the true answer. We must rather mitigate existing embargoes to make easier the exchange of products which one Nation has and the other Nation has not.

The Conference was called to better and perhaps to cure fundamental economic ills. It must not be diverted from that effort.

This, it will be recognized, was a good deal more than a declaration having to do with fiscal policy. It was a statement which implied a settled conviction about the most pressing matters then before the nation: the road to recovery, notably, but also an acceptance of economic nationalism. Recovery was to be by way of raising the price level, enlarging relief and public works, and attaining balanced budgets to curb inflation. Implied in this was a shutting off of the United States from the malign influences in London, Paris and Amsterdam. Implied also was a program of production adjusted to the American market and not dependent on exports.

Much of this was anathema to Secretary Hull and his school of liberal free traders. It was obvious that if the Secretary was to remain in the administration some fast conciliating would have to be done by the President. It was also, curiously, a rebuke to Moley, not because he would not have agreed, but because he had not been consulted, and was, in fact, negotiating a modified exchange agreement which he understood to be the President's desire.

There was, as a salty stay-at-homer remarked, "Hell to pay and no money in the till." The President had offended everyone, it seemed, with one short message. But that judgment was gradually modified in the succeeding weeks and months. He may have offended members of his official family and the statesmen but eventually his was seen to be not only a logical but a practical attitude, although it was precisely the reverse of Hull's. It was true that he had been provocative in his statement; but what seemed to me much worse was that when his position was taken he did not stick to it. He proceeded to truckle to Hull and allow him a strange leeway; and he did not go straight to his monetary goal but adopted various tangential expedients, until Keynes remarked, after a year or two, that what he had attained was merely a kind of debased gold standard--the very thing he had set out to escape.

Still, at the time and place, it was a very important paper. I should nominate it for second place among the early New Deal declarations--first place going to the Inaugural, and second place to the message accompanying the AAA as it was submitted to Congress.

I have noted some of the preliminaries in which I was more or less continuously--even if unsatisfactorily--involved. Since my notes, however, do not cover the period of the Conference, I rely on contemporary commentaries; also the reader is referred to the accounts of Raymond Moley in After Seven Years, of Cordell Hull in his Memoirs, and especially of Ernest K. Lindley, whose chapter, "The New Deal Meets the Old World," in The Roosevelt Revolution is perhaps the best account. There were unfortunate incidents throughout the meeting. They began in the early days when Moley so dramatically flew to meet the President on the Amberjack off the New England coast and then went on to London, accompanied by Herbert Bayard Swope; he landed to find a confused Conference waiting for a Presidential lead, and an enraged Hull whose fury at being displaced from the center of affairs by his Assistant Secretary was concealed from no one. The account in Time for 3 July was representative of the press dispatches:

> Progress at the World Monetary and Economic Conference began in London last week with loud wincing from Chief U.S. Delegate Cordell Hull. "Everything I do is misconstrued these days!" he wailed, then rang down a quick curtain on the comedy of contradictions in which U.S. Delegates seemed to spend most of their time repudiating each others' mimeographed proposals...

Meanwhile the conference cocked apprehensive eyes on the new, slim, swift U.S. cabin liner Manhattan as she sped toward England.

The Manhattan carried President Roosevelt's premier Braintruster, smooth, positive Professor Raymond Moley, and slashing, impulsive Herbert Bayard Swope...

In vain Professor Moley said on sailing, "I am going to make myself useful and furnish background for the Delegation." London whispers that Professor Moley, "The Isolationist," was coming to supersede Secretary Hull, dinned louder and louder until they beat like African war drums on the U.S. Delegation's sensitive ears.

This din Kansas' irrepressible William Allen White likened in London to a throb of "Moley, Lord God Almighty." While the New York Times dubbed Almighty Moley a "Professor ex machina," the wonder of his rise was neatly satirized by Frank R. Kent in the Baltimore Sun: "It must, when he tucks himself in bed at night...seem to him like a dream. Sometimes he must ask himself: 'Is it real--am I Moley?' Less than a year ago, Dr. Moley was an obscure professor at Columbia University...Today...as he sails for Europe, ensconced in the royal suite, reporters besieged him for a word, while Kings, Ambassadors, Prime Ministers, Premiers and publicists...anxiously await his arrival..."

The proceedings in London continued to be dramatized by the press; and the Conference was the contemporary sensation. Time's 10 July issue spoke of tense waiting for a message from the President. McDonald said to expectant delegates, "I will wait up...the moment I hear I shall let you all know...":

During the day before the dollar's gyrations had driven delegates of Europe's six gold-standard nations (France, Italy, Switzerland, Netherlands, Belgium and Poland) nearly frantic. They feared they would be forced off gold should the dollar fall much further...President Roosevelt, they knew, was determined to reject any pact for permanent dollar stabilization, but would he agree to a joint statement pledging the world's central banks to steady the dollar, at least for the duration of the Conference. Such a statement must be carefully worded. Locked in a big room the gold standard statesmen, dubbed "golders" by London correspondents, wrote in succession seven statements. These were carried one after another by British Chancellor of the Exchequer Neville Chamberlain into another room. There they were rejected one after another by the U.S. delegation's acting fiscal expert James P. Warburg. The eighth draft was passed. It was transmitted to the President by Professor Raymond Moley who proved, last week, a great disappointment to the Conference. Delegates had hoped they could get down to business with him and really negotiate. Instead Dr. Moley, bland and self-possessed, talked courteously with everyone but made clear that on all major issues the President must be consulted by cable...

When the President replied he fired first a pistol, then a broadside. His pistol shot was to reject the Golders' proposal for steadying the dollar with respect to gold. His broadside came two days later in a cablegram which Secretary of State Cordell Hull, vainly attempting to hide his own amazement, read to the hushed, expectant Delegates...

...Unbalanced budgets, chronic today throughout the world, became officially the Roosevelt Administration's premise for arguing that to stabilize the dollar with respect to gold would at present be premature. And precisely that point made every French delegate mad clear through as he assumed the President Roosevelt's finger was pointed squarely at France as the outstanding gold nation whose budget was not balanced. On the other hand the President came out clearly for stabilization of all currencies with respect to general purchasing power. How this could or should be done he neither said nor hinted.

Since in the Continental view there is no basis for stabilization other than gold, France was promptly joined in wrath by the Italians, Dutch, Swiss, Belgians, Poles. The view of all had already been voiced by the President of France, who normally keeps as aloof as the King of England from all issues. In Besancon, President Albert Lebrun arouse thus: "How can contracts be made and engagements signed on a monetary basis that varies with events and speculation? To speak of tariff adjustments while moneys are variable is pure Utopia."

Thus the conference faced a complete deadlock between the advice of the Presidents of the U.S. and France. Three U.S. delegates were reported to favor adjournment, as were all the "Golders," but white-thatched conference President James

Ramsey MacDonald rushed excitedly about urging the delegates
to keep on. Divine Providence, he reminded all and sundry,
must surely come to the Conference's aid if all good men would
pull together.

Meanwhile an eager, delighted Roosevelt public reread
and relished parts of the President's cablegram which the
Conference simply ignored, those parts in which he talked
turkey to the world in the tone of a brisk uncle brimming with
new ideas: "I do not relish...continuance of basic economic errors
that underlie so much of the present world depression. The
world will not long be gulled by a specious fallacy of achieving
a temporary and probably artificial stability in foreign exchange
on the part of a few countries only..."

I have my own story to tell concerning the Conference--an
unimportant one, historically, yet one which throws some light on the
events in London. Those events were spectacular; they were the center
of attention for a time, because much had been hoped for from them by
a good many harassed people.

As our conversations with successive groups of visitors had gone
on in Washington, it had become clearer and clearer to us that such
expectations as there were would be disappointed. The European
statesmen wanted something we should not and could not give them.
They were disappointed in their conversations with us; but we more
than suspected that they intended to put us on the spot in London with
the full glare of publicity upon us. If we refused what they proposed we
should be blamed for the further ills of all peoples. The politicians in all
the gold nations, but especially France, were preparing to make the most
of this opportunity. It had been a terrible shock to the French that we
had gone off gold while they were at sea on their way to Washington.
They hoped to recover some ground, and at least to put themselves in
the right with their own people, by forcing us into a stabilization
agreement in London. This would give them an advantage over us in all
the world's markets and encourage their recovery at the expense of ours.

We became warier as the conversations progressed and some of
us would have put off the conference longer if we could, not holding it
at all until some hope of success appeared. For myself, the more I
discussed these matters and thought about them, the more it seemed to
me that any stabilization agreement was impossible. The only one I
could visualize as possible for us was one for strengthening central bank
relations so that flexible management was possible. But the Europeans
wanted to tie us up; and that we could not allow.

More and more it seemed to me that we ought to turn away from
monetary discussion--fruitless in any case, and, I felt, secondary--and

center on devices for increasing trade and recovery. And, as the Conference approached, this last began to seem to me more important. I was impressed by our own beginning successes with relief, public works, NRA, AAA, and all the rest. Why not a world-wide program of this sort? And why not turn the Conference into a discussion of recovery instead of stabilization?

When we did our planning about the conduct of our delegation we were confronted by a group chosen by the President in a light-hearted mood--one for having been a campaign contributor, one for being an old fellow Democrat, one because he represented a silver state, one because he was an amenable Republican, and the Chairman because he was Secretary of State and demanded the recognition. This last being Cordell Hull, we knew he would use the platform provided by the conference to preach free trade, and we knew the President would not instruct him that he must abide by the terms of reference agreed on. And sure enough he acted as we anticipated, thus causing confusion from the first.

The point arrived at by the President was made explicit in the "bombshell" message. He still laid much stress on the balanced budget. This, in itself, is somewhat ironic considering how seldom he would achieve one for his own administration in the years ahead. In July of 1933 he was still hoping strongly enough so that he felt no misgivings about lecturing the French on the subject. And he was on the verge of deciding that the buying and selling of gold by the government was an adequate mechanism for regulating the price level; and if the price level could be regulated, the purchasing power of the dollar could be stabilized when that was desired. He would be disillusioned about this, and would become more sophisticated about the manipulation of fiscal devices--the rediscount rate, the interest rate for government issues and so on. It is impossible to say just how much confidence he had in the bolstering of consumers' purchasing power through relief or the stimulation of business activity through public works. The "compensating budget," as we learned to call it, was not yet important, at least; and, considering the stress on balancing, was perhaps not yet present in his thinking at all.

It is not important to know what any of us thought who did not succeed in influencing policy, except that the President did have numerous choices. Henry Wallace could be called an inflationist; the Treasury people were deflationists (at this time); Lewis Douglas was the budget balancer; the Cornell people (who were to persuade the President of the virtues of gold) were interested in a monetary policy which would make the AAA (which they detested) unnecessary; Bob LaFollette and I (along with others) were advocates of recovery through relief, public works, the use of tax and fiscal devices, the regulation of production and price control (as in AAA and NRA).

This does violence to some attitudes. Henry Wallace was not

doctrinaire in his inflationism; and he too favored public works and relief; also, of course, he wanted an adjustment mechanism by which such gross imbalances as that between industry and agriculture could be corrected. And Henry Wallace was coming to be a much-trusted advisor. The President recognized his strong intelligence and his disinterestedness.

It will be realized that there were many discussions among us about these matters. As the Conference came on, there was something of a crystallization. None of us knew what the President was going to say in his message, because none of us knew what he had arrived at as a conclusion. He was, just at that time, not in Washington. He had been at Campobello and sailing on the Amberjack; and, when the message was composed and sent, he was on the Indianapolis at sea. Louis Howe, who was with him, seems to have been the only person consulted.

Several of us had, however, kept in the closest touch with events. I was one of these, because I was scheduled to go to the Conference two weeks after Moley went. I was to bear messages, the latest Presidential advice, all that kind of thing. I therefore thought that I had some excuse for suggesting the kind of reply the President ought to make when Moley arrived at his compromise stabilization plan and asked for the President's approval. I drafted one. I agreed to Moley's proposal temporarily; but it suggested that a joint attack, serious and of adequate size, be made on the problem of recovery, as we were doing in the United States. I suggested that the Conference turn its attention to this. Unemployment needed to be relieved, industry stimulated, public works undertaken, etc. I did not mention a balanced budget; and I would even have suggested financial assistance in getting going the recovery program.

My effort was too late. The President's message had gone before I could see him. And my plan was not heard of again. I have not even been able to find copies or outlines of it in my surviving files and have reconstructed it purely from memory. I recall discussing it excitedly with Henry Wallace, Jerome Frank, and Dan Roper, and trying frantically to reach the President on the Indianapolis. I also recall our conversation when I did see the President a few days later. He was rather pleased with himself. He would have to do something about both Hull and Moley. Both were in a resigning mood. And he admitted that his tone and language would have been improved by advice. He listened as I expanded on the joint recovery theme. Afterward, he turned in that direction himself, perhaps somewhat influenced by Bob LaFollette, Ickes, Hopkins and myself. But that was a good deal later.

Some of the immediate repercussions were noticed in the next week's issue of Time (that for 17 July 1933):

So pained and vexed with Franklin Delano Roosevelt grew James Ramsay MacDonald that for a time last week the

British Premier spoke of the U.S. President as "that person."

Spleen boiled up bitterest around a green-topped table in one of the small private committee rooms of the World Monetary and Economic Conference... Last to arrive was U.S. delegate James M. Cox who battled so fiercely when the Conference first met to be elected Monetary Chairman. As he strolled in several minutes late Mr. Cox heard high words, realized that the other Conference officials were flaying President Roosevelt.

"Gentlemen!" cried Ohio's Cox, "I agree with you that in this grave hour absolute candor is essential. I realize that my presence may embarrass you in your exchange of views. If so, I am quite willing to withdraw."

They made him stay and listen to their views on the President's blunt refusal to stabilize the dollar in terms of gold...

Meanwhile, his sea vacation over, President Roosevelt returned to the White House to find his desk lettered with urgent cables from Chief U.S. Delegate Cordell Hull in London. In them Mr. Hull -- described by London newshawks as a "stricken man" -- revealed that the Conference steering Committee was ready to vote adjournment. Blame seemed about to fall squarely on the President. By utmost efforts Mr. Hull had barely managed to persuade the Conference steering committee to hold off until next day. What was the U.S. delegation to do? The President pondered an answer...

Cheerily independent, President Roosevelt queried Secretary Hull as to whether a ten-day recess of the Conference might do some good. By this time Conference stenographers and pages had been warned by the Secretariat that their jobs might not outlast the week...The President, still without consulting his Brain Trust, began to draft in the White House a second message to the Conference...

That night Secretary Hull was able to read to the Conference a second Roosevelt pronouncement so courteous in tone that the Continentals, whose feathers had been badly ruffled... were perceptibly smoothed down...Mr. Roosevelt again refused gold stabilization between currencies but in effect persuasively invited the world to join the U.S. on a standard of managed currency and commodity money. "Revaluation of the dollar in terms of American commodities," he wrote, "is an end from which the Government and people of the United States cannot be diverted...The exchange value of the dollar will ultimately depend upon the success of other nations in raising the prices of their own commodities in terms of their national money...

"The first task is to restore prices to a level at which industry and above all, agriculture, can function profitably and efficiently.

"The second task is to preserve the stability of this adjustment, once achieved.

"The part which gold and silver should play after adjustment has been secured would seem a further subject for consideration by the Conference.

"We conceive, therefore, that the great problems which justify the assembling of nations are as present today and as deserving of exploration as was the case a few weeks ago."...

Secretary Hull, after fresh talks with President Roosevelt, tried to inject an idea that the Conference should grapple with "price levels, credit policy, innumerable prohibitions and restrictions strangling mutually profitable trade transactions, retaliations and countless other war-breeding trade practices and methods." The steering committee, cold to this proposal, began to discuss adjourning the Conference on July 26 "for at least two months" but were halted by a fresh emotional plea from Mr. Hull...

Candidly Scot MacDonald admits that he knows next to nothing about economics. Eager last week to find out what President Roosevelt meant by a "commodity dollar" the Prime Minister invited to lunch the most eminent of Britain's more radical economists, Professor John Maynard Keynes.

Presumably they discussed the so-called "Keynes Plan." This proposes to devalue all the world's currencies between 20 and 33%...By making the respective governments' gold holdings more valuable in terms of devaluated paper, such devaluation would permit more paper money to be issued against basic stores of gold and this money would be used to promote public works and cover treasury deficits.

An essential feature of the Keynes plan is that monies should be "definitely devaluated," i.e. stabilized at their new low levels in terms of commodity prices. The sort of money which would be created under this "Keynes Plan" is similar to the "commodity dollar" of U.S. Professor Irving Fisher which President Roosevelt may well have had in mind last week. Both professors urge that governments methodically vary the gold parity of their paper money in such a way that it shall always have the same average commodity purchasing power, computed with reference to a broad commodity price index, as now kept by the U.S. Department of Labor.

Professor Keynes declared last week that President Roosevelt is "magnificently right," called his message "a challenge to us to decide whether we propose to tread the old, unfortunate paths or to explore paths new to statesmen and to bankers."...

In Washington the President received a flood of congratulations on his stand against the "European bankers." Most authoritative was a statement by the Committee for the Nation on which figure such tycoons as Remington Rand's J.H. Rand and Sears, Roebuck's Lessing J. Rosenwald. They urged not Professor Keynes' 33% devaluation but a prompt cut in the gold content of the dollar by 42.8%, "as necessary to restore the 1926 price level..."

The President may not have lost anything politically from his rude treatment of the conference and his repudiation of Moley. But he did have a problem on his hands not only with Moley -- which was not politically important -- but with an angry Hull -- and this was dangerous. The Southern Democrat had to be conciliated. There was also the small matter of infuriated European statesmen.

The treatment Hull was to receive the President had a phrase for. His intimates often heard it. He called it "buttering up." In the note to the "bombshell" message in the Public Papers Vol. II, p. 266, he said:

Secretary of State Hull by virtue of his fine practical idealism, however, succeeded in preventing immediate adjournment.

Although the Conference failed in its major objectives it did a real service by showing to the world that fundamental ills could not be cured by treating one of many difficulties.

        This was not what he said of Hull in private; nor what he said
about the Conference.

        As to James Ramsay MacDonald, who had been calling him "that
person," he sent a message of 26 July which began as follows:

> Before the recess of the Conference I want you to know
> of my sincere admiration and respect for your courage and your
> patience as its presiding officer. I feel that because of it the
> Nations of the world can continue to discuss mutual problems
> with frankness... Results are not always measured in terms of
> formal agreements...

        Toward the end of the Conference, as Ernest Lindley notes in The
Roosevelt Revolution (p. 216), there entered:

> a strangely evanescent message. Beneath his restrained,
> courteous exterior, Mr. Hull harbored a long list of objections to
> Mr. Moley and to everyone associated with Mr. Moley. Several
> persons thought they saw such a list of criticisms of Mr. Moley
> and his real or supposed friends in the form of a long cablegram
> to the President.   The message did not contain Mr. Hull's
> resignation, but the deduction was easily made.   Officially this
> message was and is non-existent.

        This last is a thing which always interested me. As I have noted,
I was supposed to follow Moley in a matter of a week or two. Naturally
when the atmosphere of comedy developed to the French farce stage, I
thought myself lucky not to be more deeply involved. Without saying
why, I simply remarked to the President that there seemed no point in my
going. He laughed; and, in fact, we spent an hilarious hour over the
goings-on in London.

        He showed me various confidential messages which were in one
pile on the corner of his desk. "None of these will ever find their way into
the history books," he said. And none have. Some were heavy and
impregnated with fury, like Hull's; some were confidential accounts of the
behavior, in lighter moments, of our Delegates.

        The Hull cablegram is not mentioned in Hull's Memoir; it does
not exist among the Hyde Park papers. Lindley was right. Officially it
was and is non-existent.

        As to what happened when Moley returned, his own accurate and
vivid account (in After Seven Years, Chapter VIII) must be read. In it he
tells how the President received him, on his return, as blandly as though

nothing had happened; but how, also, Louis Howe, intimated on their first meeting that Ray had been "taken in" by the Europeans. There is the account, also, of his leaving the Department of State, and eventually the government. For me this was a sad parting; but I could see that it had been made inevitable by what had happened in London.

Intimations of the Civilian Conservation Corps

One of the subjects closest to Mr. Roosevelt's heart was conservation; and of the many subjects subsumed under that general heading, perhaps forests would come first. He had had as his first committee assignment in the New York legislature in 1910 that on Forests, Fish, and Game. He took his duties seriously as befitted a landed gentleman from Dutchess County and a younger relative of Theodore Roosevelt. And from then on all this range of subject matter was one to which he was sensitized. On Hyde Park land, purchased for the purpose because his mother would not allow it on the old estate, he started a forestry project of his own. This part of his land had the closest supervision from its owner; and it was to his growing trees that he took favored visitors with the greatest pride.

I have told in another place that these made common ground on which our acquaintanceship could ripen. A good deal later, during his Presidency, I should be chosen to be his representative at a conservation dinner in Albany. This was perhaps a kind of reward for like-mindedness.[1]

There were, however, many other landmarks in my joint experience with him. The Forest Service would come under my immediate direction in the Department of Agriculture and we should have a good deal of happy business about it. Long before that I should have been of use to him in the matter of the Civilian Conservation Corps.

It has always amused me that so many of those close to the President should have been so awkward in their approach to the Corps. Their memoirs are almost as clumsy as their original apprehension.

[1]"The Preparation of a President," Western Political Quarterly, June, 1945.

The fact is that the President began to talk to me - and I to him - about the idea which finally crystallized as the Corps long before he was nominated. This was not one of those research subjects we had to bone up on, to make memoranda about, and to schedule for an evening of discussion. It was something we talked about eagerly in much more relaxed moments, letting it take shape pleasantly in our minds as a fine and worthy matter we could bring to fruition.

One of the things about it which has always amused me, also, is that when he first tentatively suggested that a useful relationship existed between the pool of labor represented by the idle young men of those years and the neglected national forests, I was able to startle him by saying that such a scheme had been worked out already by Mussolini in Italy. This he did not much like. But he gradually got used to Mussolini's priority and evidenced so much curiosity about it that I had, after all, to do some research--and that in spite of knowing a good deal from a visit I had made to Italy in 1928-29.

There was a likeness between the Corps and the Italian experiment which was never mentioned publicly--for obvious political reasons. And most of those whose recollections are now appearing evidence no knowledge of the connection.

When the election had been won, our anticipations could at last become more concrete. And early in December I was commissioned to begin conversations with the Foresters in Washington.

The correspondence which follows with Major Robert Y. Stuart, then Chief Forester, is not very revealing. Neither of us was putting much on paper. And I was not yet doing my duty about aides memoirs. But it does show that the scheme was one we developed gradually and was not one suddenly conceived in March of 1933 and rushed into legislation.

When it did come to the legislative stage it began to have complications we had none of us anticipated. One of these was the opposition of organized labor which had to be conciliated by the appointment of Bob Fechner as administrator. Another was the recruiting difficulty which finally involved the Department of Labor and Frances Perkins, its Secretary. Still another was the late determination to use the army for administration. The Corps, when it came into being, operated not only in the National Forests, but in the National Parks as well, and after a bit in state parks, on the public domain--in fact everywhere where there was need for reclamation of grass and timberlands, for rehabilitating and expanding recreation areas and protecting the forests from fire, flood and disease.

Its success is one of the pleasanter phases of the New Deal to recall at the distance of two decades.

December 6, 1932

Dr. Rexford G. Tugwell
Professor of Economics
Columbia University
New York, NY

Dear Dr. Tugwell:

You may find interest in portions of the attached annual report of the Forest Service for the fiscal year 1932, particularly in the discussion, "New light on the Timber Situation" (page 1) and of "Research" (page 28).

Enclosed also is a statement "Providing work for the unemployed on the National Forests," touching a matter of current interest.

Sincerely yours,

R. Y. Stuart
Forester

Enclosure

December 7, 1932

Mr. R. Y. Stuart, Forester
United States Department of Agriculture
Washington, D.C.

My dear Mr. Stuart:

I am very grateful to you for sending me the Forest Service Report and the statement about providing work for the Unemployed on the National Forests. As you know, I am very much interested and shall study the report with care.

Very truly yours,

Rexford G. Tugwell

December 14, 1932

Dr. Rexford G. Tugwell
Department of Economics
Columbia University
New York, NY

Dear Dr. Tugwell:

At the risk of appearing to take advantage of your expressed interest in forestry, I am attaching a Manual for Forest Officers, "Job-Load Analysis and Planning of Executive Work in National Forest Administration," which has just come from the press. It is an illustration of what can be done toward efficiency in government service. It has certainly worked in the Forest Service. Needless to say, any comments or suggestions you may make will be appreciated.

With best wishes,

Sincerely yours,

R. Y. Stuart
Forester

Enclosure

December 17, 1932

Major R. Y. Stuart, Forester
United States Department of Agriculture
Washington, D.C.

My dear Major Stuart:

I am indeed very much interested in the work of the Forest Service and have had a number of talks with Governor Roosevelt concerning its possibilities in the present emergency. I had great pleasure in telling him of our conversation at the Cosmos Club. I think you will find that some permissive legislation for expansion will be introduced almost immediately and I have every confidence that if it should pass, Forest Service will do its share of carrying the burden we all shall have to cooperate in during the coming months.

Sincerely yours,

Rexford G. Tugwell

June 1933 to March 1934

From June of 1933 to March of 1934 I have no orderly notes; and there will be no attempt here to fill the gap with a complete account of the events in which I had a part. It is possible, however, to summarize them; and this has been done. The following is a kind of time-table covering the period. The mere headlines of The New York Times articles on the controversial Food and Drug Bill (Tugwell Bill) indicate the progress of that ill-fated measure during this period.

June 1933 -- March 1934

June	6	Food and Drug Bill introduced by Copeland, S. 1944
	16	Public Works Administration set up by executive order[1]
	16	National Recovery Administration created by executive order--Hugh Johnson, Administrator: Special Industrial Recovery Board members-- Secretary of Commerce, Chairman, the Attorney General, Secretary of Interior, Secretary of Agriculture, Secretary of Labor, Director of the Budget, Administrator for Industrial Recovery, Chairman of the Federal Trade Commission.
	24	Address to Federation of Bar Association of Western New York, "Design for Government"

24   President asks cotton growers to cooperate in Crop Reduction[1]

26   NIRA administration over certain farm products transferred to Department of Agriculture by Executive Order[1]

27   Consumers' Counsel established in AAA[1]

30   "Cotton Exports"--radio speech

July   3   President sends cable to London Conference insisting upon larger objectives than mere currency stabilization--"Bombshell" message[1]

8   Harold L. Ickes appointed Administrator of Public Works Special Board for Public Works begins to function[1]

9   Cotton Textile Code approved--the first large one[1]

11   Executive Council set up
            The President and Cabinet
            Administrators of NIRA, FERA, AAA
            Federal Transportation Coordinator
            Governor of Farm Credit Administrator
            Chairman, Board of Reconstruction
                Finance Corporation, Home
                Owners Loan Corporation,
                Tennessee Valley Authority
            Director of Emergency Conservation
            Work
            Secretary to the President
            Assistant Secretary of the Treasury
            Frank C. Walker, Executive Secretary[1]

21   President delegates powers under NIRA relating to Subsistence Homesteads to Secretary of the Interior[1]

22   Consumers Advisory Board established in NRA[1]

24 3rd Fireside Chat "The Simple Purposes and the Solid Foundations of Our Recovery Program"[1]

27 Establishment of Central Statistical Board by Executive Order
  Secretary of the Interior
  Secretary of Agriculture
  Secretary of Commerce
  Secretary of Labor
  Governor of the Federal Reserve Board
  Administrator of NIRA
  (Isidor Lubin took charge of this office and did an able job.)[1]

Aug 4 Coal strike, called late in July, settled on appointment by President of a Board for submission of disputes pending adoption of a permanent code.[1]

4 Radio speech "Our Lands in Order"

5 Began syndicated articles--to 28 January 1934 when contract nullified as result of newspaper publishers opposition.

5 President appoints first National Labor Board for adjustment of disputes arising out of labor provisions of codes. Membership: Senator R. F. Wagner, Chairman, John L. Lewis, Louis E. Kirstein, William Green, Walter C. Teagle, Leo Wolman, Gerald Swope.[1]

12 Visit to several CCC camps with President

13 President issues statement outlining U.S. position of non-intervention with reference to forced resignation of President Machado of Cuba on 11 August.[1]

15 Start on trip through western states

19 President delegates the Federal Power Commission as an Agency of Public Works Administration[1]

Sept   7   Admiral Byrd leaves for the Antartic

               17   "Drugs Manufacturers Risk Loss if Act is
                        Changed" New York Times II, 15:4

               21   Announcement of Program for Feeding Surplus
                        Foodstuffs to Unemployed

               27   "Bureaucratic administration of amendment to
                        Pure Food law feared by P. W. West" New York
                        Times, 37:3

               30   Gardiner C. Means appointed economic advisor
                        on finance to Secretary Wallace

Oct   4   Federal Surplus Relief Corporation organized as
                        a non-stock, non-profit, membership corporation
                        under the laws of Delaware--powers granted in
                        NIRA.   Secretary   of   Agriculture   and
                        Administrators of Public Works and Emergency
                        Relief members of the Corporation.[1]

                8   "Manufacturing circles reported to be planning
                        drive against proposed revision" (food & drug)
                        New York Times II, 15:3

               11   "Tugwell bill opposed by Proprietary Association"
                        New York Times, 10:6

               15   "Tugwell bill opposed by Drug Manufacturers"
                        New York Times, 15:7

               15   Deposit Liquidation Board establish in RFC to
                        provide loans to closed banks[1]

               16   Commodity Credit Corporation formed by
                        Executive Order[1]

               17   President opens door to recognition of Russia;
                        exchange of letters with Mikhail Kalinin,
                        President of the All Union Central Executive
                        Committee[1]

29   Address to Chicago Adult Education Forum "Sound Money"

Nov   1   "British Amazed at Tugwell's speech to Chicago Forum" New York Times, 10:5

7   President's statement on negotiations over British War Debt[1]

8   Civil Works Administration created by Executive Order[1]

9   "New York Board of Trade opposes Tugwell bill" New York Times, 7:1

10   Invitation from Moley to write for Today

11   Appointment to Yale University, Research Associate in Law

12   "Advertising programs in food and drug industries retarded because of Food and Drug bills," New York Times II, 15:4

14   "President reported in favor of revision of F & D Act" New York Times, 6:2

14   Speech in Brooklyn, New York, "Prospect for the Future," Grace Church Parish House

15   F. A. Silcox appointed Chief United States Forest Service

16   Lecture McMillain Theatre, Columbia University, "Recent Trends in Economics"

16   Exchange of communications between the President and Litvinov in establishing diplomatic relations with the Union of Soviet Socialist Republics[1]

17   Creation of National Emergency Council by Executive Order, in which Special Industrial Recovery Board is merged on 19 December[1]

23   President issues statement on non-intervention
        in Cuba--Good Neighbor Policy Applied[1]

25   "The Social Philosophy of the New Deal" NBC
        with Harry Laidler, Director, League for
        Industrial Democracy

26   Lecture, Swarthmore College--"New Strength for
        the Soil"

29   Creation of Public Works Emergency Housing
        Corporation by Executive Order (this organization
        never utilized because of adverse ruling of
        Comptroller General and dissolved 14 August
        1935)[1]

Dec   1   FORTUNE article

4   Federal Alcohol Control Administration
       established by Executive Order[1]

5   President proclaims repeal of the 18th
       Amendment[1]

6   President appoints Frank C. Walker Acting
       Executive Director of the National Emergency
       Council[1]

6   President authorized statement, following
       conference with Wallace, Peek and General
       Johnson, on respective jurisdiction of AAA and
       NRA codes[1]

9   "Senate committee hearings on Food & Drug bill
       ended." New York Times, 10:8

11   George N. Peek resigns as Agricultural
       Adjustment Administrator

16   "Senator Copeland to redraft Food & Drug bill,"
       New York Times, 4:6

16   President increases powers of the National Labor

Board[1]

19   Electric Home and Farm Authority authorized--
      Arthur E. Morgan, H. A. Morgan, and David
      Lilienthal, Board of Directors[1]

19   President adds members of the Special Industrial
      Recovery Board to the National Emergency
      Council[1]

20   Calvin B. Hoover joins the staff as Economic
      Consultant

21   President ratifies London agreement on silver[1]

29   "The Place of Government in a National Land
      Program," American Economic Association,
      Philadelphia

30   Non-member banks restored to jurisdiction of
      their own state banking authorities by
      Presidential Proclamation[1]

Jan   1   Secretary of the Treasury Woodin resigns because
           of ill health; Henry Morgenthau, Jr. takes his
           place

      2   Chester C. Davis announces reorganization of
           AAA, 8 sections abolished; appoints: 3 assistants-
           -Admiral V. A. Christgau, H. R. Tolley, A. D.
           Stedman, New York Times, 8:2

      2   Radio speech with Secretary Wallace, "The Farmer
           and the New Deal," National Advisory Council on
           Radio in Education

      3   President's annual message and budget message[1]

      5   "Copeland offers revised Food & Drug bill," New
           York Times, 17:4

      6   "Roosevelt deletes clause relating to wholesale
           grocery code from act to avoid duplication," New
           York Times, 9:6

7   "National Drug Trade Conference offers substitute
         to Food & Drug bill" <u>New York Times</u>, 24:2

8   First Ambassador from the U.S.S.R. arrives

9   Reduction of pay to Federal employees continued
         by Executive Order[1]

9   <u>New York Times</u> rumors that Tugwell is to be
         made Under Secretary, 3:6

9   <u>New York Times</u> rumors that Tugwell is being
         sought for faculty of Harvard, 3:6

10   President recommends legislation to guarantee
         principle of farm mortgage bonds[1]

10   President requests Senate ratification of St.
         Lawrence treaty in Canada[1]

14   "Renewed Frontiers" Sunday <u>New York Times</u>

15   President requests legislation to organize a sound
         and adequate currency system[1]

21   President signs bill continuing and limiting the
         lending power of the Reconstruction Finance
         Corporation[1]

22   President talks with German Ambassador about
         debt payments[1]

25   Speech, Union College, Schenectady, New York,
         "The Progressive Tradition"; also published in
         <u>Atlantic Monthly</u> in February

26   Speech, University of Cincinnati, "Taking Stock"

28   "U.S. Chamber of Commerce opposes Tugwell bill
         as 'censorship'" <u>New York Times</u>, 27:4

30   First Benefit Ball for Crippled Children[1]

31   Federal Judge A. Akerman holds AAA Act unconstituational in Florida citrus fruit suit. New York Times, 1:4

31   President fixes the weight of the gold dollar by Presidential Proclamation[1]

Feb   2   Creation of the Export Import Bank of Washington. Governing body: Daniel Roper, Secretary of Commerce, Robert F. Kelly, Chief of the Division of Eastern European Affairs, State Department, Chester Davis, Administrator, AAA, Stanley Reed, General Counsel, Reconstruction Finance Corporation[1]

2   Radio speech Farm and Home Hour "Conservation"

3   "Manufacturers' Committee calls Food & Drug bull 'unAmerican'" New York Times, 30:3

5   "Wine, Women and the New Deal" Address, Women's National Democratic Club

6   President agrees to arbitrate the Peru-Ecuador boundary dispute.[1]

8   President asks for legislation to help the sugar industry[1]

9   President makes recommendation for the Securities and Exchange Commission[1]

9   "Copeland reports President has approved final draft of revised bill," New York Times, 2:5

9   President orders the Army to fly the mail because Postmaster, on 6 February had concluded that existing mail contracts with private companies were illegal and had cancelled them.[1]

10   "A. F. Baumgarten says Tugwell bill will cripple advertising in U.S." New York Times, 18:3

11   U.S. Circuit Court of Appeals stays Judge Akerman's injunction on AAA

12   "Seventeen newspapers listed as foes of Food & Drug bill," New York Times, 24:4

13   Address, Columbia University Alumni Federation; "A New Deal for the Consumer"

16   President recommends passage of the Bankhead Bill for compulsory control of cotton crop.[1]

23   President forms Advisory Council to assist in the formulation of a social and economic plan for the advancement of the people of the Virgin Islands, financed from Public Works Funds. Secretary of Agriculture and Secretary of Interior on committee.[1]

26   President recommends creation of Federal Communications Commission[1]

28   "C. W. Dunn charges Copeland exempts publishers, broadcasters and advertising agencies from penalties of Food & Drug revised bill," New York Times, 11:1

28   "Tugwell and Department of Agriculture experts to study rehabilitation in Puerto Rico" New York Times, 15:6

Mar   2   President requests authority to consummate reciprocal trade agreements for the revival of foreign trade[1]

2   President recommends legislation to grant Philippine Islands their independence[1]

4   "Copeland bill hearings" New York Times, 32:1

5   President addresses code authorities of 600 industries on the accomplishments and failings of N.R.A.[1]

5   President's report on the Inter American
Highway[1]

[1] Details to be found in The Public Papers and Addresses
of Franklin D. Roosevelt, Vol. II, III, 1933, 1934, Random
House.

This is a time, it will be seen, of getting under weigh. The laws passed during the Special Session now had to be put into operation. That session adjourned in mid-June and left all of us with the powers we had asked for to begin the fight on depression. As in all such grants of discretion, we had now to set to work at making the program specific. We had to write the regulations. When it was clear just what we would do, we had to decide how to do it. Then we could proceed. Naturally we learned as we advanced and as we learned we revised.

All in all it was a time of going forward into the new country to which the legislation pointed. None of the others had greater responsibilities of this kind than those of us in Agriculture. The farmers' depression had gone on for a decade now. Various measures for relief had been tried and had failed. We had decided on the kind of law we wanted the Congress to give us, and that had been done. That law, however, included such wide directives that there were several major possibilities for the development of actual policy. We were somewhat nearer agreement on which of these ought to be most emphasized, but we were not unanimous and there were still possibilities of serious disagreement, ones which very rapidly developed. They came to a climax late in Fall. At that time George Peek, who had been Administrator of the Agricultural Adjustment Administration resigned in an unusual flurry of public recrimination and Chester Davis became his successor.

The issue here was one of great interest to students of democracy. For we were attempting the kind of thing from which politicians instinctively shrink. We were asking a large segment of the American people to accept a discipline they were certain to resent and certain to evade if they could. And we were perfectly well aware that the process would be accompanied by shrill appeals to "freedom" and "individual rights," and cries of "regimentation" by as unprincipled a lot of demagogues as ever mounted soap-boxes.

The trouble in the farm-sector had gone on and on because no leaders had had the courage to say that what would have to be done was to reduce the production of those crops of which enormous surpluses had piled up--that is production would have to be adjusted to consumption. We hoped that as other citizens became more prosperous they would be able to buy more foods and fibers; then production could again be increased. But meanwhile the farmer would carry more than his share of the burden until adjustment was made. And so long as he did carry it, he would drag down the whole economy.

We proposed to end the evasions and futilities and go directly to the obvious solution. We had a good device for it--a democratic one. We proposed to have the farmers' own neighbors allocate the duties of reduction and accept the responsibilities of enforcement. We called it the "domestic allotment plan." It had been quite largely an invention of M.L. Wilson, but it had come out of long preliminary discussions, and it owed much to the preparatory work of such of our predecessors as W. J. Spillman.

Those of us who had accepted this method included the Secretary, Henry Wallace, as well as myself. The processors of farm products naturally were opposed. They got larger profits from a large volume of produce than from a smaller one. And they were reluctant to see the farmers established in a firmer bargaining position vis-á-vis themselves. And what processors believed was very apt to be believed by the whole business community, including the publishers of newspapers.

They were inclined to be less aggressive at the moment than was usual because it was so obvious that something drastic must be done. At the same time their influence was steadily exerted toward other methods of relief. They had been saying for years that what we must do was to re-establish foreign markets. This was wholly futile in the circumstances; but it had been the basis of the successive McNary-Haugen Acts of recent years, unaccountably vetoed by Republican presidents. It could not be said to have been tried in a determined way--by frankly dumping abroad at sacrifice prices. And because it had not been tried it served as a kind of alternative to which the more evasive could resort.

Then there was farm relief by the "marketing agreement" method. This was the processors' favorite alternative. If they could be exempted from the Anti-Trust Acts, they said, and allowed a free hand, they would be able to pay the farmers enough more to lift them altogether out of their depression. This was the claim.

So the question still was--as it had been for a long time--whether we should reduce production of the surplus crops (mostly wheat, cotton, and corn-hogs), whether we should undertake dumping abroad, or whether we should try to regularize the agricultural industry by a system of agreements. As it turned out we should do all of these things, and there was never doubt in any of our minds that each might prove useful. But there were disagreements about which should be emphasized. And then there were disagreements about how each was to be done.

In choosing George Peek to be Administrator we were doing something obvious. But, like many obvious actions, it was unwise. For he did not agree with us--that is Henry Wallace and myself--about emphasis; and he agreed even less about method. He was against the whole reduction program; and because reduction, to be a success, had to be carried out with enthusiasm and energy, his holding back was very conspicuous. Then, when it came to shaping up the marketing agreements with various processors, he objected violently to a number of provisions we thought no more than a minimum protection of the public interest. These had to do with the inspection of books and records and some fair trade practices.

Our differences with him resulted in his resignation in December.

In the press it was I who was supposed to have been the activist in unseating Peek. It was true that I did nothing to conciliate a conflict which had grown so embarrassing that only an end to it would cut our losses. Before that I had tried to be conciliatory enough. And actually I had a kind of fondness for the bluff, shrewd and persistent Peek. But these qualities were, unfortunately, consistent with an essential stupidity which finally became intolerable.

His resignation amounted to a choice on the part of the President. He hated to make it, as he always hated such choices. And he tried to smooth over the break with an Ambassadorship for Peek which was refused. But he did give him an appointment as a Foreign Trade Adviser with terms of reference which infuriated Cordell Hull and others in the Department of State. They were convinced free traders; and were intent on steering our policy as close to that line as they dared. Peek's idea was to force open particular opportunities for the sale of our products through specific deals with other governments. This too was a situation of practically open conflict from the start and ended as it had to after an embarrassing interlude.

TUGWELL DEFEATS PEEK IN DUEL OVER AAA POLICY

LEADER OF ADMINISTRATION 'LIBERALS' MANOEUVRES OPPOSITION SPEARPOINT OUT OF AGRICULTURAL COMMAND

BUT ROOSEVELT AVERTS LOSS

By offering Direction of New Foreign Trade Division to Farm Chief, He would end Dispute and Open Opportunity.

By ARTHUR KROCK.

WASHINGTON, Dec. 9.--In this week's encounter of men and

theories at the Department of Agriculture the real "winnah and new champion," as Joe Humphreys would say, is Rexford Guy Tugwell, erstwhile Professor of Economics at Columbia University. By a skillful mixture of discernment and tactics he finally manoeuvred the blunt administrator of the AAA, George N. Peek, into a position where the President had to choose between him and Secretary of Agriculture Wallace. The result was the obscuration of Mr. Peek; for practical reasons it had to be.

Friends of Professor Tugwell say that a slight tinge of alarm is now mixed with his natural pride in his achievement. This does credit to his intelligence and observation. He was long a close associate and co-worker of Professor Raymond Moley and well realizes what happened to that economist and why. "Rex," say his friends, "doesn't want to stick his chin out too far." It is explained that for this reason he induced Secretary Wallace to make the argument at the Capitol for the proposed new Pure Food and Drugs Act, which is largely the handiwork of Mr. Tugwell himself.

It was during the hearings on the tobacco code that Administrator Peek first realized that the Tugwell group in the department, possessed of ideas that seemed very wrong to him, was coming into the ascendant and must be fought immediately. Incidentally, Mr. Peek won this particular fight. He had previously asked Secretary Wallace to spare him the ministration of Jerome N. Frank, general counsel for AAA, his predecessor in the organization and one of Professor Felix Frankfurter's brightest protegés. When Mr. Wallace confessed his inability to do this, Mr. Peek promptly made over his administrator's salary to Fred Lee, his personal counsel. Through Mr. Lee's hands passed every opinion emanating from the general counsel. But not until the tobacco code was up did the administrator comprehend the number and--to him--the poisonous theories of the "liberal" group which swears by Mr. Tugwell.

At that hearing it developed that the "liberals" had permanent rather than temporary ideas for relieving society in its file. They proceeded as the besoms of inequality for all time. It was not one depression they were after; they were out to make the new world in which the old profit system and the laws of supply and demand were to be supplanted. This sounded like nonsense to Mr. Peek and he said so.

LINES OF STRATEGY LAID.

The result was so much internal argument over the agricultural codes which had been assigned to the AAA for formulation that unconscionable delays developed. Mr. Peek is a plain-spoken man, and he said plenty. He said it to, among others, some milk dealers who had been told at Detroit by one of Mr. Frank's young assistants that the government would in time take over the milk business and the grocery and meat business as well.

By that time, it was fairly clear to Mr. Tugwell, if not to Mr. Wallace, that Mr. Peek, must be jockeyed into an untenable position.

The President had not, as in the example of the NRA, made the administrator of the AAA directly responsible to him, but had put the adminstrator under the Secretary of Agriculture. Even if Mr. Peek had wanted to stay under, the departmental manoeuvring inched him away from that position. He must quit, get an independent set-up for the AAA or take a permanent back seat. The independent set-up Mr. Tugwell and his associates did not want. Mr. Wallace, being human, was persuaded that he could not at that point permit it.

It is now disputed whether the idea of solving the departmental conflict by turning over the agricultural codes to the NRA originated with Mr. Peek or Mr. Wallace. Friends of both claim it on behalf of each. At any rate, this week the administrator was talking with some newspaper men and told them that was the thing to do. He added some remarks about individuals. These somehow got back to the Secretary.

The Secretary promptly sought the President and, laying the situation before him, persuaded him to make the code transfer himself before Mr. Peek reached the press with the proposal. The President was grieved over the personalities which report had ascribed to Mr. Peek. Acting as he thought the situation required, he issued the code transfer order from the White House at midnight Wednesday.

The next day Messrs. Peek and Wallace shuttled between the White House and their offices. But the President did not lack contact also with Mr. Tugwell, with whom he is intimate and for whom he has deep liking and admiration. What to do with Mr. Peek? The President and Mr. Wallace both have affection for the administrator and appreciation for the excellent and arduous labor he has rendered. Also they do not relish the prospect of a man of his temper and vocabulary roaming critically on the outside of the administration.

MR. TUGWELL'S INSPIRATION.

So they looked around for a high office to which he could be transferred with dignity and interest for himself. At this point Mr. Tugwell had an inspiration which suggests he is still a bit of an amateur in public affairs. Francis White is retiring as Minister to Czechoslovakia. Send George Peek there! But the President, who is not an amateur, knew that he could not tempt Mr. Peek with any place except one that permits him to pursue his hobbies of getting the farmer back onto economic parity, preferably through export trade.

It was the President who thought of creating the new division for

him to head in the State Department with supervision over activities to
promote foreign markets for American agriculture and industry on the
basis of American demand for imported wines and liquours. As Mr. Peek
inclined to accept the offer, it was clear that two things would be
accomplished: he would emerge undiminished in prestige from the
dispute over policy and would enter upon the execution of his lifelong
idea of exporting farm surpluses.

Thus the departmental tempest ended, with the big wind on the
outside. Mr. Wallace had fought and won the battle of the "liberal" group,
things having reached a stage where there was nothing else he could do.
Mr. Tugwell, having engineered the struggle from a hidden position,
breathed more freely, because if Mr. Peek had won, the Assistant
Secretary's security was definitely threatened. It was in the full flush of
this victory, presumably, that he wisely decided to pull in his chin. There
had been a good deal of ground-work done, by way of inspired publicity
about the impending "revolt of the young liberals," before the battle was
joined. But there was no longer any point to intrigue.

TUGWELL'S STAR ASCENDANT.

The hero of the contest, Mr. Tugwell, is a brilliant, engaging and
good-looking young man. His manner has impelled some with whom he
has come in contact to ascribe his assurance to personal conceit. But
those who know him intimately and admire him say that this impression
is false. He tells them that he is not ambitious, and they believe him. "All
I want, when this job is done," a friend quotes Mr. Tugwell as saying
recently, "is to go back to Columbia." Before he goes he wants to make
sure that government has provided for every American dweller "a more
abundant life."

During the campaign, by some chance or other, most of the spotlight directed on the "brain trust" struck Professor Moley. Professor
Tugwell was prominent on the set also. But somehow he didn't stand out
often, and that continued throughout the first part of Mr. Roosevelt's
administration. Lately, through no wish of his own perhaps, the spotlight
has followed him about. It is not likely to leave him soon, even though,
as he says, he wants to get away from it all.*
New York Times, 8 December 1933.

- 3 -**

In this matter, I was nearer Peek's position than Hull's. And, if
I understood it, as I still think I did, nearer the President's too. The
outcome of this conflict, in which the President's hand was mostly

**Tugwell did not identify section 2 in this part of the revised diary.*

hidden, would be the Trade Agreements Act, which would be approved 12 June 1934.

At this time we were much concerned with the preliminaries in this matter. There were, during the summer and early autumn, innumerable conversations, meetings, and discussions both formal and informal. These resulted in the appointment, at the urging of several of us, of an Executive Committee on Commercial Policy early in November. One member of this Committee was the Secretary of Agriculture. But it was I, as in other instances, who was, for this purpose, the Secretary. I was faithful in attendance, and industrious in the preparation of materials--or in having them prepared by various of our Departmental experts. And it can be imagined how much effort must have gone into so intricate and controversial a duty.[1]

I may not dwell on this particular activity further here. It does, however, need saying that this was by no means the only series of interdepartmental discussions in which I was engaged. There was, for instance, the Special Industrial Recovery Board. And, also, there was the Public Works Board. There were others; but these were so important that I must mention them, even if only briefly.

The Special Industrial Recovery Board was established by executive order on 16 June 1933.[2] The Board was item 2 of the order; item 1 was Hugh Johnson and his appointment as Administrator for Industrial Recovery. It is curious that, from the first, the Board got very little attention and the Administrator got a great deal. This was probably because the Administrator was recognized to be a pretty direct representative of the President and responsible to him rather than to the Board, a situation which the President did nothing to change and much to confirm. The result was that before the year's end the Board died. Actually it was merged in the National Emergency Council; but this was merely a covering procedure for burial by night.

The Board did not die, however, before having become the focus of one of the most interesting inner controversies of the New Deal. For the majority took a firm position that the codes of fair practice for industry must not include price-fixing provisions which would continue the going policy of reducing production to maintain prices. This was based on a general theory of recovery. That theory was that although agricultural prices needed to be raised, industrial prices needed to be

---

[1]The letter creating the original committee may be found in Public Papers, Vol. II, p. 466; and the succeeding Committee, appointed after the passage of the Act is referred to in Public Papers, Vol. III, p. 113 ff.

[2]Public Papers, Vol. II, pp. 247-8.

lowered--both in the interest of reestablishing an exchange relationship which would really function.

The tendency among highly organized industries had been toward using their economic power to control prices. This tended to diminish the market for their goods and to create unemployment. It had made a not inconsiderable contribution to the depression. Also it hindered the technical advances which would reduce costs and, as costs fell, reduce prices, enlarge markets and give more employment. This, at least, was the way some of us saw it. I had had many conversations with the President about these matters and I thought I knew his mind. I thought, therefore, that in joining with those who took this view I was acting in accordance with his views too. I reckoned without political realities.

The industries whose codes came up for approval first were those which had some very bad conditions to be corrected--child labor, long hours, chaotic marketing and so on. Johnson in order to get agreement on the correction of these conditions was inclined to overlook the price-fixing clauses slipped in by industry lawyers. Moreover, Johnson had taken seriously one suggestion in the Act which rested on an old idea of simultaneous advance. It was conceived that if many industries simply agreed to start going, their manual support would sustain a permanent and rising activity. He therefore conceived the President's Reemployment Agreement and resolved to put on an all-out campaign to enlist American employees. If industries were brought quickly under codes, even if they were so imperfect that revision would soon be needed, and if a reemployment agreement was widely acted on, recovery would come with an irresistible sweep. This was the conception. And the President fell for it.

I, among others, was certain that there would not be the expected results, and I greatly feared that the reaction to failure would be disastrous. I therefore opposed these policies as strenuously as I could in all the ways open to me--including continual warnings to the President, until he obviously had tired of them and had made his choice irrevocably.

My reason for believing that the simultaneity would not actually operate lay precisely in the price relationships which were allowed industry as the reward for joining the campaign. They might all start going, but if each undertook to exploit the other by establishing monopoly prices, it would end up in a price war. This war would be won by the strongest. These would prosper by exploiting the others--also the public, including farmers. Those who lost out would not be able to continue. It was a recipe for perpetuating depression, I insisted, not for recovery.

Of course I was right. But the businessmen, with Johnson leading in a whoop-de-doo campaign, which had Presidential blessing, won the immediate right of way, and the Blue Eagle campaign was undertaken.

The Special Industrial Recovery Board was a casualty of that conflict. But in opposing itself to what proved to be a mistaken policy, one, moreover, which led directly to the disappearance of the whole agency, the Board did serve a useful purpose. And in certain of the transcripts taken at its meetings, some of the central issues of those days can be observed in process of resolution.[3]

- 4 -

My work on the Special Board for Public Works was a good deal more satisfactory, although this Board, like the Recovery Board, fell victim presently to the dislike of its Administrator for any other governance than that of the President.[4]

As a subsidiary title of the National Industrial Recovery Act, an appropriation of $3,300,000,000 was made for a public building program; and it was to supervise the disbursal of this fund that the Special Board for Public Works was created and an Administration for Public Works set up with Harold Ickes as Administrator.[5]

[3]I have a copy of these transcripts, and there is of course a copy in the library at Hyde Park.

[4]The common fate of these Boards for the control of important functions ought not, I think, to cause over-hasty generalization concerning their utility. Both, I believe, were wiser than the Administrators who resented them so bitterly. Both might have resulted in better New Deal functioning if the President had chosen to support them instead of consenting to their extinction. I need not note, perhaps, that both Hugh Johnson and Harold Ickes have defended their position. But what it amounted to, actually, was impatience with the orderly process of discussion, and objection to reversals of judgment, on the part of two peculiarly imperious personalities. The President ought not, in my judgment, to have dispensed with these Boards even if only as safeguards, and he ought to have valued their intercession.

[5]I should note that this was one of a number of measures intended to relieve unemployment. The others were important: The Federal Emergency Relief Administration with Harry Hopkins in charge; and the Civilian Conservation Corps of which I have spoken before. $500,000,000 was appropriated for emergency relief. It was to be expanded by the states under the supervision of the Federal Administrator. As things turned out, unemployment relief was generally administered by Harry Hopkins who demonstrated an ability to distribute funds rapidly (his enemies said, recklessly) and to reduce unemployment rolls through work programs. Public Works was much slower (and, Ickes said, sounder). The CCC functioned for a special group. Of all of the New Deal programs this was most generally

During that first summer, I gave a good deal of time to Public Works. Besides sitting faithfully on the Board as the representative of my Department, I worked on a number of Special Committees. One of these, on which Oscar Chapman (Assistant Secretary of Interior), and Turner Battle (Assistant Secretary of Labor), also worked, was for the quick processing of early lists of projects. Ickes gradually put together an organization for this work and relieved us of it; but even then I often carried lists to the President for his approval after they had been passed by the Board. Some of my most interesting work with the President concerned or began with these lists of projects. He fancied himself as a supervisor of plans and operations. And, actually, of course, he did have an almost unparalleled familiarity with the nation and its needs. He found himself entranced by the enlargement of this knowledge implicit in the scanning of projects put forward by Federal Agencies.[6] Also, it was useful to me as Assistant Secretary of Agriculture to have an opening now and again for explaining, in some detail, one or another phase of our operations--it might be the development of long-staple cotton in the Southwest, the improvement of cattle breeding in Florida, or the control of the corn borer, of white pine blister rust, or any one of numerous other pests. We had research and regulatory operations wherever crops were produced, processed or marketed. And almost all of them could profit from better facilities.

As a matter of fact this had a good deal to do with weaning the President away from his predisposition to center budget reductions on research. Our Department was mostly research, and Lewis Douglas was determined to eliminate more than half of it (his target for this year was a sixty percent reduction). It was curious that I had been put in agriculture originally for just this purpose and had myself become convinced that much less cutting was possible than I had thought. I had great satisfaction in carrying the President along with me in my conversion. Douglas was never converted and he and I had some rather

---

approved. Nevertheless it was abolished some years later by a Congress intent on humiliating the President. Some of the $3,300,000,000 was later allocated to Hopkins who set up the Civil Works program, the first of several quick-spending agencies he was to supervise. This was done because of the slowness of Ickes' kind of works.

[6]Our projects rather quickly and naturally divided themselves into two categories: Federal and "other"--the "other" being State, municipal, etc. Our work was mostly with proposals for Federal construction. At first we found the various agencies reluctant and over-modest, so that some of our early efforts had to go to the eliciting of more and better ones. It was amazing how this could turn into policy.

acrimonious exchanges as a result.

But Douglas' was as much a one-track mind as was Harry Byrd's. Federal spending was in itself undesirable; budget reduction was a virtue. No matter what the cause to be served, if it cost something Douglas was against it. This came from a convinced reactionary bent and was not touchable by argument. The only thing to do about Douglas was to defeat him. In several instances I had some success in this. Apparently others had, too, for like Peek, he soon found his situation intolerable and presently resigned.

Public Works got going rather slowly. It was difficult to get good projects from the states and municipalities. And Ickes insisted on almost extravagant safeguards against waste and corruption. This earned him the title of Honest Harold; but it did not relieve unemployment. In the Fall the President found it necessary to allow Harry Hopkins a good share of the works funds for a different kind of operation. This was the first of the "boondoggles"; it was also the first effective attack on unemployment.

- 5 -

Harry Hopkins did not have a Board. He was also very jealous and exclusive. But in these early days he had not yet conceived the ambitions which tormented him--as they did so many others--later on. He was a newcomer to Washington and was not one of the President's immediate circle. He was much more cooperative and modest than the man Sherwood wrote about in Roosevelt and Hopkins. I had not known him well; we had met at the Congress Hotel in Chicago during the convention; but he had stayed only briefly and had taken no part in the proceedings. He had stopped by as a matter of courtesy to his, then, boss, Jesse I. Straus, who was administrator of unemployment relief in New York State. Straus had formed a Businessmen-For-Roosevelt organization, and its headquarters were in the Congress Hotel. It was by accident that I dropped in there one day and met Harry.

But I did not meet him again until he came to Washington in May. He had had no part in the campaign; and he was, in fact, only second or third choice for the job in Washington. He knew that; and he was determined to do what he could as long as he lasted. This, he always said, would not be long. But whether he meant it I never knew. It was perhaps no more than recognition of extreme hazard. For what he was undertaking to do would very rapidly become unpopular with all those comfortable reactionaries who still thought that governmental aid ruined character. He represented the New Deal in one of its most vulnerable phases.

I was already under fire from the same sources and for much the same reasons. It was only natural that we should have a fellow feeling. At any rate we did become personal friends as well as close collaborators. As he proceeded to his first task of enlarging relief rolls and then to the improvising of his first works organization, I was a good deal depended on. I could, I suppose, be said, along with a few others, to constitute his Board. That he was in training, so to speak, for the close relationship with the President which developed as the war came on, we neither of us knew at all. But on many early occasions I did make his access to the President possible and frequently argued his cause.

Harry, in those days, offered no advice outside his own area. He was not, as I then was, a member of numerous committees, or engaged in many tasks having to do with finance, foreign trade, industrial as well as agricultural recovery, and the initiating of TVA, CCC and several other New Deal agencies. He single-mindedly devoted himself to rallying the social workers of the nation. But for him the miseries and distresses of those days would have been far more intense than they were. I became almost as well acquainted with several of his assistants. They were curiously like Harry in their approach to their work. They had no hesitation about improvisation in unorthodox ways and on an enormous scale. Their operations frightened and sometimes scandalized the Washington bureaucrats. And even I often told Harry that I was glad that he and not I had to carry his responsibilities. If that came strangely from one who was already being pictured as a destroyer of institutions precious to business men, especially, but to many others of the orthodox as well, it was nevertheless true. I spent a good deal of cautionary energy on Harry and his helpers--without, however, having much effect.

My situation had already begun to degenerate; but it was not yet clear that I should never be able to recover the academic respectability I had once had. The ruin of my reputation was completed by my sponsorship of the Food and Drug Act revision. It was done in a deliberate and methodical way with a completely cynical use of all sorts of organs of opinion and without the least scruple. Pure inventions concerning me were circulated; and a stereotype created from which I should never wholly escape.

My status at this time is pretty accurately represented in the following excerpt from KIPLINGER'S LETTER, a dope-sheet to which businessmen subscribed for "inside" information on official activities in Washington, for 27 January 1934:

> Tugwell. We get scores of inquiries about Tugwell from agricultural trades and industries, most of whom fear, distrust and dislike him, because of his reputation for radicalism.

> Here's Tugwell: He is frankly a theorist, without practical

experience either in business or in politics. He thinks there are times, such as these, when the forced application of theories will result in more practical good than the application of practical ideas, which he thinks don't go deep enough to help. He doesn't always recognize a FACT when he sees one. He is radical, or ultra-liberal, but he isn't essentially a revolutionist, and he isn't a sentimentalist. His current writings do not seem as radical as his past writings. He wants POSITIVE government action, rather than drifting. He has very little understanding of human relations in the concrete, and an utter indifference to the impression which he personally makes; he just doesn't care a damn. He is not a good politician; he would make a better adviser than a public official. His sincerity and honesty are beyond question.

But this was only the beginning in late 1933 and early 1934. I was still, at that time, able to foregather with legislators, to discuss matters of policy with fellow-economists and generally to get a fair enough hearing for whatever suggestions I had to make concerning policy. I was then thought, I believe, to be the most reliable expositor of administration intentions; and this was not only because of my close association with the President; but because what I said made sense in the circumstance. So, at least, I like to think.

The President encouraged my expository efforts. I made many speeches, wrote many articles, and even began the writing of a weekly syndicated newspaper article. Gradually, however, as my deliberate detractors began to bring their weight to bear, and as my avenues of expression closed, all this changed. I began to have fewer opportunities of any kind to speak, and when I did speak what I said was tortured into the meanings agreeable to the stereotype manufacturers. And what I wrote was no longer welcome in editorial offices.

What was happening to me was watched by the President with a kind of affectionate aloofness. He sometimes spoke of it to me; and it served to underline my loyalty to him; but as a politician there was not much he could do. He could not defend me publicly or denounce the lies and misrepresentations. He could and did show by his continued close association with me that he had confidence in me. Later on he would no longer be able to do that freely; and I too should be in a state of nerves from the massive and continuous pounding. But that stage had not yet arrived. I think he was not yet certain whether my general and vague assignment to hold together the progressives in his name was made impossible by my situation or not. He was probably not counting on it. But he did not entrust it to anyone else.

By September, however, I was visibly tired. And the President suggested the first of the working trips I was to take during the next few years. It was not by any means a vacation; but it was a change; and it was an effective restorative.

- 6 -

This trip was, for me, a kind of break with one kind of activity and an introduction of a new kind. Up to now I have been pretty much an attaché of the White House, on call for all kinds of jobs, and expected to produce solutions for all kinds of problems. In future I was to be much more closely associated with the Department and its work. After this trip, for instance, it was only on rare occations that I helped in the preparation of speeches. And it was this trip that convinced my Departmental colleagues that I was to be a serious collaborator. It was a kind of initiation.

We travelled to Glacier Park by railway, stopping in Chicago for a day at the Fair. At the Park we were met by Bureau of Public Roads people and various relays of them accompanied us all the way to Santa Fe. From Montana we went through Idaho and Washington and south through western Oregon to San Francisco. There we picked up Dr. L. I. Hewes, Deputy Chief Engineer of the Regional Headquarters of the Bureau of Public Roads who piloted us during the rest of our trip. From San Francisco we took the coast road to Los Angeles where we turned inland through southern Nevada and Utah, across northeastern Arizona into southern Colorado and then down to Santa Fe, New Mexico, where we entrained for Washington.

In the belief that I might as well educate my staff as well as myself, I added to the party my two assistants, Grace Falke and Fred Bartlett, and Jack Fleming of the Department's Information Service. Fred supplied us with background material--maps, charts, reports and incidental information on the places and folks we visited; Grace took care of our correspondence, taking notes during the long rides from one stop to the next and working on them after dinner at night; Jack drafted my speeches or edited them and took notes on those yet to be written.

In the company of state and regional representatives of the various Bureaus in the Department--Forest Service, Agricultural Economics, Agricultural Engineering, Chemistry and Soils, Animal Industry, etc.--who joined us at intervals and rode with us as far as their individual interests reached, we inspected the work in the national forests, the experiment stations, the agricultural colleges. We saw the new CCC camps, we saw the great dams being built--Grand Coulee, Boulder and Beaver--and we visited and were initiated into the exciting field of agricultural experiments--apple, citrus, date, wine, rubber, erosion control, road materials, conservation, dry farming, rice and cattle.

We should thereafter be more intelligent administrators, all of us, for our trip. We not only learned more in our thirty odd days in the field than we should ever have been able to learn in five years of reading reports and correspondence, but a letter from that part of the country would henceforth conjure up a personality, an attitude, and a warm feeling of mutual objectives and understanding far beyong its literal accounts.

It was while I was in the Northwest that I heard over the radio of Ray Moley's resignation. This began the decline of a working friendship which had become very close, and it left me much more on my own in Washington than I had been before. Until then Ray and I had been an unusual team, somewhat as Corcoran and Cohen were to be, at least as concerns our mutual confidence. We had never quarreled, we had been mutually helpful, and we had never doubted each other's loyalty to a common cause--F.D.R.

For several months my relationship with the President had been changing. I had had occasion to be useful in a number of matters about which Ray knew very little. And it no longer seemed so essential as it had to regard Ray as the chief of staff. I made the transition from pre- to post-inauguration tasks more easily. He seemed to resent the inevitable decline in our intimacy with the president--or, rather, the sharing of that intimacy with numbers of new people. For some of these, like Henry Morgenthau, he had always had a certain jealousy; others of them, he regarded almost as intruders--Ickes, for instance. They had never been heard of before, he seemed to think, and ought to be heard a good deal less of now. But his chief trouble was with his own colleagues in the Department of State. He had no respect for Cordell Hull, and, if possible, less for Phillips, Feis and others with whom he had to associate. There was not much secrecy about this; and after the fiasco of the London Economic Conference, it was inevitable that he should be pushed out; everyone could see that it must be so. After all, Hull was an entrenched Southern Democrat; and Moley had no political foundation whatever.

He handled the whole transition badly. After it was over F.D.R. spoke to me about it several times. It was a kind of thing he did not like and in which he used, as he admitted, "cowardly tactics." I was amused to discover that he knew as well as the rest of us his own very marked weakness. It was one he would never overcome. It would still be very marked as the successive transitions would be made from 1939 on in the effort to find an adequate management mechanism for war preparations.[7]

---

[7]This was the only notable fault that faithful collaborator Sam Rosenman would admit when he came to write Working With Roosevelt (1952).

Ray became more and more critical of F.D.R. until his reaction from former loyalty became an immoderate one. Fortunately by that time he and I would have few occasions to meet; but when we did there were some matters we avoided by mutual if tacit consent. My own relationship with F.D.R. had always been of a different sort. I was much more inclined to take him as he was, to expect nothing myself, and therefore not to be disappointed. I had a curious mixture of optimism about large affairs and pessimism about my own--not a bad equipment for public life. I was able to argue even with a President, and sharply too, because I had no interest in pleasing him. But I had no jealous or exclusive impulses. These were the worst traits of Moley, of Corcoran, and of Hopkins, and ones, moreover, which gave them the most pain. But Sam Rosenman, for instance, was quite free of such impulses, and I suppose he was more useful, in the long run, than any one of us.

But Sam was not around now. He would not return to the Presidential entourage, in any important way, until 1939. And as Ray faded away, I was turned to more and more. By the beginning of 1934, I was a very conspicuous person in the nation, not as a White House assistant altogether, but as the protagonist of ultra New Deal policies. I was known to have an intimate relationship with the President. I was spoken of now as "the number-one brain truster"; and I was given credit for being much more of a power than I was. But this was not something the President tried at all to discourage. He was amused to see it happen. And when I expressed apprehension about it he was reassuring. So long as I kept my sense of realities, recognized the source of the massive attacks which were building my formidable reputation, there was no need to worry.

The trouble was that it made me uncomfortable. It brought upon me pressures and responsibilities I resented and found it hard to get used to. I tried to maintain some sort of serenity in the midst of constant hubbub. Indeed, it was with the President's connivance and under his direction, that I made the effort to turn all the notoriety to some use. By constant writing and speaking, as well as by keeping constantly in touch with our friends, I sought to seize and maintain leadership of the progressive forces, not in any formal way, but by shaping a program and acting as its expositor. F.D.R. needed the progressives. He was one of them; but he could not, now that he was President, be their leader. He had to head the Democratic party; and that was a coalition whose most powerful elements were the Southern Democrats and the urban machines, neither of whom had the least sympathy for progressivism, beyond a certain tolerance for relief during recovery.

The progressives were weak because they were scattered. Olson in Minnesota, the LaFollettes in Wisconsin, Norris in Nebraska, Wheeler in Montana, Johnson in California, Wagner and LaGuardia in New York,

Cutting in New Mexico[8]--it was a list of prima donnas. But they, and what they representated, were a potential force. Besides, what they believed in was what had to be done. And what the others represented was sheer regression. If the progressives could not be marshalled, F.D.R. would have to make his way into the new domain by devious and doubtful devices, always fearful of being undercut by the reactionaries, never certain of any support.

F.D.R. was to spend most of his Presidency in futile battles, gaining small victories which ought to have been large ones, giving up important objectives to attain essential ones. And much of this was because progressivism could not succeed in transforming itself into a political movement. What I could do in the next few years was not much. But what I did was all that anyone did. No one else tried until Henry Wallace went at it after 1940; but he failed as badly as I.

I could see afterward how little chance I had had to accomplish what the President wanted. But, of course, I could not see it then. I was badly placed, for one thing. I was a subordinate appointed official rather than an elected one. But also I made the mistake of attempting too much at once--of undertaking battles on more fronts than were necessary or could be successfully fought; and once engaged, I could not withdraw. So quite quickly I would become not so much the symbol of progressivism as of a kind of crack-pot do-goodism quite foreign to my nature.

Most of this quick transition happened in 1933 and 1934. When the diary resumes in the Spring of 1934, I had become a notorious character trying to turn my notoriety to some use, but mighty uncomfortable in the role I had been forced to assume.

[8]Philip F. LaFollette, Governor of Wisconsin, 1931-33, 1935-39

Robert M. LaFollette, Jr, United States Senator from Wisconsin elected to the United States Senate to fill unexpired term of his father in 1925 and sent back again in 1928 and 1934

George W. Norris, United States Senator from Nebraska, four terms, 1913-43

Burton K. Wheeler, United States Senator from Montana, two terms, 1923-35, Progressive Party candidate for Vice President with Robert M. LaFollette in 1924

Hiram W. Johnson, United States Senator from California, three terms, 1917-35, One of the founders of the Progressive party in 1912

Fiorello H. LaGuardia, member of Congress from New York, 1917-21, 1923-33, Mayor of New York City, 1934-46

Bronson Cutting, United States Senator from New Mexico, 1927-35

A faint far cry of protest to the process of vilification was raised by the St. Louis Star and Times in January of that year but there was little indication that it had been heard.

THE NEW CITIZENSHIP*

WANTED--A new conception of public service in the United States.

The above advertisement should be inserted in every newspaper in the country, hung in the corridors of every public building, and pinned on the coat lapels of every man holding or seeking public office.

If the problems and responsibilities of the past year have made one thing clear, it is that the United States cannot go on under the old system of political spoils and its attendant inefficiency and corruption.

The Andrew Jackson-Jim Farley slogan, "To the victor belongs the spoils," must go out, or our government will go down under the terrific weight it is now compelled to sustain.

The Tammany principle of municipal graft, the Teapot Dome conception of public trust, the Postmaster General Grown theory of federal contracts, all must disappear from American life.

We have gone through a national orgy of private dishonesty topped by twelve years of winking, blinking tolerance of dishonest relations between private and public interests. And what confronts the country today?

The Roosevelt administration has undertaken one of the most gigantic tasks in human history, calling for the highest degree of combined intelligence and honesty.

Without intelligence, honesty is a minor virtue. Without honesty, intelligence is worse than useless.

---

*Editorial, St. Louis Star and Times, January 29, 1934.

To carry out this intensely difficult program, Mr. Roosevelt has chosen administrators who are doing their best to handle billions of dollars with sole regard to the national welfare. There is no greater contrast in American history than the conception of public trust held by the Harding cabinet, with its Ohio Gang and its Teapot Dome, and that of the Roosevelt executive staff as typified by Secretary Ickes, Secretary Wallace and Relief Administrator Hopkins, the three men who hold the PWA, AAA and CWA purse strings.

Yet what happens as these adminstrators extend their

organization over the country?

They find it necessary to ask a federal grand jury to indict the Democratic lieutenant governor of Iowa, on the charge of conspiracy to defraud the government in Public Works contracts.

They find it necessary to transfer CWA relief jobs to control of army officers, to get the funds out of control of city politicians and their sneaking itchy-palmed followers.

They find farmers, by the thousand or the hundred thousand, trying to figure out how they can get government money for co-operation in controlling crop surpluses and then cheat the government by escaping control in the end.

They find senators and congressmen belaboring them for patronage for "deserving Democrats," without regard to character or ability, and, when their demands are resisted, stirring up the prejudice of the ignorant against non-political elements in the administration--as in the hue and cry against college professors in government service.

They find big bankers and industrialists up to their old game, fighting for the right to ride on the necks of others, plotting to pervert the measures they cannot destroy, and destroy what they cannot pervert.

No matter how high the standards of President Roosevelt and those about him may be--cabinet officers, administrators, members of the house and senate who rise above the spoils level, honest executives scattered over the country--they will mire down unless there is a <u>general standard of honesty in the United States</u>, and a general regard for the common welfare.

The day when this country can muddle through on the grafter-eat-grafter system has gone forever. The choice is honesty plus intelligence, intelligence plus honesty, or a grand mash.

From An Administrator's Notebook

The following letters explain as much as is necessary of the reasons why I was unable to reach the American public with a weekly syndicated article after December, 1933.

UNITED FEATURE SYNDICATE
Incorporated

Monte F. Bourjaily   220 East 42nd Street
General Manager   New York

December 11, 1933

Dear Dr. Tugwell:

Herewith is first statement showing a cash balance to you on the feature "Design for Government". All promotion has been paid out now and hereafter your share on a sales basis as of today will run approximately $135.00 a four-weekly period, subject to ups and downs due to additions and cancellations.

I think you know that sales were going along quite satisfactorily until the hue and cry over the Food and Drug Bill. Since then it has seemed impossible to get any publisher to buy the feature and a number of clients have threatened to actually quit. So far as this syndicate goes we regret this only because it interferes with our sales campaign and with producing a revenue from the feature for which we think it is worth.

We are happy to handle the feature so long as you wish to write it and criticism of editors and publishers on account of your activities with regards to the Food and Drug Bill has meant nothing to us except for the loss in possible revenue.

Cordially,

/s/Monte F. Bourjaily
General Manager

Dr. Rexford Guy Tugwell
U.S. Department of Agriculture
Washington, DC

December 13, 1933

Mr. Monte Bourjaily
General Manager
United Feature Syndicate, Inc.
220 East 42nd Street
New York City

Dear Mr. Bourjaily:

Thanks for the check and your very broad-minded view of a difficult and rather disappointing situation.

Sincerely,

R. G. Tugwell

UNITED FEATURE SYNDICATE
Incorporated

Monte F. Bourjaily
General Manager
GAC:BJ

220 East 42nd Street
New York

January 26, 1934

Dear Dr. Tugwell:

I am writing to you to let you know of my deep personal regret that "Design for Government" had to be discontinued. You will recall possibly that I was not enthusiastic in the beginning about the possibilities of the feature, but as you developed the feature, I came to look more and more eagerly for your copy. It was copy that should have sold itself widely on its own merits and taken its place among leading features. It is one of the minor American tragedies that conditions exist such as those that we know about which prevented "Design for Government" getting to the wide audience that it should have reached.

The principal editorial gain in it was the pleasure of our short contact with you.

Please give my best regards to Mr. Fleming.

With heartiest good wishes,

Sincerely yours,

/s/George A. Carlin

Dr. Rexford Guy Tugwell
Department of Agriculture
Washington, D.C.

There follow a selection of representative passages from the articles written for this syndicate venture. They have to do with the issues then being discussed and with the administration of the various new laws just then being begun. They reflect the controversies among us, although, of course, it is my own view point which is put forward. They were intended to be--and to an extent were--a defense and explanation of the developing New Deal: in a way they substitute for a diary during this period.

Editor's Note

At this point in the diary, Tugwell added the following syndicated articles and addresses: "Men Without Work" (1933), "Budgetary Device" (1933), "Protecting the Public Interest" (1933), "Partnership With Industry" (1933), "Codes and Agreements" (1933), "The Responsibilities of Partnership" (Address to Iowa Bankers Association, June 27, 1934), "Things Done and Not Done" (1934), "Toward Sustained Recovery" (1934), "Commitments for Tomorrow" (1933), and "The Outlines of a Permanent Agriculture" (Radio Address, 1934). All of these materials are available in the Rexford G. Tugwell papers, Franklin D. Roosevelt Library, Hyde Park, New York.

3. Brains Trust in Policy Clash

The phrase quoted above was the headline used over a quite representative article written by Theodore C. Wallen and published in the New York Herald Tribune on 1 July 1933. Excerpts from it are reproduced below. They are not only a fair account of the situation then developing inside the administration (except that my position was not quite understood), but they indicate the kind of public knowledge there was of our affairs in Washington.

WASHINGTON, July 1. -- President Roosevelt is returning to Washington to find his official family involved in a bitter controversy over proceeding the $3,300,000,000 public works program. At the bottom of it is the same American price upswing which indirectly has becalmed the World Monetary and Economic Conference.

On the theory that the tide has been turned and the price trend is in a favorable direction, Budget Director Lewis W. Douglas is for using very little of the huge fund.

On the theory that the upswing is due as much as anything to the general expectation of extensive government spending, the "brains trust" is insistent upon putting up the funds as rapidly as they can be absorbed, say at the rate of about $500,000,000 a month, and without regard to balanced budgets, nationally or locally.

TUGWELL VIEW SEEMS WINNING

The President is to be confronted with two sharply contradictory schools of thought within his Administration. The point has been fought out behind closed doors in the last week, with indications that the "brains trust," in this instance headed by Professor Rexford G. Tugwell, Assistant

Secretary of Agriculture, is taking the upper hand in the public works administration.

Mr. Roosevelt will be called upon to decide between the two factions, which are being more sharply divided as the new Administration goes more deeply into its struggle against the depression. Involved in the issue is the apparent inconsistency of Mr. Douglas, on the one hand, carrying through his drastic deflationary program to restore public confidence in the government by wholesale dismissals of government employees, and the "brains trust" on the other hand, proceeding with a huge expansion program designed to provide new jobs by the carload.

Also involved is the question whether the government is to proceed on the theory of keeping its own budget balanced and encouraging political subdivisions to balance theirs.

TO CONFER ON CRUISER MONDAY

President Roosevelt will hold a series of conferences with his advisers aboard the cruiser Indianapolis, which will anchor off Annapolis, Md., in the forenoon of Monday, and at that time will acquaint himself with the problems that have arisen since he started his holiday two weeks ago.

Except perhaps incidentally, stabilization of the currencies will not come up at that time. Administration discussion of it will be reserved for a general conference to take place after the President has returned to Washington Tuesday afternoon, it was semi-officially announced this afternoon.

This question and others related to it will occupy the President upon his return to the White House next week. That it would not engage his attention aboard the cruiser was indicated by the fact that he had not invited Secretary of the Treasury William H. Woodin, Under Secretary Dean G. Acheson or Director of the Budget Lewis Douglas to join him at Annapolis on Monday. Nor has he invited Acting Secretary of the State William Phillips.

SECRETARY WALLACE CALLED

Instead he has asked a group of officials dealing directly with domestic matters to meet him aboard ship. Secretary of Agriculture Henry A. Wallace let it be known this morning that he had been summoned, also that it was at Annapolis that the Indianapolis will make port. Until then it had not been officially indicated where the President would land.

It appears that the President wants to know immediately how matters stand regarding farm relief, industrial control and public works. He has more interest in them, at the moment, than in stablization or any other question before the London conference.

GREAT BOND ISSUE POSSIBLE

Since the Reconstruction Finance Corporation is making advances at the rate of $130,000,000 a month and the government is committed to $900,000,000 extraordinary expenditures over and above the $3,300,000,000 public works program, a decision in favor of the "brains trust" might imply a determination to float bond issues of close to $6,000,000,000 in the next year.

The two diametrically opposite schools of thought--to balance or not to balance the budget--have collided violently during the President's absence, and especially in a meeting of the Public Works Administration Friday afternoon. At the close of the meeting a member of the more radical wing of Presidential advisers intimated that sparks had flown and that Mr. Douglas had been thrown for a loss.

Against the plan to shovel out the $3,300,000,000 as quickly as possible, by promulgating liberal rules for its distribution, the budget director, it is understood, fought for the adoption of rigid restrictions which would have the effect of preventing the distribution of the fund. Mr. Douglas, it is understood, would deny government funds for the public works of political subdivisions which failed to show balanced budgets. To those which submitted plans for sound projects and showed their budgets balanced, he would make outright grants of 30 percent of the cost of the labor and supplies of the projects, and permit the subdivisions to borrow the remaining 70 percent at, say, 4 1/2 percent interest.

PROFESSORS IGNORE BUDGET

The opposite group preferred to blink at the local budgetary condition, make the 30 percent initial grants on an extremely liberal basis and lend the rest at a low rate, say about 3 percent, with the view of getting the money into circulation as quickly as possible without much regard to whether the government ever got its money back.

The "brains trust" group makes no pretense of trying to maintain a balanced budget from year to year, but insists that it should be sufficient to balance the books every ten or fifteen years as conditions permit. In the meantime they would use the government's resources to the limit to maintain the price upswing, on the theory that prosperity, once returned, would fill the Treasury coffers and enable the government to balance the budget.

The issue involves, in general outline, the question whether to inflate sharply or only gingerly. While the "brains trust" would not stop at using the entire $3,300,000,000 its members feel that once the upswing is definitely established the use of the whole fund may not be necessary. Its members, however, are perfectly willing to use it all if necessary, and issue $6,000,000,000 bonds in the next year, whatever the effect on the budget and despite the fact that it would shoot the public debt to its all-time peak level, approaching $28,000,000,000.

WORKS BOARD COMPROMISES ON LENDING

The Public Works Board, which at best has authority only to recommend projects for the President's approval, aside from proceeding with allotments of the $400,000,000 highway sub-fund and of the $238,000,000 sub-fund earmarked for naval construction, appeared to have made a compromise on the proposed lending policy in a meeting this morning.

The board agreed to recommend 4 percent as the interest rate for advances made to non-Federal public bodies for projects under the provisions of the recovery act by which the government grants 30 percent of the cost of labor and materials in the projects by states or municipalities.

Although Secretary Ickes said that it was conceivable the whole amount might be obtained in loans from the Federal organizations he doubted that such a policy would be pursued generally. He indicated further than non-Federal projects for a time would be limited probably to enterprises of fundamental necessity to the communities, such as water works and sewage systems.

The Secretary of the Interior also insisted that non-Federal bodies "must make an effort to show that their financial affairs are put in sound condition."

Amortization of such projects for a period of "reasonable life" of the project but not to exceed thirty years also was approved as the policy to be followed by the public works administration.

The "brains trust" idea is to finance the public works program by the sale of bonds to large banks which in turn may offer them for rediscount by the Federal Reserve banks. This contemplates inflation along the lines of the World War inflation. It would have the government borrow from the Federal Reserve system on the security of the bonds received from the states and municipalities or on the backing of the actual property involved in the public works projects. The government would borrow from the big commercial banks. The big commercial banks would get the money from the Federal Reserve. The Federal Reserve, in turn, is permitted under the law to make these loans without any corresponding reduction in its ability to make other loans.

While it is pointed out that this, in large outline, is the method by which the World War was financed, the exception is cited that the object in that case was destructive whereas in this case it is the creation of real, tangible wealth.

PRICE RISE BASED ON HOPE

The feeling in the "brains trust" is that the advance in prices in the securities and commodity markets to date has been based not on concrete economic improvement so much as on speculators' belief that the government intended to carry out a huge public works and industrial control program.

In this group it is felt that if the business men of the country come to suspect that the government is going to hold down the public works program to the minimum, the speculators who have bought securities and commodities upon this hope will begin to sell. Such a reaction, this group contends, would restart a downward economic spiral in which security values would fall, banks would be weakened to the point of calling their loans, industrial liquidation would start all over again and the net effect would be a national setback.

The point is made that if, on the other hand, the businessmen of the country see that the government intends to go ahead with its plan at whatever cost as it did during the World War and will not halt its expenditures until the objective of a much higher price level is realized, they will confidently buy raw materials and hire labor. This increase in private business activity it is explained, would enable the government to slow down its own expenditures.

SPENDING PROGRAM CALLED VITAL

The "brains trust" believes, in short, that sooner or later the government must embark upon a spending program in order to bring about a price rise. If the goverment delays now, and particularly if businessmen get the idea that the government is not sure to go ahead with its plans, the good effects of the last few weeks will be dissipated and the government will have to spend more money in the end, whereas, on the other hand, if the government shows every sign of determination to pour out money at the rate of $500,000,000 a month or better, business will be so heartened that it will begin spending on its own account and the government will not need to spend the whole $3,300,000,000.

The "brains trust" is not worrying about the government's ability to raise the funds for this vast program. By its plan there would be no attempt to make sales of government bonds to the investing public. It is quite willing to leave the balancing of the budget to better times. It argues that since the depression did not come from an unbalanced budget, no more is it to be assumed that recovery will come with a balanced budget. In fact, this school of thought can see how the very zeal of balancing the budget may obstruct economic recovery under present circumstances.

In the bitter wrangling of the last week members of the "brains trust" have pointed out that the price of all goods is obviously determined by the money demand for them. With a balanced budget, money which is spent by the government is taken from the taxpayers. The taxpayers have that much less to spend. In other words, as they say, purchasing power is merely transferred from the individual citizen to the national government. The total amount of money demand for goods remains constant and there is consequently no rise in prices.

When, however, a government proceeds on an unbalanced budget, this group contends, the government spends money which, in effect, is borrowed from itself instead of being collected from the taxpayers. The purchasing power of the individual citizen has not been reduced and the purchasing power of the government is increased. Consequently, the total money demand for goods is increased and prices inevitably rise.

That is, of course, they qualify, unless the supply of goods increases enough to counterbalance the increased money demand. There is the further qualification that if individuals distrust the financial policy of the government they may reduce their purchasing power. This, they say, was the case with Mr. Hoover's experiment with the Reconstruction

Finance Corporation. It is considered less likely to recur now, since there is more confidence in banks and the hoarding crises is over.

Should the government attempt to finance its recovery program through the sale of its bonds to private individual investors, these Presidential advisers contend, the government would defeat its own end. Every investor who buys a government bond would have that much less to spend, unless, of course, he took the bond to his bank, borrowed on it and his bank took the bond to the Federal Reserve and itself borrowed on it. Should the government bonds be sold to bona fide investors who held them and did not borrow on them, the government would be cutting down the purchasing power of individual citizens as rapidly as it created purchasing power through its recovery program at Washington. And, it is pointed out, there would be no inflation.

NEWS AND COMMENT FROM THE NATIONAL CAPITAL

THE CONTROVERSY BETWEEN BUDGET DIRECTOR DOUGLAS, OF THE "TREASURY CROWD," AND REXFORD TUGWELL, SPOKESMAN FOR THE "BRAINS TRUST," OVER THE BPULIC WORKS PROGRAM

WASHINGTON -- A first-class shindy has developed inside the Roosevelt Administration. On one side is Budget Director Lewis W. Douglas. Chief of the opposing faction is Assistant Secreatry of Agriculture Rexford G. Tugwell. Each of these ambitious young men has rigid ideas about what should be done to restore prosperity, and each is determined to prevail.

The present row centers around the Administration's $3,300,000,000 public works program. Douglas wants to go slowly in spending this astronomical sum. He is mortally afraid of unbalancing the Government's credit. Tugwell, on the other hand, believes it essential that the money be shoveled out as fast as humanly possible. While President Roosevelt, on his recent vacation, was cruising leisurely along the coast of Maine, the Douglas and Tugwell factions held a series of meetings in Washington. According to participants, these conferences developed into an open, angry quarrel.

No one, however, should feel unduly disturbed at this news. Such intra-Administration friction is a necessary, even valuable, part of our system of government. In England or France, the Executive can be turned out at a moment's notice. Here in the United States, we give the President immense powers and a secure term of office. Since no President can be overthrown for four years, it is important that his official family, as nearly as possible, be representative of the whole nation. The wider the variety of opinion a President can collect around him, the more effective his Administration is likely to be.

Mr. Roosevelt took office in the midst of sharp crises. There were no differences of opinion, then, anywhere in the country. During the first weeks of March, most Americans would have painted themselves red, white and blue and stood on their heads in the middle of the street, if they had thought Mr. Roosevelt wished them to. Thomas W. Lamont and Senator Huey Long united in fervid praise of Mr. Roosevelt's policies. In Washington, Administration members were working sixteen and eighteen hours a day, and had neither time nor energy for dissension.

WHO WILL BE THE KEY MAN?

Now, somewhat after the manner of a gang of small boys around a swimming hole, Administration members are testing their respective strengths. Each man wants to know to what extent he is going to be able to shape the policies of the next four years. Who is going to be the "key man" in the Roosevelt Administration? The two leaders who have so far emerged are Messrs. Douglas and Tugwell. Douglas is top man of what is very loosely called "the Treasury crowd," which includes a good part of the Cabinet. Tugwell is acknowledged spokesman for the "brains trust" -- A. A. Berle, Mordecai Ezekiel, Donald Richberg, Jerome Frank, Leo Wolman and their fellows.

Perhaps the most influential individual, after President Roosevelt, in the whole Administration, Gen. Hugh Johnson, administrator of the National Industrial Recovery Act, is carefully refraining from adhering to any faction. General Johnson is saying nothing, and attending strictly to his own colossal job. Another one preserving complete neutrality is Assistant Secretary of State Moley, once the bright, particular star of the "brain trust." Dr. Moley no longer seems to be a "brain trust" leader, nor even a member in good standing.

It would be highly unfair to describe the present public-works controversy between Messrs. Douglas and Tugwell as solely a contest of prestige. Both men are passionately in earnest. Douglas believes that the surest contribution the Administration can make toward recovery is to abstain from further spending. Government spending inevitably means government borrowing, and he believes it is of first importance that the investment-capital market be left free for private borrowers.

TUGWELL WANTS ACTION

Douglas is a hard, lean Westerner patently a man of action. Yet in this controversy, he counsels passivity on the part of the Administration. It is Tugwell, the cloistered college professor, who demands action on a vast scale. He and his group believe there is small likelihood of private investors, within the discernible future, wishing to finance large capital expenditures. They point out that agriculture is now rapidly being placed on a profit-making basis. But this is only half the job. The Administration must do as much for American heavy industry. The quickest, surest way to revive heavy industry is by a great construction program, by which, if need be, a half billion dollars a month will be poured into the steel, engineering and machinery industries. And they urge the Administration to act at once, before the present speculative rise in the securities and commodities markets has been dissipated.

At the present moment, the controversy over public-works expenditure and the deeper dispute between the conservatism of the Douglas group and radicalism of the Tugwell followers is before President Roosevelt for decision. With knowledge of the President's uncanny skill in leadership, it is not hard to predict his course. More than any President we have had in recent times, Mr. Roosevelt appears to feel himself the representative of the whole nation, and to feel it is his job to keep the whole nation behind him. It can be predicted that he will find some way to keep both Tugwell's boldness of thought, and Douglas's aggressiveness in action at the service of his Administration.

DIOGENES

4. The "Tugwell Bill" Becomes Un-American

There occurred, during 1933, and running on into later years, what seems now like a tempest in a teapot over proposed revision of the Food and Drugs Act.

What was proposed to be done could not have seemed very drastic to the detached observer. But the patent-medicine and cosmetic manufacturers were shocked beyond sanity by the threatened changes. The shock very quickly communicated itself to the newspapers and magazines. A hitherto unrealized proportion of their revenues came from these sources. And the advertising, it appeared, would be useless, or nearly so, if anything like the reliable facts had to be disclosed.

The whole matter was strictly a New Deal sideline. But once raised, the issues involved were difficult to abandon. We had a bear by the tail.

It was a very short jump, indeed, from a threat to publishers' profits from advertising, to un-Americanism. And the publishers were not long in making it.

There was, however, a not inconsiderable interest on the other side. It was hard to bring it to bear in the Congress, many of whose members found patent-medicine campaign contributions easy and reliable, and who valued the support of local newspapers. These were more effective interests than those of consumers whose votes might or might not be affected.

A fantastic controversy blew up and ran off into all sorts of corollary effects. The effect of most interest to me, of course, was the deliberate campaign (of which I was given notice) to identify me in the public mind as a "Red."

A highlight of this campaign was reached, I suppose, when The New York Herald Tribune headed a long editorial "Rex; the Red." This made it more or less official.

The industry very quickly united to repel the threat. The following is an excerpt from The New York Herald Tribune, for Feb. 3, 1934.

INDUSTRY UNITES TO FIGHT FOOD AND DRUG BILL

Manufacturers Assail Tugwell-Copeland Measure as Despotic, Un-American

---

For Compromise Reform

Agree there is Room for Improvement in Statute

Organized opposition to the Tugwell-Copeland pure food and drug bill in Congress was formulated and expressed at a luncheon yesterday of members of the food, drug and cosmetic industries at the Biltmore. A committee of manufacturers, called the Joint Committee for Sound and Democratic Consumer Legislation, was appointed to fight provisions in the bill and keep the public "informed on all measures affecting its welfare."

Lee H. Bristol, vice-president for Bristol-Myers, Inc., manufacturers of drugs and cosmetics, spokesman for the committee, characterized the Copeland-Tugwell bill as "hasty," "bureaucratic," "dangerous" and threatening the life of the industries affected. "We are in hearty accord with the intent of the bill," he said, "but we are opposed to the form because it places bureaucratic control of three major industries -- food, drugs and cosmetics -- in the hands of an appointive government employee and his subordinates."

MEASURE CALLED "UN-AMERICAN"

"The bill is dangerous and un-American because of the unprecedented powers it places in the hands of the Secretary of Agriculture -- any Secretary of Agriculture, no matter how competent or incompetent he may be. Further, the bill sets up, in some matters, joint control by the Secretary of Agriculture and a group of departmental advisers, who can pronounce life or death over what is or what is not adulterated food, over what is or what is not sound advertising, over what is or what is not sound method of manufacture, placing in the hands of this group legislative and judicial function."

Mr. Bristol announced the personnel of the committee to take up the cudgels against the measure as follows: S. B. Colgate, president of the Colgate-Palmolive-Peet Company; K. F. MacLellan, president of the United Biscuit Company of America; Ellery W. Mann, president of Zonite Products, Inc.; Arthur R. Wendell, vice-president of Wheatena Corporation; Edward J. Noble, President of Life Savers, Inc.; Allyn McIntyre, vice-president of the Pepperell Manufacturing Company, and John W. Darr, Secretary.

While characterizing as worthy the intent of the bill to protect the public and reputable manufacturers and dealers from fake cure-alls, adulterated foods and harmful cosmetics, Mr. Bristol said that it contained elements that were dangerous to the public interests and opposed to the broad principles of democratic government.

"It is unwise and inexpedient from the public interest to rush through legislation of this sort," he said. "No emergency exists to warrant the rushing through of legislation of such vital importance. We cannot agree with Professor Tugwell, Assistant Secretary of Agriculture, that our civilization is in imminent danger of destruction unless this measure or a similar measure is adopted forthwith."

PRESENT LAW HELD AMPLE

"It is our belief," he continued, "that through careful deliberation government officials, manufacturers and consumers can work out a pure food and drugs act which will embody the principles of sound democratic legislation in the interest of all concerned."

Such a bill, said Mr. Bristol, should --

1. Protect public health by keeping high standards of purity in food, drugs, cosmetics and all other items of human consumption.

2. Encourage research and laboratory experimentation by private industry.

3. Protect the interests of industry, which has always taken the initiative in raising standards.

4. Preserve the American system of legal procedure in order that the legitimate businesses shall not suffer through possible transgressions of the illegitimate.

5. Preserve the profit motive in business to encourage more efficient methods of distribution with the resulting decrease in cost to the consumer.

6. Retain the making and administering of law in the hands of the duly elected representatives of the people."

The public was amply protected, Mr. Bristol held, by the present pure food and drug act until a satisfactory measure could be written which would afford complete protection with a minimum of injustice.

The kind of propoganda sent out by the industry committee is shown by the letter here reproduced. Copies addressed to many local druggists who resented its receipt were sent on to me. Harry Elmer Barnes, to whom this particular copy had been addressed, had apparently decided to take up the cudgels in defense of the bill for he also sent me a copy of the letter of protest he had sent to JUDGE, a humorous magazine of the period, the second paragraph of which expresses the surprise felt by most people at the attitude assumed by their favorite magazines.

JOINT COMMITTEE FOR SOUND AND DEMOCRATIC CONSUMER LEGISLATION

Suite 1639 Graybar Building, 420 Lexington Avenue, New York City

Committee   February 9th, 1934

LEE H. BRISTOL, Vice President
Bristol-Myers, Inc.

S. B. COLGATE, President
Colgate-Palmolive-Peet Co.

K. F. MACLELLAN, President
United Biscuit Co., of America

ELLERY W. MANN, President
Zonite Products, Inc.

ALLYN McINTIRE, Vice President
Pepperell Mfg. Co.

EDWARD J. NOBLE, President
Life Savers, Inc.

ARTHUR R. WENDELL, Vice President
Wheatena Corporation

JOHN W. DARR, Secretary

> Dr. Harry E. Barnes
> Post,
> Cincinnati, Ohio

My dear Dr. Barnes

An opportunity presents itself, it seems to us,
for a treatment in cartoon of a vital public issue that
has just arisen. We are presenting this material to you
for your interest, information and possible use.

Under the guise of filling a public health service,
a bill has been introduced in Congress, known as the Tugwell-
Copeland Act. This bill, while it fulfills this purpose, has
in it certain basic bureaucratic elements which threaten the
American system. The enclosed clipping indicates to you just
what this bill does. It seems to us that the American people
should be appraised of this situation.

Sincerely yours,

/s/ J. W. Darr

ORGANIZED FOR THE PURPOSE OF PROMULGATING
AUTHORITATIVE INFORMATION TO THE AMERICAN PEOPLE
ON PENDING CONSUMER LEGISLATION, AND TO INVESTIGATE
AND REPORT TO THE PUBLIC ON SOUND AND DEMOCRATIC
LEGISLATION

Harry Elmer Barnes
Auburn
R.F.D. 5, New York

To the Editor of JUDGE:

I read your editorial in the January
number of JUDGE and have received some material
circulated by patent medicine pirates from the
February issue of JUDGE.

Those of us who have admired your
courageous and statesmanlike stand on prohibition
are somewhat amazed to see you lining up behind
pirates and prisoners who make either Bishop
Cannon or Al Capone seem like martyrs to the
cause of honesty, decency and humanity.

Sincerely yours,

/s/ Harry E. Barnes

b/g

There were a few other newspaper men--but no newspapers--who
took on the Food and Drug Act revision as a cause, of whom perhaps the
most courageous were Drew Pearson and Robert Allen in their
Washington Merry-Go-Round. Heywood Broun also devoted a number of
his widely circulated columns to comment on the campaign against it.
One of his most amusing is quoted below:

The Washington Daily News--Monday--December 18, 1933

IT SEEMS TO ME * * * by Heywood Broun

If I have my way this is the last column of mine which will be written in Washington for some time. I hate to confess defeat, but the pace of the Capital is too much for me.

In a sense I should welcome a chance to browse about down here because the standards of senility are so much more indulgent than those prevailing in New York. For instance, I have seen constant references in the newspapers to the "young liberals" in the Administration. Some of these gentlemen have long white beards, but in a land where every Supreme Court Justice lives to 90 before he can be pried off the bench anything less than 70 is considered adolescent.

Quite often I have read about Rexford G. Tugwell, and in every case he was described as a youthful collegian filled with sophomoric inclinations to tear down all existing institutions. Today I met him and, naturally, my first question was, "Where are the bombs?" and immediately after that, "How old are you, Mr. Assistant Secretary?"

He said he was 42. I will admit that he could pass for less, but even if he heaped on a year or so this member of the Brain Trust is not by any accurate definition a fledgling. At 40 I was distinctly suspicious that perhaps I was not as young as I used to be. At 41 this vague foreboding became a certainty. The next year I bought myself a pair of slippers and a quilted dressing gown. Long before the age of 40 Napoleon had triumphed at Austerlitz. At a less advanced period Shelley was dead and Hannibal had crossed the Alps with elephants. Rexford G. Tugwell is 42. He is not a young man. At any rate, he knows his way about.

Again, according to the placard I have seen in public places, the charge runs, "Wanted for Socialism," and so when I was ushered into the office of the Assistant Secretary of Agriculture I extended my hand and exclaimed, "Hello, comrade! Yours for the revolution." I then sang a few bars of the Internationale. Dr. Tugwell seemed puzzled and inquired, "Have you got an appointment?" Even when I gave him a little of the secret ritual he failed to tumble. The newspapers have made a grave mistake about him. He isn't a Socialist, nor has he ever been a party member.

Fiorello LaGuardia, only recently chosen as our mayor, is flaming red if set down beside the brigadier of the Brain Trust. I have no intention of insulting an extremely intelligent and personable young man, but if I ever saw a liberal Rexford G. Tugwell is that specimen. Indeed, I would describe him as Walter Lippmann with steal structure added.

Mr. Tugwell is sincere, earnest, and he isn't fooling, but is not of the martyr mold. There isn't a trace of the fanatic about him. After all, here is a middle-aged man who existed and prospered upon the faculty of Columbia University for several years without any jam whatsoever. I have no intention of imputing to him any lack of courage. For the thing which he believes Tugwell will fight hard. But the major part of his economic philosophy is by no means a swat in the eye for the world as it now stands.

The particular bill which bears his name merely extends an accepted practice into a new field. The securities bill has already nicked into the ancient concept that a buyer must beware. Under the New Deal it is established that the motto ought to run, "Let the seller beware." I'm terribly sorry that I cannot supply the Latin equivalent.

The major purposes of the Tugwell bill are so reasonable that it is difficult to understand the position of the opposition. As things stand now there exist severe restrictions as to what may be said on the label of a nostrum. Nobody can put out sugar and water and label it as a cure for Bright's disease. But he may in many states advertise it as a cure, without let or hindrance. In most communities the claims which are put into newspaper display go far beyond the limits of the label.

I am not at all sure that candor in advertising will necessarily be costly either to publications, manufacturers or agencies. It never has been my privilege to write any copy concerning myself, although my employers have at times indulged in paid statements which certainly failed to convince me. Only the other day I saw one which, as I remember, said: "This one and only Broun." If I had prepared that copy I would have finished the sentence, and I would have chosen some large and effective type for the "thank heaven!"

Suppose a cigaret company followed this formula: "The Goodus cigaret has nothing in particular which may not be found in the products of many of its rivals. Its price is the same as that of other standard brands. There is no special trick by which it is prepared. As far as we can ascertain, the longest distance anybody ever walked to get a Goofus was 67 yards. This is no whirlwind. All we assert is that the Goofus is a pretty good cigaret. Why not smoke it?"

I suppose the question will arise, "Who on earth would think of buying a cigaret presented in this way?"

The answer is easy. I would.

But there were others less spectacular. In the midst of the affair, for instance, the following letter came to me from Irving Brant, then an Editor of The St. Louis Star and Times:

Elzey Roberts, Publisher
St. Louis Star and Times
Star Building   Star Square

IRVING BRANT
Editor of Editorial Page   February 12, 1934

Personal and
Confidential.

Dr. Rexford Tugwell,
Washington, D.C.

Dear Dr. Tugwell:

I presume you receive a good share of the propaganda that goes out to newspapers against the drug bill. The advertising "heat" against this measure has been greater than anything I have encountered in twenty-five years; in fact, I should say that it is more extensive and more intense than any ten pressure campaigns combined.

Allowing for the fact that our publisher thinks your bill is dead wrong and that you are, in general, a menace to the country, he has done pretty well in allowing, first, an editorial almost unqualifiedly supporting the measure; then, in deference to demands with which he sympathized, a suggestion of changes which did not satisfy the hammer brigade at all, and latterly, in the face of continued demands, silence. About all you can get from any newspaper which is not in an impregnable position as to advertising prestige is silence. But what disgusts me is the way in which the average newspaper plays the game of the advertising agencies without one thought of the issues involved....

I did not get enough specific information, during my brief stay in Washington last summer, to write the magazine article I was planning on the effect of political patronage upon the New Deal, but gave it a little space in the Public Works chapter of my book, "Dollars and Sense," and have dealt editorially with it a number of times, as per the inclosure, "The New Citizenship."

Hoping that David Lawrence will soon have the pleasure of announcing your appointment as Under Secretary,

I am, Yours Sincerely,
/s/ Irving Brant

Enclosed in Mr. Brant's letter were the following amusing paragraphs concerning the alternative bill got up by the industrious Drug lobby and introduced by Congressman Black.

Sample of an advertisement which apparently would not be considered false, except as to one statement, under the terms of the bill introduced by Congressman Black at the request of the drug lobby. The only false statement of fact in it is contained in the word "all" in the last sentence. Something like this might show quite vividly what sort of regulations the patent medicine people think they should be under:

"Magic Wonder Pills, manufactured by one of the leading pharmacal companies of the nation from a formula discovered by the distinguished Dr. Stippelzucker.

The laboratory experiments of Dr. Stippelzucker and his expert assistants, combined with his experience in the practice of medicine, have convinced him that Magic Wonder Pills are a complete and positive cure for all diseases of women, secret ailments, influenza, colds in the head, gangrene, suppuration, piles and in fact all other ailments known to the human race.

Dr. Stippelzucker has received unsolicited testimonials from hundreds of patients who declare that Magic Wonder Pills cured them of dropsy, diabetes and other sicknesses commonly regarded as incurable.

For sale at all drug stores."

Possibly you know that David Lawrence is sending out confidential letters to publishers, in addition to his dispatches, the letters consisting mostly of propaganda against the Roosevelt program, and including false and misleading statements about the drug bill which strongly suggest that they are paid for. In fact, it is hard to escape the conclusion that Lawrence has become a paid propagandist in many directions, using his one-time prestige to cloak a sell-out.

The time may be approaching for another lobby investigation. What you would discover if you subpoenaed the correspondence of the Thompson-Kock Advertising Agency, and got it!

From THE SURVEY, Jan 1934 p. 16

EXPERTS ALSO SPOKE

Misrepresentations so violent that it would seem to defeat its own ends is rampant in the stream of propaganda pouring out in opposition to the Tugwell Bill to revise and extend federal control of foods and drugs (see The Survey, November 1933, p.383, Radio and Rouge; December, p.414, What is Timely?). Manufacturing druggists are declaring to the trade that business will be ruined because no customer can buy so much as a coughdrop without a doctor's prescription. That claim is poppycock; the bill does not prevent anyone from getting any medicine he wants unless it contains narcotics; it does insist that he shall know what he gets. More disturbing are thinly disguised threats from manufacturers to newspapers, warning them that they will lose advertising unless they oppose the measure and hinting that two doctors have written the bill to fatten doctors' pocketbooks. And still more disturbing is the fact that a responsible group like the National Publishers' Association, representing leading national magazines, has come out in opposition to one of the basic protections the bill offers to consumers -- what the Association terms "the sponsoring of food products by the government through the compulsory branding of foods, as 'U.S. Grade A' or any other governmental designation." Now not only the government itself, but big businesses save millions of dollars each year by buying by specification, instead of having to rely on the lure of trade names, packaging and the manufacturers' ballyhoo. Advertising might well suffer if consumers were able to place less emphasis on trade names, more on impartial rating by disinterested experts. But is advertising to be the arbiter?

Again we urge Survey readers to write the U.S. Department of Agriculture for a copy of S. 1944 and read for themselves, rather than rely on newspaper reports. For example, recently The New York Herald Tribune carried an account of a hearing on the bill. The headline, first paragraph and the greater part of a column detailed the arguments of the bill's opponents, with a brief mention of the approval of the bill by the Department of Agriculture. At the very end were two sentences: "W. C. Roberts indorsed the measure on behalf of the American Federation of Labor. Others who favored it were Professors Yandell Henderson of Yale; Haven Emerson, of Columbia, and Allen Freeman of Johns Hopkins." No sentence explains that these were not only "professors" but nationally known leaders in public health, and that one of them, president of the American Public Health Association, had been designated by that body to give the Association's official support of the measure.

5. The Methodists Are Offended

On an unfortunate day in February I made a speech to the Women's National Democratic Club, which I called "Wine, Women, and the New Deal." It was a plea for temperance, and a suggestion that repeal had now made possible more civilized habits. I urged the women to take the lead in the voluntary abandonment of spirits and the substitution of wine. I pointed out the great variety of wines produced in the United States and the interest of farmers in the enlargement of their market.

As I read it over now it still seems to me to have been rather happily conceived. The way I began was like this:

> I find that there is a pretty general attitude that the men who are engaged in administering the policies of the New Deal are a pretty grim lot, that we are painfully serious and so ferociously in earnest that we take no vacation from the eternal verities. Exception is always made, in this generalization, for cheerful good temper of the President but the rest of us are usually portrayed as cadaverous fanatics or haggard heroes wrestling with stupendous problems in a spirit of humorless ferocity.

> Our problems are, of course, very large and must be dealt with in a serious temper but it would be treason to the entire spirit of the New Deal to lose sight of the fact that its objective, as stated by President Roosevelt himself, is to make possible a more abundant life for the American people. A more abundant life implies a happier

and perhaps a less hectic type of existence for the average man and woman, it implies the enjoyment of the good things of life in security and contentment, and the cultivation, through such enjoyment, of the good things of the spirit: reflection, conversation and leisure.

Instead of people arguing that we are too grim, we might justifiably contend that the Old Order has made people too grim, that the presence of physical abundance in the increasing variety, hitherto associated only with the tropics, should not imply an increasing struggle for existence among the heirs and assigns of this abundance. We see that our task is fundamentally the spiritual task of calling a halt on the intemperate national tradition of going places and doing things and labelling the result pleasure. Our political dedication to the pursuit of happiness, as one of the fundamental rights of humanity, has been too rigidly interpreted as a species of buffalo hunt or a riding to hounds, in which we either exterminated our quarry or risked breaking our own necks.

Happiness is a shy creature and can be pursued in other ways than in organizing a posse or imposing a cover-charge on those who would capture it. It must be approached delicately, or better still, encouraged to approach its pursuer, or else it takes flight, and then, if captured by swift and resolute pursuit, is swiftly slain. You may hang the trophy on your wall, but it is apt to stay there, and not again to afford you pleasure.

One of the oldest and quietest roads to contentment lies through that traditional trinity of wine, woman and song. If either bathtub gin or three-weeks whiskey is substituted for the first element in this combination, the result is best characterized by the associations we have with the word "jazz." We all know what this led to in the pre-war saloon era and we all know that the excesses of the bootleg decade produced the revulsion of national feeling which has brought back legalized alcoholic beverages. While youth and high spirits must be served, there is no sense in converting them into a moral servitude which dictates that drunkenness is the chief end of drinking or confuses intoxication with happiness. We have a chance, now that the repeal of the Eighteenth Amendment is an accomplished fact, to clamp down on these lusty juvenalia and to substitute a tradition of greater maturity.

This is the tradition of wine, used as a mild social stimulant, together with good food, good talk and good company, and, let me add, good song. "Sweet Adeline" may serve to blow off steam, but that is all it does, and it is, to my mind, an unfortunate survival of the old saloon tradition which implied that men desired to escape from the company of their womenfolk and raise the roof in each other's company. I am frank to admit that I am partial to the European tradition of open air cafes and beer-gardens, where decent men and women can drink quietly in the open air under the eyes of their neighbors and where the two sexes can exert on each other the discipline of each other's presence. Covert drinking and secret drinking is the mark of the drunkard. I prefer that anything so natural as the result of the natural process of fermentation should be treated naturally and not, through moralistic regulations, converted into a clandestine and hence artificially exciting form of sinful self-indulgence....

I think that the best lead which American women can follow is that which has been given by Mrs. Roosevelt herself. To serve wine in their own homes, to favor American wines as much as possible, to choose them with discrimination, and to assimilate their use to the habit of food. The best way in which this can be done is to try out all the varieties of American wine which are coming on the market, sparingly, and to judge them with reference to flavor, bouquet and price, rather than with reference to their ability to produce the recognizable symptoms of intoxication in the shortest possible time.

and I ended as follows:

For today we have in our possession all the elements which are necessary to that more abundant life which is the real objective of all of us. We have foods and factories, we have a highly efficient system of communication and transport, we have, above all, a patient, hard-working and self-respecting people, who are distinguished for their social good-will and for their political self-control. All we need is to find the way to the enjoyment of that heritage which lies at our hands.

It is here that the women of America can make their most vital contribution. They have it in their power to define our moral objectives and lead us into channels of good taste and good judgment. We can find a sufficient salvation here at home; it is not necessary to blame Europe or Asia for our failure to solve our own problems. The New Deal has, therefore, adopted a policy which its critics and some of its friends describe as economic nationalism, but the fundamental purpose of which is to solve our own problems in terms of our own traditions and our own resources. Such a policy in purely masculine hands has too often in the past led straight to international greed, imperialism and armed conflict. It is for the women to see that the same canons of deportment which permit a member of society to conduct his own business without destroying his neighbor shall permeate our national attitude towards other countries. Too often, we regard the welfare of another as our loss and his discomfiture as our gain, in world affairs.

The more civilized attitude is to recognize that we are all members of each other's group and that the good of one may be the good of all, unless it is achieved at the direct expense of another.

Historically, wine has been, I think, a genuinely civilizing influence in that portion of the world which stems from Europe. Historically again, women have been the custodians and transmitters of culture. Song, also has been the spontaneous expression of civilized happiness. In thinking together of wine, of women, and of song, we can lay the foundation for a deep and enduring social attitude of mutual forbearance and friendly toleration. Without such an attitude, I am convinced, it will not be easy, if indeed it is possible, for the American people to enter upon the more abundant life which is rightfully theirs.

A not inconsiderable stir followed the reporting of this speech in the press. Nearly two months later the reverberations were still going on. The Baltimore Sun on 30 April, published a dispatch from Portland,

Oregon:

DID DR. TUGWELL COMMEND "WINE, WOMAN AND SONG"?
If He Did, Methodists of Portland, Ore., Will Ask President and Wallace to Oust Him--Advice to Serve Wine Also Arouses Church

------

PORTLAND, ORE., April 29--The Congregation of Rose City Park Methodist Episcopal Church wants to know if two quotations attributed to Dr. Rexford Guy Tugwell are authentic.

If they are, the parishioners expressed belief in a vote today, the Assistant Secretary of Agriculture should resign. One statement, attributed to Dr. Tugwell by a church paper was: "One of the oldest and quietest roads to contentment lies through the conventional trinity of wine, women and song."

A second statement, that "American women should follow the example of Mrs. Roosevelt and serve wine in their homes," aroused such anger that the parishioners voted that Tugwell was "unworthy to represent the people and untrue to the traditions and standards of the American people."

The congregation voted to have the pastor, the Rev. Fred C. Taylor, ascertain whether the two statements were made by Tugwell, and if so, to write to President Roosevelt and Secretary Wallace "demanding Tugwell's resignation."

The church vote came at the close of a sermon by Mr. Taylor in which he referred to statements from the Christian Advocate, Methodist publication at San Francisco, which were said to be reprints from an article in the March issue of the Democratic Digest, of Washington, assertedly written by Tugwell.

Tugwell was quoted as saying the objective of the "New Deal" is "to make possible a more abundant life for the American people," that "the enjoyment of the good things in life lies in security and contentment," and finally that "one of the oldest and quietest roads to contentment lies through the conventional trinity of wine, woman and song."

The Rose City Park Church has some 800 members and is located in one of the better residential sections of Portland. Mr. Taylor is a Republican who has been active in a battle against beer parlors here.

I was naturally stricken with embarrassment at having associated Mrs. Roosevelt with my perfidy. I wrote to her, apologizing, and saying that if she would read the speech, she would not find it as bad as pictured. This had the result, at least, of drawing a very characteristic reply from her.

THE WHITE HOUSE
WASHINGTON

May 3, 1934

My dear Dr. Tugwell:

I am much interested in both of your speeches but how could you for a minute think that the Methodists would not expire over the title of "Wine, Women and the New Deal"? I am surprised you are not flooded from every single part of the country with letters from the W.C.T.U. I had that experience myself.

But laughing aside, I think you did a swell job in both of these speeches. However, I think I would be a little more conservative in my use of words and titles at other times. Your sense of humor does lead you into traps I am afraid!

I wish I could do as well in my speeches to young women as you did in your Dartmouth speech. It was a grand challenge and full of suggestions that ought to help their imaginations. My hat is always off to your courage.

Very sincerely yours,

/s/ Eleanor R-----

/written/ I think you get secret joy out of the fray!

It is significant that when, a few months later, the White House announced its intention to serve light wines at State dinners there were no repercussions. The San Francisco Chronicle carried a picture of the President and his family behind a dinner table of which wine appeared conspicuously (posed for the purpose, apparently) with the following details:

WASHINGTON, Nov. 8 (AP)--The White House will serve light wines at State dinners this season.

It must be light wine and American wine, in accordance with Mrs. Roosevelt's pronouncement when wine first became legal.

No more than two wine glasses will be at each plate at any dinner.

Mrs. Roosevelt referred to the custom for a wine to be served with every course, adding she did not think that plan "would be at all attractive to any of us."

6. *Intimations of Resettlement*

The Resettlement Administration would not be established until 1 May 1935. The ideas embodied in it were, however, ones which had been under discussion for a long time, especially those having to do with better uses of the land. My contribution was to be the administrative joining of efforts to do something about the situation of poor people as well as poor land. It was not new, of course, to suggest that they went together. It was, however, novel to suggest that the rehabilitation of both ought to be undertaken jointly in a Federal program.

The concept of submarginal land was one which had had a gradual evolution. By 1933 it was beginning to be widely understood how much American land had been so misused that its further cultivation was uneconomic; more than this, it had positive deleterious effects on the economy. Eroded soil was not only lost to the farms it came from; it became an expensive nuisance in the lower river valleys, in reservoirs and in silted deltas. Also submarginality was relative. Land became useless for some purposes could be devoted to others with at least some yield of values--if it could not be developed as timbers- or grass-land, it could become scenic or recreational and perhaps a refuge for our hard-pressed wild life.

One of the more conspicuous small approaches to land readjustment had been made in Tompkins County, New York, in the environs of Cornell University. There, in the hilly country devoted to farming for some three generations, erosion and competition from the

West had dragged the farmers into poverty. That country had once supported a rich stand of Weymouth pine and hardwood forest. It was now gullied, grown up to the useless vegetation characteristic of leached-out soils, and much of it in process of being abandoned. The effort there was to persuade the remaining farmers to move, gather the lands into manageable units and return them to forest. About this work the President knew a good deal and had encouraged it when he had been Governor. It was not a far departure to think of similar treatment for many other areas. Not all had the same problems. In the arid country of the West; on the short-grass plains; in the over cultivated South; in the cut-over regions of Michigan and Minnesota poor and badly-used lands waited to be put to their natural uses. But also there were millions of people who had gone down this their lands (sic) and needed help and guidance if they were to escape their rural slums and find a better life.

As I worked with the Forest Service which came under my direction in the Department of Agriculture; as I heard about the ills of share-croppers through AAA; as I watched the development, under Harry Hopkins, of a program for rural rehabilitation; as I helped establish the Soil Conservation Service; as I helped in working out controls for grazing on public lands--I gradually became more and more sensitized to the problem which seemed to me as serious as any we faced. Our lands and our people were being wasted together; it was unnecessary; we ought to do something about it. The President agreed. He was, in fact, ahead of me. He supported every suggestion which had any merit having to do with the general problem. But the efforts were scattered; there was no planned attack. We discussed it many times, going over and over the special maps I had made and studying the special conditions of each area. It was not at once apparent that something grandiose ought to be attempted. It seemed enough to coordinate the various effects of many agencies. This is the stage we were in during the year preceeding the invention of the Resettlement idea.

There was not only a good deal going on in various agencies of the New Deal to which I could give encouragement and who were glad to let me assist, there was considerable background to be explored. I had been so interested for some time that I had most of this at my command; but in spite of his interest and the work he had done as Governor, there was a good deal of information I could supply the President with. This I did and it too was the subject of many conversations between us, most agreeable ones, for on no topic did we find so much in common and so much on which we could agree.

Sometimes specific issues arose which formed convenient centers for the advancing of discussion and programming. Such a one was the seeming paradox involved in taking land out of cultivation (by AAA) at the same time that more was being added (by Reclamation). The following self-explanatory documents show how this quandary was happily escaped:

DEPARTMENT OF AGRICULTURE
Washington, D.C.

July 27, 1933

The President
  The White House

Dear Mr. President:

I was much alarmed in our conference last evening at the suggestion that large sums of Public Works money would be used for new reclamation projects. Such projects will open us up to very heavy political attack throughout the middlewest, as long as we are engaged in acreage control activities. The charge will be that the right hand of the government knows not what the left hand is doing.

Of course, it may be urged that the products produced on these new projects do not come in competition with the products of the middlewest, but in this connection, it should be remembered that all foods are ultimately competitive. Moreover the projects insofar as they produce fruits and vegetables will come into competition with the irrigation projects already established, and insofar as they produce alfalfa and live stock, they will add to the problems of the middlewest.

Because of this very dangerous political and economic background, I was much interested, therefore, in the suggestion that at every step of the move to bring new land into use, there should be a corresponding move to take marginal land out of use to such an extent as to balance productive powers. Inasmuch as most irrigated land is rather productive and the sub-marginal land is decidedly unproductive this would mean the taking out of use of five or ten acres of marginal land for each one acre of irrigated land brought in. A preliminary survey would indicate that the 30,000,000 poorest acres of marginal crop land can be acquired for about $250,000,000. The greatest part of this land is found in the eastern one-half of the United States, especially in the southeast. I can give you a rough estimate by states if you so desire.

I am wondering if it might not be fruitful for Secretary Ickes and myself to appoint a joint committee to prepare a joint program dealing with the general aspects of the problem of taking old land out of use and bringing new land into use.

                              Respectfully yours

                              /s/ H. A. Wallace
                              Secretary
Copy: Secretary Ickes

                    UNITED STATES DEPARMENT OF AGRICULTURE
                           Office of the Secretary
                               Washington

                                              November 22, 1933

                        Memorandum for Dr. Tugwell

Dear Dr. Tugwell:

        Attached are copies of the report of the inter-departmental
committee with regard to the removal of land from cultivation as
submitted to Secretary Ickes on August 31, together with copy of the
report of the Department of Agriculture on uneconomic farming
submitted to and approved by the Executive Council on October 17, 1933.

        You will note the report of the inter-departmental committee
states on page 1:

        "that the following types of projects may add to the productive
        capacity of the country:

        1.   New irrigation projects which will result in increase of
             productive land areas.

        2.   Expansion of existing projects of these types.

        3.   Rehabilitation of any project of these types on a scale
             sufficient to bring its productive capacity beyond its
             highest point during the past ten years."

Further on page 2 of its report, the committee recommends:

"that if any project of any of the types mentioned above is approved
by the Public Works Administrator and an allotment made for its

accomplishment, an offsetting allotment should be made for funds to take out of production submarginal or other inefficient agricultural lands."

The report of this Department, approved by the Executive Council states:

"As to method, the Department recommends the allocation of dollar for dollar to the proposed Land Management Company from the Public Works Fund."

These reports together indicate:

1. That not merely new projects, but projects involving extension of existing projects or material rehabilitation of existing projects are to be included, and

2. That in attempting to carry through the measurement of increased production, each dollar spent on such expansion of agricultural productivity should be matched by corresponding dollar allotment for land withdrawal.

Sincerely yours,

Mordecai Ezekiel,
Economic Adviser,
Office of the Secretary.

Enclosures (2)

P.S. Since these are file copies, I would like to ask that you return them when you have finished with them. M.E.

UNITED STATES DEPARTMENT OF AGRICULTURE
Office of the Secretary
Washington

REPORT ON UNECONOMIC FARMING
to the EXECUTIVE COUNCIL
October 17, 1933

The policy of withdrawing lands undesirable for agricultural use as rapidly as more desirable ones are brought in has progressed by now to the point of general acceptance. It remains merely to work out the method of withdrawal, the purposes to which the lands may be devoted, and the best organization for management.

As to method, the Department recommends the allocation of dollar for dollar to the proposed Land Management Company from the Public Works Fund.

As to purposes, the Department sees two general possibilities: the acquisition and transfer to other operating agencies of the government of suitable tracts; and the holding, for management purposes, of all lands acquired which are not suitable for such transfer.

As to organization, the Department recommends the choice by the Secretaries of Agriculture and the Interior of a third person who, with the,(sic) will form the directorate of the Company, and who will act as its active President.

It is the Department's opinion that this will prove a most useful and flexible mechanism. There are many purposes to be served beside that of simply withdrawing land. The Land Management Company can act in many capacities to serve these other interests. It is desired, for instance, in the soil erosion campaign, to withdraw from the possibility of private use a certain proportion of the land in each area. At the same time the people in those areas ought not to be disturbed, unless voluntarily. Here the homestead gardens ought to come in to furnish the alternative to starvation farming. The Land Management Company could be used both to provide land for the homestead gardens and to acquire and manage the eroded lands. If these happened to be within a forest area, they could be transferred to the Forest Service--or to some other operating service requiring more land. But if none were available, as would often be the case, the Corporation could retain the responsibility and continue their management in accord with national policy.

It is anticipated, however, that although the problem is, in the first instance, merely the removal of land to reduce the surpluses of agriculture, some other purpose could usually be served. Those which occur to us at once as furnishing areas to be designated immediately as preferred acquisition projects are:

1.   Lands within the area of the proposed shelter belt forest.

2.   Lands for expansion of the more crowded Indian reservations.

3.   Lands in the selenium area now being surveyed.

4.   Lands in the erosion control projects now being set up.

5. Lands in the Tennessee Valley needed for public purposes.

6. Lands for homestead gardens for others adjacent thereto which might be used for common purposes such as forest or grazing land.

It is perhaps too early to speak of the possible contribution of this Land Management Company to permanent agricultural planning. Yet it is easily seen that the contribution might be considerable. There is need to reduce our crop acreage by from 50 to 75 millions of acres and to put it under such control that a slight rise in prices will not bring it in again. Meantime it can be managed so that when and if it should be needed it will be at once available and in arable condition. The Company has therefore the possibility of becoming one of those balancing mechanisms which our economy so badly needs. It will doubtless be found wise, as time goes on, to withdraw much more land than is contemplated in this present matching program. In anticipation of this, the Company suggested here should be regarded as a permanent organization.

UNITED STATES DEPARTMENT OF AGRICULTURE
Bureau of Agricultural Economics
Washington, D.C.

July 26, 1933.

MEMORANDUM TO THE SECRETARY

Re Maps and Recommendations Relating to Sub-Marginal Lands
(Through Mr. Olsen)

Dear Mr. Secretary:

We are sending herewith three maps and a sheet of recommendations relating to submarginal lands. The three maps are as follows:

1. Natural Land Use Areas of the United States, in which the areas having notable problems of land utilization are shown in colors. An explanation is attached to this map.

2. Value of Farm Real Estate Per Acre by Counties, 1930. Much of the land in the value group of $10-$25 per acre is submarginal, and some of the land in the counties having a higher average value per acre. These low value lands in the

portion of the United States having sufficient rainfall for crop production are found mostly in the South, in the Appalachian and Ozark Mountain areas, and in the drier parts of the Great Plains region.

On this map there has been indicated also, by colors, serious erosion in areas of high grade farming land, and, separately, areas of wind erosion.

A slip giving further comment on this map is attached to the map.

3. A Soil Erosion Map, supplied by Mr. Bennett, of the Bureau of Chemistry and Soils. This is a copy of a larger map, the drafting of which is not completed. It will be noted that about 20 percent of the land area of the United States is undergoing serious erosion over cultivated and overgrazed areas. The major areas of serious erosion are located as follows:

(1) The Piedmont of Virginia, the Carolinas, Georgia and Alabama, extending onto the Coastal Plain of Mississippi and into the valleys of Tennessee.

(2) The Coastal Plain of Arkansas, Louisiana, outside the Delta, and eastern Texas, extending onto the higher lands of north central Texas and central Oklahoma.

(3) The Ohio River Valley.

(4) The Lower Missouri and Upper Mississippi river valleys.

(5) The Columbia Plateau of eastern Washington and Oregon.

Harmful erosion is widespread in the Appalachian and Ozark regions and in much of the Northern Great Plains.

Sincerely yours,

L. C. Gray,
Principal Economist in Charge,
Division of Land Economics

<u>MEMORANDUM REGARDING POLICY FOR POOR FARMING AREAS</u>

A policy for poor (submarginal) farm land should be developed not merely with reference to its relation to price control, but also to (a) stabilization of local economic life, (b) conservation of natural resources, (c) an improved grouping of population to reduce undue costs of local government, and (d) removal of necessity for providing recurringly for relief through seed loans and other subsidies.

The removal of submarginal land from cultivation implies an outlet for the present occupants by removal to better farm lands, by industrial employment, or by a combination of industrial employment with farm residence. The prospect of continued extensive unemployment would remove the last two possibilities and suggest the desirability of going slowly in the elimination of submarginal lands from cultivation, even though they provide only a subsistence standard of living, except in so far as removal of population to better farming areas is feasible.

The following program is proposed for consideration:

1. Authorize expenditure during the present fiscal year of $25,000,000 and of $50,000,000 a year for the subsequent ten years for the following purposes:

    (a) To determine what agricultural areas should be diverted to other uses in the general public interest, including areas now tax delinquent, idle farm lands, and abandoned farm areas.

    (b) To acquire such lands by outright purchase or arrange with local taxing agencies for their acquisition without cost, either for State or Federal ownership.

    (c) To determine the proper use or disposition to be made of such lands.

    (d) To facilitate the removal of present occupants of poor farm lands to other locations.

    (e) To encourage the States to make the necessary institutional and fiscal adjustments in areas where it is proposed to divert farm land to other uses.

    (f) Discourage the settlement or resettlement of poor

farm lands not publicly acquired, collaborating with the States in the application of the policy of zoning such lands. (It may be found necessary to license land settlement concerns.)

2. Establish a Committee on Land Policies under the chairmanship of an assistant Secretary of Agriculture and composed of representatives from each of the major bureaus within and without the Department having a primary interest in land policy. The function of this Committee would be the making of recommendations with reference to policies in the carrying out of the program to the various Federal bureaus and agencies concerned and to the States. This Committee should urge the establishment in each State of a corresponding responsible agency with which to collaborate in the carrying out of the program.

3. Establish a land classification Board of three to five technical men in the United States Department of Agriculture properly staffed for taking account not only of physical conditions but also economic considerations and consequences of removing poor farm land from cultivation. The Board should enlist the collaborations of the various Bureaus of the Department in supplying the necessary physical and economic data. The Board should be authorized to allot funds to the several Bureaus for these services or after the first year to recommend special appropriations for their services. It should also be authorized to cooperate with State Experiment Stations and other State institutions. The Board should bring major questions of policy to the attention of the Land Policy Committee, but should be directly responsible to the Secretary of Agriculture in carrying out the work of land classification.

For one who wishes to understand the extensive, and sometimes overlapping, efforts during 1933 and subsequently, to further the adjustment of land to its best uses, and to make provision for the people displaced in this process there are two reports which may be consulted in the National Archives. Neither is available in printed form. One was prepared in 1934 by the National Resources Board (on which I sat for the Secretary).[9] This report of 36 pages was a summary of past attempts at planning and adjustment and a survey of those at that time going

[9]Bulletin A-3 "National Land Planning Activities," National Resources Board, July 1934. The copy I have consulted was transmitted to my assistant F. P. Bartlett and was found in his file in the Archives.

forward. I quote some paragraphs of its preliminary historical section:

The agricultural depression of the last five years has had the effect of concentrating public attention upon the desirability of large scale land planning. The thesis that the depression can be traced back directly to the maladjustment between the land used for agricultural purposes and the land used for other purposes has found wide acceptance. The continued settlement of the land without plan would obviously only aggravate this maladjustment. Thus, the need for an appraisal of present land uses and the formation of a plan of future development became an immediate necessity.

Growing out of the experience with the preparation of the book entitled "What about the year 2000," a semi-official activity was developed towards the land problem. In November, 1931, a National Land Use Conference was summoned at the instance of the Secretary of Agriculture to meet in Chicago for the purpose of considering land problems. Some three hundred delegates, representing a wide variety of public and private agencies concerned with land problems, attended this Conference.

As a result of the deliberations of the Conference, two committees were established, one dealing with land use problems and the other to act in an advisory capacity, whose chief function would be to educate public opinion upon the seriousness of the problem. The first committee was known as the National Land Use Committee, the second as the National Advisory and Legislative Committee on Land Use.

During the next two years, that is, from November, 1931 to November 1933, these two committees undertook a number of studies on various problems of land use which were important in crystalizing thought on the subject. The results of these studies were published in a series of pamphlets.

With the coming of the new Administration on March 4, 1933, the movement was given new impetus. The National Planning Board was established in Public

Works Administration, charged with the duty, among other things, of preparing a plan for a plan of national development. To aid in this undertaking, the Board suggested to the Secretaries of Agriculture and Interior the appointment of a joint committee to deal with land problems, known as the Land Planning Committee. Many of the members of this Committee had also served on the National Land Use Committee and were familiar with its studies and their results. Consequently, although there was a change in organization, the movement went forward without interruption.

The Science Advisory Board was established by Executive Order of July 31, 1933, charged with the duty of aiding the organization of the Federal Agencies with technical scientific advice. At once it set up a Land Use Committee to cooperate with the National Planning Board upon the specific scientific problems that were arising in the field of land planning.

The Agricultural Adjustment Administration in the meantime had been established in the Department of Agriculture to carry out the agricultural program of the New Deal. Within its organization a section was devoted to land policy whose work coordinated with that of the Land Planning Committee of the National Planning Board.

Before the end of 1933, a program for the retirement of submarginal agricultural land was launched. To this end the Surplus Relief Corporation, a subsidiary of the Federal Emergency Relief Administration, was allotted $25,000,000 from Public Works funds, for the purpose of acquiring, through purchase, submarginal agricultural areas in various parts of the country.

Such of these areas might be used for public purposes were to be turned over to the appropriate Governmental Agency for administration. A submarginal land committee was set up to pass upon the lands to be purchased, working in cooperation with the Land Planning Committee of the National Planning Board.

On April 28, 1934, a Cabinet Committee was created by Executive Order to coordinate the work of all the Federal Land Planning Agencies. However, after a short period of two months, it was abolished on June 30th without having had time to achieve any practical results.

The National Resources Board, established on that date, superseded both the Cabinet Committee on National Land Problems and the National Planning Board, combining in a single committee the personnel of both boards. It was charged with the duty of evolving a plan for the development of national resources, to be submitted to the President on or before December 1, 1934.

Thus, the movement to which so many have contributed in the gathering of scientific data over period of half a century, now will culminate in a definite report to the President, specifying in detail a future course of development for the nation's resources.

The other especially useful report I have mentioned was not made until 1941. It was then done for the Soil Conservation Service.[10] I reproduce its first pages not only because it summarizes the various activities under way but also because it furnishes useful references to previous reports, such, for instance, as the Cornell bulletins referring to the work in Tompkins County:

CHRONOLOGY OF THE LAND UTILIZATION PROGRAM

Including Factors Leading up to Its Establishment, Agencies Conducting Program at Various Times, Authorities, and the Broader Policies Adopted

A. FACTORS LEADING UP TO THE ESTABLISHMENT OF THE PROGRAM

1. The Problem Indicated by Research and Reports

---

[10]Report of the Land Utilization Program by Philip K. Hooker. My copy is one photostated for me in the Archives from the files of the Soil Conservation Service. It was never, I believe, printed.

The basic ideas of the Land Utilization Program grew out of research work in the Bureau of Agricultural Economics of the Department of Agriculture and in a number of state universities and experiment stations, principally Wisconsin and Cornell.[11] Congress recognized the growing need for something to be done about the problem of submarginal land, when, in passing the Agricultural Marketing Act of June 15, 1929, it conferred upon the Federal Farm Board as one of its special powers, authority "to make investigations and reports and publish the same, including investigations and reports on the following: Land Utilization for agricultural purposes; reduction of the acreage of unprofitable marginal lands in cultivation;..."

Special emphasis was also given to the need for a Federal program of land utilization by the National Conference on Land Utilization held in Chicago in November 1931[12] and by the Land Planning Committee of the National Resources Board which proposed, in its report to the Board of November 15, 1934, the retirement of 75,345,000 acres of "land where physical and

[11]For a comprehensive list of reports on such work see "Bibliography on Land Utilization, 1918-36"--U.S.D.A. Misc. Pub. No. 284, January 1938.

There follows reference to a few of the earlier and more outstanding publications on land utilization as related to submarginal areas:
"Tax Delinquency in Northern Wisconsin" (Wisc.Exp.Sta.Bul.399) by B. H. Hibbard, John Swenhart, W. A. Hartman and B. W. Allin, 1928.
"Use and Taxation of Land in Lincoln County, Wisconsin" (Wisc.Exp.Sta.Bul.406) by W. A. Hartman and W. N. Sparhawk, 1929.
"The Utilization of Marginal Lands" (Cornell Exp.Sta.Bul.476) by William Allen, May 1929.
"Abandoned Farm Areas in New York" (Cornell Exp.Sta.Bul.490) by Lawrence M. Vaughn, July 1929.
"Land Utilization in Laurel County, Kentucky" (U.S.D.A. Tech.Bul.289) by C. F. Clayton and W. D. Nichols, March 1932.
"Economic Utilization of Marginal Lands in Nicolas and Webster Counties, West Virginia" (U.S.D.A. Tech.Bul.303) by Millard Peck, Bernard Frank, and Paul A. Eke, May 1932.
"Georgia Land Use Problems" (Georgia Exp.Sta.Bul.191) by W. A. Hartman and H. H. Wooten, May 1935.
"Land Utilization as a basis of Rural Economic Organization" (Vermont Exp.Sta.Bul. 357) by C. F. Clayton and L. J. Peet, June 1933.

[12]See "Proceedings of the National Conference on Land Utilization-- Chicago, Ill. Nov. 19-21, 1931." U.S. Government Printing Office, 1932.

economic conditions are so unfavorable that the land should be retired from arable farming and devoted to other uses." This acreage, involving 454,000 farms, was stated to comprise 20,163,000 acres, or 27 percent, crop land; 34,883,000 acres, or 47 percent, pasture land; and 20,298,000, acres of "other land" in farms--woodland, farmsteads, etc. The total value of these farms was estimated to be $682,909,000. Later refinements of these estimates made by the Bureau of Agricultural Economics indicate that the land which should be so retired is in excess of 86,000,000 acres.

2. Initial Attempts to Start a Federal Action Program

Proposal to Offset Increased Production from New Reclamation Activities by Purchase and Retirement of Submarginal Farm Lands

On August 31, 1933, there was submitted to Harold L. Ickes, Secretary of the Department of the Interior, by a joint committee of six, representing the Department of Agriculture and the Department of the Interior, a report formulating a "Declaration of policy with regard to the removal of lands from cultivation to an extent offsetting the increase in production areas resulting from the construction of irrigation projects." This committee was composed of the following members: M. A. Schurr, Thomas C. Havell, John F. Deeds of the Department of the Interior, and M. L. Wilson, Lewis C. Gray, and Mordecai Ezekiel of the Department of Agriculture.

This committee recommended that, for each of the following types of projects approved by the Public Works Administrator with allotments for their accomplishment, "an offsetting allotment should be made for funds to take out of production sub-marginal or other inefficient agricultural lands to an extent sufficient to offset the net increased production which it is estimated will be provided by the project approved":

"1. New irrigation, drainage, subsistence homesteads, and other projects which will result in increase of productive land areas.

2. Expansion of existing projects of these types.

3. Rehabilitation of any project of these types on a scale sufficient to bring its productive capacity beyond its

highest point during the past ten years."

Consideration Given to a Land Management Corporation

A news release appearing in the Minneapolis (Minn.) Journal of November 25, 1933, indicated that consideration was being given at that time to the establishment of "a land management corporation to carry out President Roosevelt's policy to return nonproductive land to the public domain." It was proposed, according to the news item mentioned, that the corporation would "'lease, rent, or buy outright'...so called 'marginal or submarginal' areas which the President, announcing his public land policy..., said would be taken out of cultivation as fast as good new land was brought in by drainage or irrigation projects." The item mentioned the substitution of "vast grazing preserves and similar projects...for bad land on which farming has led to poverty, debt and low standards of living." It was further stated that "Work is planned on bad lands in reforestation, erosion control and conservation of water supply. To avoid adding to crop surpluses,...lands would be sown with non-competing, soil-protecting crops, such as grass." Secretary Wallace was quoted as saying, "In changing our pattern of basic crop production, we have set upon a process which might lead in time to rational resettlement in America." This corporation was never formed.

B.   THE FIRST FUNDS FOR SUBMARGINAL LAND PURCHASE ALLOTTED TO FEDERAL SURPLUS RELIEF CORPORATION

The Land Utilization Program may be said to have begun concretely on December 28, 1933, because on that date the social board for public works adopted the following resolution: "WHEREAS the President has directed that a certain program be of projects of public works of the Surplus Relief Corporation be included in the comprehensive program and that allotment and transfer of the sum of $25,000,000 be made to said Corporation to finance the accomplishment of said projects:"

"Resolved, that the Administrator and this Board include said program of projects in the comprehensive program and allot and transfer the sum of $25,000,000 to the Surplus Relief Corporation to finance the accomplishment thereof."

This allotment, made from funds appropriated by the Fourth Deficiency Act, fiscal year 1933, for the purpose of carrying into effect the provisions of the National Industrial Recovery Act, represented the first funds ever made available specifically for the purchase of submarginal farm lands.

C. CONSIDER AMENDING AGRICULTURAL ADJUSTMENT ACT

Early in February 1934 consideration was given to the desirability of amending the Agricultural Adjustment Act so as to permit the Agricultural Administration to enter into a long-time adjustment program, including the acquisition of submarginal lands and other measures to maintain a proper balance between agricultural production in various areas, and present and prospective demands for various agricultural products. While the AAA was never given authority actually to acquire submarginal farm lands, it will be indicated in succeeding paragraphs that that Administration did play an important part in the early conduct of the LU program.

D. PROGRAM UNDER FEDERAL EMERGENCY RELIEF AND AGRICULTURAL ADJUSTMENT ADMINISTRATIONS

1. Funds Transferred from FSRC to FERA

On February 28, 1934, the Special Board for Public Works, having "found that the Federal Emergency Relief Administration is a more convenient agency to receive such transfer," referring to the $25,000,000 mentioned in the resolution of December 28, 1933, resolved that that previous resolution "be now reconsidered, and, reconsideration having been had, resolved further that the Administrator and this Board include in the comprehensive program of public works the program of projects more particularly described in the resolution of the Board of Directors of the Federal Surplus Relief Corporation, dated January 13, 1934, and allot and transfer the sum of $25,000,000 to the Federal Emergency Relief Administration to finance the accomplishment thereof."

2. Early Policies and Procedures

As Stated in FSRC Resolution of January 13, 1934

The "program of projects" described in the January 13, 1934, resolution of the Board of Directors of the FSRC indicated "that the factors of consideration in the purchase of new land shall be:

1. That the lands purchased shall be such as in general fall under subsection (c) of Section 202 of N.I.R.A. in that they shall be lands of the character heretofore purchased by the State of New York under the program developed by Governor Roosevelt for the withdrawal of submarginal lands from cultivation.

2. That they shall be lands that in total amount balance against the lands, the reclamation or improvement of which has been provided for under the comprehensive program of public works on condition that counterbalancing lands be withdrawn from cultivation.

3. That they shall be lands which are now in cultivation, producing agricultural crops at a rate of production which the Department of Agriculture specifies as submarginal, that is, giving a return that is less than is to be properly expected from the labor expended with the result that the owners remain impoverished while working with them.

4. That they shall be lands available for or suitable for development of forests, or as parts or recreation spaces, or as grazing ranges, or as bird or game refuges or as additions to Indian reservations or such that their development through planting of forests and ground cover will serve as a protection against soil erosion or for other specific public works and benefits to the people of the United States.

5. That it shall be possible to work out a definite plan of resettlement or employment of the population at present living on such lands so that

they may not become stranded or transient.

Every project accepted under this program shall meet the conditions specified in the five points mentioned above. The method of operation shall be the following:

Projects will be presented through any interested department, bureau, or section, such as the Indian Service, Biological Survey, Relief Administration or otherwise. They will be examined by the several governmental departments concerned to determine whether or not they can be handled in full satisfaction of each of the five points specified above.

It is the intention to turn the land over to a federal department for its operation for the purpose to which it is best adapted--forests, range or park--these in charge of Forestry Service, Indian Office or Park Service, and so on. The purchase of the land shall be considered the first step in the whole public works program involved and a definite plan of these continuing public works shall be provided and approved by the Board of Directors of the Corporation at the time the purchase is authorized. This plan shall indicate the type of specific public works activities that will be carried forward after purchase of the land. It is to be specific as to the type of planting, such as forest or ground cover for erosion control, and as to the use, such as range on the public domain or for Indian reservations. Land is not to be purchased the improvement of which does not all (sic) within the comprehensive program of public works as indicated above."

As Stated in Press Release of April 10, 1934

A statement outlining the program was released to the press April 10, 1934. The following quotation from that release is significant for two reasons: (1) because it indicates broadly the types of projects contemplated, and (2) because it reveals that in first conceiving the program, the close interrelation of land purchase and resettlement activities was clearly recognized--a fact that seemed later on to be lost sight of by some by virtue of the fact that responsibility for the two activities was divided in such a manner that to this day it has not been found possible to witness generally realization of land purchase and resettlement activities proceeding concurrently and concertedly. The quotation: "The plan is to set up submarginal land acquisition projects in regions, first of all, where local relief problems are most acute. But before any project is set up, or any land bought, it is imperative that acceptable plans be devised for the resettlement of the present occupants of that land, that the present occupants be given ample opportunity to approve or disapprove such plans, and that the project proceed only with the assured cooperation of the settlers and of local and state agencies."

"Those who wish to present plans for a submarginal land acquisition project, therefore, must be prepared to satisfy the Federal Government on these four points:

1. That the project includes land now used for agricultural purposes but which normally does not yield sufficient income to provide reasonably adequate living conditions for the occupants thereof.

2. That there can be a satisfactory public use for acquired land such as for forests, grazing areas, parks, recreation areas, bird or game refuges, soil stabilization, etc.

3. That the settlers now on the land will cooperate, voluntarily, in the necessary resettlement.

4. That the plans for resettlement are adequate in providing new opportunities."

3.   The Submarginal Land Committee and the Land Policy Section of AAA

From the adoption of the February 28, 1934, resolution by the Special Board for Public Works until early in July of that year, the conduct of the program was the general responsibility of the Submarginal Land Committee and the Directors of the FSRC. The Departments of Agriculture and of the Interior, the FERA, and the FSRC were all represented on the Submarginal Land Committee. Mr. Jacob Baker of the FSRC, as Chairman of the Submarginal Land Committee, was made directly responsible for the program. The planning of projects was the responsibility of the following technical agencies, depending upon the type of project involved:

Agricultural Projects

Land Policy Section, Division of Program Planning, Agricultural Adjustment Administration.

Recreational Projects

National Park Service, Department of the Interior

Indian Lands Projects

Office of Indian Affairs, Department of the Interior

The nine regional directors of the Land Policy Section of the AAA were made the regional representatives of the FERA. As to the functions of the regional representatives, Mr. Baker made the following official statement: "The Regional Representatives will serve as the coordinating medium through which all submarginal land projects in states embraced by their respective regions will be routed. Their function will be to bring the several interested agencies of the State into cooperative activity in submarginal land acquisition and to provide for the resettlement and rehabilitation of families at present occupying submarginal land acquired; the recommendation of project managers for specific projects within the states and in general the supervision of the development of the submarginal land acquisition program in the states within their several regions."

The following quotations from the minutes of a meeting of the Submarginal Land Committee, held April 16, 1934, are also significant: "It was the general understanding that the Regional Representatives would be on the payroll of the AAA, that they would give immediate priority of attention to the submarginal land program, and that such Regional Representatives would be not only agricultural technicians but men qualified to understand the social problems of relief and resettlement of population, and to represent without departmental bias the submarginal land program agreed upon by the Department of the Interior, the Department of Agriculture, the Federal Emergency Relief

Administration and the Federal Surplus Relief Corporation."

"It was further agreed upon that the Project Directors would be held responsible for the planning, execution, resettlement, and public cooperation attendant upon the setting up of individual projects."

It was pointed out at that meeting of the Submarginal Land Committee that State Relief Administrators (FERA) already had complex duties, that their time was limited, and that in order to obtain their cooperation the organization developed to carry out the submarginal land program should not be complicated. It was stated in the minutes in that meeting that "in the light of the above stated necessity for simplicity of organization, the question of expansion of personnel in the Land Division was brought up." Thus early came into the foreground the question of building up a staff in the Land Division of the FSRC to function as a separate administrative unit on submarginal land projects. Although this tendency to building up a staff apart from the technical agencies charged with the duty of organizing and developing projects never came to fruition, it early led to the establishment of a separate legal service and later to the establishment of the nucleus of other services in the Federal Emergency Relief Administration in connection with the Land Program.

4. State Rural Rehabilitation Corporations Given Responsibility for Resettlement of Families

In the late spring of 1934 action was initiated in setting up State Rural Rehabilitation Corporations under the general direction of the FERA, and the specific direction of Col. Lawrence Westbrook, Assistant Adminstrator of the FERA. There was considerable difference of opinion as to the adequacy of such corporations for caring for the resettlement of the families affected by the submarginal land purchases. However, it was finally agreed that, after plans for such resettlement had been made by the technical agencies under the direction of the regional directors of the Land Policy Section and had been agreed to by the State Relief Administrators, the State Rural Rehabilitation Corporations would be responsible, in cooperation with the LPS directors, for actually carrying out such plans.

5. Procedure and Policies Realigned Under "Director of The Land Program"

Director of the Land Program Advises LPS Regional
Directors of the New Procedures

Under the date of July 13, 1934, a letter was sent
to all regional directors of the Land Policy Section by Mr.
J. S. Lansill, who had recently been made Director of the
Land Program. Mr. Lansill's letter expresses so well the
administrative changes and the procedures and policies
adopted at the time that it is being quoted below almost
in full:

"A number of adjustments have been made within
the last few days in the administrative
organization of the Land Program. These
adjustments, the necessity for which has
developed over a period of many weeks, will add
to efficiency.

As you know, the final responsibility for the
expenditure of funds for both land acquisition
and resettlement rests in one individual, Mr.
Harry L. Hopkins, Federal Emergency Relief
Administrator. In order to head up the activities
of the field representatives and the various
technical agencies, Mr. Hopkins has placed me in
charge of the entire land program, including both
land acquisition and resettlement. Heretofore,
this authority rested with the Submarginal Land
Committee and with the Directors of the Federal
Surplus Relief Corporation. Hereafter the Land
Program will function through the Rural
Rehabilitation Division of the Federal Emergency
Relief Administration.

"Briefly, the new set-up can be summarized as
follows:

1. The Regional Representatives of The Land
Program will be charged with full responsibility
for all projects within their respective regions.
This will include the development of detailed
plans for land acquisition and resettlement
projects.

2. Detailed plans of all projects are to be approved, by: First the Regional Representative, Second, by a technical Federal Agency, Third, by the Director of The Land Program, after which orders will be issued through the required channels for expenditures of funds for land acquisition and for resettlement.

3. The use of local corporations for resettlement, as previously contemplated, is now eliminated. Instead, a single state corporation for all present governmental activities of social and economic adjustments will be organized under Colonel Lawrence Westbrook, Assistant Administrator in Charge of Rural Rehabilitation. These corporations will be known as The Rural Rehabilitation Corporation of _____ (State).

I think that everything now is straightened out to the satisfaction of all concerned. It is definitely understood that our Regional Representatives will be fully responsible for the planning of both the land acquistion and resettlement phases of the Land Program. When it comes to the executiion of the plans, these will be accomplished through the State Rehabilitation Corporations, made up of seven directors. Four of these will include the Regional Representative of The Land Program, the Field Representative of the Federal Emergency Relief Administration, the Director of the State Agricultural Extension Service, and the State Relief Administrator. These four will nominate the other three directors. The Regional Representative, as a Director of the State Rural Rehabilitation Corporation, will see that approved plans are carried out in accordance with their stipulations. If any difficulties arise, they can be ironed out here in Washington.

Colonel Westbrook, Dr. Gray, Mr. Clayton, and I are in agreement with this procedure, and we all believe that each project should represent a cooperative effort on the part of Agriculture and the Relief Agencies. This means that when it comes to the preparation of plans for resettlement, you should work very closely with the Relief Administrator and his Assistants, getting from them any help you can. It would also be advisable to secure the approval of your resettlement plan from the Relief Administrator and his Assistants, getting from them any help you can. It would also be advisable to secure the approval of your resettlement plan from the Relief Administrator, and from the State Rural Rehabilitation Corporation. The more closely we cooperate with the Relief organizations, the better it is going to be for all concerned. This does not mean, however, that you are to compromise yourself on any program which is not economically and socially sound.

We propose to give you as much help as is necessary from the standpoint of servicing the various projects in your region. In this connection, you will have the benefit of:

(1) Legal personnel, to clear titles on option

(2) Construction personnel, to aid in the planning of dwellings, etc., for resettlement

(3) Industrial personnel, to provide aid and suggestions for setting up income-producing industrial activities within resettlement areas, to supplement agricultural subsistence

(4) Educational personnel to assist in any publicity and other informational activities necessary for the accomplishment of land purchase or resettlement.

This personnel will be attached to The Land Program, and should be considered as service agencies to be drawn on by you, as your needs require.

*****

"In order to provide prompt attention to matters of policy and procedure in connection with various projects, the following men have been given full immediate responsibility for the planning of projects falling within their respective fields:

Agricultural projects--Land Policy Section of the Agricultural Adjustment Adminstration--C. F. Clayton, in charge

Recreational projects--National Park Service, Department of the Interior, Conrad L. Wirth, in charge

Indian land projects--Office of Indian Affairs, Department of the

Interior, A. C. Monahan, in charge

Wild-life projects--Bureau of Biological Survey of the Department of Agriculture, J. N. Darling, in charge."

Types of Projects and Phases and Objectives of "The Land Program" Outlined by the Director

On July 16, 1934, Mr. Lansill addressed the following memorandum, quoted in full, to the Honorable Harold L. Ickes, Secretary, Department of the Interior:

"Various conferences have been held during the past three months for the purpose of formulating a land acquisition program. Active investigation in the field by the agencies cooperating in The Land Program has led up to the necessity of reconsidering the plan and scope of The Land Program. The necessity for such reconsideration is agreed to by all land-use agencies involved in The Land Program of the Federal Emergency Relief Administration.

"As a result of these conferences in which The President, Secretary of the Interior, Secretary of Agriculture, Federal Emergency Relief Administrator, and the Governor of the Farm Credit Administration have participated, it is understood that the following program of projects will be carried out, under the authority of the Federal Emergency Relief Administration, to expend funds for these purposes.

A. Projects will be of the following major types:

(1) Demonstrational agricultural projects: These include projects in which the major use (or combination of uses) of land to be purchased, includes farming, forestry or other uses falling within the administrative jurisdiction of the Department of Agriculture.
(2) Demonstration recreational projects: These include projects in which the land to be purchased is to be used primarily for recreational purposes, as submitted by the National Park Service, Department of Interior.
(3) Demonstration Indian Lands projects: These include projects in which land to be purchased is to be used

primarily for the benefit of the Indians, under the jurisdiction of the Bureau of Indian Affairs, Department of the Interior.

(4) Demonstration Wild-Life projects: These include projects in which land to be purchased is to be used primarily to carry out the Wild-Life Program of the Biological Survey, of the Department of Agriculture.

(5) Other demonstrative projects: These will include projects which may be suggested by authorized Federal or State agencies not above named.[13]

B. The Land Program has three major phases:

(1) The purchase of land.

(2) The conversion of land purchased to a use, beneficial to the people of the United States.

(3) The permanent rehabilitation of the population at present living on land purchased.

C. The objectives of The Land Program will include:

(1) Conversion of poor land to other and more proper uses;

(2) Prevention of the misuse of land by erosion or other causes, and a restoration of land productivity;

(3) Improvement of the economic and social status of families occupying poverty farms;

(4) Improvement of the economic and social status of "industrially stranded population groups," occupying essentially rural areas, including readjustment and rehabilitation of Indian population by acquisition of lands

---

[13]Three projects--one in Wisconsin and two in New York--were established in this category, sponsored by the War Department with the idea of acquiring submarginal farm land and, after developing it partially for multiple use, including forestry, recreation, and wildlife, to make the lands available to the War Department as additions to existing reservations.

to enable them to make appropriate and constructively planned use of combined land areas in units suited to their needs;

(5) Reducing the costs of local governments and of local public institutions and services;

(6) Encouragement of land-use planning by setting up experimental projects which will serve as repeatable demonstrations of types of adjustments applicable to various regions in the United States.

D. In general, it is understood that whenever land is being misused or whenever land may be put to a different and more beneficial use, such land may be acquired under The Land Program of the Federal Emergency Relief Administration."

6. Special Board for Public Works Accepts Program of Projects Outlined by Director of The Land Program

Recognizing the desirability of the program of projects outlined in Mr. Lansill's memorandum, the Special Board for Public Works, on July 18, 1934, adopted the following resolution:

"Whereas the Administrator and this Board on February 28, 1934, adopted a resolution allotting and transferring $25,000,000 to the Federal Emergency Relief Administration to finance a program of projects described in a resolution of the Board of Directors of the Federal Surplus Corporation dated January 13, 1934; and

"Whereas it now appears that the said program of projects should be revised by substituting therefore the program of projects set forth in a memorandum to the Administrator dated July 16, 1934, signed John S. Lansill, Director, Land Program, Federal Emergency Relief Administration;

"Resolved that the Administrator and this Board amend said resolution of February 28, 1934, by substituting that program of projects described in said memorandum of the Director of the Land Program, dated July 16, 1934, for the program described in said resolution of the Board of Directors of the Surplus Relief Corporation, include the

> substituted program in the comprehensive program of
> public works, and allot and transfer to finance the
> accomplishment thereof the unexpended balance of the
> said sum of $25,000,000 allotted and transferred by said
> resolution of February 28, 1934."

Great trouble was experienced in the early stages of the land buying program, not so much in finding what land to buy, because much of this planning had been done by various agencies in the Departments of Agriculture and Interior, but simply in the mechanical work of title clearance. This was done in the Department of Justice by a division which was understaff and lethargic. Until it was completely reorganized and greatly enlarged it formed an insurmountable barrier to progress. Then, of course, when the land had been acquired, it was necessary to place it in some agency which would make the best possible use of it. And this, too, was no small undertaking.

By the time Resettlement was organized, I had had enough experience with our early uncoordinated efforts to understand that we must draw all these efforts together. As we planned submarginal land retirement it must be done also with a view to its further use for another purpose--forests, wild-life, recreation, etc., and with some notion of who was to administer it--state park or forest services, for instance. Also there must have been previously the preparation of new homes for the displaced people.

That this was not so simple an approach as the early idea of merely purchasing poor land and retiring it from production will be seen. In fact the program had little chance of succeeding unless it could be approached as a long-run effort. The simultaneous rehabilitation of land and people became a matter dear to the heart of numbers of us. But we were not to be granted the time or the suspension of judgment essential to its carrying out.

During 1933 and 1934 we were gradually approaching the synthesis represented by Resettlement. It is not, even then, being very well received. There were those, like Irving Brant, who did understand; but there were others--many of them--to whom this seemed another convenient stick with which to beat the New Deal. It was more of the "do-gooding" so hated by the reactionaries.

On 28 February 1934 The New York Herald Tribune published an informative dispatch recording the President's approval of our plans.

Roosevelt Approves Program for Marginal Land Purchase

First steps in the program for retiring poor agricultural lands from production were taken today by the Administration as President

Roosevelt approved plans prepared by three divisions of the government.

The Department of Agriculture, Interior Department and the Federal Surplus Relief Corporation were told to proceed with the program for which $25,000,000 already has been provided from public works funds. Between 3,000,000 and 5,000,000 acres will be taken first. The total area of submarginal lands has been estimated at 124,000,000 to 140,000,000 acres.

What parts of the country will receive first consideration has not yet been decided. Rexford G. Tugwell, Assistant Secretary of Agriculture, who has devoted considerable time to the land program, has mentioned parts of the Appalachian highlands, the Piedmont plateau and parts of the great plains regions near the Western Great Lakes as the most likely areas.

The President's approval covered both the immediate plans of the land-planning group and the long-range proposal which seeks to replace the present emergency program of land rental with outright purchase and conversion of the areas to use in erosion control, wild-life preserves and sanctuaries, national parks and timber growing.

Agriculture officials said sufficient funds were available to buy lands and transfer people living on them to other areas for at least a year. They expressed belief that other money would be available when needed.

The procedure to be followed will be initiated by the relief corporation. Persons living on the land will be offered several alternatives, all of which will be more attractive than the prospect of continuing to raise barely enough to eat, administration officials said.

Some of these alternatives will be transferred to subsistence homesteads where part-time employment can be obtained, or acting as caretakers for wild game areas where part of the land may be used for raising food.

When decision has been reached on transferring families, the land will be purchased and work of restoring it to a wild or semi-wild state according to the use to be made of it, will be begun by the Civilian Conservation Corps and other agencies.

The government will undertake the actual moving of families and their goods from the areas with available funds.

Somewhat earlier--30 December 1933--an editorial in The St. Louis Star Times had attempted to place the program in perspective. In sending the editorial to me Mr. Irving Brant, the editor, said: "Enclosed is an editorial on your Philadelphia address on Land Control. It was written just after I had listened to a satiric attack upon you at a Chamber of Commerce meeting, by somebody who at the same time was eulogizing President Roosevelt, so I thought it might be well to deal indirectly with that, via the land theme."

LAND CONTROL

Professor Tugwell, assistant secreatary of agriculture, predicts in an address before the American Economic Association that the time is approaching when the federal government will control the use of all land in the United States, deciding whether it is to be used for farming or for some other purpose--public forests, parks, game preserves, grazing ranges, recreation centers, etc.

A great many people, on reading the news account of Mr. Tugwell's speech, will reach a conclusion somewhat as follows:

"Mr. Tugwell is a college professor.

"Mr. Tugwell is a member of the President's 'Brain Trust.'(sic)

"This is one more example of the professor in politics. Mr. Roosevelt should steer clear of these 'Brain Trusters.' They are leading the country into socialism."

The truth of the matter is that Professor Tugwell has described, in national terms, the land-planning policy begun by Franklin D. Roosevelt as governor of New York.

Government control of the use of land has been a Roosevelt idea for years. As a governor he was for state control. As President he is for national control.

In view of the effort that will be made to put the "Brain Trust" tag on this important proposal, it may be worthwhile to record some of the evidence that this policy has long been in Mr. Roosevelt's mind.

In April, 1932, Mr.Roosevelt delivered an address containing this sentence:

> "I favor economic planning, not for this period alone but
> for our needs for a long time to come."

Commenting on that statement, The St. Louis Star said
editorially that it separated Mr. Roosevelt from the "leave things alone"
political school to which Mr. Hoover belonged, but did not necessarily
separate him from the school of thought typified by Owen D. Young, who
believed in a planned economy for the benefit of Big Business.

Mr. Roosevelt then wrote to The Star, sending several pamphlets
to show whom he would help through economic planning. One of them,
devoted to his farm policies, told of his land-planning program for New
York State and contained this statement about a statewide soil survey:

> "It reveals that thousands of acres that have been used for
> farms should be returned to forest and the state is
> following up this knowledge by a program under which
> a million acres will be retired from competition with good
> farming land and will be used instead of growing trees."

Referring to that statement, Governor Roosevelt said in his letter
to his newspaper:

> "After all, this state with its large urban populations is in
> a way a small cross-section of the country."

That furnishes complete evidence that the national program of
land control outlined by Professor Tugwell at Philadelphia this week was
in Mr. Roosevelt's brain when he made his statement, in April, 1932, that
he favored permanent economic planning for the United States. So
Professor Tugwell spoke at Philadelphia, not as a Columbia University
professor expounding dangerous professorial ideas, but as a spokesman
for and sharer of the long-held idea of the President.

An idea is an idea, no matter who holds it. If national land
control is to be condemned as dangerous, unnecessary or socialistic
coming from a member of the "Brain Trust," it is equally so coming from
the chief executive. But it doesn't seem the same. It is harder to attack
the ideas of Mr. Roosevelt than of a Columbia professor.

What is the chance that this policy will be put into effect?
Considered apart from the crisis in farming, it would be a slight chance

indeed. The need for more forests, the value of recreation grounds, game preserves, etc., would be met by a slow and haphazard increase of lands so utilized, rather than a wholesale planned withdrawal of lands unsuitable for agriculture.

But we have a situation in which crop acreage reduction is being forced upon the country. Within the past week, the forecast has been made that Europe will soon be self-sustaining in food production. Foreign food markets are gone, and gone forever. Chronic over-production of food in the United States means chronic money poverty on the farms and industrial breakdowns in the cities. The present emergency system of control, paying farmers not to plant good land, is idiotic as a permanent method.

So whether we want it or not, national land control is going to be forced onto the country. If it doesn't come in the Roosevelt administration, it will come later, after another and worse depression. All it involves, really, is systematic land purchase and management by the government. That can be pursued, as a positive course, without any compulsion whatever. Those who would rather work poor land than sell to the government could do so. Carried out on a large enough scale to cope effectually with agricultural over-production, the cost would be tremendous. However, the absence of such control cost the farmers along $7,000,000,000 in 1933, which is a pretty penny in itself.

On 3 March matters had progressed so far that I sent the President a handwritten communication as follows:

United States Department of Agriculture
Office of the Assistant Secretary

March 3, 1934

My dear Mr. President

What very few people seem to realize about this land program we have been trying to straighten out lately is that the important consideration is not land but people. This is why Harry, with his knowledge of relief areas, stranded populations, etc. ought to be as important in the picture as Agriculture and Interior. The policy steps as I see them are three--and in this order:

1. The establishment of a real alternative to poverty living--
usually a small farm plus an industrial opportunity.

2. Relocation of the people in a new environment with a
guarantee of subsistence for a period.

3. The acquisition of the land and its incorporation in some
government administrative agency.

Notice that land buying is the third step not the first.

There is rapidly growing up again the traditional fight between
Agriculture and Interior. I think Harry could mediate and do it well if he
were to head a policy committee similar to the one you set up on
commercial policy.[14]

I am leaving this morning for Puerto Rico. I had a long talk
yesterday with Harry. I am sure you do not know how serious his
financial situation is. He really has not enough money to get by on. He is
trying to devise ways and means, but he ought not to have to think of
such things now. Perhaps I shouldn't worry you with this but I know he
would never tell you, and I thought you ought to know.

As ever,

Rex

This was to support a bill which I had drafted and had carried
around to various of those whose support I wanted. Ickes and Wallace
had both been sympathetic; but there was danger that the program would

---

[14]See File 1017 Hyde Park for August 25, 1934: Letter from Henry Wallace
(undated but probably early in March 1934) to Marvin McIntyre asking the
latter to take up with the President the need for creating a special land
committee composed of representatives from Interior, Agriculture and Federal
Emergency Relief; letter from Harold Ickes to McIntyre, March 8, 1934, saying
that he has read the above letter from Wallace and concurring in his
recommendation; letter from Louis M. Howe, April 30, 1934, advising Harold
Ickes that the President had signed an Executive Order creating the Committee
on National Land Problems on April 28th. Evidently Louis Howe was
mistaken. The Public Papers contain no such Executive Order and the
President's memorandum to Secretary Wallace, which follows on the next page
would substantiate this conclusion, although there is also some indication that
he also had the impression that there was an inter-departmental committee put
to work.

become another item in the old quarrel between Agriculture and Interior. This I wanted to avoid and so suggested the policy committee with Harry Hopkins as it head.

I have not been able to find a copy of this bill. I recall very well, however, a trip to the Hill which several of us undertook in the effort to find support. We had asked Joe Robinson to assemble Pat Harrison, Jack Garner and several others. I thought I could convince them that this was a much sounder and more conservative program than we were currently administering in A.A.A. I was treated pretty badly. These powerful Democrats regarded this as an intolerably idealistic idea. They had no interest in poor farmers because they regarded their failure as their own fault. Nothing could be done with them. They were pretty well out of the way in their rural slums. The thing to do was leave them there. And as to submarginal land--that was a fancy name for useless areas nothing could be done with anyway.

The hard, contemptuous attitude I encountered was convincing. I knew we should get help from the legislative leaders. And what I ought to have done was simply to report this to the President and thereafer leave it alone.

I think I resolved to do this; but unfortunately I did not stick to the resolution. As I recall it now I was stirred up again by the President himself in the Summer of 1934. On 25 August the President sent the following memorandum to Henry Wallace.

August 25, 1934.

MEMORANDUM FOR
THE SECRETARY OF AGRICULTURE

What is the present status of the land acquisition policy about which we have so often talked?

I enclose the last word I have on it--the Director of the Budget's reply to Tugwell's plan of last March.

Is an inter-departmental committee working on it?

If not, I suggest a committee from Agriculture (as such), Forestry, A.A.A., soil erosion, public lands and F.E.R.A.

How does this tie in with the big study of the general subject of land use, public works, etc.?

F.D.R.[15]

The report from Lewis Douglas, referred to above, was, of course, adverse; but it explains the purpose. And evidently it did not discourage the President. But then he had only had my verbal report on Robinson's, Harrison's and Garner's contempt. He had, I think, never discussed the matter with them himself. A photostat copy of the Budget Director's report follows:

BUREAU OF THE BUDGET

Washington

April 3, 1934

MEMORANDUM FOR THE PRESIDENT:

I have the undated letter, received in this office March 5, 1934, which the Acting Secretary of Agriculture, Mr. Tugwell, addressed to you in explanation of legislation proposed by him relative to the establishment and execution of a long-time land policy, including broad studies of land utilization and withdrawal of submarginal land from production.

This proposed new land policy would authorize the Secretary of Agriculture:

1. To develop plans for land utilization, including determination of the best uses of land and may be studies of local government consolidations and reorganizations in cooperation with agencies of the Federal, State and local governments and private organizations.

2. To acquire lands by gift, exchange or lease using Federal appropriations where necessary.

3. To acquire tax-delinquent and other lands in possession of State and local governments or Federal, State or local government credit agencies.

[15]Hyde Park Library, FDRL: 8/18/52 copy; cdm.

4. To provide for the issuance of non-resaleable bonds to a maximum of $500,000,000 at 1-1/2 percentum per annum to mature in 40 years to be exchanged for the kind of lands mentioned in paragraph 3.

This bill would commit the Federal Government to a long-time land policy, the scope and annual cost of which is wholly indeterminate.

The Secretary of Agriculture has, however, indicated on various occasions that dependent upon a policy of economic isolation the nation would have to remove permanently from production 50,000,000 acres of good farm land or 100,000,000 acres of marginal and submarginal land, and that dependent upon a greatly liberalized international trade policy, withdrawals might be reduced to 25,000,000 acres of good farming land or 50,000,000 acres of marginal and submarginal land. Such acreage withdrawal plans, now visioned by sponsors as needing fairly prompt execution, will cost large sums of money.

Under the economic isolation policy, the reduction in good agricultural land, using a price unit as low as $75 per acre, would cost $3,750,000,000, while the reduction in marginal and submarginal land, using a price unit of $5 per acres, would cost $500,000,000. The unit cost of $75 per acre for good land by the time it was condemned and locally appraised would doubtless average $100 per acre and perhaps much higher than that, while the increases in the unit cost of marginal and submarginal lands are almost mercurial in their possibilities. Under the liberalized international trade policy, the cost of the procurement of land, good or marginal, would be reduced fifty per cent.

Incidentally, it might be asked on what basis does one consider two acres of marginal land to be the equivalent of one acre of good land in compassing the questions of land utilization and conservation? Again, if good land is to constitute much the larger withdrawals what is to be done with the marginal and submarginal lands which will then be susceptible to uncontrolled tillage? And further, it might be asked whether the present withholding from production of 43,000,000 acres of farm land at a cost of $750,000,000 per annum, which is the Agricultural Adjustment program now, is to continue beyond 1935 and how far? Also what is to prevent the reopening of these proposed public lands to settlement again just as soon as economic conditions develop the necessary pressures?

Assuming that fifty to one hundred million acres were acquired by the Federal Government and added to the 425,985,920 acres of the present public domain, the Federal Government, instead of owning one-sixth of the country, as it does now, would find itself in possession of more than one-fifth of all the land in the United States and Alaska. The question as to what is to be done with the proposed additional land acquisitions appears to be most perplexing to the Department of Agriculture which is sponsoring this remedial legislation.

In commenting upon the retirement from production of wheat, cotton, tobacco, corn and rice acreage, the Agricultural Adjustment Administration in its recent annual report states that "the removal of forty-odd million acres of land from our total crops area raises puzzling questions as to regional and commodity competition, rotations, replacement crops, use of labor and the like.... Readjustments occasioned by taking land out of production are complicated still further by the human phase of the problem.... Provision must be made to see that the hired laborers and tenants do not bear the full brunt of the adjustment. The problem becomes even more difficult when considering the retirement of large acreages of submarginal land." A study of the literature and newspaper releases prepared by the Department of Agriculture in the last few months indicates clearly that any solution of the nation's land problem is extremely empirical. Until this great problem has received at least some degree of rationalization and until the important and costly experiments now under way by the Soil Erosion Service, Subsistence Homestead Service and the Tennessee Valley Authority begin to prove something, it would seem bad administration to resort further to the United States Treasury.

The proposed legislation provides for the development and effectuation of plans for land utilization--permanent agriculture, grazing, erosion-prevention, parks, forestry, wild life restoration or conservation and other uses. The Federal Government is spending for these general purposes $658,013,996 in 1934 and $370,019,363 in 1935, as per table below:

	1934	1935
Permanent agriculture	$ 47,198,543	$ 36,095,974
Erosion-prevention	3,410,343	9,008,068
(Flood control)	85,990,400	41,509,100
National parks	18,087,700	18,431,200
Forestry and public domain	47,126,914	33,360,858
(Civilian Conservation Camps)	341,705,600	65,190,000
Wild life restoration and conservation	2,307,250	882,450
Other uses:		

(Subsistence homesteads)	9,200,000	15,800,000
(Irrigation projects)	25,709,800	66,753,200
(Rural post roads)	51,000,000	11,000,000
(Tennessee Valley Authority)	26,277,446	71,988,513
TOTAL	$658,013,996	$370,019,363

It is apparently intended that these expenditures, expanded as they are by emergency allotments during these two years, are to become permanent annual appropriations and be probably increased even above the present figures.

In proposing the issuances of $500,000,000 in bonds for the acquisitions of tax-delinquent and foreclosed lands in the possession of Federal, State and local government bodies and affiliated credit agencies, certain obstacles appear. These two classes of farm land will be procurable only in broken lots, and it will be exceedingly difficult in attempting to acquire sufficiently large areas for proper utilization to avoid the dangers that have usually arisen in acquiring national forest lands where homesteads cover the desired tract like the black squares on a checkerboard. Integration and acquisition of lands under such circumstances is very expensive on account of the poor bargaining position in which the Federal Government invariably finds itself. Moreover, tax-delinquent and foreclosed land is largely agricultural in character, and it is not understood what effective use, other than agricultural, could be made of it by the Federal Government once it was acquired, except to give it away again at some future date. This particular proposal would appear to be most difficult and troublesome to administer from whatever angle it is approached. Finally, the proposed exchange of bonds, non-resaleable and bearing only 1-1/2 per cent interest to be amortized in 40 years leaves grave doubt in the mind as to its feasibility, but this aspect of the matter might be referred to the Secretary of the Treasury for his recommendation.

It is noted that a number of additional sheets were attached to Mr. Tugwell's letter and bill, consisting of recommendations by the recently concluded Conservation Conference.

These recommendations would enlarge the expenditures for existing forest and wild life conservation activities by $62,275,000 annually. In view of the immense sums of emergency money being expended during the fiscal years 1934 and 1935, it would seem prudent to revert as quickly as possible to normal expenditure rates since by 1936 a great part of the national forests will have been improved to the point where normal maintenance would be ample to retain the gains made in conserving them by the use of emergency funds.

Summarizing, I wish to say that Mr. Tugwell's proposed bill is so indeterminate as to both scope and cost that it is directly in conflict with the Administration's financial program.

/s/ L. W. Douglas
Director

When the President's August 25th memorandum came to Wallace he suggested, as evidenced by the following photostat copy of a note to Paul H. Applyby, his assistant, that M. L. Wilson and I draft a reply. What happened was that I was deputed to talk with the President about it. It was in this conversation that he suggested the possibility of proceeding with emergency funds rather than asking for legislation. I weakly agreed. And eventually we set Resettlement on its ill-starred course.

7. *Private and Confidential*

I was mixed up in a good many ventures, take it by and large, in 1933 and early 1934. Two of these are mentioned in the surviving memorandum from the President.

They have to do with one matter which never reached accomplishment and with another which proved to be perhaps the most significant--certainly the most permanent--of the New Deal.

I seem not to have any other record of the meetings in which a number of us joined--with Harold M. Stephens, Assistant Attorney General, taking the lead--in attempt to transfer powers of incorporation from the states to the Federal government. I could not have been very useful in the technical phases of this study; but I recall that we produced a voluminous report and a statute which the President approved. It was, however, never made law. This was not a new idea; much work had been done on it already, notably in the regime of President Taft who had favored it. The obvious abuses involved in competition among states for chartering corporations seemed to call for a Federal statute.

I cannot recall why our law was never passed; but obviously in the Session of 1934 I thought we were not yet ready, a judgment which seems to have agreed with that of the President.

THE WHITE HOUSE
Memo. to the Attorney General
20 November 1933

Will you, or someone designated by you, act as chairman of a little committee to study this subject of Federal incorporation? I would suggest you consult Assistant Secretary of Agriculture Tugwell, also Mr. A. A. Berle, also internal revenue people and also possibly representatives of the Department of Commerce, NRA and AAA.

(From Official file 466)

THE WHITE HOUSE
Washington

PRIVATE AND
CONFIDENTIAL   February 28, 1934

MEMORANDUM FROM   THE PRESIDENT

FOR   THE ASSISTANT SECRETARY
                         OF AGRICULTURE

Many thanks for yours of the 24th.

I think you are absolutely right about the Federal Incorporation Statute. It should go over to the next session.

In regard to the Unemployment Insurance Bill, I have told Miss Perkins and Bob Wagner that I have no objection to its being reported by the committees, but that I do not think the adjournment of the Session should be held up by it. As you say--it will require a good deal of overhauling and would necessarily cause much debate.

As to Social Security, there was by now a committee working under the Chairmanship of Frances Perkins as was appropriate. Professor Edwin E. Witte of the University of Wisconsin was director of the studies being made. About this subject I had had conversations with the President from time to time and had developed some thoughts. There were arguments and disagreements within the larger general determination to achieve a social security scheme; and about these I shall have more to say.

Glossary

The following abbreviations were frequently used by Rexford Tugwell throughout his New Deal diary:

AAA - Agricultural Adjustment Administration
AFL - American Federation of Labor
AP - Associated Press
ARP - Advance Ratio Plan
BCS - Bank of Corporate Surpluses
BIA - Bureau of Insular Affairs
CCC - Civilian Conservation Corps
CWA - Civil Works Administration
FCA - Farm Credit Administration
F&D - Food and Drug Administration
FD/FDR- Franklin D. Roosevelt
FERA - Federal Emergency Relief Administration
FF - Felix Frankfurter
FSA - Farm Security Administration
FSRC - Federal Surplus Relief Corporation
FTC - Federal Trade Commission
GEF/GF- Grace Falke
GP - Gifford Pinchot
HA/HAW- Henry A. Wallace
HH - Harry Hopkins
HM - Henry Morgenthau
JF - Jerome Frank
LH - Louis Howe
ML/MLW- M. L. Wilson
Mrs.R - Eleanor Roosevelt
NEC - National Emergency Council
NIRA - National Industrial Recovery Act

NRA - National Recovery Administration
PR   - Puerto Rico
PW   - Public Works
PWA - Public Works Administration
RA   - Resettlement Administration
RFC - Reconstruction Finance Corporation
RGT - Rexford Guy Tugwell
TVA - Tennessee Valley Authority
USDA - United States Department of Agriculture
WPA - Works Progress Administration

The glossary which follows identifies individuals, legislation, and events mentioned in the Tugwell New Deal diary for the years, 1932-1935. Each item is described so as to assist the reader in understanding what happened during the time period in which Tugwell wrote.

Agger, Eugene - professor of economics at Rutgers University and consultant to the Resettlement Administration, 1935-1937.
Agricultural Adjustment Act - passed May 12, 1933 - designed to increase agricultural purchasing power by reducing production, to alleviate rural credit problems, and to inflate the currency if the President so desired.
Aldrich, W.W. - Chairman, Board of Directors, Chase National Bank and member of Business Advisory Council (1933).
Alexander, Will - assistant administrator, Resettlement Administration, 1935 and administrator, Farm Security Administration, 1937-1940.
Anti-Trust Acts - specifically the Sherman Anti-Trust Act (1890), Clayton Anti-Trust Act (1914), and Federal Trade Commission Act (1914). Each was designed to regulate business. During the 1930s, the anti-trust acts were closely identified with Louis Brandeis' atomistic approach to the economy. Tugwell was particularly opposed to this thinking.
Appleby, Paul - assistant to Secretary of Agriculture Henry A. Wallace, 1933-1940.
Armour, Norman - minister to Haiti (1932-1935) and minister to Canada (1935-1938).
Arnold, Thurman - assistant attorney general and director of anti-trust division, Department of Justice (1938-1943).
Astor, William Vincent - heir of Astor fortune, contributor to Al Smith (1928) and Franklin D. Roosevelt (1932). Broke with Roosevelt in 1935 over inheritance tax issue.

Atherton, Ray - career diplomat, First Secretary (London), 1924-1927, counselor of London embassy, and minister to Bulgaria (1937).

Baldwin, C. B. (Beany) - worked with Tugwell in Resettlement Administration and in replacing the Puerto Rican Reconstruction Administration with Farm Security Administration.

Ballantine, Arthur - assistant secretary of treasury, 1931-1932, under-secretary of treasury, 1932-1933.

Ballinger - Pinchot Affair - took place during the Taft administration. Ballinger, secretary of interior, fired Gifford Pinchot, Forest Service, for his criticisms of Ballinger's refusal to maintain Theodore Roosevelt's conservation programs.

Bank for Corporate Surpluses - Tugwell proposal during the drafting of the National Industrial Recovery Act in 1933. Designed to force businesses to invest profits, the BCS would be the repository for all undistributed industrial surpluses.

Bankhead Cotton Control Act - April 1934, designed to increase participation of the Agricultural Adjustment Administration in cotton programs by penalizing non-participants and contract violators and by limiting production by taxing cotton gins.

Bankhead Tenant Bill - introduced in 1935 by Senator John Bankhead of Alabama. It attempted to help tenants and farm laborers buy farms with government loans at low interest rates.

Bartlett, Frederic P. - close associate of Tugwell from the the 1920s. Assisted Tugwell in a number of activities, including the 1934 trip to Puerto Rico and later during Tugwell's term as governor of Puerto Rico (1941-1946).

Baruch, Bernard - influential businessman. Served as chairman, War Industries Board (1918), economic adviser to Woodrow Wilson (1919), and an adviser to London Economic Conference (1933).

Battle, Turner - assistant to secretary of labor (1933) and representative of secretary of labor on special board for public works.

Bean, Louis - agricultural economist and economic advisor to the secretary of agriculture, 1923-1940.

Beck, Thomas - publisher of Collier's. Advised Roosevelt on appointment for secretary of agriculture in 1933. Tugwell attempted to enlist Beck's support for pure food and drug legislation.

Bell, Daniel - director, Bureau of the Budget, 1934-1940.

Beltsville, Md - location of National Agricultural Research Center in the United States Department of Agriculture.

Berle, Adolf - co-author of The Modern Corporation and Private Property, original member of 1932 Brains Trust, and was involved in Reconstruction Finance Corporation (1933) and was assistant secretary of state (1938-1944).

Biddle, Erich - relief administrator of Pennsylvania (1932-1935).

Bingham, Robert Worth - president and publisher, Louisville Courier-Journal and Louisville Times and ambassador extraordinary and plenipotentiary to Great Britain, 1933-1937.

Black, John D. - professor of economics at Harvard University. His proposal to reduce acreage so as to raise farm prices became the basis for the Agricultural Adjustment Act.

Blaine, John - U. S. Senate, 1927-1933 (Republican, Wisconsin), member, board of Reconstruction Finance Corporation, 1933-1934.

Blaisdell, Thomas - assisted Tugwell in preparing his report on social science teaching in American universities for the social science division of the Laura Spellman-Rockefeller Foundation in 1931.

Bogdanov, Peter - chairman, board of directors, Amtorg Trading Corporation.

Bonbright, James - adviser to Governor Franklin Roosevelt in New York and later served as an American delegate to the World Power Conference in 1933.

Bourne, James - was relief administrator of Puerto Rico in early 1930s.

Brandeis, Louis (see also anti-trusts laws) - Supreme Court Justice (1916-1939), close associate of Felix Frankfurter, and philosophical leader of atomism (small business) approach to the American economy.

Bressman, Earle - special representative, United States Department of Agriculture and Tugwell associate in Puerto Rico. Worked on gaining support for the Institute of Tropical Agriculture.

Brown, Herbert - chief, U.S. Bureau of Efficiency, 1916-1933.

Brownlow, Louis - journalist and foreign correspondent. He was chairman of Roosevelt's committee on administrative management, 1936.

Bullitt, William - adviser to Woodrow Wilson, ambassador to Soviet Union (1933-1936), and ambassador to France (1936-

1940).
Bundy, Harvey - assistant secretary of state, 1931-1933.
Bureau of Corporations - established in 1903 by Theodore
Roosevelt as a way of regulating business through
investigation and publicity.
Butler, Nicholas Murray - president, Columbia University,
1920s and 1930s. Butler initially advised Tugwell not
to join the Roosevelt administration. Later, in 1937,
he was among those not willing to have Tugwell return
to Columbia.
Byrd, Harry F. - U. S. Senate, 1933-1965 (Democrat, Va), leading
conservative critic of Franklin Roosevelt and the New
Deal.
Byrnes, James F. - U. S. Senate, 1930-1941 (Democrat, South
Carolina).
Campbell, Watler G. - chief, Food and Drug Administration,
USDA, 1933-1940.
Carman, Harry - faculty member, Columbia University, 1920s.
Worked with Tugwell on Columbia University Studies.
Carr, Wilbur - assistant secretary of state, 1924-1937.
Carter, John F. - journalist and writer. Accompanied Tugwell
to Puerto Rico in 1934, special adviser to Tugwell in
USDA, 1934-1936, and helped in information program for
Resettlement Administration.
Cavers, David - professor of law, Duke University, 1931-1945.
Was legal adviser to USDA in drafting the revised food
and drug bills in 1933-1934.
Chapman, Oscar - assistant secretary of interior, 1933.
Chardón, Carlos E. - Puerto Rican agriculturalist, chancellor,
University of Puerto Rico (1930), director of Institute
of Tropical Agriculture, and author of Chardon Plan for
Puerto Rico.
Chase, Stuart - author, consultant to New Deal agencies in
1930s, and co-founder of Consumers' Research.
Christgau, Victor - served in a number of capacities in the
Agricultural Adjustment Administration, becoming assistant
administrator in 1934-1935. Was state administrator for
Works Progress Administration in Minnesota.
Civilian Conservation Corps - established March 31, 1933.
CCC placed young men to work in reforestation projects.
It was one of the most popular and successful New Deal
relief programs.
Clarke-McNary Act - passed June 7, 1924 - provided for the
protection of forest lands and reforestation of cut-over

areas.

Clemenceau, Georges - premier and minister of war, France,
    World War I and attended Versailles peace conference.

Cohen, Benjamin - instrumental in drafting Securities Act of
    1933, Securities and Exchange Act of 1934, and Public
    Utility Holding Company Act of 1935. He was a close
    adviser to Roosevelt in 1935 and a strong opponent of
    Tugwell.

Coolidge, Thomas - special assistant to secretary of treasury,
    Henry Morgenthau (1934) and under-secretary of treasury,
    1934-1936.

Cooper, William - U. S. Commissioner of Education, 1929-
    1933.

Copeland, Royal S. - U. S. Senate, 1922-1938 (Democrat, New York).
    Was a strong critic of Franklin Roosevelt, although
    he supported revised food and drug legislation in the
    1930s. The 1938 Food, Drug and Cosmetic Act was primarily
    his contribution.

Corcoran, Thomas - attorney for Reconstruction Finance Corporation
    (1932-1933), instrumental in drafting New Deal
    legislation such as Securities and Exchange Act of 1934,
    and close adviser to Roosevelt in 1935. Corcoran and Cohen
    were in some ways responsible for Tugwell's resignation in
    1936.

Cornell Group - also called "Cornellians." Led by Professor
    George Warren of Cornell University, they advised and
    influenced Roosevelt, especially through Henry Morgenthau,
    on governmental monetary manipulation.

Coss, John - faculty and administrator, Columbia University, 1920s.

Costigan, Edward P. - U. S. Senate, 1930-1936 (Democrat, VA).
    Strong supporter of the New Deal and member of the progressive
    bloc in Congress.

Costigan-Jones Sugar Bill - introduced in 1934, the bill was
    supposed to reduce tariff on imported sugar and limit
    processing taxes. Quotas were to be set up for the
    United States and Cuba, Hawaii, Puerto Rico, and
    other Latin American countries.

Coughlin, Charles - Catholic radio priest of 1930s. Initially
    supported Franklin Roosevelt, but soon became an outspoken
    opponent. In 1934, he formed the National Union for Social
    Justice.

Cramer, Lawrence - governor, Virgin Islands. Instrumental in
    passage of revised Organic Act, 1935.

Cripps, Stafford Sir - Labor member of Parliament, chairman of

Socialist League in 1930s, and ambassador to Soviet Union, 1940-42.

Cummings, Homer - attorney general, 1933-1939.

Cutting, Bronson - U. S. Senate, 1928-1935 (Republican, New Mexico). Strong supporter of New Deal who was killed in a plane crash in 1935.

Dalton, Edward Hugh - economist and member of British House of Commons, 1924-1931. Also served as under-secretary, Foreign Office, 1929-1931.

Daniels, Josephus - secretary of navy, 1913-1921, ambassador to Mexico, 1933-1941.

Davis, Chester - agricultural economist, leading advocate of McNary-Haugenism in 1920s, and administrator, AAA, 1933-1936. Davis was responsible for the "purge" of the liberals in the legal division of AAA in 1935.

Davis, Forrest - journalist of 1930s for New York World Telegram, New York Daily News, and New York Herald Tribune.

Davis, Norman H. - chairman, American delegation, Geneva Disarmament Conference, chairman, American delegation, London Naval Conference, 1935-1936, and chief U.S. delegate, Nine Power Conference, 1937. Served as an ambassador "at large" for Franklin Roosevelt.

Davison, Frederick Trubee - assistant secretary of war, 1926. Unsucessfully ran for Lt. Governor of New York in 1932.

Day, Edmund E. - associated with Laura Spellman Rockefeller Memorial Foundation, 1927-1928 and director for social sciences, 1928-1937.

Delano, Frederick - uncle of Franklin Roosevelt and close political associate. Was director of National Planning Board (1933), National Resources Board (1934), and National Resources Planning Board (1939-41).

Dern, George - head, Bureau of Insular Affairs, 1930s.

Dickinson, John - assistant secretary of commerce (1933) and assistant attorney general (1935). Headed one group working on what became the National Industrial Recovery Act.

Dodd, William E. - American ambassador to Germany, 1934.

Domestic Allotment Plan (see also Agricultural Adjustment Act) - proposed acreage reduction to relieve farm distress in the late 1920s and early 1930s. Became the basis for the AAA.

Dominguez, Francisco Lopez - chief, rural rehabilitation division, Puerto Rico Reconstruction Administration.

Douglas, Lewis - director of budget, 1933-1934. Eventually
    split with Franklin Roosevelt. Tugwell and Douglas clashed
    frequently in 1933-1934.
Douglas, Paul H. - economist and industrial relations expert,
    University of Chicago.
Dulles, John Foster - American representative to Berlin debt
    conference, 1933.
Early, Stephen - public relations specialist, assistant press
    secretary to Franklin Roosevelt, 1933-1937, press secretary,
    1941-1945.
Eccles, Marriner - special assistant to Henry Morgenthau,
    chairman of Federal Reserve Board, 1934-1948, and helped
    in drafting the Banking Act of 1935.
Eisenhower, Milton - served in USDA as editor of Yearbook of
    Agriculture and coordinator of land use programs, 1926-
    1936.
Elliot, Walter - British Minister of Agriculture after 1932 in Ramsay
    McDonald's National government.
Emergency Banking Act of 1933 - passed March 9, 1933, the law
    legalized Franklin Roosevelt's bank holiday.
Enfield, R. R. - wrote The Agricultural Crisis, 1920-1923 and
    advocated the quantity theory and proposed cooperative
    marketing of commodities.
Ezekiel, Mordecai - chief economic adviser to Henry Wallace and
    Rexford Tugwell, USDA. Played a role in drafting the AAA and
    proposed Industrial Expansion Act of 1938.
Fackenthal, Frank - assistant to Nicholas Murray Butler in 1920s and
    later provost, Columbia University, 1932-1948.
Fairchild, David - began plant exploration division in USDA and
    advised Tugwell as governor on food supply problem in Puerto
    Rico.
Falke, Grace E. - administrative assistant, Resettlement Adminis-
    tration and married Rexford Tugwell in 1938.
Farley, James - New York politician and businessman. Served as
    Roosevelt's campaign manager in 1932 and postmaster general,
    1933-1940.
Farm Organizations - the National Farmer's Union, the National
    Grange, and the American Farm Bureau Federation were the
    major farm groups which Wallace and Tugwell had to deal with
    during their tenures in the USDA.
Fechner, Robert - director, Civilian Conservation Corps, 1933-1939.
Federal Farm Board - created by Agricultural Marketing Act, 1929.
    Attempted to stabilize farm prices during Hoover's
    administration.

Federal Trade Commission (see also anti-trusts laws) - created in 1914, the FTC was supposed to regulate business by investigation and issuance of cease-desist orders.

Feis, Herbert - economic adviser, department of state, 1931-1937. Was chief technical adviser for the U.S. delegation at the London Economic Conference in 1933.

Fennelley, John - economist, National City Company in New York, 1929-1931.

Fisher, Irving - leading economist of the 1920s. Supported the early New Deal but became very critical of Roosevelt by 1934.

Fleming, John - division of information, USDA. Wrote speeches for secretary of agriculture, Henry Wallace.

Fletcher-Rayburn Bill - orginally known as the Securities Act of 1933. The bill required companies issuing stock to provide the Federal Trade Commission with information on a company's new securities. Refined in 1934 Securities and Exchange Act.

Ford, Edsel - son of Henry Ford and president of Ford Motor Company, 1919-1943.

Frank, Jerome - general counsel to AAA and leading force in liberal faction within AAA's legal division. Fired by Chester Davis during the 1935 purge. Frank was a close associate of Rexford Tugwell.

Frankfurter, Felix - professor of law, Harvard University, close adviser to Franklin Roosevelt, and close associate of Louis Brandeis. Became Supreme Court justice in 1939.

Garner, John Nance - Speaker of House of Representatives, 1931 and vice-president of the United States, 1933-1941.

Glass, Carter - U. S. Senate, 1920-1946 (Democrat, Va). Known as the "father" of the Federal Reserve system.

Glass-Steagall Banking Act - passed in 1932, the law sought to reform America's banking system by giving the Federal Reserve more power over its member banks.

Gray, Lewis - economist who served on a number of New Deal agricultural committees and who worked with Tugwell in the Resettlement Administration.

Grayson, Carey Admiral - attending physician for Woodrow Wilson and chairman of Franklin Roosevelt's inauguration committee.

Green, William - president, American Federation of Labor, 1924-1952.

Gregory, Clifford - editor, <u>Prairie Farmer</u> and associate publisher of <u>Wallace's Farmer and Iowa Homestead</u>.

Gruening, Ernest - editor, <u>New York Evening Post</u>, 1934, director, division of territories and island possessions.

U.S. Department of Interior, 1934-1939, and administrator, FERA, Puerto Rico, 1935-1937.

Haig, Robert Murray - faculty, Columbia University, 1912-1943, financial adviser to governor of Puerto Rico, 1924-1926, and president, National Tax Association, 1931-1932.

Hall, Arnold - president, University of Oregon, 1926-1932, director for government research, Brookings Institution, 1933, and Social Science Research Council, 1929-1932.

Hamilton, Walton - professor of law, Yale University, 1928 and member of National Recovery Administration, 1934-1935.

Handler, Milton - professor of law, Columbia University, 1927. Assisted Tugwell in drafting legislation on revision of pure food and drug laws.

Harriman, Averill - businessman, banker, and railroad executive. Served as special administrative assistant, National Recovery Administration, 1934.

Harriman, Henry I - New England textile manufacturer, supporter of 1920s trade association movement, and president, U.S. Chamber of Commerce, 1930s.

Harris, Reed - editor, Columbia University Daily Spectator, 1932.

Harrison, George - governor, Federal Reserve Bank of New York, 1928-1936.

Harrison, Leland - diplomat and minister, department of state, 1920s-1930s, especially in Sweden, Uraguay, and Romania.

Harrison, Pat - U.S. Senate, 1918-1941 (Democrat, MS). Served as chairman, Senate Committee on Finance, 1933-1941. Supported early New Deal programs.

Hawkes, Herbert - mathematician, dean of Columbia College, 1918-1943, and close adviser of Nicholas M. Butler.

Hawley-Smoot Tariff - passed June, 1930. Designed to help relieve American farm problems, it was one of the highest tariffs in American history up to that time.

Hayes, Brooks - special assistant to administrator of resettlement in Farm Security Administration, 1936-1942.

Henderson, Donald - Ph.D student and faculty, Columbia University, 1920s. Failing to make progress on his degree, Tugwell fired Henderson who, in turn, made his case one of academic freedom.

Henderson, Leon - director, research and planning division, National Recovery Administration, 1934-35.

Herridge, William - Canadian minister to United States, 1931-35.

Herriot, Edouard - premier, France, 1924-25, 1926, 1932, minister of foreign affairs, 1932, and minister of state, 1934-36.

Conferred with Franklin Roosevelt on French debts, disarmament, and monetary problems in 1933.

Hickok, Lorena - journalist and reporter, close friend and adviser to Eleanor Roosevelt, and worked with Harry Hopkins in Civil Works Administration.

Hiss, Alger - assistant general counsel and legislative draftsman of AAA. Served in legal division of AAA. Resigned in protest over 1935 purge.

Hobson, Asher - consulting economist, Federal Farm Board, 1929-1930, chief of foreign agricultural service, USDA, 1930-1931, and member, U.S. Council of the International Conference of Agricultural Economists, 1930-1946.

Hoover, Calvin B - economist and consultant to National Resources Committee, 1937.

Hoover, Herbert Clark - president of United States, 1928-1932.

Hopkins, Ernest - president, Dartmouth College, 1934.

Hopkins, Harry - close adviser and friend of Franklin D. Roosevelt, director, Civil Works Administration, secretary of commerce, 1938-1940.

House, Edward - intimate adviser of Woodrow Wilson.

Howard, Roy - chairman, board of directors, Scripps-Howard newspapers, 1921-1953 and head, New York World Telegram.

Howe, Louis - close adviser of Franklin D. Roosevelt, campaign strategist of 1932 and personal secretary to the President, 1933-1935.

Hull, Cordell - U.S. Senate, 1931-1933, secretary of state, 1933-1944, and responsible for Reciprocal Trade Agreements Act, 1934.

Hutchins, Robert - president, University of Chicago, 1927-1945 and Tugwell's friend and choice to serve on the National Industrial Recovery Board.

Hyde Park, New York - birthplace and home of Franklin D. Roosevelt.

Ickes, Harold - secretary of interior, 1933-1946, director, Public Works Administration, 1933, and responsible for Tugwell's association with Puerto Rico.

Ickes-Moffett Dispute - public conflict between Harold Ickes and James Moffett, director of Federal Housing Authority over low-cost housing for individuals who could not qualify for an FHA-insured loan.

Industrial Adjustment Act - Tugwell's proposal in 1935 to replace the National Recovery Administration. Essentially, the plan was to model an industrial program on the AAA.

Interstate Commerce Commission - established in 1886 to regulate the railroads initially and later all forms of transportation.

Jackson, Gardner - journalist and political activist. Served in
the AAA promoting the interests of tenant farmers and
sharecroppers. Purged in 1935 by Chester Davis.

Jacobstein, Meyer - president, First National Bank and Trust,
Rochester, New York, 1929-1933 and publisher, Rochester
Evening Journal.

Johnson, Hiram - U. S. Senate, 1916-1945 (Republican, California).
Generally a New Deal supporter, except in foreign affairs towards
the end of the 1930s.

Johnson, Hugh - director, National Recovery Administration,
1933-1934.

Joint Resolution 117 - passed by House of Representatives on
January 24, 1935 and by the Senate on March 23, 1935.
Approved by President Roosevelt on April 8, 1935.
Resolution 117, along with executive order 7027, issued
on April 30, 1935, established the Resettlement Administration.

Jones, Marvin - House of Representatives, 1910-1940 (Democrat,
Texas). Chaired agricultural committee, 1930-1940 and
was instrumental in passing several New Deal farm bills
such as the Agricultural Adjustment Act, the Soil and
Conservation Act, and Bankhead-Jones Farm Tenancy Act.

Jones-Connally Farm Relief Act - The 1934 act provided aid
to cattle raisers by designating cattle as a basic
commodity, thereby allowing federal aid to cattle ranchers.

Jump, William - USDA official and director of finance, 1922-1949.

Kellogg-Briand Pact - also called the "Pact of Paris," 1928.
Tried to outlaw war as an instrument of national policy.
Ratified by U. S. Senate on January 15, 1929.

Kennedy, Joseph - wealthy businessman and early supporter of
Franklin Roosevelt. Played a role in the creation of the
Securities and Exchange Commission. Served as SEC director,
1934-1935.

Kent, Fred I. - Chicago and New York banker. Served as adviser
and member of Business Advisory Council, 1920s-1930s.

Keynes, John Maynard - wrote The General Theory of Employment,
Interest, and Money (1936) and is considered the father of
the Keynesian revolution in economics.

Kieran, James - journalist and reporter. Coined the phrase,
"Brain Trust" for Roosevelt's 1932 advisers.

Kirk, Alan G - U. S. Navy. Was naval attaché to U. S. embassy in
London, 1930s.

Knickerbocker, Hubert - journalist and European correspondent for
Hearst's international news service in the 1920s and 1930s.

LaFollette, Philip F. - governor of Wisconsin and progressive
   leader. In 1934, he formed the Wisconsin Progressive
   Party which supported much of the New Deal.
LaFollette, Robert M. (Jr.) - U. S. Senate, 1925-1949 (Republican, WI).
   Liberal member of the Congress who was
   critical of the New Deal while playing a key role in the
   passage of important public works and relief acts.
LaGuardia, Fiorello - mayor, New York City, 1933-1935. Was a
   strong supporter of the New Deal and would later ask
   Tugwell to work with him in New York City.
Landis, James - commissioner, Federal Trade Commission, 1933 and
   chairman, Securities and Exchange Commission, 1934-1938.
Lansill, John - head, suburban resettlement division, Resettlement
   Administration, 1935-1936.
League of Nations - established after World War I and designed
   to prevent aggression among nations. Despite Woodrow
   Wilson's support, the United States did not join the
   League.
Lee, Frederic P. - special counsel to secretary of agriculture,
   1933.
Lehand, Marguerite Alice - secretary for Franklin D. Roosevelt,
   1933-1943.
Leon, René - banker and monetary expert. Influenced Franklin
   Roosevelt on gold standard and banking crisis, 1933-1934.
Liberty League - coalition of conservative Democrats and
   businessmen who opposed the New Deal, especially in 1934
   and 1936 elections. Al Smith was a member of the League.
Lilienthal, David E. - member, board of directors, Tennessee
   Valley Authority, 1933 and later chairman of the board,
   1941-1946. Tugwell did not support Lilienthal's regional
   perception of planning.
Lindley, Ernest K. - journalist and author who worked for major
   news services such as New York World, Newsweek, and the
   New York Herald Tribune in the 1930s. Close friend and
   supporter of Rexford Tugwell.
Lindsay, Ronald Sir - British ambassador extraordinary and
   plenipotentiary to the United States, 1930-1939. Strongly
   encouraged Anglo-American cooperation.
Lippmann, Walter - journalist and author who wrote syndicated
   columns throughout the 1930s. Initially supported the
   New Deal but broke with Roosevelt in 1935.
Llewellyn, Karl - professor of law, Columbia University,
   1925-1951.
London Economic Conference - June-July, 1933. Convened to help

world economy by stabilizing currencies and relieving
pressures on money markets. Roosevelt sent his famous
"bombshell" message saying that the United States would
concentrate on its own economic recovery.

Long, Boaz Walton - public relations director, National Recovery
Administration, 1933-1934 and deputy administrator, Puerto
Rico, 1934-1936.

Long, Breckinridge - U. S. ambassador to Italy, 1933-1936.

Long, Huey - Louisiana politician who served as govenor (1928-32) and
senator (1932-1935). Initially supported the New Deal, but
quickly opposed Franklin Roosevelt. In 1935, he announced
plans to run for the presidency. He was assassinated in
September 1935.

Lovell, Malcolm R. - asssistant to under-secretary of agriculture, 1933-
1934 and financial adviser to Federal Housing Authority, 1934-
1935.

Lubin, David - instrumental in founding the International
Institute of Agriculture in Rome. Served as an American
delegate to the Institute.

MacDonald, Ramsey - British Prime Minister, 1929-1935.

McBain, Howard Lee - political scientist, Columbia University.
Drafted a new electoral code for Cuba in 1933.

McCarl, John R - comptroller general of the United States,
1921-1936.

McClelland, Thomas - horticulturist, Puerto Rico.

McCrory, Samuel - chief, bureau of agricultural engineering,
USDA, 1933.

McGoldrick, Joseph - assisted Tugwell in preparing his report
on social science teaching in American universities for
the social science division of the Laura Spellman
Rockefeller Foundation in 1931.

McGrady, Edward - assistant administrator, NRA, 1933 and assistant
secretary of labor, 1933-1937.

McNary-Haugenism - popular proposal in the 1920s to relieve
agricultural depression by dumping American surpluses
abroad after the federal government had purchased the
farm commodities from the American farmer. Was not actually
tried.

Mack, Julian - Chicago lawyer and social activist. Worked for
social work causes and American Zionism.

Maltbie, Mile - public utility expert. Served as chairman,
Public Service Commission of New York and head of New
York State Department of Public Service, 1930-1939.

Mazur, Paul - economist and investment banker. Wrote on the

American economy and business throughout the 1920s and 1930s.

Means, Gardiner - co-author with Adolf Berle of The Modern Corporation and Private Property. Served as economic adviser to Henry Wallace, USDA, 1933-1935.

Mellett, Lowell - journalist and editor, Washington Daily News, 1921-1937.

Mannheimer Group - named after Dutch banker, Fritz Mannheimer. Powerful group of banking interests in 1930s.

Menéndez-Ramos, Rafael - commissioner of agriculture in Puerto Rico, 1934 and assisted in drawing up the Chardón Plan.

Merriam, Charles E. - founded Social Science Research Council and served on the National Resources Planning Board (1933-1943).

Michelson, Charles D. - state and national Democratic party leader in 1920s-1930s.

Miller, Adolph - member, Federal Reserve Board, Washington, D.C., 1914-1936.

Mills, Ogden - under-secretary of treasury, 1927-1932 and secretary of treasury, 1932-1933.

Mitchell, Wesley C. - economist, Columbia University, 1920s. Close friend and colleague of Rexford Tugwell who also served in a number of positions in the New Deal.

Moley, Raymond - political scientist and faculty, Columbia University, 1920s. Was responsible for organizing the Brains Trust. Became assistant secretary of state in 1933 and was a close adviser of Franklin Roosevelt. Left the New Deal and became editor of Today. Eventually broke with Roosevelt.

Morgenthau, Henry - close friend and neighbor of Franklin D. Roosevelt. Was secretary of treasury, 1933-1945.

Morley, Felix - journalist and editor, Washington Post, 1933-1940.

Morris, David - U. S. ambassador to Belguim and minister to the grand duchy of Luxembourg, 1933.

Morrow, Dwight - U. S. ambassador to Mexico, 1927-1931.

Moses, Robert - commissioner, New York state parks, 1934-1960. Very powerful individual who clashed with Tugwell while Tugwell was chairman of the New York City Planning Commission.

Moskowitz, Belle - campaign manager for Al Smith, 1928 presidential election.

Moulton, H. G. - president, Brookings Institution, 1927-1952.

Mundelein, George Cardinal - Catholic archbishop of Chicago, 1915-1939.

Muñoz, Marín Luis - leader of Populares Party, Puerto Rico and close associate of Rexford Tugwell (1941-1946).

Murphy, Fred P. - manager and later president, Grolier, Inc. 1915-1947.

Muscles Shoals - in Alabama. Served as predecessor to the Tennessee Valley Authority. During the 1920s, Senator George Norris consistently attempted to have government operation of Muscle Shoals, only to have Coolidge and Hoover veto the bills.

Mussolini, Benito - "El Duce," Italy, 1922-1943.

Myers, William - served on Federal Farm Board, 1933, Farm Credit Administration, 1933-1938 and Federal Farm Mortgage Corporation, 1934-1938.

National Agricultural Research Center - (see also Beltsville, Md) - Tugwell claimed personal responsibility for this USDA research facility.

National Association of Manufacturers - founded at the turn of the century, the NAM represented the interests of small business. It generally opposed the New Deal and the growth of labor unions.

National Emergency Council - originally the executive council (1933), the NEC consisted of the secretaries of labor, interior, agriculture, and commerce in addition to the directors of the Public Works Administration, the Federal Emergency Relief Administration, the Agricultural Adjustment Administration, and several other New Deal agencies. In 1934, a new National Emergency Council was set up with Donald Richberg as chairman.

National Industrial Recovery Act - passed during the "100 Days," it established the National Recovery Administration which was to serve as the New Deal prime effort to achieve industrial recovery from the depression.

National Industrial Recovery Board - resulted in September 1934 when the National Recovery Administration was reorganized after Hugh Johnson resigned as director. The NIRB tried to continue the NRA program, albeit ineffectively.

National Recovery Administration - better known as the NRA. Established in 1933 with Hugh Johnson as director, it was responsible for carrying out the provisions of the NIRA, especially in the code-making and labor provisions of the law.

National Resources Planning Board - established in 1933 under the NIRA. It was originally called the National Resources Board

and then the National Resources Committee, and later the
National Resources Planning Board. Frederick Delano,
Charles Merriam, and Wesley Mitchell all served on the
board.

New York City Planning Commission - also referred to as the
NYCPC. Tugwell was chairman, 1938-1941.

Nine-Power Pact - included the United States, Belgium,
England, China, France, Italy, Japan, the Netherlands,
and Portugal. Concluded at the Washington Naval Confernce
in 1922, the pact agreed to maintain the Open Door policy
and China's integrity.

Norbeck, Peter - U. S. Senate, 1921-1936 (Republican, SD). The
Norbeck bill, introduced in 1932, was a predecessor to the
domestic allotment plan.

Nye, Gerald - U. S. Senate, 1925-1945 (Republican, N.D.). Influential in
opposing Roosevelt's attempts to rearm the United States in the
1930s.

O'Connor, Basil (Doc) - law partner and close personal adviser to
Franklin D. Roosevelt. O'Connor screened Tugwell before he
was admitted to the Brains Trust in 1932.

Ogburn, William F. - sociologist and friend of Rexford Tugwell
in 1920s and 1930s.

Oliphant, Herman - general counsel, department of treasury,
1933-1934.

O'Neal, Edward A. - president, American Farm Bureau Federation,
1931-1947.

Ottawa Agreements - resulted from the Ottawa conference in 1932.
Agreements set up preferential tariff rates between England
and the Dominions.

Patten, Simon Nelson - teacher and friend of Rexford Tugwell.
Taught at the University of Pennsylvania, 1888-1917.

Patterson, Ernest - faculty, University of Pennsylvania.
Was chairman of the economics department at the Wharton
School when Tugwell returned for his Ph.D. in 1920.
Patterson was not an enthusiastic supporter of Tugwell.

Pearson, Frank A. - faculty, Cornell University. Advocated
the "commodity dollar theory." With Professor George
Warren, he influenced Franklin Roosevelt on monetary policy
in the early 1930s.

Pearson, Paul M. - governor, Virgin Islands, 1931-1935.

Peek, George - director, Agricultural Adjustment Administration,
1933. Peek and Tugwell clashed frequently over the domestic
allotment provisions of the AAA, resulting in Peek's resignation
in December 1933.

Peffer, Nathaniel - faculty, Columbia University and expert
in international relations, especially in the Far East.

Perkins, Frances - secretary of labor, 1933-1945. Instrumental
in labor and social security legislation.

Perkins, Milo - assistant to secretary of agriculture, Henry
Wallace, 1935. Later served in Farm Security Administration.

Phillips, William - American diplomat, 1920s and 1930s who
served as ambassador and minister to a number of countries
including the Netherlands, Luxembourg, Belguim, Canada,
Italy, and India. Also served as under-secretary of state,
1933.

Pinchot, Gifford - (see also Ballinger - Pinchot affair) - renowned
forester who helped Theodore Roosevelt put together his
conservation program. Was governor of Pennsylvania,
1923-1927, 1931-1935.

Pittman, Key - U. S. Senate, 1912-1940 (Democrat, Nevada). Played
a key role in World Monetary and Economic conference in 1933
advocating his strong support of silver.

Profitt, Charles - manager and director, Columbia University
Press, 1927-1958.

Pure Food and Drugs Law - originally passed in 1906, the law
established the Pure Food and Drug Administration in the
USDA. Tugwell attempted to revise the 1906 act by extending
the administration's authority over the food and drugs
industry. The final 1938 act was so disappointing to Tugwell
that he felt it did little of what he wanted.

Rand, James H. - president, Remington Rand Corporation.
Tugwell lunched with Rand during the interregnum and made a
serious political mistake by saying that Roosevelt would
let the banking crisis develop on its own with Hoover
bearing the responsibility for what happened.

"Recent Social Trends" - report of the President's research
committee on social trends. Edited for school and college
use by John T. Greenan.

Reconstruction Finance Corporation - established in January 1932
to help businesses in danger of collapse. Under Hoover,
the RFC proved to be a failure. Roosevelt expanded the
functions of the RFC in his New Deal.

Resettlement Administration - established in 1935 and designed
to consolidate tenant displacement programs among New Deal
agencies. Tugwell served as its first director.

Richberg, Donald - Chicago attorney and general counsel, National
Recovery Administration, 1933-1934. Replaced Hugh Johnson
after his resignation in 1934.

Riefler, Winfield - research economist, Federal Reserve Board, 1923-1935 and chairman, Central Statistical Board of America, 1933-1935.

Robinson, Joseph T. - U. S. Senate, 1913-1937 (Democrat, Arkansas). Influential in foreign affairs, playing a key role in trying to obtain Senate approval for America's joining the World Court.

Rogers, James Harvey - economist and member of economics committee, League of Nations (1933-1937) and special representative of U. S. Treasury to China, Japan, and India, 1934.

Romine, Audrey - economic adviser on securities legislation, 1933 and representative in Washington, D.C. of Standard Statistical Company.

Roosevelt, Theodore - president of the United States, 1901-1908 and uncle of Franklin D. Roosevelt.

Roper, Daniel C. - secretary of commerce, 1933-1938.

Rosenman, Samuel - political adviser and speech writer to Franklin D. Roosevelt in 1920s and 1930s. Was involved in screening Tugwell for the Brains Trust.

Rowe, Leo - faculty, University of Pennsylvania, 1920s. Taught Tugwell constitutional law.

Ruml, Beardsley - one of the original proponents of the domestic allotment proposal in the 1920s and 1930s. Later served as director, Federal Reserve Bank of New York, 1937-1941.

Rumsey, Mary - close friend of Franklin and Eleanor Roosevelt. Chairman, Consumers' Advisory Board, NRA, 1933.

Savoy, Prew - chief, tax section, office of general counsel, AAA, 1933. Also worked on sugar bill, 1934.

Schoenfeld, Hans F. Arthur - American diplomat and minister, 1920s and 1930s to Bulgaria, Costa Rica, Dominican Republic, Finland, and Hungary.

Sheets, Earl W. - chief, division of animal husbandry, USDA, 1924 through 1930s.

Sherley, Joseph - U.S. House of Representatives (Democrat, Ky), 1903-1919, director, U.S. Railroad Administration, 1919-1920 and Washington, D.C. attorney, 1930s.

Shotwell, James T. - faculty, Columbia University, 1920s and director, division of economics and history, Carnegie Endowment for International Peace, 1924-1948.

Silcox, Ferdinand A. - chief, U. S. Forest Service, 1933-1939. Close friend and supporter of Rexford Tugwell.

Silver Purchase Act - passed in 1934 and designed to bring silver into circulation through the issuance of silver certificates and coinage.

Simpson, John - president, National Farmers' Union, 1931. Advocated federally guaranteed farm prices and supporter of AAA.

Smith, Al - Democratic party leader and presidential candidate, 1928. Initially supported Franklin Roosevelt in 1932, but soon openly opposed the New Deal.

Smith, Earl C. - president, Illinois Agricultural Association, 1926-1945 and board member, American Farm Bureau Federation, 1931.

Smith, Ellison D. (Cotton Ed) - U. S. Senate, 1909-1944 (Democrat, South Carolina).

Soil Conservation Service - established by the Soil Conservation Act of 1935 and designed to protect America's soil and water resources.

Soil Erosion Service - established in 1933 in USDA.

Soule, George - editorial board, The New Republic, 1920s and friend of Rexford Tugwell.

Spillman, William J. - agricultural economist who outlined the domestic allotment plan in his book, Balancing The Farm Output in 1927.

Sprague, Oliver - Harvard economist who taught Franklin D. Roosevelt as an undergradaute at Harvard University. Later served briefly as assistant secretary of treasury, 1933.

Stephens, Waldo - faculty, Columbia University, 1920s and 1930s. Supported efforts to revive the National Recovery Administration after it was declared unconstitutional.

Stewart, Walter Wheeler - economist and governmental adviser. Served as special adviser for German reparations payments in 1931, a trustee, Rockefeller Foundation, 1931-1950, and chairman, General Education Board, 1933-1950.

Stimson, Henry - secretary of war, 1911-1913, governor general of Philippines, 1927-1929, secretary of state, 1929-1933, and responsible for Stimson Doctrine which condemned Japanese aggression in Manchuria in 1931.

Stone, Julius - director, Federal Emergency Relief Administration for Puerto Rico and Virgin Islands, 1933-1935.

Straus, Jesse - father of Robert Straus, president, R. H. Macy and Co., and ambassador to France, 1933-1936.

Straus, Robert K. - deputy administrator, NRA, 1933-1935 and deputy director, Resettlement Administration, 1935-1936.

Street, Arthur - British broadcaster and lecturer on agricultural policy, 1930s.

Strong, Lee - chief, Bureau of Plant Quarantine, 1932-1933, USDA,

chief, Bureau of Entomology, 1933-1934, USDA, and chief,
Bureau of Entomology and Plant Quarantine, 1934-1941.

Sullivan, Mark - journalist and editor, Collier's. In 1930s,
he was a strong opponent of the New Deal and a particularly
virulent critic of Rexford Tugwell.

Swope, Herbert B. - businessman and president, General Electric,
1930s.

Taber, Louis - master, National Grange, 1923-1941. Generally
supported New Deal programs but had difficulties with
National Labor Relations Act and Roosevelt's "court
packing" plan.

Tannenbaum, Frank - faculty, Columbia University, 1930s,
Latin American historian who surveyed economic conditions
in Puerto Rico in late 1920s.

Tapp, Jesse - agricultural economist, USDA, assistant administrator,
AAA, 1933-1939.

Taussig, Charles - president, American Molasses Company.
Close friend of Rexford Tugwell. Also served as a
technical adviser to World Economic Conference in
1933 and in Latin American affairs generally.

Tax and Reserve Fund - Tugwell proposal during the drafting
of the National Industrial Recovery Act. Sought to
build up a surplus reserve for industry by the use of
a processing tax.

Taylor, Carl - director, rural resettlement, Resettlement
Administration, 1935.

Taylor, Henry C. - agricultural economist and member of American
delegation to International Institute of Agriculture in
Rome, 1933-1935.

Tennessee Valley Authority - established May 18, 1933. TVA was
supposed to plan for the use and development of the Tennessee
valley. Proved to be one of the most successful New Deal
programs.

Thomas, Seth - solicitor, USDA, 1933-1935.

Thorpe, Merle - editor, The Nation's Business. Strong critic of
the New Deal, Merle Thorpe charged that the New Deal had
enacted some of the points of the Communist manifesto.

Tittman, Harold - American diplomat in 1920s and 1930s serving
in a number of embassies such as Geneva, Paris, and Rome.

Tolley, Harold R. - was member and later chief of Bureau of
Agricultural Economics, USDA, 1915-1938. Also was head,
AAA, 1936-1938.

Trade Agreement Act - passed June 12, 1934. Amended the Hawley-
Smoot tariff by giving the president the authority to make

foreign trade agreements on the basis of mutual reductions in tariffs. Strongly supported by Cordell Hull.

Trading With the Enemy Act - passed October 6, 1917. Originally designed to prevent trade with Germany. In 1933, Tugwell and other members of the Roosevelt administration attempted to use the law to justify the president's actions in the banking crisis.

Trent, Dover - assistant director, commodities division, AAA, 1934.

Tully, Grace - secretary at first to Eleanor Roosevelt and later private secretary to Franklin D. Roosevelt.

Tugwell, Charles - father of Rexford Tugwell and successful businessman in Wilson, New York.

Tugwell, Edessa - mother of Rexford Tugwell.

Tugwell, Florence Arnold - married Rexford Tugwell in 1914, divorced in 1938.

Tugwell, Marcia - Tugwell's daughter by his first wife.

Tugwell, Tanis - Tugwell's daughter by his first wife.

Valeur, Robert - faculty, Columbia University, 1930-1940. Close friend of Rexford Tugwell.

Vanderburg, Arthur - U. S. Senate, 1928-1951 (Republican, Michigan). Voted against most New Deal programs, although he co-sponsored the Federal Deposit Insurance Plan. Also known as a committed isolationist in the 1930s.

Van Hise, Charles - faculty, University of Wisconsin, before World War I. Developed concept of concentration and control which Tugwell absorbed into his own economic thinking.

Viner, Jacob - economist and special assistant, secretary of treasury, 1934.

Wagner, Robert F. - U. S. Senate, 1926-1949 (Democrat, New York). Instrumental in the passage of several major public works laws and other New Deal legislation such as the National Labor Relations Act and the Social Security Act.

Wagner-Lewis Bill - sponsored by Robert Wagner in 1934, it provided for unemployment compensation. Served as a basis for the Social Security Act of 1935.

Wallace, Henry A. - secretary of agriculture, 1933-1941. Originally, a close associate of Rexford Tugwell until the purge of 1935.

Walker, Frank - executive director, National Emergency Council, 1935.

Walsh, David I. - U. S. Senate, 1919-1947 (Democrat, MA). Co-sponsor of Walsh-Healy Public Contracts Act of 1936 which required minimum wages to be paid by companies with government contracts. Strong supporter of labor's rights.

War Industries Board - established in 1917 by Woodrow Wilson
     in order to coordinate American production during World
     War I. Came to represent the idea of "industrial self-
     government."

War Settlements Act - passed in 1928, it created a special fund
     in the American treasury for the payment of war claims
     against Germany.

Warburg, James - Wall Street banker and Democratic party supporter.
     Close adviser of Franklin Roosevelt in 1933, helped in drafting the
     National Industrial Recovery Act as well as serving as a delegate
     to the London Economic Conference. Broke with Roosevelt over
     monetary policies.

Warm Springs, Georgia - also called "the little White House."
     Franklin Roosevelt spent much time there for treatment of
     his paralysis.

Warren, George - agricultural economist, Cornell University,
     1920-38. Authored the Warren plan to purchase gold in
     large amounts so as to affect commodity prices.

Wassermann, Max - economist and statistician, USDA, 1934-1935.
     Also worked in Resettlement Adminstration, 1935-1937.

Weaver, A. J. S. - associate director, program planning division,
     AAA, 1933-1934.

Welles, Sumner - American career diplomat in 1920s and 1930s.
     Also assistant secretary of state, 1933-1937 and ambassador
     to Cuba, 1933.

West, Charles - under-secretary of interior, 1935.

Westbrook, Lawrence - director, Texas relief, 1933-1934, assistant
     administrator, FERA, 1934, director, national rural
     rehabilitation program, 1935, and WPA administrator,
     1935-1936.

Wheeler, Burton K. - U. S. Senate, 1922-1947 (Democrat, Montana).
     Supported New Deal programs in banking, Federal Reserve,
     and securities exchanges but opposed Roosevelt's "court
     packing" plan.

Wickens, D. L. - helped Tugwell, along with Mordecai Ezekiel,
     to study credit reform in 1933.

Williams, John H. - represented, along with E. E. Day, the United
     States in the Geneva conference, 1932. Also contributed to
     setting the agenda for the London Economic Conference in
     1933.

Williams, Samuel Clay - president, R. J. Reynolds Company and
     head, National Industrial Recovery Board, 1934-1935.

Willis, H. Parker - well-known economist and finance expert in
     1920s and 1930s who had worked on major legislation such as

Federal Farm Loan Act and Banking Act of 1933.

Willkie, Wendell - well-known Republican of 1920s and 1930s who opposed TVA and the Public Utility Holding Company Act of 1935. Was Republican presidential candidate in 1940.

Wilson, Milburn L. - agronomist and agricultural economist at Montana State College. Published Farm Relief and the Domestic Allotment Plan in 1933. Served in a number of official capacities in New Deal, especially in AAA and USDA.

Winship, Blanton - governor, Puerto Rico, 1934-1939.

Wirt Affair - right-wing critic of the New Deal who charged Tugwell as being the leader of a communist group in the federal government. Charges clouded Tugwell's promotion as under-secretary of agriculture in 1934.

Woodin, William - secretary of treasury, 1933-1934. Known as a fiscal conservative who urged restraint in New Deal spending programs.

Young, Owen - chairman, board of directors, General Electric, 1922-1939. Co-author of Dawes Plan and Young Plan for German reparations.

Bibliography

The purpose of this bibliography is to provide the reader with a guide for pursuing any further interest he/she may have in Rexford Tugwell. It is not intended to be a complete listing of everything Tugwell ever wrote nor is it designed to provide a detailed account of secondary literature available on either Tugwell or the New Deal. It does, however, give the specific citations to books and/or articles Tugwell mentioned in the diary as well as additional selective works which should prove helpful in understanding his thinking in the 1920s and 1930s.

For those interested in works that have been done on Tugwell, the most recent and the only complete study covering his entire life is Michael V. Namorato, <u>Rexford G. Tugwell: A Biography</u> (New York: Praeger, 1988).

Rexford G. Tugwell Papers

The personal papers of Rexford Tugwell are deposited at the Franklin D. Roosevelt Library in Hyde Park, New York. The collection is rather large, comprising 114 boxes and 9 scrapbooks. The diary represents a major part of the collection, consisting of the original entries, Tugwell's revisions, and substantial newspaper and miscellaneous inserts. In addition to the papers at the Franklin D. Roosevelt Library, there are some materials in Washington, D.C. at the National Archives, specifically in governmental agency collections such as the United States Department of Agriculture, the National Recovery Administration, and the Resettlement Administration. Tugwell also was interviewed for the Columbia Oral History Project in New York. The transcript for this interview is available on microfiche.

A more easily accessible source on Tugwell are the autobiographies which he wrote and published throughout his life. While many of Tugwell's writings contained information about his activities at

various stages of his career, the following are the most important: The
Light of Other Days (New York: Doubleday, 1962), To The Lesser Heights
of Morningside: A Memoir (Philadephia: University of Pennsylvania
Press, 1982), The Brains Trust (New York: Viking Press, 1968),
Roosevelt's Revolution: The First Year, A Personal Perspective (New
York: Macmillan, 1977), The Stricken Land: The Story of Puerto Rico
(New York: Doubleday, 1947), A Chronicle of Jeopardy, 1945-1955
(Chicago: University Press of Chicago, 1955), and Off Course: From
Truman to Nixon (New York: Praeger, 1971).

Rexford G. Tugwell Writings

The following list contains the specific citations mentioned by
Tugwell in the diary as well as a selective collection of books and articles
indicative of Tugwell's thinking in the period, 1920 - 1937:

Books/Chapters in Books

The Economic Basis of Public Interest (Menasha, Wisconsin: George
    Banta, 1922).
American Economic Life and the Means of Its Improvement, 2nd ed.,
    (New York: Harcourt, Brace, 1924). Joint Author with Thomas
    Munro and Roy E. Stryker.
"Russian Agriculture," in Soviet Russia in the Second Decade
    (New York: John Day, 1928). Edited by Rexford Tugwell,
    Stuart Chase, and Robert Dunn.
Industry's Coming of Age (New York: Harcourt, Brace, 1927).
Mr. Hoover's Economic Policy (New York: John Day, 1932).
The Industrial Discipline and the Governmental Arts (New York:
    Columbia University Press, 1933).
Essays Upon Field Husbandry in New England, and Other Papers,
    1748-1762 (New York: Columbia University Press, 1934). By
    Eliot Jared and edited by Rexford Tugwell and Harry Carman.
Redirecting Education, 2 volumes (New York: Columbia University
    Press, 1934-1935). Edited by Rexford Tugwell and Leon
    Keyserling.
The Battle For Democracy (New York: Columbia University Press,
    1935).

Articles

"The Philosophy of Despair: Outlawing the I.W.W.," New York Call
    (October 17, 1920).
"The Gipsey Strain," Pacific Review 2 (September 1921), 177-96.

"Country Life in America," Pacific Review (March 1922), 566-86.
"Economic Theory and Practice," American Economic Review,
  Supplement 13 (March 1923), 107-09.
"The Problem of Agriculture," Political Science Quarterly 39
  (December, 1924), 549-91.
"Chameleon Woods," New Republic 48 (August 25, 1926), 16-17.
"The End of Laissez-Faire," New Republic 48 (October 13, 1926),
  222.
"America's Wartime Socialism," Nation 124 (April 6, 1927),
  364-67.
"What Will Become of the Farmer?" Nation 124 (June 5, 1927),
  664-66.
"Paradox of Peace," New Republic 54 (April 18, 1928), 262-66.
"Hunger, Cold, and Candidates," New Republic 54 (May 2, 1928),
  323-25.
"Governor or President?" New Republic 54 (May 16, 1928), 381-82.
"Communist Theory vs. Russian Fact," New Republic 54 (May 16,
  1928), 367.
"Contemporary Economics," New Republic 54 (May 16, 1928), 397-98.
"Platforms and Candidates," New Republic 55 (May 30, 1928), 44-
  45.
"What is a Scientific Tariff?" New Republic 55 (June 13, 1928),
  92-93.
"That Living Constitution," New Republic 55 (June 20, 1928),
  120-22.
"Experimental Control in Russian Industry," Political Science
  Quarterly 43 (June 1928), 161-87.
"A Plank for Agriculture," New Republic 55 (July 4, 1928),
  161-63.
"Wage Pressure and Efficiency," New Republic 55 (July 11, 1928),
  196-98.
"Governor Smith's Dilemma," New Republic 55 (August 1, 1928),
  276-77.
"The Liberal Choice," New Republic 56 (September 5, 1928), 74-75.
"Banker's Banks," New Republic 57 (December 12, 1928), 95-96.
"Reflections on Farm Relief," Political Science Quarterly 43
  (December 1928), 481-97.
"Farm Relief and a Permanent Agriculture," The Annals of the
  American Academy of Political and Social Science 142
  (March 1929), 271-82.
"Agricultural Policy of France," Political Science Quarterly
  45 (June-December 1930), 214-30, 405-28, 527-47.
"The Theory of Occupational Obsolescence," Political Science
  Quarterly 46 (June 1931), 171-227.

The Diary of Rexford G. Tugwell

"Flaws in the Hoover Economic Plan," Current History 35
     (January 1932), 525-31. Written with A. T. Cutler and
     G. S. Mitchell.
"The Copeland Bill and the Food Industries," Grocery Trade News
     (October 24, 1933).
"Freedom from Fakes," Today (November 18, 1933), 6-7.
"The Farm Price Level," Fortune 8 (November 1933).
"Planned Use of the Land," Today 1 (January 20, 1934), 6-7.
"The Price Also Rises," Fortune 9 (January 1934), 70-71, 107-08.
"Should Congress Enact a New Pure Food and Drugs Law?"
     Congressional Digest 13 (March 1934), 72ff.
"America Takes Hold of Its Destiny," Today 1 (April 28, 1934),
     6-7.
"The Progressive Tradition," Atlantic Monthly 155 (April 1935),
     409-18.
"No More Frontiers," Today (June 22 and 29, 1935), 3-4, 8-9.
"National Significance of Recent Trends in Farm Population,"
     Social Forces 14 (October 1935), 1-7.
"Our New National Domain," Scribner's Magazine 99 (March 1936),
     165-68.
"New Frontier: The Story of Resettlement," Chicago Sun-Times
     (April 19, 1936).
"Why Resettlement?" Labor Information Bulletin 3 (May 1936), 1-4.
"The Future of National Planning," New Republic 89 (December 9,
     1936), 162-64.
"The Meaning of Greenbelt Towns," New Republic 90 (February 17,
     1937), 42-43.
"Co-operation and Resettlement," Current History 45 (February,
     1937), 71-76.

Index

About the Editor

MICHAEL VINCENT NAMORATO is Associate Professor of History at the University of Mississippi. He is the author of *Rexford G. Tugwell: A Biography* (Praeger 1988) and the editor of two earlier books, *The New Deal and the South* (1984) and *Have We Overcome? Race Relations Since Brown* (1979).